SIXTH BOOK OF

Junior Authors & Illustrators

Biographical Reference Books from
The H. W. Wilson Company

American Reformers

Greek and Latin Authors 800 B.C.–A.D. 1000
European Authors 1000–1900
British Authors Before 1800
British Authors of the Nineteenth Century
American Authors 1600–1900
Twentieth Century Authors
Twentieth Century Authors: First Supplement
World Authors 1950–1970
World Authors 1970–1975
World Authors 1975–1980

The Junior Book of Authors
More Junior Authors
Third Book of Junior Authors
Fourth Book of Junior Authors and Illustrators
Fifth Book of Junior Authors and Illustrators
Sixth Book of Junior Authors and Illustrators

Great Composers: 1300–1900
Composers Since 1900
Composers Since 1900: First Supplement
Musicians Since 1900
American Songwriters

Nobel Prize Winners

World Artists 1950–1980

World Film Directors: Volumes I, II

SIXTH BOOK OF
Junior Authors
& Illustrators

EDITED BY SALLY HOLMES HOLTZE

THE H. W. WILSON COMPANY • NEW YORK 1989

Library of Congress Cataloging-in-Publication Data

Main entry under title:

Sixth book of junior authors & illustrators / edited by Sally Holmes
    Holtze.
        p.   cm.
    Continues: Fifth book of junior authors & illustrators.
    Includes index.
    ISBN 0-8242-0777-7
    1. Children's literature—Bio-bibliography.   2. Illustrated books,
Children's—Bio-bibliography.   I. Holtze, Sally Holmes.   II. Fifth
book of junior authors & illustrators.
PN1009.A1S3936   1989
809'.89282—dc20   89-14815
                                                                        CIP

Preface

"I HATE WRITING ABOUT MYSELF," one author wrote to me when I requested an autobiographical sketch for this volume. "Who would want to know about my dull life?", questioned another. But despite these familiar declarations the sketches sent tell fascinating and entertaining stories of how people came to be writers and artists: how one was transfixed by an artist in his younger years, where many of them studied, how they came to realize that it was possible for them to create books for children and young adults, and even how several of them had the misconception that all writers were either "dead or living in England." This information is meaningful, even precious, to the readers who treasure their books, who feel that an author or artist is speaking directly to them.

Many of the people who have written for this book have expressed that they feel lucky to be doing what they love. Conveying a common sentiment, Dorothy Haas writes, "I consider myself blessed to have found my life's work in a field that not only brings enjoyment to me but to children as well." Sue Alexander and Diane Stanley are among the biographees who echo that idea in their words.

This is the sixth book in a series that has a long and fine tradition of introducing young readers to the writers and artists they love best. The first book of this series, *The Junior Book of Authors*, was published in 1935. A revised edition came out in 1951. *More Junior Authors* appeared in 1963. The *Third Book of Junior Authors* was published in 1972, containing the first cumulative index to the series. In 1978 the title of the *Fourth Book of Junior Authors and Illustrators* reflected, for the first time, the series' ongoing inclusion of artists as well as writers. The *Fifth Book of Junior Authors and Illustrators* was published six years ago, in 1983.

The *Sixth Book of Junior Authors and Illustrators* contains 236 sketches of authors and illustrators who have come to prominence since the publication of the previous volume. From a file of contemporary authors and illustrators, the editor compiled a preliminary list of a thousand names. As the basis for selection for this list, several aspects of a candidate's work were considered: the recommendations of reviews and criticism and the appearance of titles on various recommended lists; awards and honors won; and popularity. An advisory committee of children's and young adult literature specialists from across the country was chosen to vote on candidates from the preliminary list and was invited to suggest additional names. The committee and the editor voted for approximately 250 names.

The committee for the *Sixth Book . . .* consisted of Jane Botham, Coordinator of Children's Services, Milwaukee Public Library; Mary Mehlman Burns, Coordinator, Curriculum Library and Children's Literature Specialist, Framingham (Massachusetts) State College; Barbara Elleman, Children's Books Editor, *Booklist*, American Library Association; Barbara H. Fischer, Children's/Youth Services Consultant, Virginia State Library & Archives, Richmond; Dr. M. Jean Greenlaw, Regents Professor, University of North Texas; Roger Sutton, Associate Editor, *Bulletin of the Center for Children's Books*, University of Chicago;

and Judith Volc, Coordinator of Children's Services, Boulder Public Library, Colorado.

The sketches are arranged in alphabetical order by that version of an author or illustrator's name appearing most often on title pages. The index provides cross references for all names and pen names, not only in this volume but in all five previous volumes in the series as well. Phonetic pronunciations are supplied when necessary. When authors and illustrators have omitted from their sketches important information about themselves, such as awards or degrees, editorial additions follow their autobiographical sketches. When biographical sources disclosed contradictory information, every possible attempt was made to obtain the correct information.

The number of awards and prizes given to children's books and their creators grows each year, and editorial decisions have been made to include only those that would be of greatest interest to readers. In particular, awards voted by children were omitted; it is not that the popularity of the books with their intended audience is not valued or considered, but the rules of eligibility often result in the judgment of books by peculiar comparisons.

The SELECTED WORKS section of each sketch is by no means an attempt to provide a complete list of works; we have tried to select books that have received particularly favorable reviews or that are important to an author or illustrator's career, or that are representative of their work. That the title may be out of print is not considered. Books published by adult book departments or those not published in the U.S. are not listed in SELECTED WORKS. The ABOUT sections provide biographical references to books and articles that are likely to be generally available and that are in English. For the most part, articles that are strictly subjective have not been included.

When it has been impossible to obtain autobiographical material, biographical sketches have been compiled. When a sketch has been written by someone who knew the subject personally or who is an authority on his or her work, credit is given to the writer in the heading of the sketch. Other biographical sketches were written anonymously by the editor and by Sally Bates Goodroe, Maryclare O'Donnell Himmel, Krystal K. Irven, Karen Jameyson, Sarah Guille Kvilhaug, Claudia A. Logan, Anne Paget, Michael C. Parsons, and Gwen Salama.

The editor would like to acknowledge those who have helped in the preparation of this book, especially Bruce R. Carrick, Vice President, The H.W. Wilson Company, and Judith O'Malley, also of The H.W. Wilson Company. Thanks are also due to the editors, library promotion departments, and publicity departments of many publishing companies, and to the Children's Book Council, for maintaining a collection of contemporary books for children that are readily available for examination. The editor is also grateful to the members of the advisory committee for their thoughtful opinions and to Roslyn Corwin for her assistance.

Above all, the editor appreciates the contributions of the authors and illustrators who took time away from their work to compose sketches and who, many times, expressed their pleasure in being included in this book, which affords them a unique method of reaching their readers.

SALLY HOLMES HOLTZE
August 1, 1989

Contents

SIXTH BOOK OF

Junior Authors
& Illustrators

CHESTER AARON

May 9, 1923–

AUTHOR OF *Duchess, etc.*

Autobiographical sketch of Chester Aaron:

MY EARLIEST MEMORIES: miners and their families on the porch of my father's general store, waiting for the truck from County Relief to deliver used clothing and cans of food; the shelves of our store, empty; my parents (Russian, Polish) trying but eventually failing to adjust to this strange land and its stranger people; days and weeks of eating nothing but potatoes— fried, boiled, baked—with, on occasional Friday nights, one of our declining brood of chickens; and my own attempts to defend and deny, among the rugged mine children whom I loved and hated, my Jewishness.

That Butler, Pennsylvania, childhood in the early twenties shaped both my reading then and, later, my writing. Instead of escaping into fantasy to deny the poverty and pain and confusion, I escaped into realistic literature. I walked to town to the library and brought home Jack London and Booth Tarkington and Zane Grey. Barely into high school, I was intensely aware of the trial of Sacco and Vanzetti, of the Russian revolution, of the rise of Fascism. Fiction? I gorged on Charles Dickens and Maxim Gorki and the Italians, Levi and Silone and Moravia and Berto. A brother whom I idolized, then involved in the WPA Writers Project, alerted me to the work of James T. Farrell and Nelson Algren and Richard Wright.

Later in my life, after combat in Europe in World War II and participation in the liberation of Dachau, I was committed, in both adult and young adult fiction, to writing about social action. After twenty years of effort I finally had a story published and then a semi-autobiographical novel. An editor in New York suggested I try writing for young people because I told such wonderful stories. She guided me into one and then another success (*Better Than Laughter* and *An American Ghost*). Though reviews were not widly enthusiastic in the U.S., both novels received praise in Europe and sold well.

Traveling across the country, as I wrote more novels, I met with grade-school and high-school students. My audience, I discovered, was fascinated by my stories. I became more and more fascinated with kids as an audience.

An American Ghost later became a TV weekend special and the kids' awareness of the difference of values in television drama and novels convinced me that I should pay more attention to fiction, less to movies. I had been working on scripts. I quit. I soon realized that I was beginning to veer slowly, and not too reluctantly, toward an interest in nature and animals, toward a mix of fantasy and science fiction.

What had happened to my youth and its preoccupation with political resolutions to both political and nonpolitical problems? The evidence of man's determination to destroy himself and his world has persuaded me to worry not about what humans do to themselves but what they do to the earth and its innocent victims.

At sixty-five, I know that if I had another thirty years to write, I would concentrate on topics related to the mysteries not of the real world but of worlds we can only imagine.

I have written two novels for adults and eight novels for young adults, I am writing two more for young adults, one about a girl who is more animal than human. A sort of *Green Mansions.* In returning to the writing of adult fiction, I bring the conviction, learned from writing for young people, that *story* is the muscle, bone, and nerve to every novel. Every, for me, good novel.

———

Chester Aaron was born in Butler, Pennsylvania. He served in the U.S. Army from 1943 to 1946. He attended the University of California in Los Angeles from 1945 to 1948 and the University of California at Berkeley from 1954 to 1956, receiving his B.A. degree in 1956. He was married in 1954. He received an M.A. degree in 1977 from San Francisco State University. He has worked as an X-ray technician, as a technical writer, and as Professor of English, at Saint Mary's College in Moraga, California. He was the recipient of the Huntington Hartford Foundation Fellowship in 1950 and in 1951, and has received several grants, including a National Endowment for the Arts grant in 1976. He has written a novel for adults, *About Us*, published in 1967, and has had stories published in *North American Review* and *Texas Review.*

Duchess was named a 1982 Notable Children's Trade Book in the Field of Social Studies by a joint committee of the National Council for the Social Studies and the Children's Book Council.

SELECTED WORKS: Better Than Laughter, 1972; An American Ghost, 1973; Hello to Bodega, 1975; Spill, 1977; Catch Calico!, 1979; Gideon, 1982; Duchess, 1982; Out of Sight, Out of Mind, 1985; Lackawanna, 1986.

ABOUT: Contemporary Authors (First Revision), Vol. 21-24; (New Revision Series), Vol. 8; Something About the Author, Vol. 9; Kirkpatrick, D. L., ed. Twentieth-Century Children's Writers, 2nd ed.; Who's Who in the West, 1974-1975.

NATHAN AASENG

July 7, 1953–

AUTHOR OF *More with Less: The Future World of Buckminster Fuller*, etc.

Autobiographical sketch of Nathan Aaseng, who also writes under the pen name "Nate Aaseng":

MOST OF MY CHILDHOOD was spent in St. Louis Park, Minnesota, just a ways down the road from where Garrison Keillor grew up. I'm not quite as tall as Keillor, but I'm just as shy, and his stories about Norwegians and Lutherans, if anything, understate the environment in which I was raised. I had foolish notions of becoming an author when I was in grade school. Teachers often used the word "clever" as a comment on my papers. I took it as a compliment, but never really understood what it meant until I was a freshman at Luther College, Iowa.

That year I dreaded doing a long English paper on Homer's *Iliad.* As the deadline

Aaseng: *A W seng*

Nathan Aaseng

drew closer, I sat down to write. After grousing and agonizing for a while, it struck me that I used to think that writing was fun. What could I do to recapture the fun? I ended up making a puzzle out of it by trying to copy Homer. I wrote a long paper completely in his style of rhyme and rhythm. To my surprise, the paper came back with an *A* and that old word "clever" on it. That led me to believe that clever meant finding something to say, or a way to say it, that other people had not thought of.

Since I knew how impossible it was to get published, I worked as a research biochemist for four years after college. But I knew by then where all that "clever" stuff had come from. I was a person who saw things differently than other people. I didn't see more than others. I just saw things that most people didn't, and, to my daily shame, missed a lot of things that most people saw. It is a great advantage for such a person to be a writer and to stay out of professions where common sense is important.

I took a year out of my life to try and become a writer because it seemed to my wife and me that a person ought to *use* the talents that he or she has been given. My parents taught me that the shame is not in failure but in aiming too low. By the grace of God, I am becoming a writer.

Although I enjoy my children, I never intended to write for children. Although I enjoy sports, I never intended to write sports books. Writing for children is much harder than writing for adults, and sportswriting earns little respect. But in trying to establish myself as a full-time writer, I have tried to follow Matthew Arnold's advice, that "to the wise man, all knowledge is interesting."

My progress as a person learning to write has sometimes seemed painfully slow. I am reminded, however, that no one's life is defined solely by their profession. The roles of father of four small children, husband, friend, and community member frequently take priority.

My books so far are all part of the learning process. As I learn more, and as time becomes more my own, I look forward to being able to make words say so much more. I haven't hit the mark at which I'm aiming. If I ever do, I would like to make sure it is not because I aimed too low.

———

Nathan Aaseng was born in Park Rapids, Minnesota. He received his B.A. degree from Luther College in 1975; he was married on December 20, 1975. He worked as a microbiologist from 1975 to 1979 in Manitowoc, Wisconsin. Two of his books were chosen as Outstanding Science Trade Books for Children in their years of publication by a joint committee of the Science Teachers Association and the Children's Book Council: *Disease Fighters: The Nobel Prize in Medicine* and *More with Less: The Future World of Buckminster Fuller.*

SELECTED WORKS: Bruce Jenner: Decathalon Winner, 1979; Football's Fiercest Defenses, 1980; Winners Never Quit, 1980; Superstars Stopped Short, 1982; World-Class Marathoners, 1982; Baseball's Hottest Hitters, 1983; Basketball's Sharpshooters, 1983; Football's Hardhitting Linebackers, 1984; Supersubs of Pro Sports, 1983; Carl Lewis: Legend Chaser, 1985; Bob Geldof: The Man Behind Live Aid, 1986; More with Less: The Future World of Buckminster Fuller, 1986;

The Disease Fighters: The Nobel Prize in Medicine, 1987; From Rags to Riches: People Who Started Businesses from Scratch, 1989.

ABOUT: Contemporary Authors, Vol. 106; Something About the Author, Vol. 38.

YOSSI ABOLAFIA

June 4, 1944–

ILLUSTRATOR OF *Harry's Dog*, etc.

Autobiographical sketch of Yossi Abolafia:

I NEVER THOUGHT I'd write and illustrate books. I always wanted to be a pilot. Until this day, when I doodle, I doodle planes. All kinds.

I was born in Tiberias, on the sea of Galilee, where I attended school. But mostly I doodled. My older sister, Chana, collected some drawings of mine and took them to a local artist—Mira Laufer. She expressed a desire to teach me drawing, and so, one afternoon, I found myself in her living room, staring at a vase full of flowers. Still-life drawing doesn't appeal to me now, and it didn't much then. The minute she left the room, I climbed out of the living room window and ran for my life.

I wasn't particularly successful where school was concerned, but in the middle of high school, I transferred to a Kibbutz. It was there, on the banks of the Jordan River, that I started to take my drawing more seriously. As I recall, two things affected my development there. The first was being put in charge of illustrating and designing the school's monthly paper. The second was Beefsteak. Beefsteak was a mule. Being an agricultural school, we had a large vegetable garden which supplied us with a good portion of our food. The students were in charge of picking them; Beefsteak was in charge of carting them; I was in charge of Beefsteak.

It was a beautiful period in my life. I'd always been small, and in one year on the Kibbutz, I grew five inches taller.

At the age of seventeen, I was accepted at the Bezalel Art Academy, where I studied graphic design for the next four years. It was after that, during my three years of army service, that I began to do illustrations and cartoons for the army news magazine. On occasion, I was sent on assignment, to cover stories—mostly humorous—on army life. It was clear in my mind that I would work in cartoons and illustrations; there was one specific medium that fascinated and excited me—animation—where cartoons come to life.

In those days, believe it or not, there was no television in Israel. Finally, in 1968, when the Israel Television Authority was born, I got my chance. I was hired as a cartoonist for the News Program, and took immediately to experimenting with animation. Since no one knew much about it then, they were overjoyed with my experiments, and luckily for me, most everything I did was aired . . . even an animated weather report!

For the next few years, I worked in Israel as an animator. In 1974 I was approached by Keter Books, an Israeli Publishing House; they figured that if I could amuse adults with my drawings, then children might enjoy them in books written for children. And so, alongside my work as an animator, which brought me to Canada and the U.S., I began to illustrate other people's stories until 1984, working closely with Greenwillow Books. It was Susan Hirschman, the Editor-in-Chief of Greenwillow, who first suggested that I write my own stories. I protested, explaining that since Hebrew is my mother tongue, I was not really equipped to write stories in English! She insisted that there were stories hidden inside the illustrations, and that what I thought was a language problem was no big deal. (Since then, my English has gotten progressively gooder and gooder.)

My time and energies are divided among writing and illustrating children's books in Israel, and in New York; creating and drawing comic strips for Israeli newspapers; and most importantly, my three children, and lovely wife.

————

Harry's Visit and *Harry's Dog* were both named Notable Books by the American Library Association, in 1983 and 1984 respectively.

SELECTED WORKS WRITTEN AND ILLUSTRATED: My Three Uncles, 1984; Yanosh's Island, 1987; A Fish for Mrs. Gardenia, 1988; Leo and Emily's Zoo, 1988.

SELECTED WORKS ILLUSTRATED: Buffy and Albert, by Charlotte Pomerantz, 1982; Harry's Visit, by Barbara Ann Porte, 1983; It's Valentine's Day, by Jack Prelutsky, 1983; Harry's Dog, by Barbara Ann Porte, 1984; What I Did Last Summer, by Jack Prelutsky, 1984; Harry's Mom, 1985; My Parents Think I'm Sleeping, by Jack Prelutsky, 1985; Harry in Trouble, by Barbara Ann Porte, 1989.

ABOUT: Something About the Author, Vol. 46.

C. S. ADLER

February 23, 1932–

AUTHOR OF *The Magic of the Glits*, etc.

Autobiographical sketch of Carole Schwerdtfeger Adler:

I GOT TO WRITING through reading when I was seven years old and became an avid reader. It seemed to me that storytelling had to be the best job in the world, and so I started writing for fun. In those days we lived in the Bronx, but my childhood covered all the boroughs of New York City except one, and included the lonely periods of time essential to a writer. At thirteen I got my first rejection slip from a professional magazine.

In the fifties, getting married was the most essential part of life for most women; so I rushed through Hunter College and in 1953 grabbed a degree, with honors. I did it in three years because I was in a hurry to marry my husband, Arnold. I worked in the advertising department of Worthington

Pump in New Jersey for a couple of years and then produced twin boys. We moved around a lot in the corporate hopscotch game (my husband was an engineering manager for General Electric) and had another son while I practiced writing novels in the children's nap time. I finally sold my first short story to *American Girl*, the Girl Scout magazine, when I was thirty-one.

The seventeen teenage love stories I sold thereafter didn't make me feel like a professional writer. Instead, I became a teacher. I got an M.S. degree in education at Russell Sage College in Troy, New York, and began teaching middle school, sixth- and eighth-grade English. English teachers work too hard on their students' writing to do much of their own. The only writing I did in my eight years of teaching were snippets of prose and poetry created in saunas and on buses.

Eventually, the writing urge overcame me and I became a full-time author. I sold my first children's book when I was in my mid-forties. *The Magic of the Glits* was the name of that book. Macmillan brought it out in 1979. It won the William Allen White Award and the Golden Kite Award and had some other recognition. Twenty-six published books followed it with Macmillan, Putnam, and Clarion/Houghton Mifflin. Many of my hardcover books are out in paperback with Avon now.

I think a children's writer owes optimism to his or her readers. Children's books should not only entertain, they should be a comfort, a living-aid in some sense. Books have always been that to me in my life. I believe in the truth of fictional characters, and when I meet admirable people in my novels, it reinforces my faith in the human race. I hope that my books give something positive to my readers, and I get pleasure from the fan mail that tells me they do. In this world, it's important for children to know that things can work out well sometimes, and even if they don't, that you can survive and hope for better.

Children ask me often how my sons feel about my writing. They're very proud of my books and read them all, even though they are men now. Someday I hope my two grandchildren will read my books.

I enjoy being a writer. I love getting people's lives on paper and playing with words. Besides, writing is such a lifelong habit with me that I probably couldn't stop if I tried.

———

Carole S. Adler received an M.S. degree from Russell Sage College in 1964. She taught at Niskayuna Middle Schools in New York State from 1967 to 1977. She is a member of the Society of Children's Book Writers and the Authors Guild.

The Shell Lady's Daughter was chosen a Best Book for Young Adults for the year 1983 by the American Library Association. *With Westie and the Tin Man* was given a Child Study Children's Book Award by the Child Study Children's Book Committee at Bank Street College of Education in 1985, and *In Our House Scott Is My Brother* was named a Children's Choice Book of 1981 by the International Reading Association. *The Silver Coach* and *The Cat That Was Left Behind* were both Junior Literary Guild selections. Her books have been published in

Japan, Germany, England, Denmark, and Austria.

SELECTED WORKS: The Magic of the Glits, 1979; The Silver Coach, 1979; Shelter on Blue Barns Road, 1981; In Our House Scott Is My Brother, 1980; The Cat That Was Left Behind, 1981; Down By the River, 1981; Footsteps on the Stairs, 1982; The Shell Lady's Daughter, 1983; With Westie and the Tin Man, 1985; Split Sisters, 1986; One Sister Too Many, 1989.

ABOUT: A Directory of American Poets and Fiction Writers, 1985; Something About the Author, Vol. 26.

DAVID A. ADLER

April 10, 1947–

AUTHOR OF *Cam Jansen and the Mystery of the Monster Movie*, etc.

Autobiographical sketch of David A. Adler:

I WAS ALWAYS a dreamer. As a young boy, when I played baseball in my backyard I dreamed that a Major League scout or manager would see me make a great play and immediately sign me to play for the Yankees. I dreamed of becoming a great actor, artist, and lawyer. I did some of my dreaming, perhaps too much of it, in school.

Just last year my son had as his teacher the same teacher I had more than thirty years ago. She told me that she once complained to the assistant principal that I was such a dreamer. I didn't pay enough attention in class. According to this teacher, the assistant principal said, "Maybe one day he'll become a writer."

Well, I did become a writer. This is one of the dreams I had that came true.

I didn't start out to be a writer. I was always good in mathematics. In college I majored in econimics, and after I graduated I taught math in an intermediate school for almost nine years. While I was teaching I also went to graduate school. I was awarded a Masters in Business Administration and was beginning work on a doctorate when I wrote *A Little at a Time*. The inspiration for the story was my nephew who kept asking me questions.

Only a dreamer would send a manuscript out with the hope that it would be published. But I sent it out. The book was published by Random House, and while I continued to teach math I slowly began work on my second career. Five years after my first book was accepted for publication I left teaching to write full-time.

I've been very fortunate. I have many interests and I have been able to pursue them as a part of my work as a writer. I've written book on math, science, economics, history, Jewish holidays, riddles, and puzzles, and I've written picture books, biographies, mysteries, and adventure stories.

I am the second of six children. We were all very close in age and lived in a large house. My parents encouraged each of us to be an individual. It was their way of lessening the competition between us. As a child I was known as the family artist. Paintings and drawings I did when I was as young as twelve still hang in my parents' home. And I was creative. I drew funny signs that I taped around the house. I made up stories to entertain my younger brothers and sisters. I'm still making up stories.

———

David A. Adler was born in New York City and received his B.A. from Queens College in New York City in 1968 and his business degree in 1971. He has worked as a math teacher and a writer for a financial newsletter, and has been the senior editor of books for young readers at a publishing house for many years. He is the author of more than seventy books for young readers.

Our Golda was named a Carter G. Woodson Award Honor Book by the National Council for the Social Studies in 1985. *The Number on My Grandfather's Arm* received a Sydney Taylor Book Award as one of the best Jewish children's books of 1987 from the Association of Jewish Libraries. *A Picture Book of Jewish Holidays* was named a Notable Book of 1981 by the American Library Association. *3D, 2D, 1D* was named an Outstanding Science Trade Book for Children by a joint committe of the National Science Teachers Association and the Children's Book Council. Several of his books, including *Roman Numerals*, were named Children's Choice books by a joint committee of the International Reading Association and the CBC. *Our Golda* and *Martin Luther King, Jr.* were Notable Children's Trade Books in the Field of Social Studies in their years of publication, so named by a joint committee of the CBC and the National Council on the Social Studies.

SELECTED WORKS: 3D, 2D, 1D, 1975; A Little at a Time, 1976; Roman Numerals, 1977; A Picture Book of Jewish Holidays, 1981; Bunny Rabbit Rebus, 1983; Cam Jansen and the Mystery of the Monster Movie, 1984; Our Golda: The Story of Golda Meir, 1984; Cam Jansen and the Mystery at the Monkey House, 1985; The Fourth Floor Twins and the Disappearing Parrot Trick, 1986; Martin Luther King, Jr.: Free at Last, 1986; The Number on My Grandfather's Arm, 1987; The Fourth Floor Twins and the Sand Castle Contest, 1988; Jackie Robinson: He Was the First, 1989.

ABOUT: Contemporary Authors, Vol. 57; (New Revision Series), Vol. 7; Something About the Author, Vol. 14.

VIVIEN ALCOCK

September 23, 1924–

AUTHOR OF *The Haunting of Cassie Palmer,* etc.

Autobiographical sketch of Vivien Alcock:

I WAS BORN in Worthing, a small seaside town in the south of England. My early memories are of seagulls crying, sand between my toes, and the salty tang of the sea. I was the youngest of three sisters. Our mother was ill for as long as I can remember, in and out of hospital all the time. I think this drew the three of us closer together, though we sometimes quarrelled, as sisters will. In summer we played on the beach and fished in the rock pools when the tide went out. In winter, the sea sometimes came right over the road and we had to wade to school in gumboots.

We were all fond of painting and reading, and we used to tell each other bedtime stories at night. As I was the youngest, my turn always came last, and before I had properly begun, my sisters would be fast asleep. I sometimes wonder if this is what made me want to become a writer— perhaps I was determined to get my stories told at last.

When I was ten, my mother became terminally ill, and my father sent us to be looked after by some old family friends in Devizes, Wiltshire. It is a pretty town, with a cobbled market place, baskets of flowers hanging from every lamp post, a castle, and a canal. The first night we sat on our beds and determined to run away. We hated it. We wanted to go home. But we did not have enough money. Besides, where could we go? Our home was no longer there. I often think of this time when I am writing. What surprises me, looking back, is that my memories are by no means all miserable ones. I was often very happy there. Children are fortunately resilient. The very next morning after our arrival, the sun was shining and we discovered what we thought was a secret passage, starting from the kitchen

yard and running the length of the garden, concealed beneath a high rockery, to the old stables beyond. This and a friendly dog were enough to make us decide we would stay for a little while, just to see what it was like. In the end we stayed there until we had finished our schooling.

I studied at the Oxford School of Art for two years, intending to be a teacher, but volunteered for the army before I had finished my course. It was at the time of the Second World War and things were going badly for us. It was an impulse that took me into the recruiting centre. I can't pretend my joining the army made the slightest difference to the course of the war, but it made an enormous difference to me! I was an ambulance driver, serving in France, Belgium, and Germany. My husband, Leon Garfield, was in the medical corps, and we met in an army canteen in Belgium. He too wanted to be either a writer or an artist. As it happened, he became a writer many years before I did.

After the war, I worked as a commercial artist for several years, only stopping when our daughter Jane was born. I had never lost my love of telling stories, and there is no better audience than a child. Soon I began writing again.

Vivien Alcock was in the British Army from 1942 to 1946. Her marriage took place on October 23, 1947. She was an artist at Gestetner Ltd. (a duplicating firm) in London from 1947 to 1953, and worked as a secretary in Whiltington Hospital in London from 1953 to 1958.

The Sylvia Game, Travelers By Night, The Cukoo Sister, and *The Mysterious Mr. Ross* were named Junior Literary Guild selections. Three of her books were named Notable Books of the year by the American Library Association: *Travelers By Night* in 1985, *The Cukoo Sister* in 1986, and *The Monster Garden* in 1988. *The Haunting of Cassie Palmer* was adapted for British television.

SELECTED WORKS: The Haunting of Cassie Palmer, 1982; The Stonewalkers, 1983; The Sylvia Game, 1984; Travelers by Night, 1985; The Cuckoo Sister, 1986; Ghostly Companions: A Feast of Chilling Tales, 1987; The Mysterious Mr. Ross, 1987; The Monster Garden, 1988.

ABOUT: Contemporary Authors, Vol. 110; Kirkpatrick, D.L., ed. Twentieth-Century Children's Writers, 2nd ed.; Something About the Author, Vol. 38; Vol. 45; Times Literary Supplement November 20, 1981; July 23, 1982.

SUE ALEXANDER

August 20, 1933–

AUTHOR OF *Nadia the Willful*, etc.

Autobiographical sketch of Sue Alexander:

IT NEVER occurred to me, as I was growing up, that someday I would write books for anyone to read. Strange as it may sound, though I had started reading before I went to school, until I was twelve I didn't know that books were written by *people*. I never thought about where they came from; all I cared about was that they existed and I could read them. I read all kinds of books: poetry, plays, nonfiction ("true" books I called them), but mostly I read stories.

Stories became even more important to me in third grade, when I started to write them to tell my classmates at recess. Because I was a clumsy child, I was often left out of the games the other children played, but they would happily listen to my stories.

Once I started writing, I couldn't stop. Besides the stories I wrote to tell my classmates, I wrote poems, plays, and stories just for myself. In most of those stories, I was the main character and all the endings were happy—even though the story may have begun with something that had upset me. One of the stories I wrote then began when another girl and I had an argument and she stalked away declaring that we were no longer friends. That afternoon I wrote about two girls who had a fight, made up, and were best friends forever. Writing stories became my way of working out problems.

I read a lot then, too (I still do). Books appealed to me more than playing outside. My father often wondered if I could breathe air that didn't contain printer's ink! An apartment on the North Side of Chicago, Illinois, was my family's home during those years, though I had been born much farther west, in Tucson, Arizona. The landing of that apartment building became part of *Lila on the Landing,* as did the games I made up to play there.

I was still writing stories when I went to college, though I no longer told them to anyone. At Drake University (in Des Moines, Iowa), I enrolled in the School of Journalism, thinking it would be exciting to be a newspaper reporter. There was only one problem. Writing about something that really happened didn't stop me from using my imagination to make the event end the way I *thought* it should—instead of the way it really did. Since that isn't the way newspaper articles are written, my professor suggested that perhaps I shouldn't try to be a reporter—so I studied psychology instead.

Even after I left college I continued to write stories (it was almost as if I needed to write in order to breathe), but it wasn't until the late 1960s that I thought about making writing my life's work. By then I'd been married, had my son Glenn, been divorced, moved to California, married my husband Joel, and had two more children—Marc and Stacey.

Settling down to work in earnest, I quickly discovered that I wanted most of all to write for young people. I also discovered that the stories I'd been writing weren't good enough to be published. It wasn't until I understood that—funny or sad—a story had to begin with something that really mattered to me that I was able to sell anything I wrote.

And that's the way I've continued to write. What I care about, what I wonder about, what makes me sad, what strikes me funny—it's all there; in the stories about *Witch, Goblin and Ghost,* and *Nadia the Willful,* in *World Famous Muriel,* in every one of my books.

I feel very lucky to be able to do something I love so much.

———

Sue Alexander attended Drake University from 1950 to 1952, and Northwestern University from 1952 to 1953. She is a member of the Society of Children's Book Writers, and is on the board of directors of the Southern California Council on Literature for Children and Young People. She has been a book reviewer and contributed material to children's magazines like *Jack and Jill. Finding Your First Job* was named a nonfiction Honor Book in the 1980 Golden Kite Awards by the Society of Children's Book Writers. *Nadia the Willful* was named a 1983 Notable Children's Trade Book in the Field of Social Studies by a joint committee of the National Council on the Social Studies and the Children's Book Council.

SELECTED WORKS: Small Plays for You and a Friend, 1973; Witch, Goblin, and Sometimes Ghost, 1976; More Witch, Goblin and Ghost Stories, 1978; Finding Your First Job, 1980; Witch, Goblin, and Ghost in the Haunted Woods, 1981; Witch, Goblin, and Ghosts Book of Things To Do, 1982; Nadia the Willful, 1983; Dear Phoebe, 1984; World Famous Muriel, 1984; Witch, Goblin, and Ghost Are Back, 1985; World Famous Muriel and the Scary Dragon, 1985; Lila on the Landing, 1987.

ABOUT: Contemporary Authors, Vol. 53; (New Revision Series), Vol. 4; Something About the Author, Vol. 12.

MABEL ESTHER ALLAN

February 11, 1915–

AUTHOR OF *An Island in a Green Sea,* etc

Biographical sketch of Mabel Esther Allan, who also writes under the pen names "Jean Estoril," "Priscilla Hagon," and "Anne Pilgrim":

MABEL ESTHER ALLAN was born in Cheshire, a part of England that is south of the city of Liverpool and west of the border with Wales, in the town of Wallasey. Her mother was Priscilla (Hagon) Allan and her father James Pemberton Allan, a businessman.

She started school at the age of six and attended private schools until she was seventeen. In *To Be an Author: A Short*

Autobiography (Charles Gill & Sons, 1982, not published in the U.S.), she recalls learning to read at an early age and a childhood in which poor eyesight and a lack of books at home and at school could not discourage her desire to read.

At the age of eight, she says, she determined that she would become an author, and by the age of twelve she had composed and typed her first long book. Other novels, short stories, and poetry for children followed, and in 1939 one of her books was accepted for publication. With the coming of World War II, however, publication was delayed.

During the early part of the war she served in the Women's Land Army and then worked as a teacher. Later she was assigned as a nursery school warden responsible for several dozen children.

In 1945 she sold her first book; it was published in 1948. Writing became her full-time career, and by 1957 some of her novels were beginning to be published in the U.S. Many of these books were adventure or mystery stories, and many were set in places other than England.

Mabel Esther Allan has taken great pleasure in traveling, including many visits to the U.S. She has said that geography was a subject that did not interest her in school but that became interesting only as she was able to visit and know foreign places. Rather than write travel books, she has said, she uses her travel experiences to provide atmosphere for her novels. Her stories have been set in London, Scotland, Wales, and Ireland; in New York; and in continental European nations including France, Germany, Italy, Denmark, Holland, and Norway.

Later novels reflect broader interests than geographic ones. *A Strange Enchantment*, for example, describes a wartime England such as that she herself experienced, and *The Mills Down Below* has women's suffrage as its theme.

In her novels, she has said, she has expressed her belief that the education of young people should be based on the concept of self-discipline and that learning should be for its own sake. She has said that from the age of twelve she has pursued her career in writing through her own self-discipline. She also credits her ability to persevere in solitude while writing, her good memory, and her ability to recall the events and feelings of her own childhood.

Mabel Esther Allan has published books with a ballet theme under the name Jean Estoril and other novels under the names Anne Pilgrim and Priscilla Hagon. She has published more than 130 books, all but one of them for children. She has said that the interests of children are her own interests, since it is they for whom she writes. Her books have been translated into many languages.

Both *Island in a Green Sea* and *Time to Go Back* are autobiographical novels. *Mystery in Wales* was a runner-up for a 1972 Edgar Allan Poe Award, which is administered by the Mystery Writers of America. *An Island in a Green Sea* was an Honor Book for fiction in the 1973 Boston Globe-Horn Book Awards.

SELECTED WORKS: Mystery in Wales, 1971; An Island in a Green Sea, 1972; Time to Go Back, 1974; Romansgrove, 1975; The View Beyond My Father, 1978; A Lovely Tomorrow, 1980; The Horns of Danger, 1981; The Mills Down Below, 1981; A Strange Enchantment, 1982; A Dream of Hunger Moss, 1983.

ABOUT: Carpenter, Humphrey and Mari Prichard. The Oxford Companion to Children's Literature; Contemporary Authors, Vol. 5; (New Revision Series), Vol. 2; Vol. 18; The International Authors and Writers Who's Who, 1982; Kirkpatrick, D. L., ed. Twentieth-Century Children's Writers, 2nd ed.; Something About the Author, Vol. 5; Vol. 32; The Writers Directory 1984-86.

LEE JUDAH AMES

January 8, 1921–

AUTHOR OF *Draw 50 Animals*, etc.

Autobiographical sketch of Lee Judah Ames, who also writes and illustrates under the pen name "Jonathan David":

WHEN I WAS FIFTEEN, our family lived in the now notorious East Bronx. In the local public library where I learned to love books, I came across one that completely stunned and delighted me—Washington Irving's *Knickerbocker's History of New York*, illustrated by James Daugherty.

Those illustrations exploded in my mind. That, I decided, was it! I would be a book illustrator. About ten years ago I bought a used copy of the book. Forty years had elapsed since I had first seen it, but it still was magic. One of my few treasures.

And one of these days, I may get around to reading it.

Family stories would have you believe that I drew mothers and babies and baby carriages before I was two. I may well have been some kind of precocious child. I do seem to remember some drawings I'd made between the ages of three and four. Probably, my mind has glorified them to help feed my ego. For certain, I've been driven to draw for as long as I can remember, on brown paper bags, enameled tabletops, anywhere.

After graduating from high school, I applied for and was accepted to work at a job for Walt Disney. At that time, 1939, he was loading the studio for work on *Pinocchio* and *Fantasia*. I was eighteen and almost immediately became homesick. Three months later, I returned home. Nonetheless the experience was impressive, instructive, and altogether enthralling.

Back east, I worked at the Terrytoon Studios, for comic magazines, enlisted in the army, went through World War II, became a second lieutenant, and returned to peacetime.

It was time to fall in love. I did. Since she was foolish enough to accept, I lucked out and married Jocelyn. I designed sweaters, opened (and within a year, closed) an advertising agency, taught at what is now the School of Visual Arts, and on and on.... Then Gertrude Blumenthal (Feldman), Julian Messner's Juvenile Editor, gave me my first book-illustrating opportunity: *Three Conquistadors*, by Shannon Garst (1948).

A few years later Louise Bonino at Random House had me do pictures for *The Pony Express*, by Samuel Hopkins Adams, one of the first ten books in Bennett Cerf's Landmark series. I was a newcomer and unknown. The other nine chosen illustrators, among them Peter Spier's father, Jo Spier, were top artists of that day. One was James Daugherty, my boyhood idol! I still thrill at the memory. As the series grew, Louise had me illustrate six more titles by such authors as Sterling North, John Mason Brown, and Senator Neuberger of Oregon.

Biographies, Golden Books, Westerns, historicals, Girl Scout books, Boy Scout books, how-to's, and textbooks followed, totalling, to date, about 150 titles.

In 1955 Bill Hall at Doubleday hired Roy Gallant and me as a sort of writer-illustrator team. About five years into this lovely experience, during a workless period, Bill suggested I write a book. Thus, *Draw Draw Draw* came to be. The book did well, but Bill's department closed down and I found myself a free lancer again.

Some years later I suggested to Doubleday that I do another book, a step by step how-to-draw book. Unlike others, this one would contain MANY subjects in MANY subject areas. The title: *Draw 175 People, Places, Things and More....*

The contract came through. One hundred ninety-two pages to retail at $3.95 and be published in 1967. Delay followed delay. The title was too long and wrong. How should the subjects be sorted? A table of contents or an index or both? The editor died. A new editor took over and couldn't resolve the problems. That editor died. The next editor, understandably, wanted no part of this: "Lee, keep your first half of the advance and promise not to take the concept elsewhere. I'd like to continue living!"

Busy years followed.

I again thought of doing another book. Doubleday's newest editor, Tom Aylesworth, and I discussed ideas. He surprised me by suggesting we pick up the old contract and go with fifty drawings in one subject area rather than many subjects in many areas, retail $5.95. I said, "Tom, I like you. Please, don't give up your life for a book."

But we went with it, Tom lived, and we produced *Draw 50 Animals.* Thus the "Draw 50" series began. My reasons for being: Jocelyn, the meaning of my life. My children, Alison, Jonathan, Jonathan's wife Cindy, Alison's husband Marty, and the great grandkids: beautiful Hilary, great guy Mark, and her lovely majesty Lauren.

———

Lee Judah Ames was married on June 24, 1945. He was a second lieutenant in the U. S. Army from 1942 to 1944 and has attended Columbia University.

SELECTED WORKS WRITTEN AND ILLUSTRATED: Draw, Draw, Draw, 1962; Draw 50 Animals, 1974; Draw 50 Boats, Ships, Trucks, and Trains, 1977; Draw 50 Famous Faces, 1978; Draw 50 Famous Cartoons, 1979; Make 25 Crayon Drawings of the Circus, 1980; Draw 50 Dogs, 1981; Draw 50 Horses, 1984; Draw 50 Athletes, 1985; Draw 50 Cars, Trucks, and Motorcycles, 1986; Draw 50 Cats, 1986.

SELECTED WORKS ILLUSTRATED: Three Conquistadors, by Shannon Garst, 1948; Irish Red, Son of Big Red, by Jim Kjelgaard, 1951; Circus Parade, by Phyllis R. Fenner, 1954; Abe Lincoln, by Sterling North, 1956; The Quest of Louis Pasteur, by Pat Lauber, 1960; Great Ideas of Science, by Issac Asimov, 1969.

ABOUT: Contemporary Authors, Vol, 1; (New Revision Series), Vol. 3; (New Revision Series), Vol. 18; Kingman, Lee and others, comps. Illustrators of Children's Books: 1957-1966; 1967-1976; Something About the Author, Vol. 3; Viguers, Ruth Hill and others, comps. Illustrators of Children's Books: 1946-1956; Who's Who in America, 1984-85.

GEORGE ANCONA

December 4, 1929–

AUTHOR AND PHOTOGRAPHER OF *I Feel,* etc.

Biographical sketch of George Ancona:

GEORGE ANCONA, photographer, writer, and filmmaker, was born in New York City, the son of Mexican-born parents from the Yucatan. He was raised in the Coney Island section of the city and attended schools there. Although he was taught Spanish before English, he has said, and was immersed in his parents' native culture, the family brought him up as an American. His father's hobby was photography, and as a child Ancona began to draw by copying photographs.

While in junior and senior high school, he became interested in art. His first jobs, however, were as an assistant to an auto mechanic, to a carpenter, and to a sign painter.

During high school he attended classes at the Brooklyn Museum Art School. He also received encouragement from an enthusiastic art teacher who organized an extracurricular "Art Squad" of students and invited former students back to meet with them. After graduation, he visited Mexico for the first time, studying painting and other subjects at the Academy of San Carlos from 1949 to 1950. Back in New York, he studied at the Art Students League and at The Cooper Union.

Ancona began his professional employment in art studios, moving on to art direc-

tion for magazines and in advertising agencies. During the 1950s he worked for such publications as *Esquire* and *Seventeen*. As art director at advertising agencies, he designed ads for NBC television, among other accounts, and worked extensively in designing and directing fashion ads. And, at this time, he began making films.

In 1960, he opened his own studio in New York, as a full-time professional photographer and filmmaker. He produced photography for advertisements in a variety of magazines as well as educational documentaries and industrial films. In 1967 he won a Cine Golden Eagle Award from the Council on International Nontheatrical Events for his film *Reflections*. His *Cities of the Web* received the award in 1972.

After ten years, he moved his studio to his home in Stony Point, New York. In 1970 he published his first book for children, photographs for *Faces*. *Handtalk*, published in 1974, garnered numerous awards and honors. Most of the photographs by Ancona that have been included in his children's books have been black and white; *Handtalk* is one of the few books in color.

In his books, the photographs are displayed in different formats to match the nature of the subject matter and the age of the intended readership. The dramatized accounts of historical subjects such as those on Williamsburg, pioneer life, and the first Thanksgiving record re-created events in great detail, much as a documentary film would.

Some of his books use photography to introduce concepts to younger audiences. These often concentrate on individual faces or objects, with the visual images scattered across the pages. *I Feel*, for example, captures pertinent emotions through images that are largely self-evident and that need few captions. *Bodies* includes X-rays and images magnified by a microscope.

Ancona has an obvious fascination with people, and his books positively convey a multinational, multiracial view of American life. He often spotlights the world of work, taking delight in both the diversity of human occupation and in the pride people take in their work.

In many of his books, particularly those done with Maxine B. Rosenberg, Ancona deals with the natural questions of growing children concerning themselves and their observations of other people. *Being Adopted* paints a warm picture of children who are loved; *Living in Two Worlds* presents the subject of interracial families with warmth and honesty. Ancona is especially successful in using his photographs to treat subjects both openly and sensitively.

In addition to his books for children, Ancona has produced children's films, including some for *Sesame Street*. He has taught at art schools like Parsons School of Design and has traveled widely in his work. He and his second wife, Helen Von Sydow, a writer, have six children and are now grandparents. He is now working on his fifty-first book.

Handtalk was an Honor Book in the Younger Category of the New York Academy of Sciences Book Awards in 1975. It was also an American Library Association Notable Book of 1974 and was named a 1974 Outstanding Science Trade Book for Children by a joint committee of the National Science Teachers Association and the Children's Book Council. *And What Do You Do?* was a Junior Literary Guild selection.

It's a Baby! was an ALA Notable Book of 1979 and a Junior Literary Guild selection. *Dancing Is* was a Junior Literary Guild selection. *My Friend Leslie* was a 1983 ALA Notable Book. *Being Adopted* was a Reading Rainbow book and a 1984 ALA Notable Book. *Monster Movers* was a Junior Literary Guild selection. *Sheepdog* was named a 1985 Notable Children's Trade Book in the Field of Social Studies by a joint committee of the National Council on the Social Studies and the Children's Book Council. *Handtalk Birthday* was named a *New York Times* Best Illustrated Book of 1987. The same year, *Turtle Watch* was named an ALA Notable Book and was a Junior Literary Guild selection.

SELECTED WORKS WRITTEN AND ILLUSTRATED: And What Do You Do?, 1976; I Feel, 1977; Growing Older, 1978; It's a Baby!, 1979; Dancing Is, 1981; Monster Movers, 1983; Sheepdog, 1985; Turtle Watch, 1987; Riverkeeper, 1989.

SELECTED WORKS ILLUSTRATED: Faces, by Barbara Brenner, 1970; Bodies, by Barbara Brenner, 1973; Handtalk: An ABC of Finger Spelling and Sign Language, by Remy Charlip and Mary Beth, 1974; Grandpa Had a Windmill, Grandma Had a Churn, by Louise A. Jackson, 1977; My Friend Leslie: The Story of a Handicapped Child, by Maxine B. Rosenberg, 1983; Being Adopted, by Maxine B. Rosenberg, 1984; Living in Two Worlds, by Maxine B. Rosenberg, 1986; Making a New Home in America, by Maxine B. Rosenberg, 1986; Handtalk Birthday: A Number and Story Book in Sign Language, by Remy Charlip and Mary Beth, 1987; A Williamsburg Household, by Joan Anderson, 1988.

ABOUT: Contemporary Authors, Vol. 53; (New Revision Series), Vol. 4; Something About the Author, Vol. 12.

MARY ANDERSON

January 20, 1939–

AUTHOR OF *Who Says Nobody's Perfect?*, etc.

Autobiographical sketch of Mary Anderson:

OFTEN, when I meet people, they ask what I do. "I'm a writer," I tell them. "What do you write?" they ask. "Children's books," I reply proudly. And sometimes they'll reply, "Well, maybe someday you'll write *real* books for *real* people."

That always makes me laugh because they don't know my secret: that writing for kids is *wonderful* and I wouldn't trade it for anything. Kids are the greatest, most honest, most attentive audience a writer could ever hope to have. And if something's no good, they'll let you know it right away. If something is terrific, they'll let you know that, too. Kids keep a writer honest.

When I was growing up in a Manhattan tenement, books were my windows onto the world (as I know they were for many other poor kids). They expanded my horizon and transported me to the faraway places I never expected to see (and still haven't!). Ironically, the books I read as child weren't children's books. I didn't like children's books. When I was seven, I'd read *Heidi* and *The Adventures of Pinocchio.* Sure, I'd loved them both, but they were so terribly sad that I swore off children's books after that.

Instead, every day after school I'd hurry to the local library and drag out the largest anthologies of plays I could lift. Sometimes, I'd spend an hour just looking through the titles, crippled by indecision about which one to read first. Since I loved plays so much, I thought that meant I'd grow up to be an actress.

When I was twelve, a friend gave me a copy of *Mary Poppins*: the first children's book I'd read in five years. I loved it! Instantly, I rediscovered the enchanting world of children's books and I've been enchanted ever since!

At the time, I still didn't suspect I'd ever write—I was going to be an actress. But while studying acting, I noticed something significant: in every play in which I appeared, I kept *rewriting* my dialogue. So maybe I was a *writer*, not an actress? Maybe; but the idea of writing an entire book seemed impossible. I thought I might manage a short story, though. (So far, I've written over two dozen novels; I've never written a short story.)

And I've never been to college. That's because I was still a teenager when I got married and began to raise a family (three daughters). Although there wasn't time for college, I took lots of evening writing courses. And whenever I had spare time, I'd write. I collected a deskful of rejection slips, but I never gave up. Happily, my first full-length novel for young readers got published and I've been getting published ever since.

I love the solitude of writing. I also like the fact that I can do the laundry, fix dinner, scrub the floor and technically, still be writing (at least in my head!). Most of all, I appreciate the fact that I was able to raise my family, stay at home, and also have a career—thanks to writing. Now, whenever I'm alone, I'm never actually alone. There are always characters creeping around the corners of my mind, talking to me, introducing themselves, pouring out their problems. Some folks might call that being nutty, but I call it being a writer. And I love it!

Mary Anderson was an actress in Off-Broadway productions from 1956 to 1958. She was married March 1, 1958. She has taught creative writing with the Teachers and Writers Collaborative. *I'm Nobody! Who Are You?* and *Who Says Nobody's Perfect?* were Junior Literary Guild selections. *The Rise and Fall of a Teenage Wacko* was a Book-of-the-Month Club selection.

SELECTED WORKS: Matilda Investigates, 1973; I'm Nobody! Who Are You?, 1974; F.T.C. Superstar!, 1976; The Rise and Fall of a Teenage Wacko, 1980; That's Not My Style, 1983; Tune in Tomorrow, 1984; Catch Me, I'm Falling in Love, 1985; Do You Call That a Dream Date?, 1987; The Haunting of Hill Crest, 1987; The Leipzig Vampire, 1987; Who Says Nobody's Perfect?, 1987; The Curse of the Demon, 1989; The Missing Movie Creature, 1989.

ABOUT: Contemporary Authors, Vol. 49; (New Revision Series), Vol. 1; Vol. 16; The International Authors and Writers Who's Who, 1982; Something About the Author, Vol.7.

JAN ANDREWS

June 6, 1942–

AUTHOR OF *Very Last First Time*, etc.

Autobiographical sketch of Jan Andrews:

I HAVE THOUGHT more than once that I would probably never ever have become a writer if I had not come to Canada. Partly, in Canada I seem to have found more chances to do the things I'd never dreamed of. More especially, there is something about the land—the size and the spaces of it—that calls to me with a very particular kind of strength.

In a way, that was true right from the beginning, when I arrived from England with my husband in the city of Saskatoon on the prairies in 1963. I couldn't fully recognize it at first, though. There were too many new things to get used to; there was too much strangeness everywhere.

My first job was at a radio station in Saskatoon writing commercials, but up to that point I'd never thought about "being a writer" and still I didn't then. I kept on "not-thinking" about it too—until I began to tell stories to my children and finally had a story I liked so much I wrote it down. That eventually came to be a book called *Ella the Elephant/Ella Un Éléphant*, but long before it came to be a book—and out of the writing it down somehow—I found there were stories and stories and stories in my head.

For the most part, they have been there ever since, but there have been times too when they've gone away. I think those times are among the most frightening I'll ever live through. Not frightening the way you're frightened by a sudden danger but in a deeper, longer way.

Maybe, a little, that fear is caught up in the moment when the candle goes out and Eva is in the darkness in the story *Very Last First Time*. I'm not certain. Probably I believe that's something for each reader to find out.

I said at the beginning that an important thing for me in Canada is the land. Perhaps then I don't need to say that I'm a wilderness sort of person and go out to be in the mountains or on the rivers or in the forests whenever I can. I have travelled a lot by canoe, but I also have a kayak. I bought this because it's easier for one person so I can go and paddle and camp and travel on my own. I think being on your own is important. I talked about fear earlier but I have never been afraid when I have been in the wilderness by myself. I came to a place once where I arrived exhausted and stepped out of the kayak onto the land and suddenly felt as if I didn't know what tiredness was. Stepping out of the kayak was like coming home.

When I don't have time to get out into the wilderness I go and work in the garden. I like to find the way of it—what will grow where, what won't survive the earwigs, what has to be planted when. I hardly ever wear gardening gloves. I want to get my hands in the earth and feel it. It's all part of the same thing.

I don't only write for a living. I do research for exhibitions and provide programs for festivals and other special events. Even with these things though I feel as if I'm making stories—finding a shape for a telling, plotting the details, creating the world of it, organizing the space.

I don't know if I'll always write stories or make them or even always be a writer. But I hope so. I can't think of any other way I'd rather live.

———

Jan Andrews was born in Shoreham-by-Sea in Sussex, England. She received a B.A. degree from the University of Reading and her M.A. degree from the University of Saskatoon. Married on August 10, 1963, she has two children. In addition to being a writer, she is an editor, a researcher, and a programmer for special events. She is a member of the Writers Union of Canada and the Canadian Society of Children's Authors, Illustrators, and Performers. She received a Canada Council Grant in 1983. She is a contributor to *Cricket* and *Ahoy* magazines.

Very First Last Time was named a Notable Book of 1986 by the American Library Association and a Children's Choice book in 1987 by a joint committee of the International Reading Association and the Children's Book Council. It also earned her a nomination for the Ruth Schwartz Award from the Ontario Arts Council and the Children's Literature Prize from the Canada Council in 1986. It was a Junior Literary Guild Selection.

SELECTED WORKS: Fresh Fish . . . and Chips, 1973; Ella the Elephant/Ella un Éléphant, 1976; Very First Last Time, 1986.

ABOUT: Contemporary Authors, Vol. 122; Something About the Author, Vol. 49.

JUDIE ANGELL

JUDIE ANGELL

July 10, 1937–

AUTHOR OF *In Summertime It's Tuffy*, etc.

Biographical sketch of Judie Angell, who also writes under the pen name "Fran Arrick":

JUDIE ANGELL was born in New York City. Her father was a lawyer and her mother taught school. In December, 1964, she was married to Philip Gaberman, a music arranger and teacher who specializes in pop music and jazz music. She and her husband have two sons, and they reside in a house on a lake in South Salem, New York.

Judie Angell attended Syracuse University and received a Bachelor of Science degree in 1959. After graduating, she became an elementary school teacher in Brooklyn, New York, where she taught for four years.

She was an associate editor for *TV Guide* for two years, through 1963. Her career has also included six years of work for a television station in New York City. She worked for WNDT-TV, which is now WNET-TV, as a continuity writer for the educational station. Her work experiences have also included being a switchboard operator and a waitress. She has said that she wishes she had been a musical comedy star.

Judie Angell has a spectrum of varied interests. She likes to sing and to listen to music. She also likes to paint. She possesses a distinct fondness for cats.

She has used her childhood experiences and her experiences as a teacher in writing books for children and young adults. She has incorporated her experiences of summer camp and the diaries children keep, and writes about things she knows and remembers. She has used her background in writing her books for children and teenagers.

In her book *A Home Is to Share—and Share—and Share*, for the middle-elementary child, three children undertake the rescue of an animal shelter in danger of closing, and learn about family spirit and about adopted children. In *In Summertime It's Tuffy*, eleven-year-old Tuffy details the humorous exploits she instigates during a summer at camp. Judie Angell is not afraid to tackle the more sobering issues that affect children and young people. Divorce, adoption, and runaway children as well as the problems of "just being a teen-ager" are all subjects she has treated in her popular books. For instance, in *What's Best for You,* a split-up family copes with the problems that arise despite the fact that everyone wants the best for everyone else. *One-Way to Ansonia* is a young adult novel, the story of a strong-willed sixteen-year-old determined to improve her situation in life for herself and her baby. In the book, Angell incorporates the experiences of her grandmother, who lived in New York in the late 1800s. The book was named a 1985 Best Book for Young Adults by the American Library Association.

Judie Angell also writes under the name Fran Arrick, writing novels that concern the darker, harsher aspects of being a teenager. *Steffie Can't Come Out to Play* deals with a runaway who, filled with dreams of becoming a fashion model, falls prey to a handsome man who turns her into a prostitute. The ALA named the book a 1978 Best Book for Young Adults. *Tunnel Vision* deals with the issue of teenage suicide, and in *Chernowitz!*, anti-Semitism infects a small community and the author confronts the issue on a larger scale in our society. In *Voice of Youth Advocates,* Dorothy M. Broderick states, " . . . a book that raises that many questions must be bought and discussed. It should be in the hands of history teachers and those dealing with values education and human relations."

God's Radar deals with the biases of fundamentalist, evangelical Christians who gradually bring Roxie Cable's family under their compelling influence. This book, too, was named an ALA Best Book for Young Adults, in 1983. In addition to her novels, Angell has a short story represented in the anthology *Sixteen: Short Stories by Outstanding Writers for Young Adults,* edited by Donald R. Gallo, "Turmoil in a Blue and Beige Bedroom."

SELECTED WORKS: In Summertime It's Tuffy, 1977; Tina Gogo, 1978; Secret Selves, 1979; A Word from Our Sponsor or My Friend Alfred, 1979; What's Best for You, 1981; The Buffalo Nickel Blues Band, 1982; First the Good News, 1983; A Home Is to Share . . . and Share . . . and Share, 1984; One-Way to Ansonia, 1985.

SELECTED WORKS AS FRAN ARRICK: Steffie Can't Come Out to Play, 1978; Tunnel Vision, 1979; Chernowitz!, 1981; God's Radar, 1983.

ABOUT: Contemporary Authors, Vol. 77; Something About the Author, Vol. 22.

JOHN ARCHAMBAULT

CO-AUTHOR OF *The Ghost-Eye Tree*, etc.

Biographical sketch of John Archambault:

JOHN ARCHAMBAULT was born and raised in and near Pasadena, California. He received his B.A. degree from the University of California in 1981. He has also attended Columbia Teacher's College. His favorite book as a child was E.B. White's *Charlotte's Web*, which he now acknowledges as an influence on his writing.

He is a poet, and journalist, and a storyteller. He writes children's books with Bill Martin, Jr., and they combined their disparate childhood memories when they worked on *The Ghost-Eye Tree.* Reviewer Ann A. Flowers, writing in *The Horn Book Magazine,* called it "a splendidly theatrical book for storytelling and reading aloud." The same writer called *Knots on a Counting Rope* an "emotional, affecting . . . beautiful . . . story."

Archambault also writes poetry and educational books. He has traveled in Europe and the Middle East. He lives in Riverside, California.

The Ghost-Eye Tree was an Irma Simonton Black Honor Book for 1985, so named by the Bank Street College of Education. *The Ghost-Eye Tree* and *Barn Dance!* were named Children's Choice Books by a joint committee of the International Reading Association and the Children's Book Council, in 1986 and 1987 respectively. The two books, as well as *Knots on a Counting Rope,* were also Reading Rainbow Books. *Knots* was named a 1987 Notable Children's Trade Book in the Field of Social Studies by a joint committee of the CBC and the National Council on the Social Studies.

JOHN ARCHAMBAULT

Three videotapes of poetry and storytelling by Archambault, Bill Martin, Jr., and a guitarist have been produced by DLM Publishers.

SELECTED WORKS WRITTEN WITH BILL MARTIN, JR.: The Ghost-Eye Tree, 1985; Barn Dance!, 1986; White Dynamite and Curly Kidd, 1986; Here Are My Hands, 1987; Knots on a Counting Rope, 1987; Listen to the Rain, 1988; Up and Down on the Merry-Go-Round, 1988.

BRENT ASHABRANNER

November 3, 1921–

AUTHOR OF Dark Harvest: Migrant Farmworkers in America, etc.

Autobiographical sketch of Brent Ashabranner:

DON'T TRY to tell me that what you read as a boy doesn't influence your later life. I grew up in a small Oklahoma town; but from the time I could read, I ranged far beyond that friendly little farming community. I was hooked on books about foreign places. I devoured Kipling, practically memorized Beau Geste, and couldn't get enough of the travel adventures of Richard Halliburton. The owner of the town's tiny bookstore asked me to lug boxes around one afternoon. My reward was the pick of any book on the shelves. I remember that I took Alex Waugh's Hot Countries. It was a bit hard going for a boy of thirteen, but I had sweated for the book, and I read it.

I first tried my hand at writing at the age of eleven. Under the spell of a book called Bomba the Jungle Boy, I decided to write Barbara the Jungle Girl. By page three I was hopelessly bogged down in the plot and gave up, but it was a beginning. I never stopped writing after that. I became editor of the school newspaper and wrote most of the stories. When I was a junior in high school, I won fourth prize in a Scholastic magazine national short story writing contest. My story was about a young man who becomes a world champion professional prizefighter. I recently reread the story and, after so many years, it seemed to me not a bad imitation of Damon Runyon for a sixteen-year-old boy who had never been out of Oklahoma.

World War II got me out of Oklahoma and into the Navy for three years. I saw some of the world—Hawaii, the Philip-

Ashabranner: ASH-a-branner

pines, Japan—that I had only read about before; but after the war I came back to Oklahoma, finished my education at Oklahoma State University, and taught English there for several years. I kept on writing and published over a hundred stories and articles about the American West. It looked as if I was settling in for a career of teaching and writing in my native state.

Then, out of the blue, I had a change to go to Africa under the old Point Four foreign aid program. All of the Kipling, Wren, Halliburton, Edgar Rice Burroughs, and H. Ryder Haggard I had read as a boy came flooding back. With my wife's enthusiastic agreement, we packed our bags, convinced our two young daughters that they were in for a big adventure, and headed for Africa. We never got back to Oklahoma except for an occasional visit.

Two years in Ethiopia were followed by two in Libya, working with ministries of education in developing reading materials for their schools. Then I joined the Peace Corps staff, started the Peace Corps program in Nigeria, and was director of the Peace Corps in India when it had the world's largest program with over 750 volunteers. After that I worked for the Ford Foundation in the Philippines and Indonesia.

But no matter where I was or what I was doing, I have always had another life as a writer. The things I felt was learning about understanding other cultures and about people of different cultures understanding each other seemed worth sharing with young readers. While overseas, I wrote or coauthored a book of Ethiopian folk tales, nonfiction books about West Africa and American foreign aid around the world, a novel set in Nigeria, the retelling of a desert epic. I wrote *A Moment in History* to tell the story of the first ten years of the Peace Corps.

Since returning to the United States to live, I have devoted most of my time to writing and have concentrated on nonfiction. I now write mostly, but not exclusive-

ly, about minorities—including American Indians—and growing ethnic groups in America. I believe that my years of living and working overseas have helped me to understand better their hopes, desires, frustrations, and fears.

Writing about people whose voices need to be heard—immigrants, refugees, migrant farm workers, Native Americans—making clear that their lives have value and that they have a right to a decent life, is work that I love. I feel it is exactly what I should be doing at this point in my life.

A delightful bonus is that my family has been able to be a part of my writing. My wife Martha frequently travels with me, helps with interviews, and has taken photographs for some of my books. My daughter Melissa has collaborated with me on two books, one of which, *Into a Strange Land*, won a Christopher Award. My daughter Jennifer took all of the photographs for my recent book about the Vietnam Veterans Memorial, *Always to Remember*. Indeed, I am thinking about starting the Ashabranner family cottage industry of young readers' books.

———

Brent Ashabranner was born in Shawnee, Oklahoma and grew up in Bristow. He was in the U.S. Navy from 1942 to 1945. He received his B.S. degree in English in 1948 and his M.A. in English in 1952, both from Oklahoma State University. He taught English there for several years. He traveled under the auspices of the U.S. International Cooperation Administration and was Deputy Director of the Peace Corps in Washington, D.C. from 1967 to 1969.

Morning Star, Black Sun received the Carter G. Woodson Book Award in 1983 from the National Council for the Social Studies. *The New Americans* was named a Notable Book of 1983 by the American Library Association. *To Live in Two Worlds* was named an ALA Best Book for Young Adults of the year 1984 and received the Carter G. Woodson Book Award in 1985.

Gavriel and Jamal was an ALA Notable Book of 1984. All four of these books were selections of the Junior Literary Guild and were named Notable Children's Trade Books in the Field of Social Studies in their years of publication by a joint committee of the Children's Book Council and the National Council on the Social Studies.

Dark Harvest was named a Boston Globe-Horn Book Awards Honor Book in nonfiction in 1986. It also won a Carter G. Woodson Book Award in the same year. *Into a Strange Land* was a Junior Literary Guild selection. Both of these books, as well as *Children of the Maya*, were named ALA Notable Books and Notable Children's Trade Books in the Field of Social Studies, in their years of publication. *Children of the Maya* was also named an Honor Book for the Jane Addams Children's Book Award in 1987. *The Vanishing Border* was a Junior Literary Guild selection and a Notable Children's Trade Book in the Field of Social Studies.

Always to Remember was named a 1988 Best Books for Young Adults and a 1988 Notable Book by the ALA.

SELECTED WORKS: Morning Star, Black Sun: The Northern Cheyenne Indians and American's Energy Crisis, 1982; The New Americans: Changing Patterns in U.S. Immigration, 1983; Gavriel and Jemal: Two Boys of Jerusalem, 1984; To Live in Two Worlds: American Indian Youth Today, 1984; Dark Harvest: Migrant Farmworkers in America, 1985; Children of the Maya: A Guatemalan Indian Odyssey, 1986; The Vanishing Border: A Photographic Journey Along Our Frontier with Mexico, 1987; Always to Remember: The Story of the Vietnam Veterans Memorial, 1988.

SELECTED WORKS WITH MELISSA ASHABRANNER: Into a Strange Land: Unaccompanied Refugee Youth in America, 1987; Counting America: The Story of the U.S. Census, 1989.

ABOUT: Contemporary Authors, Vol. 5; (New Revision Series), Vol. 10; Something About the Author, Vol. 1.

LYNNE REID BANKS

AUTHOR OF *The Indian in the Cupboard,* etc.

Autobiographical sektch of Lynne Reid Banks:

OFTEN, students ask me: "When did you begin to write?" I usually reply, "When I was a lot younger than you."

I have a letter I wrote to my mother from a holiday I took when I was about seven. I described a conversation that was taking place in the same railway carriage, between another little girl and her nanny. The child had been promised that if she was good, she could have a donkey ride when they got to the seaside. Every time the train stopped, she would ask in a whiney little voice: "Is the donkey here?" "No, dear, not yet," the nurse would reply, patiently at first. "Can I see the donkey now?" "Donkey won't be here if you get off now." "Here? Here? Is the donkey here?" And so on, till the poor nanny lost patience and shouted, "If you say 'donkey' once more, I shall throw you out of the window!"

Now, I don't believe she really said that. But I wrote it, to bring the scene to a satisfactory climax. Even so early in my life, I was shaping truth to make a better story.

Perhaps because writing seemed so easy to me, as natural as breathing almost, because it was such *fun*, I never thought of it as a career. Careers had to be Serious, Earnest and Hard. I was going to be an actress like my mother. And as soon as I was old enough—after World War II, which I spent in Canada as an evacuee—I went to drama school (three of them, as a matter of fact) to learn acting, singing, dancing, and all kinds of stagecraft.

I adored every minute of it. I bore even the jealousies, the disappointments, the rivalries because they were part of being an actress. I was going to take the theatre by storm! Little did any of us know the heartbreaks and hardships ahead. Very few of us made it. The vast majority of my fellow stu-

LYNNE REID BANKS

dents left the profession—we simply couldn't make a living. But the techniques I had mastered turned out to be far more use to me in other careers, later.

When I found myself in Israel, many years later, teaching English to Hebrew-speaking children, how glad I was that I had learned to project confidence (even when I didn't feel it!) After half-a-day's training I was thrust before my first class, and all I had to help me was my knowledge of mime, movement, voice-projection, audience control, and drama. Every lesson was a performance—how else could I make them understand me? And it worked. I was more successful at teaching than I ever was on the stage—but I used all the same techniques.

And later, when I left Israel and became a full-time writer, all that experience was recycled yet again. I wrote many books about Israel. I also became a speaker. Performing again! Life is always eating its own tail!

I had learned a fundamental lesson. Nothing one ever learns is wasted. And for writers, there's something more: nothing one ever experiences or feels is wasted. Even the bad things, the negative emotions, that most people try to push away and forget: anger, bitterness, humiliation, failure, shock, grief . . . While one is suffering them, I mean at the time, a little voice is saying: "Hold on to it. Remember." Because one day you may need it. Not to write it down just as it happened to you—oh no! That would be autobiography! But to transmute it into the stuff of *fiction*, to feed it into your characters so that what moved you can move them, and in the end, move the readers.

And my children's books use all these aspects of myself and my life, as much as adult ones. Sometimes children write to me about some of the 'bad' things in the Indian in the Cupboard books. Why did Tommy and Boone's horse have to die? Why is Patrick sometimes not a good friend? Why does Boone drink and swear? Why doesn't Omri have sisters instead of brothers? Why, in other words, isn't everything perfect?

Because I'm not perfect, and because life isn't perfect—that's why. Because if I used only the nice, admirable parts of myself, instead of sometimes the spiteful, violent, hurt parts, I would be lying about the real world.

But (do I hear you say?) you lied about the nanny in the train. Not in a story, but in a letter to your mother! You wanted her to believe what wasn't true.

Oh dear. Well, the truth was, everyone in the carriage was ready to throw the whingeing little wretch out of the window. That was what I wished the nanny would say, so I made it happen in the letter and I felt better. And that says a lot about why and how I write fiction!

————

Lynne Reid Banks was born in London and was evacuated to Saskatchewan, Canada during World War II. She was educated at the Royal Academy of Dramatic Art in London, graduating in 1949, and was an actress for five years. She has worked as a journalist and was the first woman reporter on British television. In 1962 she emigrated to Israel, where she lived in a kibbutz, and was married in 1965. She has three children. Banks is the author of twenty-five books, including volumes of Jewish history. She now resides in England, where she writes full-time and occasionally acts on radio.

The Return of the Indian was a Junior Literary Guild selection. *Dark Quartet: The Story of the Brontës* was named a Best Book for Young Adults by the American Library Association for the year 1977. Her adult novel, *The L-Shaped Room*, is widely read by young adults.

SELECTED WORKS: One More River, 1973; Sarah and After: The Matriarchs, 1975; The Farthest-Away Mountain, 1977; Dark Quartet: The Story of the Brontës, 1977; My Darling Villain, 1977; The Indian in the Cupboard, 1981; The Writing on the Wall, 1982; The Return of the Indian, 1986; The Fairy Rebel, 1988; I, Houdini: The Autobiography of a Self-Educated Hamster, 1988; Melusine: A Mystery, 1989.

ABOUT: Carpenter, Humphrey and Mari Prichard, eds. The Oxford Companion to Children's Literature; Contemporary Novelists, 1976; The International Authors and Writers Who's Who, 1982; Kirkpatrick, D.L., ed. Twentieth-Century Children's Writers, 2nd ed.

JUDI BARRETT

AUTHOR OF *Cloudy with a Chance of Meatballs*, etc.

Biographical sketch of Judi Barrett:

JUDI BARRETT was born in Brooklyn. She attended Pratt Institute in Brooklyn, where she received her B.F.A. degree. She began teaching art to children and continued her education with graduate courses at the Bank Street College of Education, and pottery and painting classes at the Brooklyn Museum. She has taught art to children at Packer Collegiate Institute, a private school in Brooklyn Heights, and at Berkeley Carroll School in Brooklyn. She has also taught classes at the Brooklyn Museum and at the Metropolitan Museum of Art in Manhattan.

Since 1974, she has been a reviewer for *The New York Times*. She is also a free-lance designer. She enjoys gardening and collecting antiques, including old books, as well as new books, and attending concerts at Carnegie Hall. She lives in Brooklyn.

In her books, Barrett takes a whimsical view of the world. By starting with an idea and adding "suppose," as in "suppose animals wore clothing?" or "suppose it rained food?", she presents a new world of imaginative possibilities.

Old MacDonald Had an Apartment House was the first of her new looks at an old idea. This book was illustrated by her former husband, Ron Barrett. They collaborated on a series of books, including *Cloudy with a Chance of Meatballs*. In the book, the town of Chewandswallow gets its meals from the weather, a satisfactory arrangement until the weather turns ugly. The book was named a *New York Times* Best Illustrated Book of 1978 as well as a Children's Choice Book, designated by a joint committee of the Children's Book Council and the International Reading Association.

Her *A Snake Is Totally Tail*, which was illustrated by Lonni Sue Johnson, was selected for the Graphic Gallery, a showcase of excellent books honored by *The Horn Book Magazine*. Both *Benjamin's 365 Birthdays* and *Peter's Pocket* were named Junior Literary Guild selections. Two of her books received American Institute of Graphic Arts Book Show Awards, *Benjamin's 365 Birthdays* in 1975 and *Cloudy with a Chance of Meatballs* in 1979.

SELECTED WORKS WRITTEN AND ILLUSTRATED: What's Left?, 1983.

SELECTED WORKS WRITTEN: Old MacDonald Had an Apartment House, 1969; Animals Should Definitely *Not* Wear Clothing, 1970; An Apple a Day, 1973; Benjamin's 365 Birthdays, 1974; Peter's Pocket, 1974; I Hate to Take a Bath, 1975; I Hate to Go to Bed, 1977; The Wind Thief, 1977; Cloudy with a Chance of Meatballs, 1978; Animals Should Definitely *Not* Act Like People, 1980; A Snake Is Totally Tail, 1983; Pickles Have Pimples, 1986.

ABOUT: Contemporary Authors, Vol. 103; Horn Book November/December 1986; Something About the Author, Vol. 26; The Writers Directory 1988-90.

RON BARRETT

July 25, 1937–

ILLUSTRATOR OF *Cloudy with a Chance of Meatballs*, etc.

Autobiographical sketch of Ron Barrett:

IT MUST BE THE BRONX was a most backwards part of New York City. We didn't have children's books. At bedtime my mother read me her shopping list or laundry ticket. I can still remember *Quart of Milk and the Three Lamb Chops* and the wonderful *Seven White Shirts, No Starch.*

We had comic books. My father, James Aloysius, would leave Donald Duck comics next to my lunch plate. He wanted to work for Walt Disney, but instead of going to Hollywood, he went to pieces. He got his pieces to work in a liquor store, where he made funny signs. How could the hold-up men aim straight if they were laughing?

We had newspapers. My father introduced me to Jiggs, Snuffy Smith, Smokey Stover and all the others who lived stacked up in the little boxes on the funny pages. He drew them for me and wrote to their creators, asking for drawings, pretending to be me. And I pretended to be him.

I spent lots of time in my room, fighting World War II with crayons. (A pencil point makes a devastating hole in a Nazi dive bomber.) If I dared to go out, it was to pretend I was French twins or attend a rehearsal of my country-western band, The Hudson River Valley Boys.

After the Japanese surrendered to me, I attended the High School of Industrial Art. It was a nutty school that brought together the artistic talent of the five boroughs to dance to doo-wop, drool over *Mad* comics and become teenage commerical artists.

I was given a scholarship to the Society of Illustrators' Saturday art classes, and Ervine Metzl, the Society's president and Ludwig Bemelman's ghost artist, became my mentor. He taught me the meaning of "Snoddery Oscar" (rubber cement pickup).

At school, a teacher, J. I. Beigeleisen, arranged for me to become an apprentice in the atelier of Lucian Bernhard, a titan who stood astride modern poster design, with one foot in Munich, 1920, and one foot next to Caruso's Hair Salon on 55th Street, 1954. It was the rule that all work had to bear the mark of the artist, that all lettering look as though it were hewn out of stone.

I liked high school so much, I wanted to do it all over again, so I went to Pratt Institute. It lacked the soul of an all-city school, but it had Herschel Levit, who tried to expand our awareness of art to include Peruvian textiles and classical music, which we found impossible to dance to.

I left Pratt wanting to be an art director, not an artist. It was an exciting time to be in advertising. Art directors and writers were throwing out the pretty, superficial accretions of the 50s and creating a new advertising that was human, direct, disarming, and witty. I was fortunate to work where it was being done best, at Young & Rubicam and at Carl Ally.

I also worked at an innovative place in the evening—the kitchen table. There, with my then wife, Judith Bauman Barrett, we created *Old MacDonald Had an Apartment House* and *Animals Should Definitely* Not *Wear Clothing.*

Finally, in 1972, after twelve years of Madison Avenue, I left for a loft in New York's Little Italy, to live *la vie Boheme,* to continue to work on children's books—*Benjamin's 365 Birthdays, Bible Stories You Can't Forget (No Matter How Hard You Try)*—to write and draw for the *National Lampoon,* and to avoid the cross-fire of gangland rub-outs.

Crouching low, I accepted a consultant-ship at the Children's Television Workshop and was art director and editor of the first two years of *The Electric Company Magazine* (now *Kid City*).

Aspiring to the middle class, I moved up-town and opened my own atelier, where I teach the meaning of "Snoddery Oscar." There I've drawn *Cloudy with a Chance of Meatballs, The Daily Blab, Hi-Yo Fido* and other works of humor for children, as well as *The Encyclopedia Placematica* for adults.

By the way, I've also found the instructions for my life (some assembly required): my now wife, Barbara Schubeck, and I have become the parents of Rebecca and Jessica. Charmed, I'm sure.

———

Ron Barrett received his B.F.A. degree from Pratt Institute in Brooklyn in 1959. He was an instructor there from 1970 to 1972. His art was exhibited at the Musee Des Arts Decoratif at The Louvre in Paris in 1973.

Benjamin's 365 Birthdays appeared in the American Institute of Graphic Arts Children's Book Show for 1973/74. *Cloudy with a Chance of Meatballs* was a *New York Times* Best Illustrated Book of the Year 1978. It was also a 1979 Children's Choice Book, designated by a joint committee of the International Reading Association and the Children's Book Council. *Old MacDonald* was also in an AIGA Children's Book Show.

SELECTED WORKS WRITTEN AND ILLUSTRATED: The Daily Blab, 1981; Hi Yo, Fido!, 1984.

SELECTED WORKS ILLUSTRATED: Old MacDonald Had an Apartment House, by Judi Barrett, 1969; Animals Should Definitely *Not* Wear Clothing, by Judi Barrett, 1970; Benjamin's 365 Birthdays, by Judi Barrett, 1974; Bible Stories You Can't Forget (No Matter How Hard You Try), by Marshall Efron and Alfa-Betty Olsen, 1976; Cloudy with a Chance of Meatballs, by Judi Barrett, 1978; Animals Should Definitely *Not* Act Like People, by Judi Barrett, 1980; Chicken Trek: The Third Strange Thing that Happened to Oscar Noodleman, by Stephen Manes, 1987; Ghastlies, Goops and Pincushions, by X.J. Kennedy, 1989.

ABOUT: Kingman, Lee and other, comps. Illustrators of Children's Books: 1967-1976; Something About the Author, Vol. 14.

NICOLA BAYLEY

August 18, 1949–

COMPILER AND ILLUSTRATOR OF *Nicola Bayley's Book of Nursery Rhymes,* etc.

Biographical sketch of Nicola Bayley:

NICOLA BAYLEY was born in Singapore, but spent part of her childhood in Hampshire, England. There she attended boarding school. She had "growing pains" and wasn't allowed to participate in sports, so she was allowed to spend her afternoons in the art room. Her parents encouraged her in her artwork. She originally wanted to be a fashion designer and studied graphic design courses at St. Martin's School of Art in London. She continued her education at the Royal College of Art in London. There she was encouraged by the well-known children's book illustrator Quentin Blake. She received her diploma from the College in 1974. She was married December 21, 1979. Following graduation she worked at Jonathan Cape publishers in London and then compiled her first book, *Nicola Bayley's Book of Nursery Rhymes.* This was quickly successful, and she began her career as an illustrator with *The Tyger Voyage*.

Bayley has had her work exhibited at St. Martin's School of Art from 1967 to 1971, and at Royal College of Art Graduate Exhibitions from 1971 to 1974.

She now lives in London, working in the studio once used by Arthur Rackham. She prefers to use watercolors on cartridge paper for her illustrations, employing a technique called stippling, which consists of dotting the paint onto the surface. Bayley enjoys painting animals, but her favorite is the cat. She has only one, named Desdemona, but plans on having more.

The Patchwork Cat was named a 1982 Children's Choice Book by a joint committee of the Children's Book Council and the International Reading Association. It won a Bologna Book Fair Prize in 1983 and was named a "Commended" book by the 1981 Kate Greenway Medal judges. *The Mouldy* was a runner-up for a 1983 Kurt Maschler Award, presented by The Book Trust in London.

SELECTED WORKS COMPILED AND ILLUSTRATED: Nicola Bayley's Book of Nursery Rhymes, 1977; One Old Oxford Ox, 1977; Copycats, 1984; As I Was Going Up and Down: and Other Nonsense Rhymes, 1986; Hush-a-Bye Baby: and Other Bedtime Rhymes, 1986.

SELECTED WORKS ILLUSTRATED: The Tyger Voyage, by Richard Adams, 1976; Puss-in-Boots, adapted by Christopher Logue, 1977; La Corona and the Tin Frog, by Russell Hoban, 1981; The Patchwork Cat, by William Mayne, 1981; The Mouldy, by William Mayne, 1983.

ABOUT: Carpenter, Humphrey and Mari Prichard. The Oxford Companion to Children's Literature; Contemporary Authors, Vol. 118; Herdig, Walter, ed., Graphis 4th International Survey of Children's Book Illustration, 1979 (Publication No. 156); Kingman, Lee and others, comps. Illustrators of Children's Books: 1967-1976; Something About the Author, Vol. 41.

MONIKA BEISNER

AUTHOR AND ILLUSTRATOR OF *Secret Spells and Curious Charms*, etc.

Biographical sketch of Monika Beisner:

MONIKA BEISNER, an artist who lives in London and Malta, is the author and illustrator of a number of intriguing books for children. With an illustrative style that has been characterized as sleek and sophisticated, Beisner creates beautiful illustrations to accompany mythical texts. She provided the pictures for two books by Alison Lurie, *Fabulous Beasts* and *The Heavenly Zoo*. Of *Fabulous Beasts* Ann Flowers, in *The Horn Book Magazine*, wrote that the illustrations "glow with brilliant color . . . almost achieving the appearance of a medieval illumination." Each page is home to a variety of strange and wonderful creatures, and there is a wealth of detail in every corner of Beisner's landscapes. Patricia Dooley, wrote in *School Library Journal*, "Besides unforgettable and unexpected details of the aspect, habits and history of these creatures . . . the small, glowing, meticulous portraits leave no doubt as to the fabulous reality of the beasts described."

Beisner explored mythical themes once again in *Secret Spells and Curious Charms*, which Dooley called a "collection of magical lore in verse and prose." Included in this compilation for the novice occultist are love potions, a spell for revenge, and the formula for flying, as well as brief charms to dispel superstitions about such objects as four-leaf clovers, fig trees, eggshells, and pins. In *Growing Point*, reviewer Margery Fisher wrote, "here are snatches of country lore and popular belief on pages textured to suggest illuminated parchment, decorated with exquisite spray-painted pictures. . . . In detail and in the total visual effect of scenes, a book for the connoisseur." Children can pore over each page, discovering a new aspect of Beisner's mysterious worlds at every reading. Mary Burns of *The Horn Book Magazine* praises *Secret Spells and Curious Charms* for the "enigmatic, surreal paintings, filled with symbols and arranged in handsome, decorative patterns," and writes, "the book is not the usual compilation of folklore and learning. Rather, it demands attention and a willingness to discard linear analysis for allusion and metaphor."

Beisner's book of improbable situations, such as a sheep shearing a shepherd, *Topsy Turvy*, won the admiration of a *School Library Journal* reviewer: "this elegantly designed, imaginatively-stimulating picture book [is] reminscent of a 19th-Century miniaturist's style."

SELECTED WORKS WRITTEN AND ILLUSTRATED: Monika Beisner's Book of Riddles, 1984; Secret Spells and Curious Charms, 1985; Topsy Turvy: The Book of Upside Down, 1988.

SELECTED WORKS ILLUSTRATED: The Heavenly Zoo, by Alison Lurie, 1980; Fabulous Beasts, by Alison Lurie, 1981.

ABOUT: Herdeg, Walter, ed. Graphis 3rd International Survey of Children's Book Illustration, 1975 (Publication No. 140).

JAY BENNETT

JAY BENNETT

December 24, 1912–

AUTHOR OF *The Long Black Coat*, etc.

Biographical sketch of Jay Bennett:

IN SPITE of the fact that Jay Bennett—in his wife's words "a child who will never grow up"— readily admits he has always been "intensely interested in the young and their problems and hopes," he is not sure what in his background compelled him to turn to writing for that audience.

From the time he was born, he lived in Brooklyn, New York, with his father, a Russian immigrant; his mother; and five siblings. After a year of public schooling, Bennett enrolled in a Hebrew Institute, where students were provided with a firm grounding in Hebrew, Jewish culture, and the Old Testament along with more conventional academic subjects. It was during this time, Bennett reflects, that a "life-enduring influence" entered his life: the great Hebrew prophets. He also recalls the strong support of a teacher of English,

who impressed upon young Bennett the power and importance of literature.

Because the Hebrew Institute did not offer high school courses, he eventually transferred to a public school and then attended New York University for a few years. But partly, perhaps, because of the Depression's influence, he became disillusioned with his formal education and began wandering the country, hitching rides on highways, traveling in boxcars on freight trains, and sleeping occasionally in flophouses or even in jails, when he wanted to break the monotony. When he finally returned to New York, the Depression was still on, but Bennett was lucky enough to get another job in his string of miscellaneous positions that included working as a farmhand, factory worker, lifeguard, mailman, salesman, senior encyclopedia editor, and even writer and editor at the Office of War Information.

His writing days actually officially began with a play—begun at the age of 16 and then abandoned. But 2 years later he did start writing seriously, and for 14 years, while supporting himself in whatever way he could, working at one of the previously mentioned positions, he produced poetry, approximately 150 short stories, several novels, and 5 stage plays.

In 1969, following a long stint of writing for television and radio and creating his three adult novels, *Catacombs, Murder Money,* and *Death Is a Silent Room,* Bennett produced *Deathman, Do Not Follow Me,* his first young adult book. His concern for the reactions of the young and their ability to cope with an increasingly complex world made him intent on communicating with them. And what better way than through suspense novels?" While Bennett's books have occasionally been criticized for their lack of in-depth characterization and for their melodrama, their high achievement of successful suspense has put the author at the forefront of young adult mystery writing, earning him two Edgar Allan Poe Awards from the Mystery Writers of America for best juvenile mystery novel—in 1974 for *The Long Black Coat* and in 1975 for *The Dangling Witness.* An *English Journal* critic stated that in *Deathman, Do Not Follow Me,* "the author portrays unbearable suspense with a sinister quality, while at the same time he demonstrates a warm recognition of what constitutes the long, long thoughts of a loner." *The Horn Book Magazine* called *Pigeon* "fast-paced and exciting," and *The Long Black Coat* was labeled a "taut, uncluttered thriller," by *Kirkus Reviews. The Birthday Murderer,* according to *Publishers Weekly,* "earns high grades for its atmosphere of suspense and menace."

Bennett attempts to speak to loners in his books, trying to make them see the importance of reaching out to other people. In general, the novels spotlight a male high-school or college student who has inadvertently become involved in a murder or theft of some sort. But despite the books' subject matter, Bennett firmly attests that he abhors violence and tries never to trivialize death, as so often is done in contemporary television and cinema. For him plot occupies the most important slot; he attempts to grip his readers from the beginning and hold on to them throughout the entire story. In *Masks: A Love Story* and *I Never Said I*

Loved You he also tried his hand at love stories.

Bennett, whose works have been translated into 16 foreign languages, is married and lives with his wife in Brooklyn, New York.

SELECTED WORKS: Deathman, Do Not Follow Me, 1969; The Deadly Gift, 1969; Masks: A Love Story, 1971; The Killing Tree, 1972; The Long Black Coat, 1973; The Dangling Witness, 1974; Shadows Offstage, 1974; Say Hello to the Hit Man, 1976; The Birthday Murderer, 1977; The Pigeon, 1980; The Executioner, 1982; Slowly, Slowly I Raise the Gun, 1983; I Never Said I Loved You, 1984; To Be a Killer, 1985; The Skeleton Man, 1986; The Haunted One, 1987.

ABOUT: Contemporary Authors (New Revision Series), Vol. 5; Contemporary Literary Criticism, Vol. 35; Donelson, Kenneth L. and Alleen Pace Nilsen. Literature for Today's Young Adults; Something About the Author, Vol. 41; Something About the Author Autobiography Series, Vol. 4; Who's Who in America, 1978–1979.

BARBARA HELEN BERGER

March 1, 1945–

AUTHOR OF *Grandfather Twilight*, etc.

Autobiographical sketch of Barbara Helen Berger:

MAKING a children's book, the words and pictures together, fulfills a thought I had one day as a child. I don't know how old I was. But I do know that ever since I could hold a crayon, I loved to draw and paint. My sister and I spent many hours together drawing. It was a custom in our family to each make a special picture for our mother for Christmas. Dad took us "in secret" to his studio and gave us paints to use. Then he would frame our pictures. Mom hung them in the kitchen, year after year, until there was no more room on the wall.

Dad was working as a medical illustrator and photographer. He loves to make things and is a wonderful artist. I still use methods I first learned standing by his drawing table, watching him work, asking questions but trying not to bother him. When I was

Berger: *BER jer*

Barbara Helen Berger

old enough, he gave me small jobs to do, like retouching photographs. And he let me draw the skeleton he kept, whom we called Mr. Bones.

Meanwhile, Mom got up early in the morning to write poetry. She shared her love of language with us. Whenever she read aloud the words sang, whether she read from a Greek myth, or *Stuart Little*, or "Jabberwocky" (which she knew in French). She told me all about metaphor, rhythm, and rhyme, and how you can paint images in words.

I wrote poems too, and tried to make my own illustrated books. They were fun to make, but the little books were never what I hoped they would be. There was more to it than I knew, it seemed. One day I had a strong clear thought: "When I grow up I'm going to learn to do this. I'm going to put words and pictures together and make my own books."

First I went to college and studied art, expecially painting, because that is what I loved best. After that, for about ten years, I just painted, on my own. I had a few other jobs, to make ends meet, but before long the paintings were being shown in a gallery and people were buying them.

I worked on more than one painting at a time, and though each one was different, they were often closely related. Sometimes I felt as if they were parts of a story I didn't yet know. You could put the paintings together in different ways, and "read" the mysterious story from one picture to another. At the same time, each one seemed to have a story of its own, hidden within it. The images I loved to paint were symbols and metaphors, things that are more than they seem. Trees, stones, wings, the wise old man, the rose, pathways and doors, sky, raindrops like spheres of glass with the stars inside them.

Then one year I went to a workshop on writing books for children, led by Jane Yolen. It was a door for me, open and inviting. I stepped into that world of children's books, and began to write more and more. Words joined the pictures and at last, the thought that was so strong and clear that day as a child began to come true. It had been growing all along, slowly and quietly, like a tree, even when I did not know it. A tree doesn't bear its fruit right away, and each tree has its own way of growing. For me, it was through painting, and the "stories" hidden in things that are more than they seem.

————

Barbara Helen Berger was born in Lancaster, California, and grew up in Seattle. She received her B.F.A. degree from the University of Washington in 1968 and attended Yale Summer School of Music and Art in 1966. She also studied for a year at the Temple University Tyler School of Art in Rome, Italy. She is a member of the Society of Children's Book Writers.

Grandfather Twilight was chosen to appear in the Graphic Gallery, a showcase of excellent books honored by *The Horn Book Magazine*. *The Donkey's Dream* won the 1985 Golden Kite Award for Illustration from the Society of Children's Book Writers, and pieces from it and from *When the Sun Rose* were included in the Biennale of Illustrations at Bratislava in 1987.

SELECTED WORKS WRITTEN AND ILLUSTRATED: Animalia, 1982; Grandfather Twilight, 1984; The Donkey's Dream, 1985; When the Sun Rose, 1986.

SELECTED WORKS ILLUSTRATED: Brothers of the Wind, by Jane Yolen, 1981.

ABOUT: Horn Book December 1986.

CLAYTON BESS

December 30, 1944–

AUTHOR OF *Story for a Black Night*, etc.

Autobiographical sketch of Robert Locke, who writes under the pen name "Clayton Bess":

WHEN I WAS A KID no one ever told me I could grow up to be an author, so it never entered my head that I would. I was going to be a truck driver—that's what I thought in elementary school—so I could see the world. In junior high, I decided I'd be a gardener because I started having a love affair with green and growing things. In high school I made up my mind that I was going to be an actor, and throughout college I majored in theater and acted my brains out.

It wasn't until I went to Africa in the Peace Corps that I ever thought about writing a story, and I wouldn't have thought of it then except it was told to me, a true story about something so horrible that I couldn't forget it. You see, one of my students invited me home to dinner and to meet his mother. I'll never forget her. Her face was covered with deep scars, and her arms, and her legs, scars all over her body. She told me what had happened to her on a black night long ago. After that, black night after black night I lay awake thinking about the woman's story, until finally I told myself I'd just have to write it to get it out of my head. That story became the basis for my first book, *Story for a Black Night*, the story of a courageous woman fighting against a terrible disease. Of course, the book is differ-

ent in many ways from the true story; that is what fiction means.

It took me over ten years to get that book published. Editor after editor rejected it. What made me keep writing in the face of all that rejection? I don't know. I just know I did. And I'm glad I did.

I feel that I have a different kind of vision to offer young people. Because of my three years in Africa, I've learned that the world is a very diverse place, and there's room on the planet for all kinds of different people with different customs and different opinions. I hope my stories will open up the minds of people, young or old, to accept people's differences, to cherish them.

"Be what you wish to seem to be." That's the best advice I ever got, and it came out of a novel. Mary Renault with her novels of ancient Greece influenced me perhaps more than any other author. Her characters are noble people always trying to be nobler in a world that too often asks them to be less. It's tough, trying to be noble, but what's the alternative? Trying to be base? Trying to be ordinary? Why not go for the best *you* that you can be?

Two other people who had great influence on me are my dad and mom, Clayton and Bess Locke, who didn't want me when they found out I was on my way, and who thought I was one-mouth-too-many to feed in those hard times, but who welcomed me all the same when I was born in a little hospital in Vallejo, California, on December 30, 1944, the last of their four children.

Yes, my real name is not Clayton Bess but Robert Locke. Most people call me Bob, and some still call me Skip or Skipper, which was my nickname because, they say, I was such a bossy little kid and always trying to be skipper of the ship. I took the name Clayton Bess as my pen name because I figured I owed a tribute to two people as great as my mom and dad, who raised me with a good sense of values and open-mindedness. If you've read my novel *Tracks*, then you've met my mom and dad, or at least their personalities: they're Blue and Marge. Or if you've read *Big Man and the Burn-Out*, you'll see some parts of Clay and Bess in Sid and Hannah.

But you probably won't recognize me in any of my books. For some reason I don't write autobiographically. Maybe other people's stories are more interesting to me than my own stories. Maybe I don't see myself very clearly. Or maybe I'm just not a very interesting character. Maybe that's why I'm an actor as well as a writer, so that I can get rid of Bob Locke and get under the skin of all those marvelous characters, Hamlet, Hector, Sidney Bruhl, heroes and villains.

The stage has given me another career because, under my own name, I also write plays and screenplays.

Where do my stories come from? From imagination sometimes. And from real life, a lot. If I hear a story that happened to somebody, and if that story keeps me lying awake at night, I begin to think, "Huh oh, hold on, Bob, we're taking off again. How can we make this story juicier? " When I finally do start writing, I write hard and fast. I don't schedule a particular time to write because when I'm hot, I'm hot; you can't drag me away from the computer. And when I'm cold . . . I take a vacation. There are lots of things to do besides write. Travel. See old friends—I keep my old friends like a treasure, friends from junior high and high school, from college, from Peace Corps days. Read. Research. Watch a good movie. Or work in the garden. I love that. Weeding and seeding and harvesting. Gardening is a lot like writing, when you think about it.

————

Clayton Bess received his B.A. degree from California State University at Chico in 1965 and his M.A. degree from California State University at San Francisco in 1967. He graduated with an M.S. degree in Library Science from Simmons College in 1973. He has taught play writing and was Playwright-in-Residence at the American Conservatory Theatre in San Francisco, from 1983 to 1984. He has also worked as a teacher and as a reference librarian. He has received several acting scholarships, including two from the Oregon Shakespearean Festival in Ashland and from White Oaks Musical Theatre in Carmel Valley. He has also written plays and screenplays, including *Rose Jewel and Harmony*, produced by The Exchange for the Performing Arts in 1986, which won eight Emmy Awards, including best original script and best drama.

Story for a Black Night was honored by the Southern California Council on Literature for Children and Young People as "a contribution of cultural significance" in 1983. *Tracks* was named a Best Book for Young Adults for 1986 by the American Library Association.

SELECTED WORKS: Story for a Black Night, 1982; The Truth About the Moon, 1983; Big Man and the Burn-Out, 1985; Tracks, 1986.

LLOYD BLOOM

January 10, 1947–

ILLUSTRATOR OF *Like Jake and Me*, etc.

Biographical sketch of Lloyd Bloom:

LLOYD BLOOM was born in New York
City. He received his B.A. degree from
Hunter College in 1972 and his M.F.A. de-
gree in drawing and painting from Indiana
University at Bloomington in 1975. He also
studied at the Art Students' League from
1964 to 1967, and at New York Studio
School from 1967 to 1968. He has studied
studio painting, drawing, and sculpture.
Bloom lives in Brooklyn.

Hanna B. Zeiger, writing in *Horn Book*,
described *Yonder* as a "cyclical pattern of
a farming way of life," commenting that
"Lloyd Bloom's lush palette of verdant
green and earth tones wakens all the
senses." About *Poems for Jewish Holidays*
a *Booklist* reviewer wrote: " . . . with fine
detail and infinite depth Bloom's black-
and-white drawings capture the spirit of
traditional Orthodox observances, mod-
ernistically interpret ancient scenes, and in-
geniously entwine the past with the
present." A *School Library Journal* reviewer praised the same book's illustrations:
" . . . it is Bloom's black-and-white illustrations that make this a truly distinguished
book."

Like Jake and Me was named a 1985
Newbery Honor Book by the American Li-
brary Association. It was also named a 1985
Boston Globe-Horn Book Honor Book for
Illustration, and was named an ALA Nota-
ble Book of 1984. *Arthur, for the Very First
Time* won a 1980 Golden Kite Award for
Fiction from the Society of Children's Book
Writers, and was also a 1980 ALA Notable
Book.

Grey Cloud won a 1980 Friends of American Writers Juvenile Merit Award. *No One
Is Going to Nashville* was the 1983 winner
of the Irma Simonton Black Award given
by the Bank Street College of Education. *A
Man Named Thoreau* was a 1985 ALA Notable Book. *Poems for Jewish Holidays* won
a 1987 National Jewish Book Award for Illustration from the Jewish Welfare Board of
the Jewish Book Council. *Yonder* will be exhibited at the Biennale Illustrations Bratislava in 1989, sponsored by the
International Board on Books for Young
People.

SELECTED WORKS ILLUSTRATED: Grey Cloud, by
Charlotte Towner Graeber, 1979; Arthur, for the Very
First Time, by Patricia MacLachlan, 1980; The Maid
of the North: Feminist Folk Tales from Around the
World, by Ethel Johnston Phelps, 1981; The Green
Book, by Jill Paton Walsh, 1982; Nadia the Willful, by
Sue Alexander, 1983; No One Is Going to Nashville, by
Mavis Jukes, 1983; Like Jake and Me, by Mavis Jukes,
1984; A Man Named Thoreau, by Robert Burleigh,
1985; Poems for Jewish Holidays, sel. by Myra Cohn
Livingston, 1986; Yonder, by Tony Johnston, 1988.

ABOUT: Something About the Author, Vol. 43.

RHODA BLUMBERG

December 14, 1917–

AUTHOR OF *Commodore Perry in the Land
of the Shogun*, etc.

Autobiographical sketch of Rhoda Blumberg:

WHEN I GRADUATED from Adelphi
College in 1938, I had no thoughts about a

career and never dreamed of becoming a writer. After a year of graduate work in philosophy at Columbia University, I worked as a secretary for radio station WMCA in New York City. I shared an office with two writers who composed monologues for disc jockeys, and realized that I, too, was qualified to have a job as a writer. After submitting a sample script, I was hired to write radio scripts.

I subsequently worked as a researcher, reporter, and talent scout for various CBS and NBC radio network shows. Finding people with unique stories, strange jobs, and unusual talents became my specialty. My files were so well stocked with believe-it-or-not stories that I used the materials in them to write magazine articles about explorers, inventors, detectives, daredevils, and other remarkable personalities. I also wrote travel guides, and had free-lance assignments as a ghost writer for well-known people.

In 1975 I touched home base in the children's book field when I wrote *Sharks* (Franklin Watts). I love writing for children. This is my occupation and my very happy preoccupation. What a joy it is to find information about a captivating subject that will eventually intrigue readers. I

wrote books about pets, monsters, witches, dragons, and UFOs.

I collect books about natural history and history, and love to cull odd facts and anecdotes that are amusing. For the past five years I have been an avid history buff, willing to wade through a sea of information in my desire to find out the truth about the past. Something that happened hundreds of years ago is just as real for me as any contemporary event.

I'm a compulsive researcher who finds libraries irresistable. It's heaven to explore, examine, and choose books. I am intrigued by social history, and willingly endure monotonous diaries and poorly written journals when they reward me with surprising information about people and events.

Writing is hard work that can be frustrating. I am glued to my typewriter almost every morning. My trash basket is usually filled with discarded drafts of paragraphs and chapters that have to be rewritten. However, the joy of learning through research, and the pleasure of conveying information through writing give me tremendous satisfaction. I find great happiness studying and writing.

My husband, Gerald, and I live on a farm forty miles north of New York City, near Yorktown Heights, New York. We used to keep two cows, forty sheep, and a flock of chickens. Today the barn has become a stable for friends' horses, and for my daughter Leda's fine stallion. I have one son, Lawrence, who is my husband's law partner. I have three daughters: Rena, a teacher; Alice, a scientist; and Leda, who writes children's books. And I have nine lovely grandchildren.

———

Rhoda Blumberg was married January 7, 1945. She is a member of P.E.N. America, the Authors Guild, the Authors League of America, and the Society of Children's Book Writers.

The First Travel Guide to the Moon was named a 1980 Outstanding Science Trade

Book for Children by a joint committee of the Children's Book Council and the National Science Teachers Association.

Commodore Perry in the Land of the Shogun was named a Newbery Honor Book of 1986 by the American Library Association. It also won the Boston Globe-Horn Book Award for 1985 and the Golden Kite Award for nonfiction in 1985, and was named an ALA Notable Book of 1985. It was selected for the *Horn Book* Graphic Gallery, a showcase of excellent books honored by *The Horn Book Magazine. The Incredible Journey of Lewis and Clark* won a 1988 Christopher Award and a 1987 Golden Kite Award for nonfiction, and was an ALA Notable Book of 1987.

SELECTED WORKS: Firefighters, 1975; Sharks, 1976; First Ladies, 1977; UFO, 1977; Famine, 1978; Backyard Bestiary, 1979; The First Travel Guide to the Moon, 1980; The Truth About Dragons, 1980; Devils and Demons, 1982; Commodore Perry in the Land of the Shogun, 1985; The Incredible Journey of Lewis and Clark, 1987; The Great California Gold Rush, 1989.

ABOUT: Contemporary Authors, Vol. 65; (New Revision Series), Vol. 9; Horn Book January/February 1986; Something About the Author, Vol. 35; Who's Who of American Women, 1983-1984.

N. M. BODECKER

January 13, 1922–February 1, 1988

AUTHOR AND ILLUSTRATOR OF *It's Raining Said John Twaining,*etc.

Biographical sketch of Niels Mogens Bodecker:

N.M. BODECKER was born in Copenhagen, Denmark. He attended boarding school from the ages of ten to eighteen. His education included studies at the Technical Society School of Architecture from 1939 to 1941, the School of Applied Art from 1941 to 1944, and the School of Commerce from 1942 to 1944, all in Copenhagen. He also served in the Danish artillery from 1945 to

N.M. BODECKER

1947. His first book of Danish poetry was published in 1943, when he was nineteen. Poetry was his first love, though he also became an illustrator and then a writer for children.

Bodecker emigrated to the United States in 1952. He lived in New York City and Westport, Connecticut, before settling in Hancock, New Hampshire, in 1972. In 1952 he was married, and he had three sons. The marriage ended in 1959.

For twenty years, he worked as an illustrator while writing poetry in his free time. In 1973, he had his first book published in New York, *It's Raining Said John Twaining: Danish Nursery Rhymes*. He had translated the book for his sons. A *Horn Book Magazine* review of *John Twaining* calls the book "a fresh and beautiful, perfectly integrated picture book." The reviewer adds, "Visualizing and expanding the moods and meanings of the verses, the artist has made pictures which display a unity of spirit and an exciting variety of humor, color, composition, and design." This book was followed by *Let's Marry Said the Cherry*, which he both wrote and illustrated. The books gave him a chance to embark on a career as a writer that he had wanted for twenty-three years. During this time period, he also wrote his first English-language prose book, *Miss Jaster's Garden*, followed by *The Mushroom Center Disaster* and *Quimble Wood*.

Bodecker's greatest contribution to children's literature has been his nonsense verse. He is often compared to A.A. Milne and Edward Lear. Imagination and a sense of the absurd permeate his rhymes and wordplay.

Bodecker was author, illustrator, or contributor of illustrations to forty-five books. They have been published in many countries including Canada, England, France, Sweden, Denmark, Italy, Germany, Holland, and Spain. Illustrations by N.M. Bodecker have appeared in magazines like *The Saturday Evening Post*, *McCall's*, *Esquire*, and *The Ladies' Home Journal*.

Half Magic was placed on the American Library Association list "Notable Children's Books 1940–1970." *Miss Jaster's Garden* was named a 1972 *New York Times* Best Illustrated Book of the Year. *It's Raining Said John Twaining* won a 1974 Christopher Award and was named an ALA Notable Book of 1973. *Hurry, Hurry, Mary Dear!* won a 1977 Christopher Award.

SELECTED WORKS WRITTEN OR COMPILED AND ILLUSTRATED: Miss Jaster's Garden, 1972; It's Raining Said John Twaining: Danish Nursey Rhymes, 1973; Let's Marry Said the Cherry and Other Nonsense Poems, 1974; Hurry, Hurry, Mary Dear! and Other Nonsense Poems, 1976; A Person from Britain Whose Head Was the Shape of a Mitten and Other Limericks, 1980; The Lost String Quartet, 1981; Pigeon Cubes and Other Verse, 1982; Snowman Sniffles and Other Verse, 1983.

SELECTED WORKS WRITTEN: The Mushroom Center Disaster, 1974; Quimble Wood, 1981.

SELECTED WORKS ILLUSTRATED: Half Magic, by Edward Eager, 1954; Seven-Day Magic, by Edward Eager, 1962; Shoe Full of Shamrock, by Mary Francis Shura, 1965; Good Night, Little A.B.C., by Robert Kraus, 1973; Good Night Little One, by Robert Kraus, 1973; Good Night Richard Rabbit, by Robert Kraus, 1973.

ABOUT: Contemporary Authors, Vol. 49–52; (New Revision Series), Vol. 4; Vol. 124; Kingman, Lee and others, comps. Illustrators of Children's Books: 1957–1966; 1967–1976; Kirkpatrick, D.L., ed. Twentieth-Century Children's Writers, 2nd ed.; New York Times February 3, 1988; Publishers Weekly February 26, 1988; School Library Journal March 1988; Something About the Author, Vol. 8; Vol. 54; Shaw, John Mackay. Childhood in Poetry, 2nd supplement; Viguers, Ruth Hill and others, comps. Illustrators of Children's Books: 1946–1956; The Writers Directory 1984–86.

FELICIA BOND

July 18, 1954–

AUTHOR AND ILLUSTRATOR OF *Poinsettia and the Firefighters*, etc.

Autobiographical sketch of Felicia Bond:

THE MAKING of a picture book is an internal and an external process; the internal one being that of the imagination, full of rough edges and free associations, the external one being that of the craft, of giving shape and credibility to the ideas.

When I travel to schools and talk to the children about books and my work, I like to tell them where my ideas come from. I also show them many of the materials I use. This is my way of simplifying—and leaving unsaid—the often complicated distinctions between the internal and the external process in the creative mind.

Recently I was asked by a primary school magazine to submit to them a "message" of my choice for their young readers. I wrote the following three paragraphs. They describe as well as twenty a small part of the interior world I would draw on when writing or illustrating a book.

"I was five years old when I decided to become an artist. I liked to draw houses, animals, and the people in my family. But it was a beam of sunlight coming through my bedroom window in the late afternoon that inspired me to draw what I saw and felt as I walked into that room.

"Today, twenty-eight years later, it is still light that inspires me. In my first book,

Poinsettia and Her Family, I drew that beam of sunlight I had seen so many years before, and described it. This is how I started writing. The sunbeam needed words to go with it.

"If you look at that first book about Poinsettia you will see that it is about those same things I said I liked to draw when I was five. This is often the way it is with me. When I make a book I use ideas that come from things I cared about or was interested in when I was a child. Things like food! Or Christmas trees! Or sleeping and dreaming, making valentines, or noises in the dark! I continue to care about these things today, and although they are sometimes just small parts of my books, they are often the reason my story gets told."

———

Felicia Bond was born in Yokohama, Japan, to American parents. She received her B.F.A. degree in 1976 from the University of Texas in Austin. She lived in New York City for ten years, then moved to Austin. Before becoming a full-time artist and author, she had been a botanical illustrator, at the Spring Branch Science Center in Houston, Texas; a puppeteer in Austin, Texas,

performing at the public library; and Art Director at Margaret K. McElderry Books in New York City. She has also taught art to grade-school students and painting to adults. Her work has appeared in *Cricket* magazine and in *Family Circle* and has been translated into German, French, Danish, Japanese, and Afrikaans.

Poinsettia and Her Family was a Reading Rainbow selection in 1984, and *If You Give a Mouse a Cookie* was a selection of both the Junior Literary Guild and the Book-of-the-Month Club. *Big Red Barn* was also a Book-of-the-Month Club selection.

SELECTED WORKS WRITTEN AND ILLUSTRATED: Poinsettia and Her Family, 1981; Mary Betty Lizzie McNutt's Birthday, 1983; Four Valentines in a Rainstorm, 1983; The Halloween Performance, 1983; Christmas in the Chicken Coop, 1983; Poinsettia and the Firefighters, 1984; Wake Up, Vladimir, 1987.

SELECTED WORKS ILLUSTRATED: The Sky Is Full of Stars, by Franklyn M. Branley, 1981; How Little Porcupine Played Christmas, by Joseph Slate, 1982; Mama's Secret, by Maria Polushkin, 1984; If You Give a Mouse a Cookie, by Laura Joffe Numeroff, 1985; Big Red Barn (rev. ed), by Margaret Wise Brown, 1989.

ABOUT: Something About the Author, Vol. 49.

SUSAN BONNERS

April 8, 1947–

AUTHOR AND ILLUSTRATOR OF *A Penguin Year*, etc.

Biographical sketch of Susan Bonners:

SUSAN BONNERS was born in Chicago, Illinois, the middle child of three daughters. She learned to draw from her mother, who once worked as a commercial artist in Chicago. She watched her mother as she worked on volunteer projects or on projects for their home, and was taught some perspective drawing before grade school. During one summer in high school, she attended a figure drawing class at the Chicago Art Institute.

After receiving a B.A. degree in English in 1970 from Fordham University, where she took no art classes, she studied in Manhattan at the New York-Phoenix School of Design, from January 1971 to June 1972. She also took a summer course in painting at the National Academy of Design in Manhattan, in 1972.

"I work in children's books," she writes, "because this field offers a tremendous amount of creative freedom. Also, I have the feeling that, even if I didn't have to make a living and just painted for myself, the paintings would have a kind of narrative quality even if not attached to a particular story. I also like the limitations of a particular format (page size, number of pages, etc.). It's kind of like working out a Chinese puzzle or doing a sonnet. You have to make everything fit, once you've chosen a particular form."

Her books are illustrated with soft pencil, pen-and-ink and watercolor wash drawings. Her first book written and illustrated was *Panda*, a nonfiction picture book describing the life cycle of the panda, its habits, food, growth, and mating, with a hand-lettered text.

Bonners discusses her method of working: "I have worked in several mediums, but my favorite—which I have hardly used for professional work at all—is oil paints. (I did one book jacket in oils for a book, a YA novel, called *Rice Without Rain*, by Minfong Ho.) Right now, however, I'm working on the sketches for a book for Lothrop, a fiction storybook, that will be done entirely in oils. I also wrote the story. This will be the first fiction story I've done, if you don't count *Just in Passing*, which I plotted more than wrote.)

"I like oils because I'm a natural-born putterer. I like to work slowly and constantly readjust things. Oil paint allows one to do that easily. Watercolor, which I have used extensively when I wanted certain effects, is much more demanding and, for me, much more nerve-wracking. Also, I like to work from dark to light in a painting, build-

ing up slowly to the lightest highlights. In watercolor, the technique is the opposite, for the most part."

Since 1974, Susan Bonners has lived in Brooklyn, and she was married December 4, 1988, to a sculptor, Barry Silverman.

Panda was named a 1978 Notable Book by the American Library Association. *A Penguin Year* won a 1982 American Book Award in the children's nonfiction category and was also an ALA Notable Book. Eight of Bonners' books have been named Outstanding Science Trade Books in their years of publication by a joint committee of the National Science Teachers Association and the Children's Book Council. They are: *Animals in Your Neighborhood, Discovering What Puppies Do, What Do You Want to Know About Guppies?, Panda, A Penguin Year, A Forest Is Reborn, Rain Shadow,* and *Inside Turtle's Shell. Anybody Home?* was named a 1981 Children's Choice Book by a joint committee of the CBC and the International Reading Association.

SELECTED WORKS WRITTEN AND ILLUSTRATED: Panda, 1978; A Peguin Year, 1981; Just in Passing, 1989.

SELECTED WORKS ILLUSTRATED: Animals in Your Neighborhood, by Seymour Simon, 1976; Discovering What Puppies Do, by Seymour Simon, 1977; What Do You Want to Know About Guppies?, by Seymour Simon, 1977; Anybody Home?, by Aileen Fisher, 1980; Audubon Cat, by Mary Calhoun, 1981; A Forest Is Reborn, by James Newton, 1982; Rain Shadow, by James R. Newton, 1983; Inside Turtle's Shell and Other Poems of the Field, by Joanne Ryder, 1985; Sarah's Questions, by Harriet Ziefert, 1986.

ABOUT: Something About the Author, Vol. 48.

BARBARA BOTTNER

May 25, 1943–

AUTHOR AND ILLUSTRATOR OF *Myra*, etc.

Autobiographical sketch of Barbara Bottner:

I WAS BORN loving to dance and to paint, and while I was still very young, my mother was warned by a teacher that I was reading too many books! I was a strange child; while very outgoing, and a dedicated tomboy, I always needed tremendous amounts of 'inner' time.

Living with the pressure of a family that did not want to be together, I fled into art, music, storytelling, dance; creativity made much more sense to me than everyday life. Art was my bread and butter, my passion, my world.

I studied ballet assiduously until the advent of boys, dates, parties. My dancing fell off, but not my drawing. That was a place I could express the conflicts I lived with; a place I could make real my torments. My drawings from this period are very grotesque and I remember my mother asking: "Can't you ever draw any *happy* people?" I didn't think happy people were very interesting. I adored the German Expressionists; they existed for me alone.

I attended three different colleges in four years and was lucky in that all were valuable. For my junior year, I arranged to study abroad at the Ecole des Beaux Arts. I painted, spoke French, and soaked in the art, the ambiance of Paris and Western Europe. I was thrilled at my life! One of the Americans I knew had a brother who was a co-curator of the Guggenheim Museum. We helped him with his exhibits and gained entrance to many artists' lives and their work.

All this time, covered with linseed oil, gesso, and flecks of paint, it never dawned on me that I would eventually become a writer!

The sixties was a time of experiments. I lived on a mountaintop in Santa Barbara and painted, earning a masters degree. Then I came to New York and designed sets for an off-Broadway theater. Eventually I wanted to act myself, and joined Cafe La Mama, touring this country and Europe, in the company of gifted and now famous playwrights and actors. However, during a rehearsal, I broke my leg in three places. While recuperating, I remembered my love of visual art. That's when I decided I wanted to illustrate children's books.

The editors I met urged me to write my own stories. I resisted this idea, but when I finally did, my first book, *What Would You Do with a Giant*, was published. However, it wasn't long before I saw that by filming my drawings I could make a movie! So now I fell in love with animation. I produced my own short films and also spots for *The Electric Company*. I wrote songs for *Sesame Street*. I loved it all!

I was bursting out all over, and finally, I had to make a decision. I had never written anything longer than a story book, but I began to realize there was so much I wanted to say. During this time I had also taught kindergarten in Harlem, been a waitress, and worked with senior citizens in Bushwick, Brooklyn. I had also spent many years teaching Writing and Illustrating Children's Books at the Parson's School of Design in New York City.

I had other ingredients: I had been lonely, asked questions, examined my life, listened to people. Slowly, my courage grew: I wanted to be a writer.

All the pent-up experiences, both the lovely ones and the hurtful ones, began to find their way into my books. In my first teenage novel, *Nothing In Common*, I dug deeper, and allowed passion onto the page.

Now, my clothes are cleaner than when I was an artist. So is my house: I just got married! But writing is the hardest thing I've ever done. My mind is filled with characters and their problems; their search for joy, understanding, justice, love, victory, and wisdom to face this horrifying and magnificent world—a search very much like my own.

———

Barbara Bottner attended Boston University from 1961 to 1962 and the Ecole des Beaux Arts in France from 1963 to 1964. She received a B.S. degree from the University of Wisconsin in 1965, and an M.A. degree in painting from the University of California at Santa Barbara in 1966. She is a member of the Writers Guild of America. As a filmmaker, she has received the Cine Golden Eagle Award from the Council for International Nontheatrical Events for *Later That Night* and won a Best Film for Television Award from the International Animation Festival in Annecy, France, for *A Goat in a Boat* in 1973. She has reviewed for *The New York Times* and *The Lion and the Unicorn*. She also co-wrote, with Arlene Sidaris, "Let's Trade Moms," an ABC After-school Special.

Mean Maxine was named a Children's Choice Book of 1980 by a joint committee of the International Reading Association and the Children's Book Council. *Myra* was a Junior Literary Guild selection.

SELECTED WORKS WRITTEN AND ILLUSTRATED: What Would You Do with a Giant?, 1972; Doing the Toledo, 1977; Jungle Day, 1978; There Was Nobody There, 1978; Big Boss, Little Boss, 1978; Dumb Old Casey Is a Fat Tree, 1979; Messy, 1979; Myra, 1979; Horrible Hannah, 1980; Mean Maxine, 1980.

SELECTED WORKS WRITTEN: The World's Greatest Expert on Absolutely Everything . . . Is Crying, 1984; Nothing in Common, 1986; Zoo Song, 1987; Let Me Tell You Everything: Memories of a Lovesick Intellectual, 1989.

ABOUT: Contemporary Authors, Vol. 61–64; (New Revision Series), Vol. 8; Smith, Sharon. Women Who Make Movies; Something About the Author, Vol. 14.

IRENE BRADY

December 29, 1943–

AUTHOR AND ILLUSTRATOR OF *Wild Mouse*, etc.

Biographical sketch of Irene Brady:

IRENE BRADY was born in Ontario, Oregon. She lived on an Idaho farm as a child and, with her brother and three sisters, helped with the chores. She had an early interest in collecting and drawing animals and insects. Brady attended high school in Caldwell, Idaho.

Brady received a B.P.A. degree from the Oregon College of Art in 1975. From 1968 to 1970 she was botanical and paleontological illustrator at the Botanical Museum at Harvard University. Since 1969 she has been an illustrator and writer for *Audubon* and *Ranger Rick's Nature Magazine*. She has been a college instructor in book illustration from 1974 to 1975 in Ashland, Oregon. She has also taught Children's Literature at Southern Oregon State College in 1979, Biological Illustration at the same College in 1980, and Story Illustration at The Pacific College of Art & Design in 1988. She has lectured for ten years on illustrating books for children. Her career as an author and illustrator began in 1964.

Brady has had her work exhibited at The Cascade Wildlife Gallery in Ashland, Oregon, and at The Pacific College of Arts and Design.

Irene Brady is a member of the National Audubon Society, the National Wildlife Foundation, and Nature Conservancy. She is married and lives in Oregon on five acres set aside as a sanctuary for wildlife.

America's Horses and Ponies was Brady's

IRENE BRADY

first book. It shows thirty-eight breeds of horses drawn to scale. *Wild Mouse* won a 1978 New York Academy of Sciences Children's Science Book Award. Irene Brady won the 1986 Evelyn Sibley Lampman Award given by the Oregon Library Association. Many of Brady's books have been named Outstanding Science Trade Books for Children by a joint committee of the Children's Book Council and the National Science Teachers Association. They include *Owlet* in 1974, *Wild Mouse* in 1976; *Wild Babies* in 1979; *Forest Log* and *Have You Heard of Kangaroo Bird* in 1980, *Kangaroo Bird* in 1980; *Rajpur* in 1982; *Gorilla* in 1984, and *Lili* in 1988.

SELECTED WORKS WRITTEN AND ILLUSTRATED: America's Horses and Ponies, 1969; A Mouse Named Mus, 1972; Owlet, the Great Horned Owl, 1974; Beaver Year, 1976; Wild Mouse, 1976; Doodlebug, 1977; Elephants on the Beach, 1979; Wild Babies: A Canyon Sketchbook, 1979.

SELECTED WORKS ILLUSTRATED: Forest Log, by James R. Newton, 1980; Have You Ever Heard of a Kangaroo Bird?, by Barbara Brenner, 1980; Animal Baby-Sitters, by Frances Zweifel, 1981; Rajpur: Last of the Bengal Tigers, by Robert M. McClung, 1982; Gorilla, by Robert McClung, 1984; Peeping in the Shell: A Whooping Crane Is Hatched, by Faith McNulty, 1986; Whitetail, by Robert M. McClung, 1987; Lili: A Giant Panda of Sichuan, by Robert M. McClung, 1988.

ABOUT: Contemporary Authors (First Revision), Vol. 33; Kingman, Lee and others, comps. Illustrators of Children's Books: 1967-1976; Something About the Author, Vol. 4.

JAN BRETT

December 1, 1949–

AUTHOR AND ILLUSTRATOR OF *Annie and the Wild Animals*, etc.

Biographical sketch of Jan Brett, who also writes under the name "Jan Brett Bowler":

JAN BRETT grew up in the seacoast town of Hingham, Massachusetts where her family has lived for over three hundred years. She now lives close by, in the town of Norwell with her husband, Joseph Hearne, a member of the Boston Symphony Orchestra, and her daughter Lia.

Brett remembers, "My mother is a teacher. She encouraged her children to use their creativity. We never went to art classes, instead we were given art materials and allowed to create our own imaginary world on paper. As a child, I loved horses, and I drew pictures of them constantly. I worked many years on my horse pictures in only black and white, trying for the perfect horse."

Jan Brett's books are filled with nature and animals. "When I was little," she relates, "I had many different animals as my pets. We raised guinea pigs, rabbits, had a donkey and a horse, and the usual dogs and cats. I'll never forget my pet chicken, Delly, who used to ride on my shoulder. Now, these animals, along with many others reappear in my books."

In *Annie and the Wild Animals*, a little girl whose pet cat has disappeared in the woods is visited by a succession of wild animals. "My daughter always wanted a wolf or a moose. They are animals that are very attractive to young children, but would not make good pets. *Annie* is my way of exploring the differences between wild animals and friendly pets."

Jan Brett attended Colby-Sawyer College from 1968 to 1969 and then, in 1970, the Boston Museum of Fine Arts School. "As art students we spent most of our free time in the museum. I'm surprised to discover that images from the museum still reappear in my mind to inspire my work."

Jan Brett includes many details in her books, especially on the page borders. These ornamental borders form an integral part of the storytelling process. They enrich the mood of the story while at the same time they elaborate on the action and direction of the story.

"When I was young," she says, "I found a beautiful fossil on a beach filled with stones. Remembering my happy surprise, I try in my artwork to create a mood of discovery for the reader. It's an exercise in seeing. I like the idea of not all images being obvious. Young children are bright and curious. Their vocabulary and ability to read is limited, but often I can communicate with them with my artwork. Many of the subtle things they understand. We share a common ground, the wonder of discovery and the appreciation of nature. I create books that appeal to me, and I am pleased when children enjoy them also."

Jan Brett and her husband travel extensively. "These experiences add to my knowledge and artistic ability. From the time I was six years old," she says, "I wanted to be a children's book illustrator. The new vistas that traveling provides are reflected in my books. I realize now that writing and illustrating takes more than talent. It requires a lifelong commitment. My entire life is involved with children's books."

Some Birds Have Funny Names was named an Ambassador of Honor Book of 1983 by the English-Speaking Union. *Some Plants Have Funny Names* was named a 1984 Outstanding Science Trade Book for Children by a joint committee of the National Science Teachers Association and the Children's Book Council.

Brett's artwork has appeared in various gallery exhibits, such as the Master Eagle Gallery exhibits of children's book art in New York, the Gallery on the Green in Lexington, Massachusetts, and Main Street Gallery in Nantucket, Massachusetts.

Jan Brett keeps a horse and also has a license for piloting gliders.

SELECTED WORKS WRITTEN AND ILLUSTRATED: Fritz and the Beautiful Horses, 1981; Good Luck Sneakers, 1981; Annie and the Wild Animals, 1985; The First Dog, 1988.

SELECTED WORKS RETOLD AND ILLUSTRATED: Goldilocks and the Three Bears, 1987.

SELECTED WORKS ILLUSTRATED: Some Birds Have Funny Names, by Diana Harding Cross, 1981; Some Plants Have Funny Names, by Diana Harding Cross, 1983; Mother's Day Mice, by Eve Bunting, 1986; The Twelve Days of Chirstmas, 1986; Happy Birthday, Dear Duck, by Eve Bunting, 1988.

SELECTED WORKS ILLUSTRATED AS JAN BRETT BOWLER: Woodland Crossings, by Stephen Krensky, 1978.

ABOUT: Contemporary Authors, Vol. 116; Something About the Author, Vol. 42.

BRUCE BROOKS

1950–

Author of *The Moves Make the Man*, etc.

Autobiographical sketch of Bruce Brooks:

PERHAPS the biographical fact that implies the most about me-as-a-writer is the division of my childhood between two terrifically different places: Washington, D.C., and North Carolina. From the age of six I bounced back and forth from a tiny cool family in the very international city to a huge, warm, weird Southern clan in Carolina towns. The demands of living like this (I still live like this, come to think of it) inspired nearly all of the tricky movements of heart and mind that I feel "make" me a writer.

Most important was the investigative spirit, which informs such things as an eye for detail, an ear for voices, a quickness to analyze how people do things and why, an almost desperately open mind, and a sense of strategy. When I was a kid these were not a writer's tools—they were the tools of trying to be oneself. I *had* to use them to investigate D.C. and the South, because I was not lodged truly inside either culture, yet needed to get along naturally in both. I was half-native and half-outsider everywhere. At times I wished simply to belong in one place or the other, but most of the time I relished my freedom from the immersed habituation of the natives. There were things I loved and things I hated about life as a streetwise city boy and life as a canny grit; I would not have been able to choose between them. More than either place, I loved being able to move and adapt and choose my attributes, when they were not already determined. This has a lot in common with creating characters, empathizing with them, developing a critique of their interactions, setting them well in a place and society, and letting them be themselves. It is tremendously important for my writing.

The restlessness and curiosity have kept me happily moving ever since. After college in North Carolina (after high school in D.C.), I took off for New England. I spent a few years on the very beautiful, very strange island of Martha's Vineyard; during this time (on weekends) I also insinuated myself into Boston and Cambridge, which were only a ferry ride and a two-hour hitch-hike away. Later I moved to the Midwest, where I went to graduate school and came as close to settling as is likely for me: I lived in Iowa City for six years. In 1984, my son Alexander was born there, and my wife (an East Coaster) and I thought: "Is he an Iowan? Are we Iowans?" We immediately moved back to D.C., where we have lived for nearly five years now. But we travel a lot!

The thing I seem to need the most as a writer is the chance to grow through diverse experiments. I want to do lots of things well. I don't want to be good only at one or two, and keep writing books that emphasize established strengths: "He's a puppet-master of first-person voices" or "Her dialogue is wonderful" or "He's really got Texas down pat," which always imply "but his third-person narrative is cold" and "but her descriptive passages are skittish" and "but he couldn't write a scene anywhere north of Amarillo."

There is so much to *try*. Whenever I think up a book to do, it is a book I am incapable of writing at the outset: I learn how to pull off the trick in the process of doing it. There is something in the writing to draw out every aspect of one's wit and heart; something the "mastery" of which will require one to grow in a new direction through thinking and feeling. This applies, of course, to reading, with exactly the same power. I want to keep moving, and make my readers move, too. There are a lot of characters yet to meet, and a lot of mysterious places to visit.

————

Bruce Brooks was born in Virginia. He graduated from the University of North Carolina at Chapel Hill in 1972 and from the University of Iowa Writers' Workshop in 1980. He has been a letterpress printer and a reporter for newspapers and magazines. *The Moves Make the Man* was named a 1985 Newbery Honor Book by the American Library Association, as well as an ALA Notable Book for 1984 and a Best Book for Young Adults of 1984. It was also the 1985 Boston Globe-Horn Book Award winner for fiction. *Midnight Hour Encores* was an ALA Best Books for Young Adults for 1986.

SELECTED WORKS: The Moves Make the Man, 1984; Midnight Hour Encores, 1986; No Kidding, 1989.

ABOUT: Horn Book January/February 1986; March/April 1987; Something About the Author, Vol. 53.

ANTHONY BROWNE

September 11, 1946–

AUTHOR AND ILLUSTRATOR OF *Gorilla*, etc.

Autobiographical sketch of Anthony Browne:

Anthony Browne.

WHEN I WAS A YOUNG BOY I wanted to be a boxer, and if I couldn't do that, then I wanted to be a newspaper reporter. I suppose what I really wanted was to be like my dad—a big, powerfully built man, and I was always a small boy. He was an unusual man—he had a strong, outwardly confident manner, but also a shy, sensitive nature. He had a succession of jobs, as an art teacher, a professional boxer, a drummer and singer in a jazz band, a travelling salesman, and he was in the army for ten years. Later I found out from his diaries (he died when I was seventeen) that he'd strangled enemy guards while on patrol in North Africa during the war. I can't imagine him doing that. He was a very gentle man. He would spend hours drawing for my brother and me, he wrote poetry for us and made beautiful delicate models of castles and boats and houses. Yet he also encouraged us to play rugby and soccer and cricket, to box and wrestle, to lift weights and to run.

The schools I went to in the industrial north of England were fairly tough, and it could have been quite difficult for a boy who was small, didn't speak with the very broad local dialect, and who liked drawing and writing poetry. Being good at sport saved me from being bullied; the hours of playing games and fighting with my brother had paid off. I don't totally understand why but I concentrated on rugby and continued playing until my late twenties.

Throughout all this time of course I was drawing—mostly very detailed drawings of battles, strongly influenced by the comics I was reading at the time, and with macabre little jokes and speech bubbles in the background.

I studied graphic design for three years at Leeds College of Art and hated it. It seems that the most useful thing I learned was to keep my drawings free from thumb prints and smudges.

I left in 1967 with a hatred of the commercial art world, a morbid fascination with the insides of people's bodies, and an amibition to be the next Francis Bacon. Instead I became a medical artist, painting finely detailed watercolours of muscle, blood vessels, fat, and bone to demonstrate operational techniques. For a long time I've seen no connection between that and what I do now—but there is a very important one. I learned to tell stories in pictures. An operation is a mess—all blood, instruments and hands. Much is hidden, and a medical artist has to clean all this up, make clear what is muscle and what is fat, what is artery and what is vein—to tell the story of the operation. To decide what to show and what to leave out, what can be explained in pictures and what to explain in words. Just like a picture book.

———

Anthony Browne received his degree in graphic design in 1967. He was married July 26, 1980 and has two children. He was a medical artist at the Royal Infirmary from 1968 to 1970 and has also been a greeting card designer.

Browne received the British Library Association's Kate Greenaway Medal for *Gorilla* in 1983, which also received the 1983 Kurt Maschler Award, nicknamed the "Emil." *Gorilla* was also named one of the

Best Illustrated Children's books of the year 1985 by *The New York Times* and was a Boston Globe-Horn Book Award Honor Book in 1986. *Hansel and Gretel* received a commendation from the Kate Greenaway Medal Awards in 1981, and was placed on the International Board on Books for Young People list for 1984. He also received the Deutscher Jugend Literatur Preis in 1985 for *The Visitors Who Came to Stay. Alice's Adventures in Wonderland* was a Book-of-the-Month Club selection.

SELECTED WORKS WRITTEN AND ILLUSTRATED: Through the Magic Mirror, 1977; Bear Hunt, 1979; Look What I've Got, 1980; Gorilla, 1985; Willy the Wimp, 1985; Piggybook, 1986; Willy the Champ, 1986.

SELECTED WORKS ILLUSTRATED: Hansel and Gretel, by the Brothers Grimm, 1982; The Visitors Who Came to Stay, by Annalena McAfee, 1985; Knock, Knock! Who's There?, by Sally Grindley, 1986; Alice's Adventures in Wonderland, by Lewis Carroll, 1988; Kirsty Knows Best, by Annalena McAfee, 1988.

ABOUT: Contemporary Authors, Vol. 97; Horn Book December 1981; Something About the Author, Vol. 44; 45.

BEVERLY BUTLER

May 4, 1932–

AUTHOR OF *Light a Single Candle*, etc.

Biographical sketch of Beverly Kathleen Butler, who also writes under the pen name "Kathleen Victor":

BORN IN FOND DU LAC, Wisconsin, Beverly Butler was raised in Milwaukee. She was born into "a family that delights in books, words, and storytelling," and she remembers that books were everywhere in the household. She was given permission to read any book she wanted to read, as her mother believed that if a child were old enough to understand a book, she was old enough to read it; and if she didn't understand it, she would set it aside or learn by asking questions. As a child she enjoyed art

B everley Butler

and considered herself an artist, but came to think that her drawings were actually illustrations of story fragments that came to her.

At the age of fourteen, Beverly Butler lost her eyesight through glaucoma. In an effort to rejoin her classmates in school, she learned to type, and for practice she rewrote poems and stories she had read. Then she began to experiment, to change characters and endings, and then to invent whole stories. She spent six months at the Wisconsin School for the Visually Handicapped, graduated from Washington High School in Milwaukee, and went on to college. She received her B.A. degree from Mount Mary College in Milwaukee in 1954 and her M.A. degree from Marquette University in 1961, on a Woodrow Wilson Fellowship for Advanced Study.

From 1962 to 1974, she taught creative writing at Mount Mary College. In 1976, Butler married T.V. Olsen, an author of historical, Western, and contemporary novels. For many years she taught an annual course in writing fiction for young adults at the Rhinelander School of Arts. She also lectures at schools and libraries. Her favorite place to write is the screened deck of her home in Rhinelander, Wisconsin, where she can "enjoy the sounds of birds and insects and the wind in the trees" while she works.

Song of the Voyageur, Butler's first book, won a literary competition, and several of her books have won various awards and honors. *Light a Single Candle* won the Clara Ingram Judson Award in 1963, sponsored by the Society of Midland Authors. *My Sister's Keeper* was a Junior Literary Guild selection, and *Maggie by My Side* was named a Notable Book of 1987 by the American Library Association. Beverly Butler was named to a roster of notable Wisconsin authors by the Wisconsin Library Association in 1984.

SELECTED WORKS: Song of the Voyageur, 1955; The Lion and the Otter, 1957; The Fur Lodge, 1959; The Silver Key, 1961; Light a Single Candle, 1962; Feather in the Wind, 1965; The Wind and Me, 1971; A Gift of Gold, 1972; A Girl Named Wendy, 1976; My Sister's Keeper, 1980; Ghost Cat, 1984; Maggie by My Side, 1987.

ABOUT: Contemporary Authors, Vol. 1; (New Revision Series), Vol. 4; Foremost Women in Communications; Something About the Author, Vol. 7.

PATRICIA CALVERT

July 22, 1931–

AUTHOR OF *The Snowbird*, etc.

Biographical sketch of Patricia Calvert, who also writes under the pen name "Peter J. Freeman":

PATRICIA CALVERT was born in Great Falls, Montana, during the Great Depression. Her teenage parents were without money or employment, so her father moved the family of four into an abandoned miner's shack that he had discovered eighty miles southeast of Great Falls. Calvert says that since fish and game were plentiful in the surrounding hillsides, her father was able to provide for his family, and although the little cabin had neither windows nor a floor when they arrived, he was soon able to make it habitable.

Patricia Calvert

With her younger brother John, Calvert learned to fish in the brooks near the abandoned gold and silver mines that were scattered across the mountainsides. Later, she had a horse to ride, and a cat and dog for company, but to counter the isolation of their self-sufficient way of life, reading and storytelling soon became an important pastime for the whole family.

Calvert's Irish mother was one of ten children, and often told "sad and funny . . . and sometimes outrageous" stories about her own upbringing. Calvert decided that she, too, would like to be a storyteller, and names two books in particular that influenced her: Armstrong Sperry's *Call It Courage* and Kate Seredy's *The White Stag*. She remembers that the themes, settings, and fine prose of those books further inspired her early decision to become a writer herself.

Patricia Calvert was married to her high school sweetheart on January 27, 1951, and has two daughters. She attended college in Montana and Minnesota, and received a B.A. degree (summa cum laude) in 1976 from Winona State University in Minnesota. She has worked at several kinds of jobs, including lab clerk, cardiac lab technician, and senior editorial assistant in the Section of Publications at the Mayo Clinic. She is a member of the Society of Children's Book Writers, Children's Reading Round Table, and the American Medical Writers Association.

It was not until Calvert was a grandmother and living on a small farm in southern Minnesota that she converted a chicken coop into a writing room and sat down to write her first children's novel, *The Snowbird*. The book was named a Best Book for Young Adults for the year 1980 by the American Library Association. It also won a Friends of American Writers Juvenile Award and a Young Women's Christian Association Award for Outstanding Achievements in the Arts in 1981. *Yesterday's Daughter* also was named an ALA Best Book for Young Adults, in 1986.

Patricia Calvert is a member of the Authors Guild of the Authors League of America, and sometimes writes for such magazines as *Grit*, *The Friend*, and *National Future Farmer* under the pen name Peter J. Freeman. She is currently working on a novel of historical fiction for adults. She travels occasionally, and especially likes to go to Ireland and Scotland, where her parents' ancestors were born. She works on a new book every year and says that when she is eighty-five she plans to learn to roller-skate.

SELECTED WORKS: The Snowbird, 1980; The Money Creek Mare, 1981; The Stone Pony, 1982; Hour of the Wolf, 1983; Hadder MacColl, 1985; Yesterday's Daughter, 1986; Stranger, You and I, 1987; When Morning Comes, 1989.

ABOUT: Contemporary Authors, Vol. 105; Something About the Author, Vol. 45.

NANCY WHITE CARLSTROM

August 4, 1948–

AUTHOR OF *Jesse Bear, What Will You Wear?*, etc.

Nancy White Carlstrom

Autobiographical sketch of Nancy White Carlstrom:

IN ELEMENTARY SCHOOL I started writing poetry and then, during high school, worked in the children's department of our local library in my hometown of Washington, Pennsylvania. It was there that I began to appreciate good children's books. Also, there I discovered *Writer* magazine. As I thumbed through the latest copy, I dreamed of someday writing a book.

But first, I earned a B.A. in education at Wheaton College, taught first and second grades in Pennsylvania and Massachusetts, and spent three summers in West Africa, the West Indies, and Mexico.

In 1976 my husband, David, and I moved to Seattle, Washington, where the following spring I opened The Secret Garden Children's Bookshop. I loved matching up children of all ages with good books. But the desire to write my own books wouldn't go away, so in 1981 I enrolled in a two-week workshop with the renowned author, Jane Yolen. That was the turning point in my writing career.

Usually I get the title for a book first. Often it is many months, sometimes even years later that I actually begin the writing.

The idea is there, simmering on the back burner like a pot of stew. When the stew is ready, it can be served—but may need a little more seasoning.

When the time is right for a story, the writing comes easily. Then I give a copy to my husband or members of my writing group and they point out that the manuscript needs a little more salt, so to speak. That's when the rewriting begins.

Rhythm and rhyme are important to me as I want the words of my books to flow off the page and be easy to repeat by young children. Their participation is the final step of the creative process that may have started with something my own child said, such as "The moon came too."

After a decade in Seattle, our family moved to Fairbanks, Alaska. Many features of our life on the "edge of the Arctic" are finding their way into manuscripts and forthcoming books—moose in the garden, the northern lights, seasonal extremes and, generally, a new sense of closeness to nature.

I love growing our own pumpkins, sharing the broccoli and cauliflower with the moose, skiing in the moonlight. Walking in the woods around our log house, I might surprise a snowshoe hare, ptarmigan or great horned owl. Living in the country truly nourishes my creative spirit.

I am very thankful that I can do something as enjoyable and satisfying as writing books. With the support of my husband and sons, I can see a real connection betwen my vocation as a mother and a writer. When I am frustrated that my writing has to be done in "bits and pieces" fitting around the needs and responsibilities of family life, I remind myself that it's been within these special relationships that I have found a wealth of ideas and images for my stories and poems.

————

Nancy White Carlstrom was married September 7, 1974. She opened The Secret Garden children's book shop in Seattle,

Washington, in 1977 and managed it until 1983. She is a member of the Society of Children's Book Writers. *Jesse Bear . . . and The Moon Came, Too*, and *Better Not Get Wet, Jesse Bear* were all Junior Literary Guild selections. *Jesse Bear . . .* was also named a Children's Choice Book in 1987 by a joint committee of the International Reading Association and the Children's Book Council.

SELECTED WORKS: Jesse Bear, What Will You Wear?, 1986; The Moon Came, Too, 1987; Wild Wild Sunflower Child Anna, 1987; Better Not Get Wet, Jesse Bear, 1988; Graham Cracker Animals 1-2-3, 1989.

ABOUT: Something About the Author, Vol. 53.

SYLVIA CASSEDY

January 29, 1930–April 6, 1989

AUTHOR OF *Behind the Attic Wall*, etc.

Autobiographical sketch of Sylvia Cassedy:

ON THE WHOLE, I was not an unpopular kid. I had some good friends. I got invited to birthday parties. When I was eleven, a boy asked me to dance. But I *felt* unpopular. My good friends had better friends of their own, or seemed to. My place card at those birthday parties was somehow always at the end of the table, farthest from the hostess. The boy who asked me to dance was the shortest boy in the class; I was the shortest girl. He picked me for my size.

And so, during a childhood that a lot of kids would have probably considered pretty enviable (my family was intact; my father earned a living of sorts, even though these were Depression years; I went to private school), I spent much of my time suffering. I collected hurts. I nurtured them, almost, relishing their details in a way that most people reserve for Fourth of July parades. I took excruciating notice, for example, of how somebody's eyes would shift ever so slightly or her fingers curl into her palm as she explained why she couldn't play with

me after school that day. They were hurts that I savored.

And remembered. Not only then, but now. Except that now I don't suffer over them; I write about them. All those troubled eleven- and twelve-year-old girls in my novels are, in their way, recreations not of my actual childhood but of how I perceived it at the time and remember those perceptions now.

Probably what made my life most enviable to other kids was the school I attended—a small, private institution whose program was based on the teachings of John Dewey and the philosophy that children learn best in an atmosphere of generous freedom. A "progressive" school. To most outsiders, the atmosphere was one of outrageous abandon: We addressed our teachers—to their faces and with their approval—by slangy diminutives of their last names. Boys as well as girls took dance twice a week—not social dancing, either; the Isadora Duncan kind. Girls as well as boys took shop, and we made whatever we felt like making: I spent three months on a pair of wooden castanets, so I could be Carmen when no one was looking. In one second-grade play, it was a boy who took the part of the fairy queen; in another, all the girls were cavemen. (All of this took place in the *thirties*, by the way. Nor was it in some reclusive rural commune; the school was located in the middle of Brooklyn.)

So it was not especially surprising that by the time I was in second grade I was turning out—with the encouragement, but not the coercion, of my teachers—sizable amounts of poetry and prose. One of my first efforts was a poem called "The Clock." It went "Tick-tock, tick-tock/ Goes my little electric clock." There was more, but this was my favorite part—two lines of eminently satisfying tetrameter. Inevitably, some members of my family pointed out that electric clocks don't go tick-tock. They go bzzz. I was told to change the wording to "alarm clock." Or just plain "clock": "Tick-tock, tick-tock/ Goes my little clock." *Adults* told me to do this. I didn't know the word "scansion" then, or "meter," for that matter, but I knew a wrong line when I saw—or heard—one, and I stuck with electric. "Eschie," my teacher at the time, thought that was just fine. Anyway, it was too late to make any changes; the poem had already found its way into print—in the elegantly turned out school journal, a glossy publicaton distributed to parents and intended as the scholastic equivalent of an annual report. That was my first published work.

So that, I suppose, is why I write: I spent a lot of childhood time suffering. I *remembered* all that suffering, in what can only be described as loving detail. I went to a school where creative writing was not a class assignment—where, in fact, nothing much was a class assignment—and where the staff understood the beauty of poetic license.

————

Sylvia Cassedy was born in Brooklyn, New York. She graduated with a B.A. degree from Brooklyn College in 1951 and took writing seminars at Johns Hopkins University from 1959 to 1960. She was mar-ried and had four children. She was a second-grade teacher in the Baltimore Public Schools and taught creative writing to primary- and secondary-school students from 1970 to 1984. Silvia Cassedy died in 1989.

Behind the Attic Wall was named a Notable Book of 1983 by the American Library Association and a Children's Choice Book by a joint committee of the International Reading Association and the Children's Book Council. *M.E. and Morton* was also named an ALA Notable Book, in 1987.

SELECTED WORKS: Little Chameleon, 1966; Pierino and the Bell, 1966; Marzipan Day on Bridget Lane, 1967; In Your Own Words: A Beginner's Guide to Writing, 1979; Behind the Attic Wall, 1983; M.E. and Morton, 1987; Roomrimes, 1987; The Best Cat Suit of All, 1989.

SELECTED WORKS WITH KUNIHIRO SUETAKE: Birds, Frogs, and Moonlight, 1967.

ABOUT: Contemporary Authors, Vol. 105; (New Revision Series), Vol. 22; Something About the Author, Vol. 27.

LORINDA BRYAN CAULEY

July 2, 1951–

RETELLER AND ILLUSTRATOR OF *Goldilocks and the Three Bears*, etc.

Biographical sketch of Lorinda Bryan Cauley:

LORINDA BRYAN CAULEY was born in Washington, D.C. She cannot remember a time when she did not want to be an artist. Her parents encouraged her art, and her uncle was a muralist. The sight of him working on a ladder, transforming a plain wall into "scenery or characters from faraway places" fascinated her.

She attended Montgomery Junior College and the Rhode Island School of Design, graduating in 1974 with a B.F.A. degree. She studied painting, drawing, and sculpture there, eventually choosing illustration, enjoying that discipline because illustration

Lounda Bryan Cauley

requires a specific subject rather than the range of choices possible in painting. Cauley was married June 15, 1974 to an artist and teacher, and has three children. She enjoys long walks with her family on the beach and in the city. She lives in New York City and spends her summers in Beach Haven, New Jersey. There, she and her husband own several stores where they sell hand-screened and embroidered clothing of their own design.

Her books include retellings of folk and classic tales as well as stories she has written. She has also illustrated many books written by other authors.

The Animal Kids was named a Junior Literary Guild selection. *The Ugly Duckling* and *Puss in Boots* were Reading Rainbow Books. Three of Cauley's books were named Children's Choice Books by a joint committee of the Children's Book Council and the International Reading Association: *If You Say So, Claude* in 1981, *The Cock, the Mouse, and the Little Red Hen* in 1983, and *The Goose and the Golden Coins* in 1983. *The Town Mouse* was named a Notable Children's Trade Book in the Field of Social Studies for 1984 by a joint committee of the CBC and the National Council on the Social

Studies. *The Goodnight Circle* won a 1985 Friends of American Writers Juvenile Book Merit Award. *Goldilocks* was made into a Weston Woods filmstrip.

SELECTED WORKS WRITTEN OR RETOLD AND ILLUSTRATED: The Animal Kids, 1979; The Ugly Duckling, 1979; Goldilocks and the Three Bears, 1981; The Cock, the Mouse, and the Little Red Hen, 1982; The Goose and the Golden Coins, 1982; Jack and the Beanstalk, 1983; The Three Little Kittens, 1983; The Town Mouse and the Country Mouse, 1984; Puss in Boots, 1986; The Pancake Boy: An Old Norwegian Folk Tale, 1988; The Trouble with Tyrannosaurus Rex, 1988; Old MacDonald Had a Farm, 1989.

SELECTED WORKS ILLUSTRATED: Fairy Tales, by E.E. Cummings, 1865; If You Say So, Claude, by Joan Lowery Nixon, 1980; The Story of the Three Little Pigs, by Joseph Jacobs, 1980; The Elephant's Child, by Rudyard Kipling, 1982; The Goodnight Circle, by Carolyn Lesser, 1984; The Owl and the Pussycat, by Edward Lear, 1986.

ABOUT: Contemporary Authors, Vol. 101; Something About the Author, Vol. 43.

MIRIAM CHAIKIN

December 8, 1928–

AUTHOR OF: *I Should Worry, I Should Care*, etc.

Autobiographical sketch of Miriam Chaikin:

I WAS BORN in Jerusalem and brought to America when I was eight months of age. We, my mother, father and I, lived in Brooklyn. Through no suggestion of mine, the family grew and before long I was no longer an only child but the eldest of three. By age ten, I was the eldest of five and, because of my antiquity, when my mother could catch me, something of a surrogate parent.

My family was poor, as was our Brooklyn neighborhood. There was not a lot of joy in the streets. Contributing to the mood, for me, were the "older girls" across the street. Perhaps they were only bigger. This gang

of four or five young teenagers menaced my existence. As a Jewish child, I kept away from them. They wanted it that way. The rules were that that side of the street, their side, was off-limits to Jewish kids.

Both my parents were immigrants. They looked a little different. One day I saw my father turn the corner across the street and walk heedlessly on their side of the street. Worried, I watched. The girls, always in evidence, were sitting on a stoop. They went down from the stoop and, walking behind my father, made faces and rude signs behind his back. My father didn't know. I never told him. My humiliation was great enough.

I determined not to stand out. I wanted to be perceived as an American, so I borrowed some sounds and gestures from available models like Deanna Durbin, even Bette Davis. In the march of time, the girls left the neighborhood, some for reformatories, others for wherever the stresses of their own lives took them. I became a baby-sitter, to earn movie and candy money, and was content with my friends, my first dates, in that sweeter, more innocent time, and above all with school. I did not know it was possible to be so happy. I had already found

reading. Now, in English classes, I also found writing. I wrote poems for every occasion and spoofs of the classics we studied. My teachers, trying not to smile, said I would be a writer one day. Sometimes, but not often, I took it as a prophecy, and let my heart rejoice.

Our large family remained poor, and after high school I went to work. I spent several years in Washington, D.C., working for two United States senators. I then returned to New York, and worked for a public relations firm. Finally, after trying and trying, I got what is called an "entry level" job in publishing. As a beginner in the field, I did the donkey work, typing, filing, and answering the phone. It was worth it. I discovered children's books. As a child, I had read whatever came my way—from Dostoevsky to Street and Smith Love Stories. Fired by the wonderful world of children's books, I worked diligently to become an editor, and in time succeeded.

One day, Edna Barth, a close friend and colleague, and herself a writer, said, "Miriam, why don't you write about your roots, about growing up Jewish?" I could not believe my ears. I was an American. Did she know what she was saying? Angry as I was, she had triggered something, and I did begin to write. I later told her how angry her words had made me. Also how grateful I was to her.

Harper published my first book, *I Should Worry, I Should Care*, about Molly, a little Jewish girl growin up in Brooklyn at the start of World War II. It was not autobiographical. But I drew upon my remembered childhood and I could not have written it if I had lived some other life. There are now five Molly books.

In time, I stopped being an editor and began to write full-time. Clarion published my Jewish holidays series; and Harper, a second series as well, about Yossi, an amusing (I hope) Hasidic Jewish boy, leading a different sort of Jewish life. I have retold Bible stories and written about the Holocaust. Returning to my roots has not only educated me. It has awakened me to the riches of my heritage, and nourished me. Sometimes, as I read, or write, about some aspect of Jewish history that makes me proud, I think of the girls across the street. And I say to them: *Maybe, if you knew this, or that, you wouldn't have acted that way. How much sweeter our lives, yours and mine, could have been.*

Miriam Chaikin has been editorial director of both Bobbs-Merrill Company and Holt, Rinehart & Winston. She is a member of the Authors Guild, International P.E.N., the Authors League of America, and the Women's National Book Association. She won the Sydney Taylor "Body-of-Work" Award in 1985, which is presented by the Association of Jewish Libraries. Her *A Nightmare in History: The Holocaust 1933-1945* was named a Notable Book of 1987 by the American Library Association. Chaikin's adaptation of *Exodus*, illustrated by Charles Mikolaycak, won the 1988 National Jewish Book Award for illustrated book.

SELECTED WORKS: I Should Worry, I Should Care, 1979; Finder Weepers, 1980; Light Another Candle: The Story and Meaning of Hanukkah, 1981; Getting Even, 1982; Joshua in the Promised Land, 1982; How Yossi Beat the Evil Urge, 1983; Lower! Higher! You're a Liar!, 1984; Shake a Palm Branch: The Story and Meaning of Sukkot, 1984; Yossi Asks the Angels for Help, 1985; Aviva's Piano, 1986; Exodus, 1987; A Nightmare in History; The Holocaust 1933–1945, 1987; Friends Forever, 1988; Feathers in the Wind, 1989.

ABOUT: Contemporary Authors, Vol. 81; (New Revision Series), Vol. 14; Foremost Women in Communications, 1970; Something About the Author, Vol. 24.

AIDAN CHAMBERS

December 27, 1934–

AUTHOR OF *Breaktime*, etc.

Autobiographical sketch of Aidan Cham-

bers, who also writes under the pseudonym "Malcolm Blacklin":

I CAN REMEMBER the day—evening rather—when I first learned to read. Till then, I'd been a problem. Teachers said I was a slow-learner, and my mother worried about me. I'm still a slow-learner and my mother still worries about me.

The problem was that I could identify individual words, but I couldn't join them together into sentences. For some reason, I hadn't realised that printed words stand for sounds. That evening in winter I sat staring at a page of print, and suddenly I started to hear the words in my head, making sense. And the sense they were making was a story, with people talking in it, about an adventure on an island. Hearing those printed words suddenly making sense in my head is one of the most vivid and valued moments in my life.

Not that I became an avid reader there and then. Not at all. I was born into a working-class family in Chester-le-Street, a small town in the northeast of England close to Durham. My father was a skilled worker with wood. Like most mothers in such families, mine stayed at home, endlessly cleaning, cooking, washing clothes, and polishing the huge black iron fireplace where all our food was cooked and water was heated. We had very few books in the house—a dictionary, a do-it-yourself medical book, and a volume of *Aesop's Fables* with coloured plates scattered through it, which I stared at for hours.

Reading wasn't something any of us did for pleasure or for information. I did badly in primary school, where books weren't much in evidence either. Throughout my ninth year I was beaten twice every Friday for not being able to do well enough in mental arithmetic tests. School in Chester-le-Street was not a place you learned anything except how to avoid bullies.

When I was ten, we moved twenty-five miles south to Darlington, a place I disliked. But its education system was good. Books were put in front of me and I was encouraged to read. It was there that a new friend took me, almost by force, to the local library and made me join the children's section. That way I found W. E. Johns' Biggles books and, more important to me then and now, Richmal Crompton's William stories, and *Treasure Island* and *Wind in the Willows* and *Tom Brown's School Days* and shelves full of others.

It was a teacher who helped me become a real reader. At thirteen I was transferred late (slow-learner again) to the local, very fine grammar school, where I met P. J. Osborn, a man who truly believed that the reading and writing of literature were the most important educational, cultural, and intellectual activities anyone could be concerned with. He helped me discover the inexhaustible pleasure there is in the densest and most complex writing.

I found for myself the American writers with whom I felt at home, but it was stumbling across D. H. Lawrence and reading *Sons and Lovers* that first made me think I wanted to write, and more importantly, that I could. For Lawrence came from exactly my own cultural background and *Sons and Lovers* seemed, amazingly, to be about myself. I learned from it that you finally become a reader, and perhaps a writer too, only when you have discovered yourself in another writer's book. I finished Lawrence's novel in the middle of the night. The next day I began writing a novel set in the town where I was born. It was never finished. It never will be. Everything I've written about since has been a failed attempt to write the book I started then.

What follows is merely data. Because of Jim Osborn, I became a teacher; I taught English, trying to help boys become readers in the way Jim had helped me. During that time, I joined the Anglican church, in a new Anglican monastic order, founded specifically to work among young people. After training, I started work in a local secondary school. The boys and girls there weren't great readers, and I was responsible for their library and drama work. After a couple of years, in despair at ever finding novels they'd read and plays they'd enjoy acting, I finally wrote them some of both. And both were so successful they were soon published. I'd found an audience, a voice, and a purpose.

I wrote my first book about children and reading, *The Reluctant Reader*, started a paperback fiction list, Topliners, and began speaking at conferences and meetings all over the country. So now I had three full-time careers—monk, teacher, and writer. I was in my thirties. The crisis came in 1967, when I knew I had to decide whether to be a monk who also happened to teach, or a writer. Obviously, I chose what I knew I had chosen to be all those years before, in the middle of the night, as I finished reading *Sons and Lovers*. Not without bother, I settled down to the unpredictable, anxiety-ridden and wholly satisfying life of the freelance writer.

————

Aidan Chambers served in the Royal Navy from 1953 to 1955, and trained to be a teacher at Borough Road College, Isleworth, in London from 1955 to 1957. He is the cofounder of The Thimble Press, with his wife Nancy, whom he married March 30, 1968. The press publishes *Signal*, a critical magazine about children's books. His "Letter from England" column appeared in *The Horn Book Magazine* from 1972 to 1984, and he is the author of *Introducing Books to Children* (rev. ed., 1983). Chambers delivered the American Library Association's May Hill Arbuthnot Lecture presented April 25, 1986 at the University of Kansas at Little Rock. He received the Children's Literature Association Award for criticism in 1978, and the Eleanor Farjeon Award with Nancy Chambers in 1982. *Dance on My Grave* was named a Best Book for Young Adults by the ALA in 1983.

He is a contributor to *Books and Bookmen*, the *London Times Educational Supplement*, and *Books for Your Children*. He is the author of *Booktalk: Occasional Writing on Literature and Criticism* (1988). He is currently a visiting lecturer at Westminster College in Oxford, a playwright, and a member of the Society of Authors.

SELECTED WORKS: Breaktime, 1979; Seal Secret, 1981; Dance on My Grave, 1983; The Present Takers, 1984; Out of Time, 1985; Shades of Dark, 1986; NIK: Now I Know, 1988.

ABOUT: The Author's and Writer's Who's Who, 1971; Carpenter, Humphrey and Mari Prichard. The Oxford Companion to Children's Literature; Contemporary Authors (First Revision), Vol. 25; Vol. 12 (New Revision Series); The International Author's and Writer's Who's Who, 1982; Something About the Author, Vol. 1; Kirkpatrick, D.L., ed. Twentieth-Century Children's Writers, 2nd ed.; The Writers Directory 1984-86.

VICTORIA CHESS

November 16, 1939–

ILLUSTRATOR OF *Rolling Harvey Down the Hill*, etc.

Autobiographical sketch of Victoria Dickerson Chess:

I WAS BORN in Chicago in 1939 and

VICTORIA CHESS

brought up in a small town in Connecticut. I now live not far from there. It's a little like a sandwich, with Connecticut being the bread. Fifteen years in Manhattan and occasional forays into odd corners of the world are the tomatoes and cold cuts. I don't miss the city; I have a river at the bottom of my yard. For that matter, I have a yard. Also, plenty of other illustrators live nearby and are readily available for shop talk, complaints or congratulations.

All children draw, but I think illustrators are the ones who keep on doing it after fifth grade. I used to draw horses. Thousands and thousands of horses. I learned to draw other things by adding antlers to make them into stags, or putting trees, castles, witches, and princesses in the background. Only princes got to ride the horses. I would spend hours with a book called *How to Draw Animals*, trying to get them right. Often with little success. It was maddening. I adored the Brothers Grimm and the nineteenth-century tales of the Comtesse de Ségur. The illustrations were steel engravings, I think. They were gloomy, threatening, and to me, very exciting. That took care of the serious side of things. For fun, nothing could top *Krazy Kat* and *Pogo*.

I attended the Mary C. Wheeler School for Girls in Providence, Rhode Island. Most of my time there was spent drawing, reading unassigned books and avoiding Latin, maths, and sciences. Consequently, I was asked to leave. I then went to Là Châtelainie in St. Blâise, Switzerland. More girls. I got to get very good in French and Sneaking Out. After that, there were a few years at the School of the Museum of Fine Arts in Boston . . . where due to a rich and enjoyable social life and incomplete assignments, I was also asked to leave. I got to illustrate my first book almost by accident and discovered that there is nothing like the promise of money to develop good work habits. Twenty-five years later, I still get up every morning happy, and eager to get on with whatever assignment I have at the moment. So many people have only the recreational times in their lives to look forward to. It is such a blessing not to be among them. In the end, I work to please myself. I only hope that children will enjoy my pictures, and learn to laugh at the world and not take themselves too seriously.

———

Bugs received an American Institute of Graphic Arts Book Show Award in 1977.

SELECTED WORKS WRITTEN AND ILLUSTRATED: Alfred's Alphabet Walk, 1979; Catcards: Purrfect for Every Occasion, 1982; Poor Esme, 1982.

SELECTED WORKS WRITTEN WITH EDWARD GOREY AND ILLUSTRATED: Fletcher and Zenobia, 1967.

SELECTED WORKS ILLUSTRATED: The Animal's Peace Day, by Jan Wahl, 1970; Bugs: Poems, by Mary Ann Hoberman, 1976; The Queen of Eene, by Jack Prelutsky, 1978; Rolling Harvey Down the Hill, by Jack Prelutsky, 1980; Taking Care of Melvin, by Marjorie Weinman Sharmat, 1980; The Sheriff of Rottenshot, by Jack Prelutsky, 1982; Slugs, by David Greenberg, 1983; Bim Dooley Makes His Move, by Alice Schertle, 1984; Tales for the Perfect Child, by Florence Heide, 1985; Jim, by Hillaire Belloc, 1987; Princess Gorilla and a New Kind of Water, by Verna Aardema, 1988.

ABOUT: Contemporary Authors, Vol. 107; Kingman, Lee and others, comps. Illustrators of Children's Books: 1967-1976; Something About the Author, Vol. 33.

RUTH CHEW

April 8, 1920–

AUTHOR AND ILLUSTRATOR OF *The Wednesday Witch*, etc.

Autobiographical sketch of Ruth Silver, who writes under the pen name "Ruth Chew":

I WAS BORN in Minneapolis. My father was a newspaper reporter. The family moved to Des Moines and then, when I was three years old, to Washington, D.C., where my father edited the *Yearbook of Agriculture.* I grew up in Washington.

Before I entered first grade, I started telling myself stories. I drew pictures about the stories on any piece of paper that was blank. Teachers called on me a lot, because they thought I wasn't paying attention, but I drew and listened at the same time, and I liked being called on.

I made pictures for my book reports and biology projects. The pictures were not very good, but I always thought they were.

My best friend and I made up adventures for the dolls in our orange crate doll houses. We dressed up in things we found in my mother's ragbag. Sometimes we were Arabs, other times, "flappers" (1920s term for young women). We were the Dukes of Buckingham and York, the queens of fireflies and butterflies. As we invented the stories, we acted them, never knowing what would happen next!

In high school I majored in art and had an hour and a half of it every day. I stopped drawing on the back of my test papers. One summer, when I was fifteen, I taught myself to type while writing a book-length story about an imaginary trip to Europe.

After high school, for four blissful years I attended the Corcoran School of Art. In my last year I wrote a children's book and illustrated it. Nobody wanted to publish this.

The only work for an artist in Washington seemed to be in advertising. I worked as a fashion illustrator for department stores

Ruth Chew

and newspapers in Baltimore and Washington.

When I was twenty-three, I decided to seek my fortune in New York. I worked for a large advertising agency and then for a department store in Newark.

In April 1948 I married Aaron Ben Zion Silver, a lawyer. We have five children. When they were small I told them stories. After they were all in school I tried to return to fashion drawing, but found that I was out of date. I decided to illustrate children's books and trudged around with samples for five years before I got an assignment from Doubleday—*Three Cheers for Polly* by Carol Morse (a pseudonym).

I thought I was "in" now, but art editors said, "The drawings are all right, but we don't have a manuscript."

I went home and wrote *The Wednesday Witch* and made batches of little line drawings. It was turned down by at least ten publishers before it was accepted by Scholastic.

Beatrice de Regniers, editor of Scholastic's Lucky Book Club, made me rewrite the manuscript. She taught me everything I know about writing. She said I was a better writer than an artist. I went back to

school and studied with John Groth at the Art Students League. Then I illustrated *Shark Lady* by Ann McGovern. This book was awarded a prize for both text and illustrations.

I think I'm the luckiest person alive!

———

Ruth Chew was a student at the Corcoran School of Art from 1936 to 1940. She was an artist for the *Washington Post* from 1942 to 1943.

SELECTED WORKS WRITTEN AND ILLUSTRATED: The Wednesday Witch, 1969; No Such Thing as a Witch, 1971; Magic in the Park, 1972; What the Witch Left, 1973; The Hidden Cave, 1973; The Secret Summer, 1974; The Magic Cave, 1978; Earthstar Magic, 1979; Do-It-Yourself Magic, 1988.

SELECTED WORKS ILLUSTRATED: Three Cheers for Polly, by Carol Morse, 1967; The Questers, by E.W. Hildick, 1970; Mystery of the Ghost Bell, by Val Abbott, 1971; Shark Lady: True Adventures of Eugenie Clark, by Ann McGovern, 1979.

ABOUT: Contemporary Authors, (First Revision), Vol. 41; (New Revision Series), Vol. 14; The International Authors and Writers Who's Who, 1982; Something About the Author, Vol. 7.

ETH CLIFFORD

December 25, 1915–

AUTHOR OF *Just Tell Me When We're Dead!*, etc.

Autobiographical sketch of Eth Clifford, who also writes under the pen names "Ruth Bonn Penn" and "Ethel Rosenberg":

WHEN I WAS A CHILD, I decided that when I was grown I would be an actress, a dancer, a singer, and a criminal lawyer. I also thought it might be pleasant to be a princess, to live in a castle in some far-off land, wear fine clothes, eat chocolate without limit, and be gracious and kind to my subjects. This last daydream I soon realized was impractical. To begin with, I would have to marry a prince, and princes were in short supply in my neighborhood.

Eth Clifford

I never, ever thought I would be a writer. Writers I regarded as a race apart. They were tall, and handsome, and witty, and flawless. Then I discovered that all writers were not necessarily male. I found Louisa May Alcott, and later, Edna St. Vincent Millay, Elizabeth Barrett Browning, Emily Dickinson. But of course these women were tall and beautiful. Since I was tiny, and certainly not beautiful, I automatically disqualified myself.

Further, authors lived wildly adventurous lives. They scaled mountains, explored the underworld of seas, dived for coral in lagoons, ate exotic foods. And they spoke of their experiences with passion and delight. I could not see myself moving into such exalted circles.

Then what was left for me to write about, should I wish to be a writer?

When I was a little girl, my family lived in the country for about two years, where pines filled the air with a sharp, pervading scent; the woods were alive with birds; tiny creatures scrambled from beneath dead branches, and a silent walk on a dusty road was heady adventure. I attended a one-room schoolhouse. What I recall most vividly were the orchards—a pear orchard and

an apple orchard—that enclosed that school in aromatic parentheses. Lunchtime, I sat with my back against one of the pear trees, or an apple tree, opened my brown bag, ate lunch indifferently, and *read.*

Naturally I could not be a writer with so simple a background, but I could be, and was, a reader. As a child, a teenager, and adult . . . *always* a reader.

I wrote, of course, very early on. But that was not being a writer. When we were given assignments to write a 'composition' for English class, many a groan filled the air. I was surprised. Writing a composition beat arithmetic, which plagued me, or geography, which seemed sodden with unimportant details. Did I really care that Wisconsin was the dairy state of America? (I cared a lot about that, when my husband and daughter and I moved to Indiana, to live there for more than twenty years!)

I wrote whenever I could, threw away what I wrote, and wrote again. Then I submitted a story to a small magazine, who accepted it, *paid me for it*, and put my name on the front cover.

I was stunned. I was a writer!

I never did become an actress, a dancer, a singer, and a criminal lawyer. But I create characters, and fulfill my dreams through them. I never married that mythical prince, but I did marry a prince of a fellow, who won me instantly when he called me his 'greenpea princess'. And still does, after forty-seven years of marriage.

Isn't it remarkable that one doesn't have to be tall and beautiful and flawless to be a writer? And isn't it extraordinary to be able to say . . . *I am a writer!*

Eth Clifford was born in New York City but grew up in New Jersey, New York, and Philadelphia. She was married October 15, 1941 and has a daughter. She has also lived in Indianapolis and in Florida.

Beginning her career as a short story writer, she has also contributed to and edited language arts supplementary readers, and science and social studies texts for Compton's Encyclopedia and McGraw-Hill, among others. She has also written history texts.

Some of Eth Clifford's papers are collected in the Kerlan Collection at the University of Minnesota, the Division of Rare Books and Special Collections of the University of Wyoming, and the Bicentennial Library of California State College in California, Pennsylvania. She is a member of the Authors Guild, the Authors League of America, the Society of Children's Book Writers, and The Mystery Writers of America.

The Rocking Chair Rebellion was made into an Afterschool Special.

SELECTED WORKS: Red Is Never a Mouse, 1960; Why Is an Elephant Called an Elephant?, 1966; Burning Star, 1974; The Wild One, 1974; The Curse of the Moonraker, 1977; The Rocking Chair Rebellion, 1978; Help! I'm a Prisoner in the Library, 1979; The Killer Swan, 1980; The Dastardly Murder of Dirty Pete, 1981; Just Tell Me When We're Dead!, 1983; Harvey's Horrible Snake Disaster, 1984; The Remembering Box, 1985; The Man Who Sang in the Dark, 1987.

SELECTED WORKS AS RUTH BONN PENN: Mommies Are for Loving, 1962; Unusual Animals of the West, 1962; Simply Silly, 1964.

ABOUT (as Ethel Rosenberg): Contemporary Authors (First Revision), Vol. 29; (New Revision Series), Vol. 16; Something About the Author, Vol. 3; Who's Who of American Women, 1985-1986.

ELEANOR COERR

May 29, 1922–

AUTHOR OF *Sadako and the Thousand Paper Cranes*, etc.

Autobiographical sketch of Eleanor Beatrice Coerr, who also writes under the pen names "Eleanor B. Hicks" and "Eleanor Page":

I WAS BORN in the small town of Kamsack, Saskatchewan, Canada, but spent my growing-up years in Saskatoon, where my Dad owned a drugstore.

Coerr: rhymes with *more*

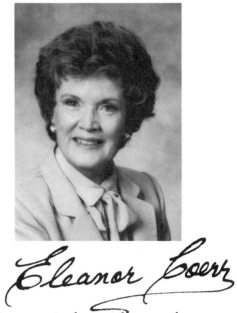

It was not in the stars for me to become an author of children's books. When I was very young, drawing was my passion, and I sketched every day after school. It seemed so easy for me that I did not think of taking art lessons, just enjoyed the hobby. Writing stories and the usual essays at school was also a pleasure, but I didn't think of that as a career.

If I had any ideas of becoming a serious artist, they were snuffed out at high school where we were all given aptitude tests. Although I was most interested in the humanities, the test showed that I was best suited for a scientific career, possibly in the medical field.

Who was I to argue with tests? My Dad sent me to the University of Saskatchewan where I struggled with biology, chemistry, and German. The only pleasure then was making drawings of the insides of frogs, or cross-sections of worms.

Finally, realizing that I would be a danger to the world at large if I became a physician, I dropped out of classes and got a job as the most junior reporter for our local newspaper.

That was the beginning of my writing career.

Since I was the youngest on staff, the job of writing a weekly column for children fell upon my shoulders. With great enthusiasm, I wrote original stories, drew the illustrations for them, and conducted a club for my readers. It was great fun; however, I had a secret desire to become a famous girl reporter and cover exciting events abroad—like wars and coronations.

That never happened. For the next fifteen years I wrote and illustrated columns for children in Canada, the United States, Jamaica, and The Philippines.

Over those busy years I managed to write and illustrate two books for children, *The Mystery of the Golden Cat*, and *Circus Day in Japan*.

At various foreign posts I turned out serious articles about the countries we lived in or visited for newspapers and magazines. For two years I was contract writer for the Voice of America. My vocabulary had to shrink to 900 words for this job, good training for the easy-to-read books I am writing now.

Children's books always fascinated me, so when we returned to the United States I earned an M.L.S. degree and obtained a position as Children's Librarian in a public library.

Like most librarians, I decided that I, too, should try my hand at writing juvenile books.

I discovered that selling a manuscript is not easy, and many of my early efforts ended up in the attic. After floundering around for a year or so, I found a hole in the library shelves on the subject of pandas, and set to work. The result was *The Biography of a Giant Panda*, my first real success.

Possibly because of my ability to write for newspapers, I find it easiest to put true facts together in an interesting way. It gives me a tremendous thrill to discover a snippet of history that fires my imagination. After a lot of research—which I love—I can put together a biography or a piece of historical fiction that might entice children to read.

Sometimes one book can change an au-

thor's life. *Sadako and the Thousand Paper Cranes*, written after our tour of duty in Japan, has been that book for me. Translated into several languages, it has moved thousands of children around the world to fold cranes as wishes for peace. Most of my "author talks" are devoted to that particular story and its background.

In the future I plan to write many more books for young readers, and hope that they will get as much pleasure from reading them as I do in researching and writing.

————

Eleanor Coerr received her B.A. degree in English Literature from American University in Washington, D.C. in 1969, and her M.L.S. from the University of Maryland in 1971. She was married in 1951; that marriage ended in divorce, and she was remarried in 1965. Her husband's career in the foreign service led to the travels that informed her books. She has taught courses in creative writing and in children's literature at Chapman College and the Monterey Peninsula College. She has visited schools in the U.S. and abroad, including the U.S.S.R. and Japan, where her story about Sadako is used as a reading tool in English classes.

Sadako and the Thousand Paper Cranes received the 1981 West Australia Young Readers Book Award for the Primary Grades from the Library Association of Australia. It is being produced for a film to be used in primary schools by Informed Democracy of Santa Cruz, California. *The Big Balloon Race* was named a 1982 Children's Choice Book by a joint committee of the Children's Book Council and the International Reading Association. *Jane Goodall* was named an Oustanding Science Trade Book for Children by a joint committee of the National Science Teachers Association and the CBC in 1976. *The Big Balloon Race* was a Reading Rainbow book. *The Josefina Story Quilt* was named a Notable Children's Trade Book in the Field of Social Studies by a joint committee of the CBC and the National Council on the Social Studies in 1986.

SELECTED WORKS WRITTEN AND ILLUSTRATED AS ELEANOR B. HICKS: Circus Day in Japan, 1954.

SELECTED WORKS WRITTEN AND ILLUSTRATED AS ELEANOR COERR: The Mystery of The Golden Cat, 1969; Biography of a Giant Panda, 1976; Jane Goodall, 1976; The Mixed-Up Mystery Smell, 1976; Sadako and the Thousand Paper Cranes, 1977; The Big Balloon Race, 1981; The Bellringer and the Pirates, 1983; The Josefina Story Quilt, 1986; Lady with a Torch, 1986; Chang's Paper Pony, 1988.

SELECTED WORKS AS ELEANOR PAGE: Snoopy, 1945.

ABOUT: Contemporary Authors (First Revision), Vol. 25-28; (New Revision), Vol. 11; Something About the Author, Vol. 1; Who's Who of American Women, 1983-1984; The Writers Directory 1984-1986.

DANIEL COHEN

March 12, 1936–

AUTHOR OF *America's Very Own Monsters*, etc.

Autobiographical sketch of Daniel Cohen:

WHEN I WAS A KID I never wanted to be a writer. It didn't seem a very practical way to make a living. Besides, I couldn't spell. I still can't. I wanted to be a zookeeper, and I have often thought that not becoming one was the biggest mistake of my life. I was supposed to go to college, and you didn't need a college degree to clean the elephant cage. Today many zookeepers do have degrees, and they do lots more than clean the elephant cage, but growing up I didn't know that. To compensate I have filled my life with a series of eccentric and spoiled dogs and cats.

A less successful compensation was my decision to become a biologist. That was a respectable business that did require college. I soon discovered that looking at cells through a microscope wasn't nearly as much fun as cleaning the elephant cage. So I drifted—and I mean drifted, for I had absolutely no plan at all—into journalism and ultimately into writing books.

It hasn't been an unhappy fate because I write about animals and zoos and other things that interest me like monsters and ghosts and ancient Egypt. It keeps me young. Here I am, a middle-aged man, and I'm a lot more concerned about the Loch Ness Monster than about the stock market or mowing the lawn.

Let's go back to the beginning. I was born in Chicago during the Great Depression. We were pretty poor, but I gather we were pretty poor before the Depression, so when it came we were ready for it.

I went to the usual public schools and finally to the Chicago branch of the University of Illinois, where I began to work on the school newspaper. That is what really turned me toward journalism. I was an editor on a magazine called *Science Digest* for about nine years before becoming a full-time free-lance writer.

I was married about two weeks after I graduated from college and over the years my wife Susan has slowly been converted to writing. She has done a number of novels on her own and more recently we have collaborated on books, not an easy thing to do I'm told, but it has worked for us.

We have one child, a daughter, Theodora, who is a drama student. No, that's not fair, she has done a lot of summer stock as well as school, so she's an actress. She thinks that what her parents do is boring, and compared to theater I daresay it is.

We have a couple of cats and current dog is a Clumber spaniel. What, you've never heard of a Clumber spaniel! Well, they weigh about seventy pounds, and snore loudly, and they....no time for that, because once I get started on dog stories I don't stop.

I write nonfiction—that is, I don't make up the stories. That's easy to understand when I'm doing a book on dinosaurs or a biography of Carl Sagan. When I write on subjects like ghosts and monsters the nonfiction label becomes a bit confusing. I'm often asked if all the ghost or UFO tales I've reported are really true, and if I believe in ghosts and ESP. I try to report accurately on what I have seen and heard. In some of my books I recount tales that I know, or strongly suspect, are legendary. I make that clear to my readers. I love a good yarn as much as the next person, but I don't try to pass a legend off as a fact. On the other hand, I don't want to take credit for a good ghost story that someone else made up.

After some twenty years as a full-time writer, and some 140 books I can say it has been fun most of the time. That about wraps it up. After all, I'm not getting paid for this, and the Clumber spaniel is getting restless.

————

Daniel Cohen graduated from the University of Illinois with a degree in Journalism in 1958. He was married February 2, 1958. From 1960 to 1969 he was managing editor of *Science Digest* magazine and has been a writer ever since. He is a member of the Author's Guild, the Audubon Society, and the Appalachian Mountain Club.

SELECTED WORKS: Secrets from Animal Graves, 1968; Vaccination and You, 1968; The Age of Giant Mammals, 1969; Animals of the City, 1969; Night Animals, 1970; Talking with Animals, 1971; Watchers in the Wild, 1972; Shaka: King of the Zulus, 1973; The Spirit of the Lord: Revivalism in America, 1975;

Young Ghosts, 1978; Famous Curses, 1979; The Tomb Robbers, 1980; The Headless Roommate and Other Tales of Terror, 1981; America's Very Own Monsters, 1982; Hiram Bingham and the Dream of Gold, 1984; Carl Sagan: Superstar Scientist, 1986; ESP, 1986; Dinosaurs, 1987; Hollywood Dinosaur, 1987; UFO's: The Third Wave, 1988.

ABOUT: Contemporary Authors, Vol. 45; (New Revision Series), Vol. 1; The International Authors and Writers Who's Who, 1982; Something About the Author, Vol. 8; Something About the Author Autobiography Series, Vol. 4.

BROCK COLE

May 29, 1938–

AUTHOR OF *The Goats*, etc.

Biographical sketch of Brock Cole:

BROCK COLE was born in Charlotte, Michigan, and his childhood was spent in the Midwest. He graduated from Kenyon College in Ohio, and received a Doctorate of Philosophy from the University of Minnesota. He later taught Philosophy at the University. Around 1975, he tired of teaching and decided to pursue his interest in writing. He thought that being able to illustrate his books would make them easier to publish, so he took up painting. He is self-taught and uses watercolors as well as black-and-white line drawings.

The father of two grown sons, Cole currently resides in Oak Park, Illinois, with his wife, who teaches Ancient History at the University of Illinois at Chicago Circle.

Cole says he hopes that young people will "keep at what you're interested in," rather than pursuing a profession that results only in monetary rewards.

The Goats, which was Cole's first novel, was the subject of an editorial by Anita Silvey in *The Horn Book Magazine*, in which she hailed the book as "an extraordinary first novel." The *Horn Book* reviewer, Nancy Vasilakis, said, "Brock Cole has written a gripping novel that is part survival story, part psychological drama, and part

Brock Cole

realistic problem novel, though these descriptions do not come close to conveying the conviction and the depth of the writing." Editor Silvey writes, "The publication of a novel like *The Goats* signifies that we are still creating children's books that affirm the human spirit and the ability of the individual to rise above adversity."

No More Baths was a Book-of-the-Month Club selection. *The King at the Door* won a 1980 Friends of American Writers Juvenile Book Merit Award. *Gaffer Samson's Luck* won the 1985 Smarties "Grand Prix" for Children's Books, given by England's Book Trust. *The Goats* won the 1988 Carl Sandburg Award, given by the Friends of Chicago Public Library. The American Library Association named *The Goats* a 1987 Best Book for Young Adults as well as a 1987 Notable Book.

SELECTED WORKS WRITTEN AND ILLUSTRATED: The King at the Door, 1979; No More Baths, 1980; Nothing But a Pig, 1981; The Winter Wren, 1984; The Giant's Toe, 1986.

SELECTED WORKS WRITTEN: The Goats, 1987.

SELECTED WORKS ILLUSTRATED: The Indian in the Cupboard, by Lynne Reid Banks, 1981; Gaffer Samson's Luck, by Jill Paton Walsh, 1985.

ABOUT: Horn Book January/February 1988; September/October 1989.

CHRIS CONOVER

February 12, 1950–

RETELLER AND ILLUSTRATOR OF *Six Little Ducks*, etc.

Autobiographical sketch of Chris Conover:

I WAS BORN in New York City. Both of my parents were artists. Books and reading were important to them, and they read to me and taught me to appreciate books. Art was important, too, and always a part of our household. I have such happy memories of waking up on Saturdays, my mother's day off from her teaching responsibilities, and smelling the pungent odor of turpentine and hearing the scratch of brushes on canvas. I would wander out and perch on the arm of a chair to watch the painting progress. Sometimes, I would teasingly insist that I could pick out a dog, a tree, or a mermaid in the big abstract canvas. And my mother would laugh, and paintings became something we shared.

Because I had no brothers and sisters, books and paintings became my companions. Naturally, I wanted to write my own stories and draw pictures for them. As a little girl, I illustrated stories on construction paper with crayons, and once even sent one to a publisher. I was thrilled to receive an encouraging letter from them, accompanied by my "manuscript."

The desire to work on children's books stayed with me. I attended the High School of Music and Art in New York City and the State University of New York at Buffalo. I did not study illustration, which was more oriented towards advertising at that time. I studied Fine Art/Printmaking. Although I liked the work, I had the feeling that I was not on the right path.

During those school years, I held several jobs as a day camp instructor, teaching art

Chris Conover *(signature)*

to young children. Perhaps it was inevitable that those experiences would shape my future.

After leaving college, my husband and I lived in Montana, where he was working towards an M.F.A. in Creative Writing. Away from any artistic influence of home or school, I just naturally gravitated toward children's book illustration.

One evening, while watching a W.C. Fields movie, I got an idea for my first book. By the end of the movie, my text was written! It was based on a song that my day-campers used to love, called "Six Little Ducks." Without formal training in illustration, I plunged into the project, guided by my instincts and the books I admired. I was tremendously excited by this new challenge, and I found the feeling that had been missing from my student work. Although the task before me was far from easy, I felt that I was doing the right work, and knew I would continue. *Six Little Ducks* did indeed get published several years later, and my love for illustration and storytelling has stayed with me. I expect to spend the rest of my life trying to capture the images in my mind with brush and paper.

———

Chris Conover attended the State University of New York in Buffalo from 1969 to 1971. She was married October 17, 1980. She is a member of the Graphics Artists Guild. She also gives lectures at children's literature conferences.

Six Little Ducks was named a Boston Globe-Horn Book Honor Book for Illustration in 1976. Three of her books won American Institute of Graphic Arts citations: *Where Did My Mother Go?*, *The Bear and the Kingbird*, and *The Beast in the Bed*.

SELECTED WORKS ADAPTED OR RETOLD AND ILLUSTRATED: Six Little Ducks, 1976; Froggie Went A-Courting, 1986; The Adventures of Simple Simon, 1987.

SELECTED WORKS ILLUSTRATED: The Wish at the Top, by Clyde Robert Bulla, 1974; Somebody Else's Child, by Roberta Silman, 1976; The School Mouse, by Dorothy J. Harris, 1977; Where Did My Mother Go?, by Edna M. Preston, 1978; The Bear and the Kingbird, by the Grimm Brothers, 1979; The Little Humpbacked Horse: A Russian Tale, adapted by Margaret Hodges, 1980; The Beast in the Bed, by Barbara Dillon, 1981.

ABOUT: Kingman, Lee and others, comps. Illustrators of Children's Books: 1967-1976; Shulevitz, Uri. Writing with Pictures; Something About the Author, Vol. 31.

PAM CONRAD

June 18, 1947–

AUTHOR OF *Prairie Songs*, etc.

Autobiographical sketch of Pam Conrad:

MY EARLIEST MEMORIES involve books and words and rhymes—little chairs in the children's library room, and my father standing in our basement apartment booming that sorrowful song about Frankie and Johnny.

And then late at night I would listen to him read *Moby Dick* to my mother, while I slept with Babar under my pillow.

I began writing when I was seven and had the chicken pox. My mother gave me

some paper and colored pencils to draw with, but instead of drawing I began writing poetry that sounded a lot like A.A. Milne. From then on, whenever I had a fever, I would write poems. This must have been quite often, because when I was twelve my father published a private collection of them all, called *Tea by the Garden Wall*.

I wrote off and on through junior high and high school, mostly love poems and stories about girls who would perform acts of great sacrifice; and then after a little college, I got married and entered one of my "silences," as Tillie Olsen would call it. I wrote only in my journal—dull, daily notations—and newsy, perky letters home from Colorado and Texas, where my husband was stationed. But it wasn't until I was back in New York and my children were in school that I returned to college and my dormant writing talent suddenly batted its eyes, stretched, yawned, and said, "Yes, now where was I?"

I met Johanna Hurwitz at the Hofstra Writer's Conference in 1981 and decided to try my hand at children's books, as I was trying everything else from magazine articles to paperback romances. With Johan-

na's encouragement, I wrote a Beverly Cleary-type book called *I Don't Live Here!*, and after twelve submissions finally sold it to E.P. Dutton.

While I was mailing this book around I began a new book. My earlier stay out West had introduced me to Nebraska, a place that both fascinated and terrified me. I had read Willa Cather, Mari Sandoz, and of course the Little House books. I had a story to tell—about a woman who moves from New York to the West, much as I had—and goes mad. But the story was too painful for me to write from her point of view. It wasn't till I found a child's voice to tell the story that it began to flow and *Prairie Songs* was written.

Since then I have found my young adult novels begin with settings. *Holding Me Here* is the house I was living in then and the town where I still live today—a nice suburban place where kids ride bicycles, take trains, and sell holiday wrapping paper. *What I Did For Roman* started with my memories of the Central Park Zoo, and the stories of a friend who used to work there as a teenager. *Taking the Ferry Home* is really Shelter Island, my favorite place on earth, and my latest novel, *My Daniel*, is a story about Nebraska told by an old woman as she walks through the Museum of Natural History.

While none of my books are particularly autobiographical, they are each about my life in one disguise or another. As it did Emmeline in *Prairie Songs*, the prairie frightened me; as Robin is affected in *Holding Me Here*, someone else's diary always calls to me; and like Darcie and Roman in the zoo book, I too stuck gravel up my nose when I was very young, risked my life on a wooden swing, and lived along the railroad tracks.

My other books for young readers are gifts to my children, based on their lives, and my picture books are sort of like spontaneous combustion or hiccoughs. They usually happen quickly without too much forethought, except for one that took three years because it's a poem that is nearly a mathematical equation.

Besides writing I have discovered the joy of teaching writing. I believe that all we write comes through us, not from us, that we're channels of sorts of hundreds of stories that are floating around in the universe. And the greatest happiness for me is when all of a sudden little parts of my life begin to take on a strange, new significance. Something slowly opens up inside me like a dam on a Nebraska river, and a story begins to unfold.

I live in Rockville Centre with my teenage daughter, who when she was little and I gave her paper to write poems, drew pictures. We intend to collaborate on a picture book one day and we hope to become the "Judds" of children's literature.

————

Pam Conrad attended Hofstra University from 1977 to 1979, and received her B.A. degree from the New School for Social Research in 1984. She was married June 25, 1967, and is now divorced. She is a member of the Society of Children's Book Writers, P.E.N., and the Author's Guild. She writes poetry, and her essays and articles have appeared in *Publishers Weekly*, *McCalls*, *Newsweek*, *Newsday*, and *The New York Times*. She teaches writing courses at Queens College.

Prairie Songs won many awards; it was named a Notable Book and a Best Book for Young Adults by the American Library Association in 1985; it was a 1986 Honor Book for fiction in the Boston Globe-Horn Book awards; it was named an Honor Book in the 1985 Society of Children's Book Writers' Golden Kite Book Awards; it received a Western Heritage Award from the National Cowboy Hall of Fame, and it won the International Reading Association Award, both in 1986. It was also named a 1985 Notable Trade Book in the Field of Social Studies by a joint committee of the National Council on the Social Studies and the Children's Book Council. *What I Did for Roman* was also named an ALA Best Book for Young Adults, in 1987.

SELECTED WORKS: I Don't Live Here!, 1983; Prairie Songs, 1985; Holding Me Here, 1986; Seven Silly Circles, 1987; What I Did for Roman, 1987; Staying Nine, 1988; Taking the Ferry Home, 1988; My Daniel, 1989; The Tub People, 1989.

ABOUT: Something About the Author, Vol. 52.

GILLIAN CROSS

December 24, 1945–

AUTHOR OF *On the Edge*, etc.

Autobiographical sketch of Gillian Clare Cross:

I CAN'T REMEMBER a time without stories. I was born on Christmas Eve, 1945, in London. It was a time of austerity and rationing in Britain, but that isn't how I remember my childhood. I remember being in a house full of books and stories. Books filled the shelves and cupboards. They were stacked in cardboard boxes and piled in heaps on the floor. Before we could read our mother made up stories to tell us and our father read stories onto tape on his big reel-to-reel tape recorder—long before commercial story cassettes were dreamt of.

I made up stories too, for my younger brother and sister, telling them out loud, drawing them and writing them down. I scrounged every spare blank page I could find and begged for paper as a birthday present.

But, as I got older, time ran out. I had a long train journey to and from school each day, with lots of homework and piano practice to fit in afterwards. Studying English Literature inhibited me, too, because I realized how clumsy my own stories were. They started to founder after the first few pages, as I brooded about "structure" and "imagery" and "characterization".

But there's always a place for stories. The place they found then was that long, boring

GILLIAN CROSS

myself, I understood that each story makes its own special demands of the story-teller. I realized—at last—that "structure" and "imagery" and "characterization" were simply necessary tools in the struggle to tell that story properly.

Since then, I have written twenty-one novels, most of which have been published. I've had a strange collection of jobs, as well: I've worked for a Member of Parliament, and for a village baker with an old-fashioned brick oven; I've taught in a school and in a University; and I've worked as a child-minder and as a clerical assistant in an office. I'm still producing "fast fiction", too, because we have four children now, and the youngest is only three. But writing that first book was what made sense of my life. From then on, I knew what I wanted to do.

———

Gillian Cross was married on May 10, 1967. She took first class honors at Somerville College in Oxford. Two of her books have been named Best Books for Young Adults in their year of publication by the American Library Association: *On the Edge* and *Chartbreaker*. The ALA also named two of her books Notable Books of the year, *On the Edge* in 1985 and *Roscoe's Leap* in 1987. The latter was also a Junior Literary Guild selection.

SELECTED WORKS: The Iron Way, 1979; Revolt at Ratcliffe's Rags, 1980; A Whisper of Lace, 1982; The Demon Headmaster, 1983; Born of the Sun, 1984; The Dark Behind the Curtain, 1984; On the Edge, 1985; The Prime Minister's Brain, 1986; Chartbreaker, 1987; Roscoe's Leap, 1987; a Map of Nowhere, 1989.

ABOUT: Carpenter, Humphrey and Mari Prichard. The Oxford Companion to Children's Literature; Contemporary Authors, Vol. 111; Kirkpatrick, D.L., ed. Twentieth-Century Children's Writers, 2nd ed.; Something About the Author, Vol. 38.

train journey to and from school. I told my friends a serial story in which they were the heroines, and they met their heroes and fulfilled their ambitions. Whatever they asked for, I put into the story, with never a thought for structure or imagery or characterization. It was "fast fiction".

For a long time, as I studied literature, all my fiction was fast. After school, I went on, first to Oxford, where I gained a B.A. in English in 1969, and then to the University of Sussex, where I wrote a thesis on G.K. Chesterton and the Decadents. I was awarded a D.Phil in 1974. But I was a mother as well as a student. By 1970 I had a son and a daughter, who adored stories. That meant more "fast fiction" of course. We had stories at bedtime, at mealtimes, even when we were walking along the road. I never had time to think about the niceties I was studying at University. The only important question in those stories was the most primitive one: "What's next?"

Then, in 1974, I finished studying. I had been in formal education for twenty-five years and suddenly it was all over and I had time to write a book. So I did. And that was when everything in my life came together, to make sense. Once I was trying to write

PAT CUMMINGS

November 9, 1950–

ILLUSTRATOR OF *My Mama Needs Me*, etc.

Autobiographical sketch of Pat Cummings:

I'VE BEEN illustrating for as long as I can remember. Of course, I didn't call it that, but when I was in the fifth grade I was doing a healthy business selling ballerina drawings during recess. They all had pinpoint waists, huge flowered tutus and legs that tapered down to needlelike toe shoes. I sold them for nickels or chocolate bars, which were acceptable forms of currency then, and did a good business. It never occurred to me to change professions.

My father was in the Army and, because we moved frequently, my brother and two sisters and I were always the "new kids of the block." Art was often an entree: I'd meet other kids working on the school yearbook or making hall posters.

My parents always encouraged me and kept me well stocked with art supplies. Their support and the satisfaction when I was little of doing a picture that was good enough to hang on the refrigerator door are no doubt the bases for the strong sense of well-being that I feel when drawing.

I think I was lucky to grow up experiencing different cultures. When I was eight we moved to Okinawa, where magic and mystery were just a part of daily life. Ghosts made the front page of the national newspaper. My friends and I ran into and from witches and water buffalos on our forays into the villages. We ate candies wrapped in paper that melted in your mouth and learned ritualistic tea ceremonies dressed in kimonos. I grew up to realize that memory is imprecise and logical explanations can suck mystery dry, but I still draw on the sense of "anything is possible" that my childhood gave me.

I remember the magical stories my mother read to us from a series called "Tales of the Rhine" when we lived in Germany. They were full of dragons and princesses in dire need of saving by a dashing prince. I thought they were heavily illustrated with detailed drawings. Finding them again as an adult, however, I saw there were very few pictures. My imagination had supplied the rest.

Being able to visualize a story as it's read is natural, but it becomes essential to an illustrator. While drawing I try to see each scene as the characters see it. I want to look around the little boy's room and see what he collects or what's hidden in his closet. Sometimes I like to see from unusual angles, perhaps from the level of a four year old whose view of an adult might just stop at the knees. I love aerial views because I have sensational flying dreams and want to recapture the perspective I have in them. There may be color combinations or patterns I want to use, and I save up pictures to pin to my desk to trigger ideas as I work.

I studied art at Pratt Institute and started to work as a free lancer while I was there. Brooklyn's Billie Holiday Theatre for Little Folks staged plays by and for kids, and I did their flyers, posters, and newspapers ads. After graduation I worked for magazines, newspapers, advertising agencies, and book publishers.

When I finally got my first children's book to illustrate, I sought out illustrator Tom Feelings in New York. I'd never met him, but I admired his work. He took the time to explain all of the technical things I needed to know and showed me the book he was working on at the time. His help made me want always to be available to others who are trying to get started.

Writing stories has made illustrating them even more enjoyable. In a fantasy like *C.L.O.U.D.S.* I could draw everything in my studio, but locate it in the sky. In *Jimmy Lee Did It*, an exposé about my younger brother Arty's imaginary friend, I got revenge for all the pranks he pulled when we were little. Using my family and friends as models makes each book more personal as well. My husband Chuku Lee is my most frequent and most underpaid model.

I grew up loving to read and look at picture books, so actually producing them is very satisfying. I still collect and read picture books from all over the world. I want children to be able to see positive reflections of themselves in my books and hopefully to find, as I always have, a little magic and mystery between the covers.

———

Pat Cummings was born in Chicago, Illinois. She graduated from Pratt Institute in Brooklyn with a B.F.A. degree in 1974. She is a member of the Black Art Directors Group of New York and the Graphic Artists Guild. Her work has been exhibited at Black Enterprise Gallery in New York in 1980 and at CRT Gallery in Hartford in 1981.

In 1984, Pat Cummings was awarded the Coretta Scott King Award for her illustrations for *My Mama Needs Me*; the book was also a Reading Rainbow book. She received an Honorable Mention for the King Award in 1983 for *Just Us Women* and in 1987 for *C.L.O.U.D.S. Just Us Women* was also named a Notable Children's Trade Book in the Field of Social Studies in 1982 by a joint committee of the Children's Book Council and the National Council on the Social Studies.

SELECTED WORKS WRITTEN AND ILLUSTRATED: Jimmy Lee Did It, 1985; C.L.O.U.D.S., 1986.

SELECTED WORKS ILLUSTRATED: Good News, by Eloise Greenfield, 1987; Just Us Women, by Jeannette Caines, 1982; My Mama Needs Me, by Mildred Pitts Walter, 1983; Fred's First Day, by Cathy Warren, 1984; Chilly Stomach, by Jeannette Caines, 1986; Springtime Bears, by Cathy Warren, 1987; I Need a Lunch Box, by Jeannette Caines, 1988; Storm in the Night, by Mary Stolz, 1988.

ABOUT: Rollock, Barbara. Black Authors and Illustrators of Children's Books; Something About the Author, Vol. 42.

LYDIA DABCOVICH

October 23, 1935–

ILLUSTRATOR OF *There Once Was a Woman Who Married a Man*, etc.

Autobiographical sketch of Lydia Dabcovich:

I WAS BORN in Bulgaria but I don't remember much about it because my parents moved to Israel (then Palestine) when I was very young. Most of the family—grandparents, aunts, uncles—had already settled there. This was during the Second World War. We left on the last ship out of Bulgaria, which was already occupied by the Germans.

A lot was going on while I was growing up—the war, the Declaration of the State of Israel, the Arab-Israeli War of 1948—but I remember the pleasant things most of all: the bright blue of the Mediterranean; the dark green of cypresses; the smell of orange trees and eucalyptus; the sound of Chopin mazurkas played by my grandmother for my sister and me to dance to . . . and books, books, books—*Winnie-the-Pooh, Dr. Dolittle, Heidi, Kim, Huck Finn*—they're all magic; illustrations by Hugh Lofting, Rackham, Cruikshank; *Great Expectations, A Tale of Two Cities*—books made whole worlds come alive.

We spent a lot of time at my grandparents' house high up on Mt. Carmel in Haifa. Around the house there were rocky fields sloping all the way down to the sea. Olive,

Lydia Dabcovich

pine, and carob trees grew in between prickly bushes, and Arab shepherds came there to graze their goats and sheep and to play on their flutes. At night one could hear jackals howling, which was both scary and exciting.

At my grandparents' there were always lots of people. Everyone spoke many languages and it was natural for them to shift from one language to another all during one meal.

My father's family had been among the founders of a kibbutz (a collective farm). Sometimes I went there to spend a few days with my cousins. The children in the kibbutz lived apart from the adults in the children's house. They had their own kitchen and dining room and everyone took turns doing chores. Visiting there made one feel grown-up and independent.

In Tel-Aviv I dreamed and doodled my way through school. I drew on anything—my first still-existing drawing is on the flyleaf of my mother's Hungarian cookbook. It's a drawing of a house which I made around the age of three. I still think it's pretty good! However, I didn't decide to become an artist until much later, after I finished high school. During my school years I had other ambitions: I took every conceivable type of dance class and spent many hours practicing splits, turning cartwheels, and planning to become a famous dancer. Later on I was going to be a musician, actress, costume designer, and zookeeper.

After high school, during my compulsory military service, I took night classes in drawing and painting. And then everything fell into place—I was going to art school to become a book illustrator. During that time I also went on a trip to Turkey and there I met my husband. He was a student of Naval architecture at M.I.T. We got married at the beginning of my second year at the Boston Museum School.

My older daughter was born after my graduation. I didn't do much serious art work until just before my second daughter was born eight years later. By then nothing could stop me. I went around "beating the pavements" with my portfolio and took every job I could get—magazines, textbooks, greeting cards. Eventually I got what I really wanted—picture books. Later I was encouraged by my editor to write some of my own. I feel very lucky to be able to earn a living doing what I like best. Picture books seem to contain everything I've always been drawn to—music and rhythm, movement and drama. Each picture book is a whole new world and I'm free to dream and doodle as much as I want.

———

Lydia Dabcovich attended the Central School of Arts and Crafts in London from 1956 to 1957 and graduated from the Boston Museum School of Fine Arts, with highest honors, in 1960. She has taught book illustration for five years at the Boston Art Institute, from 1983 to 1988. She is a member of the Graphic Artists' Guild.

There Once Was a Woman Who Married a Man was named a *New York Times* Best Illustrated Book of 1978. *Mrs. Huggins and Her Hen Hannah* was named a Children's Choice book by a joint committee of the International Reading Association and the Children's Book Council in 1985 and was also a Reading Rainbow selection.

SELECTED WORKS WRITTEN AND ILLUSTRATED: Follow the River, 1980; Sleepy Bear, 1982; Mrs. Huggins and Her Hen Hannah, 1985; Busy Beavers, 1988.

SELECTED WORKS ILLUSTRATED: There Once Was a Woman Who Married a Man, by Norma Farber, 1978; The Boy Who Would Be a Hero, by Marjorie Lewis, 1982; Animal Hedge, by Paul Fleischman, 1983; Hurry Home, Grandma!, by Arielle North Olson, 1984; Up North in Winter, by Barbara Hartley, 1986; William and Grandpa, by Alice Schertle, 1989.

ABOUT: Contemporary Authors, Vol. 124; Something About the Author, Vol. 47.

NIKI DALY

NIKI DALY

June 13, 1946–

AUTHOR OF *Not So Fast, Songololo*, etc.

Autobiographical sketch of Nicholas Daly:

I WAS BORN in Cape Town, South Africa. The first artist I knew was my Uncle Piet, who was a bit of a travelling artist. I think I first developed a deep fascination for art materials before developing an interest in actual art-making processes. Uncle Piet used Venus pencils. They were a dark racing color veined with a lighter green, tipped with a gold metal encased rubber. When they became reduced to stubs, he let me have them. He was a watercolourist and used little blocks of Windsor and Newton watercolours that were kept in a black metal case. I regarded his materials as things of mystery and magic.

We were not a very well-off family, and art materials like crayons, paints, and paper were not to be found around the house. I remember getting tremendous satisfaction out of discovering white pieces of unprinted paper like margins in books and newspapers to draw on. And it might very well have been the relationship between my drawings and the neighboring type that

formed my love of picture and type. Academically I wasn't up to much but I was adequately compensated by being able to draw and sing. I think it must have been the emotional rewards gained through art rather than cerebral satisfaction I was after.

In 1970 I left South Africa to take up a recording contract with CBS Records in London. (I was one of those art students who also had aspirations for becoming a pop star!)

I spent two years as a songwriter and recorded with CBS in London. But in 1973 during a recession in Britain my contract was not renewed, and I decided to go back to working as a designer in advertising.

During this time I came into contact with illustration of a very high quality, which was so inspiring that I decided to become a free-lance illustrator. During the mid-1970s I worked mainly for an educational publisher doing strip cartoons, using black-and-white pen-and-ink drawings. I grew to love and respect the very rich heritage of illustration that was evident in the work of illustrators like Tenniel to Edward Ardizzone, who was still living and working at that time. Great is my regret that I never visited him; this could easily have been arranged through my agent Laura Cecil, who also worked as agent for Ardizzone.

I had a special regard for illustrators of the old school who all knew how to draw and use the most basic reproducible medium of pen and ink. This group of artists included Harold Jones, Faith Jaques, Shirley Hughes, and Charles Keeping. So many of the younger illustrators seemed to have neglected good drawing for the sake of sophisticated illustrative effects.

I became a member of the Association of Illustrators in London, and at one of their functions I met a young book illustrator called Eliza Trimby. Eliza's work was most impressive. In fact it was more her attitude towards it than the actual work that I found so impressive, as well as educational. She researched everything she illustrated in the most serious and dedicated manner. Her approach to illustration was rather like the approach of the artists of the Arts and Crafts movement of the 19th Century; each book under her care became an object of beauty where illustration and decoration mingled.

In contrast, my line of work was based on quantity (as I was not very well paid for individual pieces) and a speedy, spontaneous, sketchy kind of approach. This method really suited my nature, which sometimes demands change before change is due.

Through my friendship with Eliza I changed my attitude towards illustration and decided that I should try my hand at an illustrated book. The difficulty I faced (and which all beginners face) was the overcautious art editor's concern for trying out an untested illustrator on an entire book.

To overcome this prejudice, I wrote my own story and made a mock-up book that was so finished, it looked like the real thing (endpapers, simulated type, and bound!). Eliza introduced me to a young agent, Laura Cecil, and within a week I was offered a contract by William Collins to do *The Little Girl Who Lived Down the Road*. I based the book on a day trip to the sea that my wife and I made to Brighton. The experi-

ence sparked off childhood memories of going to the sea, and my experience as a songwriter assisted the writing of the text.

Much encouraged by an award received for the illustration for my first book, I produced a second book entitled *Vim the Rag Mouse* and also illustrated Kathleen Hersom's *Maybe It's a Tiger*.

In 1979 my first son Joseph was born, and we decided to return to South Africa. To family, grandparents, and a troubled country.

During my first year back I worked on *Joseph's Other Red Sock* and started several amazing postal relationships with Laura Cecil and all the wonderful editors and publishers I have corresponded and worked with over the past nine years.

Now, I must explain what it is like to be a children's book illustrator in South Africa.

The first local job on returning introduced me to the bizarre and perverted nature of apartheid and racist mentality. I had to illustrate a poem about friendship, so I decided to introduce a black and a white child into the illustration, which seemed wholly appropriate to the poem's sentiments. The poem stated that although each child is an individual, and no matter where they are, each likes the other. The illustration made the editor blanch. It appeared that not only was such a friendship "most unlikely" but on the facing page there was an illustration of a little white girl "taking a bath!"

After this episode I realized I had two choices. I could either go back to England or stay and try and join the movement towards dismantling apartheid and educating children to be respectful and curious of children outside their own lives and experiences.

Subsequently things have changed. Some have replaced fear with love whilst others have compounded fear with hate. There is an enormous illiteracy problem among many of our black children due to poverty. Yes! Children need food before books. But the one feeds the body and the other feeds the mind and affirms the spirit of child-hood.

There is a challenge for makers of picture books in South Africa. Themes to be gathered from the lives of all South Africans are rich because life here is so strange and full of irony and pain. Our children need to have their childhoods protected and enriched with imagination, and harsh reality must be made more understandable and therefore less frightening.

My latest plan is to start a children's book division with David Philip, a publisher of many fine adult books dealing with life in Africa. It will be called Songololo Books after my book *Not So Fast, Songololo*, which I believe has added to a growing interest and respect between children of different backgrounds.

A songololo is a little black millipede that can be seen after rain has fallen and the sun has come out.

———

Niki Daly was educated at Cape Town Technikon, where he received his diploma in 1970. He has been a graphics teacher at East Ham Technical College in London. He has two sons.

The Little Girl Who Lived Down the Road won the 1978 Provincial Booksellers Award for illustration in Britain, and *Not So Fast, Songololo* won the South African Katrien Harries Award for illustration.

Selected Works Written and Illustrated: The Little Girl Who Lived Down the Road, 1978; Vim the Rag Mouse, 1979; Joseph's Other Red Sock, 1982; Leo's Christmas Surprise, 1983, Ben's Gingerbread Man, 1985; Monsters Are Like That, 1985; Teddy's Ear, 1985; Just Like Archie, 1986; Look At Me!, 1986; Not So Fast, Songololo, 1986; Thank You, Henrietta, 1986.

Selected Works Illustrated: Maybe It's a Tiger by Kathleen Hersom, 1981; I Want To See the Moon by Louis Baum, 1984.

About: Something About the Author, Vol. 37.

BARTHE DeCLEMENTS

October 8, 1920–

Author of *Nothing's Fair in Fifth Grade*, etc.

Autobiographical sketch of Barthe DeClements:

WHEN MY SON Christopher woke up from his naps, he sang. He sang and banged his head on the back of his crib. Psychologists have done research on babies who bang their heads on their cribs and have found them to be musical. Now that Christopher is grown, he still sings and he sings while he drives. When I ride with him, I wonder if I'm safe as the car slithers merrily along the road to the rhythm of his songs. But there is no way anyone could stop Christopher from singing. Or, for that matter, stop me from writing.

Many times young people ask me how I began to write or who inspired me to write or why I write. I don't know how to answer these questions. Did I make a pact to communicate that I don't remember? There are things I feel compelled to share with young people: things I have learned, things if they knew might keep them safer, perhaps make them kinder.

Some professors at the University of Washington where I studied psychology believed that people behaved in a certain way because they got rewarded for it or got attention they wanted. That may be the cause of some behaviors, but often my writing got me into trouble I didn't want. When I attended Garfield High School in Seattle, Washington, students took four subjects each semester. The other two hours in school were spent in a study hall.

There I was, a fourteen-year-old freshman in a huge long room. A man teacher sat in the middle of the room watching the students so they wouldn't make a peep while they worked on their algebra problems or learned their French verbs. I had my algebra, English, and French books in the study hall, but I never opened them be-

Barthe De Clements

cause I was in a quiet place with nobody to bother me. My mother's lips wouldn't tighten in frigid silence because she was doing the housework alone. My father couldn't say, "What do you think you are around here? An ornament? Get in the kitchen and help your mother."

On my study hall desk with my books was a notebook full of clean paper to write on. So I wrote. I wrote story after story all semester. Nobody around me knew what I was doing and nobody cared. It never occurred to me to show the stories to my English teacher. I wasn't writing for attention or to get rewarded. I was writing because I had all those luscious, quiet hours.

They didn't last, of course. They ended the day report cards came out.

Now I'm no longer young. My children are grown and I live alone. I can look over my computer, out my office window, look across the field, over the trees, and down toward the river while I think of the next sentence to write. I am supremely happy. Nobody can tell me what to do. I have all these luscious, quiet hours to write book after book. And don't ask me why I write them. Dancers dance, painters paint, singers sing, and writers write.

————

Barthe DeClements was born in Seattle. She attended Western Washington College from 1940 to 1942 and received her B.A. degree from the University of Washington in Seattle in 1944. She earned an M.Ed. degree in Educational Psychology there in 1970, and did postgraduate study from 1974 to 1975. She is divorced and has four children.

DeClements has taught school, from elementary grades to high school, in Washington and is a psychologist, having practiced from 1947 to 1948 in a clinic and from 1950 to 1955 in public schools in Seattle. She has also been a school counselor.

Barthe DeClements' extremely popular books have won many awards chosen by school children. *Nothing's Fair in Fifth Grade* was a Junior Literary Guild selection and was made into a cassette recording. Three of her books have been named Children's Choice Books by a joint committee of the International Reading Association and the Children's Book Council: . . . *Ninth Grade Blues* in 1984, *Sixth Grade Can Really Kill You* in 1986, and *Double Trouble* in 1988. *Double Trouble* was co-written with her son.

SELECTED WORKS: Nothing's Fair in Fifth Grade, 1981; How Do You Lose Those Ninth Grade Blues?, 1983; Seventeen and In-Between, 1984; Sixth Grade Can Really Kill You, 1985; I Never Asked You to Understand Me, 1986; No Place for Me, 1987; The Fourth Grade Wizards, 1988; Five Finger Discount, 1989.

SELECTED WORKS WRITTEN WITH CHRISTOPHER GREIMES: Double Trouble, 1987.

ABOUT: Contemporary Authors, Vol. 105; Something About the Author, Vol. 35.

BRUCE DEGEN

1945–

AUTHOR AND ILLUSTRATOR OF *Jamberry*, etc.

Biographical sketch of Bruce Degen:

BORN IN BROOKLYN, Bruce Degen

BRUCE DEGEN

showed an early interest in drawing and painting. This talent was encouraged by an elementary school teacher. Degen received his B.F.A. degree from The Cooper Union and a master's degree from Pratt Institute, both in New York City.

While finishing his master's degree, Degen re-evaluated his love of art and realized that the art he most wanted to create was the kind of illustrations found in children's books. He was not trained to be an illustrator and he didn't believe that illustration was much respected, but Degen followed this interest.

Along with a career including such diverse activities as advertising design, teaching art to high school age students and children's book illustration to adult students, painting scenery for opera productions, and running a lithography studio in Israel, Degen has illustrated over thirty books, including several series. These include the Commander Toad series, the Jesse Bear books, and the Forgetful Bears books. Many feature humorous touches that add to the text, particularly in the Magic School Bus series by Joanna Cole. In them, a creative science teacher, Ms. Frizzle, takes her class on a series of educational adventures.

Ms. Frizzle's clothing is only one of the details readers look for, such as a dress decorated with toothbrushes, accessorized by shoes resembling sets of teeth.

Degen has written his own books as well. *Jamberry* features nonsense about a bear who likes berries. In *Pumpkin Man*, very few words are used to tell a Halloween story.

Degen enjoys illustrating with children in mind and visiting classrooms. He encourages ideas from students, such as new clothes for Ms. Frizzle, and illustrates them. He tries to help children to develop their own talents, remembering the teacher who encouraged him.

Degen met his wife at The Cooper Union. She is a designer who paints, does magazine illustration and printmaking, and designs patchwork and needlework. Together they illustrated a collection of poems, *When It Comes to Bugs*. They live in Brooklyn Heights with their two sons.

Degen has taught a course in writing and illustrating children's books at the School of Visual Arts in New York City and has given lectures at schools and conferences.

The Magic School Bus at the Waterworks was an Honor Book in the nonfiction category of the 1987 Boston Globe-Horn Book Awards. Three of Degen's books were named Children's Choice Books by a joint committee of the International Reading Association and the Children's Book Council: *Little Chick's Big Day* in 1982, *Jamberry* in 1983, and *The Forgetful Bears Meet Mr. Memory* in 1988. Both the latter and *The Magic School Bus Inside the Human Body* were Book-of-the-Month selections.

Degen has had his work exhibited at the Master Eagle Gallery and at the Hempstead Municipal Gallery, both in New York.

SELECTED WORKS WRITTEN AND ILLUSTRATED: Aunt Possum and the Pumpkin Man, 1977; Little Witch and the Riddle, 1980; Jamberry, 1983.

SELECTED WORKS ILLUSTRATED: Commander Toad in Space, by Jane Yolen, 1980; Encyclopedia Brown's Second Book of Weird and Wonderful Facts, by Donald Sobol, 1981; Liitle Chick's Big Day, by Mary De-

Ball Kwitz, 1981; Upchuck Summer, by Joel L. Schwartz, 1982; The Josefina Story Quilt, by Eleanor Coerr, 1986; The Magic School Bus at the Waterworks, by Joanna Cole, 1986; The Forgetful Bears Meet Mr. Memory, by Larry Weinberg, 1987; The Magic School Bus Inside the Earth, by Joanna Cole, 1987; The Magic School Bus Inside the Human Body, by Joanna Cole, 1989.

SELECTED WORKS ILLUSTRATED WITH CHRIS DEGEN: When It Comes to Bugs, by Aileen Fisher, 1986.

ABOUT: Something About the Author, Vol. 47.

ETIENNE DELESSERT

January 4, 1941–

AUTHOR AND ILLUSTRATOR OF *How the Mouse Was Hit on the Head by a Stone and So Discovered the World*, etc.

Biographical sketch of Etienne Delessert:

ETIENNE DELESSERT was born in Lausanne, Switzerland. His mother died when he was a baby, and he was raised by his stepmother, who was "a great storyteller." Delessert says she influenced his creative development tremendously. The two of them acted out play-like scenarios that he continued by himself when she had to attend to other things. His father was a prominent minister who loved nature. He died when Delessert was only eighteen.

At the age of eight, the artist began to draw Disney characters and caricatures. He had classical training in Greek and Latin in school, but preferred fairy tales and fables. After high school, he worked at Studio Maffei in Lausanne for three years. He attended College Classique in Lausanne from 1951 to 1956, and Gymnase Classique, also in Lausanne, from 1957 to 1958. He served in the Swiss Army in 1961. At the age of twenty-one, he was living in Paris, working as an art director and doing editorial illustrations. He enjoyed summing up a story with a visual interpretation, a natural precursor to the art of the picture book.

In 1965, he moved to the United States.

ETIENNE DELESSERT

Tomi Ungerer had introduced him to some American publishers. At first he was discouraged by the texts presented to him to illustrate, and was reluctant to do color separations by hand, rather than have them done by a camera, which is far less time consuming. He was excited by the prospect of illustrating some books for Harlan Quist in the 1970s, and produced unusual and ground-breaking picture books for the publisher. He worked with Eugene Ionesco on several of them, and showed his work to the psychologist Jean Piaget as well. Piaget worked with Delessert on a book exploring the cognizance of a five-year-old child of the world around him, called *How the Mouse Was Hit on the Head by a Stone and So Discovered the World*. The book was later produced as a play staged in Geneva, Switzerland. He continued to work with Piaget and with children, studying the reactions of children to art.

Delessert returned to Europe in 1973, working in Paris as an art director and founding a studio where he produced animated films for children, including some produced for the U.S. television show "Sesame Street." Four years later, he established his own publishing line, Editions

Tournesol, based on his experience in book design, and production. Delessert now lives in Lausanne and in Connecticut, where he works on books for children. It takes him about three months to produce a book. He lives with his wife, a graphic designer and art director, whom he married in 1975.

Editorial illustrations by Delessert have appeared in *Atlantic Monthly, Fortune, Playboy, Punch, McCall's, Elle,* and other magazines. There have been many exhibitions of Delessert's work in galleries in the U.S. and abroad, including the Art Alliance Gallery in Philadelphia, Pennsylvania in 1970, Galerie Delpire in Paris in 1972, and Le Musée des Arts décoratifs du Louvre in Paris in 1975. He has won a Gold Medal from the Society of Illustrators in 1967 for his illustration for a *Graphis* cover. *Story Number One* was named a *New York Times* Best Illustrated Book for the year 1968, and *Just So Stories* received the same award in 1972. *How the Mouse . . .* and *Just So Stories* both appeared in American Institute of Graphic Arts Book Shows in 1972 and 1973 respectively.

Delessert received a Gold Plaque from the Biennale of Illustration of Bratislava in 1979 for two of his books, and received the prize again in 1985. In 1980 he was awarded the Hans Christian Andersen "Highly Commended Illustrator" award from the International Board on Books for Young People for the entire body of his work. His "Yok-Yok" series of books, published in Europe, was awarded First Graphic Prize of the International Exhibition of Bologna in 1981. In the *New York Times Book Review*, author-artist David Macaulay called *A Long Long Song* "a beautifully produced portfolio of some of [his] best work to date . . . the inventiveness of the imagery goes well beyond the requirements and limitations of simple narrative." The book won the 1989 First Graphic Prize of the Bologna Book Fair in 1989.

SELECTED WORKS WRITTEN AND ILLUSTRATED: How the Mouse Was Hit on the Head by a Stone and So Discovered the World, 1971; A Long Long Song, 1988.

SELECTED WORKS WRITTEN WITH ELEONORE SCHMID AND ILLUSTRATED: The Endless Party, 1967.

SELECTED WORKS ILLUSTRATED: The Secret Seller, 1968; Story Number One for Children Under Three Years of Age, by Eugene Ionesco, 1968; Story Number Two for Children Under Three Years of Age, by Eugene Ionesco, 1969; The Pony Man, by Gordon Lightfoot, 1972; Just So Stories, by Rudyard Kipling, 1972; Being Green, by Joseph G. Raposo, 1973.

ABOUT: Amstutz, Walter, ed. Who's Who in Graphic Art; Contemporary Authors (First Revision), Vol. 21-22; (New Revision Series), Vol. 13; Herdeg, Walter, ed. Graphis 3rd International Survey of Children's Book Illustration, 1975 (Publication No. 140); Graphis 4th International Survey of Children's Book Illustration, 1979 (Publication No. 156); Kingman, Lee and others, comps. Illustrators of Children's Books: 1967-1976; Something About the Author, Vol. 27; Vol. 46.

DEMI

September 2, 1942–

AUTHOR AND ILLUSTRATOR OF *LuPan, the Carpenter's Apprentice,* etc.

Biographical sketch of Charlotte Dumaresq Hunt, who also illustrates under the name "Demi Hitz":

BORN in Cambridge, Massachusetts, and christened Charlotte Dumaresq Hunt, Demi uses her childhood nickname as her pen name—perhaps an extension of her expressed desire never to grow up. The daughter of artists, the great-granddaughter of the American painter William Morris Hunt and the great-grandniece of the dean of American architects, Richard Morris Hunt, Demi grew up in a household where design and color were important and artistic self-expression was expected and encouraged.

Her father, William Morris Hunt, was a highly respected figure in theatrical circles. Among many other achievements, he founded the Cambridge Drama Festival and served as executive producer of that event for many years. As a result of her father's involvement in theater, Demi's child-

hood household hosted some of the most famous and lionized theatrical names of the day. People such as Sir John Gielgud and Marcel Marceau were part of the Hunt's lives; in this colorful atmosphere, a young girl might well feel that it was possible for her to "paint everything," as Demi did.

It was Demi's mother, Rosamond Hunt, herself a painter of note, who harnessed and directed Demi's artistic inclinations. She oversaw her daughter's artistic education, and made sure she was exposed to a wide range of artistic media—jewelry-making, ceramics, silk screening, mural painting. As a continuation of this philosophy, Demi enrolled in Immaculate Heart College in Los Angeles and received her Bachelor of Arts degree there in 1962. Founded by Sister Mary Magdalen and expanded by Sister Corita, the art program at Immaculate Heart was renowed for its eclectic and all-encompassing approach to art. Sister Corita, an enormous influence on Demi, eventually became a controversial figure who left the Church and established a worldwide reputation as an unconventional and taboo-breaking artist. The precepts of Immaculate Heart College and Corita's work have provided the foundation for Demi's work ever since.

She also had formal training at the Rhode Island School of Design in 1960 and received her Master of Arts degree from the University of Baroda in 1965, but the primary impetus in her education was simply to follow her artistic inclinations where they took her—to Brazil, as a Fulbright scholar to India from 1962 to 1963, and later to China.

Demi soaked up all she could during her travels, and one can see the result of that absorption in her work in children's books. The time she spent in India, where she saw Hindus and Buddhists drawing uncountable worshipful repetitions of the same object, is reflected in books such as Demi's *Count the Animals 1 2 3*, where each animal is drawn and redrawn up to twenty times. Demi's travels through China resulted in books such as *Liang and the Magic Paintbrush* and *Dragon Kites and Dragon-flies: A Collection of Chinese Nursery Rhymes*. Her exuberant use of color and wild designs, while seen by some reviewers as chaotic and discordant, manage to capture a child's attention and hold it.

Demi's output over the years has been prodigious, and she has more than fifty books to her credit. *Liang and the Magic Paintbrush* was named a Notable Book of 1980 by the American Library Association.

Demi's irrepressible talent has not confined itself to children's books; her murals, paintings, and silkscreen prints have been exhibited in museums and galleries in the United States and in India. She has painted murals in Mexico, walls for private homes, and the dome of St. Peter's and Paul's Church in Wilmington, California. Demi now lives in New York City.

SELECTED WORKS ILLUSTRATED AS DEMI HITZ: The Surangini Tales, by Partap Sharma, 1973; The Old China Trade: Americans in Canton, 1784–1843, by Francis Ross Carpenter, 1976.

SELECTED WORKS ILLUSTRATED AS DEMI: Dragon Night and Other Lullabies, by Jane Yolen, 1980; Light Another Candle: The Story and Meaning of Hanukkah, by Miriam Chaikin, 1981; Make Noise, Make Merry: The Story and Meaning of Purim, by Miriam Chaikin, 1983.

SELECTED WORKS WRITTEN AND ILLUSTRATED AS DEMI: LuPan, the Carpenter's Apprentice, 1978; Where Is It?, 1979; Liang and the Magic Paintbrush, 1980; Demi's Count the Animals 1 2 3, 1986; Demi's Find the Animals A B C, 1986; Dragon Kites and Dragonflies: A Collection of Chinese Nursery Rhymes, 1986; The Hallowed Horse, 1987; A Chinese Zoo, 1987; Demi's Reflective Fables, 1988.

ABOUT: Contemporary Authors, Vol. 61–64; (New Revision Series), Vol. 8; Roginski, Jim. Behind the Covers; Something About the Author, Vol. 11.

CRESCENT DRAGONWAGON

November 25, 1952–

AUTHOR OF *Half a Moon and One Whole Star*, etc.

Biographical sketch of Crescent Dragonwagon:

CRESCENT DRAGONWAGON was born Ellen Zolotow. She is the daughter of the children's book editor and writer Charlotte Zolotow and biographer and Broadway theater critic Maurice Zolotow. She grew up in Hastings-on-Hudson, New York. At the age of sixteen, she left school and was married for the first time. Her husband and she chose new names for themselves, and she chose Crescent because it means "the growing." The two chose Dragonwagon to be frivolous, but she sometimes regrets having to explain her unusual name.

In 1972, Dragonwagon moved to the town of Eureka Springs, Arkansas, in the Ozark Mountains. Her first novel, *To Take a Dare*, which was co-written with Paul Zindel, is set in this town. Her first marriage ended in divorce, and on October 20, 1978, she married Ned Shank, with whom she runs a country inn and restaurant in Eureka Springs, Arkansas. She enjoys gardening and putting up preserves at Dairy Hollow House, where the couple does much of the restoration work.

"I'm always writing," Dragonwagon says, "if not at the computer, then mentally." Besides running the inn and doing most of the cooking, she is active in the community, "beautiful quirky Eureka Springs . . . an Ozark mountain resort town founded in the 1880s. It's a good life—though cornucopia-filled-to-overflowing full. Librarians who've read my books, and kids (and their families!) who know my work, are among our guests at the inn, often. It's a privilege to meet readers face to face—also to make a living doing something I love."

Dragonwagon also enjoys reading, interior and garden designs, and old movies. She writes both picture books and novels for young readers and poetry for adults. She has written many magazine articles, for publications ranging from *McCall's* and *Ladies' Home Journal* to *New Age* and *Cosmopolitan*. With Jan Brown she co-wrote *The Dairy Hollow House Cookbook*, published in 1986, and she has written other cookbooks. She wrote a book for adults, *The Year It Rained*. She has also made many appearances at writers' conferences and library conferences, and at schools.

To Take a Dare was named a Notable Book of 1982 by the American Library Association. *Wind Rose* was named a 1976 Outstanding Science Trade Book for Children by a joint committee of the National

Science Teachers Association and the Children's Book Council, and was adapted into a film by Phoenix Films in 1983. *Half a Moon and One Whole Star* won the 1987 Coretta Scott King Award for Illustration, and was a Reading Rainbow book.

SELECTED WORKS: When Light Turns into Night, 1975; Wind Rose, 1976; Will It Be Okay?, 1977; Your Owl Friend, 1977; If You Call My Name, 1981; I Hate My Brother Harry, 1983; Katie in the Morning, 1983; Dear Miss Moshki, 1986; Half a Moon and One Whole Star, 1986; Alligator Arrived with Apples: A Potluck Alphabet Feast, 1987; Diana, Maybe, 1987; Margaret Ziegler Is Horse-Crazy, 1988.

SELECTED WORKS WRITTEN WITH PAUL ZINDEL: To Take a Dare, 1982.

ABOUT: Contemporary Authors, Vol. 65; (New Revision Series), Vol. 12; Directory of American Poets and Writers; Something About the Author, Vol. 11; Vol. 41.

HENRIK DRESCHER

December 15, 1955–

AUTHOR AND ILLUSTRATOR OF *Simon's Book*, etc.

Biographical sketch of Henrik Drescher:

HENRIK DRESCHER was born in Denmark in 1955 and spent his childhood living by the sea. He came to the U.S. with his family in 1967. By age fifteen, he knew he wanted to be an artist. His only formal art training was a semester at the Boston Museum School. He left there to travel all over the world—always drawing in notebooks he kept with him.

Drescher's art career began with editorial illustrations, to which he continues to devote about one-third of his time. His illustrations appear in publications like *Rolling Stone* and *The New York Times Book Review*. He began to illustrate children's books for reasons of economics, but found he enjoyed it.

The first book he both wrote and illustrated was *The Strange Appearance of Howard Cranebill, Jr.*, the story of a child born looking a bit different and the parents who love him. This still remains his most satisfying book, he says, because of the work he put into it: first doing the black-and-white drawings, then the color separations. Since books produced this way don't come together until actual production, "it was like a five-to-six-month drum roll" and then everything put together turned out just as he'd wanted. The book was named a Best Illustrated Book of 1982 by *The New York Times*.

Simon's Book, another of Drescher's favorites, is the story of a boy—looking somewhat like Drescher—who draws himself into a story with a scary monster. His pens and ink bottle contrive to draw him out of danger, producing a story that later becomes a book that he finds when he awakens the next morning. It was selected for the Graphic Gallery, a showcase of excellent books honored by *The Horn Book Magazine*. It was also chosen for the Reading Rainbow television program and was a *New York Times* Best Illustrated Book of 1983.

Blossom the cow asks Maggie, a little girl, if she wants to go *Looking for Santa Claus* on Christmas eve. They fly all over the world and find other white-bearded, red-suited gentlemen, but don't see Santa until they're all home again.

More subtle ties connect the pages of *Whose Furry Nose?* and *Whose Scaly Tail?*. In each book a part of an animal, Australian and African respectively, is shown on one page and then identified on the next. A boy who looks a lot like Simon swings from page to page. *Look-Alikes* returns to high adventure when dolls identical to a boy and a monkey face dangers while their counterparts watch through a window.

Drescher says his influences are everywhere. His admiration for older-style illustrators like Wanda Gag, H.A. Rev, and Laurent de Brunhoff led him to try a two-color format similar to theirs in *The Yellow Umbrella*. This wordless book, published when his son Uli was born and dedicated to him, is done in black and yellow. Janwillem van de Wetering describes the book in *The New York Times Book Review*: Monkeys at play with the umbrella "flee from evil, swoop through storms, overfly disaster, overcome, overjoy."

Drescher's illustrations have been compared to Escher or Bosch; he himself says he may be considered to be "on the edge" where conventional illustration is concerned. Although he creates with children in mind, he says his work is not modified for children, "not pedagogical."

He says, "book-making, that's what I like," book-making in many forms. His love of making books extends to his visits to schools where he makes books with children, using their own art, showing them what can be done. It also extends to an interest in artists' notebooks, his own and others'.

His upcoming plans include illustrating books by others, including a poetry collection by Jack Prelutsky. He will do the art for a video and book/tape production of Brer Rabbit to be read by Danny Glover by Rabbit Ears Productions. Drescher lives with his wife Lauren and son Uli in upstate New York. He draws every day; "you have to practice constantly," he says. He divides his time between children's and editorial illustration, painting, and notebooks.

SELECTED WORKS WRITTEN AND ILLUSTRATED: The Strange Appearance of Howard Cranebill, Jr., 1982; Simon's Book, 1983; Looking for Santa Claus, 1984; Look-Alikes, 1985; The Yellow Umbrella, 1987.

SELECTED WORKS ILLUSTRATED: All Clean, by Harriet Ziefert, 1986; All Gone!, by Harriet Ziefert, 1986; Cock-a-Doodle-Doo!, by Harriet Ziefert, 1986; Run! Run!, by Harriet Ziefert, 1986 Whose Furry Nose?: Australian Animals You'd Like to Meet, by Harriet Ziefert, 1987; Whose Scaly Tail?: African Animals You'd Like to Meet, by Harriet Ziefert, 1987.

ABOUT: Horn Book November/December 1986.

MAGGIE DUFF

January 4, 1916–

AUTHOR OF *Rum Pum Pum*, etc.

Autobiographical sketch of Maggie Duff:

NO ONE in my little hometown of Walton, Indiana, ever dreamed that I would grow up to write books when I was born. From an early age my brother and sister and I were involved in music because music teachers lived nearby, and there wasn't much else in our small town to do. We were pretty good, so expectations were high that we would all become professional musicians. But it didn't turn out quite that way. Only my sister made music a vocation. My brother became a businessman with music his avocation. And instead of becoming one, I married a professional musician. Painting and writing became my vehicles for self-expression.

As a child I was a dreamer, and dreamed of grand things. I would become a concert violinist, I dreamed, or maybe a ballerina, or maybe even an actress. But my favorite dream was that I would write books and paint pictures. Perhaps my dreams were too varied and scattered in my young days, for

it took me quite a while to arrive at the realization of THE dream. I never did aspire to be anything other than something connected with the arts. And oh, yes, as time moved on, to be a wife and mother was high on my list—another dream with creative overtones.

As I look back, I've been really blessed in realizing nearly all my childhood dreams in one way or another. While growing up, I did perform at least semiprofessionally on the violin and piano, along with my siblings. If getting paid for it means you are professional, then we were professional. I received a box of watercolors for Christmas one year and spent many happy hours tinting greeting cards, which I sold to congenial relatives and family friends. I read fairy tales voraciously, then made up stories with myself the heroine, of course (I was the lost princess rescued by the knight in shining armor). But I never started writing stories until I went to college. I was leading actress in high school plays (not, I hasten to add, because I was so great, but because the school had a very limited number of aspiring actresses). But I never did achieve anything even close to ballerina status, for my grace was virtually nonexistent. I was all awkward arms and legs.

At College (Butler University), classmates urged me to write down my stories. I continued to perform in recitals while looking enviously at art students. The study of English literature took up a lot of my time. Then I met Cloyd Duff, the young timpanist of the Indianapolis Symphony Orchestra. We fell in love and married. When Cloyd was invited to join the Cleveland Orchestra a few years later, we moved to Cleveland, Ohio, where we remained for thirty-nine years.

I started the study of art and dreamed of the books I might sometime have published. Our two children were born soon after moving to Cleveland, so much of my time was taken up in the care of, and in activities connected with, them. Not until the younger one was getting ready for college did my thoughts and efforts return to the pursuit of bookmaking. But how to go about it was the question. I took another detour. I went back to school to learn about children's literature, and wound up with a Master's Degree in Library Science. Putting it to use while our children were in college, I became a librarian for the Children's Department of Cuyahoga County Public Library, where I remained for fifteen years. During this period I did much research on folk tales, much storytelling. From these activities came the books *Johnny and His Drum, Rum Pum Pum, The Princess and the Pumpkin*, and *Dancing Turtle*. It was my husband's involvement with drums that inspired *Jonny and His Drum* and started me on research that wound up as *Rum Pum Pum*.

During this period I also started presenting puppet shows as a different form of storytelling, using folk and fairy tales as the vehicles. In travel with my husband in his work, my interest in puppets was fired up by visits to the famous Kabuki and Noh Threatres of Japan, and the wonderful puppet and marionette theatres in France, Belgium, Germany, and Austria. The Puppet Center of Cuyahoga County Library System was established, under my direction. It is still growing and flourishing.

My life reads somewhat like a fairy tale. Will that be my next story to write?

———

Maggie Duff received her A.B. degree from Butler University in 1937. She was married October 26, 1940. She received her M.L.S. degree from Case Western Reserve University in 1966 and also attended the Cleveland Institute of Art. She is the author of over sixty puppet shows for children and has contributed articles to *Top of the News*. A member of the American Library Association, she has served on the 1985 Caldecott committee. She is also a member of Mu Phi Epsilon and Pi Beta Phi.

Both *Rum Pum Pum* and *Dancing Turtle* were named Children's Choice books by a joint committee of the Children's Book Council and the International Reading Association, in 1979 and 1982 respectively.

SELECTED WORKS: Jonny and His Drum, 1972; Rum Pum Pum, 1978; The Princess and the Pumpkin, 1980; Dancing Turtle, 1981.

ABOUT: Ash, Lee, ed. Who's Who in Library Service, 4th edition; Contemporary Authors (First Revision), Vol.37; (New Revision Series), Vol. 14; Something About the Author, Vol. 37; Who's Who of American Women, 1985-1986.

EILEEN DUNLOP

October 13, 1938–

AUTHOR OF *The House on the Hill*, etc.

Autobiographical sketch of Eileen Rhona Dunlop:

WHEN I WAS growing up, in the age before television, we lived in the country, and entertainment had to be self-made. I read, and wrote stories of my own, because writing was fun, and a way of passing the time. I made no conscious decision in my early years to be a writer; when I grew up, I became a primary school teacher, and teaching has been my happy occupation all of

my adult life. However, I kept at the back of my mind the possibility that I would one day write a book; the spur actually to do so was my thirtieth birthday, a moment of truth when I decided that if I were to fulfil the intentions of youth, now was the time to get on with it. So I wrote *Robinsheugh*, a book which set out the themes and preoccupations of all my later work.

My reason for choosing to write for young readers is obvious; they had been my companions for years, and I had shared with them the books of many other writers. Why I chose to write fantasy and ghost stories is less clear to me; I have no personal belief in the supernatural. I might say that children like a ghost story, which is true, but as an adult I need a more intellectually plausible reason than that. It is that, in my work, ghosts are symbolic of certain states of mind, and of the power of the imagination to evoke very powerful images of the past. I suppose that it is because of my inevitable identification with my own people that I write most naturally in a historical and fantastical vein.

I am a Scottish writer. I have lived in Scotland all my life, and I write with most conviction when I choose Scottish themes and settings. My 'spirit of place' is very strong, and I share the deep identification of the Celts with their past. I also love, in Scottish folklore, the intertwining of chilling fantasy with humdrum reality. These are the major influences in my work.

————

Eileen Dunlop was born in Alloa, Scotland. She received a Diploma with Distinction in Primary Education from Moray House College of Education in Edinburgh, in 1959. She taught at Sunnyside School in Alloa from 1963 to 1979, and is at present teaching at Dollar Academy. She was married October 27, 1979. She is a member of the Professional Association of Teachers and of P.E.N. Scottish Centre. Her hobbies include gardening and theater. *Robinsheugh* was published for children in the U.S. under the title *Elizabeth Elizabeth*, but for adults in the U.S. under its original title.

The Maze Stone was nominated for a 1983 Edgar Allan Poe Award by the Mystery Writers of America. Both *Maze Stone* and *Clementina* received the Scottish Arts Council Book Award, in 1983 and 1986 respectively. *The House on the Hill* was a Junior Literary Guild selection, and was named a Notable Book of 1987 by the American Library Association. It was also named a "Commended" book in the 1987 Carnegie Medal Awards.

SELECTED WORKS: Elizabeth Elizabeth, 1976; The House on Mayferry Street, 1977; Fox Farm, 1979; The Maze Stone, 1983; Clementina, 1987; The House on the Hill, 1987; The Valley of the Deer, 1989.

ABOUT: Contemporary Authors, Vol. 73; (New Revision Series), Vol. 14; Something About the Author, Vol. 24; Who's Who in the World, 1980-1981; Writers Directory 1984-86.

THOMAS J. DYGARD

August 10, 1931–

AUTHOR OF *Outside Shooter*, etc.

Autobiographical sketch of Thomas J. Dygard:

WRITING ABOUT MYSELF is the hardest writing of all.

Where to begin?

Well, I was born in Little Rock, Arkansas.

And it wasn't too many years later that I knew I wanted to be a writer. I don't know the exact moment the realization dawned on me. Probably right after I learned to read. From the first, I loved reading. If only I could create something as wonderful as what I was enjoying.

The desire to write led me into journalism. First, as the twelve-year-old editor of *The Neighbor News,* a neighborhood newspaper of limited circulation and irregular publication. Then, as editor of my junior high school newspaper, and as news editor of my high school paper. Finally, at the age of seventeen, as a sports writer with the *Arkansas Gazette* in Little Rock. My first byline in the *Gazette* adorned a story about a game between two touring women's professional softball teams. Not much, but a beginning.

After working at the *Gazette* through school at Little Rock Junior College, and then the University of Arkansas, mostly writing sports, I joined the Associated Press as a newsman in the Little Rock bureau. With the AP, I've held a variety of news jobs—reporter, copy editor, correspondent, news editor, and chief of bureau—in a string of places beyond Little Rock—Detroit, Birmingham, New Orleans, Indianapolis, Chicago, and my present station, Tokyo, Japan, where I have been chief of bureau since 1985.

Along the way, I've been able to do a lot of the writing I wanted to do—covering sports ranging from Sugar Bowl football games to the Indianapolis 500-mile race, political campaigns and elections, two race riots, labor negotiations in the auto industry, hurricanes, one space shot.

I've always wanted to write fiction, and I began trying early. My first novel, blessedly never completed, was begun in grade school. I sold a short story to a magazine when I was twenty-two. I had several other false starts with novels.

Then, with an evening on my hands in a motel in Champaign, Illinois, I began writing what became my first publisehd novel, *Running Scared*.

All through the writing and rewriting of the following months, I thought I was writing an adult novel. It was only at the finish, when I stepped back and took a long look, that I knew that what I had produced was a young adult novel.

My misimpression throughout all the writing was, I decided, a stroke of great good fortune. I had, truly, written an adult novel—but for young adult readers. I had not written down to my readers, as if they were a bunch of kids. I had written right at them, as if they were adults—which they are: young adults. It was a lesson that I've repeated to myself hundreds of times in the course of writing a dozen young adult novels.

———

Thomas J. Dygard received a B.A. degree in American History from the University of Arkansas in 1953. He was married November 23, 1951, and has two children. Three of his books, *Outside Shooter*, *Point Spread*, and *Soccer Duel*, were named Junior Literary Guild selections.

SELECTED WORKS: Running Scared, 1977; Winning Kicker, 1978; Outside Shooter, 1979; Point Spread, 1980; Soccer Duel, 1981; Quarterback Walk-On, 1982; Rebound Caper, 1983; Tournament Upstart, 1984; Wilderness Peril, 1985; Halfback Tough, 1986; The Rookie Arrives, 1988.

ABOUT: Contemporary Authors, Vol. 85; (New Revision Series), Vol. 15; Something About the Author, Vol. 24; Who's Who in the Midwest, 1984-1985.

RICHARD EGIELSKI

July 16, 1952–

ILLUSTRATOR OF *Hey, Al*, etc.

Biographical sketch of Richard Egielski:

RICHARD EGIELSKI was born in Queens, New York, and grew up in Maspeth, Queens. His first artistic influences were comic books and movies on television. Books were definitely not an influence on his picture-book art; he recalls discovering picture books at an age when he was too old for them. He attended a strict parochial school until he took the initiative to enter the public school system. He submitted a portfolio in hopes of being admitted to the High School of Art and Design, and he was. It was there that he realized he wanted to be an artist.

Egielski attended Pratt Institute from 1970 to 1971, where he felt out of place, as the painting program concentrated on Abstract Expressionism, and he was working towards becoming a magazine illustrator. He transferred to the Parsons School of Design in New York, where he took a course in picture books with Maurice Sendak. In picture-book illustration, he had found "a discipline that answered all my creative needs," as he said in his Caldecott Award acceptance speech; and he attributes this, in

Richard Egielski

part, to his love of movies and the cinematic flow of picture-book narrative. He began to work professionally while at school; his drawings appeared in magazines and in *New Times* magazine. He graduated in 1974. Egielski met Denise Sadutti, also a book illustrator, at Parsons, and they were married May 8, 1977.

He did not have too much success at first with his book illustration. He took his portfolio around to publishers, and few found it suitable for the kinds of stories they wanted illustrated. Since Egielski didn't want to write his own stories, it was not until he was introduced to Arthur Yorinks, through Maurice Sendak, that he found a true collaborator.

Arthur Yorinks has said that music is very important to his writing; he will bring to Richard Egielski one or several stories and Egielski can choose one; Yorinks often tells him what piece of music he was listening to while working on the story. The books Yorinks has written and that they have completed together are sometimes inspired by writers such as Kafka, whose *Metamorphosis* influenced *Louis the Fish*. Egielski sometimes generally discusses influences with Yorinks during the illustrat-

ing of the book, which he considers unusual in the author-artist working relationship.

Hey, Al won the 1987 Caldecott Medal awarded by the American Library Association. It was also a 1986 ALA Notable Book. *Louis the Fish* was a Reading Rainbow book. Egielski received a plaque from the 1985 Biennale of Illustrations Bratislavia for *It Happened in Pinsk*. *The Porcelain Pagoda* was a 1976 American Institute of Graphic Arts Book Show book. A videotape about the working relationship of Yorinks and Egielski is distributed by Farrar, Straus & Giroux Publishers.

SELECTED WORKS ILLUSTRATED: The Porcelain Pagoda, by F. N. Monjo, 1976; The Letter, the Witch, and the Ring, by John Bellairs, 1976; Sid and Sol, by Arthur Yorinks, 1977; I Should Worry, I Should Care, by Miriam Chaikin, 1979; Louis the Fish, by Arthur Yorinks, 1980; It Happened in Pinsk, by Arthur Yorinks, 1983; Lower! Higher! You're a Liar!, by Miriam Chaikin, 1984; Amy's Eyes, by Richard Kennedy, 1985; The Little Father, by Gelett Burgess, 1985; Hey, Al, by Arthur Yorinks, 1986; Bravo, Minski, by Arthur Yorinks, 1988; Friends Forever, by Miriam Chaikin, 1988; The Tub People, by Pam Conrad, 1989.

ABOUT: Horn Book July/August 1987; Kingman, Lee and others, comps. Illustrators of Children's Books 1967-1976; New York Times Book Review January 10, 1988; Sendak, Maurice. Caldecott & Co : Notes on Books and Pictures; Something About the Author, Vol. 11; Vol. 49; Who's Who in America 1988-89.

DOUGLAS FLORIAN

March 18, 1950–

AUTHOR AND ILLUSTRATOR OF *Discovering Seashells*, etc.

Autobiographical sketch of Douglas Florian:

HOW DO YOU get to be an illustrator of children's books? Being the son of an artist certainly helps. The walls of our house were always covered with paintings, mostly landscapes, done by my father, Hal Florian. But the first time I had any idea that I might be an artist was when I was ten years old. I entered a national coloring contest where all you had to do was color in a drawing of the circus. I mailed in my entry and three months later the postman brought a brown parcel to our door. Inside was a pair of gold roller skates. I had placed second out of thousands of entries, and skated triumphantly around the neighborhood.

It wasn't until high school that art really became important to me. My father enrolled me in a painting course being given over the summer at The School of Visual Arts in New York.

The first day I walked into a large bright studio filled with paintings, drawings, easels, and the smell of linseed oil. Somehow I knew then I was going to be an artist.

Next came the hard part: learning to draw. I would use anyone and anything as a model. My goal was to do a hundred drawings a day. Slowly, very slowly, I gained control over the pencil line. My eyes started seeing shapes more clearly. And my mind discovered a new territory called imagination.

———

Douglas Florian graduated from Queens College in New York with a B.A. degree. He has had his work appear in *The New York Times* and *The New Yorker*. He is a free-lance illustrator and lives with his wife and daughter in New York City.

Discovering Seashells was placed on the International Board on Books for Young People Honour List. *A Winter Day* was named an Outstanding Science Trade Book for Children by a joint committee of the National Science Teachers Association and the Children's Book Council in 1987.

SELECTED WORKS WRITTEN AND ILLUSTRATED: A Bird Can Fly, 1980; The City, 1982; People Working, 1983; Airplane Ride, 1984; Discovering Butterflies, 1986; Discovering Trees, 1986; Discovering Frogs, 1986; Discovering Seashells, 1986; A Winter Day, 1987; A Summer Day, 1988.

SELECTED WORKS ILLUSTRATED: Tit for Tat, by Dorothy O. Van Woerkom, 1977; The Night It Rained Pancakes, by Mirra Ginsburg, 1980.

ABOUT: Something About the Author, Vol. 19; Working Parents February 1984.

MICHAEL FOREMAN

March 21, 1938–

ILLUSTRATOR OF *Hans Andersen: His Classic Fairy Tales*, etc.

Biographical sketch of Michael Foreman:

MICHAEL FOREMAN was born in Pakefield, Suffolk, England, a fishing village. He had few books available as a child, and delivered newspapers. When he was fifteen, *The Wind in the Willows* was read aloud to him, and he sees that experience as a turning point in his life. He studied painting at the Lowestoft School of Art, where he received a National Diploma in Design in 1958. In 1959 he was married, and had one child with his wife, but was later divorced. He received the Gimpel Fils Prize for a young painter in 1962. He received an A.R.C.A. degree from the Royal College of Art in 1963. He has been a lecturer in graphics at St. Martins School of Art in London from 1963 to 1965. He also lectured at the Royal College of Art in London from 1968 to 1970. He was Art Director of *Playboy* in Chicago in 1965 and *King* in London from 1966 to 1967. In 1980, Foreman was married for a second time and had another child.

Foreman, a graphic artist, has been a designer and illustrator of advertising and editorial material. In addition to creating books, he has also created animated films for television in England and Scandinavia. His work has been exhibited in Europe, America, and Japan.

He has travelled extensively, through Europe and North Africa, across Siberia by rail to Japan, and in the Far East, Australia, and America. He feels that travel has been very important to his work. Foreman won a Francis Williams Illustration Award of the Victoria and Albert Museum and the National Book League for the period of 1968 to 1972. *City of Gold* won a 1980 Carnegie Medal and was "Highly Commended" in the 1980 Kate Greenaway Awards of the British Library Association. Foreman won the Graphics Prize at the 1982 International Children's Book Fair at Bologna. He also won the 1982 Greenaway Medal. Two of his books were named Commended Books in the Greenaway Awards: *The Brothers Grimm* in 1978 and *Seasons of Splendour* in 1985. *Sleeping Beauty* won the 1982 Kurt Maschler Award (the "Emil"), administered by England's Book Trust. *Cat and Canary* was a Reading Rainbow Book.

SELECTED WORKS WRITTEN AND ILLUSTRATED: The Great Sleigh Robbery, 1968; War and Pea, 1974; Dinosaurs and All That Rubbish, 1976; Trick a Tracker, 1981; Land of Dreams, 1982; Cat & Canary, 1985; Panda and the Bushfire, 1986; Ben's Baby,1988; The Angel and the Wild Man, 1989.

SELECTED WORKS ILLUSTRATED: Private Zoo, by Georgess McHargue, 1975; Hans Andersen: His Classic Fairy Tales, 1976; Popular Folk Tales, by The Brothers Grimm, translated by Brian Alderson, 1978; Alan Garner's Fairy Tales of Gold, 1980; City of Gold and Other Stories from the Old Testament, by Peter Dickinson, 1980; The Saga of Erik the Viking, by Terry Jones, 1983; Sleeping Beauty and Other Favourite Fairytales, sel. and trans. by Angela Carter, 1984; Seasons of Splendour: Tales, Myths and Legends of India, by Madhur Jaffrey, 1985; Tales for the Telling: Irish Folk and Fairy Tales, by Edna O'Brien, 1986.

ABOUT: Amstutz, Walter, ed. Who's Who in Graphic Art; Carpenter, Humphrey and Mari Prichard. The Oxford Companion to Children's Literature; Contemporary Authors (First Revision), Vol. 21; (New Revision Series), Vol. 10; Graphis No. 187, 1977; Herdeg, Walter, ed. Graphis 4th International Survey of Children's Book Illustration, 1979 (Publication No. 156); Kingman, Lee and others, comps. Illustrators of Children's Books: 1967-1976; Kirkpatrick, D.L., ed. Twentieth-Century Children's Writers, 2nd ed.; Something About the Author, Vol. 2; Who's Who, 1983-84; The Writers Directory 1988-90.

MEM FOX

March 5, 1946–

AUTHOR OF *Possum Magic*, etc.

MEM FOX

Autobiographical sketch of Merrion Frances Fox:

ONE OF THE MOST IMPORTANT, oh, wow, fantastic events of my life was having a baby in 1971. Her name was Chloë. It's still Chloë even though she's now eighteen years old (as I write in 1989) and almost grown up.

When Chloë was newborn my husband and I decided that she could have any book she ever wanted. Her bookshelves soon creaked with wonderful books and we had a happy time reading them to her.

When she was around seven years old I noticed that most of her books were English or American. "Hey! This is crazy," I thought. "Why aren't there more beautiful Australian books for my beautiful Australian kid?" I was studying at the time, and had to write a children's book as an assignment in a Children's Literature course. I decided to write a picture book for Chloë that would make her proud to be Australian. It would be the most Australian book in the world.

The result was that *Possum Magic* was published five years and nine rejections later, in 1983. It has become a classic—the best selling children's picture book in Australia's history. Hooray, hooray.

Since then I've written many more, my favourite of which is *Koala Lou*. Why do I love it? Because it's about mothers and sisters, and loving families, and coming second in important competitions and a whole lot of other things I've experienced and cried over.

Mostly I hate writing. It's so hard to do well and so easy to do badly. What I love about writing is *having written*: that's when people say nice, warm things to me about my books and that's when my heart jumps for joy inside my rib cage!

I was born in Australia but grew up in Zimbabwe, Africa, where my parents were missionaries. I trained as an actress in London, England, 1965-1968, but never went on the stage having decided three weeks before my course finished that I'd had enough of acting after three years of it! I married Malcolm whom I'd met at drama school. We came to Australia in 1970 and have lived there ever since. I teach people who want to become teachers.

I teach them about reading and writing and literature and I love my job. I could never give it up to write full-time. I'd miss the company. I adore my students.

Just before I go—you may have read a book of mine called *Wilfrid Gordon McDonald Partridge*. In case you have, you should know that that's my father's full name. If he were here he'd send you his love. But he's not so I'll send you mine!

———

Mem Fox received a diploma from the Rose Bruford Drama School in London in 1968. She had her B.A. degree from Finders University in South Australia in 1978 and also attended the South Australian College of Advanced Education, where she received a B.Ed. degree in 1979. She was married January 2, 1969 and has two children. She has been a drama teacher and a senior lecturer at the South Australian College of Advanced Education. She is a member of Actors Equity, the Australian Society of Authors, and the National Council of Teachers of English. The New South Wales Premier's Literary Award for the Best Children's Book of 1984 was awarded to *Possum Magic*. Her *Wilfrid Gordon McDonald Partridge* was named a Notable Book of 1985 by the American Library Association. The International Board on Books for Young People placed *Possum Magic* on its Honour List for Illustration in 1986.

SELECTED WORKS: Wilfrid Gordon McDonald Partridge, 1985; Hattie and the Fox, 1988; Possum Magic, 1987; Arabella: The Smallest Girl in the World, 1987; With Love at Christmas, 1988.

ABOUT: Something About the Author, Vol. 51.

RUSSELL FREEDMAN

October 11, 1929–

AUTHOR OF *Lincoln: A Photobiography*, etc.

Autobiographical sketch of Russell Freedman:

MY PARENTS met for the first time in a San Francisco bookshop. She was a salesclerk, and he was the West Coast representative of a large publishing house. They held their first conversation over a stack of bestsellers, and soon afterward, they married. I had the good luck to grow up in a house filled with books and with the lively conversations of visiting authors.

I knew at an early age that I wanted to be a writer, like those strange wonderful men and women who sat at our dinner table and told stories that were always fascinating and sometimes hard to believe. My mother's speciality on those occasions was leg of lamb with mint jelly, the only "fancy" dish she trusted herself to cook. When Mom came home from the butcher and unwrapped a leg of lamb, I knew that another author was coming to dinner.

We lived near San Francisco's Golden Gate Park, where I loved to ride my bike

through the fog. I listened to the Lone Ranger on radio, played trombone in the school band, and collected comic books. In the fifth grade I tried my hand at writing (and drawing) some comic strips of my own. In high school I wrote mystery stories, and in college, where I majored in English literature, I became a poet. One poem won the James Phelan Award and an award of $25, the first money I ever earned for something I had written.

After college, Uncle Sam paid for my first trip overseas. I was drafted and sent to Korea, where I served with the Second Infantry Division. When I returned to San Francisco, I found a job as a cub reporter with The Associated Press. That's where I really learned to write. At the A.P., a story had to be clear, accurate, and to the point. You couldn't spend all day messing around with it. I learned to organize my thoughts, respect facts, and meet deadlines.

But I was restless. I wanted to travel, to see the world, so I went east and worked in New York as a publicity writer for *Kraft Television Theater*, *Father Knows Best*, and other network television shows. My friends thought I had a glamorous job, but I didn't think so. I wanted to write about people and things that I cared about.

One day I happened to read an article in *The New York Times* that changed my life. It was about a sixteen-year-old boy who was blind. He had invented a Braille typewriter. That seemed remarkable, but as I read on, I discovered something even more amazing: the Braille system itself, as used today all over the world, was invented in France by another sixteen-year-old blind boy, Louis Braille. The newspaper article inspired some research, and the research resulted in my first book, a collection of biographies called *Teenagers Who Made History*.

I hadn't expected to become a writer of nonfiction for young people, but that's what happened. I had wandered into the field by chance, and I felt right at home. I couldn't wait to get started on my next book.

That was in 1961. I'm happy to say that I've been a full-time writer ever since, which is exactly what I had always wanted to be. One of the best things about my work is the opportunity it gives me to explore subjects that, for some reason, excite my curiosity, my enthusiasm, or my concern. Pick a subject, a good subject, and you're sure to find kids who are interested in it.

My idea of a good time is to sit in a library somewhere, searching through the yellowing pages of old books, looking at faded photographs, hoping to find what I'm looking for. And I savor the pleasures of on-site research. Once I spent three days at a rattlesnake farm in Maryland. I watched cowboys at work in Oklahoma. And I followed in Abraham Lincoln's footsteps all the way from his log-cabin birthplace in Kentucky to Ford's Theatre in Washington, D.C., where I sat in the back row and tried to imagine the night Lincoln was shot.

Like every writer, a nonfiction writer is essentially a storyteller. Whatever my subject, I always feel that I have a story to tell that is worth telling. I want to tell it as clearly and simply and effectively as I can, in a way that will stretch the reader's imagination and make that reader care.

———

Receiving his B.A. degree from the University of California at Berkeley in 1951, Russell Freedman served in the U.S. Army Counter Intelligence Corps from 1951 to 1953. He served with the Second Infantry Division in Korea. From 1969 to 1986, he conducted writing workshops at the New School for Social Research in New York. He gave a lecture, "In Lincoln's Footsteps," at the New York Public Library in May of 1988. He is a member of the Authors League of America and the American Civil Liberties Union. The 1988 John Newbery Medal was presented to Russell Freedman by the American Library Association for *Lincoln: A Photobiography*. The book was also an ALA Notable Book for 1988 and a Society of Children's Book Writers Honor Book for nonfiction. *Children of the Wild West* was named an Honor Book in nonfiction by the 1984 Boston Globe-Horn Book Award Committee; it received a 1984 Western Heritage Award from the National Cowboy Hall of Fame and was named an ALA Notable Book of 1983. *Cowboys of the Wild West* was designated a 1985 Spur Award Honor Book, by the Western Writers of America and was an ALA Notable Book for 1985. *Immigrant Kids*, *Indian Chiefs*, and *Buffalo Hunt* were also ALA Notable Books, in 1980, 1987, and 1988 respectively, and *Indian Chiefs* and *Lincoln* were also named Best Books for Young Adults in their years of publication by the ALA. *Hanging On* was named an Honor Book in the New York Academy of Sciences Children's Science Book Awards in 1978; *Lincoln* has appeared in the *Horn Book* Graphic Gallery, a showcase of excellent books honored by the magazine.

SELECTED WORKS: Teenagers Who Made History, 1961; Jules Verne: Portrait of a Prophet, 1965; The First Days of Life, 1974; Animal Fathers, 1976; Hanging On: How Animals Carry Their Young, 1977; Getting Born, 1978; How Animals Defend Their Young, 1978; Immigrant Kids, 1980; Children of the Wild West, 1983; Rattlesnakes, 1984; Cowboys of the Wild West, 1985; Indian Chiefs, 1987; Lincoln: A Photobiography, 1987; Buffalo Hunt, 1988.

ABOUT: Contemporary Authors (First Revision), Vol. 17; (New Revision Series), Vol. 7; Horn Book January/February 1986; July/August 1988; May/June 1989; Something About the Author, Vol.16; Who's Who in the East, 1974-1975.

JOHN REYNOLDS GARDINER

December 6, 1944–

AUTHOR OF *Stone Fox*, etc.

Autobiographical sketch of John Reynolds Gardiner:

AS A BOY I was a rebel. Whatever my parents wanted me to do, I did the opposite. My mother wanted me to read. So I didn't read. She tried to bribe me, but that didn't work. The more she insisted, the more I refused. In fact, I really showed her. I didn't read my first novel until I was nineteen.

If she had just put all those books she wanted me to read into a glass case and locked it, I would have found the key and read every one of them. But, she didn't.

However, in the evenings, after I had turned off my light, she would come into my room, turn on the light, and read to me. At first, I would complain, put my hands over my ears, or pretend to be asleep, but as soon as I became interested in the story, I wouldn't want her to stop.

Nonreaders are usually poor spellers, and I was no exception. Because I couldn't spell (not to mention my grammar), I received low grades on my writing compositions. The imagination was there and so was the humor that was to appear later in my books, but my teachers didn't seem to notice, except for one who said, "You couldn't have written this." Looking back now, she had paid me a compliment, but at the time, it was far from encouraging.

When I was about to graduate from high school, my English teacher took me aside and told me quite frankly, "You'll never make it in college English."

What really gets me is that he was right!

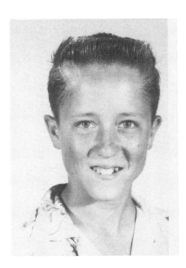

That story, by the way, became a children's book called *Stone Fox,* which is currently selling at a rate of 5,000 copies a month and has been translated into three foreign languages.

I would like to thank anyone who has ever given a beginning writer encouragement.

And thank you, Mom, for not giving up on me, for your rebel son is now a reader, a writer, and a lover of books.

———

John Reynolds Gardiner has a Masters Degree in Engineering from the University of California in Los Angeles and currently works as an engineer for McDonnell Douglas Corporation, where he predicts the temperature of satellites. He does his writing on his lunch break. He has held a variety of part-time jobs, including rock-and-roll singer and Santa Claus at a Sears store. He offers seminars in writing and marketing children's books at colleges and universities. He has traveled widely, living and working in Ireland, El Salvador, and West Germany. He is married and has three daughters.

Stone Fox has sold over 150,000 copies and won the 1987 Maud Hart Lovelace Award and the George G. Stone Center for Childrens' Books Recognition of Merit Award for the same year. It was named a Notable Book of 1980 by the American Library Association and was made into a 1987 NBC television movie.

SELECTED WORKS: Stone Fox, 1980; Top Secret, 1985; General Butterfingers, 1986.

John R. Gardiner

At UCLA I ended up in "dumbbell" English along with the foreign students, who couldn't speak English, but who could and did get better grades on their compositions than I did.

With all this "encouragement," I wrote no stories between the ages of eighteen and twenty-eight. Ten lost years.

My imagination, however, was still intact, for at this time I had started the Num Num Novelty Company, selling plastic neckties filled with water and goldfish.

My brother, recognizing my imagination, got me to enroll in a television writing class, taught by an instructor who didn't give a hoot about spelling and grammar, and my writing career began.

Six years later, after being unable to sell anything to television, I sent a story about a boy and his dog to a book publisher, and it was purchased.

Had my spelling and grammar improved? No. Were there misspelled words in the manuscript? Yes. Then why did the publisher buy it? Because the publisher knew something that my English teachers didn't, and that is that someone who may not have a good command of spelling or grammar may still be able to write a good story.

BEAU GARDNER

August 28, 1941—

AUTHOR AND ILLUSTRATOR OF *The Turn About, Think About, Look About Book*, etc.

Autobiographical sketch of Beau Gardner:

I AM a Graphic Designer by trade with a

During my second year in business, I was befriended by Louis Phillips, a writer who enticed me to collaborate on a children's book with him. He said he would write the words, and that I could create the images. Lou already was established with a publisher. We submitted our presentation. The publisher said they would publish the book . . . images only . . . no text.

After the success of the first book, I have produced at least one book a year. Four years after our initial collaboration, Lou and I finally connected together.

All in all, it has been very gratifying and a heck of a lot of fun.

———

Beau Gardner was born in Oceanside, New York. He was married in June, 1966. *Guess What?*, *The Upside Down Riddle Book*, and *The Turn About, Think About, Look About Book* were Reading Rainbow Books. Two of Gardner's books appeared in American Institute of Graphic Arts Book Shows: *The Turn About, Think About, Look About Book* in 1981 and *The Look Again . . . and Again and Again, and Again Book* in 1985. *Guess What?* was named a 1985 Outstanding Science Trade Book for Children by a joint committee of the National Science Teachers Association and the Children's Book Council.

SELECTED WORKS WRITTEN AND ILLUSTRATED: The Turn About, Think About, Look About Book, 1980; The Look Again . . . and Again and Again, and Again Book, 1984; Guess What?, 1985; Have You Ever Seen . . . ?: An ABC Book, 1986; Can You Imagine?: A Counting Book, 1987;

SELECTED WORKS ILLUSTRATED: The Upside Down Riddle Book, by Louis Phillips, 1982.

ABOUT: Something About the Author, Vol. 50.

[signature: Beau Gardner]

successful studio in midtown Manhattan. The main thrust of our business is communication graphics for large corporations.

Corporate graphics is very different from the world of children's books. But . . . I think I am drawn to children's books because they provide me with an outlet for unbridled invention and expression.

I grew up in Rockville Centre, Long Island, and attended school there. My special interests were sports, girls, and art . . . in that order. I was not a particularly good student and did just enough work to get by. After graduation from high school, I attended a junior college, the State University Agricultural and Technical Institute at Farmingdale. The entrance requirements and the price were right. I entered their Advertising Design and Art program with a special interest in technical illustration. By my second year at S.U.A.T.I., I knew I would go on to further education and a broader, more complete curriculum. I entered Pratt Institute in Brooklyn, New York. There I had four marvelous years. Upon graduation I went to work in the "real world."

After nine years of learning my trade in a leading studio in New York, I decided to open my own business.

SHEILA GARRIGUE

December 30, 1931–

AUTHOR OF *The Eternal Spring of Mr. Ito*, etc.

Sheila Garrigue

Autobiographical sketch of Sheila Garrigue:

I GREW UP an only child in a small town near London, England. It was Depression time and my mother ate poorly during her pregnancy so I developed rickets, a bone disease, which showed up as soon as I started to walk. I spent my childhood with my legs strapped into steel braces and was unable to run and play like other children. My parents read to me a great deal to help me pass the time and, once I learned to read, I became a real bookworm. I believe my first writing produced a few extra chapters to *Winnie-the-Pooh* and I also attempted extensions of the stories in a popular children's comic strip. But none of this was published or even read by anyone else but me.

When I was seven, World War II broke out in Europe. We lived near England's capital city and close to two airports likely to be bombing targets, so I was sent for safety to a country village where I lived for eight months, until an epidemic forced my return home. Although the war was still young and there were only occasional air-raids, it was felt that worse was to come and my parents sent me across the ocean to live with an uncle in Canada. This experience formed the basis for my children's novels *All the Children Were Sent Away* and *The Eternal Spring of Mr. Ito.*

I did not return to England until the war ended five years later. My first job was with a distributor of German scientific books. Several years later, I moved to an advertising agency and eventually I came to the United States, where I found a job in San Francisco. Two years after that, I moved to New York and married Paul Garrigue (pronounced like "intrigue"). By this time, I was at CBS News with Edward R. Murrow, a well-known reporter, and I continued working there until our first son was born. Looking back, I see that all these jobs had a common feature—working with words— but I still had no thought of being a writer myself.

I spent the next six years mothering two sons and a daughter. When our youngest entered first grade, I realized I could do what I wanted with my day once my chores were finished. I had always written a lot of letters and had been told they were interesting and I should try writing. So I began.

I started with short stories for children, working with a workshop group. The workshop leader encouraged me to consider a longer work, a novel. Although the length and commitment of time frightened me, I promised to try, and that is how *All the Children Were Sent Away* came into being. It took me two years to write.

The next book was *Between Friends*. This was based on my daughter's friendship with a retarded neighbor and portrayed the ups and downs of such a friendship. Once again, it took me about two years to write.

After *Between Friends*, I spent several years dealing with my mother's serious illness in faraway England. Despite difficulty in concentrating and keeping up my momentum, I got *The Eternal Spring of Mr. Ito* written and published in time for her to know it was dedicated to her.

In addition to writing, I work onstage and backstage with our local community theatre group. I also speak in schools and colleges and enjoy getting together with the budding authors I meet on these occasions. At present, I am working on several children's books and a nonfiction book for adults.

———

Sheila Garrigue was born in Bechenham, Kent, a suburb of London. She attended school in Canada and in England. She was married March 14, 1959. She is a member of the Authors Guild of Authors League of America. *The Eternal Spring of Mr. Ito* was a Junior Literary Guild selection and was named a 1985 Notable Children's Trade Book in the Field of Social Studies by a joint committee of the Children's Book Council and the National Council on the Social Studies.

SELECTED WORKS: All the Children Were Sent Away, 1976; Between Friends, 1978; The Eternal Spring of Mr. Ito, 1985.

ABOUT: Something About the Authors, Vol. 21.

MORDICAI GERSTEIN

November 25, 1935–

AUTHOR AND ILLUSTRATOR OF *The Mountains of Tibet*, etc.

Biographical sketch of Mordicai Gerstein:

BORN IN Los Angeles, California, Mordicai Gerstein grew up first in East Los Angeles, a racially mixed section of the city, and later in the San Fernando Valley, which was like the country. His mother loved painting and books, and took him to the library frequently. His father is a playwright, but had to work as a businessman until he retired, in order to support himself and his family. Young Gerstein was stimulated by stories and books and drew illustrations for them as a child.

After graduating from high school, he traveled to New Mexico to study with a

MORDICAI GERSTEIN

painter there. In the fall of 1953 he began study at Chouinard Art Institute, which lasted until 1956. After his last year there, he went to work at United Producers of America, an animation studio. He was encouraged, along with other young artists, to create films, and he painted in his spare time. In 1957 he and his then wife moved to New York, where he became interested in de Kooning and other Abstract Impressionists. He lived in a loft in Soho, and began making films. His *The Magic Ring* won the 1967 Cine Golden Eagle Award given by the Center for International Nontheatrical Events. He adapted one of his films, *The Room*, into a picture book. He made his living from commercial animation and from a cartoon he drew for the *Village Voice*, "The Inner Man."

His first children's books came from a collaboration with Elizabeth Levy on the "Something Queer" mystery series. He has since created many other books, some based on his travels abroad. He likes to work every day, setting his own schedule, and he works best in the morning. He enjoys running, drawing, painting, cooking, and reading, and visits museums frequently.

Gerstein is married for a second time and

lives with his wife in Massachusetts. He has three children. *Arnold of the Ducks* was a *New York Times* Best Illustrated Book of 1983; *The Mountains of Tibet* was given the same distinction in 1987. Both that book and *Something Queer at the Ballpark* were Junior Literary Guild selections. *Something Queer on Vacation* was named a 1981 Children's Choice Book by a joint committee of the Children's Book Council and the International Reading Association. *Arnold of the Ducks* was adapted for a CBS-TV Storybreak in 1985.

SELECTED WORKS WRITTEN AND ILLUSTRATED: Arnold of the Ducks, 1983; Follow Me!, 1983; Prince Sparrow, 1984; Roll Over!, 1984; The Room, 1984; William, Where Are You?, 1985; The Seal Mother, 1986; Tales of Pan, 1986; The Mountains of Tibet, 1987; The Sun's Day, 1989.

SELECTED WORKS ILLUSTRATED: Something Queer Is Going on, by Elizabeth Levy, 1973; Something Queer at the Ballpark, by Elizabeth Levy, 1975; Something Queer on Vacation, by Elizabeth Levy, 1980; Something Queer in Rock N' Roll, by Elizabeth Levy, 1987.

ABOUT: Something About the Author, Vol. 36; Vol. 47.

GAIL GIBBONS

August 1, 1944–

AUTHOR AND ILLUSTRATOR OF *Sun Up, Sun Down*, etc.

Biographical sketch of Gail Gibbons:

GAIL GIBBONS was born in Oak Park, Illinois. She attended schools in the three Illinois towns in which her family lived during her childhood. She studied graphic design at the University of Illinois, receiving a B.F.A. degree in 1967.

She says that her career interest in illustrating children's books was spurred by an instructor in college who was involved in that field himself. She was impressed, she says, that he was actively involved in professional work, not just in his teaching du-

ties. Her career after graduation began as a graphic artist for WCIA Television, the CBS affiliate in Champaign, Illinois. Two years later she was doing free-lance art and design work, including animation, in Chicago for NBC.

After moving to New York City in 1970 with her husband, Glenn Gibbons, she did graphics work for the local news broadcast by WNBC Television. She later became graphic artist for an hour-long NBC children's program, broadcast as *Take a Giant Step* from 1971 to 1972 and later continued as *Talk with a Giant*. Now she was illustrating for children, although not yet for children's books. She designed the graphic images for the sets behind the children and for transitions between features and commercials. Later, working for NBC's local evening news show with John Chancellor, she produced topical graphic work illustrating the newscaster's reports. Currently she designs graphics that are distributed to television programs around the country by United Press International.

These colorful, carefully interpreted graphic designs appear in her illustrations for children's books. "There's a very strong graphic play in illustration for television because it has to be so readable," she says. "And in a lot of my books I want things easily readable."

After her husband's death in an accident in 1972, she balanced her career between television work and some free-lance art. In 1975 *Willie and His Wheel Wagon*, a book that illustrated the concept of set theory for children learning new math, became her first published book.

In many of the more than forty published books that she has illustrated since, Gibbons has skillfully elucidated for curious minds how things work, what they are composed of, and what they do. Whether explaining mechanical operations, as in *Clocks and How They Go*, or service organizations, as in *The Post Office Book: Mail and How It Moves*, text and illustration complement each other, artfully simplifying complex topics.

"I was always curious, I was always driving my parents nuts," she says. This curiosity leads her to some unusual research. While preparing to write her book on clocks, she disassembled those around the house. "I still have two boxes of clock parts left," she says. Gail Gibbons says that once her interest in a subject is triggered, "one of my favorite parts is the research. For every single book I do, I have sources that I go to to make sure that what I'm saying is accurate. I know I can't rely just on the library, because things get dated."

Although she has illustrated some books for other authors, she now prefers to illustrate texts that she herself has written. "If I do only the artwork," she says, "I end up doing almost as much research to do the artwork as if I were going to write and illustrate it anyway. That's why I prefer doing my own thing."

Her research has taken her to the American Museum of Natural History for her book *Dinosaurs* and to Key West, Florida, and Woods Hole, Massachusetts, for *Sunken Treasure*. She studied a large department store in New York City for *Department Store* as well as zoos and lighthouses for other books, some still unpublished.

In addition to the research for and designing of her books, she enjoys talking with the children who are her audience. "Kids are so curious about things, so stimulating," she says. "School talks require so much energy. Kids are excited; you have to use a lot of energy just to keep up with them." Among the many honors that she has received for her books is the 1987 *Washington Post*-Children's Book Guild Award for Nonfiction. "The enormous breadth of subjects that Gail Gibbons has brought to life is astonishing," the judges said. "Her books are free-flowing fountains of information." Gibbons has written and illustrated over forty books.

Gail Gibbons and her husband Kent Ancliffe, a builder, live in Corinth, Vermont. They have two grown children. Their house, which they built themselves, sits on three acres, most of it woods and fields, but fifty acres of which is sugarbush. They have a dog, three cats, and a four-wheel drive pickup truck. *Clocks and How They Go* won a 1980 American Institute of Graphic Arts Award. *Locks and Keys* and *Tool Book* were named Outstanding Science Trade Books for Children by a joint committee of the Children's Book Council and the National Science Teachers Association, in 1980 and 1982 respectively. Two of Gibbons' books have been named American Library Association Notable Books: *Cars and How They Go* in 1983 and *The Milk Makers* in 1985.

SELECTED WORKS WRITTEN AND ILLUSTRATED: Willie and His Wheel Wagon, 1975; Clocks and How They Go, 1979; The Missing Maple Syrup Sap Mystery, 1979; Locks and Keys, 1980; Trucks, 1981; The Post Office Book: Mail and How It Moves, 1981; Tool Book, 1982; Sun Up, Sun Down, 1983; Department Store, 1984; Lights! Camera! Action!: How a Movie Is Made, 1985; The Milk Makers, 1985; Deadline!: From News to Newspaper, 1987; Dinosaurs, 1987; Zoo, 1987; Sunken Treasure, 1988.

SELECTED WORKS ILLUSTRATED: Cars and How They Go, By Joanna Cole, 1983.

ABOUT: Children's Literature Review, Vol. 8; Contemporary Authors, Vol. 69; (New Revision Series), Vol. 12; Something About the Author, Vol. 23.

JAMES CROSS GIBLIN

July 8, 1933–

AUTHOR OF *Chimney Sweeps: Yesterday and Today*, etc.

Autobiographical Sketch of James Cross Giblin:

WHEN I WAS asked once by an interviewer what I was like as a small boy, I replied: "Shy. Bookish. And probably a little spoiled."

I was born in Cleveland, Ohio, on July 8, 1933, the only child of Kelley, a lawyer and poet (unpublished), and Anna, a former teacher of high school French. Mother studied law after her marriage and passed the bar exam, but she never practiced. Instead she devoted herself to my upbringing, and was the person responsible for introducing me to children's books and reading.

When I was three, we settled into a sprawling old house in the suburban town of Painesville. The neighborhood was composed largely of retired couples, and I was the only child for blocks around. Consequently, I was left to my own devices much of the time. But I also shared from an early age in the stimulating conversations my parents had with their friends on the faculty of Lake Erie College. Those were the years before and during World War II, and the ideas and events the grownups discussed were exciting to a young boy like me. Interestingly, many of them have figured in such books of mine as *Let There Be Light*, *Milk*, and *Walls: Defenses Throughout History*.

I blossomed in high school, writing articles for the school newspaper, coediting it in my senior year, and acting in all the school plays. This pattern continued at Case Western Reserve University in Cleveland, where I received a B.A. degree in 1954. I majored in English and dramatic arts, wrote for the college paper, and acted in many of the major productions at Eldred Theatre on the Reserve campus.

But acting wasn't enough for me. I wanted to make a more direct, personal statement, so I turned to playwriting. My first published work was a one-act play, *My Bus Is Always Late* (Dramatic Publishing, 1954), and I went on to earn an M.F.A. in playwriting from Columbia University in 1955. That led to my doing an adaptation of William Styron's novel, *Lie Down in Darkness*, which was optioned for Broadway production in 1956. The option was dropped a year later, however, and at age twenty-four I was left on the sidelines— disappointed, depressed, and broke.

A job at the British Book Centre raised my spirits and proved to be the start of a career in publishing. From the Centre, I moved on to Criterion Books, where I decided to concentrate on children's books. In 1962 I joined Lothrop, Lee & Shepard Books as associate editor and stayed there until 1967, when I left to become editor-in-chief of a fledgling juvenile list at Seabury Press that grew into Clarion Books.

Although editorial work was satisfying to me, I had never lost my desire to write. So I responded enthusiastically in 1977 when I was asked to contribute a brief piece to *The New York Kid's Book*, all royalties from which were to go to the children's rooms of the New York Public Library. I

Giblin: hard *G*

chose to write about an early New York sky-scraper, the triangular Flatiron Building. That piece led to an article about skyscrapers in general for *Cricket* and then to my second children's book, *The Skyscraper Book*. Meanwhile, I'd collaborated with Dale Ferguson on a photo essay, *The Scarecrow Book*.

My books have all sprung from ideas that piqued my curiosity for one reason or another and made me want to explore them. In most instances I didn't know where the exploration would take me when I started out. For example, I thought *Walls* would be a photo essay of famous walls such as the Great Wall of China, but it turned into a history of fortification with a strong antiwar theme. And *From Hand to Mouth*, which began as a history of eating utensils, evolved into a chronicle of table manners in various cultures and epochs also.

As I pursue them, these nonfiction explorations become adventures for me. I hope my young readers are as fascinated as I am by the new facts and insights that emerge along the way.

Today I live by myself in a high-rise apartment in New York City with a marvelous view of rooftops, distant towers, and the sky. As in high school, I'm still combining writing with editing. I even indulge in a bit of performing now and then when I give lectures on writing and publishing to teachers, librarians, fellow writers—and children.

James Cross Giblin has been a contributor to *The Writer, Writer's Digest, Cricket, Highlights for Children*, and *Horn Book*, among other magazines. He is a member of the editorial board of *Children's Literature in Education*, and has had a book for adults published in 1989, *Writing Books for Young People*.

The Scarecrow Book and *The Skyscraper Book* were named Notable Children's Books by the American Library Association, for 1980 and 1981 respectively;

Chimney Sweeps won a Golden Kite Award from the Society of Children's Book Writers in 1983, was the nonfiction children's winner of the 1983 American Book Award, and was an ALA Notable Book of 1982. *The Truth About Santa Claus* was a Boston Globe-Horn Book Honor Book for 1986 in the nonfiction category and an ALA Notable Book for 1985. *Walls* won another SCBW Golden Kite Award for nonfiction, in 1984, and was a Junior Literary Guild selection. *Milk* was named an ALA Notable Book of 1986 and a Junior Literary Guild selection. *Fireworks, Picnics, and Flags* was a Junior Literary Guild selection, and *From Hand to Mouth* was an ALA Notable Book of 1987 and a Junior Literary Guild selection. *Let There Be Light* was an ALA Notable Book of 1988.

SELECTED WORKS: The Scarecrow Book, 1980; The Skyscraper Book, 1981; Chimney Sweeps: Yesterday and Today, 1982; Fireworks, Picnics, and Flags: The Story of the Fourth of July Symbols, 1983; Walls: Defenses Throughout History, 1984; The Truth About Santa Claus, 1985; Milk: The Fight for Purity, 1986; From Hand to Mouth: Or, How We Invented Knives, Forks, Spoons, and Chopsticks and the Table Manners to Go With Them, 1987; Let There Be Light: A Book About Windows, 1988.

SELECTED WORKS WITH DALE FERGUSON: The Scarecrow Book, 1980.

ABOUT: Contemporary Authors, Vol. 106; Giblin, James C. Writing Books for Young People; Horn Book December 1975; January/February 1987; School Library Journal October 1988; Something About the Author, Vol. 33.

JAMIE GILSON

July 4, 1933–

AUTHOR OF *Harvey, the Beer Can King*, etc.

Autobiographical sketch of Jamie Gilson:

"WHICH do you do most," a fifth grader in Little Rock asked me, "read or write?"

"Read," I told him. "I read a lot." When I was a child my favorite books were

Caddie Woodlawn, The Wonderful Wizard of Oz, and *Homer Price*. Now I always have at least two or three open somewhere in the house ready to be picked up again and then again. I love books. I learned to write by reading them.

My father was a flour miller. Every small midwestern town had a mill to grind the wheat brought in by local farmers. We moved a lot. Growing up in Beardstown, Illinois; Boonville, Missouri; Pittsfield, Illinois; and Independence, Missouri, I wore out library cards because I read so much, but I wrote only when I was told to.

I wasn't interested in being a writer. I didn't think of that until later. I wanted to be an actress. Every year I was in a play or two, memorizing someone else's words. I learned dramatic poems, too, and said them to women's clubs. Sometimes they paid me five dollars, which I thought was terrific.

When I went to college at Northwestern University, my major was speech and, in addition to learning about the history of western civilization, I studied acting, radio, and television. And I got a teacher's certificate.

For one year I taught speech and English to junior-high students. I doubt, however, that any of them will remember either our hand-puppet fairy tales or amazing sentence diagrams as absolute highlights of their school life.

My next job, teaching by radio, was, I think, more successful. I did my first professional writing for WBEZ, Chicago's educational radio station, preparing and directing and acting in scripts that told why the Chicago River flows backwards, how big the ferris wheel was at the Columbian Exhibition of 1893, and how awful plaque can be for your teeth.

Before writing books, I also wrote for a fine arts radio station, for Encyclopedia Britannica Films, and for a number of magazines—especially *Chicago* magazine where I wrote lots of stories about people who did wonderful things for a living like bind leather books and create candy recipes.

But I think I couldn't have written books about children if I hadn't had children of my own. My husband Jerry and I have three: Tom, Matthew, and Anne. When they were little I read to them. When they learned to read I read the books they read. I knew which ones they liked and which they didn't. They liked funny books, so I decided to try to write funny.

A boy down the block had a remarkable collection of 1,000 beer cans, all of them different. There ought to be some humor there, I thought. I interviewed him and found enough possibilities to write my first book, *Harvey, the Beer Can King*.

Most of my ideas come from watching and talking to kids in the town where I live. Our Central School has a spit pit just like the one in *Thirteen Ways to Sink a Sub*. I went with a class of local fifth graders on a pretty wacky outdoor education trip like the group took in *4B Goes Wild*. And I made lots of notes for *Hobie Hanson, You're Weird* at a pie-eating contest in a park right across the street from our house. It was during a Fourth of July celebration, a holiday I've always wanted to write about because, flags, fireworks, and all, it's my birthday.

There are funny things going on out there, and from moldy bread in lockers to inflatable giraffe boats, I'll do my best to find them.

———

Jamie Gilson was born in Beardstown, Illinois. She received her B.S. degree from Northwestern University in 1955 and was married June 19, 1955. She is a member of the Society of Children's Book Writers.

Do Bananas Chew Gum? won the 1981 Carl Sandburg Award given by the Friends of the Chicago Public Library, and along with *Can't Catch Me . . .* , it was a Junior Literary Guild selection.

SELECTED WORKS: Dial Leroi Rupert, DJ, 1979; Do Bananas Chew Gum?, 1980; Can't Catch Me, I'm the Gingerbread Man, 1981; Thirteen Ways to Sink a Sub, 1982; 4B Goes Wild, 1983; Harvey, the Beer Can King, 1983; Hello, My Name Is Scrambled Eggs, 1985; Hobie Hanson, You're Weird, 1987; Double Dog Dare, 1988.

ABOUT: Contemporary Authors, Vol. 111; Language Arts May 1983; Something About the Author, Vol. 34; Vol. 37; Who's Who of American Women, 1985-1986.

MIRRA GINSBURG

AUTHOR OF *Good Morning, Chick*, etc.

Autobiographical sketch of Mirra Ginsburg:

I WAS BORN AND SPENT my early childhood in Bobruisk, a small town in Byelorussia that seems centuries away from my present home in New York.

It was a town of small one-storey wooden houses, with only three brick buildings two storeys high. It was surrounded by woods and fields within walking distance, and we lived simply. We had no running water and no plumbing. Most streets, especially on the outskirts of town where we lived, were not paved. When it rained, barrels were put out to collect the water, for washing and cleaning. Drinking water was brought from a neighbor's well. After rains there were huge puddles in the street, where pigs, big and

little, came to wallow and luxuriate, and I loved to slosh barefoot through the mud, among the pigs. Neighboring women rinsed their wash in rivulets that ran along the board sidewalks.

Wars and revolutions, famines and epidemics shook the world, but at first our lives were relatively untouched, especially the lives of young children in remote small towns. Before long, all this was changed, but meantime flowers bloomed, orchards bore fruit, and we children spent our days as children do, playing, learning, reading (I began at four), and listening to the talk of our elders about happenings in the adult world. Like all perceptive children, I reacted to the talk and the rumors and the terrors of the time (they finally reached us, too), but this reaction was not immediately or fully realized. Oddly, there was little conscious fear. This came later, and still returns in many a nightmare.

Yet, it is strange to find how many worlds a single individual can inhabit, historically, geographically, mentally, and emotionally.

When I was about six or seven, my mother took me to visit her friends who lived at the other end of town. They also had children, and the children had a set of books with folk tales of the Caucasus, a mountainous regions in southern Russia. I opened one of the books, and I was captured for life. The magical world has stayed with me ever since, through many more books and many, many tales.

In many ways, I was fortunate in my parents (not in all ways). From my father, I learned to love animals and green growing things. As a child, I was surrounded with them. From my mother, I learned sympathy for people. From both, I learned to love books and pictures. The choices within these areas were mostly my own, and as I grew up, they became more and more my own.

I began to write early. At nine or so I began a long epic poem, imitating the Odyssey (such impertinence!), hiding in the shade of a currant bush in our garden.

After we left Russia, we lived for a time in Latvia, then Canada, finally coming to settle in the United States. Schooling was all broken up with this moving from place to place. So were friendships. When I learned English (by reading poetry, mostly Byron, Shelley, and Keats, with a dictionary) I began to write again: diaries, poems, stories (not very good ones). And when the time came to earn my own living, I turned to translation. In this, too, I was fortunate. I insisted, almost from the first, on choosing books and authors that I felt close to even if it meant more time and lower earnings. I have always believed that good work can be done only when you love what you are doing. And so I was able to translate some of the best Russian writers of the twentieth century into English, and that is a source of much joy.

After a while I also began to work with folk tales and children's books. I have loved and collected them all my life, and one day if dawned on me—there is so much richness and wit and beauty here, why not share it with American children?

I started by translating stories and tales I especially liked. Soon I began to add, to change and adapt them, so that the result was a sort of joint performance. As time went on, my books became more and more my own, sometimes merely based on a line or an idea found in Russian sources.

I dislike books that "teach a lesson" or offer "a slice of life" or tell the reader what to think. I like stories that are witty and imaginative, that are fun to write and to read, stories that open fresh poetic vistas and expand horizons, and those that are pure play, and those that are deeply meaningful without being pretentious or preachy. All these qualities are richly present in folk tales and in the best books for young readers (and listeners), and I try to keep them alive in my work.

I have also been very lucky in my editors and illustrators, so that I can say without reserve: "I love my books. They are a joy and a delight."

———

Ginsburg has translated books for adults, such as *Notes from the Underground* by Fyodor Dostoyevsky, and plays, such as those by Mikhail Bulgakov. She is a member of P.E.N.

The Chick and the Duckling was a Book-of-the-Month Club selection. *Good Morning, Chick* was named a 1981 Children's Choice Book by a joint committee of the Children's Book Council and the International Reading Association. It was also a Book-of-the-Month Club selection. *The Three Kittens* was a Junior Literary Guild selection.

SELECTED WORKS TRANSLATED, EDITED, ADAPTED, OR WRITTEN: Three Rolls and One Doughnut: Fables from Russia, 1970; The Chick and the Duckling, by V. Suteyev, 1972; The Three Kittens, by V. Suteyev, 1973; How the Sun Was Brought Back to the Sky, 1975; How Wilka Went to Sea: Folk Tales from West of the Urals, 1975; Twelve Clever Brothers and Other Fools, 1979; Good Morning, Chick, 1980; Where Does the Sun Go at Night?, 1980; Across the Stream, 1982; The Sun's Asleep Behind the Hill, 1982; Four Brave Sailors, 1987; The Chinese Mirror, 1988.

SELECTED WORKS TRANSLATED: The Diary of Nina Kosterina, by Nina Kosterina, 1969; The White Ship, by Chingiz Aitmatov, 1972; Daughter of Night, by Lydia Obukhova, 1974.

ABOUT: Contemporary Authors, Vol. 17-20; (First Revision), Vol. 17; (New Revision Series), Vol. 11; The International Authors and Writers Who's Who, 1982; Publishers Weekly November 5, 1972; Reginald, R., comp. and ed. Contemporary Science Fiction Authors; Something About the Author, Vol. 6; Who's Who of American Women, 1977-1978.

BARBARA GIRION

November 20, 1938–

AUTHOR OF *A Tangle of Roots*, etc.

Autobiographical sketch of Barbara Girion:

I'D LIKE TO be able to report that I fell out of my crib and immediately started writing, but that wouldn't be true. I grew up and went to school in Hillside, New Jersey, and while I loved books and loved to read, I hated to write, especially essays or reports—i.e., "What I did on my summer vacation"—that were assigned by teachers!

I worked after school in my father's five-and-ten-cent store, teased my younger brother, and was a gung-ho cheerleader in my high school years. Still, my favorite place was always the library, and I once tried like my favorite heroine, Francie Nolan in *A Tree Grows in Brooklyn,* to read through all the books alphabetically.

After graduating from college, where I majored in history, I married and got a job teaching seventh grade in the very same school in Hillside, N.J., that I had attended. It was eerie walking through the halls that had somehow gotten so much smaller over the years and going into the Teachers' Room (where I finally learned that teachers really didn't have such secret things to talk about)!

When my first son was born, I found it impossible to get him to take a nap unless I told him a story. So I'd stretch out on the couch and began to weave tales about the everyday things around us. I don't know if the stories were boring or my voice was, but he'd soon be asleep. It was faster than rocking him in his carriage. But I'd be wide awake and my mind would keep on with the stories. The hardest decision I've ever had to make took place on the day I decided to get these stories out of my head and onto a piece of paper.

I soon realized that I could recall all the feelings I had growing up. The happiness, the sadness, the fears, and the triumphs. After my second son and daughter came along and I was able to borrow Grandma and Grandpa to babysit, I signed up for a writers' workshop in New York City.

That became the highlight of a busy mother's week. On Wednesday nights I'd travel to class clutching my typewritten pages, heart beating madly. I'd either wind up crying all the way back home to New Jersey if my work was heavily criticized or be wildly happy if I had received some compliments.

I've never had the desire to write fantasy. I guess I'm too fascinated by the real people and happenings that surround me. All of my work so far is contemporary in nature, though the feelings my characters have are the same feelings I had growing up, and I daresay the same feelings young people will have fifty years from now. Since my personal family background is a very strong one, I like to use the generations of families in my books! I had loving and interested grandparents. Although immigrants themselves, they impressed upon me the love and reverence for books that I try to pass on to my own children.

From my own experience as a parent I know that parents are neither heroes or the completely selfish coldblooded devils that they are made out to be. I am not trying to write about the family extremes, the abusers or the staunchest, most wonderful. Somehow, I am trying to write about those of us who muddle through, who make mistakes at times but are still around with an awful lot of love to give.

I try to learn from each of my books. They are almost like my children. I try to put the very best of myself into them that I can. Then I send them out into the world where they have to stand or fall by themselves.

———

Barbara Girion was born in New York City. She was married November 27, 1957, and received her B.A. degree from Montclair State College in New Jersey in 1958. She did graduate study at Kean College and the New School for Social Research. She has been a special education instructor in addition to her seventh-grade teaching. She has also been a guest lecturer at Hofstra University in 1978 and 1978, and at the University of Rhode Island from 1980 to 1981. She is a member of the Society of Children's Book Writers and the Authors Guild. Girion has had short stories published in *Seventeen*, *Young World*, *Co-Ed*, and *Young Miss*.

A Tangle of Roots and *A Handful of Stars* were both named Best Books for Young Adults by the American Library Association in their years of publication. *Like Everybody Else* was named a Children's Choice Book for 1981 by a joint committee of the International Reading Association and the Children's Book Council.

SELECTED WORKS: The Boy with the Special Face,

1978; Joshua, the Czar and the Chicken Bone Wish, 1978; Misty and Me, 1979; A Tangle of Roots, 1979; Like Everybody Else, 1980; A Handful of Stars, 1981; In the Middle of a Rainbow, 1983; A Very Brief Season, 1984; Portfolio to Fame: Cameron's Story, 1987; Prescription for Success: Amanda's Story, 1987.

ABOUT: Contemporary Authors, Vol. 85; (New Revision Series), Vol. 15; Something About the Author, Vol. 26; Who's Who of American Women, 1981-1982; Who's Who in the East, 1983-84.

ANDREW GLASS

AUTHOR AND ILLUSTRATOR OF: *Chickpea and the Talking Cow*, etc.

Biographical sketch of Andrew Glass:

ANDREW GLASS was born in Pittsburgh, Pennsylvania, the oldest of eight children. He attended the Tyler School of Art at Temple University in Philadelphia and later studied at the School of Visual Arts in New York City.

His characteristic style is executed in various media: watercolor, pencil, and colored pencil. His effective use of shadow and light evokes sinister and joyous moods alike and enhances Bill Brittain's folkloric *The Wish Giver* and *The Devil's Donkey*. What *School Library Journal* described as his "buck-toothed, rubbery children" emerge in books like Beverly Major's *Playing Sardines*, where children pile upon children in a game.

In one of the books Glass has both written and illustrated, *Jackson Makes His Move*, a young raccoon artist experiments with a new abstract painting style. Two space creatures visit earth and so provide a new perspective for earth-dwelling readers in *My Brother Tries to Make Me Laugh*.

Glass lives in New York City, where he illustrates books, writes, and produces paintings and collages.

Two of the books Andrew Glass has illustrated have been named Newbery Honor Books by the American Library Association: *Graven Images* in 1983, and *The Wish*

ANDREW GLASS

Giver in 1984. Both books, as well as *The Devil's Donkey*, were ALA Notable Books in their years of publication. Two of his books have been named Children's Choice Books by a joint committee of the Children's Book Council and the International Reading Association: *Jackson Makes His Move* in 1983 and *Spooky Night* in 1983.

SELECTED WORKS WRITTEN AND ILLUSTRATED: Jackson Makes His Move, 1982; My Brother Tries to Make Me Laugh, 1984; Chickpea and the Talking Cow, 1987.

SELECTED WORKS ILLUSTRATED: The Devil's Donkey, by Bill Brittain, 1981; Banjo, by Robert Newton Peck, 1982; Graven Images: Three Stories, by Paul Fleischman, 1982; Spooky Night, by Natalie Savage Carlson, 1982; Battle in the Englishl Channel by Theodore Taylor, 1983; The Wish Giver: Three Tales of Coven Tree, by Bill Brittain, 1983; Spooky and the Ghost Cat, by Natalie Savage Carlson, 1985; Dr. Dredd's Wagon of Wonders, by Bill Brittain, 1987; Playing Sardines, by Beverly Major, 1988.

ABOUT: Something About the Author, Vol. 46.

JAN GREENBERG

December 29, 1942–

AUTHOR OF *No Dragons to Slay*, etc.

Autobiographical sketch of Jan Schonwald Greenberg:

WHEN I WAS about ten years old, I developed a strange eye allergy, which made my eyes water every time I went into the sunlight. The doctor told me to wear sunglasses. But I felt silly hiding behind dark glasses, so I spent that summer inside, curled up in my parents' library reading. Their bookshelves were filled with an assortment of books ranging from Plato's *Dialogues* to *Gone with the Wind*. It was there in that cozy room with a fireplace that I developed not only a love of books, but also eclectic tastes in literature. Now I read anything and everything from popular magazines to the classics. I began writing a journal during that long summer, and even now I find it helpful to jot down my thoughts every day. Some of those notes to myself have been the beginnings of a new book.

In 1964, I received a B.A. from Washington University, where I was an English major. I loved the work of many American poets, among them Walt Whitman, Emily Dickinson, and William Carlos Williams. I began reviewing the work of new poets for the *St. Louis Post-Dispatch,* which were my first published pieces. A few years later, I decided I wanted to teach, so I went back to school and completed a Master's Degree in Education. I taught English Composition at several colleges in St. Louis. The most interesting job I ever had was developing arts curricula with a group of actors, musicians, poets, and dancers. The energy and excitement engendered by my contact with these artists inspired me to develop my own creative skills. In the early seventies, my husband and I began collecting contemporary American art. We then opened a gallery, which has become a center for new art in St. Louis. Our rambling old house is filled with bright canvases and large steel sculpture on the lawn. Learning to look at art has helped me in terms of the way I perceive the world through my writing.

I began writing my first novel as a way of sharing some of my family history with my three teenage daughters. But as I began telling them about my parents and what it was like growing up in St. Louis and attending a private girls' school, I began to exaggerate and embellish the facts of my life. In other words, I used my imagination. I did it that way because it was more fun. Making things up allowed me to control certain events and characters in ways I couldn't do as a child. One hundred and fifty pages later, I had a story with a beginning, a middle, and an end. And it was a work of fiction, rather than an autobiography. Of course, the feelings that I described were real. What I discovered was that what makes autobiographical fiction work is relating an honest expression of a human emotion, not necessarily sticking to the facts. All the characters in my books represent some part of my personality. They often surprise me by behaving in ways I never suspected. I learn about myself through writing. Although I don't believe in easy solutions, I would rather have my characters walk out of a snowstorm at the end of a book, rather than into one.

My novels focus on the development of characters who face problems and have difficult relationships. Like most people, I've experienced my share of rough moments. But maintaining my sense of humor has helped me in evey aspect of my life. I hope the young people in my books reflect that attitude. After my first novel *A Season In-Between*—which is the story of a girl who must face the illness and death of her father—some people told me how brave I was to admit weakness and negative feelings in print. But writing is an act of sharing. A book is never a total figment of the imagination. It begins as a stomachache, a slight quiver of discomfort. It's like falling in and out of love. If the feeling is strong enough, a book may evolve. Or maybe not. But when something happens, and a year later I'm holding a new novel in my hand, I want to jump up and down, throw confetti, and stop everyone on the street and say, "Look what I've done."

———

Jan Greenberg received her M.A.T. degree in Communications from Webster University, St. Louis, in 1971. She has been a teacher in public schools, a book reviewer, a college instructor in English, and Director of a program to teach graduate students perception and creativity in the arts, at Webster University. She is a member of P.E.N., the Society of Children's Book Writers, the Missouri Arts Council. She also gives workshops on Aesthetic Education and Writing Books for Young Readers. *No Dragons to Slay* was named a Notable Book of 1984 by the American Library Association.

SELECTED WORKS: A Season In-Between, 1979; The Iceberg and Its Shadow, 1980; The Pig-Out Blues, 1982; No Dragons to Slay, 1984; Bye, Bye Miss American Pie, 1985; Exercises of the Heart, 1986; Just the Two of Us, 1988.

—Karen Gundersheimer

KAREN GUNDERSHEIMER

October 16, 1939–

AUTHOR AND ILLUSTRATOR OF *Happy Winter*, etc.

Autobiographical sketch of Karen Gundersheimer:

I WAS BORN feisty and grew up out of sync, both at home and at school. I set the example for what my younger sister and brother should not be: volatile, quirky, chaotic—artistic. I cannot remember a time I did not draw or paint or doodle or decorate. Of course, I did so constantly in school and, as a consequence, spent much of my time out on the bench, waiting for my attitude to improve. My mother says it happened even earlier, but my recollection is Second Grade when, in the midst of a wonderful mural project, we were summarily told to clean up, open our long-division workbooks, and buckle down. I was the lone, very loud dissenter—and promptly dismissed to the bench.

The mortification was tempered by the amazing parade before my very eyes: all those people with their weird gaits, odd postures, goofy voices. I was honing a lifelong passion for trivia, learning the value of eavesdropping: I was becoming the snoop I am today. I will gladly go to any lengths to get past the door that says "DO NOT ENTER."

The fascination for places unfamiliar took me into books—particularly those where there was trouble, danger, conflict. I loved tragedy! Those lucky orphans! Gypsies! Hobos! Adventurers—especially when their supplies ran out. . . . After some juicy story, I'd re-read it or invent even more terrible situations for these characters I'd come to know—and I mean know as if they were family.

Besides books, there was radio. Listening to "Baby Snooks" I could "see" her, crystal-clear, never dreaming it was anything but *my* vision—until that awful moment when I saw a photograph of Fanny Brice, who acted the role. A grownup! I was appalled—totally devastated. An inviolable Truth had been shattered, like the news about Santa. . . . And now, when I do invent a character, each gets a most specific "biography": how else could I know how to situate, dress, furnish, pose, etc? This absolutely involuntary, unswerving attraction to and for characters led to mimicry and later on, to acting. My debut was Grandpapa, in *Peter and the Wolf*, then a pirate in *Penzance*, and finally, Amanda, in *The Glass Menagerie*. Learning the lines and wearing outlandish costumes was exhilarating—but above all, "becoming" someone else was the Ultimate Drama.

Having grown up listening to a different drummer, I went off to Sarah Lawrence College in 1957, where beads, black stockings, and weirdness were prized. I suddenly found myself surrounded by people who had also hated dancing school, hockey, and rules—who had also been listening to madrigals and Bach when everyone else was spinning the Top 40. It never occurred to me to go to art school—nor did it dawn on me that I could combine a love of drawing

Gundersheimer: *GUNDERS high mer*

and reading into a career. I never thought of myself as "talented": it just came naturally, and I took it for granted—glad enough to be the Class Clown, Actress, Artist.

But eventually, through a series of flukey circumstances, I learned of *Cricket* magazine and, in a moment of abandon, sent off some sample sketches. I was terrified to receive an assignment, by return mail. I had no more idea about illustration than engine repair: I did not know a single, solitary thing about preparing art for reproduction. Yet all those years of sideline-snooping and mimicry had, without my realizing it, sharpened a naturally intuitive disposition. Even without my own two itchy little boys I'd have been absolutely convinced by the mother-son dialogue—so I shut the door, sat down, and did it.

I eagerly took every assignment, though few matched the quality of the first. Finally, exasperated by a third-rate poem, I thought: "If they accept *this*, I can write one, too." I did, they took it—and almost everything else I sent. Later, I spent a year doing original pieces for *Children's Digest*. Just after that, I was astonished to receive letters from Jane Feder, at Pantheon, and Elizabeth Gordon, at Harper and Row. They had seen my work in *Cricket* and had manuscripts for me to consider. I was exceptionally lucky that my editors were so patient and good-humored on the transition from articles to books. They (almost) invariably offered manuscripts with words set perfectly in their tracks, guiding and nudging me through many false starts, encouraging the idiosyncratic spin I found for those words. I learned that my fervent convictions were—are—sometimes mistaken, and that backsliding and unexpected turns are inevitable. I think one has to be very tough and get rid of beautiful details—even whole pages, if they are out of step.

Out of step has been a leitmotif of my life—but in retrospect I see how the threads began to knit together and inform my way of seeing and of thinking. For I am convinced that how a head works is at least as important, if not more so, than the ability to draw: who could ever forget Miss Clavel turning on the light and saying, "Something is not right!" And yet Bemelmans was no "great" artist, but his images are unforgettable. The images we make come from who we are, and how we think about the world. Observation was my best revenge in a world of turmoil and extremes, where I had no control. But now, at my drawing board, I can be the actress, director, stage manager, set designer, costumer—shifting and tilting the characters who emerge and, when the book is done, to be able to say, "There! That's how it *has* to be!"

———

Karen Gundersheimer was born in Boston. She graduated from Sarah Lawrence College in 1961 and studied at the Academia di Belle Arti in Florence from 1961 to 1962. She worked for Schocken Books, "as a gofer," in 1962, and was married June 23, 1963. Her two sons were born in 1964 and 1967.

Some Things Go Together won the 1984 Carolyn W. Field Award, presented by the Pennsylvania Library Association. Three of Gundersheimer's books have received American Institute of Graphic Arts Awards: *Nightdances* in 1982, *ABC—Say with Me* in 1985, and *123—Play with Me*, also in 1985. The American Library Association has named three of her books Notable Books for their years of publication: *2A Special Trade*, *Beany*, and *Happy Winter*.

SELECTED WORKS WRITTEN AND ILLUSTRATED: Happy Winter, 1982; ABC—Say with Me, 1984; 123—Play with Me, 1984; Colors to Know, 1986; Shapes to Show, 1986.

SELECTED WORKS ILLUSTRATED: The Witch Who Was Afraid of Witches, by Alice Low, 1978; Beany, by Jane Feder, 1979; A Special Trade, by Sally Wittman, 1979; Nightdances, by James Skofield, 1981; Some Things Go Together, by Charlotte Zolotow, 1983; Chocolate Mud Cake, by Harriet Ziefert, 1988; The Midnight Eaters, by Amy Hest, 1989; What Am I?, by Stephanie Calmenson, 1989.

ABOUT: Something About the Author, Vol. 44.

DOROTHY HAAS

AUTHOR OF *The Bears Upstairs*, etc.

Autobiographical sketch of Dorothy F. Haas, who also writes under the pen names "Dan McCune" and "Dee Francis":

I AM sometimes asked, "Do you write about real people?" The answer is: No, no, a thousand times no! Except for an occasional piece of nonfiction, which of course has to do with actual people, all of the characters in my books spring out of my imagination. As I write, the characters grow and develop into unique personalities. They are themselves, like nobody else; they act in certain ways and think and feel as individuals, and so the plots twist and turn as those characters live their lives. Since I admit that as I write, my characters become more intensely themselves, it is strange that nobody ever asks whether those characters are less themselves in the opening chapters of a book than in the closing chapters. The answer has to do with rewriting. One of the many reasons for writing a manuscript a second, or a third—even a fourth or fifth—time is to permit the characters to be consistently and richly themselves throughout a book, from beginning to end.

Even though the characters in my books are not copies of living persons, there is a great deal in the books that is indeed real. By reading between the lines, readers can find out a lot about the person behind the book, the author. They can discover what makes me laugh—a dog like Dilly McBean's Contrary who must be given orders in reverse—and what makes me sad—Peanut of the Peanut Butter and Jelly series and Wendy of *The Bears Upstairs* learning to cope with the death of their fathers. Readers can understand about the things I think important—such as learning to like and respect oneself as Tink does in *Tink in a Tangle* . . . sticking to one's goals as Gabby does in *To Catch a Crook* . . . taking responsibility for one's talents as Dilly McBean does . . . music . . . Oh, there is

always something about music in my books! I love music. I cannot imagine a world without music. Or a world without books.

As a child I loved to read. I lost myself in books. The world dropped away and I became the character in the book I was reading at the moment—Betsy of Dorothy Canfield Fisher's *Understood Betsy*, Anne of Green Gables fame, Sara Crewe of *The Little Princess*. I became boys, too—Tom Sawyer, Huckleberry Finn, Tarzan. This becoming the characters was simply wonderful when they were having fun. It was perfectly terrible when they were in trouble or sad or scared. How I suffered! But that's the way I read books. I did not know that other people read in other ways. I could not—nor would I have wished—to change. I still read that way! And I try to write that way, too, so that readers who are on my wavelength will be able to "become" my characters. I do my best to help by making the settings vivid and the characters' thoughts and feelings true to life.

I work in two realms, reality and fantasy. Any story is a fantasy, of course, for it's telling of something that never really happened. But some of my books deal with life in the world as it is and some contain happenings or characters that readers know at once could never actually occur or exist. Peanut and Jilly, the two little girls in the Peanut Butter and Jelly series, live in a very real world of home and school, with real problems and real delights. Fantasy never enters their world. But Dilly McBean and Wendy face astonishing elements of fantasy—Dilly in learning to control his amazing magnetism and Wendy in aiding the bears in their flight to freedom on another planet in the constellation Ursa Major, the Great Bear.

Another question frequently put to me is why I write for children. Simply, it pleases me. I enjoy the way in which reality and fantasy exist side by side in children's minds and imaginations. Writing for children permits me to share that particular childlike loveliness. I consider myself blessed to have found my life's work in a field that not only brings enjoyment to me but to children as well.

Dorothy Haas was born in Racine, Wisconsin. She received her B.S. degree from Marquette University in 1955. She has had a dual career as editor and writer of children's books, being responsible for the publication of over six hundred books. She has written over forty books herself, from picture books to nonfiction to novels. She sets some of her books in the city where she now lives, Chicago. She is a member of the READ ILLINOIS Advisory Committee to the Illinois Secretary of State and State Librarian. She is also a member of the Society of Midland Authors, the Children's Reading Round Table, and Women in Management.

The Bears Upstairs was among the 1978 Books-Across-the-Sea chosen by the English-Speaking Union. It won the German Deutscher Jugendbuchpreis for 1979. *The Secret Life of Dilly McBean* was nominated for a 1987 Edgar Allan Poe Award by the Mystery Writers of America and was also a Junior Literary Guild selection. Her books have won many awards chosen by school children.

SELECTED WORKS: Maria: Everybody Has a Name, 1966; This Little Pony, 1967; The Bears Upstairs, 1978; Poppy and the Outdoors Cat, 1981; Tink in a Tangle, 1984; The Secret Life of Dilly McBean, 1986; My First Communion, 1987; The Haunted House, 1988; New Friends, 1988; Peanut and Jilly Forever, 1988; To Catch a Crook, 1988.

ABOUT: Contemporary Authors, Vol. 5; (New Revision Series), Vol. 3; Foremost Women in Communication, 1970; Something About the Author, Vol. 43; Who's Who of American Women, 1983-1984.

MARYLIN HAFNER

December 14, 1925–

ILLUSTRATOR OF *Next Year I'll Be Special*, etc.

Biographical sketch of Marylin Hafner:

MARYLIN HAFNER was born in Brooklyn, New York. She grew up in a family of artists and musicians, in which fine arts were emphasized. She received a B.Sc. degree from Pratt Institute in 1949. She also studied at the New School for Social Research, the School of Visual Arts, and the Silvermine School of Art in Connecticut. While living in London, she studied sculpture at the Slade School, from 1965 to 1966. Access to the best periodicals and art magazines of Europe and the influence of Bauhaus-trained teachers taught her that an artist uses "all visual stimuli" from all disciplines: theater, film, architecture, book illustration, painting, and now television and video as well as animation. The artists Saul Steinberg, Paul Klee, Eric Gill, Andre Francois, and Ludwig Bemelmans are her favorites.

Early career assignments, which began while she was in art school, encompassed a wide range of graphic design: fabric and product design for R.H. Macy, display and advertising layout for B. Altman & Co., and direct mail and editorial illustration for a variety of ad agencies. Magazine illustration took precedence while her three daughters were growing up; she worked for

House Beautiful, Seventeen, and *Good Housekeeping,* among others. After leaving a staff job in the art department at *McCall's,* Hafner began working for just a few clients. She illustrated a monthly feature column for *Woman's Day* and several cookbook inserts each year for twenty-five years. She counts among mentors in the graphic design field Alexey Brodovich, Paul Rand, and Herbert Bayer. Hafner says she is "busy, busy, busy" and that she loves what she does. In 1969 she began to illustrate children's books exclusively through Publishers Graphics in Westport, Connecticut. She has contributed art to *Cricket* magazine for fifteen years. She has had one-person shows at the Bush Galleries in Boston, the most recent being in 1988. She now works from her studio in Cambridge, Massachusetts. She is a member of the Society of Illustrators and the Graphic Artist's Guild. *Next Year I'll Be Special* was named a 1982 Children's Choice Book by a joint committee of the Children's Book Council and the International Reading Association. *X Marks the Spot* was a Junior Literary Guild selection. *Sunlight* received a 1975 New York Academy of Sciences Children's Science Book Award.

SELECTED WORKS ILLUSTRATED: Bonnie Bess: The Weathervane Horse, by Alvin Tresselt, 1949; Poetry Please, by Charlotte Reynolds and Barbara Parker, 1968; X Marks the Spot, by Eleanor Felder, 1971; Water Is Wet, by Sally Cartwright, 1973; Sunlight, by Sally Cartwright, 1974; Mrs. Gaddy and the Ghost, by Wilson Gage, 1979; Next Year I'll Be Special, by Patricia Reilly Giff, 1980; My Brother, Will, by Joan Robins, 1986; M & M and the Super Child Afternoon, by Pat Ross, 1987; Dinosaurs are 568, by Jean Rogers, 1988; Happy Father's Day, by Steven Kroll, 1988.

ABOUT: Something About the Author, Vol. 7; Shaw, John Mackay. Childhood in Poetry.

MARY DOWNING HAHN

December 9, 1937–

AUTHOR OF *Daphne's Book,* etc.

Autobiographical sketch of Mary Downing Hahn:

FOR AS LONG as I can remember, I have loved to draw, read, and make up stories. At the age of three or four, I began my would-be career as an artist by illustrating a set of Winnie-the-Pooh books. Of course, Ernest Shepard had already provided sketches of Pooh and his friends, but I wasn't satisfied with them. In secret, I not only added smiling suns and more animals to Shepard's pictures, but I also colored every page.

My mother, a schoolteacher, was not happy when she discovered my artwork. After explaining the difference between coloring books and real books, she wisely supplied me with pads of drawing paper.

By the time I was seven or eight years old, I liked to make up stories and draw pictures to illustrate what was happening. Because I never wrote any words down, I can only guess at some of the sequences, but many of them seem to be about orphan boys who go out into the world and have all sorts of adventures.

Around the same time, my best friend Ann and I invented a game we called "Orphans." We used little plastic babies from our doll houses to play the parts. Like

the poor, mistreated children in my picture stories, the plastic babies ran away from the orphanage and got lost in the forest under the forsythia bush or sailed down the creek on rafts made of Popsicle sticks. Sometimes they were captured by wicked witches, sometimes they caught terrible diseases and almost died, and once they got Ann and me in big trouble because they needed a little fire to keep warm. We stole matches and made a tiny bonfire for them in the remains of a neighbor's vegetable garden. Unfortunately Bobby, their thirteen-year-old son, smelled smoke, stamped out the fire, destroyed the plastic babies' camp, and—worst of all—told our mothers.

We played the orphan game so often and so loudly that my mother grew concerned and asked me why the plastic babies had no parents. Although I don't remember what I told her, I think I know the answer to her question now. She and Ann's mother both taught at the local elementary school, and, like most teachers, they had definite ideas about the proper behavior of children. We weren't allowed to cross the train tracks at the end of our block nor were we allowed to play in the creek that meandered enticingly through College Park. The woods be-

hind our houses were off-limits as were Saturday matinees at the movie theater and trips to swimming pools because of the risk of polio. We had strict mealtimes and bedtimes, and we were expected to behave properly in public. After all, everyone in town knew our mothers.

Well, orphans had no parents to restrict their exploration of the world, so it wasn't any wonder we found them fascinating. We didn't actually want to be orphans—we just wanted more freedom.

By the time we were ten, our mothers gave up and let us play where we wanted. Losing our interest in orphans, we made up the detective game. Under the influence of Nancy Drew and the Hardy Boys, we saw potential criminals everywhere. We followed people, wrote down license numbers, watched houses, and eventually were caught searching a neighbor's garage for incriminating evidence that he was a Russian spy.

"Too much imagination," my teachers said, and my parents agreed when they saw my report cards: "Mary reads library books when she should be studying her spelling words, she looks out the window when she should be doing her math, she doodles all over her homework, her handwriting is sloppy, she doesn't pay attention."

While I was struggling through school, getting in trouble with my teachers, my neighbors, and my parents, while I was climbing trees, wading in the creek, following mysterious strangers, and scaring myself in church graveyards, I had no idea I would ever put my experiences into books. Like most kids, I thought all writers were either dead or living in England. Surely ordinary people who grew up in ordinary towns like College Park didn't become writers.

By the time I decided to put scenes from my own childhood into a book, I was almost forty years old. My greatest regret is that it took me so long to begin. I have ideas for many stories, and I wish I'd started writing them sooner.

———

Born in Washinton, D.C., Mary Downing Hahn graduated from the University of Maryland with a B.A. degree in Fine Art in 1960. She received a Master's Degree in English from the same university in 1969. She is married and has two daughters. Since 1975, she has been employed as a children's associate librarian in the Prince George's County Memorial Library System in Maryland.

Daphne's Book received the 1986 William Allen White Children's Book Award. *Wait Till Helen Comes* won the 1988 Dorothy Canfield Fisher Award. *The Jellyfish Season* was a Young Adults' Choice Book of the International Reading Association in 1987. *December Stillness* won a 1988 Child Study Children's Book Award, given by the Bank Street College of Education.

SELECTED WORKS: The Sara Summer, 1979; The Time of the Witch, 1982; Daphne's Book, 1983; The Jellyfish Season, 1985; Wait Till Helen Comes: A Ghost Story, 1986; Tallahassee Higgins, 1987; December Stillness, 1988; Following the Mystery Man, 1988; The Doll in the Garden, 1989.

ABOUT: Something About the Author, Vol. 44; Vol. 50.

EMILY HANLON

April 26, 1945–

AUTHOR OF *It's Too Late for Sorry*, etc.

Biographical sketch of Emily Hanlon:

EMILY HANLON was born in New York City. Her father's "great passion," she says, was literature. He wrote fiction and had stories published in *Esquire*, so she knew from childhood about mailing stories, with self-addressed envelopes included, to publishers for acceptance or rejection. She began writing stories herself "literally as soon as I learned to write." She submitted stories to teen magazines and continued to write, despite receiving rejections.

She attended the Dalton School and re-

ceived her B.A. degree at Barnard College, where she was a writing major, in 1967. She was married June 25, 1966, and has two children. The idea of writing professionally occurred to her when her children were small, and she began writing picture books. Her father put her in touch with the late Peggy Parish, the writer of *Amelia Bedelia* fame who was also a fifth-grade teacher at Dalton School at the time. "She taught me how to write picture books," says Hanlon.

Hanlon has been a teacher of mentally retarded adults, working at Occupation Day Center in New York from 1972 to 1974. That experience led to the book, *It's Too Late for Sorry*. She now teaches workshops in writing in Yorktown Heights, where she lives. She is also a member of the Authors League of America and the National Writers Union.

After her first attempt at being published, Hanlon became discouraged about writing. She took a short story that she had written in college to an editor who suggested she turn it into a novel. It took her a year to produce the book, but the editor did not buy it. However, after a lot of rewriting, another editor accepted the book, which became *The Swing*. She recalls another experience of receiving a rejected manuscript—complete with the inadvertent inclusion of an in-house memo, not meant for her eyes, containing negative comments. The book it described was eventually published, too.

Hanlon is an advocate of writing every day, on a regular schedule; after an early breakfast, she sits down to work from 6:30 to 12:30, a six-hour working day that has produced, for her, an average of a book each year.

Hanlon has written several books for adults, the first of which, *Binding Ties*, was not published. She calls it "autobiographical and cathartic" and says she is glad it wasn't published. Her epic novel *Petersburg* is a tale of Russia in 1905, and her new work, *The Shroud*, is set in the thirteenth century.

Emily Hanlon enjoys running and gardening, and vacationing in Maine with her husband Ned Tarasiv, who sometimes helps with the plotting of her books.

SELECTED WORKS: What If a Lion Eats Me and I Fall into a Hippopotamus' Mud Hole?, 1975; How a Horse Grew Hoarse on the Site Where He Sighted a Bare Bear, 1976; It's Too Late for Sorry, 1978; The Swing, 1979; The Wing and the Flame, 1980; Circle Home, 1981; Love Is No Excuse, 1982.

ABOUT: Contemporary Author, Vol. 77-80; Something About the Author, Vol. 15; Spotlight October 1982.

BRETT HARVEY

April 28, 1936–

AUTHOR OF *My Prairie Year*, etc.

Biographical sketch of Brett Harvey:

BRETT HARVEY was raised in Chicago, Illinois. Her mother, who died in 1965, was a successful cookbook writer, Peggy Harvey. Brett Harvey graduated from The Baldwin School, attended Northwestern University for three years, and moved to New York in 1958. She has lived in Brooklyn for twenty-five years, and has two grown children, Robert and Katie.

Harvey worked for eight years at The Feminist Press as head of publicity and promotion. She is now a free-lance journalist and book critic in addition to being a children's book writer. Her work has appeared in *The Village Voice*, *The New York Times Book Review*, and *Psychology Today*. Perhaps her journalistic background has contributed to her success in combining carefully chosen events from the past that are described in a colorful, yet informative manner for young readers.

The first book Brett Harvey wrote, *My Prairie Year*, was named a Notable Book of 1986 by the American Library Association. It is based upon the diary that belonged to the author's grandmother, Elenore Plaisted, and describes the experience of moving from Maine to the Dakota Territory in 1889. Harvey has shaped the events of the move in the form of a lengthy picture book that vividly recalls what life was like in that time and place. Through Elenore Plaisted's descriptions, Harvey carefully portrays the rigorous schedule of daily chores—one for each day but Sunday—against a backdrop of varying seasons that bring both harsh winter blizzards and the prairie fires of summer. Zena Sutherland called the descriptions "immediate and vivid" in the *Bulletin of the Center for Children's Books.* The book is illustrated by Deborah Kogan Ray.

In her second book, *Immigrant Girl*, Harvey once again combines a descriptive and informative portrait of a particular way of life while using a picture-book format. Using the voice of ten-year-old Becky, the book relates the daily life of a Jewish family who have come from Russia to escape the anti-Jewish pogroms. Rather than tell a story, the book chronicles day-to-day life as well as the sometimes deeper struggles of immigrant life. The nine members of Becky's family live in three rooms over her parents' grocery store on the Lower East Side of New York City. The book offers colorful descriptions of the tenement neighborhood as Becky narrates tales of looking after a younger brother and shopping and preparing for the Sabbath. Denise Wilms writes in *Booklist*, "Becky's references to things such as shopping on Hester Street or attending a strike rally for the women who work in the shirt factories contribute a concrete sense of time and place. . . . " Enabling the reader to appreciate a particular era is Harvey's forte, and her ability to personalize history through one character has made her books critical successes.

Cassie's Journey, like *Prairie Year*, is a story based on diary entries of pioneer women and deals with a historical event. Harvey began with Lillian Schliffel's *Women's Diaries of the Westward Journey* and, employing the narrative voice of a fictional girl who might have been on those travels, Harvey eloquently tells the heroic story of the migrant journey in the 1860s across the United States to California. The hardships on the trip are skillfully presented, along with "wonderfully homely details," according to Mary M. Burns in *The Horn Book Magazine*, who calls the account "an unpretentious gem, honest, forthright, and engaging."

Harvey has finished another book about Elenore Plaisted's life in the Dakotas, *A*

Prairie Christmas, and is also planning a book for adults about women's lives in the 1950s.

Brett Harvey is, in her own words, "an active member and passionate believer in the National Writers Union, an organization working for fair play and fair pay for all writers," and is co-chair of the Union's New York local.

SELECTED WORKS: My Prairie Year: Based on the Diary of Elenore Plaisted, 1986; Immigrant Girl: Becky of Eldridge Street, 1987; Cassie's Journey: Going West in the 1860s, 1988.

ABOUT: Contemporary Authors, Vol. 126.

JIM HASKINS

September 19, 1941–

AUTHOR OF *The Story of Stevie Wonder*, etc.

Autobiographical sketch of Jim Haskins, who also writes under the pen name "James Haskins":

I WAS BORN in Demopolis, Alabama, and spent my childhood in a house with lots of children, a household where I felt a great need for privacy. One of my favorite places was the roof of a shed behind our house. Everyone else knew I was there, especially after I started playing my trumpet up on that roof, but it somehow became my roof and no one bothered me much.

I also found privacy in books. I could be anywhere at all, but if I was reading a book I was by myself. It was hard for me to get books sometimes. In those days, Demopolis was segregated. The public library was for whites, and a black child could not go there. My mother arranged for a white lady for whom she worked to get books from the library for me. A few years ago I returned to Demopolis and visited the library, which is integrated now. I gave some of the books I had written to the library I could not visit as a child.

I attended high school in Boston, Massachusetts, and college in a variety of places. One of the colleges I attended was Alabama State University in Montgomery. It was the time of the Montgomery Bus Boycott, when black people led by Dr. Martin Luther King, Jr. refused to ride the segregated buses. I helped hand out leaflets urging black people to stay off the buses and was expelled from the college for doing so.

After graduation from college, I came to New York, where I sold newspaper advertising space and worked a stockbroker on Wall Street before I decided to become a teacher. I taught music and special education classes in Harlem, and my first book, *Diary of a Harlem Schoolteacher*, grew out of my experiences.

I tried to get my students interested in reading. It was the 1960s and college and high-school students were demonstrating against the war in Vietnam and for the civil rights of black people. My students were hearing about these events and wanted to know more about them, but there were no books written on their level. So I started writing books for young people about the Antiwar Movement and the Civil Rights Movement and the Black Power Move-

ment. After that I began writing biographies, because young people like to read about how successful people grew up and overcame barriers like poverty and racial discrimination.

By the time my first biography for young people was published, I was teaching college students. I am still teaching college courses in children's literature.

At this writing, I have published eighty books. I have written books for adults, but most of the books I write are for young people. I have written on a great variety of subjects. Lately, the books I have enjoyed doing most introduce young people to the languages and cultures of different people by using the numbers one to ten to tell about life in other countries. I feel that the young people of today will need to know more and more about the rest of the world when they grow up, and they may as well start early.

My own experience, from childhood on, is that reading books is a nice way to find your own, private world and learn about the big world at the same time. I love books, and I feel very fortunate to have been able to share this love with so many young people.

———

Jim Haskins received his B.A. degree from Georgetown University in 1960 and his B.S. degree from Alabama State University in 1962. He received an M.A. degree from the University of New Mexico in 1963. He is a Professor of English at the University of Florida at Gainesville, and lives in New York City. He has been a book editor and a book reviewer. His book for adults, *Diary of a Harlem Schoolteacher*, was published in 1969. *The Story of Stevie Wonder* won the Coretta Scott King Award in 1976, and *Lena Horne* won an honorable mention for that award in 1984. *Black Music in America* received the 1988 Carter G. Woodson Book Award of the National Council for the Social Studies and *James Van Der Zee: The Picture-Takin' Man* was named an outstanding merit book for that award in 1980. His *The Cotton Club* was made into a motion picture of the same title. *Bricktop* was chosen by the English-Speaking Union to be a Book-Across-the-Sea, and *the 60s Reader* was named an American Library Association Best Book for Young Adults of 1988.

SELECTED WORKS: Resistance: Profiles in Nonviolence, 1970; The War and the Protest: Vietnam, 1970; Fighting Shirley Chisholm, 1975; The Story of Stevie Wonder, 1976; The Cotton Club, 1977; The Life and Death of Martin Luther King, Jr., 1977; James Van Der Zee: The Picture-Takin' Man, 1979; Lena Horne, 1983; Black Music in America: A History Through Its People, 1987; Count Your Way Through China, 1987; Count Your Way Through the Arab World, 1987; Bill Cosby: America's Most Famous Father, 1988.

SELECTED WORKS WRITTEN WITH BRICKTOP: Bricktop, 1983.

SELECTED WORKS WRITTEN WITH KATHLEEN BENSON: The 60s Reader, 1988.

ABOUT: Contemporary Authors (First Revision), Vol. 33-36; Donelson, Kenneth L. and Alleen Pace Nilsen. Literature for Today's Young Adults; Page, James A., comp. Selected Black American Authors: An Illustrated Bio-Bibliography; Page, James A. and Jae Min Roh, comps., Selected Black American, African, and Caribbean Authors: A Bio-Bibliography; Something About the Author, Vol. 9; Something About the Author Autobiography Series, Vol. 4; Who's Who in the East, 1975-1976; The Writers Directory, 1980-1982.

BARBARA SHOOK HAZEN

February 4, 1930–

AUTHOR OF *The Gorilla Did It*, etc.

Autobiographical sketch of Barbara Jean Shook Hazen:

ACTORS often say their act is a cover-up. I think my writing was—and still is to a lesser degree—too. As a child I had trouble saying what I wanted to say, getting it out. I would often "think of it later." Writing is a way to put it down "later."

I also liked to read and write poetry. My first poem created quite a stir with my

Barbara Shook Hazen

teacher, being about "a horse in all his glory, who was white but not at all hoary." Only I misspelled "hoary," adding the 'w' seen on walls and bathroom stalls.

The first poem sold also created quite a stir, this time with my family. It was sold to *True Confessions*. I confessed to things I had never accomplished. I was in fifth grade.

I kept on writing—poems, diaries, short stories—through high school and college. Increasingly I hankered toward the writing life, though teachers—with a couple of significant exceptions—were not particularly encouraging.

I also wanted to be where publishing was, and made a deal with my Dayton family that I could brave the Big Apple if I went to graduate school and lived at a women's hotel. I also went to Speedwriting School at night to garner enough skill to get a foot in the door.

I did, at the *Ladies' Home Journal*, where I was a fiction/article departments girl Friday, and then Poetry Editor, because in the fifties poetry merited a department, and I had sold quite a bit to the *Journal*, among others.

The leap to children's books came when

an editor at Western Publishing, Lucille Ogle, saw and liked some of my poems and asked me to become an editor.

This was like being thrown into the ocean without the ability to swim, but I learned with the help of my Western world friends, who are still friends. (The problem was that at the *Journal* the editing was done in Philadelphia. One wrote, made decisions, and saw people in New York.)

I learned as I rode the waves and soon they became friendly. And, as I liked the feel of the water, I began writing children's books myself, although it was a long time till I again wrote in verse, rhyme not being considered fashionable.

My in-office career ended with the sixties and the birth of my son Brack.

I have been a free lancer ever since. Children's books have been the main occupation, but I am also a part-time "adult-ress," and have dipped creative toes into songwriting, TV, and consulting.

And yes, I still find it hard to say what I want to say. But I relish the process and find it increasingly enriching.

I am also increasingly aware of how much I write to and for the "child in me." Almost as a way of, belatedly, working things out, of inner exploring.

One thing I know for sure, I am on the side of the child, the un-rote response, the quirky solution. I have after-feelings about some of my books that I didn't realize at the time. I once told an IRS auditor "The Gorilla did it," as explanation for a mayhem of papers. This has not made me less disorganizationally impaired, but has raised awareness.

I also will try to grapple with more cosmic areas I have personal trouble with— such as death, divorce, sibling rivalry.

With me, exploring is a key word. I like to try far-out food combinations. I like to get on Betsy, my bike, and explore new streets, and revisit old because there's always something new to see, do, or savor. Most of the time when I write I don't know where I'm going. There's usually an itch or

snitch of an idea, but the doing shapes the end result, which usually evolves out of umpteenth variations.

I like to layer on as much as possible. Then try to make it simple, in as few words as possible.

I also follow what I see. I can't draw, but have a vivid mental eye. I am often personally surprised as to where it leads. Sometimes to the piles of begun-but-unfinished pieces in the files. Sometimes to a book. Those are the best of times.

———

Barbara Shook Hazen was born in Dayton, Ohio. She received her B.A. degree from Smith College in 1951 and her M.A. degree from Columbia University in 1952. She worked at the *Ladies' Home Journal* from 1952 to 1956 and at Western Publishing Company from 1956 to 1960. She was married December 27, 1956, and was divorced in 1966. She has one son. Barbara Shook Hazen has been a consultant for children's records at CBS Records and to *Sesame Street* magazine. She is a member of the American Society of Journalists and Authors, the Authors Guild of the Authors League of America, and Bank Street College of Education Writers Lab.

Tight Times was a Reading Rainbow book. *Even If I Did Something Awful* won a 1982 Christopher Award.

SELECTED WORKS: A Visit to the Children's Zoo, 1963; Where Do Bears Sleep?, 1970; The Gorilla Did It, 1974; Why Couldn't I Be an Only Kid Like You, Wigger, 1975; The Ups and Downs of Marvin, 1976; Gorilla Wants to Be the Baby, 1978; Tight Times, 1979; The Fat Cats, Cousin Scraggs and the Monster Mice, 1985; Fang, 1987; Step on It, Andrew, 1980; The Knight Who Was Afraid of the Dark, 1989; The Story of Santa Claus, 1989.

ABOUT: Chicago Tribune Book World February 7, 1982; Contemporary Authors, Vol. 105; (New Revision Series), Vol. 22; Something About the Author, Vol. 27.

BETSY HEARNE

October 6, 1942–

AUTHOR OF: *South Star*, etc.

Autobiographical sketch of Elizabeth Gould Hearne:

I WAS BORN in a little town down south, Wilsonville, Alabama. My father was a doctor who delivered most of the babies in the countryside, including me. I grew up playing in the pine woods around our house. It was beautiful, but it was lonely, too. There was no one my age nearby, and I used to make up stories to keep myself company. The school wasn't very good, so my mother got me a little desk and taught me how to read and write at home. She showed me how to play the piano and the harp, and we used to sing together while she worked around the house.

By the time we moved to a city and I started third grade, I was used to being alone. It was a good thing, because it was hard to make friends in a new place. Since I didn't have any kids to talk to except my older brothers, who didn't count because they were off doing other things, I kept writing. It made me feel better, but it was also interesting to play with the words, to make them sound stronger, louder, softer, faster, slower, sadder. I found out I could make them say exactly what I wanted. I was not a whiz in school, but I loved to read and was surprised to find that teachers liked what I wrote. I had to study hard in subjects like math, but reading stories and writing never seemed like work at all. Sometimes I wrote songs to sing with the harp or guitar.

By the time I was fourteen, I was almost six feet tall, which was hard for a girl. It took a long time for my confidence to catch up to my height. But it helped to travel, to find out there were all kinds of people in the world and that being different wasn't so bad. I went north to college, hitchhiked through Europe, and lived in the Middle East for a while. All the time I traveled around, I kept watching and writing—

poetry, songs, stories, diaries, letters, ideas, essays, anything that came into my head.

One of the first jobs I had was in a library, which made sense—that's where the books lived. I sang songs and told stories to children, especially stories I remembered from the south, about Brer Rabbit and his crowd. I couldn't believe that telling stories could actually be part of a real job. I went to library school so I could do it all the time. Then I got a job reading children's books and writing reviews about them in a magazine, which I've done for twenty years. I read partly to find out what happens next, partly to find out how it happens, and partly to find out how the writer lets us know how it happens. The best books always have a few surprises along the way. (The best pictures make you see something as if you've never seen it before.)

While I was reading, I was also writing. The first two children's books I wrote, *South Star* and *Home*, were about a giant girl who was trying to find out where she belonged and to prove her strength and courage as she traveled. The third book, *Eli's Ghost*, was about a boy and his friends—both natural and supernatural—getting lost in a swamp. The fourth, *Love Lines: Poetry in*

Person, for young adults, included some of the poems I worked on over a period of twenty-five years. If a poem really sings, you can live with it forever. I've written books for adults, too, some about children's books and one about the fairy tale "Beauty and the Beast," which is my favorite.

I love reading stories to children, my own and other people's. My husband tells stories, too, funny ones that I can listen to over and over. When you hear stories, you can imagine what happens, what the characters look like, how they act. It's not like TV, which shows you how everything is supposed to be. My kids like to watch television, but they also love to read. When we read together, it takes all of us into different worlds of our own, where the words sing and we can hear them ring in our heads forever.

———

Betsy Hearne graduated from the College of Wooster in Ohio in 1964. She studied at the University of Chicago, and received her M.A. in 1968 and her Ph.D. in 1985. Following her work as a storyteller and librarian, she was Book Review Editor of the children's section of *Booklist*, the American Library Association review journal, and an instructor in the Education Department of the University of Illinois at Chicago. Since 1985 she has been Editor of the *Bulletin of the Center for Children's Books* and a Faculty Member of the Graduate Library School at the University of Chicago.

Hearne has also contributed many articles and reviews to magazines like *School Library Journal*, the *New York Times Book Review*, *Signal*, and *Bookbird*. She has also written popular pieces for *McCalls*, *Parents Magazine*, and *Working Mother*. She is the coeditor of *Celebrating Children's Books: Critical Essays in Honor of Zena Sutherland*, which was published in 1981, and is the author of *Choosing Books for Children: A Commonsense Guide*, which has been published in paperback and which

she is revising for a 1989 edition. Her book *Beauty and the Beast: Visions and Revisions of an Old Tale*, will be published in 1989 as well.

Hearne has been a lecturer at many conferences about children's literature, including the International Youth Library Conference in Munich, and at many universities. She has also been a book award judge for both the American Book Awards and the National Book Awards as well as serving on the American Library Association Newbery and Caldecott Committees. She can be seen on two ALA video tapes, "Sharing Books with Young Children" (1986) and "Picture Books: Elements of Illustration and Story" (1987).

Besty Hearne was the 1982 recipient of the Children's Reading Round Table Award given by the Children's Reading Round Table of Chicago. Her *Love Lines* was named a 1987 Best Book for Young Adults by the ALA, and she won the 1987 Carl Sandburg Award, given by the Friends of the Chicago Public Library, for *Eli's Ghost*.

SELECTED WORKS: South Star, 1977; Home, 1979; Love Lines: Poetry in Person, 1987; Eli's Ghost, 1987.

ABOUT: Contemporary Authors, Vol. 114; Something About the Author, Vol. 38; Who's Who in American Libraries, 1982.

HELME HEINE

1941–

AUTHOR AND ILLUSTRATOR OF *Mr. Miller the Dog*, etc.

Biographical sketch of Helme Heine:

HELME HEINE was born in Berlin. He spent his early years there, and after completing his art studies, he traveled extensively throughout Europe and Asia, and lived in Africa for many years before settling in Munich in 1971. Heine has had a varied professional career; he has run both

HELME HEINE

a cabaret and a satirical magazine, as well as working in the professional theater as a director, actor, and stage designer.

One of Heine's early books, *King Bounce the First*, was illustrated in brightly patterned collage. Of this technique Heine wrote, "Collage is a fun technique for all those who are scared of painting, for the 'I don't know how to draw' people. . . . Extraordinary colors work best—a blue pig with letters on its belly is more fun and more appealing than a very realistic pink pig."

Helme Heine is unusually fond of the porcine set. He has said that as a child, he wanted to be a pig. He still feels a great affection for them, and even kept one for two years. *The Pigs' Wedding*, which was named one of the Best Illustrated Books of the Year 1979 by *The New York Times*, celebrates that affection. *Times* reviewer H. C.K. Rice wrote of Heine's "exuberant watercolor pictures of pigs painting one another into wedding dresses and suits . . . of pigs feasting and dancing, of pigs after a rainstorm leaping across the page into a glorious muddy bog." Heine is fond of pigs for their lack of concern about their appearance, for their excesses, especially in the

matter of eating, and also because their ungainly exterior hides sweet and intelligent creatures.

Helme Heine's delicate, evocative illustrations for *One Day in Paradise* drew praise from reviewers for contributing a very accessible version of the creation story from Genesis. *Horn Book* reviewer Elizabeth Watson called it "a simple, human, warm, and loving interpretation of the Creation story. . . . The view is traditional in the sequence of Creation and in the portrayal of God . . . it is non-traditional in depicting Adam and Eve as children and in showing God actually laboring."

Mr. Miller the Dog presented a slightly less childlike and exuberant portrait than those for which Heine is usually noted. Mr. Miller, tiring of his job as a night watchman, decides that his dog, Murphy, has a better life than he does. Murphy suggests that they trade places, and all goes so well that by the end of the story, a complete transferral has taken place. Ethel Heins of *The Horn Book* wrote, "To an adult the book might seem like a Kafkaesque spoof, to a child, pure fun." London's *Times Literary Supplement* concluded, "To the adult reader, the tale is sinister . . . but to children it is just a good joke for Mr Miller and Murphy are plump, cosy and, above all, secure.

"Anita Silvey of *The Horn Book Magazine* felt that another of Heine's works, *The Pearl*, a cautionary tale, "can be read as a political statement, but what really distinguishes it are the glorious watercolor Illustrations. . . . Helme Heine . . . is a master at creating warm, endearing creatures." Heine's strengths and charm lie in his vibrant, large-scale drawings; they sustain his widespread popularity and appeal. As *The New York Times* explained in a review of *Friends*, "what he [Heine] gives us most is a sense of joy, of irrepressible glee, of fellowship and delight."

Helme Heine has written and illustrated more than ten books, four of which have been adapted for television presentations in

Europe. Heine's work has been honored with the Bologna Fair Graphic Prize, given at the International Children's Book Fair in Bologna. In addition, *Friends* was named an Honor Book for Illustration in the 1983 Boston Globe-Horn Book Awards. Three of Heine's books were named Children's Choice Books by a joint committee of the Children's Book Council and the International Reading Association: *Mr. Miller the Dog* in 1981, *The Most Wonderful Egg in the World* in 1984, and *The Pearl* in 1986.

SELECTED WORKS: Imagine If, 1979; The Pigs' Wedding, 1979; Superhare, 1979; Merry-Go-Round, 1980; Mr. Miller the Dog, 1980; Friends, 1982; King Bounce the First, 1982; The Most Wonderful Egg in the World, 1983; The Pearl, 1985; One Day in Paradise, 1986; Seven Wild Pigs, 1988.

JUDITH HENDERSHOT

May 19, 1940–

AUTHOR OF *In Coal Country*

Autobiographical sketch of Judith Hendershot:

WHEN I WAS growing up in the little town of Neffs, Ohio, just down the road from the Willow Grove coal mine, I dreamed of one day becoming a concert pianist. Never did I imagine myself as an author, and I am still not sure that I really am one.

In Coal Country is an honest recollection of a very happy time in my life. It was easy to write about, and sometimes I'm not sure how I did it. I do know that I am hooked on writing and now that I have finally begun, I can't imagine ever giving it up.

I enjoyed books as a child, but even more than the printed word, I reveled in the stories told to my sisters, my brother, and me by our parents. They were deeply interested in the world outside our hills and recounted world and local events to us often. It was the keeping of those stories from my childhood that allowed me to see the signif-

Judith Hendershot

icance of life in a coal mining town as I grew older.

The only real writing that I did as a child was in letters to friends and family on the other side of our hills. I loved language—the way it sounded and flowed in books and in human speech.

I became interested in children's literature when I was in college the first time in the late 1950s. I enrolled in West Liberty College in West Virginia to become a teacher. It was then that I wrote my first "little" story for a group of children I was tutoring. My college professor encouraged me to do something with it. Unfortunately, I didn't know how to pursue offering my work to a publisher, and it became misplaced over the years.

In 1959 I married my husband Richard, and we moved away from coal country to the big town of Akron, Ohio. Neither Richard nor I enjoyed city life after knowing the freedom of our days roaming the beautiful hills of southeastern Ohio. When our first child was born, we moved to tiny Brimfield, where we have lived for twenty-nine years. While we raised our three children, I taught music and became a substitute teacher. When I returned to college at the University of Akron in 1973, our children were all in high school. It was then that I really discovered children's literature.

When I graduated from the university in 1975, I got a job teaching sixth grade in the school my children had attended. With my job came an added bonus—a school librarian who filled my life with new book knowledge. As I read novels and picture books to my students, ideas began to formulate in my own mind. I made myself a promise—that I would write a book of my own.

Many years went by while I continued to think about writing. Our children grew up, went to college, and got married, and still I had nothing to show for all that thinking. Then one day a new young author came to our school to speak to our students. Her ideas were very much like mine. She offered to me a challenge. I began to write and I have never stopped.

For me, the writing process is totally constructive. The time that I spend preparing to write is a building transaction in which my mind sweeps out cobwebs and replaces them with thinking energy. Though I am very content with my life, I love being immersed in an idea for a story.

As a child, I used to dream about life outside of coal country. Now that I no longer live there, I dream about being back.

———

In Coal Country was named a Notable Book of 1987 by the American Library Association. It was named a Best Illustrated Book of 1987 by *The New York Times* and won a Boston Globe-Horn Book Honor Award in the picture-book category in 1987.

SELECTED WORKS: In Coal Country, 1987.

KEVIN HENKES

November 27, 1960–

AUTHOR AND ILLUSTRATOR OF: *Chester's Way*, etc.

Autobiographical sketch of Kevin Henkes:

I'M A VERY LUCKY person. I've known for a very long time that I wanted to be an artist and a writer—and that's exactly what I do for a living. Making books is my job, but more importantly, it is what I love doing more than anything else.

All the while I was growing up I was considered an artist by my parents (Barney and Bea), my brothers (Peter, Jon, and Christopher), and my sister (Peggy). My classmates and teachers thought of me as an artist, too. I also loved books. So, when I arrived at the point in my life when I began thinking about a career, I had little trouble deciding what I wanted to do.

I was born in Racine, Wisconsin, in 1960. I left Racine in 1979 to study art at the University of Wisconsin in Madison. During the summer after my freshman year of college, when I was nineteen, I went to New York City hoping to find a publisher. I brought three portfolios of my work, a story idea, and a map of the city with me.

It was magical enough to be in New York (a place I had wished to see for myself for years), but to have Susan Hirschman at Greenwillow Books offer me a contract for a picture book was nearly too good to be true. I doubt if I'll ever forget the morning when I was given the chance to become a real, published author and illustrator.

My first book—*All Alone*—was published in 1981. Since then, I've tried to create different kinds of books, even novels. I like trying new ways to fill the pages between two covers. Experimenting with words and paint and ink keeps my job interesting.

In 1985, I married Laura Dronzek. Laura reads my stories and looks at my illustrations before anyone else does. We live in a small house in Middleton, Wisconsin. I work at my drawing table nearly every day.

When I was younger, I wondered about authors and illustrators—What did they look like? Where did they live? Did they have families? How old were they?—and now I *am* one myself. Sometimes it's hard for me to believe. I wouldn't trade it for anything.

———

Kevin Henkes was married May 18, 1985. *Chester's Way* was named a Notable Book of 1988 by the American Library Association and was a Junior Literary Guild selection. *A Weekend with Wendell* was named a Children's Choice Book of 1986 by a joint committee of the Children's Book Council and the International Reading Association.

SELECTED WORKS WRITTEN AND ILLUSTRATED: All Alone, 1981; Clean Enough, 1982; Margaret & Taylor, 1983; Return to Sender, 1984; Bailey Goes Camping, 1985; Grandpa & Bo, 1986; A Weekend with Wendell, 1986; Sheila Rae, the Brave, 1987; Two Under Par, 1987; Chester's Way, 1988; The Zebra Wall, 1988; Jessica, 1989.

SELECTED WORKS WRITTEN: Once Around the Block, 1987.

ABOUT: Contemporary Authors, Vol. 114; Publishers Weekly December 18, 1981; Something About the Author, Vol. 43.

PATRICIA HERMES

February 21, 1936–

AUTHOR OF *You Shouldn't Have to Say Good-bye*, etc.

Autobiographical sketch of Patricia Hermes:

WHEN I GROW UP, I told myself, when I was very young, I'm going to marry my father, be older than my older sister, learn to whistle, and learn to wink with just one eye. I'll go to the store alone, let the dog sleep on my bed (even if he is dusty), and buy my mom a red dress. I'll read at night, as late as I want, and never turn off my light. When I play on the swings, I won't take turns, and I'll cut out pictures from my favorite books.

Those were just some of the things I promised myself when I was very small. Some I achieved. (I CAN wink with just one eye.) And some I didn't. (My father was already married.) But the promise to read as late as I want, and to stay up all night doing it, I did achieve. Over and over and over again. Because as an adult, I am an avid reader, just as I was as a child.

As a child, I was sick frequently and spent long periods of time in hospitals. Partly because of this, partly because of other things, I was a lonely little kid—lonely, and frequently sad. But in a book, I was never lonely, never sad. Open a book, and I was surrounded by a world of people, imaginary ones, true, but imaginary ones who were sometimes more real to me than the real ones with whom I lived. I still remember Colin, from *The Secret Garden*. Colin was sickly, just as I was. But he overcame his illness. He learned to walk and he learned to play—in a garden with his friend, Mary. I read and reread *Anne of Green Gables*. Anne was an orphan, a dreamer, a child who was chastised for dreaming, who found her place in the hearts of her adopted family—and in my heart. I read the novels of Charles Dickens, as soon as I could figure out the words, but

long before I understood what all the language meant. I identified with the strange, gutsy characters in Dicken's novels. I identified with Colin. I identified with Anne.

I think it is no accident, that I who loved to read, soon learned to love to write, because the two are closely connected. I think it is also no accident that when I began to write, I began to write stories about people like me, people like the child I once was, and in many ways, still am. I've written stories of children who are ill, of parents who are leaving their children. I've written of children lonely and afraid. But because I am not—I hope—one-dimensional, and because there is more to my present life AND to my history than loneliness, I also write of the fun and nonsense and glee of childhood. I write about children who defy the odds, and win. I write of children who are wiser and saner than the adults (as sometimes—not always, but sometimes—happens in real life). And I write, frequently, of my own children. I have five of them, almost grown now, and they are the inspiration for my writing. They teach me the language of childhood that I have long forgotten. They teach me the tricks the children can play on the grown-up world. They bring love and

laughter and joy to my life, and, I hope, to my books. They appear in my books frequently—disguised, true, but they are there. And I am in my books, too—the child I once was, the child who lives in me still.

Even before I began writing books for children, I had been involved in the world of children. I taught junior and senior high school for 333 years. (All right, so it was three and a half years. But it DID feel longer.)

But the job that I love most, the one I have had for a long time now, is that of a writer of books for young people. Why do I write for young people? Partly, as I said earlier, because I am a reader, true. But there is another reason: I write because I remember what it is like to be a child, and I need to share that memory, I need to make a connection. In the beginning of this bio, I wrote of what I promised myself when I was small. Those memories are only a tiny fraction of the things I remember about childhood. I have, what a friend has called, a "dangerous" memory. (I think he means he must be careful of what he says since I never forget anything.) And in some ways, it's true. I remember vividly so many of the details of childhood, the joy and the sadness, the vulnerability, the sense of powerlessness. I need to write about it, because I need to tell the children, the children who read my books, that they are not alone. I need to tell them that someone knows what it's like to be them. My job as a writer then, as I see it, is to make the connections between my life and experiences, and their lives. It is to let them know that they are not alone. And perhaps, just perhaps, if I succeed in making that connection, I will be able to bring some ease, some joy, some laughter—and some STRENGTH—to their lives.

There is one other aspect of my job that brings me great joy. As an author, I am now often invited to speak to children in schools. I go wherever and whenever I am invited for several reasons: I love to talk to children about books. (What can be nicer than sharing something that one loves?) But also, I go, because, as I freely admit to the children, I am a SPY. I spy on the children. I listen to what they say. I watch how they act with one another and with their teachers. I look at what they wear. I sit in the cafeteria and listen to their conversations. (I even eat cafeteria food!) Because I believe that no writer is worth the paper the books are written on, if she or he is not in tune with the world of children today. Yes, feelings are universal, as is childhood, but the DETAILS of children's lives are changing today. It is important for me, as a writer, to be in touch with those changes. And it is important for a reader to know that the author is genuine, is sharing not only her life and her soul, but her knowledge of what it is to be a child today.

———

Patricia Hermes was born in Brooklyn, New York. She graduated from St. John's University in New York, with a B.A. degree in Speech and English in 1957. She married August 24, 1957, and had six children, one of whom died in infancy. She was divorced in 1984. She has lived in Delaware, Maryland, New York, Virginia, and Connecticut, and has been a teacher in a junior high school in Takoma Park, Delaware, and in a high school in Delcastle, Delaware. She has also conducted writing seminars in the Norfolk, Virginia, public schools. She has contributed articles to *Woman's Day, Life and Health, American Baby*, and other magazines. Hermes is a member of the Society of Children's Book Writers and the Authors Guild.

What If They Knew? and *Kevin Corbett Eats Flies* were named Children's Choice Books by a joint committee of the International Reading Association and the Children's Book Council, in 1981 and 1987 respectively. *A Solitary Secret* was named a 1985 Best Book for Young Adults by the American Library Association.

SELECTED WORKS: What If They Knew?, 1980; No-

body's Fault?, 1981; You Shouldn't Have to Say Goodbye, 1982; Who Will Take Care of Me?, 1983; Friends Are Like That, 1984; A Solitary Secret, 1985; Kevin Corbett Eats Flies, 1986; A Place for Jeremy, 1987; A Time to Listen: Preventing Youth Suicide, 1987; Heads, I Win, 1988.

ABOUT: Contemporary Authors, Vol. 104; Something About the Author, Vol. 31.

DOUGLAS HILL

April 6, 1935–

AUTHOR OF *Exiles of ColSec*, etc.

Autobiographical sketch of Douglas Arthur Hill, who also writes under the pen name "Martin Hillman":

I'M A CANADIAN, and I still sound like one, though I have lived more than half my life in England.

I was born in 1935 in Brandon, Manitoba, then raised in Prince Albert in northern Saskatchewan. Cruel winters, hot dry summers, lots of open wild country, not a bad place to be a kid. Except that I wasn't all that happy a kid, since I was the standard skinny bookish one with glasses who got answers right in class and couldn't play sports. So I was alone much of the time, playing my own games, wandering in my own imagination, dreaming, reading. . . .

Around the age of eleven I made two momentous discoveries. I discovered the limitless, mind-expanding universes of science fiction and fantasy—to which I became hopelessly, incurably addicted. And I discovered that when I ran out of things to read, to feed my habit, I could turn my hand to *writing* things of my own. Which was just as much fun as reading, or maybe more.

Then I grew a bit, my social and sporting life improved, so high school was okay. And I *loved* university, besottedly. I got my B.A. (Hons) in English from the University of Saskatchewan, then went to the University of Toronto to do graduate studies. Only to

find that a love of books was not by itself enough motivation for me to become a real academic.

But it *had* motivated me to keep on writing, all those years. So I dropped out and set off for London, England, the home of Eng. Lit., to seek my fortune as an *Author*.

By then, 1959, I was married—to Gail Robinson, now an established Canadian author in her own right. In London we worked at the usual odd jobs, had hard times and good times. Within a couple of years I had had a few things published— poems, stories, book reviews. In 1963 we had our son and only child, Michael. By then I had a job with a publisher of illustrated "coffee-table" books—until in 1964 I resigned and wrote a book for them: *The Supernatural*, co-authored with my friend Pat Williams.

For the next few years I was a free-lance writer of adult nonfiction—more popular folklore, some history (including *The Opening of the Canadian West*), and other subjects. It was a precarious life, as the freelance life often is, so in 1971 I began work as the literary editor of a weekly paper called *Tribune* (a job once held by George Orwell). But it was part-time; the rest of the time I went on writing.

In 1975 my wife and I co-authored a collection of "retold" North American Indian folk tales, *Coyote the Trickster*—for children. That year our marriage ended; and the book foreshadowed another change for me. Soon, with the encouragement of an editor named Jill Mackay, I began to write almost exclusively for children.

In doing so I went back to my earlier love and addiction, to write science fiction and fantasy for the twelve-to-fourteen age group. And a few smaller books for younger ones. Above all, with this change, I had the joy of finding where I feel I belong. As a storyteller for kids, I've had the most productive, most rewarding, most completely contented time of my professional life.

Even so, another few years and nearly twenty books later, more change has come upon me. I'm entirely free lance again; and I've begun writing "adult" science-fiction novels. But these books are classed as "adult" because of length, and not much else. They are intended as entertainments—farcically comic space adventures. And I hope the kids will read them too.

I haven't abandoned children's books, and I'm sure I never will. I simply enjoy them too much. Along with the spin-offs— like meeting the kids themselves, and the people associated with books. It's a specialized and amazingly dedicated subculture, the world of children's books. And I think I've become as addicted to it as I am to the wonders of science fiction.

———

Douglas Hill received his B.A. degree in 1957 and did graduate work from 1957 to 1959. He was Editor at Aldus Books in London from 1962 to 1964, and was on the *Tribune* from 1971 to 1984. He has been science fiction advisor to several publishers. He has written poems and articles for such magazines as *Poetry Review, New Statesman, The Guardian*, and *Times Literary Supplement*. He has had stories in anthologies like Aidan Chambers' *Out of Time* and Diana Wynne Jones' *Hidden*

Turnings. He reviews children's fiction for *The Guardian.* Two of his science fiction books for adults are *The Fraxilly Fracas* and *The Colloghi Conspiracy.*

SELECTED WORKS: Galactic Warlord, 1980; Deathwing Over Veynaa, 1981; Day of the Starwind, 1982; The Huntsman, 1982; Warriors of the Wasteland, 1983; Young Legionary, 1983; Alien Citadel, 1984; Exiles of ColSec, 1984; The Caves of Klydor, 1985; ColSec Rebellion, 1985; Blade of the Poisoner, 1987; Master of Fiends, 1988.

SELECTED WORKS WRITTEN WITH GAIL ROBINSON: Coyote the Trickster, 1976.

ABOUT: Author's and Writer's Who's Who, 1971; Contemporary Authors, Vol. 53; (New Revision Series), Vol. 15; Contemporary Poets, 1970; Reginald, R., comp. and ed. Contemporary Science Fiction Authors; Something About the Author, Vol. 39; The Writers Directory 1988-90.

ERIC HILL

ERIC HILL

1927–

AUTHOR AND ILLUSTRATOR OF *Where's Spot?*, etc.

Biographical sketch of Eric Hill:

ERIC HILL was born in London, England. At the age of twelve he was sent to the country to escape the World War II blitz, but chose to return to the city instead. He was fascinated by the aircraft he saw and began to draw them. He left school as soon as he could and found a job at age fifteen as a messenger and general sweeping-up boy at a commercial art studio. There he received the only art training he ever had when a cartoonist named Wilhelm Timyn took an interest in him. He continues in the style he learned there to use clear line and no detail.

With time out for a short stint in the Royal Air Force, Hill pursued his art career in cartooning, in advertising, and finally as a free-lance artist. It was when he was working out of his home that his young son Christopher saw and enjoyed some of his advertising work in which a man raised his hat to reveal what was beneath. The two-year-old was fascinated.

Hill had seen how children enjoy working with their hands. He had noted that most books were too complex for toddlers, with too-small print and illustrations that were too detailed. So Hill decided to create a book for Christopher. Because he loved dogs, he wrote and drew a story of a mother dog, Sally, looking for her puppy in what was essentially a game of hide-and-seek. The book had large print and simple line drawings; it had flaps that Christopher could lift, thereby participating in the storytelling. The result was a dummy for *Where's Spot?*.

It would have stayed on Hill's desk if a friend's daughter, a literary agent, hadn't brought it to a book fair in Frankfurt. Heinemann published the book in England, where it quickly topped the children's bestseller list. In 1980, Putnam bought the U.S. rights, and Spot became a hit in America as well. Soon Hill left his free-lance business to become a full-time children's author. He now lives in Tucson, Arizona.

Since the first book, Spot's life has mirrored that of a young child. He took a walk of discovery in *Spot's First Walk.* He has gone to the zoo, to school, and to the beach. Spot books are translated into over forty-four languages and are popular all over the world. He takes the name of the most common name for dogs in each language: Puppe in Finnish, Korochan in Japanese, Smot in Welsh.

BBC TV in England produced thirteen five-minute cartoons featuring Spot. *Where's Spot?* was a runner-up for a 1981 Mother Goose Award, sponsored by the British book club Books for Children. The American Library Association has named three of Hill's books Notable Books in their years of publication: *Where's Spot?*, *Spot's First Walk*, and *Spot's Birthday Party*.

SELECTED WORKS WRITTEN AND ILLUSTRATED: Where's Spot?, 1980; Spot's First Walk, 1981; Spot's Birthday Party, 1982; My Pets, 1983; Spot's First Christmas, 1983; Here's Spot!, 1984; Spot Goes to School, 1984; Spot Goes to the Beach, 1985; Spot Goes to the Circus, 1986; Spot Looks at Colors, 1986; Spot's Big Book of Words, 1988.

ABOUT: Children's Literature Review, Vol. 13; Horn Book September/October 1987; Publishers Weekly July 25, 1986; Something About the Author, Vol. 53.

RONALD HIMLER

October 16, 1937–

ILLUSTRATOR OF *Dakota Dugout*, etc.

Biographical sketch of Ronald Norbert Himler:

RONALD HIMLER was born in Cleveland, Ohio, and spent his childhood in the Garfield Heights section of Cleveland. In 1960, Himler received a diploma from the Cleveland Institute of Art, where he studied watercolor, life studies, oil painting, and sculpture. After graduation that year, he entered the Cranbrook Academy of Art in Bloomfield Hills, Michigan, for further study in painting, completing his studies there in 1961. Himler briefly attended Hunter College as well as New York University for two years—from 1968 to 1970.

On June 18, 1972, Himler married Ann Danowitz; the couple has two children, Daniel and Anna.

Himler spent his early childhood years painting at his grandmother's dining room table on Sunday afternoons. Drawing has always been a part of his life; Himler feels, in fact, that he was chosen by art long before he chose art. Himler worked at a variety of jobs searching for the form, place, and meaning of art in his life. He worked as a technical sculptor at General Motors Technical Center in Warren, Michigan, and as a toy designer and sculptor for Transogram Company in New York, New York, and Remco Industries in Newark, New Jersey, before entering the field of children's book illustration in 1970. In illustration, Himler feels that he has finally found the proper role of art in his life. He says that the art that chose him has now become an integrated part of his makeup. Though he still struggles with questions regarding the needs that art fulfills in himself and to what extent his art fulfills the needs of others, Himler feels at home with children's book illustration.

Himler has lived in New York City and Tucson, Arizona; in Tucson and surrounding areas, he discovered Southwestern culture and developed a special interest in American Indian culture and lore. This interest is exemplified in many of Himler's illustrations, such as those in *Coyote Dreams*. Two of Himler's books illustrated with this influence were chosen for awards. *Indian Harvests* was a Children's Book Showcase Book in 1975. Other Himler works have also been well received. Both *Baby* and *Rocket in My Pocket* received American Institute of Graphic Arts awards in 1972, and *Dakota Dugout* was an American Library Association Notable Book of 1985.

Himler has worked successfully with other authors as well as on his own. Of Arnold Adoff's *I Am the Running Girl*, a poem describing a young girl's joy in running, the *Bulletin of the Center for Children's Books* states, "Himler's pencil sketches echo the concentration and the elation of the running girl through whom the poet speaks." The Council on Interracial Books for Children 1980 *Bulletin* described the book as a "fine merger of poetry, content and art."

A *School Library Journal* review of Himler's *Wake Up, Jeremiah*, described Himler's drawings as "an impressionistic sort of realism reminiscent of Andrew Wyeth. The pictures and words combine to portray simply and joyfully the wonder of a common miracle."

In a 1972 review of *Glad Day*, Jean Valentine of *Book World* summed up Himler's talents: "What distinguishes this collection even more than the poems is the drawings: mostly cheerful, certainly, but not recklessly so, these odd, magical pictures, with their dreamlike wackiness of scale and direction, show that, like all the very best children's authors and illustrators, Himler has not forgotten his childhood."

SELECTED WORKS WRITTEN OR SELECTED AND ILLUSTRATED: The Girl on the Yellow Giraffe, 1972; Glad Day, 1972; Wake Up, Jeremiah, 1979.

SELECTED WORKS ILLUSTRATED: Baby, by Fran Manushkin, 1972; Rocket in My Pocket (rev. ed), by Carl A. Withers, 1972; Indian Harvests, by William C. Grimm, 1974; Sadako and the Thousand Paper Cranes, by Eleanor Coerr, 1977; I am the Running Girl, by Arnold Adoff, 1979; Inside My Feet: The Story of a Giant, by Richard Kenney, 1979; Dakota Dugout, by Ann Turner, 1985; Eli's Ghost, by Betsy Gould Hearne, 1987; Coyote Dreams, by Susan Nunes, 1988; The King of Prussia and a Peanut Butter Sandwich, by Alice Fleming, 1988.

SELECTED WORKS WRITTEN WITH ANN HIMLER AND ILLUSTRATED: Little Owl, Keeper of the Trees, 1974.

ABOUT: Contemporary Authors, Vol. 53–56; (New Revision Series); Vol. 5; Kingman, Lee and others, comps. Illustrators of Children's Books: 1967–1976; Something About the Author, Vol. 6.

ANNA GROSSNICKLE HINES

July 13, 1946–

AUTHOR AND ILLUSTRATOR OF *Daddy Makes the Best Spaghetti*, etc.

Anna Grossnickle Hines

Autobiographical sketch of Anna Grossnickle Hines:

WHEN I WAS SEVEN years old I remember sitting in my daddy's big chair looking at a Little Golden Book version of *Heidi*. I loved books and I loved to draw and suddenly I knew what I wanted to do when I grew up. I wanted to make picture books for boys and girls. I told my mother. She said, "If that's what you want to do, then that's what you should do."

It wasn't that easy. I had to learn a lot about drawing and writing and books and children and publishers. I went to college to study art, but there weren't any classes about illustrating children's books. Some people even told me that children's books weren't "real art," and that I should choose a more important career. But I didn't agree. Pictures on walls are nice, but I like pictures to curl up with, to share on a lap or even take to bed with you. I think the art in children's books is some of the most important art in the world. So I stuck with my dreams and studied as best I could by reading and practicing on my own.

I did other things along the way, such as teaching school and getting married and having three daughters. I always read lots of books to them and to the kids I taught. I noticed what they liked about the books and what I liked and which books seemed to be extra-special.

At first I didn't think I had any good ideas for stories. I thought I'd let somebody else do the writing and I'd just be the illustrator. But as I read the books, helped kids learn, watched them play and played with them, I started seeing more about the world the way young people see it. I remembered things about myself when I was a child and how I felt as a little girl. And I started writing poems and then stories. At first I was shy about sharing them, but finally I got brave enough to show them to a few good friends. My friends liked them, so I got braver and shared them with more people.

I found out how to send the stories to publishing companies that might make one of them into a real book. At first I mostly wrote during the summers, when I wasn't teaching school. I'd send a story to a publishing company and get a nice letter back, saying something like, "we like the way you write and the way you draw, but this story isn't right for us. Send us something else." So I'd send that story to another publishing company, and send a new story to the first publishing company. Then I'd get two nice letters back. I kept doing that until I had about one hundred of those nice letters.

By that time I had stopped teaching school. My youngest child was just a baby and I was home taking care of her and her sisters, and baking and sewing and gardening . . . and writing stories whenever I found the time.

Until one day, I realized that I was fooling myself. I was telling myself, "See all these nice letters. If I had the time I could be a 'real' author-illustrator." As long as I didn't try my best, I could say that I could have succeeded if I didn't have to do all those other important things. But if I really tried my very best and never got a book published, then I would have failed. Right then I knew that I had to try my best. If I didn't, it would be the biggest failure of all.

So I wrote or drew every day, even if it was for just a few minutes. I let the rest of the family help with the dusting and vacuuming and cooking. Pretty soon I felt like a "real" author-illustrator, and about a year after that I got a call from one of those publishing companies saying they wanted to make one of my stories into a real book. That was one of the happiest days of my life.

Now I have lots of published books, and I'm still learning things and trying to do my best to make the books better and better. Parts of this job are frustrating, but mostly it's just as much fun as I always thought it would be, and I'm very glad that I didn't give up my dream.

———

Born in Cincinnati, Ohio, Anna Grossnickle Hines was the oldest of seven children. She moved to Los Angeles as a child. Her first marriage ended in divorce, and she was married for a second time June 19, 1976. She attended San Fernando Valley State College at Northridge for three years as an art major, taught preschool in Los Angeles City Children's Centers for two years, then received her B.A. and M.A. degrees in Human Development from Pacific Oaks College in Pasadena. Hines has since taught elementary school. She is a member of the Society of Children's Book Writers and the California Reading Association.

Daddy Makes the Best Spaghetti was named a Children's Choice Book of 1987 by a joint committee of the International Reading Association and the Children's Book Council and a Junior Literary Guild selection. *Come to the Meadow* was also a Junior Literary Guild selection.

SELECTED WORKS WRITTEN AND ILLUSTRATED: Taste the Raindrops, 1983; Come to the Meadow, 1984; Maybe a Band-Aid Will Help, 1984; Bethany for Real, 1985; All by Myself, 1985; Don't Worry I'll Find You, 1986; Daddy Makes the Best Spaghetti, 1986; I'll Tell You What They Say, 1987; It's Just Me, Emily, 1987; Grandma Gets Grumpy, 1988; Boys Are Yucko!, 1989; Sky All Around, 1989; They Really Like Me, 1989.

ABOUT: Contemporary Authors, Vol. 114; Something About the Author, Vol. 45; Vol. 51.

MARY ANN HOBERMAN

August 12, 1930–

AUTHOR OF *A House Is a House for Me*, etc.

Autobiographical sketch of Mary Ann Hoberman:

I KNEW I was going to be a writer even before I knew how to write! I think I was about four years old when I first understood that many of the stories I loved so much had been made up by real people, with real names, rather than having always been here, like the moon or the sky. I decided then that when I grew up I would write stories, too, that would be printed in books for other people to read. But meanwhile I didn't wait to grow up or even to learn how to write. . . . I started right away to make up stories and poems and songs in my head, which I told to myself or to my little brother.

We had a favorite game . . . it was called "drawing pictures and telling stories." I would draw something and tell my brother a story about it. When something new happened, I would draw another picture next to the old one and tell about that. Sometimes my brother would tell me what should happen and I would put that into the story. When we were done, the page was covered with rows of pictures, a little like a comic book without any writing. But the words were all in our heads and we could tell the stories again and again, just by looking at the pictures.

We had a swing in our backyard and I would swing back and forth, up and down, for hours at a time, making up songs that I sang to myself. It was the rhythm of the swinging that got me started and gave me my ideas and put the tunes in my head. As I swung higher and higher and faster and faster, I would sing louder and louder until

I was shouting my songs out at the top of my voice and my mother would come out to see what was happening. Then I would let the swing slow down and the rhythm would get slower and my song would get softer and more dreamy and the afternoon would drift away.

Many years later, when I grew up, a long time after I had learned how to write, I did become a writer, just as I had decided when I was four years old. I saw my stories and poems and songs printed in books just like those I loved so much when I was a little girl. But I still make things up in my head before I write them down. And even though I no longer spend my afternoons in a swing, my poems and songs still begin in the rhythms that I feel when I take my daily walk, kicking up the autumn leaves or crunching through the snow or watching my bare feet make footprints in the sand.

People often ask me where I have found my ideas for my children's books. As the mother of four children (now grown up themselves), I am assumed to have found my primary inspiration in them, in observing their interests and growth. But while I did begin writing for children in large part because I was at home for many years raising a family, most of my ideas have originated in memories of my own childhood and in my own early interests and pastimes. As a younger woman I had almost total recall of myself as a child; and even now, when I am a grandmother and the years on which I draw for my stories and poems are half a century behind me, I still can tell you the names of every one of my elementary school teachers, where I sat in each classroom, who my friends (and enemies) were, and how I felt about myself, my family, and my world. In many ways, despite the sorrows and pain of childhood, I loved being a child; and as a child I was already aware that childhood was fleeting and that I must never forget what it felt like to be new in the world.

And I never have.

———

Mary Ann Hoberman was born in Stamford, Connecticut. She received a B.A. degree, magna cum laude, at Smith College in 1951. She studied history and was both Phi Beta Kappa and a Sophia Smith Scholar. She was married February 4, 1951. She has been a newspaper reporter, an editor in a children's book department, a poetry consultant and, in various Greenwich, Connecticut, schools, a poet-in-the-schools. She has given lectures and readings on children's poetry and literature for schools, libraries, clubs, and the media since 1960. She was program coordinator at C.G. Jung Center in New York in 1981 and Adjunct Professor at Fairfield University from 1980 to 1983. She is currently enrolled in a doctoral English Program at Yale University. Hoberman has had her poetry for adults published in *The Southern Poetry Review*, *Small Pond*, and *Harper's*. She also writes plays and is founder of a children's theater in Connecticut.

A House Is a House for Me won a 1983 American Book Award, in the children's paperback category. *Bugs* received a 1976 American Institute of Graphic Arts Award.

SELECTED WORKS: All My Shoes Come in Two's, 1957; Hello and Good-by, 1959; What Jim Knew, 1963; A Little Book of Little Beasts, 1973; The Raucous Auk, 1973; Bugs, 1976; I Like Old Clothes, 1976; A House Is a House for Me, 1978; Yellow Butter, Purple Jelly, Red Jam, Black Bread, 1981; The Cozy Book, 1982; Mr. and Mrs. Muddle, 1988.

ABOUT: Contemporary Author, Vol. 41-44; (First Revision), Vol. 41; Shaw, John Mackay. Childhood in Poetry, 2nd supplement; Something About the Author, Vol. 5.

WILLIAM H. HOOKS

November 14, 1921–

AUTHOR OF *Crossing the Line*, etc.

Biographical sketch of William Harris Hooks:

WILLIAM HARRIS HOOKS was born in Whiteville, North Carolina. His father was a farmer in the coastal Tidewater country. He served in the United States Army in the Medical Corps from 1942 to 1946, where he attained the rank of technical sergeant.

Hooks graduated from the University of North Carolina with a B.A. degree in 1948. He received an M.A. degree in 1950, also from the University of North Carolina. His academic achievements include membership in Phi Beta Kappa. Further studies included attendance at the American Theatre Wing, as well as the New School for Social Research and Bank Street College of Education. He makes his home in a brownstone in Greenwich Village in New York City.

The career of William H. Hooks reflects his many and varied talents and interests. In 1949, he taught high school History and Social Studies in Chapel Hill, North Carolina. In 1950, he was an instructor of Dance and History at the Hampton Institute in Hampton, Virginia. For four years, from 1960 to 1964, he was a choreographer at the Opera Workshop. During the next five years he owned a dance studio in New York City. From 1970 to 1972, he was on the staff of the Publications Division of Bank Street

College. He became chairman of the Publications and Communications Division of the Bank Street College of Education in 1972.

He has attained many artistic and aesthetic accomplishments in addition to his career as a writer. His achievements include the vice-presidency of Ballet Concepts, Inc., and he has been a choreographer for Paramount Pictures and some Off-Broadway productions, as well as for his own dance company.

William H. Hooks has been both an educational consultant to ABC Afterschool Specials as well as ABC Saturday morning children's programs. He has been involved in thirteen outdoor historical dramas, including *Unto These Hills*, a historical play depicting the history of the Cherokee Indian Nation.

In the publishing arena, he has been managing editor of Bank Street College's revised edition of "Bank Street Readers." In addition to writing for young people, he has also been a reviewer for *Dance Digest* and has written scripts for the children's television program *Captain Kangaroo*.

Hooks uses his North Carolina background to combine literature with folk tales and folk wisdom. In *Moss Gown*, he has retold a Southern folk tale, sometimes known as "Cap o' Rushes" or "Rush Cape." The retelling includes elements of "Cinderella" and *King Lear*. Candace is sent away from home by her father after she fails to flatter him as much or as well as her two sisters have.

The Mystery on Bleeker Street details the strange occurrences at the Star Hotel in a New York story of friendship, kidnapping, and detective work for middle elementary school children.

Mean Jake and the Devils is a collection of stories explaining customs, superstitions, and natural phenomena. Mary M. Burns writes in *Horn Book*, "The . . . retelling . . . has the freshness and vitality which a master raconteur can impart to familiar materials."

Continuing his theme of stories involving his North Carolina background, *Circle of Fire* tells the story of Harrison Hawkins, a white boy, eleven years old and growing up on the rural North Carolina coast, the Tidewater area where Hooks was born. When gypsies camp on his family's property, Harrison learns of an impending Ku Klux Klan attack on them. The story involves Harrison's struggle with his conscience as he suspects his own father is in on the plot. Booklist stated, "the ethical decisions inherent in the plot give readers a sense both of history and of moral obligation." Nancy Sheridan in *Horn Book* calls this book "a powerful, lingering tale of shattered innocence and changing relationships."

In *Crossing the Line*, a younger Harrison Hawkins loves to spent time listening to stories spun by an old Black woman named Little Hattie. When Hattie disappears and Horatio, her nephew, is shot, the Hawkins family becomes involved in a score they feel they must settle.

In addition to his books and novels for children, Hooks has written a nonfiction book for adults with co-author Ellen Galinsky, *The New Extended Family: Day Care That Works*.

Selected Works: The Seventeen Gerbils of Class 4-A, 1976; Doug Meets the Nutcracker, 1977; Crossing the Line, 1978; The Mystery on Bleeker Street, 1980; Mean Jake and the Devils, 1981; Circle of Fire, 1982; Three Rounds with Rabbit, 1984; Moss Gown, 1987; A Flight of Dazzle Angels, 1988; The Legend of the White Doe, 1988.

About: Contemporary Authors, Vol. 81-84; (New Revision Series), Vol. 19; Something About the Author, Vol. 16.

DEBORAH HOWE

August 12, 1946–June 3, 1978

Co-Author of *Bunnicula: A Rabbit-Tale of Mystery*, etc.

Biographical sketch of Deborah Howe:

DEBORAH HOWE

DEBORAH HOWE was born in Boston, Massachusetts, lived briefly in Denver and then moved to Riverdale, New York. Her father, Lester Smith, was a well-known newscaster for WWOR radio in New York. Her family supported her interest in the arts, because the arts were an important part of their lives.

Howe studied acting and received a B. F.A. degree at Boston University in 1968. There she met James Howe, her future husband, and they were married September 28, 1969. The two moved to New York City to pursue careers in show business, and Howe worked as an actress from 1969 to 1978.

James Howe says that his late wife's interest in writing grew directly out of her love of reading. From her childhood, she was a voracious reader, frequently reading ten or more books a week. She loved all sorts of books: classics, nonfiction, and popular genre books such as mysteries, horror novels, and historical novels. She had written very little before she and her husband began writing *Bunnicula: A Rabbit-Tale of Mystery*, "just for the fun of it" according to James Howe. During the time that they began writing *Bunnicula*, the couple dis-

covered that Deborah Howe had cancer. The two finished *Bunnicula* and also wrote *Teddy Bear's Scrapbook* together before her death in 1978.

Bunnicula is an extremely popular book for middle- elementary grade schools; it has won many awards voted upon by school children. In the mystery-comedy, a vampire rabbit preys upon vegetables instead of people. He sucks the color from the Monroe family's tomatoes. Chester, the family cat, observes these phenomena and confides his fears to Harold, the family dog, who humors him while investigating the strange occurrences. The book's equally popular sequels include James Howe's *Howliday Inn*, *The Celery Stalks at Midnight*, and *Nighty-Nightmare*.

Bunnicula received the 1981 Dorothy Canfield Fisher Award. It was also named a Notable Book of 1979 by the American Library Association, was a Junior Literary Guild selection, and was made into a recording, a TV special, and a videocassette. *Teddy Bear's Scrapbook* was a Junior Literary Guild selection.

SELECTED WORKS WRITTEN WITH JAMES HOWE: Bunnicula: A Rabbit-Tale of Mystery, 1979; Teddy Bear's Scrapbook, 1980.

ABOUT: Contemporary Authors, Vol. 105; Something About the Author, Vol. 29.

JAMES HOWE

August 2, 1946–

CO-AUTHOR OF *Bunnicula: A Rabbit-Tale of Mystery*, etc.

Autobiographical sketch of James Howe:

I WAS BORN in Oneida, New York on August 2, 1946, the youngest of four brothers. My bloodlines are mostly English, Scotch, and German, but my roots grow deep in American soil. One of my father's ancestors was hanged as a witch in Salem, Massachusetts, in the late 1600s. She's mentioned in

James Howe

Arthur Miller's play about the Salem witch trials, *The Crucible*. On my mother's side is Benjamin Rush, the "father of American psychiatry" and one of the signers of the Declaration of Independence. My mother never let my father forget which side was witch.

It is not this heritage that inspired me to be a writer, however—unless having an alleged witch in the family predisposed me to write the sorts of things I do. More likely, my turning out to be a writer has to do with a childhood spent making up stories, first on my feet with friends and toys; then, when I knew how, on paper. Words played an important part in my growing up. Not only the written word (there were books all over the house; when they didn't fit on the shelves they were stacked haphazardly on the floor), but words that flew through the air—jokes, riddles, puns. My family was always playing with words. It is little wonder that even after I got serious about writing, I've had a hard time getting serious about words.

I moved from Oneida when I was two and spent the next ten years in Webster, a small town in upstate New York. There I established the Vampire Legion (a club with

a membership of exactly three), wrote and edited its newspaper, *The Gory Gazette*, and distributed another newsletter to the neighbors that was full of family gossip. When my parents found out, that publication went out of print—fast! I was encouraged in no uncertain terms to put my writing energies to use elsewhere.

And I did. I wrote plays, poetry, short stories, and letters to my brothers, all of whom had left home by the time I was ten. Soon I decided I wanted to be—no, not a writer, but an actor. You see, as much as I loved writing plays, I loved performing in them even more. My dream was to be a child star. Since my hero was the great English actor, Sir Laurence Olivier, I decided I should change my name to Sir Reginald Windsor. (I didn't know the "sir" part came with being knighted.) I imagined movie after movie in which I would star. And being a stickler for details, even in my fantasies, I thought them out from opening credits to final fade-out. I didn't realize it, but I was writing even then.

I held onto my goal of being an actor long after becoming a child star was no longer likely. After graduating in 1964 from Niskayuna High School (in Schenectady, New York, where my family moved when I was twelve), I went to Boston University, majored in acting and received a Bachelor of Fine Arts degree in 1968. The following year, I married a college classmate, Deborah Smith, and we moved to New York City to pursue careers in show business.

It didn't take long for me to realize I was never going to be Sir Laurence Olivier—or even Sir Reginald Windsor. And though I went on to earn a Master of Arts degree in theater from Hunter College in 1977, I found myself drawn more and more to what I had first loved doing as a kid—writing.

Debbie and I wrote *Bunnicula* in 1977-78 just for the fun of it. We never imagined it would be the popular children's book it became nor that it would launch my career as a writer for children.

After Debbie died of cancer in 1978, I went on to write several sequels to *Bunnicula*, as well as other mysteries, picture books, serious novels, and nonfiction. In 1981, I left my job as a literary and theatrical agent to pursue writing full-time.

Also in 1981, I married Betsy Imershein, a photographer with whom I've collaborated so far on one children's book, *When You Go to Kindergarten*, and one child, a daughter, Zoe, born November 22, 1987.

Sometimes I wonder what it would have been like if I'd become a famous child actor. Maybe I'll write a book about it one day. But I can't imagine my parents would have been any more proud of Sir Reginald Windsor than they are of their son, the writer—especially now that they don't have that newsletter to worry about anymore.

———

James Howe is a member of the Authors Guild, P.E.N. American Center, the Mystery Writers of America, the Society of Children's Book Writers, and Writers Guild of America, East.

James and Deborah Howe's *Bunnicula* and its sequels (*Howliday Inn, Celery . . .* , and *Nighty-Nightmare*) are extremely popular middle elementary-grade novels. They have won many awards chosen by school children. *Bunnicula* was named a Notable Book of 1979 by the American Library Association and was a Junior Literary Guild selection, and was made into a recording, a TV special, and a videocassettte. *Howliday Inn, Celery . . .* , and *Nighty-Nightmare* were also made into recordings, and the latter was a Book-of-the-Month Club selection.

Teddy Bear's Scrapbook was a Junior Literary Guild selection. *The Hospital Book*, a realistic photo-essay about what a hospital stay is like, was named a Notable Book of 1981 by the ALA and a 1981 Outstanding Science Trade Book for Children by a joint committee of the National Science Teachers Association and the Children's Book Council. It was also a 1981 Boston Globe-

Horn Book Award Honor Book for nonfiction, and was nominated for the 1982 American Book Awards in the children's nonfiction category.

SELECTED WORKS: The Hospital Book, 1981; Howliday Inn, 1982; A Night Without Stars, 1983; The Celery Stalks at Midnight, 1983; The Day the Teacher Went Bananas, 1984; Morgan's Zoo, 1984; What Eric Knew, 1985; Eat Your Poison, Dear, 1986; Stage Fright, 1986; There's a Monster Under My Bed, 1986; When You Go to Kindergarten, 1986; I Wish I Were A Butterfly, 1987; Nighty-Nightmare, 1987; The Fright Before Christmas, 1988; Scared Silly, 1989.

SELECTED WORKS WRITTEN WITH DEBORAH HOWE: Bunnicula: A Rabbit-Tale of Mystery, 1979; Teddy Bear's Scrapbook, 1980.

ABOUT: Contemporary Authors, Vol. 105; Horn Book March/April 1985; Publishers Weekly February 24, 1984; School Library Journal August 1987; Something About the Author, Vol. 29; Teaching K-8 February 1987.

JANNI HOWKER

July 6, 1957–

AUTHOR OF *Badger on the Barge*, etc.

Autobiographical sketch of Janni Howker:

I AM the middle one of three sisters, add my parents to this sum and you'll see a family of five. Now, imagine us sitting around a tea-table upon which is a rhubarb pie which my mother is scrupulously dividing into five equal pieces and your picture will come clearer. Katy, my younger sister, is sulking because she's still too little to be allowed out to play in that twilight-zone of after-tea escape, and Carole and I are casting each other furtive glances over the milk jug, because we're going out to Venom Wood to see if any more aliens have landed. . . .

Like all children, my sister and I were born into a world where *anything* might happen, and if it was left to us, it usually did! We weren't at all surprised when the first men walked on the moon—only disap-

Janni Howker

pointed that the aliens seemed to have missed the rendezvous!

Until I was thirteen, my Dad was an officer in the R.A.F. This meant that, as a family, we were moved from air-base to air-base, from school to school. I think that this made us a close family, and my sisters and I partly avoided the problem of always being strangers in strange places by playing imaginative games; games which often ended up with us all being scared witless. It only took the tiniest scrap of information to filter down to us from the adult world and we were off. One bitterly cold winter we heard that a panther had escaped from a local zoo. . . . Of course, every paw print in the snow, every barking dog, every shadow on our curtains became a cause for delicious terror. . . .

Imaginative we might have been, but we were also living in the strange, abnormal streets of 'Married Quarters'. There were no old people on these streets, no handicapped people, no pubs—only the apparently neat lives of officers and their families. In fact, my Mum and Dad had come from a very different world, a world we moved back to when my father finally returned to Civvy Street and brought us all back to the North

of England. Here we were confronted at last with their real roots, and ours—grandparents who had ground their way into old age in the cotton mills of Lancashire; Great Aunt Winnie, who had raised my father, and from whom we had probably inherited our imaginations, worked in a light-bulb factory all her life, dyed her hair red until she was well into her seventies, believed in ghosts, had been crossed in love, and sang sentimental twenties tunes like a quavery, operatic whistling kettle.

At the age of thirteen, then, I moved out of the world of make-believe and into the world of talk, of family. Now all these relatives lived or were buried within a twenty-mile radius and we had come *home*. No longer intrigued by aliens or witches, I wanted to know why no one ever mentioned Great Uncle Stephen; what that fierce electric current of silence was when my parents' marriage was mentioned (my mother, daughter of a Protestant Orangeman millworker, had married a Catholic), why my Grandad had to have special shoes (his feet were deformed by splinters—having worked barefoot in the mill). Perhaps if I'd grown up with all of this around me, I'd have taken less notice. At last I discovered where my own North Lancashire accent came from, and what it was that had driven my parents out of the back streets of their childhoods, and what strong tie it was that brought them back.

At fourteen, I started writing. Ten years later I wrote the stories in *Badger on the Barge*—each of which was dedicated to a member of my family, and each of which contains some small portion of a family secret. No one else in my family, past or present, writes—although it would not surprise me at all if one day my elder sister took up a pen.

Now, at thirty-one, I live in a terraced house in Lancaster—the sort of house my grandparents lived in. Now, in adulthood, I've shared similar fears, difficulties and joys—unemployment, deaths, births, and marriage. I am reaching an age when I too have stories of my own to tell, but theirs still haunt me—the horses in the stables behind Great Granddaddy Charlie's house, the tarantula spider in Grandad Jack's waistcoat pocket, the death of my gentle grandmother from 'melancholia'. . . .

As I see around me families 'splintered' by the demands of the modern world, it sometimes seems to me that many children have little sense of *place*, of family history, and thus, in a way, there seems to be a whole area of *memory* missing, and without memory people become disconnected, even to the extent of becoming aliens to themselves.

I hope that in reading my stories they can at least share in the complex, funny, sometimes frightening business of family, where anger and love, hatred and humour, and a sulking little sister may all be sitting down at the same table for tea.

———

Janni Howker spent her childhood in Norfolk, Suffolk, Lincolnshire, and Cumbria counties in England. She received a B.A. degree with Honors from Lancaster University in 1980, and an M.A. degree in 1984. She has edited a poetry magazine for the Brewery Arts Centre in Kendal and has helped to establish writing workshops at the Trades Hall in Lancaster. She later worked in a hospital for the mentally ill, was a research assistant at the Lancaster University Sociology Department, was a Census Officer and a Park Attendant. In addition to writing, she gives readings, is a tutor, and conducts workshops. "Janni Howker —Storyteller" was presented on Thames TV in 1985. *Badger* was a screenplay for ITV in 1987, and *Nature of the Beast* was made into a full-length film for Film on 4/ British Screen, released in 1988. Janni Howker is a member of The Society of Authors and the Northern Association of Writers in Education.

Badger on the Barge won the 1985 International Reading Association Award and was commended in the Whitbread Literary

Awards and the Carnegie Medal Awards, both in 1985. *The Nature of the Beast* won the Young Observer Teenage Fiction Prize in 1985, the Whitbread Award in the children's fiction category in 1985, and the Silver Pencil Award in Holland in 1987. It was also highly commended in the 1986 Carnegie Medal Awards. *Isaac Campion* was named a Boston Globe-Horn Book Honor Book for fiction in 1987, was highly commended in the 1987 Carnegie Medal Awards, and won the Somerset Maugham Award in 1987. *Badger* and *Isaac Campion* were named Best Book of the Year in their years of American publication by the American Library Association; *Nature of the Beast* was a 1985 ALA Notable Book.

SELECTED WORKS: Badger on the Barge and Other Stories, 1985; The Nature of the Beast, 1985; Isaac Campion, 1987.

ABOUT: Children's Literature Review, Vol. 14; Something About the Author, Vol. 46.

DEAN HUGHES

August 24, 1943–

AUTHOR OF *Switching Tracks*, etc

Biographical sketch of Dean Hughes:

DEAN HUGHES was born in Ogden, Utah. As a child, he remembers himself as always reading. He told people that he wanted to be a writer when he grew up. Although he was active in sports and other school activities, he says he "entered" stories to leave the "less real" world behind. He began to write stories, and wrote a novel the year he graduated from high school.

He attended Weber State College, writing another novel and receiving a B. A. degree in 1967. He was a missionary for two years. He went on to obtain an M. A. degree in creative writing in 1968 and a Ph.D. degree from the University of Washington in 1972. Hughes returned to school for postdoctoral study at Stanford Universi-

ty in the summer of 1975 and at Yale University in the summer of 1978. He was married November 23, 1966, and has three children.

Hughes was Associate Professor of English at Central Missouri State University from 1972 to 1980. He wrote another novel while he was teaching. The College where he was teaching had an annual children's literature festival. He became interested in children's literature, and as he is a Mormon, he became interested in and wrote about the expulsion of the Mormons from Jackson County, Missouri, in the 1830s. He has since written seven fictional books backed with Mormon history, and has also written *The Mormon Church: A Basic History*.

Hughes also writes lighthearted books about Nutty Nutsell, the main character in his popular books for eight-to-twelve-year-old readers. *Switching Tracks* and *Family Pose* are more serious stories, according to the author, and are read by older children.

Hughes has moved back to the Wasatch Range of the Rocky Mountains in Utah, and given up his teaching position. He is a speaker and workshop leader at writing conferences. He is a member of the Children's Literature Association, the Society of Children's Book Writers, and the Authors Guild.

Switching Tracks was named a 1982 Notable Children's Trade Book in the Field of Social Studies by a joint committee of the Children's Book Council and the National Council on the Social Studies.

SELECTED WORKS: Nutty for President, 1981; Honestly, Myron, 1982; Switching Tracks, 1982; Millie Willenheimer and the Chestnut Corporation, 1983; Nutty and the Case of the Mastermind Thief, 1985; Nutty and the Case of the Ski-Slope Spy, 1985; Nutty Can't Miss, 1987; Theo Zephyr, 1987; Nutty Knows All, 1988; Family Pose, 1989.

ABOUT: Contemporary Authors, Vol. 106; Something About the Author, Vol. 33.

MONICA HUGHES

November 3, 1925–

AUTHOR OF *Hunter in the Dark*, etc.

Autobiographical sketch of Monica Hughes:

THOUGH I WAS BORN in Liverpool, England, my family moved to Egypt when I was only a few months old, and I lived in that hot colourful country for the next six years. I found a return to a London suburb and then to a grey granite house in cold windy Edinburgh very depressing, and I began to lead a secret life at my local library.

My first allegiance was to the novels of E. Nesbit, but not far behind were the nineteenth-century adventure writers, Alexandre Dumas, Anthony Hope, R.L. Stevenson, Rider Haggard, Baroness Orczy and, of course, the master of science fiction writing, Jules Verne. As I devoured their books I dreamed of being a writer myself.

My father, who was a mathematician and an amateur astronomer, gave me Sir James Jeans' *The Mysterious Universe*, which opened my eyes to the magic of the skies, as E. Nesbit had opened them to the magic of amulets and psammeads. During World

Monica Hughes

War II, when I was a meteorologist in the Royal Naval Service, I used to go out onto the airfield at night to take readings and marvel at the miracle of the night sky, unspoiled by city lights since the blackout was strictly enforced.

After the war I trained as a dress designer in London and then went to work in Southern Rhodesia (now Zimbabwe) for two years, where, among other wonders, I saw the stars of the Southern Hemisphere for the first time and experienced that incredible view into the centre of the Milky Way Galaxy. All this time I was writing 'when the mood struck me', but I never got anything published.

I decided to visit another part of the British Commonwealth—Canada—on my way to Australia, where I hoped to live. Here I have stayed, occasionally dreaming of sunny Australian beaches when the weather hits forty below zero, but happy to be a Canadian. I worked at the National Research Council as a lab technician, married, and had four children.

We moved from Ontario to our present home in Edmonton, Alberta, and I persisted in this 'dream' of writing. In 1971 I decided to stop 'dreaming' and writing only when

I was 'inspired'. I committed myself to writing, for young people, for four hours a day for a year. At the end of the year I had some terrible stories and a science fiction novel called *Crisis on Conshelf Ten*, inspired by Jacques Cousteau's experiment with an undersea habitat, which he called Conshelf One.

During the years that followed I continued to learn my craft. I still write regularly every morning and, though I have graduated from a typewriter to a word processor, I still write my first draft on loose-leaf paper with a black Bic pen, as I did back in 1971.

When I look back on a life filled with dreams and rejection slips, I am amazed that I have finally managed to become a writer, with twenty published novels and a file full of ideas. Yet each new book is still a risk, a venture into unknown territory, which is both terrifying and wonderful.

———

Monica Hughes graduated from the Convent of the Holy Child Jesus in Harrogate, Yorkshire, in 1942 and attended Edinburgh University from 1942 to 1943. She was married April 22, 1957 and has four children. She has been writer-in-residence at several universities and libraries, including the University of Alberta, from 1984 to 1985. She is a member of the Alberta Writers Federation.

The Vicky Metcalf Award was presented to Monica Hughes in 1981 for the body of her work, by the Canadian Authors Association. The same organization presented her with the Vicky Metcalf Short Story Award in 1983, and she has had stories anthologized in such collections as *Out of Time*, edited by Aidan Chambers.

The Keeper of the Isis Light was placed on the Honour List of the International Board on Books for Young People in 1982, and was named a Best Book for Young Adults in 1981 by the American Library Association. *The Guardian of Isis* and *Hunter in the Dark* won Canada Council Children's

Literature Prizes, in 1981 and 1982 respectively. *Ring-Rise, Ring-Set* was a runner-up for the 1983 Guardian Award. *Hunter in the Dark* won the 1983 Young Adult Canadian Book Award and was named a Best Book for Young Adults for the year 1983 by the ALA.

SELECTED WORKS: Crisis on Conshelf Ten, 1977; The Ghost Dance Caper, 1978; Beyond the Dark River, 1981; The Keeper of the Isis Light, 1981; The Guardian of Isis, 1982; Ring-Rise, Ring-Set, 1982; Hunter in the Dark, 1983; Devil on My Back, 1985; The Dream Catcher, 1987; Sandwriter, 1988.

ABOUT: Carpenter, Humphrey and Mari Prichard. The Oxford Companion to Children's Literature; Contemporary Authors, Vol. 77; Kirkpatrick. D.L., ed. Twentieth-Century Children's Writers, 2nd ed.; Something About the Author, Vol. 15; The Writers Directory 1984-1986.

THACHER HURD

March 6, 1949–

AUTHOR AND ILLUSTRATOR OF *Mama Don't Allow*, etc.

Autobiographical sketch of Thacher Hurd:

I FEEL fortunate to have grown up with parents who made children's books. My mother wrote and my father illustrated many children's books, both together and with other authors and illustrators. There was always a feeling of creativity in our house, and encouragement for anything artistic.

I have strong memories of the house in Vermont where we lived until I was six: A wide green lawn sloping down to a river filled with rocky pools to swim in, summer nights when we caught fireflies in a jar, my father's studio on a hill above our home. Clem's studio was a cosy place to go, a place to watch him work on books. His work table was made from an old door on top of two sawhorses, his chair was a vinyl fifties model. All around were piles of rice paper, driftwood, block-printing ink rolled out, dummies and drawings in profusion. The smell of inks and paints and papers filled the room.

In the midst of it all stood Clem at his table, muttering a tuneless tune, his hands covered with ink, his mind absorbed in the rhythms of working, trying a print over and over until he got it just the way he wanted it. He would give me my own paints and paper, and I would sit on the floor painting, content in that well-ordered confusion. Out of the corner of my eye I could watch him working, never hurrying or looking for the easy way through a picture, but exploring each idea with deliberate steadiness. I loved to sit in that atmosphere and watch Clem work.

And so it was from Clem, and from my mother Edith, that I first got my love of doing books. Their lives seemed charmed, and as I grew up I think I knew that eventually I would write my own books.

Yet when I started college I had no thought of becoming an artist. I just started doodling in English class. The doodling became so fascinating that I took an art class. And for me that was it, it just opened up a whole new way of seeing the world.

My first books, *The Old Chair* and *The*

Quiet Evening, were influenced by my parents, and by the books of Margaret Wise Brown. But then in *Hobo Dog* and *Axle the Freeway Cat* I began to see that I could find my own voice and go my own way in books. Slowly, with each book that I did, my colors grew brighter and the stories roamed further afield. Music began to creep into my books, whether I wanted it or not, perhaps because I am secretly a frustrated musician who once played in a rock band called the New Tokaloma Swamp Band, and who can barely carry a tune.

One day on the radio I heard the old jazz song, "Mama Don't Allow." Immediately I thought: "*That* would make a book." I loved the rebelliousness of the song, and it sparked me to write something that was raucous and loud. But it took me several years and many rewritings of the story before it would become a book. For me, the creation of a book is a long series of changes, revisions, and convolutions.

A picture book must be an adventure, with a plot that is tight and a sense of surprise at each turning of the page. As an author I like to be surprised, to discover new ideas with each rewriting of a manuscript. Each book is a journey to someplace undiscovered; the book itself, when published, is only a road map. The real joy is the exploration itself: the creation of the book.

———

Thacher Hurd was born in Burlington, Vermont. He attended the University of California at Berkeley from 1967 to 1968 and received his B.F.A. degree from The California College of Arts and Crafts in Oakland in 1972. He was married June 12, 1976. Hurd has been a builder, a designer, and an apprentice printer. With his wife Olivia, he founded The Peaceable Kingdom Press, which publishes posters and cards from children's book illustrations. Thacher Hurd has two children.

Mama Don't Allow won the 1985 Boston Globe-Horn Book Award for Illustration and was a Reading Rainbow book. *Mystery on the Docks* was also a Reading Rainbow book.

SELECTED WORKS WRITTEN AND ILLUSTRATED: The Old Chair, 1978; The Quiet Evening, 1978; Hobo Dog, 1980; Axle the Freeway Cat, 1981; Mystery on the Docks, 1983; Mama Don't Allow, 1984; Pea Patch Jig, 1986; Blackberry Ramble, 1989.

SELECTED WORKS ILLUSTRATED: Mattie and the Chicken Thief, by Ida Luttrell, 1988; Wheel Away!, by Dayle Ann Dodds, 1989.

ABOUT: Contemporary Authors, Vol. 106; Horn Book January/February 1986; Oakland Tribune, November 26, 1981; Something About the Author, Vol. 45; Vol. 46.

BELINDA HURMENCE

August 20, 1921–

AUTHOR OF *Tancy*, etc.

Autobiographical sketch of Belinda Hurmence:

MY PARENTS and both sets of my grandparents homesteaded in the Oklahoma Indian Territory, in the Kiowa-Comanche-Apache lands known among those tribes as the Big Pasture. My mother's people came into the O.T., as it was called, in three covered wagons the year before Oklahoma became one of the United States. My father's family also arrived prior to statehood with all their household goods, their horse Grady, and Pat, the dog, in a freight car over the Frisco Road.

Perhaps because I came from pioneer stock, the frontier qualities of initiative and endurance strongly attract me, and the main characters of my books tend to be pioneers in their own way. I have written several books about American blacks, whom I regard as the nation's unsung pioneers. My new book *The Nightwalker*, although it is a contemporary novel, dips deep into the rugged lives of North Carolina's early settlers.

Ever since I reached the age of conscious-

Hurmence: *HER mons*

Belinda Hurmence

ness, I wanted to be a writer; I have always written, by whatever means came to hand. I grew up in the Southwest, studied under the Southwestern writer, J. Frank Dobie, at the University of Texas, and when I graduated, set out for Manhattan in search of the literary life.

New York astonished me. I had been warned of the big city's cold arrogance; instead I met there easy and openhearted people, at work and in the neighborhoods where I lived, on the east side, west side, uptown, downtown, midtown, and the Village. I felt at home right away; there I married a chemical engineer named Howard Hurmence in the prosaic, but to me romantic, setting of City Hall. Our daughter Leslie, like many a small-town girl elsewhere, lives less than three miles from where she was born, the old Gotham Hospital in Manhattan. Howard and I moved to the beautiful state of North Carolina many years ago, but we love New York as much as ever and visit there whenever we can.

In New York I worked first as an editor at *Mademoiselle*, and later at a dynamic but short-lived publication called *Flair*. In those days I wrote in longhand, standing up on a crowded subway on my way to work. My boss, George Davis, the distinguished managing editor of those magazines, and of *Vanity Fair* before them, read my stories and encouraged me, but it wasn't until I focused on books for young people that my writing more or less "jelled."

For me, writing was then—and still is—a slow, wringing process, and the business of getting my first book published was even slower and more grueling. Today, I write on a word processor, but even so, the electronic age works very little faster for me than the stone age.

Marketing my work does come a bit easier now, and sometimes I wish I had been smart enough to recognize my niche earlier. Mostly, though, looking back on the difficulties of my apprentice years, I see that they were just that—apprentice years. So I continue to plug along and urge myself, much as I urge struggling writers at all stages, not to give up prematurely.

———

Belinda Hurmence graduated from the University of Texas in 1942. She was married in 1948. *Tough Tiffany* was named a Notable Book of 1980 by the American Library Association. *Tancy* won the Golden Kite Award for fiction in 1984 from the Society of Children's Book Writers. It was also named a 1984 Notable Children's Book in the Field of Social Studies by a joint committee of the Children's Book Council and the National Council for the Social Studies.

SELECTED WORKS: Tough Tiffany, 1980; A Girl Called Boy, 1982; My Folks Don't Want Me to Talk About Slavery, 1984; Tancy, 1984; The Nightwalker, 1988; Before Freedom, 1989.

JOHANNA HURWITZ

October 9, 1937–

AUTHOR OF *Aldo Applesauce*, etc.

Autobiographical sketch of Johanna Hurwitz:

ONE OF MY earliest memories is of taking a book from a low shelf I could reach. I opened the book and held it as I had seen my parents do. I pretended that I was reading. It is quite possible that I held the book upside-down because I was only about three at the time. But even then I knew that reading was a wonderful activity that I wanted to be able to do by myself. I don't remember the actual process of learning, but the act of reading filled countless hours of my childhood. I have always loved books!

I grew up in the Bronx in New York City. The walls of our apartment were crowded with bookshelves because both of my parents were bibliophiles. (They actually met in a bookstore!) My father often took me with him when he went browsing in secondhand bookshops in Manhattan and from him I learned to love the smell and feel of old books. I also spent many hours every week at the local branch of the New York Public Library and belonged to a reading club there called the Melrose Bookworms. The first poems and stories I ever wrote were read aloud to my fellow members and transcribed into the club scrapbook. Those early stories were generally derivative of whatever book I had read most recently.

That is why although I had two loving parents I often wrote sad stories about orphans. I thought my own everyday life was dull and boring. I wished that I lived somewhere exotic like Nebraska or Minnesota or Mississippi. Those were places I learned about by sending a postcard to the states' Chambers of Commerce and receiving in return colorful folders and maps. I had a whole carton of those travel brochures under my bed. I thought if I studied them enough, I could set my stories in those other more interesting places.

When I was fifteen, my family moved to Queens, another part of New York City. There I had new libraries to explore, new friends to make, and new schools to attend. But my goals had already been set. I knew that someday I would work in a library and that I would write books that would be on the library shelves.

After high school, I attended Queens College and Columbia University. In 1959, I became a children's librarian with the New York Public Library. I was proud to sit side by side at library meetings with the librarian who had led the Melrose Bookworms. In 1961, I married Uri Hurwitz, a writer and college teacher. I was impressed that he could read books in four different languages! Our children Nomi and Beni were born in 1964 and 1966 respectively. For ten years we lived in an apartment in Manhattan and it is out of our many experiences there that my first book *Busybody Nora* evolved. All the stories about Nora and her little brother Teddy and their friend Russell are fiction, and yet they would never have been written if we had not lived in that apartment building and had certain experiences that closely resemble those that I recorded.

In 1974, we moved to Great Neck, a Long Island suburb of New York. Although it is just a few miles away from the city, for the first time in my life I found myself living in a large area of private homes, tending a garden, driving in car pools, making fires in my fireplace, etc. These experiences have found their way into print, too, in *Aldo Applesauce* and *Aldo Ice Cream*.

It seems as if all my fiction has grown out of real experiences. Whether it is my children's passion for baseball (*Baseball Fever*), my own childhood at the end of World War II (*Once I Was a Plum Tree*), my mother's childhood (*The Rabbi's Girls*) or a summer vacation in Vermont (*Yellow Blue Jay*), I have found ample material close at hand. Even my cats and their fleas have made it into a book (*Hurricane Elaine*).

It took me many years to realize that my everyday life contained the substance for the books I fantasized I would write. Nowadays I have even spent time visiting in Nebraska, Minnesota, and Mississippi as well as many other states and foreign countries. Still I continue to write about the life I know best—my own. When I was twelve I received a check for fifty cents for my first published work. It was a poem that said: "For me to read a book is still/And always will be quite a thrill." It concluded, "And what is more, I'll read until I'm grown/And then I'll write books of my own."

I was right!

———

Johanna Hurwitz received her B.A. degree from Queens College in 1958 and her M.L.S. from Columbia University in 1959. She was married February 19, 1962. In addition to being a children's librarian, she has also lectured on children's literature at Queens Collge of the City of New York. She is a member of the American Library Association, the Authors Guild, P.E.N., and Amnesty International.

Rip-Roaring Russell was named a Notable Book of 1983 by the American Library Association. *Aldo Applesauce* was named a Children's Choice Book of 1979 by a joint committee of the International Reading Association and the Children's Book Council.

SELECTED WORKS: Busybody Nora, 1976; Much Ado About Aldo, 1978; Aldo Applesauce, 1979; Once I Was a Plum Tree, 1980; Aldo Ice Cream, 1981; Baseball Fever, 1981; The Rabbi's Girls, 1982; Rip-Roaring Rus-

sell, 1983; DeDe Takes Charge!, 1984; The Hot and Cold Summer, 1984; The Adventures of Ali Baba Bernstein, 1985; Hurricane Elaine, 1986; Yellow Blue Jay, 1986; Class Clown, 1987; Russell Sprouts, 1987; Teacher's Pet, 1988.

ABOUT: Contemporary Authors, Vol. 65; (New Revision Series), Vol. 10; Lee, Joel M., ed. Who's Who in Library and Information Services; Something About the Author, Vol. 20.

WARWICK HUTTON

July 17, 1939–

RETELLER AND ILLUSTRATOR OF *Jonah and the Great Fish*, etc.

Biographical sketch of Warwick Hutton:

WARWICK HUTTON was born in England, the son of an artist, John Hutton, and Helen Hutton, nee Blair. He was educated at the Colchester Art School, and received an N.D.D. diploma in 1961. He was married August 26, 1965, and has two children. Hutton was a visiting lecturer at Cambridge College of Art and Technology in 1972, and at Morley College from 1973 to 1975. Hutton is a full-time artist. When he is not involved in illustrating, he carries out commissions for glass engravings for churches, homes, and civic buildings, using a large-scale glass engraving technique invented by his father. He is a member of the Cambridge Society of Painters and Sculptors.

Hutton has illustrated a number of retellings of popular folk tales, among them *Sleeping Beauty*, *The Tinderbox*, *The Selkie Girl*, and *The Silver Cow*, which was named a 1983 Notable Book by the American Library Association. *The Nose Tree* was named a Best Illustrated Book of 1981 by the *New York Times*.

The Horn Book Magazine calls Hutton's *Beauty and the Beast* "not simply another version of a well-loved tale but a work of art," and comments, "The backgrounds are designed like massive stage sets." *The New*

WARWICK HUTTON

York Times Book Review praised Hutton, saying, "Warwick Hutton . . . has done a skillful job of paring the often-told tale to something like its essential form. . . . Mr. Hutton . . . paints with a voluptuary's fine concern for the ripeness of things." Another *Times* reviewer states, "In the strange and gaudy world of children's picture books, Warwick Hutton is something of a rarity. He is an honest artist. He can draw beautifully and he is not ashamed of it."

Of Susan Cooper's *The Selkie Girl, School Library Journal* reports, "Hutton's watercolors match and extend Cooper's narrative in the best traditional 'picture story book' fashion." *The Horn Book Magazine* spoke of Hutton "capturing both the beauty and the bittersweet quality of an ancient legend."

Hutton prefers to adapt the book texts, then spend a good deal of time planning and exploring the illustrative elements of the story. He tries to use models, real objects, and landscapes, and likes to draw and paint his way gradually into a story, thoroughly immersing himself in the process. Hutton has characterized his books as not only for children.

In additional to the folk tales, Hutton has retold and illustrated a number of Biblical stories. *Adam and Eve, Moses in the Bulrushes,* and *Jonah and the Great Fish* are among Hutton's favorites. *Horn Book* published a speech given at the Boston Globe-Horn Book Awards on October 1, 1984. In the piece, "How *Jonah and the Great Fish* Began," he wrote, "I had already been painting a number of religious pictures, and since the Old Testament stories of Noah and his great Ark and Jonah inside a whale's stomach had always fascinated me, I decided to sit down to try and draw them both. Neither as a child nor an adult had I ever seen a satisfactory set of pictures for these two stories. No one seemed to read the Bible text properly." As part of his research, Hutton worked out the measurements of cubits to correctly portray the size of the ark.

The Horn Book Magazine, in a review of *Moses in the Bulrushes,* told of the great "eloquence" of Hutton's illustrations, of "the placement and scale of the figures . . . dominating the page and larger-than-life, speak[ing] volumes about the heroism of the acts committed by each of these women." A *School Library Journal* reviewer wrote, "Hutton's magnificent pen and watercolor illustrations suggest both the domestic and the historic dimensions of the tale while delighting the eye with tender greens, vibrant blues and palpable air." The book was a 1976 ALA Notable Book.

Jonah and the Great Fish was awarded the 1974 Boston Globe-Horn Book Award for illustration. It was also named a *New York Times* Best Illustrated Book of 1984. Of its making, Hutton wrote, "I found out, to my surprise, that Jonah was never swallowed by a whale. The word *whale* never appears. It was always a "great fish. . . . I bought a ten-inch whiting from the fishmonger, propped its mouth open with a match stick, and started to draw."

Hutton feels strongly about the importance of publishers' responsibility in choosing which books to publish; he says that, "[as] the waves breaking on the desert island shore . . . are silent because there's no one there to hear them, writers, illustrators, and their books don't exist unless there is a publisher to notice them."

Hutton is also the author of *Making Woodcuts*, a book published for adults. He resides in England with his family.

SELECTED WORKS RETOLD AND ILLUSTRATED: Noah and the Great Flood, 1977; The Sleeping Beauty, 1979; The Nose Tree, 1980; Jonah and the Great Fish, 1984; Beauty and the Beast, 1985; Moses in the Bulrushes, 1986; Adam and Eve, 1987; Theseus and the Minotaur, 1989.

SELECTED WORKS ILLUSTRATED: The Silver Cow: A Welsh Tale, by Susan Cooper, 1983; The Selkie Girl, retold by Susan Cooper, 1986; The Tinderbox, by Hans Christian Andersen, 1988.

ABOUT: Contemporary Authors, (New Revision Series), Vol. 9; Horn Book January/February 1985; Something About the Author, Vol. 20; The Writers Directory 1988–90.

"HADLEY IRWIN"

CO-AUTHORS OF *Abby, My Love*, etc.

Biographical sketch of Annabelle Bowen Irwin and Lee Hadley:

THE NAME Hadley Irwin represents the writing of two women, Annabelle Bowen Irwin and Lee Hadley. By combining their talents, Irwin and Hadley claim they write better stories than those they could create individually. Even when they visit schools to speak to students, three chairs are placed in front of the crowd: one for Ann Irwin, one for Lee Hadley, and the other for Hadley Irwin, the dual author who writes their books. Sharing a similiar background, both Irwin and Hadley grew up and live in Iowa.

Annabelle Bowen Irwin was born October 8, 1915, in Peterson, Iowa, the daughter of a farmer and a teacher. She was one of four children, two boys and two girls. She graduated with her B.A. degree from Morningside College in 1937. She married Keith C. Irwin, a businessman, on May 29, 1943, and had four children. Irwin contin-

ued teaching high school from 1937 until 1967, when she finished her M.A. degree from the University of Iowa. From 1968 to 1970, Irwin was an English instructor at Midwestern College in Denison, Iowa. In 1970 Irwin became an associate professor of English at Iowa State University, and she remained there until her retirement in 1985.

Lee Hadley was also the daughter of a farmer, growing up in Earlham, Iowa. She was born October 10, 1934, and was one of four children, two boys and two girls. From 1955 to 1958 Lee Hadley worked in a department store, Younkers of Des Moines, as a copywriter. Like her collaborator, Ann Irwin, Lee Hadley was an English teacher in De Soto, Iowa, from 1959 to 1960, after which she enrolled in the University of Wisconsin in Madison to finish her M.A. degree in 1961. After completing her masters, Hadley taught school in Monmouth, New Jersey, for three years, and then taught at Ocean County Community College in Toms River, New Jersey, from 1965 to 1968. Since 1969 Lee Hadley has been at Iowa State University in Ames, Iowa, as an associate professor of English.

The two women met in 1973 in the English Department at Iowa State. After collaborating on two professional assignments for the University, Irwin and Hadley discovered that they enjoyed writing together and decided to try to write a novel. They chose the genderless name, Hadley Irwin, for their book's author. They enjoy their cooperative writing relationship, and find they balance each other, allowing the ideas and words to flow easily for their books. Hadley and Irwin write each day from eight o'clock in the morning until one o'clock in the afternoon, or until they have completed eight pages.

Respecting the young adult for whom they write, Irwin and Hadley create realistic novels about life's experiences, covering such themes as incest, divorce, cross-cultural issues, and cross-generational relationships. Humor is also an essential element in the personalities of the authors, and is reflected in the stories they write. Hadley and Irwin claim they are not moralists, but rather they try to explain to young adults how to view and cope with the strange, confusing world in which we live.

In 1981 the Jane Addams Peace Association named *We Are Mesquakie, We Are One* an Honor Book in their Children's Book Awards. *What About Grandma?* was named a 1982 Notable Children's Trade Book in the Field of Social Studies by a joint committee of the National Council on the Social Studies and the Children's Book Council. It was also named a 1982 Best Book for Young Adults by the American Library Association. *Abby, My Love* was a 1985 Best Book for Young Adults, and was included in the ALA list, "Best of the Best Books for Young Adults, 1966–1986." It was also named a Notable Children's Trade Book by the aforementioned social studies committee, in 1985, and a 1986 Children's Choice Book, by a joint committee of the CBC and the International Reading Association.

The most controversial theme Hadley Irwin writes about is incest in the award-winning *Abby, My Love.* The authors do not dwell on the details of the abuse, but rather deal with the behavioral effects of the abuse, and how the victim and the support group deal with the problem. Social workers and a former student of Irwin and Hadley who grew up as an abused child helped to supply the background information for the authors. Their approach is positive and constructive in spite of the tragic theme.

During the school year, Irwin and Hadley meet at their apartment near the Iowa State University campus to write their books for young adults. The apartment and its telephone are both listed under the name Hadley Irwin.

SELECTED WORKS: The Lilith Summer, 1979; We are Mesquakie, We Are One, 1980; Bring to a Boil and Separate, 1981; Moon and Me, 1981; What About Grandma?, 1982; I Be Somebody, 1984; Abby, My Love, 1985; Kim/Kimi, 1987; So Long at the Fair, 1988.

ABOUT: Children's Literature in Education Winter 1987; Contemporary Authors, Vol. 101; Something About the Author, Vol. 44.

PAUL B. JANECZKO

July 25, 1945–

AUTHOR OF *Poetspeak*, etc.

Autobiographical sketch of Paul Bryan Janeczko, who also writes under the pen name "P. Wolny":

I DIDN'T start out to be a writer. I started out as a kid in New Jersey who had two major goals in life: (1) survive one more year of delivering newspapers without being attacked by thugs from the public high school and Ike, a one-eyed, crazed dog that lurked in the bushes at the top of the hill, and (2) become more than a weak-hitting, third-string catcher on our Little League team. I failed at both.

In grammar school I still wasn't interested in creative writing. I had other things on my mind. Things that I wondered about.

Janeczko: *ja NES ko*

For example, I wondered why all nuns had such beautiful handwriting? I wondered what Ozzie Nelson did for a living. You always saw him hanging around the house wearing a tie and a cardigan sweater, but he never seemed to go to work.

It wasn't until after grammar school that I began to write when I didn't have to. In high school I wrote a few articles for our school newspaper. No hard-hitting investigative pieces about strange things appearing in the school lunch or anything like that, but at least I was writing for a real audience. In college and graduate school—as an English major—I wrote some poetry for the literary magazine.

Armed with a master's degree, I began teaching high school in 1968. I also began writing articles and reviews for educational journals. While I received no money for the pieces I wrote, I did get three things that are invaluable to a young writer: experience, practice, and an audience.

While I was doing the educational writing in the seventies, I began what became my first unpublished novel. I discovered that the urge to write pesters you like a pebble in your shoe. The only way to find relief is to write. And so, I wrote. And wrote. And

wrote before *Loads of Codes and Secret Ciphers* was published in 1984. I had always been a sucker for cloak-and-dagger stuff, so that book was a lot of fun to research and write. My first published novel—I'd written at least half a dozen unpublished ones before it—was *Bridges to Cross.* While most of what happens in the novel is fiction, the central idea is based on my experiences in a Catholic high school in New Jersey.

In addition to the two books that I've written, I've edited nine poetry anthologies. Even though the books contain the work of other writers, putting together a good anthology is much like writing a novel. I want every collection to tell its own story.

I'm still writing, working on a new children's novel and another nonfiction book. I can't see why I'd ever stop. Writing has allowed me to fashion completely new worlds. When I write fiction, I can make things turn out any way I like. At times that seems to be the best thing about writing. The poet Philip Booth said a very interesting thing about poetry, but I find it applies to fiction as well. He said that a good poem "makes the world more inhabitable . . . stretches not toward mere pleasure, but toward joy. It changes the world slightly in favor of being alive and being human." If I've done my job—writing about believable people facing real problems—my readers will feel alive when they read my work.

———

Paul B. Janeczko received his A.B. degree from St. Francis College in Biddeford, Maine, in 1967 and his M.A. degree from John Carroll University in 1970. He is a member of the National Council of Teachers of English and the New England Association of Teachers of English. He lives in Maine, where he works with the Maine Freeze Committee and the local chapter of Educators for Social Responsibility to stop nuclear power and the arms race.

The American Library Association named six of Paul B. Janeczko's books Best

Book for Young Adults in their years of publication: *Don't Forget to Fly, Poetspeak, Strings, Pocket Poems, Going Over to Your Place,* and *The Music of What Happens. Poetspeak* was also named a Books-Across-the-Sea Honor Book in the 1984 Ambassador Book Awards given by the English-Speaking Union.

SELECTED WORKS COMPILED: The Crystal Image, 1977; Postcard Poems: A Collection of Poetry for Sharing, 1979; Don't Forget to Fly, 1981; Poetspeak: In Their Work, About Their Work, 1983; Strings: A Gathering of Family Poems, 1984; Pocket Poems: Selected for a Journey, 1985; Going Over to Your Place, 1987; This Delicious Day: 65 Poems, 1987; The Music of What Happens: Poems That Tell Stories, 1988.

SELECTED WORKS WRITTEN: Loads of Codes and Secret Ciphers, 1984; Bridges to Cross, 1986.

ABOUT: Something About the Author, Vol. 53.

TONY JOHNSTON

January 30, 1942–

AUTHOR OF *The Quilt Story*, etc.

Biographical sketch of Susan T. Johnston:

TONY JOHNSTON was born in Los Angeles, California. Christened Susan, she is the daughter of David L. Taylor, a professional golfer, and Ruth Taylor. Johnston attended the University of California at Berkeley from 1959 to 1960. She received a Bachelor of Arts degree in History in 1963 and a Master of Arts degree in Education in 1964 from Stanford University. After receiving her master's, Johnston taught in the public elementary schools in Pasadena, California, for two years. On June 25, 1966, she married Roger Johnston, a banker, with whom she has two daughters, Jennifer and Samantha. Johnston worked for a number of years in publishing: she was an editing supervisor at McGraw-Hill Publishing from 1966 to 1968 and a copy editor for children's books at Harper & Row Publishers. In addition to working with children, John-

TONY JOHNSTON

ston's interests include cooking, archaeology, and collecting dance masks and Latin American textiles, as well as enjoying sports such as tennis.

After living in New York for many years, Johnston and her family moved to Mexico City. Being a native Californian, she is intrigued by the magic and mystery of a snowy winter's eve and the freshness of the following day. In fact, one of her most memorable Christmases was one spent in New Hampshire. This experience provided the inspiration for a number of the popular *Mole and Troll* stories, as well as for *Five Little Foxes and the Snow. Night Noises and other Mole and Troll Stories* received a starred *Booklist* review that described the engaging twosome: "Mole and Troll are two of the more worthwhile recurring easy-reader actors: they're ingenuous and distinct, and they regularly show evidence of a remarkable likeness-of-soul to their audience. The dialogue is fresh and plentiful throughout."

Johnston collaborated successfully with popular artist Tomie dePaola on a number of titles, among them: *Four Scary Stories, Pages of Music, Odd Jobs,* and most notably, *The Quilt Story,* which was named a

1986 Children's Choice Book by a joint committee of the Children's Book Council and the International Reading Association. The *Bulletin of the Center for Children's Books* applauded the winning combination of dePaola and Johnston, saying, "The story is soberly told . . . and its solemnity is matched by the illustrations, technically proficient in composition and the use of color. . . ."

More recently, Johnston worked with Lloyd Bloom on a tale of the passage of generations entitled *Yonder.* This story developed from a special family tradition. An orchard of fruit trees stands behind a house that Johnston knows well; each tree is planted in part to commemorate the births and passings of members of her family.

Among the other illustrators of her books are Ed Young, Diane Stanley, Cyndy Szekeres, Giulio Maestro, and Wallace Tripp.

Tony Johnston has returned to California once again, where she devotes her time to her family and to writing.

SELECTED WORKS: The Adventures of Mole and Troll, 1972; Mole and Troll Trim the Tree, 1974; Fig Tale, 1974; Five Little Foxes and the Snow, 1977; Night Noises and Other Mole and Troll Stories, 1977; Odd Jobs, 1977; Four Scary Stories, 1978; Happy Birthday Mole and Troll, 1979; Little Mouse Nibbling, 1979; The Quilt Story, 1985; Whale Song, 1987; Pages of Music, 1988; Yonder, 1988.

ABOUT: Contemporary Authors (First Revision), Vol. 41-44; Something About the Author, Vol. 8.

WILLIAM JOYCE

December 11, 1957–

AUTHOR AND ILLUSTRATOR OF *Dinosaur Bob* and *His Adventures with the Family Lizardo*, etc.

Biographical sketch of William Joyce:

AS A CHILD, William Joyce showed an interest in drawing, and was encouraged by his parents. He remembers wanting to

WILLIAM JOYCE

create picture books at the age of five after he read *Where the Wild Things Are* by Maurice Sendak. He read many stories and watched movies, particularly horror movies, which gave him a feeling for how to tell a story. He also had a childhood fascination with cartoons, comic books, and science fiction, and points out that he is among the first generation to be raised "by the TV set." He also thought a lot about the space program, as he grew up in the 1960s, and says that his books are set "vaguely in this rounded past," meaning that cars, appliances, and other familiar objects had a rounded shape then.

Combining his interests in film and in illustrating, he earned a degree in filmmaking and illustrating from Southern Methodist University in Dallas. Film study gave him the background for telling a story through a series of images, similar to the way a picture-book story is told.

Before graduating from school, William Joyce sent his portfolio to Random House and had interviews there and with several other publishers. He received assignments right away, and has since been an illustrator and author of children's books.

George Shrinks, the first book he both

wrote and illustrated, tells the story of a boy who temporarily shrinks to the size of a mouse. Joyce recalls the films *King Kong* and *The Incredible Shrinking Man* and the story "Tom Thumb" and the book *The Borrowers* as contributing influences.

For *Dinosaur Bob*, the author-artist cites the movie *The Beast from 20,000 Fathoms* and the novel *The Great Gatsby* as sources of inspiration. The friendly dinosaur is a family pet in the story.

Joyce acknowledges the influences of Maurice Sendak, N.C. Wyeth, and cartoonist Harold Gray. His own stories evolve from pictures and a story layout to writing the actual prose. He finds this difficult because the prose must be simple, but the words must hold the reader's interest.

Joyce's most successful work is a picture book about comments on his work, "When I was kid, I used to dream about what it would be like to have a dinosaur. Now as an adult I write books about them, so what I dreamt has become what I do. So, if you pay attention to your dreams, in a way they can come true."

Joyce has contributed illustrations to magazines such as *Louisiana Life Magazine* and *Spy*. He also writes film criticism.

William Joyce lives with his wife in Shreveport, Louisiana. Elizabeth Joyce is a lawyer working as a social worker, running a job training center for underpriveleged youths.

Dinosaur Bob and *George Shrinks* are Reading Rainbow Books, and *Dinosaur Bob* is a Book-of-the-Month Club selection.

SELECTED WORKS WRITTEN AND ILLUSTRATED: George Shrinks, 1985; Dinosaur Bob and His Adventures with the Family Lazardo, 1988.

SELECTED WORKS ILLUSTRATED: My First Book of Nursery Tales: Five Favorite Bedtime Tales, retold by Marianna Mayer, 1983; Tammy and the Gigantic Fish, by Catherine and James Gray, 1983; Mother Goose, 1984; Waiting-for-Spring Stories, by Bethany Roberts, 1984; Shoes, by Elizabeth Winthrop, 1986; Humphrey's Bear, by Jan Wahl, 1987.

ABOUT: Bulletin (Newsletter of the Children's Literature Assembly of the National Council of Teachers of English) Fall 1987; Something About the Author, Vol. 46.

MAVIS JUKES

May 3, 1947–

AUTHOR OF *Like Jake and Me*, etc.

Autobiographical sketch of Mavis Jukes:

I GREW UP in the fifties, when girls didn't know that girls grew up to be anything; so I didn't make plans to be a writer.

And my childhood would never have fit the childhood-of-a-writer profile: I wasn't a loner. I didn't read much; I preferred to leaf through the Montgomery Ward catalog, looking at people in nightgowns and slippers.

There was only one book I liked: *The Border Boys on the Trail*. My favorite part was when the guy was galloping along on a horse and yelling, "You double-doggone dash beblinkered son of a sidewinder!"

Brother.

What a jerk.

Good thing my dash beblinkered big brother, Ken, had the sense to modify *The Border Boys* and make it . . . more interesting. He hollowed out the pages and installed an ignition coil from an O and R model airplane engine. It had an actual spark plug—very valuable and rare. Then he covered the book with foil and wrote SEX on the front with red nail polish—you would be shocked if you'd opened it.

And I'm talking: REALLY SHOCKED.

Nice girls—pretty ones, who wore corkscrew curls and socks that matched—wouldn't have passed around a book like that. And they wouldn't have joined My Brother's Gang, like I did; they would have joined 4-H—where Mrs. Hoppman taught such useful skills as: How to decorate fish-food containers with felt and sequins; and: How to make green jello with grated cabbage in it.

Ick!

It was much better going to My Brother's Gang meetings, where we chewed Blackjack gum and threw rotten apples at Don and Kitty Coates.

But not just anyone could be a member. Joining My Brother's Gang involved a kind of boot-camp initiation ritual that began with jumping off the high end of the pighut roof and ended with, maybe, ten years of searching abandoned project sites for lost box wrenches and gooseneck pliers.

How many purple burrs can be stuck to one poodle? How difficult is it to maintain control of a motorcycle made out of a bicycle and a lawnmower engine? The answers to these and other questions had to be determined by gang members in the field.

But WHO WERE the other gang members—I mean, besides me? I didn't have time to wonder; there was a hole out there that needed to be dug.

Deep.

Cash and bootlegged whiskey were reported to have been buried in the vicinity of that hole. I had to get to it! Before Don and Kitty Coates did!

I don't know exactly how old I was when I discovered that I was the only one in my brother's gang.

That even he had quit.

But I was probably eleven or twelve, and the only thing I had left to learn in life was how to whistle through my teeth—I could drive a Packard and fly a J-3 Piper Cub; I didn't need a gang.

I was on my way someplace; I didn't know where. And I can't tell you how I ended up being a writer, just that I did.

———

Mavis Jukes was born in Nyack, New York, and grew up in New City, New York, and Princeton, New Jersey. She graduated from the University of California with a B.A. degree in Art. She taught school for five years, earned a Doctor of Jurisprudence degree from Golden Gate University, and became a member of the California bar in 1979. She married Robert Hudson in 1976. She has two daughters and two adult stepsons.

No One Is Going to Nashville won the Bank Street College of Education's Irma Simonton Black Award in 1983. *Like Jake and Me* was designated a Newbery Honor Book in 1985 by the American Library Association, and an Honor Book for fiction in the 1985 Boston Globe-Horn Book Awards. Both *Like Jake and Me* and *Blackberries in the Dark* were named ALA Notable Books in their years of publication, and were both named Notable Children's Trade Books in the Field of Social Studies by a joint committee of the National Council on the Social Studies and the Children's Book Council, in 1984 and 1985 respectively.

SELECTED WORKS: No One Is Going to Nashville, 1983; Like Jake and Me, 1984; Blackberries in the Dark, 1985; Lights Around the Palm, 1987; Getting Even, 1988.

ABOUT: Something About the Author, Vol. 43.

X. J. KENNEDY

August 21, 1929–

AUTHOR OF *Ghastlies, Goops & Pincushions*, etc.

Autobiographical sketch of Joseph Charles Kennedy, who writes under the pen name "X.J. Kennedy":

I WAS BORN of nice, well-behaved parents in the industrial town of Dover, New Jersey, thirty-five miles from New York.

I didn't begin by wanting to be a writer, but by wanting to be a cartoonist. With this aim, I turned out dozens of hand-drawn comic books—imitations of *Superman* and *Batman*, mostly. My friends agreed that I had a bright future in cartooning ahead of me, but in truth I wasn't good enough. I had trouble drawing the same character twice. By high school, I had given up on comic books and had started reading science fiction magazines like *Planet Stories*. Back then, their covers sported huge green-spotted octopi wringing the juice out of unlucky spaceships. The first time my mother found a pile of these magazines in my dresser drawer, she marched them and me down to the furnace and made me feed them to the flames. But by and by she relented, and I bought more of the stuff. I imitated the science fiction I read, sometimes sending out my efforts in the mail, but eight years went by before I sold any stories to paying magazines.

For four years after college I was a sailor in the Navy, making cruises on destroyers in the Atlantic and Mediterranean, taking pictures of other sailors for their hometown newspapers. This light duty left me plenty of time to write, so I began writing poems. While still a sailor I sold two poems to a magazine, *The New Yorker*, and felt encouraged. Eventually, in 1961, a book of my verse for adults came out. By then I had begun teaching English in colleges, first at the University of Michigan, later at Tufts University, near Boston.

In the early 1970s, I was feeling down in the dumps about my poetry for adults. I had continued to write in rhyme and regular rhythm, and that was no longer fashionable. Then along came inspiring letters from two generous ladies: first, Myra Cohn Livingston, the California poet and anthologist for children, who had spied two kids' poems (in that first adult book) and asked if there were more. She mentioned me to Margaret K. McElderry, the children's book editor and publisher, who invited a whole collection. The result was *One Winter Night in August* in 1975, and I've been scribbling happily for kids ever since. These scribblings have included one novel so far, *The Owlstone Crown*, which began as a story told aloud to our own kids during a rain-lashed vacation on Cape Cod.

Today I live in Bedford, Massachusetts, a town that has stayed fairly quiet since the local farmers stopped shooting at British redcoats. There, our five children have gone to school, and my wife Dorothy and I work together writing college textbooks. These are our main bread and butter. Dorothy and I have done one children's book together, *Knock at a Star: A Child's Intro-duction to Poetry*. It's writing for kids that's the most fun of all.

X.J. Kennedy received his B.S. degree from Seton Hall University in 1950 and his M.A. degree from Columbia University in 1951. He has also done graduate work at the Unversity of Paris, receiving a certificate in 1956, and at the University of Michigan. He was in the Navy from 1951 to 1955. He was married January 30, 1962. He is a member of the Authors Guild, P.E.N., Phi Beta Kappa, and the Children's Literature Association.

His first collection of poetry for adults, *Nude Descending a Staircase*, won the Lamont Award of the Academy of American Poets. He has written college textbooks, including *An Introduction to Poetry*, and until 1979 was Professor of English at Tufts University. He has also been poetry editor of *The Paris Review*. He now writes full-time. His verse has appeared in 160 anthologies and magazines, including *The Atlantic* and *The New Yorker*, and he has received a Guggenheim Fellowship and a Los Angeles *Times* Book Award for Poetry. *The Forgetful Wishing Well* was named a Notable Book of 1985 by the American Library Association.

SELECTED WORKS: One Winter Night in August, 1975; The Phantom Ice Cream Man, 1979; Did Adam Name the Vinegarroon?, 1982; The Owlstone Crown, 1983; The Forgetful Wishing Well: Poems for Young People, 1985; Brats, 1986; Ghastlies, Goops and Pincushions, 1989.

SELECTED WORKS WITH DOROTHY M. KENNEDY: Knock at a Star: A Child's Introduction to Poetry, 1982.

ABOUT: Contemporary Authors (First Revision), Vol. 1; (New Revision), Vol. 4; Contemporary Authors Autobiography Series, Vol. 9; Contemporary Literary Criticism, Vol. 8; Contemporary Poets, 1985; Dictionary of Literary Biography, Vol. 5; Shaw, John Mackay. Childhood in Poetry, 2nd supplement; Something About the Author, Vol. 14; Who's Who in America, 1986-1987; World Authors: 1950–1970.

Dick King-Smith [signature]

DICK KING-SMITH

March 27, 1922–

AUTHOR OF *Babe: The Gallant Pig*, etc.

Autobiographical sketch of Dick King-Smith:

TO MY SURPRISE, I became a children's author at the age of fifty-six. This comparatively late start is explained by the fact that, prior to that age, I had been earning my living in other ways and had not had the remotest thought of writing stories for children.

I was born in the county of Gloucestershire in the West of England, in a house precisely three and a third miles as the crow flies from my present cottage. Apart from war service, I have never lived further from my birthplace than eight miles. I am, you might say, a parochial man.

In 1941, at the age of nineteen, I joined the Grenadier Guards.

In 1943, I married.

Also in 1943 I landed at Salerno, in the invasion of Italy by Allied troops.

In 1944 I was gravely wounded, just south of Florence, by a German paratrooper who threw a nasty thing at me.

In 1946, I was invalided out of the army.

Between 1947 and 1967 (when the bank manager intervened) we farmed (near my birthplace, of course).

Then things began to get tricky. Six months selling aluminised asbestos fire-fighting suits was followed by three years working in a shoe factory. Then I trained to be a teacher, took a Bachelor of Education degree at the age of fifty-three, taught in a primary school for seven years, and retired at the age of sixty, in 1972.

'Retirement'—which is a very pleasurable condition—consists of writing lots of children's books—to make up for lost time—numbering at the time of writing about thirty; and doing a couple of small stints as a presenter on children's TV which led, in 1988, to my writing and presenting a new children's series on Yorkshire Television, called *Tumbledown Farm*. A second series is in the making.

In the course of this chequered career, three children were born—in 1945, 1948, and 1953—two girls and a boy, and between them they have presented my wife Myrle and myself with ten grandchildren. If we make it to February 1993, we ought to have a pretty good Golden Wedding celebration.

Words have always fascinated me, and I've always attempted to write poetry in one form or another, but not till my fifties did an idea for a children's novel (inspired by a real-life incident during the farming years) start to take shape in my mind. This idea, after a great deal of editorial help, advice, and encouragement, led eventually to my first book, *The Fox Busters*, which, to my delight, is to be published in America, by Dell, to join my other books from Atheneum, Crown, Greenwillow, Harper & Row, and Viking.

A hobby, says my dictionary, is 'a favourite pursuit followed as an amusement.'

I'm a lucky man. At last, my work is my hobby.

———

Dick King-Smith was born in Bitton, Gloucestershire. He was educated at Marlborough College, Wiltshire, from 1935 to 1940. His education degree was from the University of Bristol in 1975. *Pigs Might Fly*, published as *Daggie Dogfoot* in England, was a runner-up for the 1981 Guardian Award; *The Sheep-pig*, which has not been published in the U.S., won the Guardian Award in 1984. *Babe: The Gallant Pig* was named an Honor Book in fiction by the Boston Globe-Horn Book Award committee in 1985. *Babe: The Gallant Pig* and *Harry's Mad* were both named Notable Books by the American Library Association, in 1985 and 1987 respectively.

SELECTED WORKS: The Mouse Butcher, 1982; Pigs Might Fly, 1982; Magnus Powermouse, 1984; Babe: The Gallant Pig, 1985; The Queen's Nose, 1985; Farmer Bungle Forgets, 1987; Harry's Mad, 1987; Cuckoobush Farm, 1988; The Fox Busters, 1988; Martin's Mice, 1989.

ABOUT: Contemporary Authors, Vol. 105.; Kirkpatrick, D.L., Twentieth-Century Children's Writers, 2nd ed.; Something About the Author, Vol. 38.

R. R. KNUDSON

June 1, 1932–

AUTHOR OF *Zanballer*, etc.

Biographical sketch of Rozanne Ruth Knudson:

ROZANNE R. KNUDSON has always loved sports. This author of numerous popular sports novels and sports biographies for children and young adults has played ball since she was five years old, when her dad used to toss baseballs in her direction. Her father used to shoot hoops with her after arriving home from his office. A versatile ath-

Knudson: *NUDE son*

lete, she has been a baseball first baseman and catcher. She has played basketball, hockey, tennis, golf, and squash. Her hobbies include skiing and skin diving as well as amateur birdwatching.

The descendant of Mormon pioneers, she was born in Washington, D.C. Her father, a lawyer, had been an all-American basketball player, despite having contracted polio when he was a child. Helping her to develop a life-long love of reading and books, her mother taught her to read when she was four years old. She spent a lot of her time when she was young reading, playing ball, or playing the piano. Knudson was raised in Arlington, Virginia, and she attended Si dwell Friends School in nearby Washington, D.C.

She received a B.A. from Brigham Young University in 1954. She received a M.A. degree with honors from the University of Georgia in 1955. A doctorate was awarded to her by Stanford University in 1967.

Knudson worked as an English teacher in Florida Public High Schools from 1957 to 1960. She has also taught in schools in California and New York. From 1965 to 1967, she was an assistant professor of English at Purdue University, which is located in Lafayette, Indiana. She was the Supervisor of English in the Hicksville Schools in Hicksville, New York, from 1967 to 1970. She became an assistant professor of English at York College in Jamaica, New York, part of the City University of New York, from 1970 to 1972. She has taught students from the junior high age level through graduate school. In 1987, she was writer-in-residence at Kean College in New Jersey.

She lives in a house that overlooks Long Island Sound in Sea Cliff, New York.

Her professional interests include membership in the National Council of Teachers of English and the American Civil Liberties Union as well as the Authors League of America.

She writes under the name R.R. Knudson. Knudson has stated that she never really in-

tended to be a writer. When she left for college, she intended to learn to be a sports coach. Somewhere along the way to the library, she fell in love with novels and put aside sports for books. She loves to read, preferring fiction and poetry. She usually manages to read through more than one book every day.

Because she has been active in the world of academia, she has written articles for professional journals, as well as reviews. When she was still in graduate school she was helping professors to write. She was also a ghost writer to help earn her way through graduate school. She has co-authored an English textbook, written numerous articles on schoolbook censorship, and ghost-written books for athletes and written reviews of sports books.

Her first novel, *Zanballer*, was written in only thirty-eight days, at the suggestion of a colleague who felt the lack of young adult novels about female athletes. *Zanballer* introduces a character named Suzanne Hagen and her friend Arthur Rinehart. They join forces to form a girls' football team when the school gym collapses, effectively ending their basketball season, and thereby forcing the girls into ballet and folk-dancing lessons. Along the way, readers learn about football plays, conditioning, and rules; and Zan, Rinehart and company get a new gymnasium and modern locker room facilities for the girls. This novel about a girl who would rather play ball than sit on the sidelines like the other girls is "somewhat autobiographical." *School Library Journal* states, "The team . . . faces discrimination, hassling and heckling, but manages to keep cool even when the chauvinists descend en masse." The publication of *Zanballer* led to Knudson's decision to become a full-time writer.

Suzanne and Rinehart tackle basketball in *Zanbanger*. When Zan is tossed off the girl's basketball team because she doesn't "play like a lady," the case ends up in court and the judge rules that Zan may play on the boys' team.

In *Zanboomer*, Suzanne damages her shoulder playing baseball and ends up in the hospital, temporarily ending her baseball career. Rinehart, her best friend and personal coach, won't let her give up, however, and designs a program for her that involves running.

Continuing her writing about running, Knudson takes Zan to the Olympics in *Zan Hagen's Marathon*. Other books about running include *Fox Running* and *Speed*.

Knudson's interest in weightlifting and bodybuilding led to a novel for young people in which Arthur Rinehart is given "one last chance" to succeed in a sport by his friend and successful athlete Zan Hagen. *Booklist* reviewed the book as "One of the most satisfying, original 'weak-kid-makes-good' stories to come along . . . Knudson's style is clipped and defined, letting humor and the affection between her two main characters glide effortlessly off the page."

American Sports Poems was selected as a 1988 Best Book for Young Adults by the American Library Association. Knudson has also written sports biographies for young people about Babe Didrikson Zaharias and Martina Navratilova.

SELECTED WORKS: Zanballer, 1972; Fox Running, 1977; Zanbanger, 1977; Zanboomer, 1978; Rinehart Lifts, 1981; Speed, 1983; Zan Hagen's Marathon, 1984; Babe Didrikson: Athlete of the Century, 1985; Martina Navratilova: Tennis Power, 1986; Rinehart Shouts, 1987.

SELECTED WORKS EDITED WITH MAY SWENSON: American Sports Poems, 1988.

ABOUT: Contemporary Authors (First Revision), Vol. 33; (New Revision Series), Vol. 15; Foremost Women in Communications, 1970; Publishers Weekly April 16, 1973; Something About the Author, Vol. 7; Who's Who of American Women, 1974-1975; The Writers Directory 1984-86.

STEPHEN KRENSKY

November 25, 1953–

AUTHOR OF *The Dragon Circle*, etc.

Autobiographical sketch of Stephen Krensky:

AT A TIME like this, when I'm supposed to be writing about myself, I feel very uncomfortable and scuff the floor with my shoe. If I were an explorer mapping rain forests, I would have a lot to say. If I were a scientist developing rare vaccines, there would be much to talk about. I would feel somewhat better if I could at least settle for discussing my Mysterious Past. The problem is I never had one.

The plain truth is that I'm a happily married guy with two sons, a large mortgage, a chicken in every pot and two cars without a garage. I didn't plan to end up this way. These things just happen. As I boy, I never thought about being a writer. I did, however, want to be an astonomer in the fourth grade, a cartoonist in the fifth, and a superhero always. Like other children I was often asked "What do you want to be when you grow up?" At one point I began answering "A philanthropist," which usually led to an awkward silence and no further questions.

Even though I didn't do much writing when I was younger, I still spent a lot of time making up stories in my head. I especially liked to do this before I went to sleep at night. One of my favorite games was to think hard about a character—Robin Hood or Gandalf, for example—just before I dozed off. My hope was to stimulate a dream involving one of these characters and myself in some great adventure. Sometimes this worked. Then again, sometimes I had dreams about taking a test I hadn't studied for.

I started writing stories for children while in college, something I backed into after becoming interested in illustrating children's books. But I was much more comfortable writing than drawing, and so I stuck with

that. Over the years my writing has taken many forms—from fantasy to realism, from fiction to nonfiction. For me writing is as much a craft as an art. I've rarely been struck by lightning bolts of inspiration. Mostly I have to roll up my sleeves and tell myself to get started. Sometimes I write a story from beginning to end, sometimes I just keep making up bits and pieces until a story starts to take shape. I never know how many drafts of a manuscript I'll do before I'm finished. I just keep revising until I stop seeing things to fix. The final result is a book for me which is also a book for children. Some people, I guess, think of writing for children as a stepping stone to writing for adults. I think of it simply as writing the kind of stories I like best.

———

Stephen Krensky was born in Boston, Massachusetts, and grew up in nearby Lexington. He earned his B.A. in English literature from Hamilton College in upstate New York in 1975. Since 1976 he has been a freelance writer specializing in books for children. He has also written dozens of book reviews and articles for magazines and newspapers, including *The New York Times Book Review* and the *Boston Globe*. He adapted his novel *The Wilder Summer* for a Home Box Office Family Playhouse special and has also worked on other children's television projects. *Dinosaurs, Beware!* was a 1987 American Library Association Notable Book.

Stephen Krensky lives with his wife, Joan, and their two sons, Andrew and Peter, in Lexington, Massachusetts.

SELECTED WORKS: The Dragon Circle, 1977; A Troll in Passing, 1980; The Witching Hour, 1981; Dinosaurs, Beware!, 1982; Perfect Pigs, 1983; The Wilder Summer, 1983; A Ghostly Business, 1984; Maiden Voyage, 1985; Scoop After Scoop, 1986; Lionel at Large, 1986; Big Time Bears, 1989.

ABOUT: Something About the Author, Vol. 47; Contemporary Authors, Vols. 73-76; (New Revision Series), Vol. 13.

KATHRYN LASKY

June 24, 1944–

AUTHOR OF *Sugaring Time*, etc.

Biographical sketch of Kathryn Lasky Knight:

KATHRYN LASKY was born in Indianapolis, Indiana. She was educated at, according to her, a very old-fashioned all-girls school. The writing taught there was nonfiction, and not creative. This situation did not particularly suit a compulsive story maker, as Lasky saw herself. She graduated from the University of Michigan in 1966 with a B.A. degree. She also received a master's degree from Wheelock College in 1977.

Even though she was reluctant to share her stories with her parents, and later with her husband, she realized a certain freedom in being a writer. She mainly writes fiction, and even when writing nonfiction, looks for a real story, rather than just facts. She enjoys being her own boss, setting her own hours, and being able to wear anything she likes to work.

Lasky writes for both young children and

Kathryn Lasky

teenagers. Her *Jem's Island* draws on her own family's experiences; it is the story of her husband, who is an expert kayakist, as is his father and brothers. The book is about a boy's first kayaking adventure.

The literary bent runs in Lasky's family. Christopher Knight, Lasky's husband, is a photographer and filmmaker, and has illustrated several of Lasky's books with photographs. Even their young son, Max, born in 1977, is an aspiring author. During her pregnancy with Max's sister Meribah, who was born in 1982, Max wanted to write a book about becoming a big brother. For several months, his parents recorded his thoughts and feelings about having a new baby in the house. Those words were paired with his father's photographs to make his own book, *A Baby for Max*.

Kathryn Lasky also writes books for adults, such as *Trace Elements* and *The Widow of Oz*, under the name Kathryn Lasky Knight. She is a contributor to *Horn Book* and *Sail* magazines.

Sugaring Time, with photographs by Christopher Knight, was named a 1985 Newbery Honor Book by the American Library Association. *The Weaver's Gift* was the 1981 Boston Globe-Horn Book Award

nonfiction winner. Lasky has had four of her books named Notable Books by the ALA: *The Night Journey* and *The Weaver's Gift* in 1981; *Sugaring Time* in 1984; and *Puppeteer* in 1985. The ALA also named several of her books Best Books for Young Adults: *Beyond the Divide* in 1983; *Prank* in 1984, and *Pageant* in 1986. *The Night Journey* won the 1982 Association of Jewish Libraries Sydney Taylor Book Award in the Older Children category. Kathryn Lasky received the 1986 *Washington Post/* Children's Book Guild Nonfiction Award for the body of her work.

SELECTED WORKS: Agatha's Alphabet, 1975; I Have Four Names for My Grandfather, 1976; Tugboats Never Sleep, 1977; Tall Ships, 1978; Dollmaker: The Eyelight and the Shadow, 1981; The Night Journey, 1981; The Weaver's Gift, 1981; Jem's Island, 1982; Beyond the Divide, 1983; Sugaring Time, 1984; Home Free, 1985; Puppeteer, 1985; Night Journey, 1986; Pageant, 1986; Sugaring Time, 1986; The Bone Wars, 1988; Sea Swan, 1988.

ABOUT: Contemporary Authors, Vol. 69-72; (New Revision Series), Vol. 11; Horn Book September/ October 1985; Something About the Author, Vol. 13.

LOUISE LAWRENCE

June 5, 1943–

AUTHOR OF *Children of the Dust*, etc.

Autobiographical sketch of Elizabeth Rhoda Holden, who writes under the pen name "Louise Lawrence":

I WAS BORN in Leatherhead, Surrey, during the last years of the war, which I do not remember. I was the elder daughter of a bricklayer and a cook, somewhat out of place in what was to become the English stock-broker belt. Looking back, I doubt if it was my 'humble' origins or my parents' comparative poverty that made my years at junior school such a hideous experience. It was more the kind of child I was, I guess, someone difficult and different and apt to tell uncomfortable truths at inappropriate

Louise Lawrence

qualities that had been branded as bad, judged and condemned, and my potential academic cleverness that never materialised. I wanted to be ordinary and unnoticed. So I left school at seventeen, worked in a bank and a succession of libraries, married and had children. It was not much fun living in a remote farmhouse with only toddlers to converse with. I missed my contact with books and people, and feared to exist with only myself inside my own head.

I had never dreamed of being a writer, but one day, while I was washing dishes, an idea for a book simply dropped into my mind seemingly from nowhere. And so I wrote it down. And so I began. Writing became an escape route. I was deeply unhappy in the 'real' world, so escaped into fantasy worlds where I ceased to exist and fictional characters took over. The fifth book was *Andra*, which was published.

After that I decided to become a professional writer, left my husband, and set out to survive alone. With three children it was not easy to make ends meet. I had to supplement my income by doing all manner of undesirable jobs, slave labour for low wages. And writing books was no longer an escape but a necessity. Now I was using fantasy worlds and fictional characters as a way of examining my understanding of the real world, human emotions, and social situations. It was a way of facing up to things.

Right now I am married again, happily, and my children have flown the nest. Still in the Forest of Dean, I am busy helping to restore an old house and wonder if I need to go on writing. Yet it remains a strange and magical process, and it was never I who chose to write the books but the books that chose me to write them. Each one came to me unasked for, like watching a film being projected onto a screen inside my head . . . plot, setting, names, characters . . . the whole story from beginning to end compelling me to write it. I assume it is a process, that it will go on happening and I shall continue to write down what I see whenever it is given to me. Only the em-

times. Adults told lies, I discovered, and in order to avoid punishment it was best if I told lies as well. Childhood in Leatherhead is definitely a time I would prefer to forget about.

In any case, home to me was always the Forest of Dean in Gloucestershire, where my grandfather lived and where we went to avoid the bombing and for holidays after the war. We moved to live there permanently when I was eleven years old. It was a land of wooded hills and quarries, small coal mines and rural industries, bad roads and shabby cottages. I spent the rest of my childhood roaming the countryside, when I was not engrossed in schoolwork or listening to the tales my grandfather told me. He had the power to frighten me witless. He peopled the hills with giants and fairies and mythical beasts, monsters of his own ghoulish imagination. And he fostered mine— taught me of trees and flowers, how to dabble in ponds, where the birds nested, and how to distinguish their songs. He taught me to recognise constellations and name the stars. And my mother instilled in me a love of poetry. It was all a beginning.

Never-the-less, I was glad to be done with childhood. I longed to put behind me those phasis will change as the world changes around me and I myself change in maturity and understanding. And who knows what the next book will be or why I shall write it?

———

Louise Lawrence was Assistant Librarian at Gloucestershire County Library from 1960 to 1964, and at Forest of Dean branches from 1969 to 1971. *Andra* was published in England in 1971. She was married for a second time on August 28, 1987.

Calling B for Butterfly and *Children of the Dust* were both named Best Books for Young Adults by the American Library Association, in 1982 and 1985 respectively.

SELECTED WORKS: Andra, 1971; The Power of Stars, 1972; Sing and Scatter Daisies, 1977; Star Lord, 1978; Cat Call, 1980; The Earth Witch, 1981; Calling B for Butterfly, 1982; The Dram Road, 1983; Children of the Dust, 1985; Moonwind, 1986; The Warriors of Taan, 1988;

ABOUT: Contemporary Authors, Vol. 97; Kirkpatrick, D.L., ed. Twentieth-Century Children's Writers, 2nd ed.; Something About the Author, Vol. 38.

DON LAWSON

May 20, 1917–

AUTHOR OF *The United States in the Vietnam War*, etc.

Autobiographical sketch of Donald Elmer Lawson:

I WAS BORN IN CHICAGO but grew up in the Chicago suburb of Downers Grove, Illinois. It was then a small, idyllic town, and the twenties and thirties were stimulating times. I like to think I captured some of this atmosphere many years later in my autobiographical first published novel, *A Brand for the Burning*.

I wanted to be a writer from the time my sixth-grade report on our trip to Chicago's Lincoln Park Zoo was published in the local

weekly newspaper. In high school I reported sports for that paper, wrote for the school weekly newspaper, and helped start the first literary magazine.

One of my high school English teachers—whom I later married—took a special interest in my writing and encouraged me to attend Iowa's Cornell College, where they had a highly regarded writing program. At Cornell I worked on the school paper, was a campus correspondent for the Des Moines *Register*, edited the annual, and had numerous stories published in the college magazine, *The Husk*. Several of these stories were cited as noteworthy in the O'Brien best short story annuals.

After graduating from Cornell (where I was later awarded an honorary Litt. D. degree), I attended the Writers' Workshop at the University of Iowa where we were fortunate to have Robert Penn Warren as a visiting instructor.

Just before World War II began, I edited a weekly newspaper in northern Iowa for a year. At nights and on the weekends I continued to write, but with no success at being published.

During World War II I served with the U.S. Army Air Force in counterintelligence, putting in three years overseas in England and on the Continent. Midway through the war one of my short stories, "The Channel Island Girl," was awarded first prize in *Story* magazine's Armed Forces Contest. My first sale!

After the war I sold additional stories to *Story, Colliers, Family Circle, Argosy, Adventure*, and other magazines. I also took a year off—while my good and loyal wife supported us—to write a novel. This first novel finally sold—some fifteen years later and following half-a-dozen rewrites.

In the late 1940s I went to work as a staff editor for *Compton's Encyclopedia*. Eventually I got to be editor in chief of Compton's, but I continued to write nights and weekends. Several articles I did for Compton's got me interested in the possibility of writing books for young people, an idea that had never before occurred to me. My first book in this field was, *Young People in the White House*, which I later revised several times. After that I did one on *The United States in World War II*, mainly because at that time—late fifties and early sixties—there simply was nothing available for young people on World War II.

There quickly followed books on all of the other American wars—eleven in all, under the umbrella title *The Young People's History of America's Wars*. One of the titles in this series, *The United States in World War I*, has been continuously in print since 1963. Another, *The United States in the Vietnam War*, was chosen by the American Library Association as a Best Book for Young Adults, was a *School Library Journal* Best Book of the year, and was a Notable Children's Trade Book in the Field of Social Studies, all in 1981.

In between war books I did a number of others—I believe my title total is now about forty—almost all in the area of American history. Among then, *FDR's New Deal* was an ALA Notable Children's Book of 1979, and several have been cited by the National Council for the Social Studies.

Young people frequently ask me how they can get to be writers. My answer always is, "By writing. It's easy to talk about, but it's tough to sit down on a regular schedule in your room and face that blank sheet of paper. There is no lonelier feeling in the world. But there's no more rewarding feeling than to get something written, something you're proud of, on that formerly blank sheet." I also tell young would-be writers to read, read everything they can get their hands on, because reading will stand them in good stead for the rest of their lives, whether or not they become successful writers. I can't imagine not being able to read. I think I could get by—barely—without writing. But not reading? Life wouldn't be worthwhile.

Don Lawson received his Cornell College degree from the Mt. Vernon, Iowa, school in 1939. He received his honary Litt.D. degree in 1970 and attended the University of Iowa Writers' Workshop in 1939 and 1940. His armed services career spanned 1944 and 1945, and he worked for Compton's from 1946 to 1973. When Lawson left the company, he was a vice president. He has since worked at United Educators, Inc., in Illinois. He is a member of the Authors Guild, the Society of Midland Authors, the Chicago Press Club, and Phi Beta Kappa. The Social Studies Awards cited are judged by a joint committee of the National Council on the Social Studies and the Children's Book Council. *An Album of the Vietnam War* also received this award in 1986, and was named an Honor Book in the 1987 Jefferson Cup Awards presented by the Virginia Library Association.

SELECTED WORKS: A Brand for the Burning, 1961; Young People in the White House, 1961; The United States in World War I, 1963; The United States in World War II, 1963; FDR's New Deal, 1979; The United States in the Vietnam War, 1981; The French Resistance, 1984; The KGB, 1984; The Eagle and the Dragon: The History of U.S.-China Relations, 1985; An Album of the Vietnam War, 1986; Libya and Qaddafi (rev. ed.), 1987; The Abraham Lincoln Brigade: Americans Fighting Fascism in the Spanish Civil War, 1989; Presidential Scandals, 1989.

ABOUT: Contemporary Authors (New Revision Series), Vol. 2; Leaders in Education; Something About the Author, Vol. 9; Who's Who in America, 1988-89; Who's Who in the Midwest, 1984-85.

ERROL LE CAIN

March 5, 1941–January 3, 1989

ILLUSTRATOR OF *Hiawatha's Childhood*, etc.

Biographical sketch of Errol John Le Cain:

ERROL LE CAIN was born in Singapore, the son of John and Muriel (Kronenburgh) Le Cain. He attended St. Joseph's Institution in Singapore and spent his childhood in the Far East travelling extensively through Japan, Hong Kong, and Saigon. During World War II, Le Cain was evacuated to India, where he lived for five years. He married Dean Alison Thomson in December, 1976, and has one child.

At the age of fourteen, Le Cain made an animated film called *The Enchanted Mouse,* and a year later he made another, *The Goatherd,* which caught the eye of an Asian executive representing Pearl and Dean, an advertising agency. The executive eventually brought him to London to work in the firm's studio.

Le Cain later joined Richard Williams Studios in London as a designer and animator, working on such films as *Casino Royale, The Charge of the Light Brigade, Prudence and the Pill,* and others. During his tenure at Richard Williams, he also won a 1963 *Amateur Cine World* Ten Best Award for his cartoon *Victoria's Rocking Horse.* More recently, Le Cain worked with BBC Television on their productions of Hans Christian Andersen's *The Snow Queen,* George Macdonald's *The Light Princess,* and E. Nesbit's *The Mystery of the Disappearing Schoolgirls.*

Errol Le Cain first became fascinated with myths and legends during his early life in the East, an interest he later extended to the legends of the "exotic West." *King Arthur's Sword* was his first children's book. It began as an elaborate storyboard for a film that Le Cain wanted to make. Creating the book made him realize that children's books would be his medium. The designs for the book were based on medieval manuscripts, and he used intricate borders on the book's pages.

In 1969, Le Cain wrote and illustrated *The Cabbage Princess,* which received a 1969 Honor distinction in the British Library Association's Kate Greenaway Medal Awards. Le Cain felt less comfortable as an author, however, regarding himself as a creator of images; therefore, his later work in children's books was as illustrator. Some of Le Cain's most characteristic work is found in his illustrations for legends and fairy tales. *Briar Rose* (published as *Thorn Rose* in Britain) was a Commended Book in the 1975 Greenaway Medal Awards as well as named to the International Board on Books for Young People Honor List for illustration. *The Twelve Dancing Princesses* was a Greenaway Medal Commended Book in 1978. *Hiawatha's Childhood* won Le Cain the Kate Greenaway Medal in 1984.

Le Cain collaborated with Rosemary Harris on a number of successful works. She wrote his obituary for *The Guardian* in 1989 and commented, "It's hard to describe Errol's extreme involvement with his painting—it was an almost bodily thing, which dominated all his waking thoughts. Pictures flowed out of him as though his fingers were the brush and the other end of the handle was in his mind. . . . He would invent strange techniques to get his effects— like dipping the whole picture in the bath. He could deal with the charming and poetic and the sinister and macabre with equal ease. His powers of invention seemed never-ending."

John Cech of the *Bulletin of the Center for Children's Books* reviewed *The Three Magic Gifts*: "[This] is a thoroughly enjoyable book, precisely because neither the artist nor the reteller takes casually his share of the responsibility for shaping a unified book."

Le Cain once wrote of children's books, "I feel one should not be too dogmatic when talking of picture books. The range available to children should be as wide as possible and the traditional classics should have their place with contemporary works. Back-street slums and fairytale castles must all be there. It is too easy to impose one's own opinions, thus narrowing and limiting a child's imagination.

"I think the first task of an illustrator is to be in full sympathy with the writer," he wrote. "No matter how splendid and exciting the drawings may be, if they work against the mood of the story the picture book is a failure. I am all for illustrations with a lot of relevant detail so that the child can discover fresh things with every look. And I like bold 'simple' pictures which are humorous or dramatic, subtly underlining and extending the story, giving the young imagination something to feed on. . . . My idea of the perfect picture book is one with an imaginative text, simply told, and where the words and drawings belong to each other inseparably."

Errol Le Cain died on January 3, 1989 after a long illness at the age of forty-seven. He left behind a legacy of work, both in illustration and in film. Rosemary Harris also wrote, "His imaginative genius was of the type that fires imagination in others. It is a tragic thing that someone so gifted should die so comparatively young. . . . Although deeply saddened . . . at the loss he will be to his family, his friends and the world of illustration, I cannot help remembering the old phrase that 'Life is long, if it is fulfilled.'"

SELECTED WORKS WRITTEN OR RETOLD AND ILLUSTRATED: King Arthur's Sword, 1968; The Cabbage Princess, 1969; The White Cat, 1973.

SELECTED WORKS ILLUSTRATED: Cinderella, or The Glass Slipper, by Charles Perrault, 1971; Briar Rose, by the Grimm Brothers, 1975; The Twelve Dancing Princesses, by the Grimm Brothers, 1978; The Snow Queen, by Hans Christian Andersen: A New Adapted Version by Naomi Lewis, 1979; The Three Magic Gifts, by James Riordan, 1980; Aladdin and the Won-derful Lamp, by Andrew Lang, 1981; Molly Whuppie, by Walter de la Mare, 1983; Hiawatha's Childhood, by Henry Wadsworth Longfellow, 1984; Growltiger's Last Stand and Other Poems, by T.S. Eliot, 1987; The Enchanter's Daughter, by Antonia Barber, 1988.

ABOUT: The Authors and Writers Who's Who, 1971; Contemporary Authors (First Revision), Vol. 33; (New Revision Series), Vol. 13; Guardian (London) January 6, 1989; Herdeg, Walter, ed. Graphis 3rd International Survey of Children's Book Illustration, 1975 (Publication No. 140); Kingman, Lee and others, comps. Illustrators of Children's Books: 1967-76; Shaw, John Mackay. Childhood in Poetry, 2nd supplement; Something About the Author, Vol. 6.

CAROL LERNER

July 6, 1927–

AUTHOR AND ILLUSTRATOR OF *Seasons of the Tallgrass Prairie*, etc.

Autobiographical sketch of Carol Lerner:

I FEEL a little pang of wonder when I read about authors and illustrators who knew their destiny from the day they left the cradle. That pang might be mixed with a little envy. I was very slow in finding my way into this work.

Probably the acme of my early artistic expression was in eighth grade. Selected students were periodically excused from class routines to work on the brown paper "mural" stretched across the blackboard at the back of the room. It was bliss to stand there blending colored pastels while those not chosen struggled through recitations. But my single art class in high school did not give much satisfaction and it convinced me that I should look to express myself in other directions.

I attended the college of the University of Chicago. At that time, this rare school permitted no undergraduate majors but instead exposed all students to a representative array of academic disciplines. This made perfect sense to me educationally because I still had so much to learn. The fact that it postponed specializa-

Carol Lerner

tion for a few more years was an added bonus. I loved being at the University and I wasn't ready to leave it after graduation. I remained there as a graduate student in the history department. I chose history because it seemed the most comprehensive field, since it includes everything that has ever happened.

After graduate school, there were some years of travel, and marriage and then children. As my kids grew up and the chores that are part of child rearing began to lighten, I began to think practically about my vocational options. Some new interests that had developed during those years of raising kids pointed out my direction.

The bulk of our family activities focused on the natural world. One of my kids wrote, published, and distributed a monthly nature magazine. The other transformed their room into a natural history museum and filled every crevice with specimens of bone, shell, and rock. My husband and I discovered the educational program at the Morton Arboretum and attended classes there for years. I studied botanical illustration at the Arboretum and developed a competent pen technique.

After considering lines of work that would draw on these skills and interests, I decided to try my hand at writing and illustrating nonfiction books for children. I set to work and wrote some pieces, made simple illustrations, and began mailing them out to publishers.

After a couple of years of this, with little to show except a fat rejection file, an editor offered me the opportunity to illustrate another writer's book (Robert M. McClung's *Peeper, First Voice of Spring*). The next year, that same house accepted one of my own manuscripts for publication.

I'm delighted to have found such an interesting job to do. Perhaps what I like best about it is the variety of the work: research, writing, designing the illustrations, and finally executing them. To compensate for my late start, I hope to continue making books for as long as I can still hike in the woods and hold the watercolor brush with a firm hand.

———

Carol Lerner was born in Chicago. She received her B.A. degree from the University of Chicago in 1950, and her M.A. degree in 1954. She married on October 30, 1954. Her work has been exhibited at the Museum of Science and Industry in Chicago, at Yeshiva University Museum in New York City, at Illinois State Museum, and other places; she has had one-person shows at Morton Arboretum in Lisle, Illinois, at the Chicago Botanic Garden in Glencoe, and at Arnold Arboretum of Harvard University, and elsewhere.

Many of her books were named Outstanding Science Trade Books for Children by a joint committee of the National Science Teachers Association and the Children's Book Council: *Peeper* in 1977, *Green Darner* and *Seasons of the Tallgrass Prairie* in 1980, *A Biblical Garden* in 1982, *The 100-Year-Old Cactus* in 1983, *Pitcher Plants* in 1983, *Tree Flowers* in 1984, and *A Forest Year* in 1987, and *Moonseed and Mistletoe* in 1988. The American Library Association deemed four of her books Notable Books for their years of publication: *Seasons of the Tallgrass Prairie, A Biblical Garden, Pitcher Plants,* and *Tree Flowers. Seasons* was an Ambassador Honor Book of the English-Speaking Union for 1980, and *Pitcher Plants* won the 1984 Carl Sandburg Award for Children's Literature. *Peeper* won the 1977 nonfiction Golden Kite Award from the Society of Children's Book Writers.

SELECTED WORKS WRITTEN AND ILLUSTRATED: On the Forest Edge, 1978; Flowers of a Woodland Spring, 1979; Seasons of the Tallgrass Prairie, 1980; A Biblical Garden, 1982; Pitcher Plants: The Elegant Insect Traps, 1983; A Forest Year, 1987; Moonseed and Mistletoe: A Book of Poisonous Wild Plants, 1988; Plant Families, 1989.

SELECTED WORKS ILLUSTRATED: Peeper, First Voice of Spring, by Robert McClung, 1977; Green Darner, The Story of a Dragonfly, by Robert McClung, 1980; Sphinx: The Story of a Caterpillar, by Robert McClung, 1981; The 100-Year-Old Cactus, by Anita Holmes, 1983; Tree Flowers, by Millicent Selsam, 1984.

ABOUT: Contemporary Authors, Vol. 102; Something About the Author, Vol. 33.

BIJOU Le TORD

January 15, 1945–

AUTHOR AND ILLUSTRATOR OF *Rabbit Seeds,* etc.

Biographical sketch of Bijou Le Tord:

BIJOU Le TORD was born in Saint-Raphael, France. She grew up in a house where she was surrounded by art. Her father was a painter and her mother modeled for him. At an early age, she learned to be alone and spent many hours drawing and painting. She also began to cut out type from magazines and put it together with pictures. By the time she was seven she had written and illustrated stories for herself. She knew then that she wanted to be a writer. Her mother encouraged her by supplying art books, natural history books, and

American picture books. She once visited Paris with her mother for a month, staying at a hotel five minutes' walk from where Colette lived. She looked at the windows of Colette's apartment every day, saying to herself, "Imagine, a writer lived there!"

She was educated at the Ecole des Beaux Arts in Lyon, France. Because of her familiarity with American writers, she always assumed she would come to the United States. At the age of eighteen she arrived in New York to design silk textiles for couture designers like Oscar de la Renta and Bill Blass. She continued to design for several years, then taught at the Fashion Institute of Technology for three years. At this time she began to write and illustrate children's books.

Her first book, *A Perfect Place to Be,* is about the craft, songs, and music of American folk art. She wrote it after becoming aware of what America meant to her. Many of her books are about life's experiences. *My Grandma Leonie* tells the story of a child who deals with her grief over her grandmother's death by remembering the special times they shared together. This was based on her own experiences with her grandmother.

Le Tord likes to work long hours at her desk, every day. Her illustrations range from black-and-white line drawings to her favorite medium, watercolors. She uses the colors that will set the right mood for the book rather than trying to duplicate exactly those in nature, and it takes her from six months to a year to write and illustrate a book. She now lives in Sag Harbor, New York, which is on the waterfront like her childhood home on the French Riviera. Here she has opportunities to observe nature.

Le Tord enjoys poetry, the fine arts, travel, music, and people. *The Generous Cow* received a 1977 American Institute of Graphic Arts Award. *Joseph and Nellie* was named a 1986 Notable Children's Trade Book in the Field of Social Studies by a joint committee of the Children's Book Council and the National Council on the Social Studies.

SELECTED WORKS WRITTEN AND ILLUSTRATED: A Perfect Place to Be, 1976; The Generous Cow, 1977; Nice and Cozy, 1980; Picking and Weaving, 1980; Arf, Boo, Click: An Alphabet of Sounds, 1981; Rabbit Seeds, 1983; Good Wood Bear, 1985; Joseph and Nellie, 1986; My Grandma Leonie, 1987; The Little Hills of Nazareth, 1988.

ABOUT: Contemporary Authors, Vol. 65; Sag Harbor Express December 15, 1988; Something About the Author, Vol. 49.

BETTY LEVIN

September 10, 1927–

AUTHOR OF *A Griffon's Nest*, etc.

Autobiographical sketch of Betty Levin:

FOR A LONG TIME my youngest daughter, Jennifer, couldn't believe I really wrote while she was in school. Surely no mother in her right mind would sit all day long at a typewriter pounding on the keys. Then one day when there was a heating problem in school and all the children were bussed home early, Jennifer surprised me at my

typewriter. She was amazed. So it was true! I *was* a writer.

"What did you think I do all day?" I asked her.

"What anyone would do," she told me. "Sit in front of the TV and eat candy. Of course," she added, "I knew you'd do chores first."

Chores were believable because Jennifer and her older sisters grew up helping to feed the farm animals and muck out the barn. But for me writing was a private activity; I needed to be alone for it. Only when a book is ready to be sent to the publisher is it given over to the scrutiny of the family. My husband and children have always been wonderfully supportive, and even Jennifer—now grown—helps me to believe in my writing.

When I was very young, when all I knew was that I loved stories (hearing and reading them and making them up), a teacher criticized me for stealing an idea for one of my stories from a book. I can still remember feeling as though that made my story worthless. As a teacher and a parent, I have always accepted what my students and my children have written on their terms. I have encouraged them to learn from books they admire.

I still have one of my first stories. I wrote and illustrated it when I was around six years old. It was about a lion cub, and I suspect it was strongly influenced by Kipling's *Jungle Books*, which were read aloud to me and my older brothers, and also by *Winnie-the-Pooh*—an unlikely combination.

All of my earliest stories were about animals. By the time I was in high school I was writing about people and places—short stories and poetry for the school magazine. But much later, when Kathy, my first child, was ready for stories, I began to write about animals again. *The Zoo Conspiracy* was the first book written for my children that was published. My middle daughter, Bara, thought up its title.

Some of my books spring from incidents of my childhood. *A Binding Spell* came out of the time my brothers and a neighbhor boy rebuilt the skeleton of an old wagon. They said I was too young to help. Besides, I was a girl. So I turned to the real farm horses down the road and to imaginary ones.

Other books start from images or places. *The Keeping-Room* is set in a town like the one I have lived in for many years. It reflects my habit of looking beneath the surface appearances to picture what time has buried. Some of the people I write about might have been my neighbors in an earlier century.

In *The Ice Bear* I used history to invent a place and time. In *The Trouble With Gramary* I stuck to the present to explore a family and community in the throes of change. This book is about people I have never met, although I might have known them and would have cared deeply about them. Long after a book is finished, its characters become people in my past and are as real to me as friends who have drifted out of my life.

———

Betty Levin was born in New York City. She married on August 3, 1947 and had three children. She received her B.A. degree from the University of Rochester in 1949, her M.A. from Radcliffe College in 1951, and her A.M.T. degree from Harvard University in 1951. Levin has been a research assistant at Boston's Museum of Fine Arts, and a fellow at the Harvard Graduate Schools of Education. She has also been a literature instructor at Emmanuel College, Radcliffe, and Simmons College in Boston. She received a Fellowship in Creative Writing at Radcliffe Institute from 1968 to 1970. She is now a special instructor in children's literature at Simmons College. She is a member of the Authors Guild, Masterworks Chorale, the Middlesex Sheep Breeders Association, and the Society of Radcliffe. Her manuscripts are housed in the Kerlan collection at the University of Minnesota.

The Trouble with Gramary won the 1988 Judy Lopez Memorial Award of the Women's National Book Association of Los Angeles.

SELECTED WORKS: The Zoo Conspiracy, 1973; The Sword of Culann, 1973; A Griffon's Nest, 1975; The Forespoken, 1976; Landfall, 1979; The Beast on the Brink, 1980; The Keeping-Room, 1981; A Binding Spell, 1984; Put on My Crown, 1985; The Ice Bear, 1986; The Trouble with Gramary, 1988.

ABOUT: Contemporary Authors, Vol. 65; (New Revision Series), Vol. 9; Kirkpatrick, D. L., ed. Twentieth-Century Children's Writers, 2nd ed.; Something About the Author, Vol. 19.

RIKI LEVINSON

AUTHOR OF *Watch the Stars Come Out*, etc.

Autobiographical sketch of Riki Levinson:

CREATIVE WRITING and Geometry were my favorite courses in high school. An odd combination, surely, but that's what I liked the most. But when I graduated I received a scholarship in Art, and went to The Cooper Union School of Art and Sciences.

It wasn't until September 1983 that I sat

Riki Levinson

down for the very first time and wrote a picture-book story. It became *Watch the Stars Come Out.*

I was born in Brooklyn, New York. I have four brothers—two older, and two younger.

When I was about seven my mother went to work. It was very unusual for a woman to go to business at the time. My mother was my role model.

Until I was about ten, my father was a jewelry designer. I know my talent for art is from him. When we moved to Flatbush my father became a cantor in a synagogue. He had a beautiful voice. Our family loved to sing.

All my books are about family, for it is the most important part of my life.

Watch the Stars Come Out was about my imagining what it was like when my mother came to America as a little girl. *I* love to watch the stars. And *I Go with My Family to Grandma's* was about our family going to my grandparents' home in Williamsburg, Brooklyn. I have many aunts and uncles, and loads of cousins. It was so much fun for me there.

DinnieAbbieSister-r-r-r! (my mother always called our names in a stream) is my remembering what it was like—how I felt—

as the younger sibling—trying to "catch up" with my older brothers. Although we had very little money, my redheaded mother made everything seem like fun. She really did dance in the rain—just as I wrote in the story.

Touch! Touch! was inspired by my own daughter, Gerry, when she was a toddler. She loved to touch everything.

And the book most recently published, *Our Home Is the Sea*, is the first that I wrote about someone else's family—an Asian family. I have been in Hong Kong fifteen times, each time for a few weeks. My job as Associate Publisher/Art Director takes me there to supervise the printing of the full-color picture books. I feel quite at home in Hong Kong.

There is so much that I share with Chinese people—a deep love of family, and respect for tradition.

My husband Mort, an attorney, always encouraged me to do anything I had a mind to try. If not for him I doubt that I would have become an author. For when I told him that I had an idea for a story but didn't know how to write, he said so wisely, "Don't worry about writing, just put it down."

That's what I do. I don't agonize over it. I just write as it comes to me. When the words and sounds fill my head to bursting I don't have a choice—I have to sit down and write.

My stories are about family. I doubt that my writing would have been so readily accepted for publication ten to fifteen years ago. Family wasn't "in" then. The fact that there weren't enough stories about family really bothered me. I had no idea then that ultimately I would contribute to filling this void.

And when I write I don't think of where I will submit a story. I don't write to be published. I write because I want to—have to.

I am an artist because it's natural to me—always has been since my earliest memory. And now I write because it, too, seems so natural to me. It is the most relaxing part of my life.

———

Riki Levinson received her four-year certificate from The Cooper Union in 1943. She has been a free-lance designer and is currently Associate Publisher/Art Director of Children's Books at E.P. Dutton Publishers. She is a member of the American Institute of Graphic Arts and the Authors Guild.

Except for *Touch! Touch!*, all of Levinson's books have been named Notable Children's Trade Books in the Field of Social Studies by a joint committee of the National Council on the Social Studies and the Children's Book Council, all in their years of publication. *Stars* was named a 1985 Notable Book by the American Library Association and was a Reading Rainbow book. *I Go with My Family* was an Honor Book in the 1987 Jefferson Cup Awards of the Virginia Library Association and appeared in the 1987 AIGA Book Show. *Watch the Stars Come Out* and *I Go With My Family* have both been made into filmstrips.

SELECTED WORKS: Watch the Stars Come Out, 1985; I Go with My Family to Grandma's, 1986; DinnieAbbieSister-r-r!, 1987; Touch! Touch!, 1987; Our Home Is the Sea, 1988.

ABOUT: Contemporary Authors, Vol. 121; Something About the Author, Vol. 49; Vol. 52.

ANNE LINDBERGH

October 2, 1940–

AUTHOR OF *The People in Pineapple Place*, etc.

Biographical sketch of Anne Lindbergh, who has also written under the name "Anne Lindbergh Feydy":

ANNE LINDBERGH was born in New York City, the daughter of aviator Charles A. Lindbergh and writer Anne Morrow Lindbergh. She grew up in Connecticut in a house filled with books, and her parents, both writers, instilled in her the idea that one could write books as well as read them. She remembers making up stories with her

siblings. She attended Radcliffe College and the Sorbonne in Paris. For fifteen years, she lived in Paris. She has two children and lives on a farm in Vermont.

Anne Lindbergh has contributed short stories to *Vogue* and *Redbook*. She has also had her poetry published.

Some of Anne Lindbergh's fiction includes time travel or fantasy. *The People in Pineapple Place* has a Washington, D.C., locale and involves a ten-year-old boy who slips back in time while exploring a neighborhood after moving there. *School Library Journal* calls *Bailey's Window* "an engaging fantasy full of magic and mischief with a solid base of reality," calling the dialogue natural with a generous sprinkling of humor. *Booklist* calls *The Hunky-Dory Dairy* "a lightweight fantasy with strong appeal" and comments, "her character portrayals, sense of dialogue, and background detail are smoothly accomplished and diverting."

SELECTED WORKS: The People in Pineapple Place, 1982; Nobody's Orphan, 1983; Bailey's Window, 1984; The Worry Week, 1985; The Hunky-Dory Dairy, 1986; The Shadow on the Dial, 1987; Next Time, Take Care, 1988; The Prisoner of Pineapple Place, 1988.

SELECTED WORKS WRITTEN AS ANNE LINDBERGH FEYDY: Osprey Island, 1974.

ABOUT: Contemporary Authors, Vol. 113; Vol. 115; Something About the Author, Vol. 35; Washington Post Magazine February 6, 1983; Washington Post March 18, 1983.

BARBRO LINDGREN

March 18, 1937–

AUTHOR OF *The Wild Baby*, etc.

Autobiographical sketch of Barbro Lindgren:

I WAS BORN in Stockholm, where I still live. After senior high school I studied art at Konstfackskolan for five years.

When I was a child there were three things that absorbed me: music, art, and literature. I played the piano and sang, I drew and painted, and I wrote a lot of novels and poems as soon as I had learnt how to spell. Well, I had yet another interest—nature. Nature has always been an inspiration to me in my painting as well as in my writing. For a long time it seemed as if art should be my profession as I found it easier than writing. It was much more difficult to write really well—the way I wanted it to be.

In 1959 I married a friend from art school, and it was when I expected our first child (we now have two grown-up boys) that I decided to make a last effort at writing, and I said to myself: If this fails, I'll never try writing again . . .

I tried to write about sorrow and death and complicated love affairs, but even I myself could see that it was no good. And I felt it was too early for me to write about such things, when I had no experience of them yet. . . . So I started to write about things I really knew about instead. And the only thing I knew anything about was my childhood! When I had written a few chapters I sent them to Rabén & Sjögren, where Astrid Lindgren was children's books editor at that time. She answered my letter and gave me a lot of good advice, because, as she wrote: "There is something in your writ-

ing that rings true. But in writing you have to follow certain rules if you want people to read your books!"

I followed her advice and the next year my first book was published (1965). Since then I have been writing all the time, and it is obvious that I express myself much better in writing than in painting, so I continue writing prose and poetry for children and grown-ups. I write about what I see and hear. About my life and what is happening all around. I have a feeling that I am always "pinching" from reality and then I re-make it in my own way. Humour is very important, I think, in literature, for children as well as for grown-ups. I want to make the language full of music (instead of playing the piano, I guess).

I often write about people who are different in some way or another, people who cannot easily manage in this hard world. Deep in my heart I am fighting and writing for the weak, I guess, against oppression of any kind.

I like Mozart and stuffed cabbage rolls and tracks of wild birds and I always write by hand.

———

Barbro Lindgren has been a commercial artist and designer. She has received the Expressens Heffaklump, the Astrid Lindgren Prize, and the Nils Holgersson Plaque in Sweden for her work.

SELECTED WORKS: Hilding's Summer, 1967; Let's Be Gorillas!, 1976; The Wild Baby, 1981; Sam's Car, 1982; Sam's Cookie, 1982; Sam's Teddy Bear, 1982; Sam's Ball, 1983; Sam's Bath, 1983; Sam's Lamp, 1983; The Wild Baby Goes to Sea, 1983; A Worm's Tale, 1988.

ABOUT: Something About the Author, Vol. 46.

JANET TAYLOR LISLE

February 13, 1947–

AUTHOR OF *Sirens and Spies*, etc.

Autobiographical sketch of Janet Taylor Lisle:

I GREW UP in Farmington, Connecticut, the eldest and the only girl in a family of five children. My brothers ranged in age from two to fifteen years younger than I. They ranged in temperament from pacifist to warlord, and displayed in general such differing personalities that I believe I must have taken up my role as "compromiser" and "neutral observer" early on. Questions of who was right and who was wrong, what was true and what was false, who did this, and who said that, arose daily in our house, and being oldest, I was often visited by the necessity of making up solutions, if only for a little peace and quiet.

Later, I went away from home to a girls' boarding school. When I had finished high school there, I went on to college and, except for holidays and vacations, never really lived at home again. But my sense of being an eye at the center of the storm, of being a watcher and a listener to many voices, stayed with me. In college, I was a good essay-writer but a bad debater. I could deftly describe the arguments surrounding an issue. When it came to taking sides, to speaking out powerfully for one position over

another, I grew muddled and weak. These were days in which the Vietnam war was underway, and political feeling ran high in nearly all of my friends. There were moments when I, too, was electrified by what seemed to be one crystal-clear view of events. Then I would march in an antiwar rally or participate in a hunger strike. I would argue hotly during a lunch-hour conversation. All too often, though, I found myself beginning to see the opposition's point of view. Yes, that was true, I'd admit. Well, yes, I could see how that might be understood. And so, before long, my strong opinions were eroded and I was back to watching, listening. Wishy-washy, incapable of firm conviction, I thought I was by the time I graduated from Smith College in 1969, a disappointment especially since Smith was particularly noted for sharpening women's minds.

After college, I moved to Atlanta, Georgia, to become a member of VISTA (Volunteers in Service to America), a federally funded corps of young professionals hired to work in low-income American neighborhoods. There I helped set up food-buying cooperatives in the city's public housing projects, and heard an array of new voices.

Lisle: *LYLE*

By 1971, I was a journalism student at Georgia State University, and a year later I went to work for local newspapers, a trained observer now, a listener with a tape recorder in my pocket and an ability to take notes at lightening speed. It was the beginning of a reporting career that lasted ten years and taught me a great deal about writing.

One thing journalism couldn't teach me was how to write fiction. I'd been one of the book-enthralled as a child, and a fiction junkie at college masquerading under the respectable title of "English Major." I still read daily and, as I typed my news articles, I couldn't resist trying out a bit of "voice" here, a whimsical pause there. I moved away from news reporting into the less fact-driven "human interest" or "feature" story. But even features didn't give me enough room for the different styles of writing I suddenly needed to practice, or for the wider subject matter I wanted.

After thirty years of listening, I still wasn't attracted by the sound of a particular voice, but the idea of inventing scenes in which arguments might occur, the idea of seeing over the heads of individuals to broader views of life, rang wonderful bells in my head. At this point, I began writing stories and novels seriously. I've been lucky enough to publish my work, four novels for children so far.

———

Janet Taylor Lisle is married and has a daughter. *Sirens and Spies* was named an American Library Association Notable Book of 1985 as well as an ALA Best Book for Young Adults of 1985. *The Great Dimpole Oak* was an Honor Book in the 1987 Golden Kite Awards.

SELECTED WORKS: The Dancing Cats of Applesap, 1984; Sirens and Spies, 1985; The Great Dimpole Oak, 1987; Afternoon of the Elves, 1989.

ABOUT: Horn Book November/December 1988; Something About the Author, Vol. 47.

THOMAS LOCKER

1937–

AUTHOR AND ILLUSTRATOR OF *Where the River Begins*, etc.

Biographical sketch of Thomas Locker:

ALREADY a painter of note who had exhibited widely in the United States and Europe when his first children's book was published in 1984, Thomas Locker garnered immediate recognition for the sweeping pastoral scenes that filled *Where the River Begins*. Unmistakably influenced by ninetheenth-century European Romanticism and the American Hudson River School, Locker's work offers vast, idealized landscapes that dwarf the people, animals, and objects that move through them. *Where the River Begins*—the story of the quest of two young boys and their grandfather for the source of the river on which they live—was followed quickly by *The Mare on the Hill* and *Sailing with the Wind*. The former follows the efforts of the two boys from Locker's first book as they attempt over the course of a year to befriend a skittish mare. The latter is the story of a young girl's day-long journey with her uncle down the river near her house to the sea and back.

Critics were virtually unanimous in their praise for Locker's lush landscapes, and all three books received awards for excellence: *Where the River Begins* was named a *New York Times* Best Illustrated Book of 1984 and an Outstanding Science Trade Book for Children of 1984 by a joint committee of the National Science Teachers Association and the Children's Book Council, *The Mare on the Hill* received Honorable Mention at the Bologna Book Fair, *Sailing with the Wind* was an American Institute of Graphic Arts Book in 1987 and a Reading Rainbow book.

Betsy Hearne, writing in the *Bulletin of the Center for Children's Books*, displayed sentiment common to many reviews when she observed, "The paintings . . . set a

Thomas Locker

monumental tone. . . . The overall vision is of an America the Beautiful, with sweeping natural panoramas untouched by factory or highway. That perspective at once moves and stills a viewer of any age." Ethel L. Heins, writing in the *Horn Book*, said of Locker's work, "Its limpid beauty and exquisite detail are—to paraphrase Emerson—their own excuse for being. Reminiscent of the work of great landscape painters, like Turner, Constable, and the American George Inness. . . . "

While many reviewers reveled in the beauty of Locker's settings, some of those same reviewers questioned its ultimate appeal for children. Specifically, many critics expressed concern over Locker's treatment of the characters in his illustrations, fearing that children would not be able to identify with the tiny, stiff people that he typically paints. The texts of Locker's works created some problems for reviewers as well. Amanda J. Williams noted in *School Library Journal* that "the text seems stiff and slightly stilted at times, and the language never rises to the level of the illustrations. . . . " However, other critics felt that Locker's quiet texts provided the perfect counterpoint for his dazzling illustrations.

Locker's latest works seem destined to evoke similiar praise and criticism. In *Family Farm*, the illustrator moves his setting from the Northeast to the Midwest to depict life on a struggling farm. In *Booklist*, Denise M. Wilms found "Locker's trademark landscape paintings still dominate and are as lovely as ever, but he's also showing skill with smaller scale views. The story's main characters, seen at close range, are drawn quite successfully. . . . The book won a 1989 Christopher Award.

In addition to the five works he has both written and illustrated, Locker illustrated Marianna Mayer's adaptation of Hans Christian Andersen's *The Ugly Duckling*, and a retelling of a Dutch tale, *The Boy Who Held Back the Sea*.

SELECTED WORKS WRITTEN AND ILLUSTRATED: Where the River Begins, 1984; The Mare on the Hill, 1985; Sailing with the Wind, 1986; Family Farm, 1988; Rip Van Winkle, 1988.

SELECTED WORKS ILLUSTRATED: The Ugly Duckling, by Hans Christian Andersen, adapted by Marianna Mayer, 1986; The Boy Who Held Back the Sea, retold by Lenny Hort, 1987.

ABOUT: Children's Literature Review, Vol. 14; Sutherland, Zena and May Hill Arbuthnot, eds. Children and Books, 7th ed.

BETTE BAO LORD

November 3, 1938–

AUTHOR OF *In the Year of the Boar and Jackie Robinson*, etc.

Biographical sketch of Bette Bao Lord:

BETTE BAO LORD was born in Shanghai, China, in 1938. Her father was a Kuomintang official, which provided her the life of an upper-class Chinese. In 1946 she emigrated with her family to the United States, when her father was assigned a tour of duty there. She graduated from Tufts University in 1959 and received a master's degree from the Fletcher School of Law and Diplo-

BETTE BAO LORD

macy in 1960. She became a naturalized citizen of the U.S. in 1964.

Lord's younger sister stayed behind in China with relatives, and it was not until sixteen years later, when the Communists won the Chinese civil war, that she was able to join her family in the U.S. *Eighth Moon: The True Story of a Young Girl's Life*, Lord's first book, chronicled her sister's life in China and her reunion with the family. Co-written with her sister, it was published for adults in 1974 and was translated into several foreign languages.

Lord was Assistant to the Director of the East-West Cultural Exchange in Hawaii from 1961 to 1962. She was Program Officer for the Fulbright Exchange Program for Senior Scholars from 1962 to 1963. From 1964 to 1973, Lord taught and performed modern dance in Geneva and Washington, D.C. During that time, she was also Conference Director of the National Conference for the Associated Councils of the Arts, from 1970 to 1971.

Lord's husband, Winston Lord, is former Ambassador to the People's Republic of China, and in 1973, when he was principal advisor to Henry Kissinger during the China opening, she returned to her native land.

Her reunion with her relatives gave her the idea for her best-selling book for adults, *Spring Moon: A Novel of China*. The story tells of the events between 1892, when the Chinese empire is crumbling, to 1972, when the revolution is complete. She describes through the eyes of nine-year-old Spring Moon the household of a centuries-old clan of scholar-landowners: their rituals, beliefs, Confucian conformity, devotion to family, and the roles ancestors still play in contemporary China. The book was nominated for a 1982 American Book Award and was translated into twenty languages. It was a main selection of the Literary Guild and will be made into a motion picture.

Lord then wrote a children's book based on her experiences when she came to America. She writes about why she produced the book *In the Year of the Boar and Jackie Robinson*: She wanted to remember "the fun and the fright of being a Chinese Immigrant dumped into the fifth grade at P.S. 8 [a New York City public school] without speaking a word of English, without knowing another soul."

In the novel, Shirley Temple Wong is the girl who is misunderstood because she makes good grades. After an encounter with a school bully, Mabel, who then invites her to play stickball, the Chinese girl enters a whole new world. Shirley develops Dodger fever with a vengeance. Later that school year, she presents the key to P.S. 8 to Jackie Robinson. Through it all, Shirley remembers her relatives in China as her own family celebrates the traditional Chinese holidays as well as American ones. As the birth of another child in the family approaches, she realizes the importance of passing on the Chinese language and traditions. The book was named a 1984 Notable Book by the American Library Association. It also won the 1985 Jefferson Cup Award from the Virginia Library Association.

Lord has received two honorary doctorates, in Humanities in 1985 from Notre Dame University, and in Letters from Tufts in 1982. She received the Woman of the Year Award from Chinatown Planning Council in 1982. She is a member of the Council on Foreign Relations, of P.E.N., and of the Authors Guild. She is also a board member of the Asia Foundation and the President's Council of the Asia Society.

Like Shirley, Lord and her family enjoy the heritage of two cultures.

SELECTED WORKS: In the Year of the Boar and Jackie Robinson, 1984.

ABOUT: Contemporary Authors, Vol. 197; New York Times Book Review October 25, 1981; New Yorker November 23, 1981; Publishers Weekly October 30, 1981.

ALICE LOW

June 5, 1926–

AUTHOR OF *The Macmillan Book of Greek Gods and Heroes*, etc.

Autobiographical sketch of Alice Low:

I GREW UP in New York City surrounded by "the arts" and people in them. I was imaginative and creative, but it took a while before I realized that writing would be my vocation.

My mother wrote children's books, and her friends included artists, writers, editors, and musicians. There were shelves of books, too. My favorites were the beautiful limited editions. I was too young to read them, but pored over the illustrations, fine paper, and print. I liked children's books, but I wasn't a real bookworm. That came after college. It was the illustrations that drew me to books.

At Birch Wathen School I adored singing and was "talented" in art. I loved making books in lower school—simple ones at first. I sketched Queen Nefertiti at the Metropolitan Museum for my Egypt book and made a newspaper called *Goings On on Mountown Olympus* for Greece. I still have my sixth-grade book on artists of the Middle

Ages. I block printed the endpapers, made a velvet cover, and bound the parchment pages that I'd decorated. I was going to be an artist!

Then came A.A. Milne's poems, the Benéts' *A Book of Americans*, and best of all, Gilbert and Sullivan. I knew almost all the words and still do. I wrote light verse for every occasion and lyrics for shows at Smith College, where I majored in art and minored in English. I would be an artist *and* a lyricist!

Then, because I loved children, I taught school. I wrote the story and lyrics for a children's musical, put on by my class. I wanted to write lyrics for children's records, and later I did.

My first children's book was inspired by my young nephew, who kept packing to go on a trip. I sent the rhyming ms. to Little Golden Records, but Little Golden *Books* published it. After my first child was born, they published another, based on what my son, Andy, saw out the window. More books in verse and poems were published by Random House and Pantheon.

My three children inspired other books such as *All Through the Town*, based on doing errands with them. But more than that, my children jogged my memory of my own childhood feelings, which I drew on repeatedly. *The Witch Who Was Afraid of Witches* reflected my feelings of being the younger sister, and my novel for girls, *Kallie's Corner*, enabled me to live vicariously in a Greenwich Village house with stairs and a back yard.

I studied short-story writing at Columbia University and gained a sense of freedom, scribbling a first draft from the subconscious, letting the characters take over, seldom knowing where they would lead me. I still write this way, though it means many drafts—finding the buried story, reshaping and cutting. This combination of freedom and control makes writing very satisfying.

Seventeen accepted two of my short stories, and my book of short stories for young adults, *At Jasper's House*, was published soon after.

I have written books for every age, depending on the characters and the ideas that come with them. I write mainly fiction because I am interested in people and their feelings, *and* I like to tell a good story. Why do I write about witches sometimes? Probably because with witches, anything can happen. Each book is an exploration, both difficult and exhilarating.

I have also reviewed children's books for the *New York Times*, been editor of Children's Choice Book Club and edited reading programs, taught creative writing, critiqued for publishers, and researched, written, and produced filmstrips. Now I am working on two anthologies for children.

Thank goodness I didn't major in math, as one college interviewer suggested!

———

Alice Low received her B.A. degree from Smith College in 1947. She was married March 25, 1949. She is a member of P.E.N. American Center, The Society of Children's Book Writers, the Authors Guild of Authors League of America, and the American Society of Composers, Authors, and Publishers. *The Macmillan Book of Greek Gods and*

Heroes was named a Literary Guild selection. *Greek Gods* was also named a 1985 Notable Children's Trade Book in the Field of Social Studies by a joint committee of the National Council on the Social Studies and the Children's Book Council. *The Witch Who Was Afraid of Witches* was made into an animated film by the Learning Corporation of America. *Herbert's Treasure* was a Junior Literary Guild selection.

SELECTED WORKS: Summer, 1963; At Jasper's House, 1968; Kallie's Corner, 1978; Herbert's Treasure, 1971; David's Windows, 1974; The Witch Who Was Afraid of Witches, 1978; Genie and the Witch's Spells, 1982; All Around the Farm, 1984; All Through the Town, 1984; The Macmillan Book of Greek Gods and Heroes, 1985; Who Lives in the Sea, 1987.

ABOUT: Contemporary Authors Vol. 61-64; (New Revision Series), Vol. 8; Something About the Author, Vol. 11.

JANET LUNN

December 28, 1928–

AUTHOR OF *The Root Cellar*, etc.

Autobiographical sketch of Janet Lunn:

I WAS BORN in Dallas, Texas. We lived in Texas for six more months, then moved back north where our family had come from. We lived in Norwich, Vermont, until I was ten years old. Although I lived in Hillier, Ontario, Canada, and I have lived in Vancouver, Toronto, and the suburbs of New York City, I still belong to Vermont in a lot of ways. The hills in *Shadow in Hawthorn Bay* are, for me, as much those Vermont hills as they are the Highlands of Scotland. And my picture book, *Amos's Sweater*, is actually about an old Norwich sheep. That countryside manages to find its way, somehow, into everything I write.

As for writing, I have always been a storyteller. My mother, father, and much later, my husband all declared I had an overactive imagination. I think I began making up stories from the moment I could talk. I

Janet Lunn [signature]

don't believe anyone considered my unceasing chatter about what I heard in the brook or saw in the trees or on the hills as leading to a career as a writer anymore than they did my compulsion to read everything the Norwich Library could provide. They were grateful, of course, that I could read, as I was a bit slow getting started at it. I don't suppose they would have been delighted, though, to learn that, as a result of the stories I was reading, I was planning to travel back in time and hunt the Psammead when I grew up. I have never found the Psammead but I have managed to go back in time in three of my books (and a planned fourth).

I graduated from high school in Montclair, New Jersey, in 1946 and started university at Queen's in Kingston, Ontario—Canada seemed such an exotic country to me in those days. There I met Richard Lunn (he sat behind me in first-year English) and got married instead of completing my degree. Sometimes I think about going back to finish it but, every time I do, another book demands to be written and I do that instead.

We had five children in rapid succession. Eric was born in 1950, Jeffrey, in 1951, Alec

in 1953, Kate in 1956 and John in 1958. I loved raising children. Our household was the kind children from small families loved to visit. "All the bodies eat there," a small boy told his mother indignantly one day when she insisted that he come home for dinner. Another said to me admiringly, "Something's always happening here!"

In and around all the bodies and the happenings I began to write. I wrote stories and articles for magazines, I wrote reviews of children's books for newspapers and radio and, in 1968, I published my first book. I was almost forty years old. I am a timid person, and I think my late start at book writing is like my early approach to swimming. All one day I watched my sisters and my brother and friends splash about in the lake. At about four in the afternoon, when everyone else was tired and ready to go home, I had worked up the courage to put my toe in the water. But now my toe has gotten wet, so to speak, I find I love the exercise and I mean to go on writing until I have run out of stories to tell.

My husband died in 1987. I live with my stories and two cats in the old farmhouse I wrote about in *The Root Cellar* beside the bay I have called Hawthorn Bay in two books. Sometimes I still miss the hills of Vermont, but I have lived in Lake Ontario country for almost forty years. I am at home here, now. I have hitched my imagination and my stories to this landscape.

———

Janet Lunn married in 1950. She spent three years at Queen's University, Kingston, Ontario, from 1947 to 1950. With her husband, she co-wrote a history of Prince Edward County, Ontario. She also writes short stories, magazine articles, book reviews, and radio talks and interviews. She has been an editor and a literary consultant for school readers, and has conducted writers' workshops with the Ontario Arts Council. She was writer-in-residence at the Regina Public Library, 1982-1983, and is currently writer-in-residence at the Kitchener Public

Library. Janet Lunn is a member of the Writer's Union of Canada, of which she was chair, 1984-1985; and of the Canadian Society of Children's Authors, Illustrators, and Performers; and of P.E.N. International.

The Twelve Dancing Princesses was named one of the ten best children's books of 1979 by the Canadian Library Association. *The Root Cellar* and *Shadow in Hawthorn Bay* were each named Canadian Library Association Books of the Year in their year of publication. *The Root Cellar* was named a Notable Book of 1983 by the American Library Association, was named a Outstanding Science Trade Book for Children by a joint committee of the National Science Teachers Association and the Children's Book Council, and was on the Honour List of the International Board on Books for Young People in 1984. *Shadow* received the 1986 Canada Council Award for children's literature. Lunn received the Vicky Metcalf Award for her body of work in 1981.

SELECTED WORKS: Twin Spell, 1968; The Twelve Dancing Princesses, 1979; The Root Cellar, 1983; Shadow in Hawthorn Bay, 1987.

ABOUT: Canadian Who's Who, 1985; Contemporary Authors (First Revision), Vol. 33; Horn Book December 1969; McDonough, Irma, ed. Profiles; Something About the Author, Vol. 4; Toye, William, ed. The Oxford Companion to Canadian Literature; Who's Who in American Women, 1975-1976; Who's Who in Canadian Literature, 1985-1986.

SUSE MacDONALD

March 3, 1940–

AUTHOR AND ILLUSTRATOR OF *Alphabatics,* etc.

Autobiographical sketch of Susan Kelsey MacDonald, who writes under the pen name "Suse MacDonald":

I CAN'T REMEMBER when I first knew that I was an artist, because it was something that happened gradually.

Suse: rhymes with *news*

I grew up in Glencoe, Illinois. My father was a professor at Northwestern University. My mother was a writer. We spent summers on an old farm in Weston, Vermont. My first art teacher was Churchill Ettinger, a Vermont artist who showed me how to visually transfer and translate the world before me to my paper. I can't remember how long I studied with him but by the time I entered college, I knew that art would be a focus in my life.

Since both of the colleges I attended were liberal arts schools, the courses offered were in the fine arts. No one talked about commercial art. It was considered a waste of one's talents.

I didn't think much about all that then. I just took courses: life drawing, painting, printmaking, ceramics. I even made sculptures out of car parts. Nothing I tried felt quite right. I knew I was an artist but where did I fit?

After college, I married, and my husband Stuart and I settled in New York City. I decided to find a job using my artistic talents. After a number of interviews, I contacted Charles Halgren at Caru Studios and discovered that he hired artists to illustrate textbooks from time to time. That sounded like the perfect job for me, so I called him every two weeks for the next nine months. Finally, a new biology book came in and I was employed to do pen-and-ink illustrations for it.

I stayed at Caru for five years. It was a wonderful time. The studio employed thirty artists, photographers, draftsmen, and even typesetters (This was before computers, and type was set by hand.). I learned all about the commercial side of art and discovered what a fascinating world it was.

Then my husband and I moved back to the family farm in Weston, Vermont, and took over a construction company. Our move came at a time when I was beginning to feel a lack of growth in my work. I'd done illustrations for all kinds of science texts and was uncertain what to do next. So I was enthusiastic about our move and our new business. I did some office work and architectural design work and drafting, and we raised two children.

However, as time went on, I needed new challenges. Somehow I was off the track. When my second child entered first grade, the time had come to quit my job and return to school. At first I thought I would become an architect. I was good at architectural design and as an architect I could continue to contribute to our business.

I looked around, found the Boston Architectural Center and went down for an interview. While I was visiting a class on that first evening, I realized very suddenly (it was like being hit by lightning) that it was not architecture that interested me, it was illustration. So my search continued, but now I was looking at art schools.

I enrolled in two schools, the New England School of Art and Design and the Art Institute. By taking courses at both, I was able to organize three days of classes each week.

After I began my studies my focus shifted. I no longer wanted to draw things just as they were, I wanted to look at them in new ways: to abstract them. Bill Oakes, one of my teachers, gave me lots of encourage-

ment in this new direction. He wanted his students to question and get away from thinking in preconceived ways. As I studied with him my work began to change.

I also enrolled in Marion Parry's class in children's book writing and illustration at Radcliffe. It was in that seminar that I really became involved in children's books and decided that was where I wanted to concentrate my energies.

After I completed my studies in Boston, I took my portfolio with a variety of picture and story ideas to New York for appointments with editors and art directors at publishing houses. I had a total of forty-seven interviews over a three-year period. I kept offering different ideas and suggestions for books. None was taken. But the situation changed with *Alphabatics*.

I showed the illustrations for just three letters, A, B, and E, to Bradbury Press, a Macmillan imprint. The idea was accepted, and my career as a children's book illustrator began.

Alphabatics is an idea that came to me while taking topography in art school. In the course, I worked exclusively with letter forms, shrinking and expanding them and manipulating their shapes in various ways. I was intrigued by the process and felt there were possibilities for a book. However, it was several years before I worked out the idea.

Publishing this book, my first, was very exciting. I love the picture-book format and feel it offers me challenging opportunities for creative illustration.

My next two books, done in collaboration with Bill Oakes, evidence my interest in challenging the minds of young people and my belief that books can change how one sees the world.

————

Suse MacDonald attended Chatham College from 1958 to 1960 and completed her B.F.A. degree at the State University of Iowa in 1962. She was married July 14, 1962. *Alphabatics* was designated a 1987

Caldecott Honor Book by the American Library Association. It also won the 1987 Golden Kite Award for Illustration, given by the Society of Children's Book Writers. It was named a Notable Trade Book in 1987 by the National Council of Teachers of English, a Junior Literary Guild selection, and a Notable Book of 1986 by the ALA.

Selected Works Written and Illustrated: Alphabatics, 1986; Numblers, 1988; Puzzlers, 1989.

About: Something About the Author, Vol. 54.

PATRICIA MacLACHLAN

March 3, 1938–

Author of *Sarah, Plain, and Tall*, etc.

Biographical sketch of Patricia MacLachlan:

ALTHOUGH Patricia MacLachlan didn't officially put pen to paper until the age of thirty-five—after her three children were all in school—her Cheyenne, Wyoming, childhood was heavily populated with stories and storybook characters. Her parents, she writes, invited her into books. "We read them, discussed them, reread them, and acted out the parts. I can still feel the goose bumps as I, in the fur of Peter Rabbit, fled from the garden and Mr. McGregor— played with great ferocity by my father— to the coat closet." Like Minna in her novel *The Facts and Fictions of Minna Pratt*, Patricia MacLachlan also loved music, and lessons filled the agenda as well.

After spending a few years in Minnesota, she traveled to the East Coast to attend the University of Connecticut. She subsequently married psychologist Robert MacLachlan and had three children. From the very beginning her family has always come before anything else. For some time she also served on the board of a family agency, where her contributions included writing a series of journalistic pieces concerning adoption and foster mothers.

PATRICIA MacLACHLAN

Clearly this concern for families and for children has shaped Patricia MacLachlan's writing career. One of her earliest books, *Mama One, Mama Two*, focuses on a foster mother. That interest, she has stated, combined with a strong commitment to literature for children, compelled her to begin writing children's books. In an article in *The New York Times Book Review*, MacLachlan comments that she writes "as a participant, to see what will happen. . . . I see that I write books about brothers and sisters, about what makes up a family, what works and what is nurturing." Before her first title, *The Sick Day*, appeared in 1979, she was voraciously reading thirty to forty children's books per week.

That first title appeared in 1977 and was followed by a number of other books in rapid succession—nearly one a year, in fact, and most of them do involve families in one way or another. They also, as she freely admits in an article for *The Horn Book*, frequently include autobiographical elements: "Like Cassie [in her novel *Cassie Binegar*] I spent hours in hidden places listening to conversations I was not meant to hear. . . . I do know . . . that Aunt Elda and Uncle Wrisby in *Arthur, For the Very First time* are my mother and father."

Then, in 1985 Harper & Row published what *Booklist* called "a near-perfect miniature novel" and what *The New York Times* termed "the simplest of love stories expressed in the simplest of prose." MacLachlan's *Sarah, Plain and Tall*, fifty-six pages of nearly flawless prose, is simple enough to be understood by younger readers and yet has also earned a large and devoted audience among older readers and adults. In 1986 the book received the John Newbery Medal from the American Library Association. The title grew, as MacLachlan revealed in her Newbery acceptance speech, "out of the heroics of a common life"—the ideas emerging from an incident in her family's history and the impetus for writing the book coming from a trip that she, her husband, and her children took to the prairies where she had been born. The novel itself is set on the prairie during the nineteenth century, as a young girl describes how a mail-order bride from Maine came to live with her and her brother and widowed father. It is written in the same gentle, quietly touching and humorous style that characterizes MacLachlan's writing in general.

Sarah, Plain and Tall, perhaps not surprinsingly, has captured numerous other awards and honors, among them the 1985 Scott O'Dell Award for Historical Fiction for Children, the 1986 Christopher Award, the 1986 Jefferson Cup Award of the Virginia Library Association, and the 1985 Golden Kite Award for fiction.

But her popularity and critical acclaim have scarcely been limited to *Sarah, Plain and Tall*. A string of awards and honors winds throughout the MacLachlan canon: *Unclaimed Treasures* was named both a 1984 Boston Globe-Horn Book Honor Book for fiction and an ALA Notable Children's Book for 1984; *Arthur, For the Very First Time* earned a 1980 Golden Kite Award for fiction from the Society of Children's Book Writers along with a place on the 1980 ALA list of Notable Books. *Through Grandpa's Eyes*, a Reading Rainbow book, and *Mama One, Mama Two* both were named Notable Children's Trade Books in The Field of Social Studies by the National Council on the Social Studies and the Children's Book Council in their years of publication. *The Facts and Fictions of Minna Pratt* followed *Sarah, Plain Tall* chronologically, and, as a *New York Times* review points out, any book coming on the heels of a Newberry winner is bound to be compared with the earlier work. Yet this title survived the test with flying colors, receiving starred reviews and making an appearance on ALA's 1988 list of Notable Children's Books.

In addition to writing and lecturing, Patricia MacLachlan teaches a course in children's literature at Smith College and lectures frequently to adult audiences throughout Massachusetts. She lives with her family in Massachusetts, moving back and forth between their 1793 saltbox home in Leeds and a second house on Cape Cod—"juggling," as Natallie Babbitt so adroitly stated in an article about her in *The Horn Book*, "various roles as wife, mother, and writer with grace but, thank goodness, without any annoying symptoms of 'Super-Momism'."

SELECTED WORKS: The Sick Day, 1979; Through Grandpa's Eyes, 1980; Arthur, For the Very First Time, 1980; Moon Stars, Frogs, and Friends, 1980; Mama One, Mama Two, 1982; Tomorrow's Wizard, 1982; Cassie Binegar, 1982; Seven Kisses in a Row, 1983; Unclaimed Treasures, 1984; Sarah, Plain and Tall, 1985; The Facts and Fictions of Minna Pratt, 1988

ABOUT: Contemporary Authors, Vol. 118; The Horn Book Magazine, January/February 1986; July/August 1986; New York Times Book Review June 29, 1986; Something About the Author, Vol. 42.

BETSY MAESTRO

January 5, 1944–

AUTHOR OF *Harriet Goes to the Circus*, etc.

Biographical sketch of Betsy Maestro:

BETSY MAESTRO was born in Brooklyn,

New York. Her involvement with children's books harkens back to her own childhood, when her mother taught nursery school and filled their home with books of all kinds. During her years at Southern Connecticut State College she worked as a student teacher in a nursery school. She pursued an early childhood education degree, receiving a B.S. degree in 1964 and a M.S. degree in Elementary Guidance in 1970. She taught kindergarten and first grade in the East Haven, Connecticut schools for eleven years.

Through the years Maestro had many ideas for children's books, but says she never got around to writing them. When she married her second husband, Giulio Maestro, in 1972, they began to collaborate on books. He was an established writer and illustrator of children's books, and she found this an opportunity to start working on children's books. By 1986 they had published thirty books together.

Her specialty is writing nonfiction books for young children. Some teach specific concepts. For example, her book *Traffic* focuses on a magenta car that goes under, over, left, right, etc. to teach the idea of opposites. *On the Town: A Book of Clothing Words* shows the outfits worn by a man and

elephant for a day of activities that includes swimming, tennis, and sleep.

The Story of the Statue of Liberty, about the planning, modeling, and erecting of the Statue of Liberty, was written for children between the ages of three and eight. The author wanted to bring the statue to life so that young readers could fit it into a larger historical picture later. A second historical book, *A More Perfect Union: The Story of Our Constitution*, was written so that young readers all across America would understand the bicentennial celebration in 1976.

Betsy Maestro feels lucky to be able to enjoy her work so much. She likes to get positive comments from teachers and librarians as well as from the children when she and her husband, Giulio, visit schools. Picture books are a passion with her; her house is "filled to the brim" with them; Maestro is a member of the Connecticut and the National Education Associations.

Harriet Goes to the Circus was named a 1978 Children's Choice Book by a joint committee of the Children's Book Council and the International Reading Association. *Ferryboat* was named a 1986 Notable Children's Trade Book in the Field of Social Studies by a joint committee of the CBC and the National Council on the Social Studies. Both *Where Is My Friend?* and *Ferryboat* were Junior Literary Guild selections. The American Library Association named *Traffic* and *A More Perfect Union* Notable Books, in 1981 and 1987 respectively.

SELECTED WORKS: Where Is My Friend?: A Word Concept Book, 1976; Harriet Goes to the Circus: A Number Concept Book, 1977; Harriet Reads Signs and More Signs: A Word Concept Book, 1981; Traffic: A Book of Opposites, 1981; On the Town: A Book of Clothing Words, 1983; Harriet at Play, 1984; Camping Out: A Book of Action Words, 1985; Ferryboat, 1986; The Story of the Statue of Liberty, 1986; A More Perfect Union: The Story of Our Constitution, 1987; Taxi: A Book of City Words, 1989.

ABOUT: Contemporary Authors, Vol. 61; (New Revision Series), Vol. 8; Shaw, John Mackay. Childhood in Poetry, 2nd supplement; Something About the Author, Vol. 30; Who's Who in American Art, 1984; The Writers Directory 1980-82.

GIULIO MAESTRO

May 6, 1942–

ILLUSTRATOR OF *The Story of the Statue of Liberty*, etc.

Biographical sketch of Giulio Maestro:

GIULIO MAESTRO was born in and grew up in Greenwich Village in New York City. He always liked to draw and knew as a child that he would be an artist when he grew up. His first ambition was to be a cartoonist like Walt Disney or Walt Kelly, creator of the comic strip Pogo. He attended the Little Red School House, Elisabeth Irwin High School, and the High School of Music and Art. At The Cooper Union School of Art, where he received a B.F.A. degree in 1964, and at Pratt Graphics Center, he studied design, lettering, painting, and printmaking. After graduating he spent five years, from 1964 to 1969, in the advertising field, designing promotional materials such as brochures, mailers, and advertisements, as well as record album covers, menus, games, and product packages.

In 1969 Maestro became a free-lance artist, illustrating book jackets, trade books, school textbooks, and primarily books for children. Many of his books and illustrations have been exhibited by the New York Society of Illustrators, the American Institute of Graphic Arts, and the Art Directors Club of New York. His first picture book illustrated was published in 1969, and since then he has illustrated over a hundred books.

Maestro has worked on many books with his wife Betsy Maestro, whom he married in 1972. He painted the brightly colored illustrations in the Harriet board books series, for example, and used watercolors to record the creation of the Statue of Liberty for young children in *The Story of the Statue of Liberty*. In another nonfiction book for young children, *A More Perfect Union*, Maestro painted historically accurate watercolors to capture the spirit of the Found-

ing Fathers and the times. He feels children are visual learners, so he tried to do this two ways: by making the scenes of the delegates very concrete and by communicating extra information about the era in the street scenes, which do not have any descriptive text.

In addition to painting, Giulio Maestro enjoys reading and traveling, which he has done extensively in Europe since childhood.

Harriet Goes to the Circus was named a 1978 Children's Choice Book by a joint committee of the International Reading Association and the Children's Book Council. *Moonkey* received the same distinction in 1982. *Ferryboat* was named a 1986 Notable Children's Trade Book in the Field of Social Studies by a joint committee of the CBC and the National Council on the Social Studies. *Where Is My Friend?* and *Ferryboat* were named Junior Literary Guild selections. The American Library Association named *Traffic* and *A More Perfect Union* Notable Books, in 1981 and 1987 respectively.

SELECTED WORKS ILLUSTRATED: The Beginning of the Armadillos, by Rudyard Kipling, 1970; Three Kittens, translated by Mirra Ginsburg, 1973; Where Is My Friend?: A Word Concept Book, by Betsy Maestro,

Giulio: *JOO lee o*

1976; Harriet Goes to the Circus: A Number Concept Book, by Besty Maestro, 1977; Moonkey, by Mike Thaler, 1981; Traffic: A Book of Opposites, by Betsy Maestro, 1981; Train Whistles, by Helen Roney Sattler, 1985; Ferryboat, by Betsy Maestro,1986; The Story of the Statue of Liberty, by Betsy Maestro, 1986; A More Perfect Union: The Story of Our Constitution, by Betsy Maestro, 1987; The Beginning of the Earth, by Franklyn M. Branley, (rev. ed), 1988; Taxi: A Book of City Words, by Betsy Maestro, 1989.

ABOUT: Contemporary Authors, Vol. 57; Kingman, Lee and others, comps. Illustrators of Children's Books: 1967-1976; Something About the Author, Vol. 8; Who's Who in American Art, 1984; The Writers Directory 1980-82.

MICHELLE MAGORIAN

November 6, 1947–

AUTHOR OF *Good Night, Mr. Tom*, etc.

Biographical sketch of Michelle Magorian:

PORTSMOUTH, ENGLAND, was the birthplace of prize-winning novelist for young adults Michelle Magorian. Her childhood was spent in such faraway places as Singapore and Perth, Australia. She received a Diploma in Speech and Drama from Rose Branford College of Speech and Drama in 1969. She also received a certificate in Film Studies from London University in 1984. She was married in 1987 and lives in London, England.

Trained professionally as an actress, a dancer, and a teacher, Magorian has toured with British companies. She has also worked in repertory theater. In addition, she has expert training in the art of the mime. Her mime training was taken at the world-famous École Internationale de Mime in Paris where she studied for two years. This training facility is run by the noted French mime Marcel Marceau.

Writing has always been a spare-time activity for her. A song she heard during an appearance in a musical was the inspiration for a short story that soon led to other stories in which the characters of Willie Beech and old Tom Oakley began to take shape. In this short story, the main characters meet. Magorian has stated, "I had to know what happened—so I wrote the book." She persisted in her writing, quietly continuing to work on what was to become her novel *Good Morning, Mr. Tom*, but not telling anyone about it. She had already written for her theater company, coming up with original horror stories and plays.

Interested in attempting to write for children, she showed her manuscript to her writing teacher, the novelist Dulan Barber. He encouraged her to send the manuscript to a publisher.

Good Night, Mr. Tom was a smashing success, garnering awards both in England and in the United States. The theme of the novel is the healing that the two main characters bring to each other. Old, crotchety Tom Oakley, a reclusive man who has never recovered emotionally from the loss of his wife and child, reluctantly takes sickly Willie Beech into his home when children from London are evacuated into his village during World War II. It soon becomes apparent from the marks and bruises on his malnourished body that Willie is a victim of his mother's brutal abuse.

At first, the lonely and fearful child is terrified by everything about the unfamiliar country village, from Old Tom's aging dog to the farm animals. But with Tom's gentle care, he comes to learn that life can be different from his experience of beatings and harsh words. He finds friendship at school and, in the midst of friendship and love, learns to read and to draw, and learns not to fear.

His idyllic life with Old Tom is drawn swiftly to a close when a telegram from his mother summons him back to the squalor and nightmare of his London home. The terror of his life as he returns to his mother is powerfully drawn by Magorian. *The Bulletin of the Center for Children's Books* said, "The ending is tense, dramatic, believable, and satisfying, a happy ending to a touching story of love. Magorian uses dialogue and dialect well, giving local color as well as using them to establish character. Save for the reflection of the current interest in the problems of child abuse, this is an old-fashioned story with timeless appeal."

The New York Times stated, "The story's fascination lies in the genuine exultation we experience seeing a pitifully stunted and deprived human being blossom into a loving, trusting and capable young boy . . . Willie's sad but eventually triumphant story is told very effectively, with the stark matter-of-factness of a Grimms' fairy tale. Miss Magorian is a welcome new voice."

Good Night, Mr. Tom was the winner of the 1982 International Reading Association Children's Book Award. It was a 1982 American Library Association Notable Book, as well as a 1982 ALA Best Book for Young Adults. It won the British Guardian Award for Children's Literature in 1982 and was a "Commended book" the 1981 Carnegie Medal presentations.

Magorian published her second novel for young adults in 1984. *Back Home* introduces the character of Virginia Dickinson, who acquires the nickname "Rusty" when she spends five years in America, safe from the ravages of World War II England. The story centers on her adjustment as she returns home to her mother in England. Both mother and daughter must adjust to five years of different experiences. Rusty must adjust to a postwar England, rationing, a now-foreign school, and a once-passive mother who out of necessity has trained herself to be an expert mechanic. *School Library Journal* praised Magorian's portrayal of "the difficulty of empathetic communications between people of different cultures, between the generations, between the sexes, and between children moving through different stages of childhood." The book has been made into a film for television.

SELECTED WORKS: Good Night, Mr. Tom, 1982; Back Home, 1984.

BILL MARTIN, JR.

1916–

AUTHOR OF *The Ghost-Eye Tree*, etc.

Biographical sketch of William Ivan Martin, Jr.:

BILL MARTIN, JR. grew up in Kansas in an environment rich in folklore and storytelling. His grandmother was a particular influence upon him, telling him stories of the Martin family history.

After graduation from Kansas State Teachers College of Emporia, Martin taught English, Journalism, and Dramatics in the St. John and Newton, Kansas, high schools. He received his master's and doctoral degrees from Northwestern University, where he studied reading, creative writing, and elementary education.

Martin has served as principal of Crow Island Elementary School in Winnetka, Illinois, and as editor of elementary classroom materials for Holt, Rinehart and Winston, beginning in 1960. He has been a lecturer and storyteller at many Universities and Colleges, including the University of Den-

ver, the University of Missouri at Kansas City, and the University of Virginia.

Martin also appeared in two television series for educational television, "The Storyteller" in 1955 and "Bill Martin," filmed in 1968. In addition to his trade books for children, Martin collaborated with Peggy Brogan on *Sounds of Language*, a literary-based reading program for grades kindergarten through eight; the Owl Books, a set of ten social studies books; and *The Human Connection*, a treatise on children, schools, and language, published by the Association for Elementary/Kindergarten/Nursery Education.

Bill Martin, Jr. believes that language is essentially oral and that the sounds of sentences are more imporant than the sounds of individual words within the sentences. He has said, "Reading instruction is best when it helps children verbalize and refine their intuitive knowledge about language and how it works." Three videotapes of poetry and storytelling by Martin, John Archambault, and a guitarist have been produced by DLM Publishers, *Smile Every Mile*, *Sing Your Way Home*, and *Brighten Your Road*. Bill Martin, Jr. lives in New York City.

Brown Bear, The Ghost-Eye Tree, and *Barn Dance!* were named Children's Choice Books by a joint committee of the Children's Book Council and the International Reading Association, in 1985, 1986, and 1987 respectively. The latter two were also Reading Rainbow books. *Knots on a Counting Rope* was named a 1987 Notable Children's Trade Book in the Field of Social Studies by a joint committee of the CBC and the National Council on the Social Studies.

SELECTED WORKS WRITTEN WITH JOHN ARCHAMBAULT: The Ghost-Eye Tree, 1985; Barn Dance!, 1986; White Dynamite and Curly Kidd, 1986; Here Are My Hands, 1987; Knots on a Counting Rope, 1987; Listen to the Rain, 1988; Up and Down on the Merry-Go-Round, 1988.

SELECTED WORKS WRITTEN: Brown Bear, Brown Bear, What Do You See?, 1984.

ABOUT: Contemporary Authors, Vol. 117; Language Arts, May 1982; Something About the Author, Vol. 40.

TOSHI MARUKI

February 11, 1912–

AUTHOR AND ILLUSTRATOR OF *Hiroshima No Pika*, etc.

Biographical sketch of Toshi Maruki:

TOSHI MARUKI, nee Akamatsu, was born near the north end of Ishikari Plain in Chippubetsu, Hokkaido, Japan. Her mother's grandfather had taken the family there to establish Zenshoji Temple. From childhood, she wished to be an artist; she saw herself as always messy with paints. In the early 1930s, she completed four years of studying Western art at Joshi Bijutsu Art College in Tokyo. When she learned to paint, she used oils, as in the West. She became a substitute teacher at Ichikawa Elementary School in Chiba. In 1933 her work was accepted for an exhibition. In 1937, Maruki became tutor to the children of a diplomat, and spent a year in Moscow. The following year, she

TOSHI MARUKI

had a one-person show in Tokyo called "Moscow Ten."

As she wanted to be "a female Gauguin," she traveled to the southern islands of the Pacific, making many sketches. She found a tiny, uninhabited island that she wanted to buy. Its price was fifty thousand yen; she went back to Tokyo to earn the money.

Maruki had more one-person shows, and joined the Bijutsu Bunka Kyokai Art Association; however, as she worked toward her goal, she met her future husband and co-artist, Iri Maruki. In 1941, they married. This began a long partnership of work, in travel, and in political activism.

After the United States dropped the atomic bomb on Hiroshima in 1945, the couple traveled to that city, staying with her husband Iri Maruki's family and working to rescue bomb victims. "We were surrounded by corpses fallen and piled," she writes. "I was affected by the remaining radiation and quite suffered from the illness it brought." This experience resulted in their joint creation of The Hiroshima Panels, which were completed in 1955 and have been exhibited in countries all over the world, including China and the Soviet Union. A documentary film was made

about the panels. In 1953 they received the Sekai Heiwa Bunka Sho World Peace and Culture Prize from the World Peace Council.

In 1956, Toshi Akamatsu changed her name to Toshi Maruki. In 1964, after a move to Matsudo, Chiba, the pair criticized the Japanese Communist Party and advised changes; with fellow members, they were expelled from the party. They continued to show their work, and the Maruki Gallery for the Hiroshima Panels in Higashimatsuyama, Saitama, opened in 1967. A catalog, *The Hiroshima Panels*, was published in 1974.

Maruki turned to Japanese tools with which to paint. She continued to exhibit her own work and to create books, but the couple went to Europe in 1975, making hundreds of sketches in preparation for a major endeavor entitled Auschwitz. A two-person exhibition of five hundred sketches opened at Nagai Gallery in 1977. Maruki and her husband also created major artworks influenced by the tragedy of Minamata, where citizens contracted mercury poisoning from the industrial waste from Kyushu's Chisso Factory in 1956, and about the city of Nagasaki and the battle of Okinawa. Their work is exhibited widely in Japan, China, and Europe.

In 1987 Maruki's health failed, and she underwent surgery for the implantation of a pacemaker. In 1988 both Iri and Toshi Maruki traveled to Boston to receive Honorary Doctoral Degrees of Fine Arts from Massachusetts College of Art in Boston.

Maruki's most famous work in the United States is her book *Hiroshima No Pika*, published here in 1982. It recounts the experience of seven-year-old Mii and her parents on and after August 6, 1945. *The Horn Book Magazine* review stated that the book "recounts in explicit detail the environmental consequences, the absolute devastation, the struggle for sheer survival, the long human agony." A *School Library Journal* reviewer commented, "this haunting—and ironically beautiful—interpretation of a subject of acute concern and decidedly current interest insure *Hiroshima No Pika* a place in every collection."

Translated into many languages and published in countries all over the world, the book won the 1983 Jane Addams Children's Book Award from the Jane Addams Peace Association, the 1983 Mildred L. Batchelder Award from the American Library Association, and the Ehon Nippon Taisho, the Japan Picture Book Grand Prize. It was also named an Honor Book in the 1983 Boston Globe-Horn Book Awards, and a 1982 ALA Notable Book.

"The Atomic Bomb is a peril to the Earth!", Maruki writes. "This I have been crying out for such a long time . . . But perhaps the Earth can still be saved." She advocates banning all nuclear weapons and closing nuclear power plants, and discontinuing the use of detergents and synthetic fibers, fertilizers, and chemicals.

"Organic gardening must commence," she says, "and all labor must be done in obedience to the ceaseless ecological cycles of the universe. There is great work ahead of us."

SELECTED WORKS: Hiroshima No Pika, 1982.

ABOUT: Kingman, Lee and others, comps. Illustrators of Children's Books: 1967-1976.

JEAN MARZOLLO

June 24, 1942–

AUTHOR OF *Halfway Down Paddy Lane*, etc.

Autobiographical sketch of Jean Marzollo:

MY FAVORITE BOOK when I was young was *Many Moons* by James Thurber. I liked it because it was funny, imaginative, sad with a happy ending, and full of interesting words. I still like books that are funny and sad and full of interesting words.

And I still love the use of the human imagination to solve problems. Using your

imagination is like singing. If you're relaxed, you can do it. You can't really make ideas and songs happen; you can only let them happen when they do.

I carry paper and pencils around with me so that I can write down good ideas when I get them. They occur in the oddest places, often when I'm driving or riding on a train. The vibration of the moving vehicle is relaxing, I think. I have to hold onto the idea in my head until I can write it down. If I'm driving I'll ask someone with me in the car to write an idea down for me and stick it in my pocketbook.

When I was young, I liked to play office. I liked to sit at my desk and use my papers, pencils, pens, stapler, construction paper, glue, and hole puncher. I still like to play office, and many times I feel as happy going to work in my attic office in the morning as I did when I was playing office in third grade.

Probably it was the combination of liking words, my imagination, and office supplies that led me to be a writer.

Today I write things for people of all ages. I write picture books for young children, easy-to-read books for slightly older children, novels for even older children, and many books and articles for parents. I enjoy switching from one type of project to another because I like to use a variety of writing styles.

———

Jean Marzollo was born in Manchester, Connecticut. She received her B.A. degree from the University of Connecticut in 1964 and her M.A.T. degree from Harvard University in 1965. She was a teacher in Arlington, Massachusetts, from 1965 to 1966 and Assistant Director of Project Upward Bound at Harvard. She has also been Director of Publications at the National Commission on Resources for Youth and editor of Scholastic's magazine for children, *Let's Find Out*. She has written books for parents, such as *Learning Through Play* and *The New Kindergarten*. She has also had articles published in *Parents*, *Redbook*, and *Mademoiselle*.She was a member of the Elementary School Study Group for U.S. Secretary of Education William Bennett in 1986. She was married in 1969 and has two children.

Halfway Down Paddy Lane was named a Best Book for Young Adults for the year 1981 by the American Library Association. *Close Your Eyes* was a Junior Literary Guild selection.

SELECTED WORKS: Close Your Eyes, 1978; Amy Goes Fishing, 1980; Uproar on Hollercat Hill, 1980; Do You Love Me, Harvey Burns?, 1983; Doll House Christmas, 1986; The Rebus Treasury, 1986; The Three Little Kittens, 1986; Cannonball Chris, 1987; Soccer Sam, 1987; Red Ribbon Rosie, 1988; The Pizza Pie Slugger, 1989.

SELECTED WORKS WRITTEN WITH CLAUDIO MARZOLLO: Jed Junior's Space Patrol, 1982; Robin of Bray, 1982; Blue Sun Ben, 1983; Red Sun Girl, 1983; Ruthie's Rude Friends, 1984.

ABOUT: Contemporary Authors, Vol. 81; (New Revision Series), Vol. 15; Something About the Author, Vol. 29.

CHRISTINE McDONNELL

July 3, 1949–

AUTHOR OF *Don't Be Mad, Ivy*, etc.

Autobiographical sketch of Christine McDonnell:

WHEN I WAS little, the people around me were always reading. My parents, my aunt, and my uncle were book readers, always reading in the living room or falling asleep with a book spread open. My grandmother was a newspaper reader, and she read me fairy tales, Uncle Wiggly stories, and Old Mother West Wind books. My favorite was Andersen's "The Little Match Girl," not a cheerful choice, but I loved it anyway.

Every Sunday I walked with my uncle to Lane's Variety Store, where we bought the ice cream for Sunday night dessert. Every Sunday my uncle let me pick a book to buy—never a comic—always a book. I still remember those Golden Books.

In first grade I didn't learn to read. Since I was tall, I sat in the back of the room and spent my time playing with the children seated around me. When my mother discovered that I couldn't read, she tutored me every night that summer. By second grade, I was a reader! By third grade I had become the kind of reader who gets lost in a book. In school we were allowed to read books when we'd finished our work. I was reading *Toby Tyler*, waiting for math to start. In the middle of the chapter, Mr. Stubbs, Toby's monkey, died. I couldn't stop reading, or crying! I read right into the middle of the next lesson.

Many of the books I loved I inherited from my older sisters and brother: *Stuart Little* and *Charlotte's Web*, the Shoe books by Noel Streatfield, Marguerite Henry's horse stories. I broke an ankle when I was nine and had to go all night before it could be set. My sister Regina read me *Circus Shoes* most of the night, until I finally fell asleep, the pain numbed by the story.

When I was eleven, I went to boarding school. The Middle School library, a pan-

elled room the size of a large closet, was the only escape from the chilly, endless evening study hall. I read through it, sampling every type of book. I read Victorian books like *The Coral Island* and *The Secret Garden,* all the Alcott books, family stories by Nesbit and Enright, fantasy, sports, adventure, anything! It's not surprising that my first job was as a children's librarian in New York City.

I was in my late twenties when I began to write, first trying adult stories, hopelessly mired in description. I stumbled upon the first chapters of *Don't be Mad, Ivy* after hearing Arnold Lobel and Uri Schulevitz describe the ideal picture-book text. "It has no description," they said. I went home, curious to try writing without description. The result of the experiment was my first book. It is very autobiographical. Ivy is me, except the artist didn't give her a gap between her front teeth and curly hair. From my own memories, I then stretched out to include ideas I found when watching my children, and the students in my classes. Now I work mostly from my imaginaiton, but memory and observation keep my writing truthful, I hope.

My husband is an artist, and also a baker, a teacher, a father. The creative processes of writing and painting are parallel, in some ways. They both require risks, and an element of confusion—moving on instinct. We both have bouts of self-doubt, and can recognize when the other is being too self-critical. We both try to work hard and to keep growing in our work.

We have three children. The oldest, Garth, my stepson, was the inspiration for *Toad Food and Measle Soup.* The younger two were born in Korea. Soo Ae joined our family when she was four, and Doo Wook joined us when he was three. I don't write directly about my children's lives. They are fine writers and I hope some day they'll tell their own stories. But living with children informs my writing in every way. They remind me of my own childhood, and of the daily dramas and traumas of growing up, as well as of the comedy.

In my work, I am interested in the adventure of day-to-day life experiences, and how we grow. I am interested in relationships—friendships, being enemies, being in a family, especially a family that changes. And I like humor, even in serious books. In my family, telling a funny story was considered the highest art, and even at a young age I learned to transform ordinary events into funny stories so I would have something to say at dinner. It's a useful skill, and I use it still.

———

Born in Southampton, New York, Christine McDonnell received her B.A. degree from Barnard College in 1972 and her M. L.S. from Columbia in 1973. She worked as a Children's Librarian for the New York Public Library from 1972 to 1975. A junior high school librarian in Arlington, Massachusetts from 1976 to 1979, she was an Assistant Professor of Education at Simmons College from 1979 to 1982. She was Director of Community Programs at the Center for the Study of Children's Literature at Simmons from 1979 to 1980. Since 1982 she has also been a teacher, at Pierce School in

Brookline, Massachusetts, and at Brookline High School. McDonnell is a contributor to *Horn Book* magazine.

SELECTED WORKS: Don't Be Mad, Ivy, 1981; Toad Food and Measle Soup, 1982; Lucky Charms and Birthday Wishes, 1984; Count Me In, 1986; Just for the Summer, 1987.

ABOUT: Contemporary Authors, Vol. 107; Lee, Joel M., ed. Who's Who in Library and Information Services; Something About the Author, Vol. 34.

BRUCE McMILLAN

May 10, 1947–

AUTHOR AND PHOTOGRAPHIC ILLUSTRATOR OF *Counting Wildflowers*, etc.

Autobiographical sketch of Bruce McMillan:

I STARTED PREPARING myself for my career as a photographer and writer when I started playing with blocks. I certainly wasn't aware of it at the time. We are all arrangers. We arrange things because it pleases us. As children, we arrange blocks. I do the same thing now that I did as a child. There's only one difference. Now, instead of using blocks, I arrange words and photographs. I arrange what's in a sentence and what's in a photograph so that it pleases me. When it does, I want to share it with everyone and I do. I do this with my books. I do this when I speak at schools.

As a youngster, I wasn't required to write much in school, but I loved to read. I'd go to my library and discover a book and then read all the books written by that particular author. Through reading I learned an appreciation for words. Now, I not only enjoy reading other people's words, I enjoy writing my own. I enjoy playing with words and their visual imagery as I did with *Puniddles*.

I owe my father thanks for getting me started in photography. He gave me my first professional camera, a Rolleicord,

when I was in the fourth grade. I tended to be more creative than he thought I should be. He wasn't too happy when I tried to photograph a burning candle . . . from above! I learned my photography skills hands-on. I took pictures for the school paper. I made a pinhole camera out of cardboard and took a picture of the school. In high school when I couldn't afford senior pictures, I made self-portraits to trade with other seniors. Using a top hat and some charcoal for a beard I became Abe Lincoln, or using a sheet I became Lawrence of Arabia. I always try to turn what seems to be a disadvantage into an advantage.

When I work on my photo-illustrated books I do many jobs. I become an entire Hollywood production crew. Although I received my college degree in biology, it was my work-study job in public television during college that held my interest. Starting as a photographer, I soon became a director, then a producer. In that job I learned organization skills. I learned how to originate, coordinate, direct, and light a production. I worked on all types of programming, including children's programs.

After three years in television, I "retired" to an island off the coast of Maine. I was the island's caretaker. This left plenty of time to work at something I still felt deficient in, my writing skills. I spent two years working towards improving my writing. At the conclusion of my stay, I photographed and wrote my first published work, an article titled "Our Winters on a Maine Island." I also wrote my first book, a book about lobstering. I photographed my five-year-old son, Brett, while he had a *Finestkind O'Day*.

I like to challenge myself. When I moved ashore to Shapleigh I challenged myself to do two things. One was to build my career as a creator of books. I photographed my next book. I challenged myself to do a completely different type of book. It became *The Alphabet Symphony*. The other challenge involved a nonbook project, though I approached it the same way I approach my books. I learned everything I could about my subject. I studied everything I could. Then, using my mind and my own two hands, I designed and built a house. Twelve years later I completed my task. Perseverance. It's now my home. This is where I work and live.

I live with Julio, a beagle who strayed by and decided to stay, and two cats from animal shelters. One of them is Pixie, the kitten in *Kitten Can* . . . . I'm allergic to animals so I wasn't quite finished with building houses. I built them their own cozy house next to mine.

My biology background and interest in nature has not been abandoned during my book career journey. My interest in the sea became *Finestkind O'Day: Lobstering in Maine*. My interest in apples led me to plant fifty trees while writing *Apples, How They Grow*. *Counting Wildflowers* was my own taxonomy lesson and *Growing Colors* was an extension of my interest in orchards and gardens.

I live in a rural setting. My books reflect that. They also reflect much more about me than that. Many people don't realize that I've already written my autobiography. It's *The Remarkable Riderless Runaway Tricycle*. I'm not the little boy in the story.

I'm the tricycle. The tricycle shows great perseverance as well as having fun along its journey. I've also shown great perseverance in my career. No matter what others thought, just like the tricycle, I had to believe in myself. I've had fun along the way, too. Parts of me are in all my books.

I enjoy life. I've been told that I could have fun with a turnip. It was meant as a compliment, I think. Three books into my career I realized that I made books with happy endings. It wasn't a conscious decision. It was a reflection of me. I love a happy ending. I've consciously followed it since then. Even *Puniddles* has a happy ending—hoe, hoe, hoe.

I enjoy working on books because each book is uniquely challenging. I've done three types of photographic books, challenging myself with each type. I've done documentaries such as *Finestkind O'Day* and *Making Sneakers*. I've done another type of book where I've mixed the reality of photo-illustration with a fantasy-like story as I did in *The Remarkable Riderless Runaway Tricycle* and *The Ghost Doll*. Finally, I've done yet another type of book. This type of book looks deceptively simple. It isn't. It's the concept book.

Documentaries are the simplest type of photo-illustrated book to do. Events happen and are recorded as they happen in front of the camera. The event flows through the camera and onto the film. The photographer captures this event. The second type of book is more complex. More of a challenge is involved in mixing the reality of photography with fantasy. The third type of book, the concept book, poses another kind of challenge. The event that will eventually happen originates in the photo-illustrator's mind. He is more than an illustrator. The book starts as an idea, as a concept. It's this idea that is going to be photographed. It flows from his mind, and out to what he creates in front of him. Then it flows back through the camera, and finally onto the film. The simple books about color, *Growing Colors*, counting, *Counting*

Wildflowers, or wetness, *Dry or Wet?*, are quite complex and work on many levels. I enjoy the mental challenge these books pose.

I love being inside my head. It's a delightful place to be. It's especially wonderful when I'm thinking and working on a book, challenging myself, playing games with myself. It gets so active up there that I can hardly keep up with the activity of my neurons. Working on a book makes me feel happy. It's the same feeling I used to get as a youngster when my neurons were rapidly firing inside my head as my mental appetite was devouring a delicious book.

Bruce McMillan was born in Boston, was raised in Maine, and graduated from Kennebunk High School. In 1969 he graduated from the University of Maine at Orono with a Bachelor of Science in Biology. He has one child. He teaches a course on children's books at the University of Southern Maine and is a member of the Author's Guild. His photographs have appeared in exhibits at universities throughout the country and in magazines like *Life* and *People*. He is the author of two humorous books for adults, *Punography* and *Punography Too*.

Two of McMillan's books have been named Notable Books by the American Library Association, *Here a Chick, There a Chick* in 1983 and *Counting Wildflowers* in 1986. . . . *Runaway Tricycle* was made into a motion picture.

SELECTED WORKS WRITTEN AND ILLUSTRATED: Finestkind O'Day: Lobstering in Maine, 1977; The Alphabet Symphony, 1977; The Remarkable Riderless Runaway Tricycle, 1978; Apples, How They Grow, 1979; Ghost Doll, 1983; Here A Chick, There a Chick, 1983; Kitten Can . . . , 1984; Counting Wildflowers, 1986; Dry or Wet?, 1988; Growing Colors, 1988; Fire Engine Shapes, 1988; Super, Super, Superwords, 1989.

SELECTED WORKS WRITTEN WITH BRETT MCMILLAN AND ILLUSTRATED: Puniddles, 1982.

SELECTED WORKS ILLUSTRATED: Everything Grows, by Raffi, 1989.

ABOUT: Contemporary Authors, Vol. 73; Something About the Author, Vol. 22.

GLORIA D. MIKLOWITZ

May 18, 1927–

AUTHOR OF *Did You Hear What Happened to Andrea?*, etc.

Autobiographical sketch of Gloria D. Miklowitz:

IN THIRD GRADE, after nearly failing second because I daydreamed too much, I wrote a story called "My Brother GooGoo." Its success at school brought me family attention and from then on I, the middle child of five, was called "The Writer."

Once I learned to read I devoured any book I could get my hands on. In high school I took journalism and wrote for the school paper. In college, I majored in English and on graduation assumed that the only choices an English major had were reporting and advertising. In fact, the only job I could get was as secretary at Bantam Books.

Shortly afterwards I married and moved first to Pittsburgh, then to Socorro, New Mexico, and finally to Pasadena, California, where the Naval Ordnance Test Station hired me as a secretary. When a film branch was started, I persuaded the director to train me to write the scripts they needed—on rockets and torpedoes.

I wrote technical films for five years, but when my first and then second son was born, I left my job to be full-time mother. By the time my oldest was three I was reading an average of ten books a week to him and his younger brother. The scriptwriting experience had taught me to write visually and succinctly, so I turned to writing picture books. The first book sale, *Barefoot Boy*, led to other books for young readers, then to middle-grade books, and finally to writing what I like to write most—books for teens.

Miklowitz: *MICK lo witz*

Gloria D. Miklowitz (signature)

I seem to have a social conscience (perhaps typical of my Jewish heritage) and many of my young adult novels are about social issues—prejudice, in *The War Between the Classes*; vigilantism, in *The Emerson High Vigilantes*; child abuse, in *Secrets Not Meant to Be Kept*; nuclear war, in *After the Bomb* and its sequel; steroids, in *Anything to Win*, etc. Since I can't have lived all the experiences of my characters, I do a lot of research to understand what teenagers would do in situations I put them into on paper. When writing *The Love Bombers*, for example, I stayed briefly with the 'Moonies' so I could write credibly about someone going into a religious cult. When writing the "bomb" books I spoke with police, fire department people, emergency hospital personnel, and many others who would be involved in the event of a nuclear disaster.

I have been fortunate in that three of my books have become Afterschool Specials, probably because of the importance of their themes, and another is under contract for a TV special.

Often I get letters from readers who ask how I could make my characters seem just like kids they know. I think it's because we all feel the same way when afraid, or happy, or sad—no matter what our age, so when my characters are afraid, or happy, etc., I just recall how I have felt.

I never thought, when I graduated from college, that I would write *books*, teach writing, speak at schools and conventions. It seems a miracle, but miracles are often self-made, I think. While some small talent is needed, it's only a small part of the recipe. A writer must also have curiosity, 'sticking' power for the times when rejection comes, or when the story stalls, a fondness for words, and above all, when writing for children—a genuine love for and nonjudgmental attitude toward the reader.

———

Gloria D. Miklowitz was born in New York City. She attended Hunter College from 1944 to 1945, and received her B.A. degree from the University of Michigan in 1948. She was married August 28, 1948. She is a member of P.E.N. International and the California Writers Guild.

Movie Stunts and the People Who Do Them was named a Children's Choice book in 1981 by a joint committee of the International Reading Asssociation and the Children's Book Council.

SELECTED WORKS: Did You Hear What Happened to Andrea?, 1979; Movie Stunts and the People Who Do Them, 1980; The Love Bombers, 1980; Close to the Edge, 1983; The Day the Senior Class Got Married, 1983; After the Bomb, 1985; The War Between the Classes, 1985; Love Story, Take Three, 1986; After the Bomb: Week One, 1987; Secrets Not Meant to Be Kept, 1987; The Emerson High Vigilantes, 1988; Anything to Win, 1989.

ABOUT: Biography Index, Vol. 9; Contemporary Authors (First Revision), Vol 25; (New Revision Series), Vol. 10; The International Authors and Writers Who's Who, 1982; Something About the Author, Vol. 4; Who's Who of American Women, 1981-1982; The Writers Directory, 1984-1986.

EDNA MILLER

EDNA MILLER

March 8, 1920–

AUTHOR AND ILLUSTRATOR OF *Mousekin's Christmas Eve*, etc.

Biographical sketch of Edna Anita Miller:

EDNA MILLER, the originator of the Mousekin series, was born in Weehawken, New Jersey. She grew up in New York with her parents and older sister in an apartment that overlooked Central Park. Another important site in her childhood was the American Museum of Natural History, which was conveniently situated next door to her home. The museum served as a second home to Miller and was largely responsible for her lifelong interest in zoology and natural history. As an apartment dweller she was prevented from having a dog; however turtles, rabbits, mice, and a small alligator provided substitutes. Miller's early drawing career began with sketches of her favorite animals from the zoo in Central Park.

She attended grammar school and Julia Richman High School in New York City.

With a scholarship, she attended Traphagen School of Fashion in New York City from 1938 to 1940, where she studied fashion, textile design, and illustration. Miller began her career as a designer for a New York sportswear manufacturer. In 1946 she married Ted Miller, an architect and cartographer. Together, they built a house in the Ramapo Hills north of New York City, overlooking a woodland landscape filled with animals. The couple travelled extensively in Europe, North Africa, Mexico, and the United States.

Miller's career as an illustrator began after the birth of their son. Her first assignments were illustrating high-school textbooks. At the same time she continued to assist her husband in his work as a historical cartographer. That marriage ended in divorce in 1971.

The idea for the first Mousekin book came when her son reached school age. Shortly after Halloween, Miller observed a small white-footed mouse exploring a pumpkin that had been placed outside. Over a period of weeks Miller continued to observe the mouse as well as the slow decay of the jack-o'-lantern. This incident provided the inspiration for *Mousekin's Golden House*. Since this first publication, there have been numerous books involving Mousekin, whose adventures take him through woodlands where he encounters other forest animals.

Miller was remarried, but her husband died in 1972. She currently lives in Vermont, where she continues to write for a new generation that includes her grandchildren.

Mousekin's Close Call was named a 1979 Children's Choice Book by a joint committee of the Children's Book Council and the International Reading Association.

SELECTED WORKS WRITTEN AND ILLUSTRATED: Mousekin's Golden House, 1964; Mousekin's Christmas Eve, 1965; Mousekin's Family, 1969; Mousekin's ABC, 1972; Mousekin's Woodland Birthday, 1974; Pebbles: A Pack Rat, 1976; Mousekin's Close Call, 1978; Jumping Bean, 1979; Mousekin's Fables, 1982;

Frederick Ferdinand Fox, 1987; Mousekin's Easter Basket, 1987.

ABOUT: Contemporary Authors, Vol. 106; Vol. 112; Kingman, Lee and others, comps. Illustrators of Children's Books: 1957-1966; Something About the Author, Vol. 29.

LILLIAN MORRISON

October 27, 1917–

AUTHOR OF *Rhythm Road*, etc.

Autobiographical sketch of Lillian Morrison:

I WAS BORN in Jersey City, New Jersey, just across the Hudson River from New York. My parents were immigrants from Russia and had to struggle to make a living for our family. I have an older sister and a brother about a year younger than I. Because we moved often, depending on our economic fortunes, I went to six different elementary schools. I liked some schools more than others, but I didn't mind all the moving. It meant a new block, a new neighborhood to explore.

Mine was a city childhood, and our playground was the street. We jumped rope, roller-skated, took turns racing around the block, timing each other, and played almost every kind of ball game—bounce ball, stoop ball, box ball, stick ball. We saved picture cards of baseball players and boxers and went to movies on Saturday afternoons. My brother and I were close friends and shared in most of these activities. Many of the poems in my book *The Sidewalk Racer* came out of the experiences in those years.

But it was not only the active life I enjoyed. There were the rhymes and chants I heard on the street and in the schoolyard. "Marguerite, go wash your feet, the Board of Health's across the street." I think I was four years old when I heard that, with great pleasure in the rhyme and beat. Then there were the jump-rope rhymes, the bounce ball rhymes, and I still remember the

strange thrill of the sound of "1, 2, 3, Ringaleevio!" (a wild form of Hide-and-Seek played over many city blocks) echoing through the night. Also I loved to read. My father was an avid reader and would often quote Shakespeare and read Poe's "The Raven" and "The Bells" to us. It was from my mother, on the other hand, that I got my "folk sense," what with her rich store of catchy proverbs, folk sayings, and songs from the old country.

My interest in sports and reading continued in high school. But, unlike many poets, I did not write poems as a teenager. I was definitely sensitive to sound and rhythm, however, and would get goose bumps at school assemblies when we yelled "Boom get a rat trap bigger than a cat trap" for our football team. At Douglass College, Rutgers, where I was on scholarships and waited on tables, I majored in mathematics (thus, *Overheard in a Bubble Chamber and Other Science Poems* many years later). It wasn't until I had graduated and took a job in The New York Public Library—a lucky accident of Fate—that I became an insatiable reader of poetry and began to write poems of my own. And in writing, I often experienced the same feelings of excitement that I had as a child running fast, jumping high, or catching a difficult fly ball. There was the same aiming for perfection, the attempt to do something skillful and graceful.

Early in my library career, I worked with young people in the Aguilar Branch in East Harlem. My first book *Yours Till Niagara Falls*, a collection of autograph verse, came out of my contact with these boys and girls. This book did well and was the beginning of a serious interest in rhymed folklore of all kinds—charms, spells, riddles, etc. More collections followed. Meanwhile my library work was absorbing and varied. I gave talks in high schools all over the city, and eventually I was put in charge of work with teenagers for The New York Public Library's branch system. But I was always writing in my free time.

In 1967, *The Ghosts of Jersey City*, the first book of my own poems, was published. Since then I have continued to write and publish poetry and to read and collect the poetry of others, for poetry is a very important part of my life.

———

Lillian Morrison received her B.S. degree in 1938 and earned her library degree from Columbia University in 1942. She was General Editor of Crowell's Poets Series and Crowell's Poems of the World Series from 1964 to 1974. She served as Coordinator of Young Adult Services at the NYPL from 1969 to 1982. She has contributed poetry to *Sports Illustrated, Atlantic, Poetry Northwest, Images,* and other magazines and journals. She is a member of the Authors League of America, the Poetry Society of America, P.E.N., and Phi Beta Kappa.

Sprints and Distances was placed on the list of American Library Association Notable Books of 1940 through 1970. *The Ghosts of Jersey City* was chosen by the English-Speaking Union to be an American Ambassador Book. In 1987 Morrison was awarded the ALA Grolier Award for contributions to

stimulating young people's interest in reading. *Rhythm Road* was named a 1988 Best Book for Young Adults and a Notable Book of 1988 by the ALA.

SELECTED WORKS: The Ghosts of Jersey City, and Other Poems, 1967; The Sidewalk Racer and Other Poems of Sports and Motion, 1977; Who Would Marry a Mineral?, 1978; Overheard in a Bubble Chamber and Other Science Poems, 1981; The Break Dance Kids: Poems of Sports, Motion and Locomotion, 1985.

SELECTED WORKS COMPILED: Yours Till Niagara Falls, 1950; Black Within and Red Without: A Book of Riddles, 1953; Touch Blue, 1958; Sprints and Distances: Sports in Poetry and the Poetry in Sport, 1965; Best Wishes, Amen: A New Collection of Autograph Verse, 1974; Rhythm Road: Poems to Move To, 1988.

ABOUT: Contemporary Authors Vol. 9; (New Revision Series), Vol. 7; Hopkins, Lee Bennett. Books Are by People; Hudson Dispatch September 25, 1979; Lee, Joel M., ed. Who's Who in Library and Information Services; Something About the Author, Vol. 3.

BARRY MOSER

October 15, 1940–

ILLUSTRATOR OF *In the Beginning: Creation Stories from Around the World*, etc.

Autobiographical sketch of Barry Moser:

I WAS BORN in Chattanooga, Tennessee. At home I learned to love and to be loved. I learned to touch, to be touched, and to be comfortable with nudity. I was taught to be pleasant and generous to visitors and strangers. I was taught to love Italian opera, musical comedies, Eddie Duchin, and Fats Waller. I was also taught to be a racist, to be anti-Catholic, anti-Semitic, and xenophobic. As Oscar Hammerstein put it, I was taught "to fear people whose eyes are oddly made and whose skin is a different shade . . . to hate all the people my relatives hate."

At my Uncle Bob's house, I learned the rudiments of craftsmanship in his woodworking shop. He taught me, when I was a very small boy, that "when a job is first be-

gun, never leave it 'til it's done . . . be the labor large or small, do it well or not at all." He harped about my work being "half-assed." He took my projects apart, and put them back together again to show how to do the job right. Despite his impatience, he taught me to take more time with my projects, he encouraged my fledgling inclinations, he built my first drawing table for me, and he gave me some grit.

I despised elementary school. Like Tom Sawyer, I was adept at inventing maladies to keep me at home. I was an academic dunce and something of a social pariah. I cared little for terrorizing smaller kids, I did not run very fast, kick very high, jump very far, nor play ball very well. When choosing up sides for a game, I was the last one chosen. I preferred the girls' side of the playground to the boys', and I've preferred the company of women ever since. All in all, my school days were undistinguished, except for drawing.

In 1952, I went to The Baylor School, a Southern military academy that sought to educate the young Southern gentleman in matters military, athletic, and academic. I was taught to diagram sentences; to dissect frogs, cats, and chickens; to be quiet; to line

up; and not to question authority. My drawing skills were no longer a source of praise and success. In fact, drawing was a cause for criticism and discipline—I was once busted from the rank of Cadet Corporal to the rank of Cadet Private for drawing a naked woman on a blank page of my Spanish textbook.

In 1958, after six more undistinguished years, I graduated from Baylor, still preferring drawing naked women to playing football, and went to Auburn University, in Auburn, Alabama, to major in Industrial Design.

At Auburn I had my first drawing and design lessons. I discovered rubber cement and rub-on letters. I learned that more is less and less is more, and that form follows function.

In 1960 I returned home and finished my baccalaureate at the University of Chattanooga, as a painting major. George Cress, my mentor, taught me to use "the broad stroke," literally, insisting that I paint with a #24 brush. He taught me to reduce subject matter to essential forms until only form remained. He encouraged me to look at, and study, and revere, the paintings of Cezanne, Braque, Kline, Shahn, Gottlieb, and Rothko.

I graduated in 1962, and found a job teaching mechanical drawing and typing at the McCallie School—another military school in Chattanooga. In 1967, disenfranchised and full of bitterness toward the xenophobia, anti-Semitism, anti-Catholicism, racism, and sexism on which I had been weaned, and with which I was now weary, impatient, and intolerant, I packed up my young family and lit out for New England, to teach at Williston Academy in Easthampton, Massachusetts. Over the next fifteen years, I would teach myself how to make etchings and wood engravings; how to set, space, and print type; and I would teach courses in drawing, life drawing, printmaking, art history, calligraphy, design, and typography.

In 1969, I met Leonard Baskin, who taught me to draw better than I already did, to persevere in my work in the search for perfection (echoing my Uncle Bob), and how to hold an engraving tool. More importantly it seems to me these many years later, I met his pressman, Harold McGrath, who taught me, by example and by the nature of printing, to be more patient, to be unimpressed with what I could do, and how to print wood engravings and type better than I already could. Correlative to those associations I designed and printed my first book, James Abbott McNeil Whistler's essay, *The Red Rag*. That was 1969. Twenty years later, I have over a hundred and twenty books to my credit, and I am twenty years older.

———

Barry Moser has illustrated some of the greatest classics of literature for adults, such as *The Divine Comedy of Dante Alighieri*, *Moby Dick*, and *Frankenstein*.

Lewis Carroll's Alice's Adventures in Wonderland won a 1983 American Book Award for pictorial design. *Jump!* was named a Notable Book of 1986 by the American Library Association. *Jump Again!* was named a *New York Times* Best Illustrated Book of 1987. *In the Beginning* was named a 1989 Newbery Medal Honor Book and a Notable Book of 1988 by the ALA. *Around the World in Eighty Days* was a Book-of-the-Month Club selection.

SELECTED WORKS ILLUSTRATED: *Lewis Carroll's Alice's Adventures in Wonderland*, 1982; *Jump!: The Adventures of Brer Rabbit*, by Joel Chandler Harris, 1986; *The Wonderful Wizard of Oz*, by Frank Baum, 1986; *Jump Again!: More Adventures of Brer Rabbit*, by Joel Chandler Harris, 1987; *Around the World in Eighty Days*, by Jules Verne, 1988; *Casey at the Bat*, by Ernest Lawrence Thayer, 1988; *In the Beginning: Creation Stories from Around the World*, retold by Virginia Hamilton, 1988; *East of the Sun and West of the Moon*, adapted by Nancy Willard, 1989.

ABOUT: Horn Book March/April 1987; November/December 1987; Publishers Weekly March 3, 1989; Who's Who in American Art, 1986.

JÖRG MÜLLER

AUTHOR AND ILLUSTRATOR OF *The Changing City*, etc.

Biographical sketch of Jörg Müller:

BORN IN LAUSANNE, Jörg Müller is a popular artist in his native country of Switzerland. Young Müller studied graphic arts at the Arts and Crafts School in Biel, Switzerland. After his studies were completed, he moved to Paris where, for several years, he worked at advertising agencies. In the late seventies, Müller provided the illustrations for two books adapted by Jörg Steiner. The first, *The Bear Who Wanted to Be a Bear*, was a cleanly illustrated tale of a bear who, as the title explains, simply wanted to be a bear. Steiner and Müller again collaborated on *Rabbit Island*, which was awarded the Mildred L. Batchelder Award in 1979. Mary M. Burns, reviewing *Rabbit Island* for *The Horn Book Magazine*, characterized the tale as "a sophisticated statement reflecting the neo-Romantic view of a postindustrialized society." Müller's full-color illustrations, rendered, as Burns says, "in a manner reminiscent of Dürer," are "executed in a meticulously detailed photorealistic style, [and] effectively contrast a mechanistic environment with the enchantment of the unspoiled natural landscape in a visual accompaniment to a modern talking beast tale." Ann Conrad Lammers translated the book.

Müller's penchant for contrasting the unspoiled natural world with the ugliness of industrial society is strongly evident in his unique, two-part series, *The Changing Countryside* and *The Changing City*. Each is a portfolio of fold-out illustrations; *The Changing Countryside* exposes the changes that occur as a farming community becomes a suburb. *The Changing City* depicts the physical changes in a European city over a period of twenty-three years, each picture portraying scenes three years apart. Müller plunged headlong into this project, compiling extensive research with the help of Heinz Ledergerber. The finished product is an outstanding achievement, a remarkable demonstration of an urgent, contemporary environmental problem. Ann Flowers wrote in *Horn Book*, "the industrial buildings [are] remarkable for their coldly repellent modern architecture. . . . although European in conception and presentation, the significance of the pictures is universal." This sentiment was evidently echoed by others as both *The Changing City* and *The Changing Countryside* received Special Honorable Mentions for "nonbook illustration" in the 1977 Boston Globe-Horn Book Awards. In addition, both books were named American Library Association Notable Books of 1977 and Notable Trade Books in the Field of Social Studies by a joint committee of the Children's Book Council and the National Council on the Social Studies.

Müller's illustrative style has been called vigorous and independent-minded; an example of this quality appears in his illustrations for Loriot's retelling of Prokofiev's *Peter and the Wolf*. The large-format, lavishly illustrated book was the first choice of a jury of children at the 1986 International Children's Book Fair in Bologna. It was also named Children's Choice Book of 1987, by a joint committee of the CBC and the International Reading Association.

Recently, Jörg Müller bought and restored an old farmhouse in Burgund, Switzerland, where he now makes his home.

SELECTED WORKS WRITTEN AND ILLUSTRATED: The Changing City, 1977; The Changing Countryside, 1977.

SELECTED WORKS ILLUSTRATED: The Bear Who Wanted to Be a Bear, by Jörg Steiner, 1977; Rabbit Island, by Jörg Steiner, 1978; Peter and the Wolf, by Sergei Prokofiev, retold by Loriot, 1986.

ABOUT: Herdeg, Walter, ed. Graphis 4th International Survey of Children's Book Illustration, 1979 (Publication No. 156); Kingman, Lee and others, com ps. Illustrators of Children's Books: 1967-1976.

ROXIE MUNRO

September 5, 1945–

AUTHOR AND ILLUSTRATOR OF *The Inside-Outside Book of New York City*, etc.

Biographical sketch of Roxie Munro:

BORN in Mineral Wells, Texas, Roxie Munro spent her childhood "reading and daydreaming." Her parents encouraged her to draw, to read, and to make toys. For many years, her family took long car trips for vacations, visiting the South, the Northeast, and the West, touring cities and countryside. Perhaps for this reason, she sees her art as "developing from perception." She writes, "I see paintings everywhere. My mind organizes reality."

A strong memory of Munro's is the artwork in a childhood favorite book of fairy tales by Hans Christian Andersen, illustrated by Arthur Szyk. Munro describes seeking out her childhood books when she was in her late thirties, and being amazed to have such a familiarity with them. She writes, "I am certain that my work is influenced by those early impressions of rich color, ornate patterns, dynamic use of space."

Munro grew up in the Chesapeake Bay area. She attended the University of Maryland in College Park from 1963 to 1965; the Maryland Institute College of Art in Baltimore from 1965 to 1966, and the University of Hawaii in Honolulu from 1966 to 1969, receiving her B.F.A. degree in Painting in 1969. She did graduate work in Painting at the Ohio University in Athens, 1969-1970, and in Photography at the University of Hawaii, 1970-1971.

From 1971 to 1975, she was a dress designer and manufacturer in Washington, D.C., and had her own company. She then worked as a free-lance illustrator, primarily for television, doing courtroom drawings. She has done editorial work for *The New Yorker*, *The Washington Post*, *U.S. News and World Report*, and other publications. In 1980, she won a Yaddo Fellowship in

JILL MURPHY

painting, and in 1981, she moved to New York City. In 1984 she began her first work on books. Since 1971, she has also worked on a series of large oil paintings, which have been exhibited in various solo shows, such as at the Delaware Art Museum, and in numerous group exhibitions. She was married in 1986 to Swedish artist-photographer Bo Zaunders.

For over ten years, Roxie Munro has been a free-lance illustrator. She has illustrated twelve covers for *The New Yorker* and has contributed spot illustrations to the magazine. Her *Inside-Outside Book of New York City* was on the 1985 *New York Times* list of Best Illustrated Children's Books.

SELECTED WORKS: Color New York, 1985; The Inside-Outside Book of New York City, 1985; Architects Make Zigzags: Looking at Architecture from A to Z, 1986; The Inside-Outside Book of Washington, D.C., 1987; Christmastime in New York City, 1987; Blimps, 1989; The Inside-Outside Book of London, 1989.

JILL MURPHY

July 5, 1949–

AUTHOR OF *Peace At Last*, etc.

Biographical Sketch of Jill Murphy:

JILL MURPHY, born in London, England, maintains she inherited her ability to draw from her engineer father, and her belief in that ability from her mother. Her mother encouraged her to be observant and to write and draw her observations from an early age. Murphy would write down stories, draw pictures for them, and staple them into little books. She wanted to do this to the virtual exclusion of her schoolwork; while this inclination did not please her teachers, her mother saw promise in the miniature masterpieces and this fortified Murphy's desire to be a writer and illustrator. She attended art schools in Chelsea, Croyden, and Camberwell.

Murphy has sustained close contact with the child she was, and with children in general, and so understands what children like and how they think. She uses the same method for writing as she did when she was ten—writing out her stories in a school exercise book—and she took care of children for many years, first in a children's home and then in a private home. She also makes frequent visits to schools.

Murphy's first foray into the world of children's books was a work for middle readers, *The Worst Witch*, which she wrote and illustrated. Felicity Trotman, writing in *Twentieth-Century Children's Writers*, said of this and two subsequent titles, *The Worst Witch Strikes Again* and *A Bad Spell for the Worst Witch*: "Jill Murphy has a particular talent for writing stories that appeal to children who have learned the basic skill of reading and want something bright and enticing to make them enjoy books thenceforward—an art more difficult than it might seem." When Murphy applied this "particular talent" to picture books, she met with equal success. *Peace at Last*, the introduction to the bear family featured in *What Next, Baby Bear?*, was a Children's Choice Book of 1981, so named by a joint committee of the Children's Book Council and the International Reading Association. It was also a Kate Greenaway Award Commended Book, designated by the British Library Association in 1981, and was adapted for BBC television. *The Worst Witch* was also on BBC-TV. *Five Minutes' Peace* and *All In One Piece*, the latter a Junior Literary Guild selection, provide telling peeks into the lives of Mr. and Mrs. Large and their three obstreperous elephant children.

Murphy has traveled all over Europe and lived in villages in Ghana and Togo. She now lives in London with her dog, who is used in television commercials.

SELECTED WORKS WRITTEN AND ILLUSTRATED: The Worst Witch, 1974; The Worst Witch Strikes Again, 1980; Peace at Last, 1980; A Bad Spell for the Worst Witch, 1982; On the Way Home, 1982; What Next, Baby Bear?, 1984; Five Minutes' Peace, 1986; All in One Piece, 1987; The Last Dinosaurs, 1988; Worlds Apart, 1989.

ABOUT: Contemporary Authors, Vol. 105; Kirkpatrick, D.L., ed. Twentieth-Century Children's Writers, 2nd ed; Something About the Author, Vol. 37; The Writers Directory 1988–1990.

SHIRLEY ROUSSEAU MURPHY

May 20, 1928–

AUTHOR OF *The Joining of the Stone*, etc.

Autobiographical sketch of Shirley Rousseau Murphy:

WHEN I WAS SMALL I spent a lot of time in my grandparents' house, and what a place to dream. From the windows I could hear the sea pounding, and hear freight trains blasting their whistles as they chugged through our small town. The house was filled with wonderful furniture carved with trees and dragons winding round the legs. And I could find, in the flower patterns of the bright rugs, strange beasts and faces peering out. On the wall hung a wooden monkey that played music when you wound it up; and there was a little iron panther that, my grandfather told me, ate real food. The food that he put in its mouth before bedtime was always gone in the morning.

In the upstairs hall, lined with books, I spent hours sprawled on the rug reading, and looking at fascinating drawings in botany and geology books. My own drawings were of the places and animals I made up as I told myself stories. My mother was an artist, so even though we didn't have much money in those Depression years, she saw that I had pencils and paints and paper.

There was no television then, so I had time for imagining. I was an only child, too. What I missed in companionship I made up for by inventing my own entertainment.

But there was another side to my childhood. My father was a horse trainer. He taught me to handle and work with all kinds of horses. He was demanding, making me do everything exactly right. He expected a lot of me, so I did more than I thought I could. With my father I didn't dream, I paid attention!

He taught me not to quit in the middle of a job just because I was tired or cold or hungry. To stop in the middle of training could ruin a good horse. I learned to keep on until I had accomplished what I had set out to do.

So I was half dreamer, half very demanding of myself. Maybe the two parts together were what I needed to be an artist and a writer.

I went to art school, and I was an artist for many years. But I still thought about writing stories. When I was thirty-five I decided to try. I put away my paints, bought a typewriter, and got to work. I was working at a job, too, in a library. I wrote my first four manuscripts at night and on weekends.

I discovered quickly that I had to learn many new skills, many new ways of thinking. I wanted to write fantasy, but that is hardest of all. My dreams were strong, I knew what I wanted to do, but it took years before I could do it the way I wanted. I'm still learning, still tackling new things, and that, to me, is the greatest adventure.

If I had it to do over I'd add one thing to my life. I'd learn, in my early teens, a steady way to support myself before my painting and writing began to do that. What freedom that would have given me. I would go to trade school during the summers, learning a skill that would help pay my way through college and later allow me to write at night. Maybe I would be a plumber or an electrician. What good money they make, and they're always in demand. Then I would be both dreamer and

practical, just as I started out, and doing what I wanted to do.

––––––

Shirley Rousseau Murphy was born in Oakland, California. She received an A.A. degree from the California School of Fine Arts in 1951 and was married August 5, 1951. She has been a designer and an interior decorator, and is a painter and sculptor. She has had her artwork exhibited, in juried and one-person shows, from 1957 to 1963. These exhibits include shows at the California Water Color Society and museums in San Francisco, Richmond, Oakland, and Los Angeles. She has received awards for her sculpture and paintings.

Murphy's work is included in the anthology *Anywhere, Anywhen*, edited by Sylvia Engdahl. *The Flight of the Fox* was a Junior Literary Guild selection.

SELECTED WORKS: The Sand Ponies, 1967; The Ring of Fire, 1977; Silver Woven in My Hair, 1977; The Flight of the Fox, 1978; The Pig Who Could Conjure the Wind, 1978; The Castle of Hape, 1980; Caves of Fire and Ice, 1980; The Joining of the Stone, 1981; Tattie's River Journey, 1983; Valentine for a Dragon, 1984; Nightpool, 1986; The Ivory Lyre, 1987; The Dragonbards, 1988.

ABOUT: Contemporary Authors (First Revision), Vol. 21; (New Revision Series), Vol 13; Something About the Author, Vol. 36; Who's Who of American Women, 1977-1978; The Writers Directory 1984-86.

ROBERT NEWMAN

JUNE 3, 1909–December 7, 1988

AUTHOR OF *The Case of the Baker Street Irregular: A Sherlock Holmes Story*, etc.

Biographical sketch of Robert Howard Newman:

ROBERT NEWMAN was born in New York City. He attended Brown University from 1927 to 1928. He worked as an assistant superintendent on Gramercy Park, and lived in a basement room, writing and selling his first poems and short stories. In 1936 he married Dorothy Vrayder, who is also a writer. They had one daughter. He and his wife lived in Stonington, Connecticut, until his death in 1988.

Contributing to radio shows, beginning in 1936, was part of his early writing career. During World War II he continued in the radio field, working for the Office of War Information. For President Franklin Delano Roosevelt's re-election campaign in 1944, Newman was in charge of the radio portions.

He wrote for several media, with articles for magazines as well as plays for the movies, radio, and television. He wrote two books for adults before switching in the 1960s to stories for young people.

Newman's published writing for children consists primarily of novels written for a middle and upper elementary school readership. Most of his books are either mystery or fantasy stories, although some include children with gifts that can be described as psychic phenomena. In *The Boy Who Could Fly*, for example, the two young brothers can communicate telepathically. In *Night Spell*, which was nominated for the Edgar Allan Poe Award in 1978, two young friends begin to dream identical dreams.

Merlin's Mistake and its sequel, *The Testing of Tertius*, are fantasies that build on and extend the legends of King Arthur and his famous wizard. In both books, brave young characters undertake quests in which they are tested in many adventures by conflicts between the light and the dark, between good and evil. Unexplained phenomena, best described as magic, play an important role in these books as well as in *The Shattered Stone*, in which two young people and a prince search for a prophesied means of bringing peace to their lands.

Newman's most extended work is his nine-book series of mystery and adventure stories in which two children in Victorian London assist first Sherlock Holmes and later Scotland Yard in solving crimes. Sara and

Andrew share the same urge as have countless adults and children, as Andrew's mother puts it, "the itch to play detective."

Beginning with *The Case of the Baker Street Irregular: A Sherlock Holmes Story*, the two children find themselves either on the spot when crimes occur or connected with people involved in the crimes. Although they are sometimes in the way, more often they are in a position to contribute, through their intelligence, cleverness, or research, to the solving of these crimes. The book was named a 1978 Notable Book by the American Library Association.

In this series Newman re-creates a realistically authentic historical setting, with descriptions, language, and plot that bring to life the time and place. He includes items of daily life and social customs unfamiliar to most readers without overwhelming them with arcane language or regionalisms. By including real persons and events in his plots, George Bernard Shaw as a young drama critic, for example, or the touring Buffalo Bill's Wild West Show, Newman expands for young readers their knowledge of the history of the times on both sides of the Atlantic.

In his work Newman creates children of great resourcefulness, children with strong bonds to companions of a similar age as well as to understanding adults. Whether in fantastical quest or detective work, they exhibit strong values that are reinforced both through events and by adults who serve as role models.

Newman has said that his interest in writing for children developed from his daughter's active response to the stories he read to her when she was young, and that he considers himself a storyteller who imparts pleasure through fantasy rather than through social statement. Newman died in December, 1988, after a long illness.

SELECTED WORKS: The Boy Who Could Fly, 1967; Merlin's Mistake, 1970; The Testing of Tertius, 1973; Shattered Stone, 1975; Night Spell, 1977; The Case of the Baker Street Irregular: A Sherlock Holmes Story, 1978; The Case of the Vanishing Corpse, 1980; The

Case of the Somerville Secret, 1981; The Case of the
Threatened King, 1982; The Case of the Etruscan
Treasure, 1983; The Case of the of the Frightened
Friend, 1984; The Case of the Murdered Players, 1985;
The Case of the Indian Curse, 1986; The Case of the
Watching Boy, 1987.

ABOUT: Contemporary Authors (First Revision), Vol.
1-4; (New Revision Series), Vol. 4; Vol. 19; Kirkpatrick,
D.L., ed. Twentieth-Century Children's Writers, 2nd
ed.; Something About the Author, Vol. 4.

SUZANNE NEWTON

October 8, 1936–

AUTHOR OF *I Will Call It Georgie's Blues*,
etc.

Autobiographical sketch of Suzanne Newton:

SUZANNE NEWTON is writing this about
herself, but she's writing in third person
(she) instead of first person (I). She has discovered that people write more freely
about themselves when it feels as though
they are telling about someone else.

She has spent all her life in North Carolina. Although she has been living in Raleigh,
the Capital City, since 1960, she thinks of
herself as a small-town or rural person.
Those are the kinds of places she lived in
the first two dozen years of her life. All of
her novels are set in little towns or country
settlements where people know each other
very well—maybe too well. In real life that
may be annoying, but for the purposes of
storytelling, Suzanne Newton thinks that
people who tend to each other's business are
far more interesting to write about than
those who remain separate and above it all.

She did not know, on the top floor of her
brain, that she was going to be a writer
someday, but the basement of her brain
knew from the beginning and maneuvered
things nicely so that it would come to pass.
She loved stories, and learned to read when
she was four so that she wouldn't have to
wait until some busy grown-up had time to

read to her. She started school in third grade
because in those far-off days nobody knew
exactly what to do with a first grader who
already knew how to read (she couldn't do
much of anything else—she was still printing in capitals when her classmates were
writing in cursive, and arithmetic was a
great mystery to her). But she did like to
write poems and make up stories. In the
third grade she filled a Blue Horse composition book with rhyming poems. In the
eighth grade she wrote romantic stories in
a larger notebook and illustrated them, but
these were not for anyone else to see.

Of course, since the top of her brain
didn't know she was going to become a
writer, she was thinking about other things
she'd rather be: a dancer, a concert pianist,
an actress, a doctor, an artist, or someone
else famous. But by the time she finished
college, having become more practical, she
had settled on being an English teacher.
Unfortunately, after she tried it for a while,
she didn't think she was a very good teacher. By that time she was married and had
begun having children—four of them. During those years she started writing in earnest, or at least as earnestly as one can when
she has four children under the age of six.

One month before her fourth baby was born, she sold a story to a magazine. She was thrilled beyond speaking. Maybe—just maybe—she could sell another one! She started thinking of herself as a writer. She even put the word "writer" in the little box on her income tax return.

She continued to write short stories, poems, and magazine articles for adults. Meanwhile, she and her children made regular trips to the public library, reading all the books they could take away. She read a great many books for young people during that time, especially the ones her own children recommended. She decided to write a short story for a children's magazine, using an idea she'd gotten from her father many years before. Strangely, the story grew until it was too long to be a short story. It became a book called *Purro and the Prattleberries*, a fantasy about a cat who has ambitions to be human without giving up his catness. When it was accepted for publication she knew she had found what she wanted to do.

She has been writing for young people ever since. As her children grew older, so did the characters in her books—to a point. Now her children are grown and she even has a grandchild. But the young people in her books are still hanging around in their early-to-mid teens, busy discovering who they are and how they want to be.

Suzanne Newton has learned how to be a teacher. She teaches college students how to write fiction and works as a writer in North Carolina's Artists-in-Schools program. The teaching helps her stay in touch with the people who read her books.

If you asked her, she would tell you she is a happy person, because she is doing exactly what she loves to do. Her life as a writer is so satisfying that most of the time she feels as though she has become a dancer, a concert pianist, an actress, a doctor, or an artist.

————

Suzanne Newton was born in Bunnlevel, North Carolina. She graduated with a B.A.

degree from Duke University in 1957. She was married June 9, 1957. She has worked in the Artists-in-Schools program since North Carolina began it in 1971. She currently spends about thirteen weeks each year traveling around the state to work in public schools as a visiting writer and teacher. She has also been one of Meredith College's visiting professors of creative writing since 1982. Newton is a member of the North Carolina Writer's Conference and the Authors Guild. She has contributed poetry and articles to *Parents', Human Voice Quarterly*, and *Southern Poetry Review*.

Three of her books have been named Junior Literary Guild selections: *C/O Arnold's Corners*, . . . *William Thomas*, and . . . *Georgie's Blues*. The latter book was an American Library Association Notable Book of 1983, an ALA Best Book for Young Adults of 1983, and an ALA Best of the Best Books for Young Adults, 1966-1986.

SELECTED WORKS: Purro and the Prattleberries, 1971; C/O Arnold's Corners, 1974; What Are You Up To, William Thomas?, 1977; Reubella and the Old Focus Home, 1978; M.V. Sexton Speaking, 1981; I Will Call It Georgie's Blues, 1983; An End to Perfect, 1984; A Place Between, 1986.

ABOUT: Contemporary Authors (First Revision), Vol 41; (New Revision Series), Vol. 14; Contemporary Literary Criticism, Vol. 35; Directory of American Poets and Fiction Writers; The International Authors and Writers Who's Who, 1977; Something About the Author, Vol. 5; The Writers Diretory 1984-85.

TRINKA HAKES NOBLE

AUTHOR AND ILLUSTRATOR OF *Apple Tree Christmas*, etc.

Biographical sketch of Trinka Hakes Noble:

TRINKA HAKES NOBLE grew up on a small farm in rural southern Michigan, one of seven children. She attended classes in a one-room schoolhouse until she was in the fifth grade, and she was the only person in her grade. She remembers always being interested in art, and began studying art

TRINKA HAKES NOBLE

thor's childhood in rural Michigan. An apple tree is lost during a terrible winter storm, and the girl who loved the tree is despondent.

Trinka Hakes Noble lives in Upper Montclair, New Jersey, with her husband and daughter.

The Day Jimmy's Boa Ate the Wash was named a 1980 Notable Book by the American Library Association and a 1981 Children's Choice Book by a joint committee of the Children's Book Council and the International Reading Association. *Apple Tree Christmas* was a Junior Literary Guild selection.

SELECTED WORKS WRITTEN AND ILLUSTRATED: The King's Tea, 1979; Hansy's Mermaid, 1983; Apple Tree Christmas, 1984.

SELECTED WORKS WRITTEN: The Day Jimmy's Boa Ate the Wash, 1980; Jimmy's Boa Bounces Back, 1984; Meanwhile, Back at the Ranch, 1987.

SELECTED WORKS ILLUSTRATED: The Witch Who Lost Her Shadow, by Mary Calhoun, 1979; Karin's Christmas Walk, by Susan Pearson, 1980; Will You Take Me to Town on Strawberry Day?, by Marilyn Singer, 1981.

ABOUT: Contemporary Authors, Vol. 116; Something About the Author, Vol. 37.

when she was twelve. After she graduated from high school, she worked in Chicago for a year in order to save money to attend Michigan State University.

Upon graduation, Noble taught art in Michigan, Virginia, and Rhode Island before moving to the New York City area. She continued her education and studied illustration with well-known artist Uri Shulevitz at his Advanced Workshop in Greenwich Village, New York City. In addition, she attended the New School for Social Research.

In 1979 her first book, *The King's Tea*, was published. The tale recounts the snowballing effects of how a cup of tea for the king was ruined by spoiled milk. In 1980, *The Day Jimmy's Boa Ate the Wash* was published, a book *School Library Journal* called "fine, funny and full of pep." The sequel, *Jimmy's Boa Bounces Back*, like the first book, was illustrated by Steven Kellogg. With *Hansy's Mermaid*, the author charted new territory: the picture-book text is the fantasy of how a storm brings a mermaid to a Dutch family. The family's young son understands how sad the mermaid is when she is away from her watery home, and he helps her to go back to the sea.

Apple Tree Christmas reflects the au-

ZIBBY ONEAL

March 17, 1934–

AUTHOR OF *The Language of Goldfish*, etc.

Autobiographical sketch of Elizabeth Oneal, who writes under the name "Zibby Oneal":

I GREW UP in a house in the middle of the Middle West where books were considered as necessary to life as food. My mother carried a book with her wherever she went just in case she might find a spare moment for reading. My parents read aloud to one another in the evening, and every night before bedtime they read to my sister and me. There were toppling stacks of books on ev-

ery flat surface in the house. The public library was very nearly our second home. It is not so surprising that I became a writer.

Briefly, when I was small, I thought about becoming a surgeon like my father. Sometimes he would let me stand on a stool beside him in the operating room to watch him work. I was interested in this all right. I never felt the least bit queasy. But my heart belonged to storytelling.

For another few years I thought I might be a painter. My father taught me something about painting. Together we went out on Saturday expeditions with our watercolors. This, too, was something I loved to do, but not as much as telling stories.

I told myself stories all the time. When I was old enough I began to write them down. While my friends learned to roller skate and jump rope and play jacks, I wrote. While they got up games of Kick the Can and Run, Sheep, Run, I sat beneath a tree in our backyard, making up stories. I think that if a child of mine behaved that way, I'd worry—nowadays we set such store by being well-rounded—but I don't believe my parents ever worried. They let me alone to pursue my singleminded path without much comment. For this I have always been grateful to them.

Well, I never *did* learn to jump rope or skate, but little by little I learned something about writing. In college, at Stanford University, I took every creative writing course offered. I married, had two children, and all the while kept writing. When the children were old enough to want stories, I began to write a few for them, and that is the way that I discovered the pleasures in writing for young people. I had never tried doing that before.

As my children grew older, so did the characters I wrote about. Eventually everyone reached adolescence, but, unlike my children, my characters have remained there. Adolescence strikes me as a deeply interesting time of life. So much is happening for the first time then. So much that we later take for granted is, then, brand new. There is rich material here for fiction.

I would like to think that young adult fiction also provides a writer with the opportunity to make some difference in a reader's life. If adolescence can be exhilarating, it can also be confusing. A book may, perhaps, sometimes speak to that confusion, may offer encouragement by example at a time when encouragement is needed. This, at least, is what I hope a book can do.

When I am not writing, I often teach courses in writing at the University of Michigan in Ann Arbor, where I now live. Teaching makes a good change from the solitude of the typewriter and gives me a chance to spend time with young people only a little older than the characters I write about. I love these classes. We talk and talk about writing books. Sometimes in the midst of these discussions I find myself thinking about how almost sinfully lucky it is to be able to spend a life engrossed in the occupation one loves best.

———

Zibby Oneal was born in Omaha, Nebraska. She attended Stanford University from 1952 to 1955 and graduated from the University of Michigan in 1966. She was married December 27, 1955. *The Lan-*

guage of Goldfish was named an American Library Association "Best of the Best" book for the years 1970-1982. *A Formal Feeling* won the Christopher Award in 1983 and was also an ALA "Best of the Best" book for 1970-1982. *In Summer Light* won the Boston Globe-Horn Book Award for Fiction in 1986. All three books were named ALA Best Books for Young Adults and Notable Books of the Year by the ALA in their years of publication.

SELECTED WORKS: War Work, 1971; The Improbable Adventures of Marvelous O'Hara Soapstone, 1972; Turtle and Snail, 1978; The Language of Goldfish, 1980; A Formal Feeling, 1982; In Summer Light, 1985; Grandma Moses: Painter of Rural America, 1986; Maude and Walter, 1986.

ABOUT: Children's Literature Review, Vol. 13; Contemporary Authors, Vol. 106; Horn Book January/February 1987; Something About the Author, Vol. 30.

JAN ORMEROD

JAN ORMEROD

September 23, 1946–

AUTHOR AND ILLUSTRATOR OF *Sunlight*, etc.

Biographical sketch of Jan Ormerod:

BORN IN Bunbury, Western Australia, Jan Ormerod was among the first of the wave of Australian writers and illustrators whose works began coming to the attention of American publishers and critics in the early part of the 1980s. Formerly a secondary-school art teacher and lecturer in drawing and basic design at the university level, Ormerod received her training at the Western Australia Institute of Technology, where she acquired an associateship in graphic design in 1966 and in art teaching in 1973; she received her teacher's certificate in 1967 from the Claremont Teachers College in Perth.

Praised in *The New York Times Book Review* for her "delicate watercolors [that] plunge their readers into the middle of a family, letting them feel their love and lives," Ormerod's work won quick recognition and wide acceptance in this country. Her first book, *Sunshine*, made something of an awards sweep in Australia when it received not only the 1982 Australian Picture Book of the Year Award from the Children's Book Council of Australia, but the 1982 Mother Goose Award as well, administered by the book club Books for Children. It was named a "Highly Commended" book by the Kate Greenaway Award Committee in 1981; upon publication in this country it was named a Notable Book by the American Library Association. A wordless book that chronicles the start of a little girl's day, *Sunshine* was followed by *Moonlight*, in which the same little girl's day is brought to a close. It was also an ALA Notable Book, of 1982. Of *Moonlight*, Kicki Moxon wrote in the *Times Literary Supplement* that, though wordless, the book is "nonetheless eloquent—and would lose much of [its] impact if accompanied by a story."

Ormerod's sure hand in depicting family relationships provides the foundation for all of her picture books. *101 Things to Do with a Baby* is an expressive introduction for siblings on the best and worst of life with a new baby; *The Story of Chicken Licken* presents the familiar story in the unusual setting of a school theatrical production. The "Jan Ormerod Baby Book" series began with a collection of four books that center on the relationship between a toddler and a father. Robert Wool, writing in *The New York Times Book Review*, praises Ormerod for her "novelist's eye for detail and her painter's grasp of nuance." He goes on to say, "There is no parent who has not gone through something like [what the author depicts] and looking at the whole charade replayed in Miss Ormerod's marvelous, soft, figurative drawing, you smile with recognition." Those first four titles, as well as the succeeding four in the series, were all named ALA Notable Books in their years of publication.

Ormerod now lives in Northampton, England, with her husband and children.

SELECTED WORKS WRITTEN AND ILLUSTRATED: Sunshine, 1981; Moonlight, 1982; 101 Things to Do with a Baby, 1984; Dad's Back, 1985; Messy Baby, 1985; Reading, 1985; Sleeping, 1985; The Story of Chicken Licken, 1985; Bend and Stretch, 1987; Making Friends, 1987; Mom's Home, 1987; This Little Nose, 1987; Kitten Day, 1989.

SELECTED WORKS ILLUSTRATED: Rhymes Around the Day, compiled by Pat Thompson, 1983; Eat Up, Gemma, by Sarah Hayes, 1988.

ABOUT: Contemporary Authors, Vol. 113; Something About the Author, Vol. 44.

GAIL OWENS

March 13, 1939–

ILLUSTRATOR OF *That Julia Redfern*, etc.

Biographical sketch of Gail Owens:

GAIL OWENS was born in Detroit, Michigan, and spent her childhood there. She read a great deal, and she began drawing at an early age. She received special permission to take a life-drawing class when she was a girl. While in high school, she began working as a free-lance artist for department stores, doing fashion illustration be-

cause it involved drawing the human figure. She says she received her best art instruction before she was eighteen. She does not name the schools she attended after that time, because she was disappointed with them.

Owens moved to Brooklyn and began raising her two children, working as a commercial artist: layout person, graphic designer, art director, and illustrator in New York City advertising agencies. After thirteen years there, she moved her family to upstate New York, where she began her career as an illustrator. At first, she illustrated magazine articles and her early few books and commuted to her Manhattan job. Eventually, she was able to work solely as a free-lance illustrator, and now spends all of her working time on books for children.

Owens employs children to be models for her illustrations. She says that she hardly ever has contact with the author of a book before it is published, and comments on the changes occurring in publishing that affect her work, such as dealing with several people instead of one, as in the past, who could supply information she needs to begin illustrating a book.

Fog in the Meadow received a 1980 New Jersey Institute of Technology New Jersey Authors Award. *The Cybil War* was named a 1982 Children's Choice Book by a joint committee of the Children's Book Council and the International Reading Association. *That Julia Redfern* was named a 1982 Notable Book by the American Library Association. Six of the books Owens illustrated were Junior Literary Guild selections: *Julia and the Hand of God*, *A Horse for X.Y.Z.*, *Hail, Hail Camp Timberwood*, *Safe as the Grave*, *The Paper Caper*, and *Goodbye Sammy*.

SELECTED WORKS ILLUSTRATED: A Horse for X.Y.Z., by Louise Moeri, 1977; Julia and the Hand of God, by Eleanor Cameron, 1977; Hail, Hail Camp Timberwood, by Ellen Conford, 1978; Fog in the Meadow, by Joanne Ryder, 1979; Safe as the Grave, by Caroline B. Cooney, 1979; The Cybil War, by Betsy Byars, 1981; The Paper Caper, by Caroline B. Cooney, 1981; A Bundle of Sticks, by Pat Rhoads Mauser, 1982; That Julia Redfern, by Eleanor Cameron, 1982; The Hot and Cold Summer, by Johanna Hurwitz, 1984; Julia's Magic, by Eleanor Cameron, 1984 Encyclopedia Brown and the Case of the Treasure Hunt, by Donald Sobol, 1988; Goodbye Sammy, by Liza Ketchum Murrow, 1989.

ABOUT: Kingman, Lee and others, comps. Illustrators of Children's Books: 1967-1976; Something About the Author, Vol. 54.

BARBARA PARK

April 27, 1947–

AUTHOR OF *Skinnybones*, etc.

Biographical sketch of Barbara Park:

BORN IN MOUNT HOLLY, New Jersey, Barbara Park was the daughter of a merchant and a secretary. From 1965 to 1967 she attended Rider College, later finishing her B.S. in 1969 at the University of Alabama. She married Richard A. Park on June 28, 1969. Making her home in Phoenix, Arizona, Park has raised two sons and continues her writing career.

Humor permeates Barbara Park's books for children. Her goal in her writing is to entertain. Park says that having two sons has influenced her writing, keeping her tuned into situations that are humorous to children. Park feels that by preserving and nurturing the child in her own personality, she inspires the creativity in herself. Knowing that her books make children laugh gives Park satisfaction.

In her first book, *Don't Make Me Smile*, Charlie has to deal with his parents' divorce. While divorce is a serious subject, the book is filled with humor, creating a balance between sadness and laughter. The main character is described as an exasperating and funny kid who is likeable to the reader as he gradually accepts all the changes in his life.

In *Operation: Dump the Chump*, children can relate to the sibling rivalry theme in the story. An older brother, Oscar Win-

kle, schemes about how he can get rid of his little brother for the summer.

Skinnybones, Park's most popular book for children, deals with another zany child, Alex Frankovitch, and Little League. Alex is a terrible baseball player, but following his attempts make the readers laugh. *Skinnybones* has won many children's book awards chosen by children. In 1988 Park wrote a sequel to *Skinnybones* called *Almost Starring Skinnybones*.

Beanpole is a story about a tall seventh-grade girl. Although she usually writes about boys, Park does not believe there is much difference between boys and girls emotionally, and considers herself a writer about children.

Barbara Park's character specialty is the underdog in life, the child who is not in control or popular. This type of character is a better vehicle for humor. If adults did not take themselves so seriously, Park believes the world would be a more relaxed place to live. Young readers benefit from the fact that Barbara Park has never completely let go of her childhood.

SELECTED WORKS: Don't Make Me Smile, 1981; Operation: Dump the Chump, 1982; Skinnybones, 1982; Beanpole, 1983; Buddies, 1985; The Kid in the Red

Jacket, 1987; Almost Starring Skinnybones, 1988; My Mother Got Married (and Other Disasters), 1989.

ABOUT: Contemporary Authors, Vol. 113; Something About the Author, Vol. 35; Vol. 40.

RUTH PARK

AUTHOR OF *Playing Beatie Bow*, etc.

Autobiographical sketch of Rosina Ruth Lucia Park:

MANY YEARS AGO I was born in that green, snowcapped archipelago called New Zealand, and I'm very glad I was. Probably I am a writer because I had a singular childhood. My first seven years I spent all alone in the forest, like a possum or a bear-cub. It was rain forest, pathless, dense; its light was a dim green twilight. How did I get there?

My father was a bridge-builder and road-maker; he drove some of the first roads through the forested Crown lands of northern New Zealand. My mother and I travelled with him, living in tents beside mountain streams lively with trout and eels. My father's head was crammed with the savage hero tales of his ancestral land, Scotland. How lucky I was that he had the gift of storytelling! You must imagine lamplight, owls hoo-hooing, the tent fly cracking with frost, and myself, this bear-cub child, listening to the stories I would play out by myself in the bush, next day. I developed an imagination both rich and rowdy. But there was one thing I had not imagined. When I went to school at last, I was totally astounded, almost frightened, to see children playing together. I hadn't known they did that!

Though I loved school, I wasn't at all interested in children's games. However, I learned how to pretend, and became on the surface just another kid, though inside I knew I wasn't. This didn't make me happy. I really believed I was a changeling. (We didn't know the word 'alien' then, otherwise I would have thought I had been dropped by a Rigelian spaceship.) I longed to be like everyone else, but my solitary early life had made me different somehow. My friends were almost all Maori children, little forest creatures like myself, anxiously pretending to be civilised.

By the time I was eight I was writing. I entered all kinds of verse and story competitions, and when I was eleven I won one of these. My story was published. This went straight to my head. I saw my life's work laid out before me, and have never stopped writing since. I think, even at the age of eleven, I felt comfortable writing, more the real person I knew I was.

I was educated mainly in Auckland. I did an external university degree while I worked as a journalist, on the *Auckland Star*. At this time I also did a great deal of freelance writing—mostly unsuccessful, I fear. There were few markets in New Zealand for a free lance, so I submitted work to journals all over the world. Nobody had a larger mail of internationally returned typescripts than I did! When I was nineteen I became editor of a very large children's section on my newspaper. It was really like a small newspaper in itself. Here I learned a great deal about what children like to read, as opposed to what they're told they ought to like. I made a vow then that I would always be true to child readers; I'd never write for publishers, or editors or critics, or to win prizes. I would just write as best I could for children.

The time came when I knew I had to leave my green islands and find a wider world, so I went to Australia and married D'Arcy Niland, a young short-story writer. For a while we led a wandering life. I saw a little of this vast, magnificent land, and was captured for ever by its noble indifference to humankind. I felt that one day this continent would give a shrug and shake all the humans off into the sea. But it would still be its own self. That's what I call *identity*.

D'Arcy and I wrote everything that came to hand—stories, films, radio plays and television plays, and then adult novels. Literary work was not well-paid; we had to work very hard, and we were often very poor. But we had five good children, and a happy life.

D'Arcy died suddenly when he was forty-seven, but he had already achieved a great deal. Our children grew up—two quite famous book illustrators, a librarian, a physicist, and a musician. I found work that took me to many countries, Norway, Japan, Egypt, and Britain. This work was mostly television, film, and sometimes special assignments in journalism. But gradually I was able to concentrate more and more on writing for children, though I don't find the latter easy at all.

Most adult writing is designed to expand the reader's inner world, but children's writing is largely the reverse. For the child the doors of imaginative vision open outwards; the content of the story is the marvellous world beyond those doors, and one's technique and style are what opens them. My ambition is to open the magic casements for kids to help them grow, to feel strong, just a little.

Now I'm quite an old woman, I find I haven't changed much. I spend part of the time living amongst giant trees, on a little island green as mint and about as big as a handkerchief—Norfolk Island, which is a thousand kilometres off the coast of Australia. I still tell myself and other people stories. I still think the earth is a marvellous home for me and everyone else. I hope you do, too.

———

Ruth Park was born in Auckland and married in 1942. She attended both St. Benedict's College and the University of Auckland. She also writes books for adults, the best known of which is *The Harp in the South*. She is the author of the "Muddle-Headed Wombat" series of children's books, which are not published in the U.S. Her autobiography, *The Drums Go Bang*, was published in Australia in 1956. Park has lived in Europe, Egypt, and Norfolk Island and other Pacific countries.

The Australian Children's Book Council named *Playing Beatie Bow* the 1981 Book of the Year. It also won the 1982 Boston Globe-Horn Book Award for fiction and was a 1982 runner-up for the Guardian Award. The International Board on Books for Young People named the book an Honor Book for 1982. It was made into a film in 1986, produced by the South Australian Film Corporation.

SELECTED WORKS: The Ship's Cat, 1961; The Road to Christmas, 1962; Uncle Matt's Mountain, 1962; Shaky Island, 1962; Airlift for Grandee, 1964; The Secret of the Maori Cave, 1964; The Road Under the Sea, 1966; Ten-Cent Island, 1968; When the Wind Changed, 1980; Playing Beatie Bow, 1981.

ABOUT: The Authors and Writers Who's Who, 1971; Carpenter, Humphrey and Mari Prichard. The Oxford Companion to Children's Literature; Contemporary Authors, Vol. 105; Kirkpatrick, D.L., ed. Twentieth-Century Children's Writers, 2nd ed.; Something About the Author, Vol. 25; The Writers Directory 1984-86.

Dorothy H Patent

DOROTHY HINSHAW PATENT

April 30, 1940–

AUTHOR OF *Evolution Goes On Every Day*, etc.

Autobiographical sketch of Dorothy Hinshaw Patent:

I HAVE ALWAYS loved animals. When I was just a toddler, my family bought a puppy; they had to keep him caged to protect him from my overly enthusiastic love. When I got a little older, I would head out on my bike each spring to the toad pond and gather jars and jars of tadpoles. I didn't know how to keep them properly, so most of them died. But each year, I'd go back and collect more. When I was a fifth grader, I fell in love with tropical fish, although I still loved frogs and toads and kept them as pets whenever I could catch them. My room became a miniature zoo, with aquariums full of fish, frogs, snakes, and lizards. I was an unusual girl.

I'm not one of those people who always wanted to be an author. I came to writing "sideways," through my love of animals, my scientific training, and my desire to use my mind. I met my husband and married while I was a graduate student, studying zoology, and had my two sons by the time I received my Ph.D. We spent a year in Detroit doing research and then a year in Naples, Italy. After that, my husband got a job at a college in North Carolina. There was no possibility of work for me, so I was faced with a dilemma—what to do with myself? I wanted to be at home with my children, but I also wanted to use my scientific training in a positive way. My friends always told me I explained scientific things well and in an interesting fashion, and I'd always been a good writer. Maybe the thing to do was write books about animals for children.

I went to the library and studied children's animal books. At that time, "life cycle" books were popular, so I wrote one on bumblebees, creatures that children encounter but knew little about. I sent it off to Holiday House. My manuscript was rejected because they weren't going to publish any more books of that type. But Ed Lindemann, the science editor, liked my writing. The following year, just after we had moved to Montana, Ed wrote and said Holiday wanted a book about the weasel family. If I was interested, I should put together a sample chapter and an outline. They liked my work and sent me my first contract. I've been writing for Holiday House ever since, even though I now also work for several other publishers as well.

Why is writing nature books for children a rewarding career? There are several things I love about it. First of all, I hate routine work. I hate doing the same thing over and over again, a requirement in most kinds of jobs. But each book is a new topic, a new look at the world, a new chance to meet interesting people and encounter wonderful creatures. There is very little routine in what I do. Writing enables me to share my love of nature with children and to inform them about some important issues. As our world gets more and more crowded, wild things are getting progressively squeezed out. I believe the earth is for all life, not just people. But in order to preserve nature, we must manage it, and manage it well. This involves hard choices based on carefully gathered information and an understanding of ecological principles. By helping children learn about such things, I hope I'm able to encourage them to be educated, responsible citizens of the world.

———

Born in Rochester, Minnesota, Dorothy Hinshaw Patent received her B.A. degree from Stanford University in 1962. She was married March 21, 1964. She took her M.A. in 1965 and her Ph.D. in 1968 from the University of California at Berkeley. She was a post-doctorate fellow at Sinai Hospital and a researcher at Stazione Zoologica in Naples, Italy, from 1970 to 1971. In the Department of Zoology, she is a faculty affiliate at the University of Montana in Missoula, and has been Acting Assistant Professor there. She is a member of the Author's Guild, the American Institute of Biological Sciences, and the Society of Children's Book Writers.

Evolution Goes On Every Day was an Honor Book in the 1977 Golden Kite Awards given by the Society of Children's Book Writers. *The Lives of Spiders* won the 1980 Golden Kite Award for nonfiction. *Spider Magic* was named a Notable Book of 1982 by the American Library Association. The American Nature Study Society Board awarded the 1986 Eva L. Gordon Award to Dorothy Hinshaw Patent as an author of outstanding science literature for children.

SELECTED WORKS: Evolution Goes On Every Day, 1977; Animal and Plant Mimicry, 1978; The World of Worms, 1978; Sizes and Shapes in Nature—What They Mean, 1979; Bacteria: How They Affect Other Living Things, 1980; The Lives of Spiders, 1980; Horses of America, 1981; A Picture Book of Cows, 1982; Spider Magic, 1982; Thoroughbred Horses, 1985; All About Whales, 1987; Dolphins and Porpoises, 1987; Appaloosa Horses, 1988; Babies!, 1988.

ABOUT: Contemporary Authors, Vol. 61; (New Revision Series), Vol. 9; Something About the Author, Vol. 22.

DIANE PATERSON

July 23, 1946–

AUTHOR AND ILLUSTRATOR OF *Smile for Auntie*, etc.

Biographical sketch of Diane R. Cole Paterson:

BORN IN Brooklyn, Diane Paterson is the daughter of A.R. and T.E. Cole. She grew up in Brooklyn, Long Island, West Virginia, and Maine. She attended Pratt Institute in Brooklyn from 1966 to 1968. She was married and has two children, but her marriage ended in divorce in 1978. She once lived in a barn on top of a hill in Barryville, New York, and now lives in High Falls, New York.

Paterson's illustrations for children are infused with humor, sometimes because of their cartoonish nature. In a review of *Kitty*, *School Library Journal* reviewer Nancy Palmer writes, "Paterson's colorful pen-and-wash illustrations fashion much of the fun; their clear, comically detailed depictions of outrageous situations perfectly complement the persona Kitty creates in her diary." Paterson has also done illustrations for magazines and textbooks.

Paterson recalls her childhood vividly and draws upon this experience in creating her books for children. For example, her *Smile for Auntie* reflects this memory, depicting a huge aunt looming above, begging for a kiss hello.

She is a member of the Authors Guild. She enjoys swimming, gardening, and painting.

SELECTED WORKS WRITTEN AND ILLUSTRATED: The Biggest Snowstorm Ever, 1974; Eat!, 1975; Smile for Auntie, 1976; If I Were a Toad, 1977; Wretched Rachel, 1979; The Bathtub Ocean, 1979; Soap and Suds, 1984; Kitty: A Cat's Diary, by Robyn Supraner, 1986.

SELECTED WORKS ILLUSTRATED: Fiona's Bee, by Beverly Keller, 1975; Monnie Hates Lydia, by Susan Pearson, 1975; Kittens for Nothing, by Robert Krauss, 1976; Skunk for a Day, by Roger Caras, 1976; The Bravest Babysitter, by Barbara Greenberg, 1977; Too Many Books!, by Caroline Feller Bauer 1984.

ABOUT: Contemporary Authors, Vol. 101; Kingman, Lee and others, comps. Illustrators of Children's Books: 1967-1976; Something About the Author, Vol. 33.

GARY PAULSEN

May 17, 1939–

AUTHOR OF *Dogsong*, etc.

Biographical sketch of Gary Paulsen:

GARY PAULSEN was born in Minneapolis, Minnesota. His parents are of Swedish descent. He attended Bemidji College in 1957-58. He also studied at the University of Colorado in 1976. He joined the army in 1958 and rose to the rank of sergeant before his discharge in May, 1962. He has worked as a teacher, an electronic field engineer, an actor, a director, a rancher, and a singer before he became a full-time writer. He worked at these various jobs in order to support himself while pursuing a career as a writer, "barely getting by" and "starving." He says that he has realized that poverty is a condition of writing as an art form. Gary Paulsen was married to an artist on May 5, 1971. It was his third marriage. He has one son.

The author leads an active life and, as a hobby, runs dogsleds. He has competed twice in the Iditarod Sled Dog Race from Anchorage to Nome, Alaska. The setting of *Dogsong* recalls that race. Paulsen once survived a Pacific storm in a fiberglass sailboat, and wrote a book drawing on that experience. *The Voyage of the Frog* is the survival story of a young Californian whose twenty-two foot sailboat is blown off course in a gale, leaving him to battle weather, the dangerous wake of a passing oil tanker, and shark attacks.

The author has also written two plays, several hundred magazine articles, short stories, and a variety of nonfiction books. He likes to write for young people because of their lack of artistic biases.

Paulsen takes an interest in community and political affairs. He works with nuclear disarmament causes and plans to collaborate on a book with a Soviet writer. Gary Paulsen lives in Becida, Minnesota. Two of his novels have been named Newbery Honor Books by the American Library Association: *Dogsong* in 1986 and *Hatchet* in 1988. *Tracker* won a 1985 Society of Midland Authors Award. Three of his books have been named ALA Notable Books in their years of publication: *Dogsong*, *The Crossing*, and *Hatchet*. *Dancing Carl*, *Tracker*, *Dogsong*, *The Crossing*, and *The Island* were all named ALA Best Books, each in their years of publication. *Dogsong* was also named a Notable Children's Trade Book in the Field of Social Studies by a joint committee of the Children's Book Council and the National Council on the Social Studies.

SELECTED WORKS: The Man Who Climbed the Mountain, 1976; Winterkill, 1977; Dancing Carl, 1983; Tracker, 1984; Dogsong, 1985; Sentries, 1986; The Crossing, 1987; Hatchet, 1987; The Island, 1988; The Voyage of the Frog, 1989.

ABOUT: Contemporary Authors, Vol. 73-76; Something About the Author, Vol. 22; Vol. 50; Vol. 54; Voice of Youth Advocates August/October 1986; Writer's Digest January 1980.

LILA PERL

AUTHOR OF *Fat Glenda's Summer Romance*, etc.

Autobiographical sketch of Lila Perl:

I WAS BORN in Brooklyn, which always used to be good for a laugh (I don't know if it still is). I had what I felt was a perfectly ordinary childhood. And I never dreamed that I would grow up to be a writer.

Today, when I talk to groups of young people in the schools, they ask me why it surprises me that I've become a writer of children's books. I explain that when *I* was a child we never met any "real, live authors" anywhere, much less in our classrooms. In fact, all the authors whose books I read were either dead or British (and often dead as well). That pretty much took in my favorites—Louisa May Alcott and Charles Dickens.

Like most serious kids in those days, I read a lot, and often the same books, over and over. Writing, on the other hand, seemed a pretentious thing to do. The earliest thing I can remember having written was a limerick for a grade-school assignment. It was a little strained, but it went:

The subject that I hate the most,
Is one of which I cannot boast.
  Though I work at it hard,
  When I look at my card,
My geometry mark is the lowest.

I started another limerick that I liked better, but I don't remember ever finishing it. It began:

The thing I hate doing the most,
Is scraping the burnt off the toast. . . .

Entering college as a quivering, immature fifteen-year-old didn't advance my self-confidence about being a writer one bit. In fact, it probably delayed my attempts at a literary career by a good ten years. At the hands of a curmudgeon professor who claimed that she ate "a freshman every morning for breakfast," I got *C*'s on most of my theme papers.

Becoming a published writer didn't really start for me until I was married, with children of grade-school age. Why does somebody choose a writing career rather than some other kind of work? Speaking for myself, I *could* say that I liked the hours and also the opportunity to be at home for my children. That isn't intended to sound flip. At that time, not as many mothers as today went out to work, and I'm still a firm believer in the value of a parent being on hand for growing youngsters.

But, of course, there are deeper reasons for giving oneself to writing. For me, writing is having a second life. It's a "place" where I can go, a "world" that I can control. I love making order out of chaos. And that's what writing really is. Fiction is taking the raw material of life and reworking it into a story that has a beginning, a middle, and an end, that has drama, suspense, and purpose. Life often does not. The writing of nonfiction, too, is a craft wherein patterns are made evident where no patterns appear to exist.

Today, forty-five books later, I realize that writing has become something of an addiction. A day when I haven't written something fresh and new is seldom a really good day for me. Nor do I ever feel totally confident that I can "pull off" each new project. My "second life" is one that presents me with a never-ending stream of challenges. But then that, too, is why I became a writer. If I'd wanted to do the same thing over and over I suppose I could have gone to work on an assembly line. I'm glad I didn't.

———

Lila Perl received her B.A. degree from Brooklyn College and did graduate work at the School of Education, New York University, and Teachers College at Columbia University. She has been a Golden Kite Award judge for the Society of Children's Book Writers, of which she is a member, and has given writing workshops for the Society at Bank Street College. She has taught writing for children at the Hofstra University Summer Writers' Conference and at the Vassar Institute of Publishing and Writing. She is a fellow of the MacDowell Colony. Lila Perl is married and has two grown children.

Junk Food, Fast Food, Health Food was an Honor Book for nonfiction in the 1981 Boston Globe-Horn Book Awards. Five of Lila Perl's books have been named Notable Children's Trade Books in the Field of Social Studies for their years of publication; the award is given by a joint committe of the Children's Book Council and the National Council on the Social Studies. The books chosen include *Slumps, Grunts, and Snickerdoodles* and *Hunter's Stew and Hangtown Fry*. Both *The Hamburger Book* and *Mummies, Tombs, and Treasure* were named Outstanding Science Trade Books

for Children by a joint committee of the Children's Book Council and the National Science Teachers Association, for 1974 and 1987 respectively. The American Library Association has designated some of her books Notable Books of the year of their publication; these include *American Regional Foods and Festivals* in 1965 and *Red Flannel Hash and Shoo-Fly Pie* in 1963.

SELECTED WORKS: Red Flannel Hash and Shoo-Fly Pie, 1963; American Regional Foods and Festivals, 1965; Me and Fat Glenda, 1972; The Hamburger Book: All About Hamburgers and Hamburger Cookery, 1974; That Crazy April, 1974; Slumps, Grunts, and Snickerdoodles: What Colonial America Ate and Why, 1975; Hunter's Stew and Hangtown Fry: What Pioneer America Ate and Why, 1977; Junk Food, Fast Food, Health Food, 1980; Annabelle Starr, E.S.P., 1983; Fat Glenda's Summer Romance, 1986; Mummies, Tombs, and Treasure, 1987; The Secret Diary of Katie Dinkerhoff, 1987; Don't Sing Before Breakfast, Don't Sleep in the Moonlight, 1988.

ABOUT: Contemporary Authors (First Revision), Vol. 33; Something About the Author, Vol. 6.

P. J. PETERSEN

October 23, 1941–

AUTHOR OF *Would You Settle for Improbable?*, etc.

Autobiographical sketch of Peter James Petersen:

I GREW UP on a prune farm in California, six miles from the tiny town of Geyserville. It was an interesting place to live, but I didn't realize that as a boy. I wanted to go somewhere else—anywhere except a prune farm.

Because actual travel was impossible, I settled for travelling through books— reading about people whose lives were different from mine. My source of books was the branch library in Geyserville with its three shelves of children's books. I read everything on the shelves before the Bookmobile arrived with a new supply. (The library had a limit of five books per person, but an

understanding librarian let me check out an extra five—supposedly for my brother.)

While we worked on the farm, I often told my younger brothers the stories I had read. I often changed the stories, though, especially the endings that involved a marriage and living happily ever after. Sometimes I made up my own stories and was delighted to find that my brothers couldn't always tell the difference between my creations and "real" ones.

By the age of eight, I had decided to become a writer, but when I told people, they laughed. Boys from Geyserville became farmers or mechanics or insurance salesmen—not writers. I never changed my mind about writing, but after a while I did quit announcing my plans.

In high school and college I wrote short stories, but I saw those as exercises. I really wanted to write novels. In fact, the day I finished college, I moved to a tiny room in a run-down section of San Francisco and began work on a novel.

At the age of twenty-three, after several false starts, I finished my first novel. I thought it was nearly perfect, but none of the publishers agreed. After it was rejected by six firms, I shoved it into a drawer. It is still there somewhere, buried under thousands of other pages.

Thirteen years and several million words later, I was very discouraged. I hadn't sold a word—not even a greeting card verse. I hadn't even tried to publish anything for years. Without realizing it, I had come to believe what I had been told as a child: Boys from Geyserville don't become writers.

My break came when my daughter, a seventh grader at the time, began bringing me the books she was reading. After reading a few and discussing them with her, I decided to write a novel for her. I had never written for young people before, but I decided it was worth a try. At least I'd have one reader, which was more than I'd had up until then.

Everything was different that time. I was no longer writing for some editor in some New York office; I was writing for my daughter. I couldn't quit when things got hard; my reader was waiting—and not very patiently.

As I worked on that book, which eventually became *Would You Settle for Improbable?*, writing was suddenly fun again. I was laughing at the jokes, wincing at the painful parts. It was like the old days, when I was out in the prune orchard telling stories to my brothers.

I had finally discovered where I belonged.

———

P. J. Petersen was born in Santa Rosa, California. He received an A.B. degree in creative writing from Stanford University in 1962 and an M.A. degree in English literature from San Francisco State College in 1964. He also received a Ph.D. degree, in American literature, in 1972 from the University of New Mexico He was married July 6, 1963. He is now a Professor of English at Shasta College.

Would You Settle for Improbable? and *Nobody Else Can Walk It for You* were both named Young Adult Best Books of the Year, in 1981 and 1982 respectively, by the

American Library Association. Four of his books have been named Junior Literary Guild selections: *Here's to the Sophomores, Going for the Big One, Good-bye to Good Ol' Charlie,* and *The Freshman Detective Blues.* . . . *Improbable* was adapted into a feature film.

SELECTED WORKS: Would You Settle for Improbable?, 1981; Nobody Else Can Walk It for You, 1982; The Boll Weevil Express, 1983; Here's to the Sophomores, 1984; Corky and the Brothers Cool, 1985; Going for the Big One, 1986; The Freshman Detective Blues, 1987; Good-bye to Good Ol' Charlie, 1987; How Can You Hijack a Cave?, 1988.

ABOUT: Contemporary Authors, Vol. 112; Something About the Author, Vol. 43; Vol. 48.

SUSAN BETH PFEFFER

February 17, 1948–

AUTHOR OF *Kid Power*, etc.

Autobiographical sketch of Susan Beth Pfeffer:

IT WASN'T UNTIL I was six that I knew I wanted to be a writer. From birth to four, I suppose my ambitions mostly focused on surviving the indignities of infancy—diapers and drooling and silverware management and tripping (I always seemed to be falling down something). At four, I knew just where my future lay. I was going to be a cowgirl. I had a cowgirl outfit, complete with cowgirl skirt, cowgirl blouse, cowgirl vest, cowgirl hat, and best of all, cowgirl gun. When you have an older brother, any sort of weapon is appreciated.

By five, I'd outgrown the cowgirl outfit, and thus the dream died. I think around then I began a lifelong yearning to be Queen of England, a job that I, a Jewish girl in the suburbs of New York, had as much chance of attaining as cowgirl. It's a shame. As a grown-up, I realize my cowgirl fantasies were a bit off base (among other things, cowgirls don't wear skirts), but Queen of England is a job I could handle with great aplomb (I look wonderful in crowns).

When I turned six, my father, a lawyer, had his first book published, and he had the good sense to dedicate it to my mother, my brother, and me. I had just learned how to read, and I would sit on the living room radiator, and read over and over again the title page and the dedication. Thus, I saw the words Pfeffer and Susan in print, and I was struck by how really fine they looked. Pfeffer. Susan. All those *f*'s and *s*'s. So naturally I decided to become a writer. I started my career with *Dookie The Cookie*, four action-packed pages about a talking Oreo cookie who falls in love with a pair of scissors named Sally. My mother loved it, or at least had the good heart to claim to. I was launched.

I wrote straight throughout school (and frequently during school, rather than paying attention), and except for a brief peculiar episode my freshman year at NYU when I wanted to be a Great Film Director, kept planning to be a writer when I grew up. Ultimately, I grew up, and my last semester in college, I wrote my first book, *Just Morgan*. The first publishing house that saw it accepted it, and while the next few years had their ups and downs, I was a professional writer by the time I was twenty-one, and I've been one ever since.

Now that I think about it, things really did work out best. Poor Prince Charles still isn't King of England, and he's been waiting forty years for a chance to put on that crown. Maybe someone should suggest writing children's books as an alternative career.

P.S. I have no trouble pronouncing Pfeffer, although the rest of the world seems to. It's just like Pepper only with *F*'s where you usually say *P*. This is not a coincidence since Pfeffer means pepper in German.

———

Susan Beth Pfeffer was born in New York City and grew up in Woodmere, Long Island. She graduated from New York University with a B.A. degree in 1969. She has been an English instructor at Orange County Community College in Middletown, New York.

About David was named a Best Book for Young Adults in 1980 by the American Library Association and *The Year Without Michael* received the same distinction in 1987. Both *Just Between Us* and *What Do You Do When Your Mouth Won't Open* were named Junior Literary Guild selections.

SELECTED WORKS: Just Morgan, 1970; Better Than All Right, 1972; Kid Power, 1977; About David, 1980; Just Between Us, 1980; What Do You Do When Your Mouth Won't Open, 1981; Starting with Melodie, 1982; Courage, Dana, 1983; Getting Even, 1986; Hard Times High, 1986; The Year Without Michael, 1987; Rewind to Yesterday, 1988; Thea at Sixteen, 1988; Turning Thirteen, 1988.

ABOUT: Contemporary Authors (First Revision), Vol. 29; Library Journal July 1, 1970; Something About the Author, Vol. 4; Who's Who in the East, 1981-1982; Who's Who of American Women, 1977-1978; The Writers Directory 1984-1986.

MEREDITH ANN PIERCE

July 5, 1958–

AUTHOR OF *The Darkangel*, etc.

Meredith Ann Pierce

Autobiographical sketch of Meredith Ann Pierce:

AS LONG as I can remember, I've been making up stories, although I didn't always know I'd wind up as a writer. My brother taught me to write when I was about three, so right from the start, I was scribbling away, mostly the adventures of my stuffed animal collection. I had dozens of plush "buddies" who obligingly enacted stories all day long. Later, the buddies were joined by an array of Barbie dolls and model horses.

My brothers and sister and I collaborated on endless narrative games that lasted months or years. The earliest was "Hansel and Gretel and the Magic Trailer." My older brother was Hansel. I was Gretel. Our bunk bed—which we envisioned as having been hurled through the wall of our bedroom during a hurricane and having miraculously acquired a working, no-fuel-required jet engine—became the Magic Trailer.

The Magic Trailer remained in continuous flight, whisking its hapless occupants all over the world. Occasionally it dipped close enough to the ocean's surface so that the orphans could fish with their bare hands. Fruit, similarly obtained by buzzing orchards, supplemented the tedious diet of raw seafood.

The arrival of my sister and younger brother on the scene added the characters of Buzzie and Buzz, similarly orphaned and wafted into the upper atmosphere by gale force winds to be deposited on the Magic Trailer to the surprise of all. The Magic Trailer was getting crowded. It began taking furloughs by dropping off its occupants on deserted islands for a few weeks before whizzing back to collect them. Always a furious rush to scramble aboard before we ran out of beach and the Magic Trailer zoomed away forever.

There were other games: the Jungle Game, for one, which included a black panther named Shah, who was the as-yet-unrevealed king of the forest and who wore a glowing ruby on a chain around his neck. I was Shah. My brother was Scar, a wise and kindly bear. My sister and younger brother were leopards. A horrible sea-serpent living in a nearby pool was always attempting to devour the companions, burn down the forest, and other atrocities. We also played the Witch Game, Slaves in India, Swiss Family Robinson, Old Yeller.

Eventually, the Unicorn Game phased in. It comprised not only me and my siblings but most of the neighborhood children as well. (This story, by the way, provided the basis for my third novel, *Birth of the Firebringer*, which revolves around a band of proud, tough unicorns menaced by gryphons and wyverns.) The Unicorn Game placed at my disposal a new pool of neighborhood talent. Better than siblings. Better even than buddies and Barbie dolls. I began writing and directing plays, roaming the block to round up enough semi-willing victims to form a cast. About half of these plays progressed far enough to be performed for parents, who yawned and applauded vigorously.

It wasn't until I reached college, though, that I realized there was a commercial market for this sort of thing. I could make a living at it. I could become a writer. I had an excellent teacher named Joy Anderson, who helped me channel my out-of-control imagination into coherent storylines and hone my writing style. She taught me that to be a writer a person needs two things: imagination to supply the raw material for the story and the craft of words, which are the means of expressing and communicating a story to others.

————

Meredith Ann Pierce was born in Seattle, Washington. She received her B.A. degree in 1978 and her M.A. degree in 1980 from the University of Florida. She was a Jane Tinkham Broughton Fellow in Writing for Children at the Bread Loaf Writers' Conference in 1984 and received a State of Florida Individual Artist's Fellowship Special Award for Children's Literature in 1987.

Her first novel, *The Darkangel*, won the International Reading Association Children's Book Award in 1983. It was also placed on the American Library Association's Best of the Best Books 1970–1982. *The Woman Who Loved Reindeer* was designated an ALA Best Book for Young Adults in 1985. She plans to write two more in the trilogy that began with the *Birth of the Firebringer*. "Rampion", a novella, appears in Andre Norton's anthology *Four from the Witch World*, a 1989 book.

SELECTED WORKS: The Darkangel, 1982; A Gathering of Gargoyles, 1984; Birth of the Firebringer, 1985; The Woman Who Loved Reindeer, 1985; Where the Wild Geese Go, 1988; The Pearl of the Soul of the World, 1989.

ABOUT: Contemporary Authors, Vol. 108; Horn Book January/February 1988. Something About the Author, Vol. 48.

JERRY PINKNEY

December 22, 1939–

ILLUSTRATOR OF *Mirandy and Brother Wind*, etc.

Autobiographical sketch of Jerry Pinkney:

I'VE LOVED TO DRAW as long as I can remember, and in elementary school my teachers were very supportive. I often handled different projects through drawing. I was never an adept speller, but when I sat down to draw, if something didn't work, I made it work. I was assigned many projects that had to do with drawing. This made me feel special.

I worked at a local newspaper stand and always took along my sketch pad and pencils to draw the store display windows and the people passing by. One day, the cartoonist John Liney saw me drawing and invited me to his studio. He gave me supplies and introduced me to the possibility of making a living at drawing and inspired me as a young artist.

All through grade school I continued to draw as much as I could. After school I took drawing and painting classes. Upon graduation from high school, I was awarded a scholarship to the Philadelphia College of Art.

In 1960 I married and moved to Boston, Massachusetts. My first job was illustrating studio cards. A few years later I was employed by a design studio as an Illustrator-Designer. It was there that I illustrated my first book, an African folk tale, and my eyes were opened to the world of books. I can still remember, after months of work, waiting for the printed book to arrive; and when it did arrive, the touch, the scent, and the sound of opening a book for the first time. I knew at once that this was what I wanted to do. In 1964 two other artists and I opened Kaleidoscope Studio. Today a resident of Croton-on-Hudson, New York, I work as a free-lance illustrator.

Some twenty books later, I realize that I have something important to contribute, especially in the area of portraying black people. My growing-up experiences, my family, the neighborhood, and the music have all found their way to my drawing board. I also have the opportunity to travel across the country speaking to young people in grade schools, colleges, and universities about the field of illustration.

The research for my projects is endless and is fascinating. I spend lots of time in the public libraries and have an extensive library in my studio. I can't help but reflect on the little boy who wasn't a terrific reader. As an illustrator, I've had to develop my ability to understand and interpret the information that I read. I've had to work very hard to achieve this.

I like to put a lot of information in my illustrations. That's why extensive research is such a key part of my work. When the research is completed, I begin a series of pencil sketches. These sketches highlight incidents that I select to illustrate in the finished work. If the text requires people, I often use my family or find models to act out manuscripts while Polaroid photographs are taken. With the photographs, a more finished sketch is done. The finished sketch is presented to the client. Upon approval the final illustration is done.

Working as an illustrator is very rewarding. One of the advantages is the opportunity to work at home. My wife and four children have played a large role in my work process. Three of our four children are now working in creative arts fields. My wife assists me in finding models, assembling costumes, and performing various clerical duties.

For the last three years, I've been teaching at the University of Delaware as an Associate Professor of Art. This enables me to participate in the development of new artists.

———

Jerry Pinkney was born in Philadelphia. He was married in 1960. He studied at the University of the Arts in Philadelphia on an art scholarship. He was Visiting Critic at the Rhode Island School of Design in Providence from 1969 to 1970 and Associate Professor at Pratt Institute in Brooklyn from 1986 to 1987. He has also been Distinguished Visiting Professor at the University of Delaware in Newark for two years in addition to being an Associate Professor of Art. He is a member of the Society of Illustrators and the Graphic Artists Guild. Pinkney has served on the U.S. Postal Service Citizens Stamp Advisory Committee since 1982. He has been commissioned to create eleven commemorative stamps, including Benjamin Banneker in 1980 and Mary McLeod Bethune in 1985. He has also been invited to join the NASA Artist Team for the Space Shuttle Columbia. He has illustrated many limited edition classics for Franklin Library and has done illustration for *National Geographic*, and other magazines, and for corporate clients. He has also had his work exhibited at one-man shows, such as his 1988 Retrospective at the Philadelphia Afro-American Historical and Cultural Museum, and at many group shows. Pinkney has been a speaker at many colleges, universities, and museums.

Jerry Pinkney has received many awards for his work; these include a 1979 Certificate of Achievement from the NAACP in Westchester, Citizen of the Year 1980 from Kappa Alpha Psi Fraternity, and a Certificate of Achievement in 1980 from the Westchester Urban League.

Roll of Thunder won the 1977 Newbery Award from the American Library Association, was a National Book Award finalist in 1977, and was a Boston Globe-Horn Book fiction Honor Book for 1977. *Childtimes* was a Boston Globe-Horn Book Award nonfiction Honor Book of 1980. *Patchwork Quilt* won the 1986 Coretta Scott King Award for illustration, as did *Half a Moon and One Whole Star* in 1987. *Quilt* also won a 1986 Christopher Award. *Mirandy and Brother Wind* won the King award in 1989, and was also an ALA 1989 Caldecott Honor Book. *More Tales of Uncle Remus* and *Mirandy* were 1988 ALA Notable Books. *The Patchwork Quilt*, and *Yagua Days* were Reading Rainbow books.

SELECTED WORKS ILLUSTRATED: Song of the Trees, by Mildred D. Taylor, 1975; Roll of Thunder, Hear My Cry, by Mildred D. Taylor, 1976; Yagua Days, by Cruz Martel, 1976; Mary McLeod Bethune, by Eloise Greenfield, 1977; Childtimes: A Three-Generation Memoir, by Eloise Greenfield, 1979; Jahdu, by Virginia Hamilton, 1980; The Patchwork Quilt, by Valerie Flournoy, 1985; Half a Moon and One Whole Star, by Crescent Dragonwagon, 1986; The Tales of Uncle Remus, retold by Julius Lester, 1987; Wild Wild Sunflower Child Anna, by Nancy White Carlstrom, 1987; Mirandy and Brother Wind, by Patricia C. McKissack, 1988; More Tales of Uncle Remus, retold by Julius Lester, 1988; Rabbit Makes a Monkey Out of Lion, by Verna Aardema, 1989.

ABOUT: American Artist May/June 1982; Cederholm, Theresa Dickason, comp. and ed. Afro-American Artists; Horn Book March/April 1988; Kingman, Lee and others, comps. Illustrators of Children's Books: 1957-1966; 1967-1976; New York Times (Westchester Section) February 26, 1978; December 13, 1988; Rollock, Barbara. Black Authors and Illustrators of Children's Books; Something About the Author, Vol. 32; Vol. 41; Who's Who in American Art, 1986.

HELEN PLOTZ

March 20, 1913–

ANTHOLOGIST OF *Gladly Learn and Gladly Teach*, etc.

Autobiographical sketch of Helen Ratnoff Plotz:

I HAVE LIVED in Brooklyn all my life. I was born in 1913 to a doctor and a teacher and was graduated from Vassar College in 1933. "My Father Was A Doctor" was published in *Commentary*. I have written various essays on children and poetry and have won a Robert Frost Poetry Prize.

In 1933, I was married to a young doctor, Milton Plotz, who became a clinical professor of medicine at Downstate University of Medicine. His book was *Coronary Heart Diseases*. He died in 1962.

We had four children: Elizabeth, Vassar '58; Paul, Harvard '58; Sarah, Vassar '65; and John, Harvard '71. Elizabeth became a medical librarian, Paul, a researcher in medicine at the National Institute of Health, Sarah, a solicitor in London, and John, a lawyer. All are married; I have five grandsons and two granddaughters.

For forty-five years, I have reviewed children's books for the Child Study Children's Book Committee. It has been a most rewarding and enriching experience. I have also talked at various schools and have taught a brief course on Children's Literature at St. Joseph's College, Brooklyn.

I became an anthologist of poetry, a career that began with my first collection:

Imagination's Other Place: Poems of Science and Mathematics, published in 1955. A magnificent review by Louise Seaman Bechtel in the *Herald Tribune* helped to launch me. The book, on the relationship between poetry and science, came into being as a result of Milton's and the children's lively discussions and of my rigorous training at Vassar.

After the first book, other topics suggested themselves, and each anthology is built around a theme: religion, music and dance, family, the American ideal, and others. Like all of us, I have learned much over the years, and I am grateful for the enduring friendship of my editors, Elizabeth Riley of Thomas Y. Crowell Company and Ada Shearon of Greenwillow Books.

———

Gladly Learn was selected to be an Ambassador of Honor Book by the English-Speaking Union in 1983.

SELECTED WORKS AS COMPILER: Imagination's Other Place: Poems of Science and Mathematics, 1955; The Earth Is the Lord's: Poems of the Spirit, 1965; Poems from the German, 1967; Untune the Sky: Poems of Music and the Dance, 1957; The Marvelous Light: Poets and Poetry, 1970; As I Walked Out One Evening: A Book of Ballads, 1976; This Powerful Rhyme: A Book of Sonnets, 1979; Gladly Learn and Gladly Teach: Poems of the School Experience, 1981; Eye's Delight: Poems of Art and Architecture, 1983.

SELECTED WORKS AS EDITOR: The Gift Outright: America to Her Poets, 1977; Life Hungers to Abound: Poems of the Family, 1978.

ABOUT: Childhood in Poetry, 1976; Contemporary Authors, Vol. 9; (New Revision Series), Vol. 8; Something About the Author, Vol. 38.

MARIA POLUSHKIN

TRANSLATOR OF *An Old Tale Carved Out of Stone*, etc.

Biographical sketch of Maria Polushkin Robbins:

MARIA POLUSHKIN was born in Russia

and emigrated with her parents to the United States. The family always spoke Russian at home. She attended Hunter College. She became an editor and married Ken Robbins, an editor and photographer who illustrates children's books with his photographs.

Her career as a children's author began as a translator. Her first translation was a Russian story by Anatolii Aleksin, *A Late-Born Child*. Although translation turned out to be more difficult than she had expected, she found it to be creative and rewarding. Her next translation was *An Old Tale Carved Out of Stone* by Aleksandr Linevski. This posed fresh challenges, which she surmounted, and the book won the Mildred L. Batchelder Award for translation in 1975. The book was also named a Notable Book of 1973 by the American Library Association.

In 1974, Polushkin gave a speech at a program sponsored by the International Board on Books for Young People during the ALA Midwinter Conference. "A Few Words on Translation" was reprinted in the June 1974 *Horn Book*. She believes translation to be "more like a creative art than a science," and describes the process. Polushkin's work took a new direction when she worked on a picture book for her next project. Though at first she based her picture books on Russian folk tales, she eventually began to write her own stories. One of these illustrates her typically lighthearted style: *Mother, Mother I Want Another*. The title represents a child's plea while avoiding bedtime. He wants another kiss, but his mother thinks he wants another mother, and brings him one after another.

Polushkin enjoys cooking, and has written several cookbooks including *The Dumpling Cookbook*. She also runs a small movie theater and likes acting in theater groups. Her other hobbies include gardening, embroidery, and pottery. She lives in East Hampton, New York.

SELECTED WORKS WRITTEN: Bubba and Bubba, 1976; The Little Hen and the Giant, 1977; Mother, I Want Another, 1978; Morning, 1983; Mama's Secret, 1984; Baby Brother Blues, 1987; Kitten in Trouble, 1988; Who Said Meow? (rev. ed.), 1988.

SELECTED WORKS TRANSLATED: A Late-Born Child, by Anatolii Aleksin, 1971; An Old Tale Carved Out of Stone, by Aleksandr Linevski, 1973; Who Said Meow?, by Vladimir Grigorevich Suteyev, 1975.

ABOUT: Horn Book June 1974.

CHARLOTTE POMERANTZ

July 24, 1930–

AUTHOR OF *The Princess and the Admiral*, etc.

Autobiographical sketch of Charlotte Pomerantz:

SOME YEARS BACK, I read an essay by a well-known author who said that he was determined to be a writer long before he had anything he wanted to write about. It was the other way 'round with me. As far back as I can remember, I have liked to write, with no thought of being a writer.

All through elementary school, I wrote stories for the enthusiastic audience that was my family. Curiously, I read almost nothing other than schoolbooks. Even as a young child, I'm told that I never sat still long enough to be read to. Happily, my own children loved to snuggle against me and listen—surely one of the sweetest rituals of parenthood.

I wrote my first poem on hearing the death of President Franklin D. Roosevelt announced over the school loudspeaker. I'm not sure why I thought it was a poem. It didn't rhyme and I had never seen a poem that didn't rhyme. Perhaps I sensed that strong feelings expressed in short sentences were something other than a story.

My first brush with literary criticism came in my last year of elementary school. Miss Snow, my beautiful English teacher with snow-white hair, read one of my stories aloud to the class and asked them to

Charlotte Pomerantz

comment. At the end of the day, I had some twenty signed pieces of paper which read, "Gee, Charlie [my then nickname], that was a good story . . . I liked it alot . . . It made me laugh out loud . . . the ending was a surprise. . . . "

I don't recall the story, but I do recall the pure happiness with which I read these comments. These were not my parents; this was a whole classroom of kids who hardly knew me. Perhaps this is the kind of reassurance that one looks for in a writer's workshop.

In New Rochelle High School, I wanted to work on the school paper, but I didn't make it. I couldn't fit my thoughts into the Where-Why-Who-What-When formula of the opening paragaph of a news story. I regret not having mastered this discipline.

In college a few of my stories appeared in the college magazine, but it wasn't 'till after graduation that I wrote my first children's story. It was about the hierarchy of personnel in a zoo, which roughly paralleled the department store where I worked. Some years later, a friend, looking over my stories, suggested submitting this one to the publisher. I did, and after drastic editing, it was published. Looking back, I don't think

it was as simple as beginner's luck. Without knowing it, I had served a long apprenticeship. Even when writing a letter, I couldn't toss off a chatty note, sprinkled with exclamation points. It usually took several drafts to put my thoughts on paper and I would never—never!—use exclamation points unless there was something to exclaim about.

Encouraged by the acceptance of one children's book, I wrote and submitted others. Although a few were published before I was married and had children, I found that my children provided rich, raw material. When they were very young, I started making notes of what they said, scribbling on whatever was at hand: scraps of paper, shopping lists, the margins of newspapers. I was charmed by their use of words and their sober hilarious attempts to impose grammatical logic onto the English language. The notes, later typed into notebooks, have served as a guide to memory and a spur to invention. I recommend the keeping of a journal to all who would write and remember.

———

Charlotte Pomerantz was born in Brooklyn. When she was three, her family moved to New Rochelle, New York. At sixteen, she spent a year in Europe, where her father was deputy chief counsel at the Nuremberg Trials. On their return, they lived in Manhattan, where she graduated from Walden School. She received a B.A. degree from Sarah Lawrence College in 1953, then worked as a sales person, a waitress, a researcher, a copy editor, and an editor. She was married November 12, 1966, and has two children. Pomerantz has had stories, poems, and articles printed in anthologies, in *Publishers Weekly*, in *The New York Times Book Review*, and in children's and adult magazines. She is the editor of *A Quarter Century of Un-Americana*, a pictorial history of the House Committee on Un-American Activities, and is also the coauthor of book and lyrics for a musical, *Eureka!*, performed in 1979 at Lincoln Center in New York City.

Posy received a 1984 Christopher Award and was named a Junior Literary Guild selection. Two of her other books were JLG selections: *The Half-Birthday Party* and *The Mango Tooth. The Tamarindo Puppy* was named a 1980 Notable Book by the American Library Association and a Reading Rainbow Book. *If I Had a Paka* was cited as an Honor Book in the 1983 Jane Addams Children's Book Awards given by Jane Addams Peace Association, and *The Princess and the Admiral* won the Award in 1975.

SELECTED WORKS: Why You Look Like You, 1969; The Day They Parachuted Cats on Borneo, 1971; The Piggy in the Puddle, 1974; The Princess and the Admiral, 1974; Detective Poufy's First Case, 1976; The Mango Tooth, 1977; The Downtown Fairy Godmother, 1978; The Tamarindo Puppy and Other Poems, 1980; If I Had a Paka: Poems in Eleven Languages, 1982; Posy, 1983; All Asleep, 1984; The Half-Birthday Party, 1984; One Duck, Another Duck, 1984; Where's the Bear?, 1984; Whiff, Sniff, Nibble and Chew: The Gingerbread Boy Retold, 1984; Timothy Tall Feather, 1986; The Chalk Doll, 1989; Flap Your Wings and Try, 1989.

ABOUT: Contemporary Authors, Vol. 85; (New Revision Series), Vol. 16; Language Arts March 15, 1976; February 2, 1976; February 1, 1977; September 1977; November 1, 1978; Something About the Author, Vol. 20; Who's Who in America, 1984-85.

BARBARA ANN PORTE

May 18, 1943–

AUTHOR AND ILLUSTRATOR OF *Harry's Visit*, etc.

Autobiographical sketch of Barbara Ann Porte-Thomas:

I WAS BORN in New York City in 1943. I began school at P.S. 72, which has long since been torn down. I have two sisters, one older and one younger. Some of the "adventures" we experienced growing up that are related in my books include: falling into a lake on a bicycle, being chased by a swarm of angry bees, digging holes in Cen-

Barbara Ann Porte-Thomas

tral Park hoping to reach China, and owning, briefly, a biting dog.

We all took turns helping in our father's drugstore. It was just around the corner from where we lived. By age four, I could roll pennies, make change, and keep the candy counter stocked. The times I liked best, though, were spent in the small back room, behind the sign that read "Prescriptions." Here I sat, perched on a high stool, at the counter where my father mixed medicines. He showed me how to weigh powdered, colored chemicals onto waxed paper, and fold the paper in half over it, forming ridges. Then I tapped opened, empty, gelatin capsules against the powder until the capsules were full. I pretended I was a pharmacist. When business was slow, sometimes we ate sugared pastries and listened to the radio.

Sometimes, my father told stories. He made them up for my sisters and me, about detectives who solved mysteries in faraway places, about chimpanzees as smart as people, and also stories about himself when he was our age. My sisters and I became storytellers, too. We also were readers.

Reading was encouraged in our house. Our mother read us books, chapter after chapter, night after night, even after we knew how to read for ourselves. Two favorite ones which I still have, despite countless moves and my own inclination to throw everything out, are: *The Wonderful Adventures of Nils* by Selma Lagerlof and *The Jungle Book* by Rudyard Kipling. I also loved folk and fairy tales. I spent years of my childhood pretending to be this character or that in one of my books. It was good practice for becoming a writer.

Though, in my family, we could hardly conceive of life without books, no one actually believed a sane person would plan to earn a living writing them. Stories were one thing, and economics was another. Therefore, I went to college, in Iowa and Michigan, to learn how to do something. I majored in agriculture, surely a useful science. First in Europe, married and with two young children, then back in New York, however, being a farmer didn't turn out a very practical choice. I went back to school and became a librarian. This was a good profession for a person like me; so many books after all.

Even so, and regardless of stages, student, wife, mother, librarian, I took my father's advice: "Read something every day and write something every day," he told us every day, "whatever else you do with your lives." I never lost sight of my life as a writer. The day my youngest child finished college, and I could afford to risk a more precarious sort of income, I left my very good job to write full time. This is my life: wake up, eat breakfast, write, eat lunch, take a walk and think about my writing, come home, read, eat dinner, revise what I wrote earlier, go to sleep. The next morning, I get up and do it all again. I'm never bored. Awake and asleep, configurations of words shape worlds in my head. It is, for me, a fine and satisfying way of life.

———

Barbara Ann Porte attended Iowa State University in Ames, received her B.S. degree from Michigan State University in 1965, and received her M.S. degree from the Palmer School of Library and Information Science at Long Island University in 1969. She has written stories and poetry for adults that have appeared in such journals as *Green's Magazine* in Canada and *Karamu*. She has had reviews and essays published in *The New York Times*, *Children's Literature in Education*, and *School Library Journal*, among others, and has written a novel for adults called *Mirra Durante*.

Harry's Visit and *Harry's Dog* were named Notable Books by the American Library Association, in 1983 and 1984 respectively. The two books, as well as *Ruthann and Her Pig*, are Junior Literary Guild selections.

SELECTED WORKS: Harry's Visit, 1983; Jesse's Ghost and Other Stories, 1983; Harry's Dog, 1984; Harry's Mom, 1985; The Kidnapping of Aunt Elizabeth, 1985; I Only Made Up the Roses, 1987; Harry in Trouble, 1989; Ruthann and Her Pig, 1989; The Take-Along Dog, 1989.

ABOUT: School Library Journal March 1989; Something About the Author, Vol. 45.

ELISE PRIMAVERA

May 19, 1954–

ILLUSTRATOR OF *Make Way for Sam Houston*, etc.

Autobiographical sketch of Elise Primavera:

I WAS BORN in West Long Branch, which is a town situated near the ocean, commonly referred to as the "Jersey Shore." When I was very young we used to spend the entire summer at the beach. But all this changed on a seemingly innocent Sunday drive to visit a horse farm. I remember being put up on a pony's back for the first time and thinking this is it—this is all I ever want to do!

From the time of about eight years old I

Elise Primavera

lived and breathed horses. This was only interrupted in the fifth grade by a series of illnesses ending with a bout of rheumatic fever. I attribute my keeping still long enough to develop an interest in drawing to this year of sickness.

I didn't grow up saying I wanted to become a children's book illustrator. In fact the thought never crossed my mind until after I was out of college. I spent all my time, before school, after school, and on weekends, with the horses, and months would pass before I would even think of picking up a pencil. Even when I was at Moore College of Art in Philadelphia, I would take the train home each Friday afternoon to New Jersey, ride from Friday to Sunday, and then sadly take the train back on Sunday night. All this time it seemed as though there was this great conflict going on between my riding and my artwork, but looking back I see that the two really balanced each other and that they weren't as far apart as I at times felt they were. I think many of the things that I learned from being involved in a sport—discipline, sacrifice, working towards a goal, organizing my time—I was able to apply when I began doing books. When I look at my work now I

can see all the things that I'm conscious of while I'm doing a painting—movement, gesture, and rhythm—are all things that I brought with me from my riding days. All that time spent around horses and barns provided me with valuable information about animals—and not only how they look but their psychology as well.

It wasn't until I graduated from college and started working as a fashion illustrator, which had been my major, that I realized I was in the wrong profession. More and more I found myself in the children's books section of book stores. At the time I was living in Pennsylvania near the Brandywine Museum. I was intrigued by the paintings of N.C. Wyeth, Howard Pyle, Jessie Wilcox Smith, and all the other artists that made up the Brandywine School. My interest in this pretty much signaled the end of my days as a competitive rider. I moved back to New Jersey in order to be near New York City, where I could continue my education.

This move that I had made really felt like a completely new life. My focus for the first time was not riding but trying to improve as an artist. I continued to ride, but not on the same scale as before. I began taking classes at the Art Students League in New York City with Jack Henderson, a teacher I had studied with at Moore and whose influence I feel very strongly. At this time I began to put together a portfolio for children's books. It took about two years before I was able to show anything; in the meantime I was still doing fashion illustrations as well. In 1980 I was given my first book to do and have been working away at books ever since.

With each book I've tried first of all to convey the mood that the author intended, this is why much of my work looks different from book to book. I've also covered a fairly broad range of age groups as well as of subject matter. It's only just recently that I've begun to feel as though I've found a style or voice that best represents me as an artist. I'm also finding that I've developed a way of working that doesn't change from one book to the next. This entails gathering as much reference from every source imaginable. I like to gather everything around me—objects, photographs, books—and then when I feel as though I'm completely saturated with the subject I like to begin the dummy. For a book of poems about witches that I just completed, I spent a lot of time in the local costume store. By the time the book was finished my studio was a jumble of witches' hats, rubber skeletons, black bats, plastic frogs, hairy spiders, and fright wigs. Some books seem to take on a life of their own at that point. It's sometimes strange for even me to walk into my studio and wonder how all this ever happened!

I live in New York City now and as far away as you can get from the life style I grew up believing I'd lead. I never fulfilled my dream of riding in the Olympics. But I like to think that all that time and effort that went towards that dream has come to serve me now in a way I never thought possible.

Elise Primavera received her B.F.A. degree from Moore College of Art in 1976.

Selected Works Written and Illustrated: Basil and Maggie, 1983.

Selected Works Illustrated: Always Abigail, by Joyce Saint Peter, 1981; The Mermaid's Cape, by Margaret Wetterer, 1981; The Snug Little House, by Eila Moorhouse Lewis, 1981; The Giant's Apprentice, by Margaret Wetterer, 1982; The Bollo Caper: A Furry Tale for All Ages, by Art Buchwald, 1983; Santa and Alex, by Delia Ephron, 1983; Uncle George Washington and Harriot's Guitar, by Miriam Anne Bourne, 1983; Grandma's House, by Elaine Moore, 1985; Make Way for Sam Houston, by Jean Fritz, 1986; Hobie Hanson, You're Weird, by Jamie Gilson, 1987; Double Dog Dare, by Jamie Gilson, 1988; Grandma's Promise, by Elaine Moore, 1988.

About: Roginski, Jim. Behind the Covers: Interviews with Authors and Illustrators of Books for Children and Young Adults; Something About the Author, Vol. 48.

PHILIP PULLMAN

October 19, 1946–

Author of *Shadow in the North*, etc.

Autobiographical sketch of Philip Pullman:

I WAS BORN in 1946 in Norwich, Norfolk. A lot of my life before I was ten was spent on board ship. My father and then my stepfather were both in the Royal Air Force, and my mother and my brother and I seemed to be constantly following them around the world by sea. In those days, that was the way you travelled long distance. We went to South Africa and Australia; we went through the Suez Canal, we went to Bombay and Aden and Columbo and Las Palmas.

And some time on board one of those ships I learned to read. I remember very well the first words I read: they were *Peninsular and Oriental Steam Navigation Company*, and I read those because I was in the bath and they were woven into the towels. I remember clearly seeing those mysterious red shapes changing into sounds as my mother said them for me.

One of the first books that some sensible person gave me was Rudyard Kipling's *Just So Stories*, and when I came to the verse about the *P & O*, I knew exactly what it meant.

The biggest influence on me was my grandfather. He was a clergyman in the Church of England, and a wonderful storyteller. He made places more exciting by making up stories about them and by giving them names. Nowadays I know that the names he used were borrowed from early Western movies or from Hiawatha: a stretch of road we sometimes drove along was The Trail of the Lonesome Pine; a mill stream we played beside was Laughing Water. I didn't know where they came from then; all that mattered was that they were strange, they were romantic and unusual. My grandfather died before I published my first children's book, but I still measure what I write against his judgement.

Philip Pullman

I don't know why so much of what I write seems to demand to be set in Victorian London. If I try (not very hard) I can find ways of relating that time to this: new technologies, nationalism, feminism, terrorism, were all affecting people's lives then as they do now. But that's only part of the reason I write about that period. The main reason, I think, is that my stories come out of atmosphere—out of smells and shapes and colours but especially out of language. The language of late Victorian London is one I know and I'm at home in, in a way that I'm not familiar with the way they spoke in the time of Shakespeare or in medieval Scotland or in ancient Greece. I know how modern teenagers speak, too. One of my books (*How to Be Cool*) started from the way the main characters speak; the story came afterwards.

For a long time I used to teach in school. I don't any more; most of my time now is spent writing. But I'm still interested in everything that goes on in schools—not only the official stuff, like education, but the unofficial stuff as well, like styles and fashions and crazes, like who's *really* in charge of the class. It's never the teacher, incidentally. Teachers are there to teach, not lead, and

the ones who think they're the leader of the pack have got it wildly wrong.

As well as my novels, I've written stage plays and television scripts. I like writing plays. Writing novels is a solitary business, but working in the theatre or for TV brings you into contact with other people. Then, if you do go mad, you go mad in a different way.

I married my wife, Jude, in 1970. We have two sons, Jamie and Tom. They are my best critics. Very often when I'm stuck with a plot, or when I don't think a book is going quite right, I ask Jude to read it. She invariably sees what's gone wrong and helps me get it going in the right direction.

My favourite TV show is *Sergeant Bilko*, and my favourite movie stars are Laurel and Hardy. They did what they did so perfectly that you can watch it a hundred times and still love it. If I could do something half as good as their best, I'd be happy.

———

Philip Pullman attended schools in Southern Rhodesia, South Australia, and in England before he was eleven; after that age he was educated at Ysgol Ardudwy, Harlech, in North Wales. He then went to Oxford, where he attended Exeter College and read English. He took his B.A. in 1968. In addition to writing and teaching, he has worked in a library, in shops, in factories, and in restaurants. He now lives in Oxford, England.

The Ruby in the Smoke won the 1988 International Reading Association Award Both *Ruby* and *Shadow in the North* were named Best Books for Young Adults for their years of publication by the American Library Association. *How To Be Cool*, published in England, was a British TV show in 1988. Pullman wrote a novel for adults, *Galatea*, published in 1979.

SELECTED WORKS: Count Karlstein, 1983; The Ruby in the Smoke, 1987; Shadow in the North, 1988.

RAFFI

July 8, 1948–

AUTHOR OF *Shake My Sillies Out*, etc.

Biographical sketch of Raffi Cavoukian:

RAFFI was born in Cairo, Egypt, to Armenian parents. He emigrated with his family to Canada when he was ten years old, in 1958. He learned guitar at the age of sixteen, and taught himself songs, beginning with The Beatles' music. He admired folk music like that of Bob Dylan, Joan Baez, and Pete Seeger.

He enrolled in the University of Toronto and began singing in coffee houses and clubs in the late 1960s. His repertoire included original songs, some comedy material, and songs written by artists such as Joni Mitchell. Raffi wrote a song about Debi Pike, a kindergarten teacher and a high-school sweetheart he was missing, and invited her to the club to hear it. She came, and they were married in 1976. In 1974, he was asked to sing for children in a Toronto nursery school. His then future wife taught him some North American children's songs, like "The Eensy Weensy Spider," and he tried using songs like these with the children. He found that he had a talent for entertaining small children with music. Raffi discovered a dearth of quality children's recordings, so he worked with his wife, several other teachers, and a musician to produce his first record. *Singable Songs for the Very Young* by Raffi came out on the record label Troubadour in 1976. The album contains a mix of traditional songs and original ones. It was a great success in Canada, and remains his best-selling album. He has always sought to produce his records and his shows with the same fine technical expertise that is applied to records and concert staging for adults.

To date, Raffi has produced eight record albums that have sold over four million copies in the U.S. and Canada. From 1987 to 1988 he played over 150 live performances in 70 cities, all in sold-out venues. He has had concert videos broadcast on The Disney

Channel of cable television, and almost 500,000 copies of his songbooks and picture books are in print.

In 1983, Raffi was awarded the Order of Canada from the Canadian government for contributing to the betterment of its children. *Everything Grows*, another album, was nominated for a Grammy Award in 1988. It represents his usual mix of styles from folk-rock to country. Raffi's records are sold both in toy stores and book stores. He turns down, however, any offer to promote merchandise, do commercials, or become a cartoon character, as he doesn't want to exploit children.

Raffi feels that the key to choosing the right material for his two- to eight-year-old audience is the love of children and respect for them as an audience. His subject matter includes children's everyday life, such as peanut-butter sandwiches, bathing, animals, and humor. "Appreciation of the natural world, children's self-esteem, and love in the family" are themes Raffi treats in the songs he writes. He assiduously avoids stereotypes, violence, and negativity in his songs. He has been a featured presenter at early childhood and educational conferences, including an American Library Association conference in 1988. Troubadour, his record company, has a division, Troubadour Learning, that publishes guides to using the songs in classrooms.

"Raffi Songs to Read" is a series of books that combine the lyrics of Raffi's songs with illustrations by well-known artists. Raffi hopes to use singing as a bridge to reading. Raffi and his wife have no children of their own, but they do have a dog named Bundles. The couple spend a great deal of their time researching children's literature and education books.

SELECTED WORKS: Down by the Bay, 1987; The Raffi Singable Songbook, 1987; The Second Raffi Songbook, 1987; One Light, One Sun, 1988; The Raffi Christmas Treasury: Fourteen Illustrated Songs and Musical Arrangements, 1988; Shake My Sillies Out, 1988; Wheels on the Bus, 1988; Everything Grows, 1989; Five Little Ducks, 1989; The Raffi Everything Grows Songbook, 1989; Tingalayo, 1989.

ABOUT: Christian Science Monitor February 10, 1987; Los Angeles Times February 11, 1987; Parenting May 1987; Spies, Karen. Raffi: The Children's Voice; Washington Post November 9, 1987.

JOAN ELMA RAHN

February 5, 1929–

AUTHOR AND ILLUSTRATOR OF *Plants that Changed History*, etc.

Biographical sketch of Joan Elma Rahn:

JOAN ELMA RAHN was born in Cleveland, Ohio, into a strict German family that emphasized learning rather than physical activity. She spent a lot of childhood time daydreaming, and developed a love of learning that has continued throughout her life. She once resolved to learn all there is to know. She received a B.S. degree from Western Reserve University in 1950, and she received her M.A. degree in 1952 and her Ph.D. in 1956 from Columbia University.

Rahn was an assistant professor at Thiel College in Greenville, Pennsylvania, from

JOAN ELMA RAHN

1956 to 1958; she was associate professor of biology there from 1958 to 1959. She then taught botany at Ohio State University in Columbus from 1959 to 1960, and at International School of America. From 1961 to 1967 she taught biology at Lake Forest College in Illinois, and at Elgin Community College. She became a free-lance writer and photographer in 1967.

Rahn enjoys new experiences. She has traveled all over the world, and her photographic essays have been published in *National Wildlife* magazine. Her photographs have appeared in *National Geographic* and *Encyclopaedia Britannica*. She has also been a member of the editorial advisory board and a contributing editor to *World of Science*. Now she devotes her time to writing and often to illustrating books for young people. Each book gives her a chance to learn something new about herself and to interest young readers in subjects she has found fascinating.

Rahn is a member of the American Institute of Biological Sciences, the Botanical Society of America, the American Association for the Advancement of Science, and Sigma Xi, among other professional organizations.

Plants That Changed History was named

a 1982 Notable Children's Trade Book in the Field of Social Studies by a joint committee of the National Council on the Social Studies and the Children's Book Council. Seven of her books have been named Outstanding Science Trade Books by a joint committee of the National Science Teachers Association and the CBC: *Seeing What Plants Do, How Plants Travel, Grocery Store Botany, How Plants Are Pollinated, Seven Ways to Collect Plants, Traps and Lures . . .* , and *Plants Up Close.* Each book received the citation in its year of publication. *How Plants Travel* received an Honorable Mention award from the New York Academy of Science Children's Book Science Awards in 1973.

SELECTED WORKS WRITTEN AND ILLUSTRATED: Seven Ways to Collect Plants, 1978; Watch It Grow, Watch It Change, 1978; Traps and Lures in the Living World, 1980; Eyes & Seeing, 1981; Plants Up Close, 1981; Plants That Changed History, 1982; Keeping Warm, Keeping Cool, 1983; Ears, Hearing, and Balance, 1984; More Plants That Changed History, 1985; Animals That Changed History, 1986.

SELECTED WORKS WRITTEN: Seeing What Plants Do, 1972; How Plants Travel, 1973; Grocery Store Botany, 1974; How Plants Are Pollinated, 1975; More About What Plants Do, 1975; The Metric System, 1976; Grocery Store Zoology: Bones and Muscles, 1977.

ABOUT: Contemporary Authors (First Revision), Vol. 37; (New Revision Series), Vol. 13; Something About the Author, Vol. 27.

TED RAND

December 27, 1915–

ILLUSTRATOR OF *The Ghost-Eye Tree,* etc.

Autobiographical sketch of Ted Rand:

THE FIRST MOMENT I felt an irresistable urge to draw a picture was at about four or five, when I saw the illustrations in the family Bible. They were dramatic engravings of subjects like The Parting Of The Red Sea, The Hanging Gardens Of Babylon, The Destruction Of The Temple, etc. And

from that time on, I've never stopped drawing. A pencil and a piece of paper have a magnetic attraction for me. I found myself doing the holiday decorations all through grade school. I did pumpkins, witches, turkeys, Santas, hearts, and so forth—and got out of class to do them. By the time I got to high school I knew how to use what skills I had to my advantage.

Out of high school, I took a handful of figure drawings to a department store and was hired to draw for newspaper advertisements. It is a great training ground. I eventually became a free-lance illustrator, primarily in advertising, interrupted only by a four-year stint as an aerial navigator in the Navy during World War II.

I taught illustration in the art department of the University of Washington for over twenty years, while also working as a free lancer. My first book illustrations came as a result of a series of paintings done from a pack trip on the coast of Washington. Supreme Court Justice William O. Douglas, a great conservationist, organized the group to protest construction of an unecessary road through one of the last great rain forests on the Olympic Peninsula. The paintings were shown in the New York Society of Illustrators Annual, and from that I had assignments for a number of textbook illustrations, inlcuding two series of wildlife books for Encyclopaedia Britannica's Educational Division.

I have had a number of one-man shows of paintings and have paintings in the collections of the Seattle Art Museum and many corporations and private collections. I've done many commemorative portraits including governors, corporation heads, presidents of universities, etc., as well as those for individuals. Among portrait commissions were three kings of Saudi Arabia, which were hung in a personal 747 aircraft built for King Khalid.

But not until about four years ago did I begin what has become an all-consuming and absorbing part of the art profession— that is illustrating children's books. I can honestly say that I have never enjoyed anything as much. The technical freedom, the opportunity to work in a great variety of styles, the people I work with, the common goal of getting children to read, all these combine to put this at the top of my list. I no longer accept portrait commissions, nor am I painting for exhibitions. There are so many challenges in the children's book field that I have time for nothing else.

I enjoy talking to schools and especially getting to know teachers and librarians. My wife, Gloria, and I are now collaborating on picture books, which has been a particular pleasure.

I spend a great deal of time in libraries, accumulating accurate reference material. Preparation and research take at least two-thirds of the total time to produce a picture book.

Our daughter Theresa is a medical illustrator in heart surgery and our son Martin manufacturers weights for medical rehabilitation that are of his own design.

I was born on Mercer Island, Washington, where my wife and I now live. I have had no formal training, about which I can only say that the self-taught person has a fool for a student and a fool for a teacher.

———

Ted Rand attended Cornish School in Seattle after graduating from high school. He was married May 1, 1948.

The Ghost-Eye Tree was an Irma Simonton Black Award Honor Book for 1985, so named by the Bank Street College of Education. It was also named a 1986 Children's Choice Book by a joint committee of the International Reading Association and the Children's Book Council. Both *Barn Dance!* and *Knots on a Counting Rope* were Reading Rainbow books. *Knots* was also named a Notable Trade Book in the Field of Social Studies by a joint committee of the CBC and the National Council on the Social Studies for 1987.

SELECTED WORKS ILLUSTRATED: The Ghost-Eye Tree, by Bill Martin, Jr. and John Archambault, 1985; Barn Dance!, by Bill Martin, Jr. and John Archambault, 1986; White Dynamite and Curly Kidd, by Bill Martin, Jr. and John Archambault, 1986; Here Are My Hands, by Bill Martin, Jr. and John Archambault, 1987; Knots on a Counting Rope, by Bill Martin, Jr. and John Archambault, 1987; Whiffle Squeak, by Caron Lee Cohen, 1987; The Hornbeam Tree and Other Poems, by Charles Norman, 1988; Once When I Was Scared, by Helena Clare Pittman, 1988; The Sun, the Wind and the Rain, by Lisa Westberg Peters, 1988; Up and Down on the Merry-Go-Round, by Bill Martin, Jr. and John Archambault, 1988; The Jumblies, by Edward Lear, 1989; A Little Excitement, by Marc Harshmany, 1989; Salty Dog, by Gloria Rand, 1989.

FLORENCE ENGEL RANDALL

October 18, 1917–

AUTHOR OF *The Almost Year*, etc.

Biographical sketch of Florence Engel Randall:

FLORENCE ENGEL RANDALL was born in Brooklyn, New York. She was a student at New York University in 1937. She was married on November 5, 1939, and had three children. She always wanted to be a writer, and sold her first story at the age of eighteen. However, she put her writing aside for years. When her third child was

FLORENCE ENGEL RANDALL

four years old, Randall's brother gave an old typewriter to the family. She greeted the gift with joy and set it up in the family laundry room, where she produced her first novel, *Hedgerow*, a book for adults that was published in 1967. Her method of writing consists of an attempt to produce three pages a day, working five or six hours a day. Randall also paints and plays the piano, and enjoys gardening.

The Almost Year began as an attempt to write a supernatural story, and Randall did a great deal of research into Ouija boards, seances, and other manifestations of the occult. She studied poltergeists, and conceived the idea of an angry, unhappy girl moving into a family's house. This idea coincided with the introduction of busing into the community where Randall lives, and it took two years for her to complete the story of a fifteen-year-old black girl who comes to stay with a white family in an affluent suburb after the death of her mother. The book was named a 1971 Best Book for Young Adults by the American Library Association.

The Watcher in the Woods is a suspense story of a visitor from another planet that is spying on a girl who has moved into a new house. *All the Sky Together* is the first-person story of a lonely, idealistic girl who ignores the advice of those who warn her away from her relationships with two wealthy, attractive, but uncaring teenagers, whose actions lead to tragedy. Nancy B. Hammond, writing in *The Horn Book Magazine*, called the protagonist's "struggle for independence . . . poignant and credible."

Randall's stories have appeared in magazines like *Harper's, Good Housekeeping, Redbook, Cosmopolitan, Seventeen,* and others. In addition to *Hedgerow*, she has written two other books for adults, *The Place of Sapphires* and *Haldane Station.* She has written several articles for *The Writer* describing the process of writing.

A Watcher in the Woods was made into a film by Walt Disney Productions.

SELECTED WORKS: The Almost Year, 1971; The Watcher in the Woods, 1976; All the Sky Together, 1983.

ABOUT: Contemporary Authors (First Revision), Vol. 41; The International Authors and Writers Who's Who, 1980; Something About the Author, Vol. 5; Who's Who of American Women, 1981-1982; The Writer March 1968; January 1972; The Writers Directory 1988-90.

WILSON RAWLS

September 24, 1913–December 16, 1984

AUTHOR OF *Where the Red Fern Grows,* etc.

Biographical sketch of Woodrow Wilson Rawls by Sophie Rawls:

WILSON RAWLS was born in 1913 in Scraper, Oklahoma. He grew up on the farm he described in his novels. Because there were no schools in that area when he was growing up, his mother taught her children how to read and write. Wilson's grandmother would order books for his mother and she would read the stories to them. She taught them to read by having

WILSON RAWLS

each of them take turns reading from the books after she had first read the stories to them.

Wilson Rawls was still quite young when his grandmother ordered *The Call of the Wild.* When they were finished with the book, his mother gave it to him. It was his first "very own" book. He loved it so much, he carried it with him wherever he went and read a page or two every chance he had.

One day he got the idea that it would be wonderful if he could write a story like *Call of the Wild.* He was about ten years old at the time. From that day for the rest of his life, he knew he wanted to be a writer. He told his father of his dream and asked him if he thought Wilson could be one. His father said he didn't know anything about writing, but told him that if that was what he wanted and he didn't give up, he could do it. His father added that he thought he would need an education to be a writer.

Because he had very little schooling, Rawls decided to get an education by reading books he got from the library. He developed a great appetite for every kind of subject from his reading. His love of reading stayed with him throughout his life.

Wilson started his writing by trying to describe the sounds he heard, and the places and things around his home. His first writing was in the dust of the country road and the sand banks along the river.

The family moved from the farm to Tahlequah, Oklahoma, when Wilson was about fifteen years old. Soon afterward, the Depression hit the country. He left home and crisscrossed the country looking for work. His family also left Oklahoma for California, but their old car broke down just outside of Albuquerque. His father got a job to pay for repairs. They liked the place and ended up settling there.

Wilson kept writing no matter where he traveled. Because he was ashamed of his spelling, grammar, and punctuation, he did not show his writing to anyone. However, he did not throw anything away—he saved his stories in an old trunk in his father's workshop.

Just before we got married, Wilson made a trip to his mother's home (his father had died a few years earlier) and destroyed all his manuscripts. He had decided that he would forget his dream of being a writer. He returned to Idaho Falls, Idaho, and we were married on August 23, 1958. Later that year, he found he couldn't put aside his dream. He told me that he had always wanted to be a writer. I encouraged him to rewrite one of his stories. I told him I could help him with his spelling, grammar, and punctuation.

The story Wilson decided to rewrite was the one based on his boyhood life. He named it "The Secret of the Red Fern." After a year of work on it, he sent it to *The Saturday Evening Post.* They rejected it. I then sent it to *The Ladies' Home Journal.* The *Journal* editors decided it didn't suit their magazine and asked for permission to send it to *The Saturday Evening Post.* This time, the *Post* accepted it and published the story as a three-part serial under the title "The Hounds of Youth." They published it again in 1986.

The novel was published in hardcover in

1961 by Doubleday as *Where the Red Fern Grows*. His second book, *Summer of the Monkeys*, was published by Doubleday in 1976. Both books have won numerous awards, particularly awards voted upon by children. *Summer of the Monkeys* won the 1979 William Allen White Award, and *Where the Red Fern Grows* was a Literary Guild selection. That book was also made into a motion picture by Doty-Dayton Productions and released in March 1974.

After the publication of his first novel, Wilson started to visit schools, speaking to the children, telling them about his childhood. He encouraged them to hang on to their dreams, that they could come true. His dreams did, and so could theirs, if they didn't give up, no matter how tough it may be.

Wilson continued the visits until he became ill in the fall of 1983. During those years, his trips took him to schools in twenty-two states, mostly in the West and South. He was a featured speaker at many teacher and librarian conventions as well.

Wilson Rawls was a member of the Authors Guild. His papers were donated to the Cherokee National Historical Society in Tahlequah, Oklahoma, in 1986. An exhibit of memorabilia and other materials, "The Wilson Rawls Collection," was held there in Spring 1987.

We had no children, but Wilson felt he had many children in the fans who loved his novels. He had one regret, that he couldn't take a copy of his book to his father and say, "It took a long time, Dad, but I made it."

SELECTED WORKS: Where the Red Fern Grows, 1961; Summer of the Monkeys, 1976.

ABOUT: Contemporary Authors, Vol. 1; (New Revision Series), Vol. 5; The International Authors and Writers Who's Who, 1982; Library Journal February 1961; Salt Lake City Tribune April 7, 1974; Something About the Author, Vol. 22; Who's Who in the West, 1965.

DEBORAH KOGAN RAY

August 31, 1940–

AUTHOR AND ILLUSTRATOR OF *My Dog, Trip*, etc.

Autobiographical sketch of Deborah Raphaela Kogan, who writes under the pen name "Deborah Kogan Ray":

PEOPLE stayed to their own streets where I grew up in Philadelphia. When I was a little girl, Carpenter Street was my whole world. There were lots of children on our block. We played alley games behind the long rows of houses. There was always a "Baby in the Air" or stickball game to join. I was good at games, but I felt like an outsider. Mostly, I loved to read and draw pictures.

The summer I was eight, I heard about an arts and crafts program at the playground in the park that was two blocks away. I begged my mother to let me go.

The first day I went to the playground, I was teased about my small size and pushed off the jungle gym, and my dime for water ice was taken. I ran home crying, but I returned the next day. By the end of the summer I had finished several potholders and a lariat keychain, and had been accepted as one of the playground group because of my bravery in leaping off the swings when hitting the "bumps."

It was pure stubborness that kept me returning to the playground that summer. Now I'm glad I did.

From the playground I explored further into Cobbs Creek Park. The park became my special place. I sat by the creek for hours. I followed its path beyond the park to where the city ended. When I was older, I rode my bike up back roads into marshlands where egret and heron lived in reedy grass. In that city park I first learned to love the natural world. Things of nature have remained the subject of my work as an artist.

As long as I can remember, I saw my thoughts in pictures. When I was twelve, I decided I would become an aritst. I took ex-

tra art classes in school. Senior year, I drew all the pictures for my yearbook. I loved being the class artist. I felt like a "somebody." I didn't know then that compliments and being noticed had nothing to do with being an artist.

When I graduated from high school, I was awarded a scholarship. I enrolled at the Philadelphia College of Art. They had commercial art courses. I knew I had to earn a living and I had vague thoughts of studying fabric design. Within a few months, I knew this was not what I wanted to do. The next year, I transferred to the Pennsylvania Academy of Fine Arts to study painting. I supported myself waiting on tables, modeling for art classes, and fitting corsets in a lingerie shop.

I finished art school with my baby daughter attending classes with me.

Since leaving art school, I've had many exhibitions of my paintings in galleries and museums. My paintings are of moving water, leaves, and plants. I paint in watercolors and acrylics. I draw and make prints.

I never studied how to be an illustrator. I got interested in making pictures for books reading stories to my two daughters when they were little girls.

The first book I illustrated was a story by a famous Russian author who lived a long time ago. I decided to illustrate the story when it made me see wonderful, bright pictures in my mind. *The Fair at Sorochintsi* was published in 1969. It led to my illustrating many other books. In illustrating children's books, I found another audience for my work.

My transition to writing was slow. I got the idea for the first story I wrote when I heard my older daughter telling her friend about our trip to the zoo. Karen was seven years old then, and she was twenty when *Sunday Morning We Went to the Zoo* was published in 1981.

Sometimes I write about things that happened to my children. Sometimes I mix bits and pieces together. I begin with something that happened, but set it in another place, as in the story of *My Dog, Trip*. Sometimes I write about things that happened in my own childhood. What I write is taken from experience. My stories are about the things that happen inside us. These are the things that are important to me.

———

Deborah Kogan Ray was married July 8, 1960; she has two children. That marriage ended in divorce in 1981. She studied at the Philadelphia College of Art from 1958 to 1959, at the University of Pennsylvania from 1959 to 1961, at the Pennsylvania Academy of the Fine Arts from 1959 to 1962, and at the Albert C. Barnes Foundation from 1962 to 1964. She received a Louis Comfort Tiffany Foundation Fellowship in Painting in 1968 and a Mabel Rush Homer Award in 1968. She also won the Philadelphia Art Directors Award for design and book illustration in 1970. Her work is in the art collections of the Free Library of Philadelphia, the University of Minnesota, the Library of Congress, and Carnegie-Mellon University, among other places. She is a member of the Artists Equity Association and the Authors Guild. *The Winter Picnic* appeared in the American Institute of

Graphic Arts Show in 1970. *Little Tree* won a Carolyn W. Field Award from the Pennsylvania Library Association in 1988. Ray won the 1987 Drexel Citation from Drexel University, and *My Prairie Year* was named a Notable Book of 1986 by the American Library Association.

SELECTED WORKS ADAPTED AND ILLUSTRATED AS DEBORAH RAY: The Fair at Sorochintsi: A Nikolai Gogol Story Retold, 1969.

SELECTED WORKS WRITTEN AND ILLUSTRATED AS DEBORAH KOGAN RAY: Sunday Morning We Went to the Zoo, 1981; Fog Drift Morning, 1983; The Cloud, 1984; My Dog, Trip, 1987.

SELECTED WORKS ILLUSTRATED AS DEBORAH RAY: The Winter Picnic, by Robert Welber, 1970; I Have a Sister/My Sister Is Deaf, by Jeanne Whitehouse Peterson, 1977.

SELECTED WORKS ILLUSTRATED AS DEBORAH KOGAN RAY: Through Grandpa's Eyes, by Patricia MacLachlan, 1980; The White Marble, by Charlotte Zolotow, 1982; My Prairie Year: Based on the Diary of Eleanor Plaisted, by Brett Harvey, 1986; Diana, Maybe, by Crescent Dragonwagon, 1987; Little Tree, by E.E. Cummings, 1987; Cassie's Journey: Going West in the 1860s, by Brett Harvey, 1988; Chang's Paper Pony, by Eleanor Coerr, 1988; The Hokey Pokey Man, by Steven Kroll, 1989; Peter, Goodnight, by Allison Weir, 1989.

ABOUT: Contemporary Authors, Vol. 57-60; Something About the Author, Vol. 50; Who's Who in American Art, 1984.

CHARLES ROBINSON

June 25, 1931–

ILLUSTRATOR OF *A Taste of Blackberries*, etc.

Biographical sketch of Charles Robinson:

CHARLES ROBINSON was born in Morristown, New Jersey. He received his A.B. degree from Harvard University in 1953. He served in the Signal Corps of the U.S. Army from 1953 to 1954. He received an L.L.B. degree from the University of Virginia Law School in 1958. He was married August 17, 1957. Robinson was employed in various business positions from 1954 to 1968. He worked as a securities analyst at Fiduciary Trust Company in New York, as a law associate at McCarter & English, a law firm in Newark; and was an attorney at Mutual Insurance Company in Newark for eight years.

After ten years of legal work, Robinson realized that his interests lay in art, not in law. Children's book illustration, he says, seemed "at that time and twenty-one years later" to be a perfect vehicle for a person like himself who loves to paint and draw in a fairly realistic manner. He also enjoys being his own boss, his "wonderfully appreciative audience—the children," and "an unusually well motivated and nice group of people to work with—the editors and art directors."

Robinson is a member of the New Jersey Watercolor Society. He has three children and lives in New Jersey.

Journey to America won the 1970 Jewish Welfare Board Jewish Book Council National Jewish Book Award. It was also a Junior Literary Guild selection. In 1971 he received the Society of Illustrators Gold Medal for illustrating the cover of *Audubon: The Man Who Painted Birds. An Island in the Green Sea* won a 1973 Boston Globe-Horn Book Honor Award for fiction. *Fleet-Footed Florence* was named a 1982 Children's Choice Book by a joint committee of the International Reading Association and the Children's Book Council. Both *Ike and Mama and the Block Wedding* and *Ike and Mama and the Seven Surprises* won Association of Jewish Libraries Sydney Taylor Book Awards, in 1980 and 1986 respectively.

SELECTED WORKS WRITTEN AND ILLUSTRATED: Yuri and the Mooneygoats, 1969; New Kid in Town, 1975.

SELECTED WORKS ILLUSTRATED: The Daybreakers, by Jane Louise Curry, 1970; Journey to America, by Sonia Levitin, 1970; An Island in the Green Sea, by Mabel Esther Allan, 1972; The Mountain of Truth, by Dale Carlson, 1972; A Taste of Blackberries, by Doris Buchanan Smith, 1973; The Birthday Visitor, by

Yoshiko Uchida, 1975; All the Money in the World, by William Brittain, 1979; Ike and Mama and the Block Wedding, by Carol Snyder, 1979; Fleet-Footed Florence, by Marylin Sachs, 1981; Ike and Mama and the Seven Surprises, by Carol Snyder, 1985; Grandma Drives a Motor Bed, by Diane Johnston Hamm, 1987; Kitty from the Start, by Judy Delton, 1987; Soup on Fire, by Robert Newton Peck, 1987; The Ghost in Tent 19, by Jim and Jane O'Connor, 1988.

ABOUT: Contemporary Authors, Vol. 49–52; (New Revision Series), Vol. 2; Kingman, Lee and others, comps. Illustrators of Children's Books: 1967-1976; Something About the Author, Vol. 6.

COLBY RODOWSKY

February 26, 1932–

AUTHOR OF *The Gathering Room*, etc.

Autobiographical sketch of Colby Rodowsky:

I WAS BORN in Baltimore, Maryland, and lived, for a while, in a house across the street from where I live now. In between those two houses, however, I lived in New York and Washington, D.C., and spent a lot of time on the Eastern shore of Virginia. In between those two houses, I also grew up, went to college (where I majored in English), taught school, (third grade and then Special Education), got married, had six children, drove car pools, made Christmas cookies and Hallowe'en costumes, walked the dogs, fed the cats, and took my children to the library. I also read a lot.

As an only child I spent a great deal of time either in the company of adults or by myself. I don't remember being lonely and I learned at an early age to value being alone. Even now, though the family has grown to include a daughter-in-law, four sons-in-law, and assorted grandchildren, I still like to go off by myself from time to time for a swim, a walk, or a trip to a museum. Sometimes, in these solitary jaunts, I get ideas for my books and stories.

When my youngest child was in elementary school I decided to do something I'd always wanted to do. It was then that I started to write, working at a desk in the corner of my bedroom and hardly daring to tell anyone what I was doing. I used to think my family thought I was writing very long grocery lists.

In 1976 my first book was published. This was followed by another, and another, and then another. Eventually, after our oldest daughter married and moved away, I turned her room into an office and began to feel like a "real" writer.

Looking back on the books I've written, I see lots of things that have to do with my own life. All of my main characters (the boys as well as the girls) have little bits of myself in them. I was a solitary child much as Mudge (*The Gathering Room*), Henley (*H, My Name Is Henley*), and Slug October (*Evy-Ivy-Over* and *Julie's Daughter*) were solitary children. The way Dorrie (*What About Me?*) felt about New York was the way *I* felt about New York, and Drew's (*Keeping Time*) favorite places in downtown Baltimore are *my* favorite places. Sarey-Ann Littleton (*Fitchett's Folly*) wants adventure just as I did, as I do. And Sydney Downie (*Sydney, Herself*) has a collossal imagination, as I hope I have.

Many places from my childhood keep turning up in my books. Dorrie's apartment in *What About Me?* is the apartment I lived in in New York, and Aunt Mercy's house in *H, My Name Is Henley* is the house my grandmother used to live in. The town in *Evy-Ivy-Over* is the same town where I spent a part of every summer while I was growing up and *P.S. Write Soon* features special Baltimore neighborhoods.

While many of the things in my books are real—and right out of my childhood—many others are made-up. After all, I never actually climbed the rigging of a sailing ship the way Drew did in *Keeping Time*. I never lived in the gatehouse of a cemetery, as Mudge did in *The Gathering Room*, or thought that my father was a rock star, as Sydney did in *Sydney, Herself.*

But then maybe it's this ability to mix fact and fancy that makes writing books so much fun.

————

Colby Rodowsky received her B.A. degree from the College of Notre Dame of Maryland in 1953. She was married August 7, 1954.

The Gathering Room was named a Notable Book of the year 1981 by the American Library Associaton and a Notable Children's Trade Book in the Field of Social Studies for the same year by a joint committee of the Children's Book Council and the National Council on the Social Studies. *Julie's Daughter* was named a Best Book for Young Adults for the year 1985 by the ALA.

SELECTED WORKS: What About Me?, 1976; Evy-Ivy-Over, 1978; P.S. Write Soon, 1978; The Gathering Room, 1981; H, My Name Is Henley, 1982; Keeping Time, 1983; Julie's Daughter, 1985; Fitchett's Folly, 1987; Sydney, Herself, 1989.

ABOUT: Contemporary Authors, Vol. 69; Something About the Author, Vol. 21.

STEPHEN ROOS

February 9, 1945–

AUTHOR OF *My Horrible Secret*, etc.

Autobiographical sketch of Stephen Kelley Roos:

WELL, naturally, I blame it on my parents. They made it look irresistible.

They were writers. They wrote mostly in collaboration with each other and mostly detective stories. I loved to eavesdrop as they plotted their stories. How to explain the lipstick on the cigarette smoldering in Jeremy's ashtray? What about the scar hidden under Catherine's pearls? Why would eleven people want to bludgeon to death anyone as sweet as Françoise? Writing, as far as I was concerned, was a lot more gripping than second grade.

The hours were better too. When my sister and I left for school, Mom and Dad were still dawdling over their coffee and the New York *Herald-Tribune*. When we got home, they might be playing Scrabble. They might even have gone to the movies.

There were times I wished my mother and father were more like other kids' parents. I wished their lives were tidier, more regular, more normal—whatever that means. But all along, I knew there was something very special, sometimes even wondrous, about them, about us, about the way we lived, and I knew it was because they wrote.

Like any number of other writers (but certainly not all), I got started early. I wrote my first play, *Dead Moment*, when I was nine. Thanks to an inordinately long intermission and an interminable segment of on-stage cocoa-making, my four- or five-page script took almost forty minutes to perform. I thought it was a smash and I thought that made me a writer.

But I didn't stick with it. I got frightened along the way and stopped writing. I worked with writers instead of writing. Then when I was in my middle thirties, I knew it was time to start again. Considering

Connecticut, attended Loomis School in Windsor, Connecticut, and graduated from Yale University in 1967. After working in the promotion and editorial departments at Harper & Row publishers from 1968 to 1980, he began writing for children. In 1986 he received the Charlie May Simon Book Award from the Arkansas State Education Department for *My Horrible Secret*.

SELECTED WORKS: My Horrible Secret, 1983; The Terrible Truth, 1983; My Secret Admirer, 1984; Confessions of a Wayward Preppie, 1986; The Fair-Weather Friends, 1987; Thirteenth Summer, 1987; My Favorite Ghost, 1988; You'll Miss Me When I'm Gone, 1988; "And the Winner Is . . . ", 1989.

SELECTED WORKS WITH KELLEY ROOS: The Incredible Cat Cap, 1985; The Mystery of the Condo Cat, 1989.

ABOUT: Contemporary Authors, Vol. 112; Something About the Author, Vol. 41.

how I have hedged my bets in life, it amazes me how calm and collected I was about quitting publishing and setting out to write stories of my own.

I had barely enough money to last out a year. I had no job to return to. I had no manuscript as yet "in progress." And I had a very realistic (i.e., pessimistic) sense of my chances of ever getting published. But I had the same sense of fun and confidence I'd had years before when I sat down at my mother's Underwood upright and started that play.

It's hard for me to be indifferent to the response my books generate. It's hard not to want to make some impact. In writing for children, that can come out in a subtle but insidious urge to "teach." I try consciously to resist that urge, but it's there always. Lately, though, I have asked my writing to teach me. I have tried to be open and willing enough to let it do just that. And it's happening and making me more excited about my writing than I ever thought I could be.

———

Stephen Roos was born in New York City and grew up there and in New Canaan,

TONY ROSS

August 10, 1938–

RETELLER AND ILLUSTRATOR OF *Jack and the Beanstalk*, etc.

Biographical sketch of Tony Ross:

TONY ROSS was born in London, England, the son of a magician, Eric Turle Lee, and Effie Ross. As a child, he received books at Christmastime, and remembers the artwork of Beatrix Potter, E.H. Shepard, Arthur Rackham, and Edward Ardizzone from that time. At the age of eight, he was impressed by the illustrations of Gustave Doré for *Don Quixote*.

He was trained as an etcher and has a fondness for graphic rather than fine artists. He studied at the Liverpool College of Art, where he received diplomas in 1960 and 1961. After completing his education, Ross worked as a graphic designer for Smith Kline and French Laboratories from 1962 to 1964, an art director at Brunnings Advertising in 1965, as lecturer at Manchester

TONY ROSS

Polytechnic, in Manchester, from 1965 to 1972, and as a senior lecturer in illustration there since 1972. Ross is a consultant in graphic design as well as a member of the Society of Industrial Artists and Designers. He also contributes cartoons to magazines like *Punch*. He is divorced. The couple had three children, Philippa, George, and Alexandra. At present Ross resides in Anglesey, where he devotes his full attention to illustrating and writing.

Ross has said that a children's illustrator creates worlds for children. This philosophy is evident in his wacky treatment of some familiar tales as well as in the tales he creates. *Jack and the Beanstalk*, adapted and illustrated by Ross, was reviewed by Patricia Dooley in *School Library Journal*. She wrote, "Most of the original tale is intact, but the insouciant, conversational tone and the slightly wacky pictures make it seem as if Ross were making it all up as he goes along."

Another familiar fable, *Lazy Jack*, received similar treatment at the hands of Tony Ross. Both *Lazy Jack* and *I'm Coming to Get You!* were named Children's Choice Books by a joint committee of the Children's Book Council and the Internaitonal Reading Association, in 1985 and 1987 respectively. Reviewers of both *Lazy Jack* and *Jack and the Beanstalk* cited Ross' offbeat humor as "Monty Pythonish." The *Bulletin of the Center for Children's Books* stated, "The tale is tongue-in-cheek, the art absurd, the overall effect a super-silly read-aloud. . . . " It is clear that Ross' professed delight at making children laugh is a crucial component of his work.

One of Ross's strengths is in creating seemingly normal children who have extraordinary, colorful adventures. A continuing character in some of Ross' books is Hugo, a boy who meets up with a strange variety of creatures in *Hugo and Oddsock*, *Hugo and the Man Who Stole Colors*, and *Hugo and the Wicked Winter*. Another super-hero—in this case super-heroine—is Jezebel, of *Super Dooper Jezebel* fame. Jezebel is a perfectly perfect little girl in *almost* every way, and she gets her comeuppance in the end. Ross' daughter and her imaginary friend provided the inspiration for the rollicking *Oscar Got All the Blame*. Ross' *I Want My Potty* appeared on the 1986 list of Commended Books in the Kate Greenaway Awards.

SELECTED WORKS WRITTEN OR RETOLD AND ILLUSTRATED: Hugo and the Man Who Stole Colors, 1977; Hugo and the Wicked Winter, 1977; Hugo and Oddsock, 1978; Jack and the Beanstalk, 1980; I'm Coming to Get You!, 1984; I Want My Potty, 1986; Foxy Fables, 1986; Lazy Jack, 1986; Jack the Giantkiller, 1987; Stone Soup, 1987; Oscar Got All the Blame, 1988; Super Dooper Jezebel, 1988; I Want a Cat, 1989.

SELECTED WORKS ILLUSTRATED: Terrible Tuesday, by Hazel Townson, 1986; Meanwhile Back at the Ranch, by Trinka Hakes Noble, 1987; The Knight Who Was Afraid of the Dark, by Barbara Shook Hazen, 1989.

ABOUT: Carpenter, Humphrey and Mari Prichard. The Oxford Companion to Children's Literature; Contemporary Authors, Vol. 77-80; Herdeg, Walter, ed. Graphis 4th International Survey of Children's Book Illustration, 1979 (Publication No. 156); The International Authors and Writers Who's Who, 1982; Something About the Author, Vol. 17.

MARGARET ROSTKOWSKI

January 12, 1945–

AUTHOR OF *After the Dancing Days*, etc.

Autobiographical sketch of Margaret Rostkowski:

I CAME TO WRITING relatively late in life, not beginning *After the Dancing Days* until I was thirty-seven. Yet, I am not sorry that I put off writing so long, for I believe that everything in my life up to now has been a preparation for writing, an accumulation of moments worth reconstructing on paper.

As a child I was a reader: *Little Women* when I was ten, *War and Peace* when I was sixteen, volumes of historical fiction I checked out from our Carnegie Free Library. We lived in the foothills of the Wasatch Mountains and our backward was literally sagebrush, rock, and rattlesnake. My mother's constant refrain was "put down your book and go outside and play, you'll ruin your eyes." She was right about the eyes, and maybe I should have spent more time in the woods, as they are now the setting for much of my writing.

I use family stories in my books. My mother's and father's families have lived in the Kansas City area since before the Civil War. My mother had young uncles who fought in World War I, who were gassed, who caught measles, and my father's father rode a motorcycle to his teaching job. All these were woven into *After the Dancing Days*. The facts were important, but more vital for the writing were the feelings that moved these family stories: the fear I see in the face of a great-aunt standing between her two brothers who are about to go to France, the joy in the faces of my mother and her sister, little girls of seven and nine, sitting on the grass on either side of their uncle, back safe from France.

I find families fascinating to write about, living as I do in a family that is so close we often grate on each other. I do not write *about* my family, but again, I use the emotions that permeate any family to bring my characters to life. Now, as mother and aunt of teenagers, I see family life from many perspectives: child, parent, sister, aunt, wife, daughter. I have never liked books for young people that portray adults as ineffectual or evil, instead of people still struggling to learn the best way to lead their lives. We all struggle, every day, and if we are lucky, we all learn, every day.

My formal writing education began in high school, when a wonderful man, George Taylor, taught me all the important things I needed to know about writing and teaching writing. In the years between high school and that January day that I began *After the Dancing Days*, I attended Middlebury College in Vermont and the University of Kansas, married, taught school, traveled, loved all the animals and friends that entered my life—I got ready for writing.

And now I write—at cost to a lot of other things. My son David and husband Chuck keep the house going so I can stare at my computer screen or take long walks through the foothills (to which I have returned, never feeling at home anywhere else) trying to work out just why the characters are acting that way. And my students have learned NEVER to say their writing is OK the way it is, so they don't need to revise. It is the revising time when I do the hard work, when I find the feeling that is buried beneath the surface of the moment.

———

Margaret Rostkowski was born in Little Rock, Arkansas. She received her B.A. degree in History from Middlebury College in 1967 and received an M.A. degree in Teaching from the University of Kansas in 1971. She is a high school teacher, and is married and has one son. *After the Dancing Days* has won many honors and awards: the 1987 International Reading Association Children's Book Award, the 1987 Jefferson Cup Award from the Virginia Library Association, and the 1986 Golden Kite Award for fiction. It was a Junior Literary Guild selection and was named a 1986 Best Book for Young Adults and a Notable Book of 1986 by the American Library Association. It was also named a 1986 Notable Children's Trade Book in the Field of Social Studies by a joint committe of the National Council on the Social Studies and the Children's Book Council.

SELECTED WORKS: After the Dancing Days, 1986; Both Sides Now, 1989.

LOIS RUBY

September 11, 1942–

AUTHOR OF *Arriving at a Place You've Never Left*, etc.

Autobiographical sketch of Lois Ruby:

I HAVE NEVER been a collector of things—ideas, characters, names, yes, but not of *things*. And yet, I look around my office, which is a 10-foot square box in my home, and I see that I am surrounded by pigs. There are pig calendars from years past, pigs stuffed in fur and plaid coats, pigs

cast in iron, molded in plaster, and drawn in crayon. How did this happen to me, a person who avoids clutter and sentimentality? Well, I wrote a book called *Pig-Out Inn*, and on its cover are three weird-looking pigs with luminous blue eyes, and ever since then, people have showered me with swine. At this rate, I shall have to move to a larger box.

Two sad little black eyes rimmed in pink stare down on me and remind me that pigs have gotten a bum rap. "We're intelligent," the eyes say. "We're not dirty or lazy. Our skin is enough like yours that it's used for human skin grafts. Give us a break." And maybe that's what I like about pigs. They're so like people.

I grew up in San Francisco and never actually came face to face with a pig until I went to the Kansas State Fair after my children were teenagers. Maybe if I had read children's stories at the right time, I would have been introduced to Wilbur, in *Charlotte's Web*, way before my sophomore year in college. But in my weekly trips to the library as a child, my main goal was to get as far away from the mean, unsmiling librarian as possible. She was near the children's room, so I turned left, away from her, to the adult reading room. Later, I showed *her*. I became a librarian.

I worked for the Dallas Public Library in the Young Adult Department, which was how I first began to read books about teenagers. And what a discovery! What's this? I missed adolescence? Why, somehow all those excursions to the adult reading room and none to shopping malls and video arcades zoomed me right past the teen years. But then, as a married woman reading those young adult books, I could recapture something I never knew I'd lost. What's more, I found out I could write books like those I was reading. And it was easy, and it was fun.

Getting published was another matter. It was not easy and not fun. As my three sons got older, they asked me what I was going to be when I grew up.

"Oh," I said, horrified at the insensitivity of the question, "but I'm already grown, and I'm a writer."

"No," my oldest replied. "I mean like a taxi cab driver, who gets paid for it."

Now my sons, David, Kenn, and Jeff, are nearly launched. One is in college, the other two almost ready to fly. I am still not a taxi cab driver, and maybe they think I'll never grow up to be a success. But I have a wonderful husband who was in my Spanish class the very first day of college in 1960, and three healthy, bright sons who have that most precious of qualities, a sense of humor, and clean Kansas air, and my books, and my fountain pen, and an endless supply of one-side-used paper, the other side of which will become stories. And I have my pigs.

What more could a woman ask?

———

Lois Ruby was born in San Francisco. She received her B.A. degree from the University of California at Berkeley in 1964 and her M.A. degree from California State University at San Jose in 1968. She was a young adult librarian at Dallas Public Library from 1965 to 1967. She was an art and museum librarian at the University of Missouri

in Columbia for a year in 1967, and has been a writer since 1973. She is also a youth group advisor. Ruby is a member of the American Library Association, the Association of Jewish Libraries, and the Church and Synagogue Library Association. *Arriving at a Place You've Never Left* was named a 1977 Best Book for Young Adults by the American Library Association, and *Two Truths in My Pocket* was named a Notable Children's Trade Book in the Field of Social Studies by a joint committee of the National Council on the Social Studies and the Children's Book Council in 1982.

SELECTED WORKS: Arriving at a Place You've Never Left, 1977; What Do You Do in Quicksand?, 1979; Two Truths in My Pocket, 1982; This Old Man, 1984; Pig-Out Inn, 1987.

ABOUT: Contemporary Authors, Vol. 97-100; Something About the Author, Vol. 34; Vol. 35.

IVY RUCKMAN

May 25, 1931–

AUTHOR OF *Night of the Twisters*, etc.

Autobiographical sketch of Ivy Ruckman:

"WHAT made you think you could become a writer?" asks an eleven-year-old boy in a letter.

Well, ummmmmm. I stop and scratch my head as puzzled people do in cartoons. I think back. I begin to ask myself "what if" sorts of things. I bet you've done the same.

Have you wondered what it would be like to be the firstborn in your family instead of the last? Or to be the opposite sex? Or to be as rich as some of the people you see on TV? I'm sitting here at my keyboard wondering all these things . . . about me. I come back to the boy's question: What *was* it, there in Nebraska during the poverty of the thirties, that made me think I could become an author some day?

One can never find a precise answer to that question, heredity being what it is, but

I suspect there are clues in those wonderings if we examine them.

Had I been the firstborn in our family (instead of the last of seven), I mightn't have had the play time I did—the unstructured, unsupervised play time, during which imagination or my legs took me wherever I wanted to go. What freedom! Until captured by school, I was free as the wind. Leisure and play are important in the development of a writer's imagination. Maybe I was lucky being the youngest in the family.

Had I been raised with more sisters than brothers, I might have behaved demurely and learned to cook. I might have enjoyed dusting furniture and playing with dolls. As it was, I identified—as we say—with my five older brothers. I grew up prefering "boy games," dreaming of becoming a trapeze artist or a bronc rider, an explorer or a pioneer like my homesteading grandparents. Later, in my teens, I thought seriously of becoming an artist, an actor, or a great evangelist. My brother Bill, my closest friend, never said, "You're a girl, you can't do that." He treated me as an equal, which helped me believe in myself and my dreams.

I also learned survival techniques, important to a female minority in a family of big boys; I learned to wheedle, cajole, trade my dessert for something I valued more, and "tell" when it seemed to my advantage.

Had I been born into wealth or privilege, who knows? I mightn't have learned persistence if life had been too easy. Or toughness, which an author needs to face rejection. Or sharing, which makes a good listener of a writer. Or taking pleasure in little things because there aren't so many big ones.

Of course we had books and games and pets during those years, but most of our entertainment was simple and homemade. In our family, we loved storytelling above all else. Probably because our father's stories were riveting—mischief-filled, action-packed adventures from his own childhood as a minister's son in Nebraska's ranch country.

Happily, there was always someone around to listen to my stories, too. I can remember hurrying home from school with the most outrageous tales of what went on at Morton Elementary that day. My mother would listen and exclaim until I was sure I'd relieved her drudgery. For years, I thought she believed the wild fictions I made up for her.

In due course, I left my fortunate childhood and grew up to be someone who loves books, theater, conversation, and almost any activity that takes place outdoors. I graduated from college, moved to Wyoming to teach high school, married, and have since raised three children of my own. Between babies and teaching jobs, while my mountain-climbing family ranged from one peak to another, I began writing stories for children and teenagers.

"What made me think I could be a writer?" the boy still asks.

Undoubtedly some-of-the-above. But more, of course. There were teachers who encouraged me, books that inspired me, early publication, and a rich life (the other kind of rich), that left me with feelings and experiences I wanted to share with readers.

Today, ten books later, I spend nearly as much time in travel and speaking as I do in writing. Sometimes, in a school auditorium full of students, I look for a scrawny little girl who can't sit still, whose eyes are neon bright with excitement, and I know she's kin—someone who'd rather read or dream up stories than eat. Before long, I'm pretty sure she'll throw her arm in the air and dare to ask, "What made you think you could ever be a writer when you grew up?"

That will make me smile. And I'll think, There she is, Ivy Ruckman at age seven or nine or thirteen—burning with curiosity, full of stories, needing center stage more than she needs sleep. And I'll want to do it all over again . . . from the beginning.

Writing books for kids has been almost agreeable life for me. I hope there will be many more books—and readers like you to go with them.

———

Ivy Ruckman was born in Hastings, Nebraska. She received her B.A. degree from Hastings College in 1953 and studied further at the University of Utah from 1963 to 1965. She was an English teacher in Casper, Wyoming, from 1953 to 1957 and also taught high school in Salt Lake City, Utah, from 1970 to 1972. She is a member of the Society of Children's Book Writers and the Southeastern Advocates of Literature for Young People. She has been writing full-time since 1974. She also speaks and gives workshops at literature and library conferences.

Night of the Twisters was a Junior Literary Guild selection and was named a 1984 Outstanding Science Trade Book for Children by a joint committee of the National Science Teachers Association and the Children's Book Council. It was also serialized in *Cricket* magazine and was named a 1984 Children's Choice Book by a joint committee of the CBC and the International Reading Association. *This Is Your Captain Speaking* was designated a 1987 Notable Children's Trade Book in the Field of Social Studies by a joint committee of the National Council on the Social Studies and the CBC. In 1984 Ivy Ruckman received an Outstanding Alumni Award from Hastings College, and received the 1985 Mountain Plains Library Association Literary Contribution Award for the body of her work.

SELECTED WORKS: Melba the Brain, 1979; The Hunger Scream, 1983; In a Class by Herself, 1983; What's an Average Kid Like Me Doing Way Up Here?, 1983; Night of the Twisters, 1984; This Is Your Captain Speaking, 1987; No Way Out, 1988; Who Invited the Undertaker?, 1989.

ABOUT: Contemporary Authors, Vol. 111; Something About the Author, Vol. 37.

JOANNE RYDER

September 16, 1946–

AUTHOR OF *The Snail's Spell*, etc.

Autobiographical sketch of Joanne Ryder:

WHEN I VISIT SCHOOLS, children often ask me why I like to write about animals. Perhaps it's because I was an only child; and when I was young in rural New Jersey, there weren't many other children living nearby. But there were animals everywhere, even salamanders in our basement when it rained, so they became my first friends. Also, my parents enjoyed observing nature, and I had an assortment of pets from rabbits to chickens, hamsters, ducks, and fish.

I liked taking walks with my father through the woods. We would always bring back armloads of treasures—rocks and leaves and, sometimes, even a wandering box turtle. Now I live in California, and I still like taking walks. What I bring back now are ideas for stories and poems.

Today, for example, I walked through Golden Gate Park in San Francisco. It was a holiday weekend, and I took along some peanuts and made friends with several squirrels. Then I found a new path I had

JOANNE RYDER

never taken before, and along the way I discovered a shallow pond. I sat on the dirt path and fed tiny bits of peanuts to the thin, fast minnows that darted close to shore. Soon three big carp appeared from under lily pads, circling closer to see what the excitement was all about. And then suddenly, silently, a heron landed a few feet away. The bird stood without moving, just watching me. I felt we were playing a game of statues, each waiting for the other to move. The heron won, for I moved first! When I left, it was still standing, watching the water and hunting for the tiny fish that swam above the mud.

Books often begin in my mind as pictures. Two fish circling slowly, almost touching. A pigeon bobbing quickly, plucking peanuts from the path. I try to find just the right words to create a picture for my reader, and by adding more and more scenes I share an experience I have had or perhaps would like to have. Either before or after I write my first draft, I try to check all my facts. I graduated from journalism school, and I want to be sure that my work is accurate as well as poetic. What kind of heron did I see? What would the carp eat in this small pond? There are books by my bed

right now about squirrels and a pile of books on my desk about birds. Someday the pictures I have in my mind of today will be part of a story or a poem you may read.

I like nature and animals, but I do like writing about children too. And I like to write about wishes and dreams. My book *The Night Flight* comes from my own experiences as a child when we moved from the country to New York City. I began to dream that I could fly through the streets of a town, just as Anna does in my story. Those flying dreams were always my favorite ones!

Writers wonder about things. I wonder what it would be like to be someone else for a little while. What would it be like to be a different person or a different animal? A squirrel, a heron, or a girl who flies through the night. There are so many fascinating possibilities, so many pictures to see and describe, so many stories to imagine and tell. I hope that I can keep on exploring the world around me and sharing what I find with children through my books.

————

Joanne Ryder was born in Morristown, New Jersey. She grew up in New York and New Jersey. She graduated from Wisconsin's Marquette University with a journalism degree in 1968, and then returned to New York to become a children's book editor and writer. In 1984 she moved to San Francisco, California, where she writes fulltime. She has worked as a docent at the San Francisco zoo.

Simon Underground was a 1977 Children's Book Showcase Book. *The Snail's Spell* won a 1983 New York Academy of Sciences Children's Science Book Award. *Fog in the Meadow* was named a 1980 Children's Choice Book by a joint committee of the Children's Book Council and the International Reading Association. Three of Ryder's books have been named Outstanding Science Trade Books for Children by a joint committee of the CBC and the National Science Teachers Association: *Fog in the*

Meadow in 1979, *Inside Turtle's Shell* in 1985, and *Step into the Night* in 1988. *The Night Flight* was a Book-of-the-Month Club selection. *Step into the Night* and *Mockingbird Morning* were Junior Literary Guild selections.

SELECTED WORKS: Simon Underground, 1976; Fireflies, 1977; A Wet and Sandy Day, 1977; Fog in the Meadow, 1979; The Spiders Dance, 1981; Beach Party, 1982; The Snail's Spell, 1982; Inside Turtle's Shell and Other Poems of the Field, 1985; The Night Flight, 1985; Chipmunk Song, 1987; Step into the Night, 1988; White Bear, Ice Bear, 1989; Mockingbird Morning, 1989; Under the Moon, 1989.

ABOUT: Childhood Education February 1988; Contemporary Authors, Vol. 112; St. Helena (California) Star March 3, 1987; Something About the Author, Vol. 34.

CYNTHIA RYLANT

June 6, 1954–

AUTHOR OF *The Relatives Came*, etc.

Autobiographical sketch of Cynthia Rylant:

WHEN I WAS growing up in a small town in West Virginia, I didn't do much reading because there just weren't that many books around. No public library, no money to buy books—no bookstores, anyway. But I loved comic books and could get those at the drugstore—three for a quarter—plus Danny Alderman who lived behind me used to trade me a big pile of his for a big pile of mine. So my training as a writer began with Archie and Jughead and The Fantastic Four. As I got older, I left comic books behind for sappy paperback romances, and it wasn't until I went away to college that I began to read what most people call "good literature."

I don't know why I became a writer. I didn't write much as a child. The only stories I ever tried were called "My Adventures with the Beatles." That was in sixth grade when I was madly in love with Paul McCartney. But that's the only time I can

recall ever writing creatively on my own time—otherwise, I just did it for dumb school assignments like everybody else.

My parents split up when I was four years old and after that I lived with my grandparents for nearly four years, until I was in third grade. It's that time that seems to have sunk thickest into my brain and my heart and much of what I saw and heard then has come into my books. My first book, *When I Was Young in the Mountains*—is about those years I lived with my grandparents. And *Night in the Country, This Year's Garden, The Relatives Came* . . . , all these came from my memories of those four years. It was hard for me, being away from my parents during that time, and so maybe everything I felt during that time I felt more intensely. And when you write stories, it's always your most intense feelings that come out. At least it's so for me.

So many of my books are directly connected to my real life, especially my childhood. A lot of *A Blue-Eyed Daisy* is about things that really happened to me—how I got my first kiss, a school bus accident, going deer hunting, worrying whether a parent would die. And all of the poems in my book *Waiting to Waltz: A Childhood* are true, and about me from age eight to fourteen.

But the more I write, it seems the more willing I am to get closer to my real life today, who I am today. I wrote a book called *A Kindness* about people who are learning to let go of each other, learning not to try to control each other. That's something I have to work hard on in my own life because I can be very insecure sometimes. And I wrote an autobiography, called *But I'll Be Back Again*, which has in it some personal lessons I've learned recently, not just twenty years ago. I think the best writing is that which is most personal, most revealing. Because we all, I think, long mostly for the same things and are afraid mostly of the same things and we all want someone to write about all of this so we won't feel too crazy or alone.

I like being a writer but I don't know if I'll be one all of my life. It seems like a long time to keep writing books, a whole lifetime. But I'm grateful that I'll be leaving something important and beautiful on the earth for other people, something honest for them to read.

———

Cynthia Rylant was born in Hopewell, Virginia. She received her B.A. degree from Morris Harvey College in 1975 and her M.A. degree from Marshall University in 1976. She also received an M.L.S. degree in 1981 from Kent State University. She taught English part-time at Marshall University, Ohio University at Ironton, and the University of Akron. *A Fine White Dust* was a Newbery Honor Book for 1987, an award given by the American Library Association. *When I Was Young in the Mountains* was a Caldecott Honor Book in 1983, and *The Relatives Came* was a Caldecott Honor Book in 1986. Three of her books were Junior Literary Guild selections: *Henry and Mudge in the Green Time*, *All I See*, and *Night in the Country*. *Birthday Presents* and *A Blue-Eyed Daisy* were named Children's Choice books by a joint committee of the International Reading Association and the Children's Book Council. *The Relatives Came* was named a Notable Children's Trade Book in the Field of Social Studies for 1985 by a joint committee of the National Council on the Social Studies and the Children's Book Council. Four of her books were named Notable Books of their years of publication, and two of her books were named Best Books for Young Adults by the ALA: *A Fine White Dust* for 1986, and *A Kindness* for 1988.

SELECTED WORKS: Miss Maggie, 1983; This Year's Garden, 1984; Waiting to Waltz: A Childhood, 1984; A Blue-Eyed Daisy, 1985; The Relatives Came, 1985; Every Living Thing, 1985; Night in the Country, 1986; Birthday Presents, 1987; Children of Christmas: Stories for the Season, 1987; A Fine White Dust, 1987; Henry and Mudge in the Green Time, 1987; All I See, 1988; A Kindness, 1988; But I'll Be Back Again: An Album, 1989; Mr. Griggs' Work, 1989.

ABOUT: Horn Book November/December 1987; Rylant, Cynthia. But I'll Be Back Again: An Album; Something About the Author, Vol. 44.

SVEND OTTO S.

1916–

AUTHOR AND ILLUSTRATOR OF *The Fir Tree*, etc.

Biographical sketch of Svend Otto Sørensen:

SVEND OTTO S. was born in Copenhagen but lived in Falster, Denmark, with his grandparents from the ages of eighteen months to eight years. He remembers his grandmother as being bright and optimistic, and his grandfather, who was a railway worker, as "strict and serious." When he was five, his mother bought for him an edition of Hans Christian Andersen tales with illustrations by Wilhelm Pedersen and Fröhlich. She read the tales aloud to him and he was very impressed by what he could read between the lines.

At the age of three, he drew a picture of

himself in a giant coat, a picture that he calls a protest against being bundled up. He drew horses, too, following the example of an uncle who drew. He recalls being "haunted" by powerful pictures. When in school, he learned that one could have a career as an illustrator, and he was encouraged by one teacher. Eventually this assistance landed him at the Art School of Bizzie Høyer, where he studied on scholarship for three years. From there he went to London, first attending a drawing school and later "wandering about and drawing everywhere." He began supporting himself at the age of seventeen.

As a young illustrator, Svend Otto S. worked hard to show his work to publishers. He eventually earned enough to make a living, though in 1959 he wanted to give up drawing entirely. He might put in a great deal of work on a book cover only to have it rejected. He says that he didn't get the books he wanted to illustrate and that no one wanted what he wanted to draw. He thought about emigration to Canada, and about being a teacher. After doing book covers and suffering through this discouraging phase, however, he began to get a great deal of work.

In 1964 he requested of Paul Ringhof at Gyldendal publishers that he be allowed to illustrate Grimm stories, and Ringhof later edited books that S. wrote and illustrated.

S. has illustrated many fairy tales. "Illustrations," he says, "should be a visual extension to the text." He conducts research to create the historical atmosphere required by the story. He lets the quality of the story determine his medium. He counts among authors who have influenced him Fournier, Istrati, Grimm, Andersen, Hermann Bang, Kafka, and Martin A. Hansen.

Svend Otto S. won the 1978 Hans Christian Andersen Illustrator Medal in the Awards administered by the International Board on Books for Young People. He also was "Highly Commended" in those awards in 1976. He received a Plaque in 1979 in the Biennale of Illustrations Bratislava competition of Czechoslovakia. *The Runaway Pancake* was named a 1981 Children's Choice Book by a joint committee of the International Reading Association and the Children's Book Council. In his Andersen Medal acceptance speech, he said that an illustrator is "an artist . . . who loves literature as much as illustration. . . . I want to arouse compassion and warmth between people. I believe that compassion is the foundation of all political understanding, and that humour can bridge a great many opposing interests."

Svend Otto S. is married and has three daughters.

SELECTED WORKS WRITTEN AND ILLUSTRATED: Tim and Trisha, 1977; Taxi Dog, 1978; A Christmas Book, 1982; The Giant Fish and Other Stories, 1982.

SELECTED WORKS ILLUSTRATED: The Fir Tree, by Hans Christian Andersen, 1971; Tom Thumb, by the Brothers Grimm, 1976; The Brave Little Tailor, by the Brothers Grimm, 1979; The Runaway Pancake, by P.C. Asbjörnsen and J. Moe, 1980; Trust in the Unexpected, by Gunnel Linde, 1984; My Nightingale Is Singing, by Astrid Lindgren, 1986; The Princess and the Sun, Moon and Stars, retold by Bjarne Reuter, 1987.

ABOUT: Bookbird No. 1, 1979; Carpenter, Humphrey and Mari Prichard. The Oxford Companion to Children's Literature; Kingman, Lee and others, comps. Illustrators of Children's Books: 1967-1976.

JUDITH ST. GEORGE

February 26, 1931–

AUTHOR OF *The Brooklyn Bridge: They Said It Couldn't Be Built*, etc.

Autobiographical sketch of Judith St. George:

LOOKING BACK to the child that was me, I see a skinny kid (my brother called me "The only girl in the world without a shadow") who loved two things above all else, books and sports.

When I was growing up our family either had no money to travel during the Depres-

Judith St. George

sion or no gasoline during World War II. It didn't matter to me because I traveled everywhere I wanted to go anyway, back in time to frontier Wisconsin with Caddie Woodlawn or to that wondrous land of Oz or to Mary's Secret Garden. Like all sensible travelers, once I'd left on a trip, I couldn't be reached, not by the phone, the dinner bell or even my mother calling me to set the table (I especially couldn't hear that).

As for sports, since I came from a family of athletes, I can't take any credit for, ahem, being the only girl on the boys' sixth-grade baseball team. And surprisingly enough, being an ex-tomboy has stood me in good stead as a writer and researcher. I've hiked to the top of the presidents' four heads on Mount Rushmore to research *The Mount Rushmore Story*; and for *Panama Canal: Gateway to the World*, in order to make a transit of the Panama Canal, I had to climb up a thirty-foot rope ladder at night to board a ship that was underway!

Tomboy or not, the skinny kid that was me was afraid of just about everything— afraid of the dark, afraid of strange noises at night, afraid of being in the house alone. At bedtime, I used to jump into bed from the doorway so that whatever was hiding under the bed couldn't grab my ankles. Maybe I was full of fears because I grew up in a big, old creaky house that had a secret back stairway and was all dark panelling. Or maybe it was because the same imagination that took me traveling to all sorts of places in books filled my mind with hobgoblins.

Now, as an adult, I spend lots of time alone (even at night), I don't mind going into an empty house, and I never worry about strange noises. But I've *never, ever* forgotten the fears that used to haunt me, and so I like to write books for kids who perhaps have fears of their own but who also enjoy a scary book because they know that at the end, the morning light will vanquish the nighttime shadows.

Do I write anything but mysteries? Well, yes and no. All of my books, even my non-fiction, are mysterious or scary in some way. After all, the men building the Brooklyn Bridge had to work from little swings 135 feet above the windy East River, and if that isn't scary, I don't know what is. And what could be more mysterious than trying to build a fifty-mile-long canal through the swamps, jungles, and mountain ranges of Panama? So no matter what kind of book I write, I hope that it will be picked up by some skinny kid who likes a goose bumpy story and who is willing to travel with me to unknown shores.

———

Judith St. George was born in Westfield, New Jersey. She received her B.A. degree from Smith College in 1952. She married on June 5, 1954 and has four children. She has led an adult course, "Writing for Children," through Rutgers University Extension Division, has been a New Jersey delegate to a White House Conference on Libraries and Information Services and a Commissioner to the Brooklyn Bridge Centennial Commission. She is a member of the Author's Guild, the Rutgers University Advisory Council on Children's Literature, and the Mystery Writers of America.

The Halloween Pumpkin Smasher was nominated for a 1979 Edgar Allan Poe Award from the Mystery Writers of America. *The Brooklyn Bridge* was named a Notable Book of 1982 by the American Library Association and a Junior Literary Guild selection. It was also an American Book Award Honor Book for 1982 and a Golden Kite Honor Book for nonfiction in 1982. Four of her other books were named JLG selections: *By George, Bloomers!, Amazing Voyage, In the Shadow of the Bear,* and *What's Happening.* The latter was named a best juvenile novel of 1986 by the journal *Voice of Youth Advocates. Mount Rushmore* won a 1986 Christopher Award, was a Golden Kite Honor Book for nonfiction in 1985, was an ALA Notable Book of 1985, and was named a 1985 Notable Children's Trade Book in the Field of Social Studies by a joint committee of the National Council on the Social Studies and the Children's Book Council. *Haunted* was named a Children's Choice book by a joint committee of the CBC and the International Reading Association.

SELECTED WORKS: By George, Bloomers!, 1976; The Halloween Pumpkin Smasher, 1978; The Amazing Voyage of the New Orleans, 1980; Haunted, 1980; Call Me Margo, 1981; The Mysterious Girl in the Garden, 1981; The Brooklyn Bridge: They Said It Couldn't Be Built, 1982; In the Shadow of the Bear, 1983; The Mount Rushmore Story, 1985; What's Happening to My Junior Year?, 1986; Who's Scared? Not Me!, 1987; Panama Canal: Gateway to the World, 1989.

ABOUT: Contemporary Authors, Vol. 69; (New Revision Series), Vol. 14; Journal of Youth Services in Libraries Fall 1987; Something About the Author, Vol. 13.

OTTO R. SALASSI

October 2, 1939–

AUTHOR OF *Jimmy D., Sidewinder, and Me,* etc.

Autobiographical sketch of Otto Russell Salassi:

BE CAREFUL what you want, Thoreau advised, because you will surely get it. And good advice it was, but it came too late for me. By the time I heard it, I already wanted to be a writer, and that's why I'm not rich, in the Baseball Hall of Fame, or running for President. Ever since those lazy summer afternoons when my young friends and I sat around the front porch and played a card game called "Authors," I have dreamed I was one, and instead of them saying "Give me all your Hawthornes" they'd someday look at my picture and say, "Give me all your Salassis." Pretty heady stuff for a nine-year-old.

If I had to blame somebody for never getting to be either rich or President, I guess I'd blame my mother, who belonged to a book-of-the-month club, and when she wasn't busy having kids or cooking and cleaning up after them, was always reading books. She taught me that reading was fun, and gave me a sense of humor by telling me some of the outrageous things that went on in them . . . books like *Cheaper By the Dozen,* and *No Time for Sargeants.*

Then, too, I'd have to blame my many teachers who taught me how to read and think about what I read, and the librarians who gave me books and were just as much a kid as I was.

Finally, I guess I'd have to blame the city of Vicksburg, Mississippi, and the time I grew up in. In 1949, when I was ten, there was a great public library—one I could walk to—with a dark, castlelike air about it; and downstairs in the children's room were stuffed animals; a bear, an eagle, raccoons, skunks, snakes, foxes, you name it, and they were real, mounted in a wall case that was as long as the room and decorated like the deep woods. There was also a human skeleton for us to wonder at, and a dead person, a mummy. When I got older and started going upstairs, it wasn't nearly as much fun.

The city itself was so steeped in history that it defies description. Every house was older than the Civil War, and so there would be stories about a Yankee spy being hung in them, or Confederate gold being hidden somewhere. One of my family's rented apartments was in a house that was part of the wall of an outdoor wrestling arena, and became the setting for *On the Ropes*.

There was also the old courthouse which was right across the street, and Fort Hill which guarded the city from attack by river gunboat, then there was the river itself, and the bridge that provided the test for the boys in *And Nobody Knew They Were There*.

Best of all there was Crowley's, the pool hall where my high school chums and I were schooled in cursing, smoking, fighting, telling tall tales, bragging about our conquests, and the other arts of manly adulthood. I put the blame most squarely on that pool hall, which I renamed Hoot's in *Jimmy D., Sidewinder, and Me*.

I guess I should also blame the whole state of Mississippi for liking writers so much and honoring them as heroes of the highest order. In every English classroom I sat in, there was a large literary map of the state with the names of the famous writers and little pictures from their most famous books. The state was covered; every city

had a writer, it seemed, who it could claim as its own . . . every city except Vicksburg. By 1954, my fourteenth year, the year I broke my arm and couldn't play baseball, the year I joined the National Guard, and learned to drive, the year I read *Johnny Tremain*, and *The Amboy Dukes*, and moved into the adult world of *I, the Jury*, and *Battle Cry*, I had already decided that I wanted to be a writer on that map more than anything in the world.

Now I'm not sure that any of it still exists; the city, the bridge or the river, the teachers, the time, Crowley's, the idea of Confederate gold, or even the map...except in my own mind. But there it is, bright as ever, and so what I do is try to re-create it in my books, like some lost world that was glorious, and maybe interest some kids who like to read about things that are outrageous, and don't necessarily give a hoot about being either rich, or President.

———

Otto Salassi joined the Air Force after high school and served as a mechanic on Atlas missle launch crews at Cape Canaveral and Vandenburg AFB. He received his B.S. degree from Memphis State University in 1967 and his M.L.S. from George Peabody College in 1968. He worked as a librarian in colleges in Tennessee, Minnesota, and New York, and had some short stories published in literary quarterlies. He then went back to school to obtain an M.F.A. degree from the University of Arkansas in 1978. He now works part-time in a university library. He was married in 1965 and has two children.

The American Library Association named *On the Ropes* and *Jimmy D., Sidewinder, and Me* Best Books for Young Adults in their years of publication.

SELECTED WORKS: On the Ropes, 1981; And Nobody Knew They Were There, 1984; Jimmy D., Sidewinder, and Me, 1987.

ABOUT: Arkansas Gazette May 4, 1981; Contemporary Authors, Vol. 106; Something About the Author, Vol. 38.

JOAN SANDIN

April 30, 1942–

AUTHOR AND ILLUSTRATOR OF *The Long Way to a New Land*, etc.

Autobiographical sketch of Joan Sandin:

I WAS BORN in Watertown, Wisconsin in 1942. It was Moving Day and my mother has never forgiven me! We did quite a bit of moving those first few years, but by the time I was old enough to start school, we had settled in Tucson, Arizona. I lived there from first grade through college, and now, twenty-five years later, I'm living there again, this time with my children. I love the desert, the climate, and the informality of the place.

As a child I was always drawing pictures. The first story I illustrated was one my brother wrote. (It was a hard one to illustrate, since everything happened in a dark cave.) I loved making things too: filmstrips for my magic lantern, holiday cards and decorations, fancy 3-D gift wraps. And I liked to write stories.

At the University of Arizona I majored in art. During school vacations I worked in restaurants, and after graduation I traveled all over Europe on the money I'd saved. I lived in Madrid for six months, teaching English and learning Spanish.

In 1965 I arrived in New York. I had no job and no place to live, and I knew no one. It was a lonely time. I waited tables and went to all the wrong places with an overflowing portfolio of drawings. On a visit home, my former illustration teacher helped me streamline my portfolio, and back in New York I got my first book to illustrate! I threw away my waitress shoes and moved to a fifth-floor walk-up in the Village. I was now a illustrator of children's books!

My marriage in 1971 to Sigfrid Leijonhufvud, a Swedish journalist, brought me to Stockholm. Our two children, Jonas and Jenny, were born there. I lived in Sweden for fourteen years, visiting the States whenever I could. During that time I worked as a free lancer for both American and Swedish publishers.

Although I had illustrated dozens of children's books, it wasn't until this time that I wrote (and illustrated) one of my own. *The Long Way to a New Land* is the story of a Swedish family who emigrate to America in 1868. (My own grandfather had been a Swedish emigrant, coming to this country in 1883.) A second book about the emigrants' journey to Minnesota (*The Long Way Westward*) is planned for publication by Harper & Row (and by Rabén & Sjögren in Sweden) in 1989. I am now working on a third book about the same family. I received several grants from the Swedish Writers' Fund for this project, which required a great deal of research for both story and pictures.

I translate children's books from the Swedish to English too, and I have written some twenty books in simple Swedish for beginning readers. One of my books is written with only nine letters of the alphabet!

I divorced in 1986 and moved back to the States a few years later. I now live in Tucson with my children and with Happy, the cat who adopted us. I'm lucky enough to have my studio in the back yard and to make my own hours. But I'm even luckier to be able to work with something I enjoy as much as writing and drawing!

————

Joan Sandin received a B.F.A. degree in 1964 from the University of Arizona. She lived in Sweden for fourteen years. She has received travel and work grants from Författarfonden (The Swedish Writers' Fund), and an exhibition grant from Bildkonstnärsfonden, The Swedish Artists' Fund. She has written or illustrated thirty-six books published in the United States and in Sweden. She has had one-person shows in Sweden and in the U.S., of the illustrations for *The Long Way to a New Land*, and has art represented in The Kerlan Collection. Sandin is a member of FST, The Swedish Society of Illustrators.

Joan Sandin also translates books, and her translation of *Linnea's Windowsill Garden*, by Christina Björk, was named a Notable Book of 1988 by the American Library Association. *Crocodile and Hen* was honored by the American Institute of Graphic Arts in 1970. *Hill of Fire, The Lemming Condition, . . . New Land*, and *Time for Uncle Joe* were named Notable Children's Trade Books in the Field of Social Studies by a joint committee of the National Council on the Social Studies and the Children's Book Council, each in their years of publication. *Woodchuck* was named a 1974 Outstanding Science Trade Book for Children by a joint committee of the National Science Teachers Association and the CBC. *The Mysterious Red Tape Gang* was nominated for a 1975 Edgar Allan Poe Award by the Mystery Writers of America. *Daniel's Duck* was a 1979 ALA Notable Book. . . . *New Land* was named an ALA Notable Book of 1981 and a Reading Rainbow book. *Hill of Fire* was also a Reading Rainbow Book.

SELECTED WORKS WRITTEN AND ILLUSTRATED: The Long Way to a New Land, 1981; The Long Way Westward, 1989.

SELECTED WORKS ILLUSTRATED: Crocodile and Hen, by Joan Lexau, 1969; Hill of Fire, by Thomas Lewis, 1971; Small Wolf, by Nathaniel Benchley, 1972; The Mysterious Red Tape Gang, by Joan Lowery Nixon, 1974; Woodchuck, by Faith McNulty, 1974; The Lemming Condition, by Alan Arkin, 1976; Bird, by Liesel Moak Skorpen, 1976; Clipper Ship, by Tom Lewis, 1978; Daniel's Duck, by Clyde Bulla, 1979; Time for Uncle Joe, by Nancy Jewell, 1981; Trouble at the Mines, by Doreen Rappaport, 1987; House of a Mouse, by Aileen Fisher, 1988.

ABOUT: Kingman, Lee and others, comps. Illustrators of Children's Books: 1967-1976; Something About the Author, Vol. 12.

PAMELA SARGENT

March 20, 1948–

AUTHOR OF *Earthseed*, etc.

Autobiographical sketch of Pamela Sargent:

I WAS a near-sighted child, which may have had as much to do with my becoming a writer as anything else. I was myopic even before entering school, and squinted my way through first grade and part of second before a teacher noticed that my academic problems might be the result of poor vision. Putting on a pair of glasses for the first time was a revelation. A blurred world suddenly became clear; indistinct shapes were sharply defined.

Before that, I had some strange ideas about the world. People's faces were only flesh-colored blobs unless I got close enough to see eyes, noses, and mouths. I used to feel my own face, amazed to find that my facial features didn't disappear when no one was near me. I was constantly bumping into things I couldn't see until too late, and getting hit by objects that appeared out of nowhere. I didn't know that you could see that someone might be angry or upset by reading the expression on his face. The world was a chaotic place, full of unseen dangers and events I could not predict, even after I learned to rely on my hearing to give me some warning. I couldn't understand how

Pamela Sargent

things worked, but longed for order, so made up stories for myself to explain what was actually going on.

Reading, however, was a skill I could learn, and I mastered it before starting school; I could hold a book close enough to make out the words. I didn't get into the habit of watching a lot of television, since a TV set was only another window revealing blurred, indistinct shapes. Reading became my primary source of entertainment, and learning to write—crouched over paper, my eyes only a couple of inches from the pencil—gave me a way to bring order into my world.

By the time I got my glasses, I had developed the habits of reading and writing, pleasures that remained even after I could see properly. But my glasses also revealed another truth; the world wasn't what I had believed it to be. This was a useful lesson. Too many people fall into a mental myopia, thinking that what they've been taught to believe reflects the truth. They never learn to look at the world through the lenses of curiosity, questions, and doubts in order to discover what can't be so easily seen.

Most of my writing has been science fiction and fantasy, a form that, by distancing

the reader from our world as it is, can also bring certain aspects of it into sharper focus. In my first young adult novel, *Earthseed*, I tell of teenagers growing up aboard a spaceship, with the ship's computer mind as their only parent. They learn that much of what the ship tells them is misleading or deceptive, and must confront the truth about themselves before they can leave the ship. In another novel, *Alien Child*, my main character is a girl raised by an alien. She is, it seems, the last person on Earth; she must not only discover what has happened to her people, but must also learn what it is to be human. Such science-fictional ideas can metaphorically illuminate the dilemmas of youth; a genre sometimes unfairly labeled "escape fiction" can give us a sense of our own possibilities.

Perhaps if I had seen the world clearly from the start, I wouldn't have had so many questions about it later, the kinds of questions a writer can explore in stories. I'm still, in a way, that child, learning how to see through the lenses my writing has given me.

———

Pamela Sargent was born in Ithaca, New York. She attended the State University of New York at Binghamton, where she earned a B.A. degree in 1968 and an M.A. degree in 1970, both in philosophy. She also studied ancient history and Greek. She has worked as a sales clerk, solderer, fine assembly worker, typist in a library, receptionist, and teaching asssistant in philosophy at her alma mater. Her first published story was written while in college. Her short stories have appeared in magazines and anthologies, and two of her books are story collections: *Starshadows* and *The Best of Pamela Sargent*. Pamela Sargent has written many novels published by adult book departments, such as *Cloned Lives*, *Venus of Dreams*, and *The Shore of Women*. She also edits story anthologies. She is a member of the Fiction Writers of America, the Authors Guild, and Amnesty International U.S.A.

Earthseed and *Women of Wonder* were both named Best Books for Young Adults in their years of publication by the American Library Association.

SELECTED WORKS: Earthseed, 1983; Eye of the Comet, 1984; Homesmind, 1984; Alien Child, 1988.

SELECTED WORKS EDITED: Women of Wonder, 1975; Bio-Futures, 1976; More Women of Wonder, 1976; The New Women of Wonder, 1978.

ABOUT: Contemporary Authors, Vol. 61; (New Revision Series), Vol. 8; Dictionary of Literary Biography, Vol. 8; English Journal May 1978; Science Fiction Encyclopedia; Something About the Author, Vol. 29; Twentieth-Century Science Fiction Writers; The Writers Directory 1984-1986.

SARAH SARGENT

March 15, 1937–

Author of Weird Henry Berg, etc.

Autobiographical sketch of Sarah Sargent:

I AM a middle-aged woman who lives in Oshkosh, Wisconsin. True. But suppose I were a dragon who lived in a cave in Wales or a girl who had to figure out what to do when a very strange creature crawled out of a basement drain? Suppose I were a young boy who was suddenly handed a blue ball that could make him the most powerful person in the world?

I like to look at questions like that, which might strike some people as silly. If you did have a glowing blue ball with incredible powers, you could do amazing tricks and dazzle your friends (and enemies). You could have money piled to the ceiling. Owning something like that would go way past winning every sort of lottery around. But would there be any catches to having so much power? Would you be any different yourself? Telling the story of Jonas McFee gives me the chance to try out the possibility, not just think about it.

When I think back over my life, as I have started to do since it hit me that I must be

at least half through it, I think of people and places I have known in books I've read almost as much as those from my "real" life. I've always read lots of books—when I was a child I read both "adult" and "children's" books and I still do. When I was a child, not being considered a person because I was young used to infuriate me.

My family—I have a husband and two children who are grown-up—has always had animals around and they have been important in my books, too. We've lived with cats and dogs, hamsters, guinea pigs, rabbits, and lizards. I think it's important to respect animals, not just to look at them as belonging to people.

Because writing stories makes me have to imagine as best I can how other people or even other kinds of creatures entirely might think and feel, I think I keep curious about the world. Reading books I see what a wonderful variety of ways of seeing and thinking people have. What's great about life is the chance to wonder and ask questions and explore mysteries, not looking for THE ANSWER, but for the possible answers that various ways of seeing suggest.

Writing, for me anyway, means going over the same pages over and over and making changes and throwing away piles of horrible stuff that didn't work. That is hard. Seeing me sweating and grinding my teeth and obviously feeling rotten about what awful junk I was writing, my daughter asked me once, "How can you say you LIKE to do that?"

I guess the answer is partly that writing is fun *because* it is hard. I don't mean because it builds character or some dumb thing like that. I mean because it forces you to be as clear and straight as you can be in the way you see and hear. It makes you go back again and again in your imagination and ask, "Is that the way it sounds? Is that what it tastes like? Would she feel exactly like that?"

It's hard to be bored by a world that you stare into and sniff at and puzzle over in that way. For me, and I suspect for most writers, life may be at times depressing or frightening or disgusting, but almost never dull.

———

Sarah Sargent was born in Roanoke, Virginia. She received her B.A. degree from Randolph-Macon Woman's College in 1959 and an M.A. degree from Yale University in 1961. She was married August 25, 1962. She taught English at the University of North Dakota from 1961 to 1962, at the University of Vermont from 1963 to 1967, the next year at the University of Minnesota, and from 1968 to 1972 and 1975 to 1978 at the University of Wisconsin at Oshkosh. *Weird Henry Berg* was a Junior Literary Guild selection and a 1981 winner of a Friends of American Writers Juvenile Book Merit Award. *Secret Lies* was named a Notable Book of 1981 by the American Library Association. The story Sarah Sargent describes in her autobiographical sketch occurs in *Jonas McFee, A.T.P.*

SELECTED WORKS: Edward Troy and the Witch Cat, 1978; Weird Henry Berg, 1980; Secret Lies, 1981; Edge of Darkness, 1982; Lure of the Dark, 1984; Watermusic, 1986; Jonas McFee, A.T.P., 1989.

ABOUT: Contemporary Authors, Vol. 106; Something About the Author, Vol. 41; Vol. 44, Who's Who of American Women, 1987–1988.

HELEN RONEY SATTLER

March 2, 1921–

AUTHOR OF *Dinosaurs of North America,* etc.

Autobiographical sketch of Helen Roney Sattler:

MOTHER, and sometimes my older sister, used to read to my brothers and me every night. My favorite stories were about wild animals. I grew up on a farm, and I thought it would be wonderful to have a wild animal for a pet. But I never did. My father taught us to appreciate nature and never allowed us to keep wild creatures. However, there were plenty of pets to be found among the farm animals. Besides the cats and dogs, my favorites were Nicodemus, a chicken; Oscar, a pig; Ferdinand, a calf; and Sam, the goat. Sam is the hero of *No Place For a Goat.*

My first home was a farm just outside of Newton, Iowa, the town where I was born. When I was eight we moved to another farm in Polk County, Missouri.

Being a middle child, between two brothers, I was a bit of a tomboy. I was adventuresome and had lots of self-confidence. I loved to explore and thought I could do anything anyone else could, and usually did. Nearly drowning, falling off a bluff, or being bitten by a copperhead snake, didn't daunt me. These personality traits have been helpful in my writing.

I attended small, one-room schools for the first eight grades. After graduating from high school, I studied to be a teacher, graduating from Southwest Missouri State College in 1946. I taught fifth and sixth graders in small, rural communities until my doctor told me I must stop or lose my health. Then I became a children's librarian because I

Roney: rhymes with *pony*

loved books as well as children. Then I was offered a job as sixth-grade teacher in an oil company's school in Aruba, Netherlands Antilles. I could not resist an opportunity to explore new territory and accepted. It was there I met my husband, Robert. In 1952 Robert went to work with Phillips Petroleum Company in Bartlesville, Oklahoma. We have lived here ever since. We have two children, a son and a daughter.

Although I loved books and read constantly, I never planned to be a writer. I started writing after I injured my back and was confined to bed for six months. I couldn't just lay there and do nothing, so I started writing short stories and articles. I sold my first story, "David's Surprise," to *Instructor* magazine and I've been writing ever since.

My grandson, who has lived with us for much of his life, has been the inspiration behind many of my books. It was he who asked me to write about dinosaurs.

Researching my nonfiction books satisfies my thirst for knowledge and exploration. It gives me an excuse to go places that I would not otherwise go—such as whale watching and on an African safari. It is fun to create the kind of nature books I loved to read as a child.

———

Helen Roney Sattler was married September 30, 1950. She was a teacher from 1941 to 1948, and a librarian for one year. She is a member of the Authors League of America, the Authors Guild, and the Society of Children's Book Writers.

Dinosaurs of North America was named an Honor Book in the nonfiction category of the 1982 Boston Globe-Horn Book Awards. It also was named an Honor Book for nonfiction in the Golden Kite Awards in 1981, given by the Society of Children's Book Writers. Along with eight of her other books, it was named an Oustanding Science Trade Book for Children in its year of publication by a joint committee of the National Science Teachers Association and the Children's Book Council. *The Illustrated Dinosaur Dictionary* won the 1983 Golden Kite Award for nonfiction.

No Place for a Goat was named a Children's Choice Book for 1981 by a joint committee of the Children's Book Council and the International Reading Association. Eight of Sattler's books have been named Notable Books of the year of their publication by the American Library Association; they include *Dinosaurs of North America*, *Whales*, and *Hominids*.

SELECTED WORKS WRITTEN: Dinosaurs of North America, 1981; The Illustrated Dinosaur Dictionary, 1983; Baby Dinosaurs,1984; Fish Facts and Bird Brains: Animal Intelligence, 1984; Pterosaurs, The Flying Reptiles, 1985; Train Whistles, 1985; Sharks, the Super Fish, 1986; Recipes for Art and Craft Materials (rev. ed.), 1977; Whales, the Nomads of the Sea, 1987; Hominids: A Look Back at Our Ancestors, 1988; Tyrannosaurus Rex and Its Kin, 1989.

ABOUT: Contemporary Authors (First Revision), Vol. 33; (New Revision Series), Vol. 14; Something About the Author, Vol. 4.

ALLEN SAY

August 28, 1937–

AUTHOR OF *The Boy of the Three-Year Nap*, etc.

Biographical sketch of Allen Say:

ALLEN SAY, who was born in Yokohama, Japan, evidently felt his artistic yearnings early on. At the age of only twelve he apprenticed himself to a famous Japanese cartoonist for training before going to California four years later. His subsequent, more diverse educational experiences included studies at Aoyama Gakuin in Tokyo, the Chouinard Art Institute, the Los Angeles Art Center School, the University of California at Berkeley, and San Francisco Art Institute. He has spent the majority of his adult life working professionally as a writer, an illustrator, and a photographer and enjoying his hobbies of fly fishing and collecting rare children's books.

ALLEN SAY

Say's first book of illustrations appeared in the 1968 publication of *A Canticle to the Waterbirds*, written by Brother Antoninus. During the next fifteen years Say created art for several picture books, among them a series of black and white and yellow paintings for Eve Bunting's text in *Magic and the Night River*, concerning a young Japanese boy's relationship with his grandfather. But the artist's first substantial critical recognition came in 1982 with the appearance of *The Bicycle Man*, both written and illustrated by Say. Set in post-World War II Japan, the book, with its elegant pen-and-ink and watercolor illustrations, tells of an unusual and delightful encounter between two American soldiers, one white and the other with "a face as black as the earth," and a group of Japanese school children, resulting in a wonderful friendship. Both *Booklist* and *Kirkus Reviews* acknowledged the title's success with starred reviews.

Two years later Say illustrated another popular, critically successful title, *How My Parents Learned to Eat*, written by Ina Friedman—a look at the crossing of cultures through a lesson in manners. In this title, a Reading Rainbow selection and

winner of the 1985 Christopher Medal, soft, full-color artwork extends the text, "capturing nuances of Japanese culture," as *School Library Journal* pointed out.

Although he has garnered most of his acclaim through his picture books, Say also tried his hand at writing novels, several of which have been well received. In *The Ink-Keeper's Apprentice* he writes a convincing and perhaps semiautobiographical tale of a Japanese teenager who apprentices himself to a well-known comic-strip artist. As a *Horn Book* reviewer commented, "The dialogue is lively, the characters are sharply drawn, and the episodes of the loose, realistic narrative are significant events in the maturing of a self-reliant Japanese adolescent." The book was named a Notable Book of 1979 and a Best Book for Young Adults of 1979 by the American Library Association.

By the mid-1980s Say had made a tentative decision to devote himself completely to professional photography, rather than to children's books. A phone call from Houghton Mifflin, however, persuaded him to take up his brush one more time to illustrate a children's story written by Dianne Snyder. He completed the artwork for *The Boy of the Three-Year Nap* on his fiftieth birthday, and the union of art and text won the 1988 Boston Globe-Horn Book Award for picture book. In addition, the book—an adaptation of a Japanese folk tale that describes how lazy Taro's clever mother outsmarts her son—became a 1989 Caldecott Honor Book for illustration, and appeared on the 1988 ALA list of Notable Children's Books. While the illustrations in some of his earlier books were somewhat restrained, the artwork in this book—while clearly influenced by Japanese painting—has what one reviewer called a "felicitous robustness," with its stronger colors and use of angles.

Later in 1988 *A River Dream*, written and illustrated by Say, was also published. In this contemporary fantasy, complete with a clear moral message, the author-artist focuses on fly fishing, one of his own favorite pastimes. Through a dream sequence young Mark comes to learn that the killing of fish does not have to be a part of fishing for sport. While Say's written text is perfectly competent, it is his rich, full-page paintings that distinguish this work and which, in fact, placed the book on the *New York Times* list of the ten Best Illustrated Children's Books of 1988. So although Say had declared that *The Boy of the Three-Year Nap* was going to be his "last fling" with children's books, he once again had become a very firm part of the children's literature world and continues to create books in his California home, where he lives with his wife and daughter.

In his Boston Globe-Horn Book acceptance speech, the author-artist comments, "I look at my work as a personal tree-ring, a growth record. It is wonderful to be my age and realize that I am growing as an artist."

SELECTED WORKS ILLUSTRATED: A Canticle to the Waterbirds, by Brother Antoninus, 1968; Two Ways of Seeing, edited by Nilson Pinney, 1971; Magic and the Night, River by Eve Bunting, 1978; The Lucky Yak, by Annetta Lawson, 1980; How My Parents Learned to Eat, by Ian Friedman, 1984; The Boy of the Three-Year Nap, by Dianne Snyder, 1988.

SELECTED WORKS WRITTEN AND ILLUSTRATED: Dr. Smith's Safari, 1973; Once Under the Cherry Blossom Tree, 1974; The Feast of Lanterns, 1976; The Ink-Keeper's Apprentice, 1979; The Bicycle Man, 1982; A River Dream, 1988.

ABOUT: Contemporary Authors, Vol. 29; Horn Book March/April 1989; Something About the Author, Vol. 28.

AMY SCHWARTZ

April 2, 1954–

AUTHOR AND ILLUSTRATOR OF *Oma and Bobo*, etc.

Autobiographical sketch of Amy Schwartz:

SEVERAL YEARS AGO I got together

with a childhood friend and we exchanged reminiscences. She told me that in the fourth grade I had said that I wanted to write and illustrate children's books when I grew up. It certainly has not felt like a straight line from then to now, but my interest in children's books has always been with me.

As a child I was a prolific reader. Though I continue my reading as an adult, and with great enjoyment, I don't think I will ever be able to duplicate the total immersion in books that I felt when I was young. I remember a period of reading *Little Women*, over and over and over again. I would finish the book, and immediately begin again with Jo grumbling on page one, "Christmas won't be Christmas without any presents." After school I memorized poems on my own, and studiously read books by authors whose last initials were near the end of the alphabet, as I believed their books to be the most advanced.

Recently while at the branch library near the house I grew up in, I browsed through the picture book section and found books I hadn't looked at in over twenty-five years. As I looked at *The Painted Pig* by Elizabeth Morrow, and *Pantaloni* by Bettina, I felt jolted by reawakened emotions. The unique world presented in each of them had been quite real to me as a child. I had interpreted the style of the art in each book as belonging not to the illustrator, but to the world of the story itself.

Both reading and drawing were encouraged in my home. My grandmother and I went on bus expeditions downtown, which included story hour at the Main Children's Room of the San Diego Public Library. My mother also took me to the library, and enrolled me in art classes at the Fine Arts Museum. And sometimes she took out her pastels and we drew together. Today when I visit my parents we still sometimes hold a story evening, where each family member chooses a short story to read aloud to the others.

I also liked to write when I was young, but this evaporated when I reached adolescence. As term papers became the order of the day, I lost all confidence.

After graduating from high school, I attended Antioch College in Yellow Springs, Ohio, before transferring to the California College of Arts and Crafts in Oakland, California, from which I received my B.F.A. in 1976.

At that time I had no idea of what I would do for a living. I held a series of odd jobs, but I continued to keep up my drawing. I was mainly doing portraits of friends and other personal drawings. Gradually I began doing some free-lance illustration. Guide books, sports books, and greeting cards were among the illustration jobs I took on.

While still living in the Bay Area, I took an evening class in writing and illustrating children's books. The subject interested me as nothing else had, and I decided that this was the field I wanted to pursue. I very bravely sent samples of my artwork to children's book editors in New York, and then went to New York myself, with my portfolio.

My plan was to illustrate picture books; I had no intention of doing any writing. But while making the rounds of publishers, a number of editors told me that it might be easiest for me to break into the field if I also wrote. I enrolled in another children's book writing course, in New York, and wrote my first two books, *Bea and Mr. Jones* and *Begin at the Beginning*.

I now write and illustrate children's books full-time. I write about half of the books that I illustrate. My books usually start with a combination of memories from childhood, and thoughts and experiences from my life at the present.

I draw heavily upon my family when I write. My book *Oma and Bobo* (Bradbury), is about the relationship between my grandmother and our family dog. My grandmother shows up one way or another in several of my books. Oma lived with my family and I felt very close to her. The book took quite a while for me to write, but I stayed with it because my main character was so dear to me.

Recently I illustrated a picture book written by my father, Henry Schwartz, called *How I Captured a Dinosaur* (Orchard). For me, this was a special collaboration, and when I first read the story, I was amused to recognize in Albert, my father's dinosaur hero, none other than Bobo—again—our intrepid family dog.

Amy Schwartz was born in San Diego, California. She taught art at the elementary level, worked in publishing, and did editorial illustration before publishing her first picture book in 1982. *Mrs. Moskowitz* received a 1985 Association of Jewish Libraries Sydney Taylor Book Award for best picture book. It also won the 1985 Jewish Welfare Board Jewish Book Council Jewish Book Award for an illustrated children's book. Several of Amy Schwartz's books have been named Notable Books by the American Library Association: *The Purple Coat* in 1986, *Oma and Bobo* in 1987, and *Annabelle Swift, Kindergartner*, in 1988. *The Witch Who Lived Down the Hall* was a Junior Literary Guild selection. *Crack of*

Dawn Walkers and . . . *Aunt Essie* were named Children's Choice Books by a joint committee of the International Reading Association and the Children's Book Council, both in 1985. *The Purple Coat* won a 1987 Christopher Award.

SELECTED WORKS WRITTEN AND ILLUSTRATED: Bea and Mrs. Jones, 1982; Begin at the Beginning, 1983; Mrs. Moskowitz and the Sabbath Candlesticks, 1984; Her Majesty, Aunt Essie, 1984; Yossel Zissel and the Wisdom of Chelm, 1986; Oma and Bobo, 1987; Annabelle Swift, Kindergartner, 1988.

SELECTED WORKS ILLUSTRATED: The Crack of Dawn Walkers, by Amy Hest, 1984; Jane Martin, Dog Detective, by Eve Bunting, 1984; The Night Flight, by Joanne Ryder, 1985; The Witch Who Lives Down the Hall, by Donna Guthrie, 1985; The Purple Coat, by Amy Hest, 1986; How I Captured a Dinosaur, by Henry Schwartz, 1989.

ABOUT: Contemporary Authors, Vol. 110; Something About the Author, Vol. 41; Vol. 47.

DAVID M. SCHWARTZ

November 29, 1951

AUTHOR OF *How Much Is a Million?*, etc.

Autobiographical sketch of David M. Schwartz:

I GREW UP in the 1960s on Long Island, which, I realized one day, is the only place in the United States where people must travel west to get to New York City. I did plenty of traveling in that direction because "The City," as we called it, had a lot more to hold my interest than "The Island." I wanted either the plays, concerts, museums, and excitement of the city or the mountains, woods, fields, and tranquility of the country, but I wasn't nearly as enthusiastic about life in the suburbs. I guess I had a bad case of "the grass is always greener on the other side of the fence."

But some activities transported me mentally to different worlds, no matter where I was physically. My mind took me far away when I was looking down a microscope at blood cells (rudely extracted from my own finger) or through a telescope at the moon or planets or stars. The tiny things and the enormous things of this universe were what fascinated me most. Compared to them, I discovered with astonishment, I was both a giant and a midget at the same time.

In junior high school, I was thrilled that nighttime star-gazing was part of my Earth Science course. Those evenings really set my mind to work, and afterwards I delighted in asking questions that no one could answer, questions that were springboards for thought rather than problems to be solved with facts alone. "What's at the end of the universe?" I wondered out loud, as the teacher threw me a dirty look for not raising my hand. If there was a wall there . . . sure, I knew it was impossible, but just suppose . . . if there *was* a wall there, what would be on the other side of the wall? Now the teacher was really mad, because I was being silly, but I really wanted to know. Or at least I wanted to think about it.

And I wondered about the hugh number of stars in the sky, and how far they were from Earth. Imagining such distances filled my mind with marvelous fantasies, yet these were real numbers, not science fiction. Could you count all the stars, I mused, and if you could, how long would it take? How long would it take to visit them all, if you could do *that*? I also wanted to understand the size of the heavenly bodies—not just to *know* that the Earth is some 8,000 miles in diameter, and Jupiter is 88,000 miles and the Sun 865,000 miles—but to have a *feel* for how much those distances really are. This was a particularly troubling concept for me because I thought of the Earth as incomprehensibly large. Why, I had once ridden my bicycle twenty-five miles and that seemed *so* far, yet twenty-five miles was hardly *anything* on the globe.

I never did any serious writing in those days, nor did I think I ever would, for I was going to be a scientist, not a writer. Well, it didn't turn out that way, and after trying several careers I ended as a journalist. One clear spring night I glanced up at the stars. There they were, just as beautiful and numerous and incomprehensible as they had been during my childhood. I suddenly regained the sense of awe I had felt when I was younger, contemplating their magnitude, and I thought I would write a book to instill that kind of awe in children. When I started writing I found I had to use lots of big numbers—millions, billions, trillions—numbers that most people (adults as well as kids) don't really understand. I decided to do something about that. So evolved my first book for children, *How Much Is a Million?*.

After the book came out, I found that many of its readers seemed most interested in knowing about millions of dollars, rather than millions of miles or millions of stars. All right, I figured, I'd write a book about money, but one that would show readers more than just how much a million dollars is. *If You Made a Million* covers many concepts about money, but most importantly, it raises the point that making money means making choices—the children in the book discover, for example, that if they actually *did* make a lot of money they could use it to take a fabulous trip . . . or to buy land to preserve an endangered animal.

It's not only the vastness of things that can fill a young (or older) mind with awe. It would take me more than a lifetime to write about even a fraction of the many unbelievable (yet true!) ways of plants and animals. I've just begun to cover a few of them in the *Hidden Life* books. The close-up photographs by Dwight Kuhn illustrate the exquisitely beautiful and complex world of common creatures that are so small or so shy that we usually pass them by without notice. And, of course, awe is to be found not just in natural history, but in human history and human culture as well. Wherever there's something worth thinking about—and where isn't there?—there's a subject for a book I'd like to write to help children see our world with the sense of wonder it deserves.

I guess I'll just need several lifetimes to cover them all.

————

David M. Schwartz graduated from Cornell University in 1973 with a degree in Biology. He also completed a graduate elementary teacher education program at The Prospect School in North Bennington, Vermont, resulting in teacher certification in 1974. He writes articles as well as books, and has contributed to *Smithsonian, Audubon, National Wildlife,* and *International Wildlife.* He has also cowritten a series of travel/restaurant guidebooks called *The Interstate Gourmet.* Schwartz is a writing tutor at Yale University and lives in North Haven, Connecticut.

How Much Is a Million? was named a Notable Book of 1985 by the American Library Association and was designated a Children's Choice book of 1985 by a joint committee of the International Reading Association and the Children's Book Council. The book also won a Boston Globe–Horn Book Honor Book Award for illustration in 1985, and the illustrator is Steven Kellogg.

SELECTED WORKS: How Much Is a Million?, 1985; The Hidden Life of the Forest, 1988; The Hidden Life of the Meadow, 1988; The Hidden Life of the Pond, 1988; If You Made a Million, 1989.

ABOUT: Contemporary Authors, Vol. 118.

JACK DENTON SCOTT

1915–

AUTHOR OF *The Book of the Pig*, etc.

Biographical sketch of Jack Denton Scott:

JACK DENTON SCOTT grew up in Elmira, New York. When he was sixteen, he had his first short story published. When he was nineteen, he had his first article published in a magazine, and he has been a writer ever since, including over two thousand articles and a dozen books. During World War II, he was a war correspondent, traveling with soldiers and pilots in Europe, Egypt, and Africa. Once, the plane he was riding in was shot down over England, and he landed safely in the ocean.

Scott reads a great deal and admires Graham Greene particularly, for his clarity, his insight, and his careful research. The kinds of books Scott writes vary widely; he writes novels, natural history, travel books, cookbooks (he is a member of the Cordon Bleu de France), children's books, and essays. He and his wife, Maria Luisa Scott, have collaborated on cookbooks. He and his "teammate," photographer Ozzie Sweet, have traveled together to many countries to produce their nature books for children. Scott's intent is both to entertain and to inform.

Scott and his wife have traveled around the world about fifteen times; from 1959 to 1964 alone, they traveled over 600,000 miles. He draws from his travels for his art; for example, *Elephant Grass*, a novel he wrote, has as its setting a wild region at the foothills of the Himalaya mountains. He wrote a travel book for adults called *Passport to Adventure*. He has warned of

JACK DENTON SCOTT

the impending extinction of some of the wild animals he observes and writes about. Typical words of praise for his work can be exemplified by a *Bulletin of the Center for Children's Books* review of *Moose* that stated, "The writing is serious but not dry, dignified but not formal, and imbued with naturalist Scott's own enthusiastic interest in the subject." President John F. Kennedy once commented on one of his books for adults, *The Duluth Mongoose*, describing the rescue of a captive Indian mongoose from death: a "classic example of government by the people."

Scott wrote a syndicated adventure column for *The New York Herald Tribune*. He is a contributor to *Smithsonian* magazine. He and his wife live in Corning, New York.

Discovering the Mysterious Egret was a 1978 ALA Notable Book. Two of his books were selected for the *School Library Journal* "Best of the Best 1966-1978" list: *City of Birds and Beasts* and *Loggerhead Turtle*. *Discovering the American Stork* was named a Notable Book of 1976 by the American Library Association and was chosen for the 1976 American Institute of Graphic Arts Book Show. *Little Dogs of the*

Prairie was a 1977 ALA Notable Book, as were both *The Book of the Pig* and *Moose* in 1981. Among his books that were named Junior Literary Guild selections are *Canada Geese, The Gulls of Smuttynose Island, Island of Wild Horses, The Book of the Goat,* and *Swans.* Many of his books have been named Oustanding Science Trade Books for Children by a joint committee of the Children's Book Council and the National Science Teachers Association. These include *Loggerhead Turtle* in 1974, *Return of the Buffalo* in 1976, *Little Dogs . . .* in 1977, *Island of Wild Horses* in 1978, *The Book of the Pig* and *Moose* in 1981, *Orphans from the Sea* in 1982, *The Fur Seals of Pribilof* in 1983, and *Alligator* in 1984.

SELECTED WORKS: Loggerhead Turtle: Survivor from the Sea, 1974; Canada Geese, 1976; Discovering the American Stork, 1976; Return of the Buffalo, 1976; The Gulls of Smuttynose Island, 1977; Little Dogs of the Prairie, 1977; City of Birds and Beasts: Behind the Scenes at the Bronx Zoo, 1978; Discovering the Mysterious Egret, 1978; Island of Wild Horses, 1978; The Book of the Goat, 1979; The Submarine Bird, 1980; The Book of the Pig, 1981; Moose, 1981; Orphans from the Sea, 1982; The Fur Seals of Pribilof, 1983; Alligator, 1984; Swans, 1987;

ABOUT: Contemporary Authors, Vol. 108; Library Journal February 1, 1969; Something About the Author, Vol. 31.

TOR SEIDLER

June 26, 1952–

AUTHOR OF *Terpin,* etc.

Autobiographical sketch of Tor Seidler:

I LIVED IN Burlington, Vermont, till I was eleven, then Seattle, Washington. My parents were divorced (and remarried) when I was very young, so growing up involved adapting to two very different sets of family as well as to two coasts. My mother and stepfather, who brought me up, were seriously involved in the theater. In Vermont,

my stepfather founded a Shakespeare festival; in Seattle, a theater devoted to contemporary plays. Some of my favorite early memories are of watching rehearsals of *Henry IV, Part One* and *Richard III.*

Another early memory is of a family vacation at a dude ranch in Colorado when I was six. One afternoon, a guide took a group of the guests' children on a hike, and somewhere along the trail I stopped, looked up at the way the sunlight was leaking down through the giant evergreens, and thought with great solemnity, "I'll always remember this moment, as long as I live." Another recollection, from a few years later—toward the end of my fourth- or fifth-grade year—is of pulling a thin blue book out of a bookshelf one day after school and taking it up the pine-needly path to the big rock at the top of the woods we lived in. I don't think I understood the book at all (*The Bridge of San Luis Rey* by Thornton Wilder); I certainly don't remember much about it. But I do remember how it electrified me. The words seemed more real than the rock, more mysterious than the lake (Lake Champlain) shimmering away through the pines.

From that early age on I really never

doubted that I wanted to be a writer, but for some reason I never wrote anything. In school I concentrated on math and sciences and competing in sports. Even at Stanford I took only one creative writing class. Still, I moved to New York City not long after graduation, assuming that within a year or so I'd produce a wonderful, poetic novel, a sort of Portrait of the Artist as a Young American. That was quite a while ago, and needless to say it hasn't happened. But I've kept trying.

Tor Seidler was born in Littleton, New Hampshire. He received his B.A. degree from Stanford University in 1972. He was a free-lance contributor to Harcourt Brace Janovich's Language Arts program from 1976 to 1978 and has been a full-time writer since 1978. *The Dulcimer Boy* won a Washington State Governor's Award in 1980 for fiction.

SELECTED WORKS: The Dulcimer Boy, 1979; Terpin, 1982; A Rat's Tale, 1986; The Tar Pit, 1987.

ABOUT: Something About the Author, Vol. 46; Vol. 52.

GEORGE SHANNON

February 14, 1952–

AUTHOR OF *The Piney Woods Peddler*, etc.

Autobiographical sketch of George William Bones Shannon:

WHEN SOMEONE asks when I started writing stories I give them five true answers. Each or all are true depending on one's point of view. The first time I wrote a story and had it published as a book was in 1981 when I was twenty-nine. The first time I submitted a story to an editor in hopes it would be published was when I was sixteen. The first time I remember writing stories for pleasure rather than homework was in the seventh grade. The first time I remember writing stories on paper was in elementary school. But even before that I was making up stories when I played like most children do. I just never stopped and hope I never do.

My early years of making stories were lived in Kansas villages—Caldwell and Kingman—surrounded by wheat, heat, and books. My mother read to me (we had no TV for a long time), and my father, who loves history, told me family tales. I often got books as presents and we were familiar faces at the public library. I had my own Golden Books but could also look at my parent's books. Two of theirs I looked at a lot were *Modern Prints and Drawings* by Paul Sachs and *The New Yorker 25th Anniversary Album, 1925–1950*.

Teachers in the seventh, tenth, and twelfth grades encouraged my writing. Their support made me write more and more on my own, and as with most things, the more I practiced the better I got. In college I studied children's literature and then worked for five years as a children's librarian. Reading and sharing the best of children's literature helped me learn more about stories, what ones I thought were best, and why. Reading still helps my writing

grow. I read stories sometimes, but my favorite books are essays on literature and art.

In 1978 I stopped working as a librarian
and devoted myself full time to telling stories and writing books. I was lucky. Despite
a pile of rejection slips (that continues to
grow), Greenwillow accepted my first book
twelve months later. When my first copy of
my first book arrived (*The Gang and Mrs.
Higgins*), I was too excited to fall asleep that
night. I kept shining the flashlight across
the room to look at the book's cover just one
more time.

Ten years and sixteen books later it is still
exciting to see a new book for the first time.
But even more exciting are the days when
a new idea takes root and I can feel it begin
to grow into a story. On those days everything feels new and full of possibility.

———

George Shannon received his B.A. degree
from Western Kentucky University in
1974. He received his M.S.L.S. degree in
1976. He was a children's librarian in Kentucky towns from 1973 to 1978. He is the
author of *Folk Literature and Children: An
Annotated Bibliography of Secondary
Materials*, published in 1981, and he has
written a 1989 book about the children's
book author and illustrator Arnold Lobel.
He is a contributor to *The Horn Book
Magazine*, *Children's Literature in
Education*, and *Catholic Library World*.

The Piney Woods Peddler was named a
Notable Book of 1981 by the American Li-
brary Association and a 1982 Children's
Choice Book by a joint committee of the In-
ternational Reading Association and the
Children's Book Council.

SELECTED WORKS: The Gang and Mrs. Higgins,
1981; The Piney Woods Peddler, 1981; Lizard's Song,
1981; Dance Away, 1982; The Surprise, 1983; Bean
Boy, 1984; O I Love, 1985; Stories to Solve: Folktales
from Around the World, 1985; Sea Gifts, 1989; Un-
lived Affections, 1989.

ABOUT: Contemporary Authors, Vol. 106; Something About the Author, Vol. 35.

MITCHELL SHARMAT

April 18, 1927–

AUTHOR OF *Gregory, the Terrible Eater*,
etc.

Autobiographical sketch of Mitchell Sharmat:

IF I HADN'T caught a cold, I probably
wouldn't have become a children's author,
or any other kind of author for that matter.

I was born in Brookline, Massachusetts, to
Lucille and Leon Sharmat. My father had
majored in English at college and wanted
me to become a writer. My mother had also
majored in English, but she was concerned
with my getting through the second grade.
My own early ambition was to become a
freight elevator operator at my grandfather's furniture showroom.

When I entered the second grade, my father insisted that I write a composition a
day. As an incentive he said he'd pay me a
nickel for each one. Every composition had
to be at least one hundred words and had
to be finished by the time he got home for
supper, so we could discuss it before I went
to bed.

When I asked him what I could write
about every day, he replied, "Anything you
want. Your life experiences." So I wrote
about going to school, the policeman at the
corner, the gang I belonged to that terror-
ized the lunch recess, the dog who walked
to school with me every day.

About the third week, new ideas became
pretty hard to come by, and I got discouraged. I just didn't seem to have enough life
experiences. My father got mad, and I quit
writing for him. It was forty-three years before I tried again. Maybe it took me that
long to have enough life experiences and to
recognize them.

In the intervening forty-three years I
managed to graduate from the second
grade and then, eventually, college. I
worked on a farm, did a stint in the Navy,
worked for four major retail chains, and
formed my own real estate business.

In February of 1956 I was between jobs, having just been fired from one and about to start another. Since I hadn't had a real vacation in some time and wouldn't qualify for one for another year, I decided to take a trip before starting my new job. In those days I had a passion for skiing, and so I planned to go to Stowe, Vermont. Then three days before I was scheduled to leave, I caught a stubborn cold.

That cold changed my whole life. Instead of Vermont, I went to Florida, where I met a young lady, Marjorie Weinman, who very much wanted to be an author. She'd already published a couple of articles and had just finished writing a book. I didn't take her writing too seriously at the time, so I didn't hold it against her. A year later we were married and in time had two children.

We enrolled the children in the Corner Nursery School. The school gave us a suggested reading list, and I went out and purchased a half dozen books from the list. The kids loved them, and Marjorie was so enthralled that she began writing children's books herself. A few years later her first children's book was published. As they say, the rest is history.

Through the years Marjorie has consulted with me when she had problems with her own writing. As a result I've picked up by osmosis a pretty good idea of how to write for children. Couple that knowledge with some of the frustrations of my childhood plus a personal quirky way of looking at the world, and the result has been an extensive part-time career that I can't sneeze at.

Our children are now grown and starting part-time literary careers of their own. Craig, who is a musician, co-wrote with Marjorie *Nate the Great and the Musical Note*, to be published by Putnam. Andrew, who is a real-estate appraiser, has written *Smedge*, published in fall 1989 by Macmillan.

Very rarely in history has one miserable cold meant so many good books for so many children.

———

Mitchell Sharmat received his A.B. degree from Harvard in 1949. He married Marjorie Weinman February 24, 1957. He served in the Navy from 1945 to 1946. His books for children include picture books, easy readers, and a novel, and he is also a contributor to basal reading programs. With his wife, Marjorie Weinman Sharmat, he has written books in a series about Olivia Sharp, "Agent for Secrets."

Three of Sharmat's books were named Children's Choice Books by a joint committee of the Children's Book Council and the International Reading Association: *I Am Not a Pest* in 1980, *The Day I Was Born* in 1981, and *Gregory, the Terrible Eater* in 1981. The latter was also a Reading Rainbow book.

SELECTED WORKS WRITTEN: Reddy Rattler and Easy Eagle, 1979; Come Home, Wilma, 1980; Gregory, the Terrible Eater, 1980; Spring Talk, 1981; Gorilla's House, 1982; The Seven Sloppy Days of Phineas Pig, 1983; Sherman Is a Slowpoke, 1988; A Girl of Many Parts, 1988.

SELECTED WORKS WRITTEN WITH MARJORIE WEINMAN SHARMAT: I Am Not a Pest, 1979; The Day I Was Born, 1980; The Pizza Monster, 1989; The Princess of the Fillmore Street School, 1989.

ABOUT: Contemporary Authors, Vol. 104; Something About the Author, Vol. 33.

SUSAN SHREVE

May 2, 1939-

AUTHOR OF *Family Secrets*, etc.

Biographical sketch of Susan Richards Shreve:

BORN IN TOLEDO, Ohio, Susan Shreve says she "grew up in a house full of stories." Her father was a crime reporter and broadcaster, and she remembers anticipating his return home from work so that she could hear the latest stories he had to tell. When Shreve was three, the family moved from Ohio to Washington, D.C., and she was struck by a succession of serious illnesses that made her the center of drama, as she puts it. She listened to soap operas on the radio and made up extravagant stories. At age nine, she began a theater in her living room, writing, directing, and starring in plays that earned enough money for sweets for the Lollipop Patch, a neighborhood hideout she shared with the other actors.

At the age of eighteen, Shreve wrote an autobiographical novel she calls "boring." She received the advice of a New York editor to go out and learn about the world, and then to write books. Instead, she wrote another book that did not sell, and went to college. She received her B.A. degree, magna cum laude, from the University of Pennsylvania in 1961. She was married May 26, 1962. Shreve taught English in private schools in Cheshire, England, from 1962 to 1963, and from 1963 to 1972 taught school in Rosemont, Pennsylvania, Washington, D.C., and Philadelphia. During this time, she and her husband had four children, and she went back to school, receiving an M.A. degree from the University of Virginia in 1969. She and her husband founded a school together, the Community Learning Center, an alternative school in Philadel-phia, which opened in 1972. The two then moved to Houston, Texas, while he trained to become a family therapist. It wasn't until Shreve was thirty that she began to write again, first for adults and then for children.

Shreve says she likes to write stories about families, and often writes about a rebellious character, because that's the kind of child she was. She writes about two hours a day, then works in her position as Associate Professor of Literature at George Mason University in Fairfax, Virginia, where she has been since 1976. She is a member of P.E.N. and Phi Beta Kappa.

The titles Shreve wrote for adults include *Children of Power*, published in 1979, and *Miracle Play*, published in 1981.

Family Secrets was named a 1979 Notable Book by the American Library Association, and was also named a 1979 Notable Children's Trade Book in the Field of Social Studies, chosen by a joint committee of the Children's Book Council and the National Council on the Social Studies. *The Masquerade* was named an ALA Best Book for Young Adults for 1980. *Lucy Forever and Miss Rosetree, Shrinks* won a 1988 Edgar Allan Poe Award given by The Mystery Writers of America.

SELECTED WORKS: The Nightmares of Geranium Street, 1977; Loveletters, 1978; Family Secrets: Five Very Important Stories, 1979; The Masquerade, 1980; The Bad Dreams of a Good Girl, 1982; The Revolution of Mary Leary, 1982; The Flunking of Joshua T. Bates, 1984; How I Saved the World on Purpose, 1985; Lucy Forever and Miss Rosetree, Shrinks, 1987.

ABOUT: Contemporary Authors, Vol. 49-52; (New Revision Series), Vol. 5; Contemporary Literary Criticism, Vol. 23; Directory of American Poets and Fiction Writers; Something About the Author, Vol. 41; Vol. 46; The Writers Directory 1984-86.

MARILYN SINGER

October 3, 1948–

AUTHOR OF *It Can't Hurt Forever*, etc.

Autobiographical sketch of Marilyn Singer:

A LOT OF PEOPLE have asked me why I write books for children and young adults, and I've given them a lot of answers. Here are some of them:

1. Kids are interesting to write about and for.

2. If you understand the child in yourself, you can understand the grown-up better. I want to understand myself better.

3. There's nothing else I know how to do.

All of these answers are pretty much true. But now I think the truest, most honest answer I can give is that I write books for children and young adults because I like to.

That doesn't mean I like to all the time. Sometimes I get very tired of writing. Sometimes I even get fed up. But there really isn't any other job I want to do more in the world than write books.

One of the people who made me most want to write was my Rumanian grandmother with whom I shared a bedroom, first in the Bronx, then on Long Island, until I was twelve. My grandmother couldn't read or write, but she told me wonderful stories—fairy tales, folk tales, fables, and bits of autobiography—some of which I can remember to this day. I especially remember *how* she told me them—they poured out of her like music; they *sang*. Now whenever I sit down to write anything, one of the things I ask myself is, does it sing?

Another person who has influenced my writing is my husband, Steven Aronson, whom I married in 1971. When we met, I was teaching high school English in New York City. I had a rough time teaching. I didn't get along with the administration. Steven encouraged me to quit, and I did in 1973. I didn't know what to do for a living then. I vaguely thought that I'd write for some magazines. Steve got me some work writing teacher's guides, program notes, and catalogues on film. That kind of writing sharpened my technical and research skills. At the same time, I started fooling around with small stories about the Porkers and Beans and other nutty characters. I read the stories to Steve, and he proceeded to laugh himself silly. I decided that was a good sign.

Among the other people who've helped me become a writer are many friends, relatives, editors, and other writers. I read a lot, and my favorite writer, the one I read over and over, is William Shakespeare. In many of my books, I've put quotes from his plays and poems. *Ghost Host* has some bits from

Macbeth. Storm Rising contains lines from the sonnets. And my whole novel *The Course of True Love Never Did Run Smooth* is about a high school production-ing of Shakespeare's *A Midsummer Night's Dream.* I guess you could say I'm one of the man's big fans.

As to what I put in my books, I draw on my childhood experiences (among these, the heart surgery I had at eight, which is the basis for *It Can't Hurt Forever*), my travels around the U.S. and Europe, my dreams, interests, and studies. I've been particularly influenced by having been a young adult in the 1960s and by a more recent involvement with Taoist meditation, yoga, and other Asian philosophies and practices. I'm an avid reader of mysteries, a longtime bird watcher and animal nut, a *Star-Trek*-er and a movie maniac—and all of these (pre-) occupations are reflected in my work.

So, I hope this tells you something about why and what I write. I think I've been pretty lucky so far to have a career I like. I plan to go on being lucky.

———

Marilyn Singer attended the University of Reading from 1967 to 1968 and received her B.A. degree from Queens College in 1969. She also received an M.A. degree in Media Ecology in 1979 from New York University, where, among other courses, she studied screenwriting with Terry Southern. She married Steven Aronson on July 31, 1971. She has written teachers' guides, catalogues, and program notes on film and filmstrips, among them the guides for Jacob Bronowski's *The Ascent of Man* and David Attenborough's *The Tribal Eye.* She is editor of *A History of American Avant-Garde Cinema.* She has also written scripts for *The Electric Company* and curated a series of avant-garde films for children, *Superfilmshow!.* Her poetry has appeared in magazines such as *Yes, Encore,* and *Corduroy.*

The Dog Who Insisted He Wasn't was named a Children's Choice Book by a joint committee of the International Reading Association and the Children's Book Council in 1977. *It Can't Hurt Forever* was named a 1979 Children's Choice Book and won the 1983 Maud Hart Lovelace Award from the Friends of the Minnesota Valley Regional Library. *The Course of True Love . . .* was named a 1983 American Library Association Best Book for Young Adults. *Archer Armadillo's Secret Room* and *Lizzie Silver of Sherwood Forest* were Junior Literary Guild selections. *Ghost Host* was a 1988 Children's Choice Book.

SELECTED WORKS: The Dog Who Insisted He Wasn't, 1976; It Can't Hurt Forever, 1978; The First Few Friends, 1981; Tarantulas on the Brain, 1982; The Course of True Love Never Did Run Smooth, 1983; The Fido Frame-Up, 1983; Leroy Is Missing, 1984; Archer Armadillo's Secret Room, 1985; A Clue in Code, 1985; Lizzie Silver of Sherwood Forest, 1986; Ghost Host, 1987; The Lightey Club, 1987; The Hoax on You, 1989; Storm Rising, 1989; Turtle in July, 1989.

ABOUT: Contemporary Authors, Vol. 65; (New Revision Series), Vol. 9; Roginski, Jim. Behind the Covers: Interviews with Authors and Illustrators of Books for Children and Young Adults; Something About the Author, Vol. 38; Vol. 48.

PETER SIS

May 11, 1949–

AUTHOR AND ILLUSTRATOR OF *Rainbow Rhino,* etc.

Autobiographical sketch of Peter Sis:

I WAS BORN in the middle of the century, and grew up in the magical city of Prague, Czechoslovakia, in the heart of Europe. Prague, "the city of a hundred towers," mysterious castles, palaces, churches, synagogues, narrow streets, cobblestones, and the medieval Charles bridge. Prague, the home of stories, myths, and legends, the Golem and Franz Kafka.

My father was a filmmaker and explorer and brought back many interesting things from his travels in Tibet, Borneo, and all

over the world. He would tell us wonderful stories and legends about the Dalai Lama, dajaks, and Satchmo.

From early on, I was encouraged to make pictures by my mother and father, both artists, and by their artist friends. I was not always encouraged at school, where I used to draw little pictures on everything, for everybody, usually in the middle of class.

I remember with great fondness what I thought of as the largest bookstore imaginable. It was our library at home. My mother's father designed railway stations in Cleveland and Chicago in the 1930s, and my mother lived in the United States as a little girl. Besides many other books of the time, my grandfather brought back with him all the Sunday cartoons from the Chicago newspapers, bound in one large volume. I guess the book was about as large as I was. I remember stretching myself over a page, and panel by panel devouring Little Orphan Annie, Mutt and Jeff, Krazy Kat, and the one with the little cable car. In a way, I wish I hadn't loved the book so much. If I hadn't worn it out it might still be in existence.

I remember sometimes becoming so involved with a picture that I didn't notice that the night was just about over. Then I would place the picture next to my bed so that I could see it first thing when I awoke.

Today, as an adult and professional, I try to anticipate when I might have to work all night and avoid it if it is possible. But I still often get up at night to look at the picture I have just finished.

I went from art school to art school, and had some wonderful teachers, especially J. Trnka, who was a famous illustrator and animator.

I was lucky to have Quentin Blake as a tutor at London's Royal College of Art. I had already become involved with animated films. After my film *Heads* won a prize in Berlin in 1980, I did a series of illustrations for TV in Zurich, Switzerland, and then another film in London, and before I knew it, I found myself working on a film in Los Angeles. But what I really wanted was to illustrate my own stories and turn them into animated films.

On the advice of a wonderful friend, Josine Ianco, I wrote to Maurice Sendak, hardly expecting him to write back. He didn't. He telephoned, first from the East Coast and then from Los Angeles where he had come to be honored by the American Library Association. By then I had a hazy idea that I should go East to meet with children's book publishers. To my surprise, Mr. Sendak, after seeing my portfolio, right then and there in the last hours of the ALA Conference introduced me to Ava Weiss. I showed her my work and she in turn introduced me to Susan Hirschman and Greenwillow. Shortly afterwards, I started to work on my first book, *Bean Boy*, by George Shannon. I moved to New York and here I am, writing about it, five years and sixteen books later.

———

Peter Sis was born in Brno, Moravia. While in art school, he worked as a disc jockey. He contributes illustrations to *The New York Times*. Sis is a member of the American Institute of Graphic Arts, the Graphic Artists Guild, and the ASIFA.

The Whipping Boy, which Sis illustrated, won the 1987 Newbery Medal from the American Library Association. *Rainbow Rhino* was named a *New York Times* Best Illustrated Book of 1987.

SELECTED WORKS WRITTEN AND ILLUSTRATED: Rainbow Rhino, 1987; Waving, 1988; Going Up!: A Color Counting Book, 1989.

SELECTED WORKS ILLUSTRATED: Bean Boy, by George Shannon, 1984; Stories to Solve: Folktales from Around the World, by George Shannon, 1985; Three Yellow Dogs, by Caron Lee Cohen, 1986; The Whipping Boy, by Sid Fleischman, 1986; City Night, by Eve Rice, 1987; Alphabet Soup, by Kate Banks, 1988; The Scarebird, by Sid Fleischman, 1988.

DAVID SMALL

February 12, 1945–

AUTHOR AND ILLUSTRATOR OF *Imogene's Antlers*, etc.

Autobiographical sketch of David Small:

I WAS BORN and raised in Detroit. My father was a doctor—a radiologist in a big hospital there. Many of my early memories are set in the X-ray department of that hospital, in those twilit rooms full of huge machines and glowing screens that revealed the insides of people. I can't help but think that these early encounters with people-as-skeletons encouraged my later interest in anatomy, as well as a rather dark creative vision.

As a child I spent most of my time playing alone. We had no TV until I was eight or nine, so I read a lot and drew pictures endlessly. Also, I had been ill a lot, and the bedridden life encourages use of the imagination. I was not so much shy as I was wary of others; I preferred my own company.

My mother tried to encourage my artistic talent by taking me to Saturday morning art classes. How I loathed those lessons! They never taught anything I was interested in, such as cartooning or drawing animals. Week after week we were set to the

task of making ashtrays out of gritty clay, or to painting with evil-smelling poster paints on pieces of cheap paper. My lack of enthusiasm for these projects must have been apparent; the teacher never recognized my ability, and my mother could not understand her failure.

One good thing about those Saturday classes: they were given at the Detroit Art Institute. From a child's perspective, it was a palace filled with works of art, suits of armor, and fantastic decorations from different historical periods. The hours I spent in that wonderful museum bolstered the view I have so far held: that the work of an artist is noble and worthy, and that art—by changing the way we see—can direct our lives.

I struggled through many schools, gaining mediocre grades but being pushed along by several teachers who recognized the intelligence and creative spirit in me. Except in English classes, I never felt comfortable in school. With rare exceptions, the art curriculum was given with such ineptitude and indifference, I had no use for it. Then, in college, I found a real home in the Art Department at Wayne State University. They had a great faculty there, in drawing, painting, and printmaking. I felt I had been suddenly washed ashore in a country where people spoke my own language. I felt alive. I grew stronger. I knew that in this world of art I could find a place. The work never tired me. In fact, I couldn't find enough hours in the day to learn what I needed to know in order to make the kind of pictures I wanted to create.

Of all the things I do now as an artist, the creation of children's picture books is the most pleasurable. There is a sense of godlike satisfaction in being the whole show, both author and artist! There is also a lot of happiness to be found in collaboration with other authors. Since I take this work very seriously, the real problem is in finding suitable projects. I am of the opinion that there are far too many books on the market today. I want to make a real contribution to children's literature, not simply add to the growing heap.

———

David Small received his B.F.A. degree from Wayne State University in Detroit in 1968 and his M.F.A. degree from Yale University in 1972. He was Assistant Professor of Art at the State University of New York, Fredonia College, from 1972 to 1978, and at Kalamazoo College from 1978 to 1982. Currently, he is a free-lance artist and illustrator. His editorial drawings appear in newspapers in New York, Boston, and Chicago. He is married to a writer and between them they have five children.

Imogene's Antlers was a Reading Rainbow book. *Mean Chickens . . .* was named a Notable Book for Children in the Field of Social Studies by a joint committee of the National Council on the Social Studies and the Children's Book Council in 1983. *Company's Coming* was named a Notable Book of 1988 by the American Library Association.

SELECTED WORKS WRITTEN AND ILLUSTRATED: Eulalie and the Hopping Head, 1982; Imogene's Antlers, 1985; Paper John, 1987.

SELECTED WORKS ILLUSTRATED: Gulliver's Travels, by Jonathan Swift, 1983; Mean Chickens and Wild Cucumbers, by Nathan Zimelman, 1983; Anna and the Seven Swans, by Maida Silverman, 1984; The Kuklapolitan Players Present: The Dragon Who Lived Downstairs, by Burr Tillstrom, 1984; The Christmas Box, by Eve Merriam, 1985; Company's Coming, by Arthur Yorinks, 1988; American Politics: How It Really Works, by Milton Meltzer, 1989; As: A Surfeit of Similes, by Norton Juster, 1989.

ABOUT: Something About the Author, Vol. 46; Vol. 50.

ROBERT KIMMEL SMITH

July 31, 1930–

AUTHOR OF *The War with Grandpa*, etc.

Autobiographical sketch of Robert Kimmel Smith:

WHEN I WAS EIGHT years old I had an illness that forced me to stay in bed for three solid months. Strange as it sounds, I didn't really mind. I had my radio, I had my tiny toy airplane to fly on dangerous missions across the mountain ranges and the blankets over my knees. Best of all, I had my books.

I always loved reading. My favorite stories had to have a hero I admired, one I could root for when things went against him, and, of course, a happy ending. That's my favorite kind of story even now, where all comes right at the end.

When I was about ten I began writing little stories, poems, and sketches, but somehow I could never make them as good as the ones I read. I made the mistake early on of showing my mother one of my stories. She praised it too much, which embarassed me. I knew the story wasn't very good, and from then on I kept all my stories hidden away in a drawer and never showed them to anyone.

Writers became my heroes. To be able to put down on paper words having the power to entertain, to make people laugh and cry, that seemed like a great thing to do with my

Robert Kimmel Smith

By luck and persuasion, I got a job in advertising. For fifteen years I wrote ads and commercials, learning how to put words together, and writing a few short stories in my spare time. But I still wanted to write books.

In 1970, encouraged by Claire, I took a year off to see if I could actually do what I'd dreamed about for so long. I took a bedtime story I'd made up for our daughter, Heidi, and in a month of furious writing had a manuscript. It took two years and seven submissions, but *Chocolate Fever* is still the best known of my children's books.

In 1973 I had a comic novel published that was successful enough for me to know I'd never have to go back to advertising. Since then I've written a few plays and TV scripts and had eight other books published. My work has brought me many rewards and awards, but none was greater than the mere fact that I was at last a full-time writer.

It was a long and twisting road, filled with frustration, rejection, and disappointment. But now I rarely think of the bad times; what I remember are all the good things that writing has brought to me. In many ways my life is like my favorite kind of story, in which the hero tries to achieve a worthwhile end, and faces challenge and disappointment, but it all comes out right in the end.

————

Robert Kimmel Smith was born in Brooklyn. He attended Brooklyn College from 1947 to 1948. He was in the Army from 1951 to 1953. Smith married September 4, 1954, and has two children. From 1957 to 1965, he was a copywriter at an ad agency, and was a partner and creative director at Smith & Toback ad agency from 1967 to 1970. He has written novels for adults, like *Jane's House*, which was named an American Library Association Best Book of 1982. He has written plays and TV scripts, and adapted *Chocolate Fever* for a 1986 CBS Storybreak TV show. He is a member of the Authors Guild, the Writers Guild, and the Dramatists Guild.

life. But when, as a teenager, I told my parents of my ambition, they were not at all pleased. "There's no way you can ever make a living being a writer," I remember my father telling me.

I was crushed, but I kept my feelings hidden away. Okay, I said in my secret soul, I'll just have to work at something else to make money, and in my spare time I'll write.

I went off to Brooklyn College to become a doctor—my parents' greatest wish—and left a short time later having failed every math course known to man. I was eighteen years old and thought myself a complete failure.

I drifted through a number of jobs until the Army drafted me and sent me to Berlin, Germany. Somewhow I found the time to read every novel in the small barracks library, about two hundred of them. Then came the turning point in my life. I met a brilliant young woman, Claire Medney, who was an English major at the college where I'd failed so miserably. Claire loved books and writing as much as I did, and to impress her, I began writing stories again. We were married a year later and Claire became my editor, counsellor, the mother of our two children, and in time, my literary agent as well.

The War with Grandpa won a 1987 William Allan White Children's Book Award, and has won many state awards chosen by school children.

SELECTED WORKS: Chocolate Fever, 1972; Jelly Belly, 1981; The War with Grandpa, 1984; Mostly Michael, 1987; Bobby Baseball, 1989.

ABOUT: Contemporary Authors, Vol. 61; (New Revision Series), Vol. 8; Kaye, Phyllis Johnson. National Playwrights Directory; Something About the Author, Vol. 12; Who's Who in the East, 1981-1982.

JERRY SPINELLI

February 1, 1941–

AUTHOR OF *Space Station Seventh Grade*, etc.

Autobiographical sketch of Jerry Spinelli:

I WAS BORN in Norristown, Pennsylvania, in 1941. For most of my kid years, we lived in a brick rowhouse in the West End.

I did the usual kid stuff: rode my bike, played chew-the-peg, flipped baseball cards, skimmed flat stones across Stony Creek, cracked twin popsicles, caught poison ivy, wondered about girls, thought stuff that I would never say out loud.

When I was sixteen, my high school football team won a big game. That night I wrote a poem about it. The poem was published in the local newspaper, and right about then I stopped wanting to become a Major League shortstop and started wanting to become a writer.

But first I became a grown-up. And I thought, as most grown-ups do: Okay, now on to the important stuff.

So I tried writing grown-up novels about important stuff. Nobody wanted them.

In my thirties I married another writer, known to young readers as Eileen Spinelli. Not only did she bring a wagonload of published poems and stories to the marriage, she brought a half-dozen kids. Instant fatherhood.

One night one of our angels snuck into the refrigerator and swiped the fried chicken that I was saving for lunch the next day. When I discovered the chicken was gone, I did what I had done after the big football victory: I wrote about it.

I didn't know it at the time, but I had begun to write my first published novel, *Space Station Seventh Grade*. By the time it was finished, hardly anything in it had to do with my grown-up, "important" years. It was all from the West End days.

And I began to see that in my own memories and in the kids around me, I had all the material I needed for a schoolbagful of books. I saw that each kid is a population unto him- or herself, and that a child's bedroom is as much a window to the universe as an orbiting telescope or a philosopher's study.

————

Jerry Spinelli enjoys writing about "the adventure" that comprises typical experiences of children and young people: "cruising a mall without a parent," "overnighting it," or "the thousand landfalls of our adolescence."

Spinelli attended Eisenhower High

School in Norristown, Pennsylvania, and received his A.B. degree in 1963 from Gettysburg College. He received an M.A. degree from Johns Hopkins University in 1964. He served in the Naval Reserve from 1966 to 1972 and was married May 21, 1977. He and his wife have seven children.

SELECTED WORKS: Space Station Seventh Grade, 1982; Who Put That Hair in My Toothbrush?, 1984; Night of the Whale, 1985; Jason and Marceline, 1986; Dump Days, 1988.

ABOUT: Contemporary Authors, Vol. 111; School Library Journal August 1988; October 1988; November 1988; Something About the Author, Vol. 39.

TRICIA SPRINGSTUBB

September 15, 1950–

AUTHOR OF *Give and Take*, etc.

Autobiographical sketch of Tricia Springstubb:

I GREW UP in a very small house with a very large family. Our rooms were crowded with voices—arguments, laughter, whispers, shouts. There was always a line for the bathroom, always an argument over who'd gotten the biggest piece of cake, always someone opening your bedroom door saying, "Well, it's *my* room, too!" Privacy? Not in our vocabulary.

But if there weren't many secrets in our house, there were lots of stories. What my father had said to his boss that morning. How my baby sister had poured cooking oil across the kitchen floor so she could "ice skate." The trials and tribulations of my Irish grandmother, who'd been rich enough one year to hire a live-in maid, so poor the next she had to cut up my grandfather's suits to make skirts for her daughters. My next door neighbor told us about her childhood in Italy, and the woman from up the street wept in our kitchen because her husband was so mean. Stories, stories, stories, and me with my eyes and ears wide open.

If it was a story I wasn't supposed to hear, I'd hide behind a door or flatten myself against a wall, eavesdropping.

There were lots of books, too. Every week my mother and I went to the public library and came home with great armloads. My mother loved to read, and she'd sit up late into the night, when all her children were finally asleep and the house was quiet. In the morning, getting us ready for school, she'd be as grumpy as anything. I wished she'd be more cheerful, like the mothers on TV, but I knew how she felt. Many nights, when she made me turn off my light and stop reading, I'd take the book in bed with me. I remember sleeping with *Little Women*, and later with *Gone with the Wind*.

I was the oldest child, and my parents had great hopes for me. I tried not to disappoint them. For a long time I thought I would be a teacher when I grew up. In college I changed my mind and decided to be a social worker. I studied sociology, and my favorite part was reading the case histories—more stories.

After college I worked with children. I taught in Head Start, and I was a housemother to adolescent girls who had emotional problems. I did a lot more listening. Somewhere along the line I began to write my own stories. Just for myself, I thought. I never really expected anyone else would want to read them. But then somewhere a little further along the line, my husband persuaded me to send them off to an editor. Long before my first story appeared in print, I knew I'd found what I wanted to do with the rest of my life. I'd found the voice that was mine alone.

Sometimes when I write I find myself laughing out loud. More often, I chew up pens and drink too much coffee. That's because, when I write, I'm trying to find out what I really, really think about life. It's hard. Telling the truth always is. But I still can't believe how lucky I am to be a writer. One of the best parts of my job is getting letters from my readers and knowing that my words came alive and meant something to someone else.

And that is the story of how a little girl who loved stories more than anything grew up to be a storyteller.

————

Tricia Springstubb was born in New York City. She received her B.A. degree from the State University of New York at Albany in 1972. She was married on August 18, 1973. She says she has worked at "every job imaginable," including selling shower curtains and teaching archery. She is the mother of three daughters. Springstubb has contributed fiction to *Redbook, McCall's,* and *Woman's Day.* Her work has also been excerpted in *Seventeen.* She is a member of the Authors Guild.

Which Way to the Nearest Wilderness? was a Junior Literary Guild selection.

SELECTED WORKS: My Minnie Is a Jewel, 1980; The Blueberry Troll, 1981; Give and Take, 1981; The Magic Guinea Pig, 1982; The Moon on a String, 1982; Which Way to the Nearest Wilderness?, 1984; Eunice Gottlieb and the Unwhitewashed Truth About Life, 1987; Eunice (the Egg Salad) Gottlieb, 1988; With a Name Like LuLu, Who Needs More Trouble?, 1989.

ABOUT: Contemporary Authors, Vol. 105; Directory of American Poets and Fiction Writers; Something About the Author, Vol. 40; Vol. 46.

DIANE STANLEY

December 27, 1943–

AUTHOR AND ILLUSTRATOR OF *Peter the Great,* etc.

Autobiographical sketch of Diane Stanley Vennema, who has also written under the names "Diane Zuromskis" and "Diane Stanley Zuromskis":

MY EARLIEST YEARS were spent in New York City, where my mother and I lived in an apartment on Perry Street. Coming there from Abilene, Texas (where I was born), New York seemed like the most exciting place there ever was. We weren't going to miss anything, and I don't think we did.

Mother's friends were writers, actors, artists, and musicians, and they led fascinating lives. They talked about all sorts of things, and I loved to listen.

My mother is a creative person, and it was natural for her to encourage my creativity. She read to me a lot—and not just children's books, but all sorts of things. She took me to the theatre (I think I saw *Peter Pan* with Mary Martin eight or nine times!). We sang duets. We wrote books together (she would type up my words and I would draw the pictures). We went to art galleries and talked about the pictures. Mother taught me to take an interest in words, and where they came from. She corrected my grammar and taught me that language is a beautiful and precise thing. And she wrote a book and got it published (a murder mystery, *Murder Leaves a Ring*), which taught me that books are written by ordinary people who like words and are willing to work hard.

In spite of all this, it took me a long time to discover what I really wanted to do with my life. In college I found that I wanted to

study everything—history, psychology, biology, literature. It wasn't until my senior year that I finally took an art course—and it was a revelation! Drawing was the most natural thing in the world for me. I don't mean that everything about it was easy. But it felt like what I was born to do.

My teacher called me into his office at the end of the year. "I have a present for you," he said. "Hold out your hand." I did, and with two fingers he put something invisible into my palm. "You have talent," he said.

That is when I first thought about being an artist. I decided to be a medical illustrator, because my drawing style was so detailed and realistic. I spent a year in Edinburgh, Scotland, going to art school in a building that looked like a castle and had a view of a real one. On my vacations I traveled all over Europe. Over New Year's I visited Russia, a trip that years later would bring me to write *Peter the Great.*

I got a master's degree from Johns Hopkins in medical illustration, and went to work in my chosen field. I found I didn't like it very much.

By that time I was the mother of two little girls and, of course, I read to them a lot.

That was when I fell in love with children's books. I practically camped out in the library. I brought home piles of books and studied them. Then I began to draw and paint pictures that looked like children's book art.

When I had enough work to show, I took it to a publisher in Boston. To my delight, he asked me to do a book for his company— that was one of the happiest days of my life.

That first book was *The Farmer in the Dell,* and I went on to illustrate many more. After a while, I began to write them, too, beginning with *The Conversation Club.*

As a writer and illustrator of children's books, I have been able to explore many different subjects, places, and times. In *A Country Tale* I tried to convey, both in my writing and in the pictures, the world of Victorian England. In *Captain Whiz-Bang* I relived my mother's childhood in America of the 1920s, '30s and '40s. I also got to do a comic strip for that one. *Peter the Great* took me to Tsarist Russia, *Shaka* to South Africa. *Birdsong Lullaby* took place in the imagination of the child I used to be.

Every book is an adventure. The time I spend writing and painting is joyful. The joy is not in having the finished book in my hand after all that work—the joy is in the making of the book.

Looking back, it seems as if I've been preparing all my life to do the work I do today. It's odd that it took me thirty-five years to find it, but now that I have I know that it will be my work for a lifetime. How lucky I am!

———

Diane Stanley received her B.A. degree in history and political science from Trinity University in San Antonio, Texas, in 1965. She did postgraduate work at the University of Texas and at Edinburgh College of Art in Scotland and traveled through Russia, Greece, and Israel. Her first marriage was May 30, 1970, and ended in divorce. In 1970 she received her M.A. degree from Johns Hopkins. Stanley has worked as a graphic designer for Dell Publishing Company and was art director for children's books for G.P. Putnam's Sons and Coward, McCann & Geoghegan, Inc. Her second marriage was September 8, 1979, to Peter Vennema, and she has three children. She has taught classes in illustration through Rice University, and visits schools and libraries to talk about her work.

The Farmer in the Dell was named a 1979 Children's Choice Book by a joint committee of the International Reading Association and the Children's Book Council. *Fiddle-I-Fee* was a Junior Literary Guild selection, as were *Sleeping Ugly* and *The Conversation Club*. Several of her books were named Notable Children's Trade Books in the Field of Social Studies by a joint committee of the National Council on the Social Studies and the CBC: *The Month Brothers* and *The Conversation Club* in 1983, *A Country Tale* in 1985, and *Peter the Great* in 1986. *All Wet!* was named an Outstanding Science Trade Book for Children by a joint committee of the CBC and the National Science Teachers Association in 1985. *Peter the Great* was an American Library Association Notable Book of 1986 and an Honor Book in the 1987 Golden Kite Awards of the Society of Children's Book Writers. *Captain Whiz-Bang* was a Book-of-the-Month Club selection, and *Shaka* was a *New York Times* Best Illustrated Book of 1988.

SELECTED WORKS WRITTEN AND ILLUSTRATED AS DIANE STANLEY: Fiddle-I-Fee: A American Chant, 1979; The Conversation Club, 1983; A Country Tale, 1985; Birdsong Lullaby, 1985; Peter the Great, 1986; Captain Whiz-Bang, 1987.

SELECTED WORKS WRITTEN WITH PETER VENNEMA AND ILLUSTRATED: Shaka: King of the Zulus, 1988.

SELECTED WORKS ILLUSTRATED AS DIANE STANLEY: Onions, Onions, by Toni Hormann, 1981; Sleeping Ugly, by Jane Yolen, 1981; Little Orphant Annie, by James Whitcomb Riley, 1983; The Month Brothers: A Slavic Tale, retold by Samuel Marshak, 1983; All Wet! All Wet!, by James Skofield, 1984.

SELECTED WORKS ILLUSTRATED AS DIANE ZUROMSKIS

: or Diane Stanley Zuromskis: The Farmer in the Dell, 1978; Half-a-Ball-of-Kenki: An Ashanti Tale Retold, by Verna Aardema, 1979.

ABOUT: Contemporary Authors, Vol. 112; Something About the Author, Vol. 32; Vol. 37.

JANET STEVENS

1953–

ILLUSTRATOR OF *Lucretia the Unbearable*, etc.

Biographical sketch of Janet Stevens:

JANET STEVENS was born in Dallas, Texas. Her father was a naval officer, so she grew up in many places, such as Italy and Hawaii. She has always been interested in art. As a child, she felt her brother and sister were smarter than she was, and she "found her niche" in art.

She received her B.F.A. degree from the University of Colorado in 1975 and began her career by designing fabric. She has also been an artist in the advertising field and an architectural illustrator. During 1977 she went to the Illustrator's Workshop in New York and became interested in children's book illustration. She was not successful at first, so she worked in advertising and design. In 1978 she attended another workshop, with Tomie dePaola. He encouraged her and showed her work to an editor. Stevens loves animals and frequently draws them in her books. Recently she has designed illustrations for animated children's television specials, but she continues to do books.

Stevens says that retelling is the closest she comes to writing. She has adapted the work of Edward Lear, Aesop, Hans Christian Andersen, and others for her books.

Janet Stevens lives in Boulder, Colorado, with her husband and her two children. She enjoys camping, skiing, biking, and the outdoors.

SELECTED WORKS RETOLD AND ILLUSTRATED: The

JANET STEVENS

Princess and the Pea, 1982; The Owl and the Pussycat, 1983; The Emperor's New Clothes, 1985; The House That Jack Built, 1985; Androcles and the Lion: An Aesop Fable, 1989.

SELECTED WORKS ILLUSTRATED: Callooh! Callay! Holiday Poems for Young Readers, by Myra Cohn Livingston, 1978; Lucretia the Unbearable, by Marjorie Weinman Sharmat, 1981; Sasha the Silly, by Marjorie Weinman Sharmat, 1984; The Cabbages Are Chasing the Rabbits, by Arnold Adoff, 1985; The Big Bunny and the Magic Show, by Steven Kroll, 1986; The Quangle Wangle's Hat, by Edward Lear, 1988.

TODD STRASSER

May 5, 1950–

AUTHOR OF *Friends Till the End*, etc.

Autobiographical sketch of Todd Strasser, who also writes under the name "Morton Rhue":

FOURTH GRADE was a big year for me. For the first time in my life my hands were large enough to grip a football at the laces and throw a decent spiral. Since I was the first kid on my block to be able to do this, I became the quarterback for all our after-school games.

Fourth grade also marked my first crush. I fell in love with my teacher, Mrs. Berk. Mrs. Berk came from California and was young (for a teacher), blond, and pretty. She also liked science and animals, as did I. Unlike my mother, Mrs. Berk thought it was great that I owned three horned lizards, two newts, a painted turtle, and a water snake. Then again, Mrs. Berk didn't have to live with their daily escape attempts. My mother did.

During the winter of fourth grade, Mrs. Berk told my mother I was behind in my reading skills and that if I didn't catch up I might have to repeat fourth grade. My mother came home and told me I was going to a reading tutor after school.

This was not good news. Seven hours of school a day was enough, and going to a reading tutor meant I would have less time to play football and pursue Dulcie Kornfield (To be honest, this didn't take up much of my time, since she hated me). Still, it was better than repeating fourth grade, so I went.

My tutor's name was Mrs. Stamper, and each time I went to her house she let me eat pretzel sticks and ginger ale. These (junk) foods were banned in my own home, and while I can't say I looked forward to my weekly visits to Mrs. Stamper's, they did make being tutored a more palatable experience for me. By the time school ended the following June, there was no more talk of my being held back.

When I look back to fourth grade I see the beginnings of the person I am today. Athletics are still important to me, as are outside interests and hobbies. I am also very involved with my family. Mrs. Stamper certainly left her mark: I love to read. However, if someone had told me in the fourth grade, or even in high school or college that I would someday make a living as a writer, I would have told them they were crazy. It still astonishes me that this is what I do.

People say I must be very disciplined to write everyday, but I'm not. If my wife brings home a bag of potato chips and says we have to save them for company, I'll eat them anyway. Discipline has very little to do with why I write. I write because I love to write and because I need to write. I've given up trying to understand why. All I know is that when I don't write I become a cranky, miserable person.

One of my goals is to become proficient in several types of writing, and for many different age groups. I would find it boring to do only one kind of writing and for only one age group. I usually have four or five projects going at the same time. Right now I am working on a screenplay. When I finish it I will go back to a juvenile book that I began last year. My second novel for adults is half-finished and I have plans for two more books for young adults.

One of my most surprising aspects of becoming a writer, for me, has been the development of a parallel career as a public speaker. Each year I am asked to speak about writing to students at schools and to teachers and librarians at conferences. I find that I love entertaining a crowd almost as mush as I love writing. This seems odd to me, since speaking forces me to be very extroverted while writing is essentially an introverted task. Perhaps they complement each other.

Sometimes when I visit a school a kid will ask me if I ever regret becoming a writer or if there is another career I wish I'd tried. One thing about being a writer is that you can have as many careers as you want. In the past year, for instance, I have dived for sunken treasure, gone into the Federal Witness Protection program, and become a lawyer and a professional model. Of course I didn't really do all those things, instead I researched and wrote about them. But when I wrote, it felt as if I'd actually done them. Tomorrow I might decide to write about hunting in Alaska, or being a computer hacker, or an actor. That, to me, is the greatest part of being a writer.

———

Todd Strasser was born in New York City. He graduated from Beloit College with a B.A. degree in 1974. He was married on July 2, 1981. He has been a reporter with the *Times Herald Record* of Middletown, New York, an advertising copywriter, an *Esquire* magazine researcher, and has owned a fortune cookie company. He has been a freelance writer since 1975. He has written one novel for adults, *The Family Man. The Wave* is a novelization from a teleplay by Johnny Dawkins. He has also written novelizations for motion pictures, such as *Ferris Bueller's Day Off* and *The Pink Cadillac.* Three of Strasser's books chronicle the story of a rock band called Coming Attractions: *Rock 'n' Roll Nights, Turn It Up!,* and *Wildlife.*

Friends Till the End was named a 1981 Best Book for Young Adults by the American Library Association, and also appeared on the ALA "Best of the Best Books for Young Adults 1966-1986" list. *Rock 'n' Roll Nights* was also named an ALA Best Book for Young Adults, in 1982. Both *Workin' for Peanuts* and *A Very Touchy Subject* were made into movies for television. *The Accident* was nominated for a 1988 Edgar Allen Poe Award by The Mystery Writers of America.

SELECTED WORKS: Angel Dust Blues, 1979; Friends Till the End, 1981; Rock 'n' Roll Nights, 1982; Workin' for Peanuts, 1983; The Complete Computer Popularity Program, 1984; Turn It Up!, 1984; A Very Touchy Subject, 1985; The Mall from Outer Space, 1987; Wildlife, 1987; The Accident, 1988; Beyond The Reef, 1989; Moving Target, 1989 .

SELECTED WORKS AS MORTON RHUE: The Wave, 1981.

ABOUT: Contemporary Authors, Vol. 117; Horn Book March/April 1986; Roginski, Jim. Behind the Covers: Interviews with Authors and Illustrators of Books for Children and Young Adults; Something About the Author, Vol. 41; Vol. 45.

OZZIE SWEET

OZZIE SWEET

September 10, 1918–

PHOTOGRAPHER OF *Canada Geese*, etc.

Biographical sketch of Oscar "Ozzie" Cowan Sweet:

OZZIE SWEET was born in Stamford, Connecticut. At the age of fourteen, Ozzie Sweet began taking pictures of wildlife in the Adirondacks. He attended the Art Center in Los Angeles to study sculpture, but his interest in photography was stronger, and he began to learn commercial photography. To earn extra money, he played bit parts in movies. He took advantage of the opportunity to study lighting and makeup on the sets. He served in the Army Air Corps as a photographic officer. He was married in 1942. His wife died in 1970, and he was married for a second time in 1973. He worked for *Newsweek* magazine in Washington, D.C. and took photographs of many famous people, such as Ingrid Bergman, Albert Einstein, and Andrei Gromyko.

Ozzie Sweet is now a free-lance photographer with 1,800 covers for magazines to his credit. He has a steady assignment photographing major league baseball spring training in Florida. In addition to the photographs he produces for his books for children, he also sells his work for calendars, posters, jigsaw puzzles, record album covers, and book jackets. He once had a catastrophic fire in which he lost his entire color transparency and black-and-white negative file, but he began working a day later. He recommends camera clubs, workshops, and short seminars as good ways to learn the craft and profession of photography. He also writes, "there is no substitute for experiences to be gained in working with a professional photographer, no matter how menial the work."

Sweet had the choice of recording any side of life, but chose to cover "the warm and sunny side of life." He says, "I've always tried to find and develop ideas that would invite the viewer to smile and feel good. . . . If sometimes my touch is felt miles away a year later, that's when photography is meaningful." Sweet spends his spare time photographing wildlife, "waiting, observing, and photographing." This talent and enthusiasm has led to the creation of many fine photographic nature books for children, produced with writer Jack Denton Scott.

When Sweet is not traveling, he lives in a two-hundred-year-old farmhouse with his wife Diane in a village in New Hampshire.

Discovering the Mysterious Egret was a 1978 ALA Notable Book. Two of Scott's books were selected for the *School Library Journal* "Best of the Best 1966-1978" list: *City of Birds and Beasts* and *Loggerhead Turtle*. *Discovering the American Stork* was named a Notable Book of 1976 by the American Library Association and was chosen for the 1976 American Institute of Graphic Arts Book Show. *Little Dogs of the Prairie* was a 1977 ALA Notable Book, as were both *The Book of the Pig* and *Moose* in 1981. Among his books that were named Junior Literary Guild selections are *Canada Geese*, *The Gulls of Smuttynose Island*, *Island of Wild Horses*, *The Book of the Goat*, and *Swans*. Many of Sweet's books have been named Outstanding Science Trade Books for Children by a joint committee of the Children's Book Council and the National Science Teachers Association. These include *Loggerhead Turtle* in 1974, *Return of the Buffalo* in 1976, *Little Dogs...* in 1977, *Island of Wild Horses* in 1978, *The Book of the Pig* and *Moose* in 1981, *Orphans from the Sea* in 1982, *The Fur Seals of Pribilof* in 1983, and *Alligator* in 1984.

SELECTED WORKS PHOTOGRAPHED: Loggerhead Turtle: Survivor from the Sea, by Jack Denton Scott, 1974; Canada Geese, by Jack Denton Scott, 1976; Discovering the American Stork, by Jack Denton Scott, 1976; Return of the Buffalo, by Jack Denton Scott, 1976; The Gulls of Smuttynose Island, by Jack Denton Scott, 1977; Little Dogs of the Prairie, by Jack Denton Scott, 1977; City of Birds and Beasts: Behind the Scenes at the Bronx Zoo, by Jack Denton Scott, 1978; Discovering the Mysterious Egret, by Jack Denton Scott, 1978; Island of Wild Horses, by Jack Denton Scott, 1978; The Book of the Goat, by Jack Denton Scott, 1979; The Submarine Bird, by Jack Denton Scott, 1980; The Book of the Pig, by Jack Denton Scott, 1981; Moose, by Jack Denton Scott, 1981; Orphans from the Sea, by Jack Denton Scott, 1982; The Fur Seals of Pribilof, by Jack Denton Scott, 1983; Alligator, by Jack Denton Scott, 1984; The Swans, by Jack Denton Scott, 1987.

ABOUT: Popular Photography October 1976.

NANCY TAFURI

November 14, 1946–

AUTHOR AND ILLUSTRATOR OF *Have You Seen My Duckling?*, etc.

Biographical sketch of Nancy Tafuri:

NANCY TAFURI'S father was a naval officer assigned to various places. As a result, she and her mother spent considerable time together when Tafuri was a child, reading many of her favorite books over and over again. She also learned to enjoy her own company, and spent hours coloring and painting.

Tafuri decided on an artistic career and entered the School of Visual Arts in New York. Her primary focus was on children's book illustration, but her course of study also included graphic design, book design, typography, and painting. Her future husband, Tom, was also taking the same courses.

She graduated in 1967, and was an assistant art director at Simon & Schuster from 1967 to 1969. The two were married on June 14, 1969. In 1971 they formed One Plus One Studio, where they do trade and paperback book jacket designs, photography, logos, and movie design. After many years of trying, Tafuri was given the chance to illustrate children's books. One of her first was *The Piney Woods Peddler* by George Shannon. Her husband modelled for the peddler, and many of the other characters are based on people she met in Pennsylvania, where she went to live in a stone mill for several months while working on the book's illustrations. Her graphic design business has done well, so she is able to devote more time to creating children's books. Tafuri's medium is concentrated colored inks with black line. She has always loved nature, so she enjoys producing books about ducks, rabbits, mice, and fairies.

Have You Seen My Duckling? was named a 1985 Caldecott Honor Book by the American Library Association. *The Piney Woods Peddler* was named a 1982 Chil-

dren's Choice Book by a joint committee of the Children's Book Council and the International Reading Association. *If I Had a Paka* was a 1983 Honor Book in the Jane Addams Children's Book Awards of the Jane Addams Peace Association.

Three of her books have been named ALA Notable Books: *The Piney Woods Peddler* in 1981, *Across the Stream* in 1982, and *Have You Seen My Duckling?* in 1984.

SELECTED WORKS WRITTEN AND ILLUSTRATED: All Year Long, 1983; Early Morning in the Barn, 1983; Have You Seen My Duckling?, 1984; Rabbit's Morning, 1985; Who's Counting, 1986; Junglewalk, 1988; Spots, Feathers, and Curly Tails, 1988; The Ball Bounced, 1989.

SELECTED WORKS ILLUSTRATED: My Hands Can, by Jean Holzenthaler, 1977; The Piney Woods Peddler, by George Shannon, 1981; Across the Stream, by Mirra Ginsburg, 1982; If I Had a Paka: Poems in Eleven Languages, by Charlotte Pomerantz, 1982; The Song, by Charlotte Zolotow, 1982; All Asleep, by Charlotte Pomerantz, 1984; Nata, by Helen V. Griffith, 1985; Flap Your Wings and Try, by Charlotte Pomerantz, 1989.

ABOUT: Contemporary Authors, Vol. 118; Something About the Author, Vol. 39.

PEGGY THOMSON

November 6, 1922–

AUTHOR OF *Auks, Rocks and the Odd Dinosaur*, etc.

Autobiographical sketch of Peggy Bebie Thomson:

RIGHT OUT OF SCHOOL my first assignment at my first job, on *Life* magazine, was to cover Raritan, New Jersey's homecoming festivities for its young Marine sergeant Johnny Basilone. In the midst of World War II this was an occasion to celebrate, for Johnny was safely home, and in saving his comrades he'd won a soldier's highest prize, the Congressional Medal of Honor. I found myself standing in the Basilones' bathtub holding lights while the photographer took pictures of our amiable hero in his undershirt lathering his chin, also nicely showing off his tattoos. Later while the bands played I ran along the parade route borrowing stepladders from people's basements to give us good overviews. So this was a writer's life! I liked it.

In later years, while living in Washington, I became a free-lance writer for newspapers and magazines. I wrote articles about wild beach plums and the blue-blooded horseshoe crabs and about White House children's toys and the good times of Georgia high-school students who interviewed old-timers in the mountain coves around Rabun Gap and recorded them for *Foxfire* magazine. More and more as I wrote about young people's activities, I knew I wanted to write for young people. And so I had to work at it, to learn to write simply and clearly: not only that, but as author Jan Adkins puts it, with the mysteries of life intact.

Museum People is my invitation to meet behind-the-scenes people of the kind who dazzle me with their quirky interests and special skills and their odd, interesting, satisfying jobs. *Auks, Rocks and the Odd Dinosaur: Inside Stories from the Smithsonian's Museum of Natural History* proposes the

notion that—to people who puzzle out the clues—a bird, a boat, a stone, or the jawbone of a mouse holds stories to be read just as if it were a book. It has stories about its beginnings or about the people who found it or made it or fixed it or studied it or about the people who cherished it. Again museum people are being celebrated, along with a well-trained guard dog, Max. *Keepers and Creatures at the National Zoo* is my look at the lucky men and women who have the best of the zoo jobs, closest to the animals. Now I'm writing about life in a big old gritty but beloved Chinese city.

For me the jolly parts of writing are the re-re-re-writing at the very end of a project and the research at the start. At the end you're coasting home free. In the research you're happily clattering about—watching, listening, snooping, and settling into libraries to read yellow clippings and brittle old letters. I hope readers get from me at least an inkling of why nonfiction writers do not fret unduly over the handicap of not being able to write fiction.

In the course of a week I visit Washington's Potato Museum, honoring the lowly spud through history, in films, on coins, on postage stamps and in art. I also meet a zookeeper who got her career start dissecting mosquitoes (picture it!) and another who records red-panda baby talk on tape, and a third who is thrilled because the gorilla who spits with exquisite aim has taken to missing her, she thinks on purpose. The glimpses of such things lowly and cosmic are the stuff of articles and books, but: How soggy will my potatoes become once I've written them into paragraphs and, in my words on paper, will a degree of affection survive when I describe great ape's spit? A nonfiction writer ponders that always and stays reasonably humble.

———

Peggy Thomson was born in St. Louis, Missouri, of Swiss parents. She received a B.A. degree with high honors from Swarthmore College in 1943 and was elected to Phi Beta Kappa. She was a researcher at *Life* magazine from 1943 to 1947 and a part-time writer for *Washington Post Magazine* from 1964 to 1967. She was married on May 11, 1945 and has three children. She has been a free-lance writer since the 1960s, with articles in such publications as *The Washington Post, The New York Times*, The *Christian Science Monitor*, and the *Smithsonian*. Thomson is a member of the Children's Book Guild of Washington, D.C., and Washington Independent Writers.

Auks, Rocks and the Odd Dinosaur was the nonfiction winner of the 1986 Boston Globe-Horn Book Awards and was named a Notable Book of 1985 by the American Library Association.

SELECTED WORKS: On Reading Palms, 1974; Museum People, Collectors and Keepers, 1977; Auks, Rocks and the Odd Dinosaur: Inside Stories from the Smithsonian's Museum of Natural History, 1985; Keepers and Creatures at the National Zoo, 1988.

SELECTED WORKS WITH EDWARDS PARK: Pilot and the Lion Cub, Odd Tales from the Smithsonian, 1988.

CRYSTAL THRASHER

December 5, 1921–

AUTHOR OF *The Dark Didn't Catch Me*, etc.

Autobiographical sketch of Crystal Faye Thrasher:

I WAS BORN in the small limestone mining town of Oolitic, Indiana. My earliest memories are of making up stories about the pictures that hung on the living room wall. One that I remember distinctly was "Highland Lassie." In my stories she was kidnapped by Indians, stolen by the Gypsies, shanghaied by pirates, and finally adopted by a family in Indiana. That's how we happened to have her picture, I told my two little brothers. Then I started to school and discovered books. I read every book I could get my hands on, newspapers, magazines, cereal boxes, sign boards; if it had writing on it, I read it. The summer that I was twelve years old, I worked three months for eight dollars and all the books that I could carry home from my employer's attic. The eight dollars bought school books for my first year in high school that fall. A few of the attic books are still with me.

When I was seventeen years old I married Joseph Thrasher. We had three children by the time I was twenty-one, Carol and Joe on my eighteenth and nineteenth birthdays, and Jan in July two years later. My children are the very best gift my husband ever gave me. In April of '89 we celebrated our fiftieth anniversary.

For the first fifteen years of my married life my husband's work took him away from home for weeks on end. We would barely get settled in one place when he'd be transferred to another. The children and I were alone in more than ten states and twenty cities during those years. We kind of grew up together. They taught me patience, love, and understanding, and I thought them how to survive in the world. (Keep the doors locked, windows closed, and don't sit on strange toilet seats!)

Crystal Thrasher

We learned to love books and each other. There were times when books were the only friends we had in those stange places. When we couldn't get books, I wrote poems and short stories for the kids. Or I would sit with them in the evening and tell them stories about Greene County, where I had lived as a child. They didn't always believe the stories, but they laughed in the right places. Years later, when I was taking writing classes at Indiana University and complaining that I didn't know what to write about, Carol said to me, "Lay some of those stories about Greene County on them. The ones you used to tell us kids." And that's what I did.

I was fifty years old when I decided to write a book for my five grandchildren. I didn't think of publishing it. I just wanted them to know what it was like when I was a child of their age. At that time I still believed that published books were written by a special breed of people . . . just a little less than gods, not by ordinary human beings like myself. In my writing class at I.U. I was told that I could write well enough to be published. All I had to do was finish the book and find a publisher. I had worked as a waitress, clerk, and general handy-to-have-around person for years, so I thought, why not try it. Writing books sounded easier than the things I'd been doing, and a lot more fun. I quit my job and told everyone that I was going to write a book. When my children heard it, they gave me a new typewriter, paper, pens and pencils, and an encyclopedia, and wished me well!

In the years since then, I have never worked harder, nor enjoyed anything more than the books I have written for the children.

When Carol, Joe, and Jan were teenagers they gave me a book for my birthday with a note that read, 'To Mom. For if all your material things were taken away, a book would absorb your loneliness and restore your hope." Books and children have been my whole life. And I couldn't have spent it in better company.

Crystal Thrasher was married April 22, 1939. She attended the University of Indiana from 1972 to 1973.

Between Dark and Daylight won a 1980 Friends of American Writers Juvenile Book Merit Award. *End of a Dark Road* was named a 1982 Notable Children's Trade Book in the Field of Social Studies by a joint committee of the Children's Book Council and the National Council on the Social Studies.

SELECTED WORKS: The Dark Didn't Catch Me, 1975; Between Dark and Daylight, 1979; Julie's Summer, 1981; End of a Dark Road, 1982; A Taste of Daylight, 1984.

ABOUT: Contemporary Authors, Vol. 61; (New Revision Series), Vol. 8; Something About the Author, Vol. 27.

JUDITH THURMAN

October 28, 1946–

AUTHOR OF *Flashlight and Other Poems,* etc.

Biographical sketch of Judith Thurman:

JUDITH THURMAN was born in New York City. She received her A.B. degree from Brandeis University in 1967. Since 1972, she has been a writer and poet. From 1973 to 1975, she was an adjunct lecturer at Brooklyn College of the City University of New York.

Judith Thurman speaks four languages and has traveled extensively. In the seventies she spent five years living in Europe, writing and working as a cook, tutor, and interpreter. She is a poet who is particularly interested in poetry by women.

Thurman's poems for children in *Flashlight and Other Poems* were described by Beryl Robinson in *The Horn Book Magazine*: "Although the brief poems in this joyous little collection are based chiefly on aspects of the city child's experience, their appeal is universal, for they illuminate many familiar subjects and feelings."

To See the World Afresh contains poetry from, for the most part, the 1960s. It anthologizes poets like Marianne Moore and Denise Levertov and poets from around the world, including those from Greece, Japan, Guatemala, and Yugoslavia.

I Became Alone contains poems and brief biographies of five poets: Sappho, Louise Labé, Anne Bradstreet, Juana Ines de la Cruz, and Emily Dickinson. Five women from different cultures and centuries are gathered together because, Thurman writes, of each woman's "identity as a creator—an identity that put her whole life into focus. . . . "

In 1980, Thurman was named a National Endowment for the Humanities fellow. She is the author of a biography for adults, *Isak Dinesen: The Life of a Storyteller*, published in 1982. Katha Pollitt, writing in *The New York Times*, called the book "a model biography." It won the American Book Award for Biography in 1983 and has been translated into eleven languages. She is also a contributor of translations to *Penguin Women Poets* and has had poems appear in anthologies. She is a contributor to *The New Yorker, Ms., The New York Times,* and *Mademoiselle*. She has also written a screenplay for public television, on Emily Dickinson's poetry.

Two of Thurman's books have been named Notable Books by the American Library Association: *To See the World Afresh* in 1974 and *Flashlight and Other Poems* in 1976. *The Magic Lantern* was a Junior Literary Guild selection.

SELECTED WORKS: I Became Alone—Five Women Poets, 1975; Flashlight and Other Poems, 1976; I'd Like to Try a Monster's Eye, 1977; Lost and Found, 1978.

SELECTED WORKS COMPILED WITH LILLIAN MOORE: To See the World Afresh, 1974.

SELECTED WORKS WRITTEN WITH JONATHAN DAVID: The Magic Lantern: How Movies Got to Move, 1978.

ABOUT: Contemporary Author, Vol. 49; (New Revision Series), Vol. 1; Directory of American Poets and Fiction Writers; Something About the Author, Vol. 33; Who's Who of American Women, 1987-1988.

JEANNE TITHERINGTON

May 23, 1951–

AUTHOR AND ILLUSTRATOR OF *Pumpkin, Pumpkin*, etc.

Biographical sketch of Jeanne Titherington:

JEANNE TITHERINGTON was born in New York City, but has spent most of her life in Maine. From the age of ten, she knew she wanted to be an artist. She attended art school, first at Pratt Institute in Brooklyn, from 1970 to 1971. She graduated from the Portland School of Art in 1973 and from the University of Maine in 1975. She majored in painting, though she comments that she was classified as a painting major because no one could figure out how else to classify her artwork. She was making "Joseph Cornell-like box constructions, with collage, found objects, and drawings."

When she graduated from college, she couldn't afford large enough living quarters

JEANNE TITHERINGTON

to house all her "wonderful junk" used in her constructions, so she turned to drawing. She had her work exhibited several times in the next few years, and was encouraged by a friend to try book illustration. From her home in Maine, she made an "unorganized" visit to New York, then to Boston, carrying her work in a paper shopping bag. She got her first job illustrating a book for children. "With the help and encouragement of Susan Hirschman," she says, referring to the Editor in Chief of Greenwillow Books, she is now writing children's books as well. Titherington's illustrations were exhibited at the Justin Schiller gallery in Manhattan in 1983. She has also had her work shown at Manhattan's Master Eagle Gallery.

Jeanne Titherington lives in Rockland, Maine, with her husband and daughter. "I love what I do and I feel truly blessed in the life I have," she comments. She says that her work combines many of her interests: " . . . art, of course; language; fairy tales and mythology; day and night dreams; the world of the child.

"'The world of the child,'" she notes, "is a deeply personal interest for me; I think, in a way, that I have never grown up. I guess I hope I never will."

In the books she writes and illustrates, she is known for her quiet and subtle realistic illustrations and stories that speak to a preschooler's concerns: a new sibling, separation, and the like. She prefers working with pencil and colored pencil. Jeanne Titherington is a member of the Author's Guild.

Big World, Small World juxtaposes the adult's and the child's perspective. *Pumpkin, Pumpkin* follows a young boy as he plants, grows, and harvests a pumpkin, ending with the carving of the Halloween jack-o-lantern, and the saving of seeds for the next spring. *A Place for Ben* tells how a child reacts to a new sibling, while *Where Are You Going, Emma?* describes a child's early adventure in being alone.

Pumpkin, Pumpkin received a 1987 New York Academy of Sciences Children's Science Book Award. It was also named a 1987 Children's Choice Book by a joint committee of the Children's Book Council and the International Reading Association. In 1984 Titherington was named a Silver Medallist by the Society of Illustrators, for *The Story-Teller*. *A Taste for Quiet* won a 1983 New Jersey Institute of Technology New Jersey Authors Award.

SELECTED WORKS WRITTEN AND ILLUSTRATED: Big World, Small World, 1985; Pumpkin, Pumpkin, 1986; A Place for Ben, 1987; Where Are You Going, Emma?, 1988; A Child's Prayer, 1989.

SELECTED WORKS ILLUSTRATED: The Chronicles of Pantouflia, by Andrew Lang, 1981; The Story-Teller, by Saki, 1982; A Taste for Quiet and Other Disquieting Tales, by Judith Gorog, 1982; It's Snowing! It's Snowing!, by Jack Prelutsky, 1984.

STEPHANIE S. TOLAN

October 25, 1942–

AUTHOR OF *The Great Skinner Strike*, etc.

Autobiographical sketch of Stephanie S. Tolan:

I WAS BORN in Canton, Ohio, on October 25, 1942, and my mother (who had been a

librarian before she became a mother) must have begun reading to me on October 26th. At least, I don't remember a time when books weren't important in my family, so important that I taught myself to read just to keep up with everybody else. Reading aloud was something we did often, and I especially remember *David Copperfield*, which Mom read to us (my sister was fifteen, my brother thirteen, and I eight) while my father was away finding a place for us to live in Kenosha, Wisconsin, where we were about to move. I was too young to really understand *David Copperfield*, but some of those characters (Uriah Heep, Betsey Trotwood, and Micawber) seemed to come alive right there in the house with us, and I've never forgotten them. I've always suspected that my writer-self was really born during the reading of that book.

The next year, when my fourth-grade teacher in Wisconsin asked us all to write stories, my ambition to be a writer bloomed. My story, about a how a baby volcano was responsible for the first Fourth of July celebration, was historically and geographically disastrous and poorly spelled, but I loved it, and have it still. I'd known the magic of little black marks on paper that could become whole worlds, but I'd never considered the possibility of making that magic myself. Writing was as much fun as reading!

In sixth grade my teacher told my mother I'd never amount to anything because I was interested in too many things, and that same year my first two manuscripts (one poem, one story) were turned down by *Jack and Jill* and *The Saturday Evening Post*. It was a bad year! But somehow, I survived, and my seventh-grade English teacher let me give a book report on a book I'd made up (though I hadn't had the energy to write it all down). The other kids wanted to know where to get that book, so it seemed to me I had a chance. I wrote through high school (often when I was supposed to be translating Latin), then majored in creative writing in college.

When I graduated, I discovered that a diploma didn't make one a writer. So, while I went to graduate school, began teaching composition, married Robert Warren Tolan, and became stepmother to Robert Jr., Andrew, and Patrick, I kept writing. It wasn't long before I'd published my first poem and my first play and had begun to understand that my sixth-grade teacher had been wrong. I wrote poetry for the next ten years; then, when our son, R.J., was in nursery school, I began writing a book. Through our four boys, I'd rediscovered children's literature, and it occurred to me that I wanted to write for the kind of flashlight-under-the-covers young reader I'd been. From the day in 1976 when I wrote the first sentence of *Grandpa—And Me*, I've been trying to do just that.

I'm still interested in far too many things, but the joy of that is being able to put some of those things into books that might make magic for kids. Sometimes I write stories about what is sad or scary, sometimes about what is happy or funny, but I always try to write about what is important to me. I hope that those things will turn out to be important for some of my readers, too.

———

Stephanie S. Tolan received her B.A. degree in Creative Writing from Purdue University in 1964 and her M.A. degree in English in 1967. She was married December 19, 1964. She has been a lecturer in English at Indiana University at Fort Wayne, an Instructor at Purdue University in Fort Wayne, and a faculty member at New York State University in Buffalo, at Franklin and Marshall College in Lancaster, Pennsylvania, and at the University of Cincinnati.

From 1965 to 1980, she taught English and Theatre Arts, and is currently on the faculty of the Institute of Children's Literature. She has been a writer-in-residence at several high schools and was a Delegate to the Second Annual Symposium on Children's Literature and Art, in the Soviet Union in 1987. She has also been an actress, and has had her plays performed and her poetry published in anthologies and in journals like *Roanoke Review* and *Oregonian Verse*. She is a member of the Authors Guild of the Authors League of America.

Currently, Tolan is both a writer and a consultant to parents of exceptionally gifted children. She has written books, like *Guiding the Gifted Child*, and magazine articles on the subject. She also gives speeches on the topic and was keynote speaker at the First National Conference for Exceptionally Gifted, in 1987.

Stephanie Tolan received a Fellowship in Children's Literature from Bread Loaf Writer's Conference in 1980. She received a certificate for her contributions to the literary arts in the state and in the nation from the Ohio Arts Council in 1981. She has also received Individual Artist Fellowships from the Ohio Council, in 1978 and 1981.

The Great Skinner Strike was made into an ABC Afterschool Special. *Grandpa—and Me* was named a 1978 Notable Children's Trade Book in the Field of Social Studies by a joint committee of the National Council on the Social Studies and the Children's Book Council; *The Liberation of Tansy Warner* won the same honor in 1980.

SELECTED WORKS: Grandpa—and Me, 1978; The Last of Eden, 1980; The Liberation of Tansy Warner, 1980; No Safe Harbors, 1981; The Great Skinner Strike, 1983; The Great Skinner Getaway, 1987; A Good Courage, 1988; The Great Skinner Homestead, 1988.

ABOUT: Contemporary Authors, Vol. 77; (New Revision Series), Vol. 15; Directory of American Poets and Fiction Writers; Horn Book May/June 1986; Something About the Author, Vol. 38.

ANN TOMPERT

January 11, 1918–

AUTHOR OF *Little Fox Goes to the End of the World*, etc.

Biographical sketch of Ann Tompert:

ANN TOMPERT was born in Detroit, Michigan, and grew up on a small farm near there. She remembers helping her father sell vegetables at a roadside stand at the age of six. After her mother died when Tompert was twelve years old, she and her two younger sisters were raised by her father. They had little money, and she recalls her father painting a pair of black shoes white when she had to have a pair of white shoes for a school procession.

Books were very important to Tompert, and after reading *Little Women*, she decided that she wanted to be a writer. She was encouraged in school by a teacher who praised a short story she wrote.

She graduated summa cum laude from Siena Heights College with a B.A. degree in 1938. She also did graduate work at Wayne State University from 1941 to 1946. She then began a teaching career, starting out at a two-room country school. She taught elementary school and junior and senior high school English from 1938 to 1959 in various towns and cities in Michigan. She was married March 31, 1951.

During her early teaching years, she says she didn't work at writing "seriously," but thought she could write books that were as good as those she was using in class. She began to try to sell her work, and after three years, sold her first story to *Jack and Jill* magazine. Since 1959 she has been a full-time writer, and is a member of the Society of Children's Book Writers. In addition to her books for children, she has contributed articles on writing to the bulletin of the Chicago-based Children's Reading Round Table, of which she is a member. Her work has also been published in *Wee Wisdom*, *The Friend*, and *Highlights* magazines.

Tompert and her husband, a retired social service worker, live in Port Huron, Michigan. She enjoys gardening, reading, and making quilts and baskets. She also belongs to the Detroit Women Writers, Alpha Delta Kappa, and Friends of the St. Clair County Library.

Little Fox appeared on the *School Library Journal* "Best of the Best 1966-1978" list that appeared in the December 1979 *SLJ*. It was also named a Notable Book of 1976 by the American Library Association. *Little Otter Remembers* was named a Children's Choice Book by a joint committee of the International Reading Association and the Children's Book Council in 1978. *Charlotte and Charles* won the 1980 Woodward Park (Brooklyn) School Annual Book Award, and was a runner-up for the 1980 Irma Simonton Black Award given by Bank Street College of Education.

SELECTED WORKS: What Makes My Cat Purr?, 1965; It May Come In Handy Someday, 1975; Little Fox Goes to the End of the World, 1976; Little Otter Remembers, 1977; Badger on His Own, 1978; Charlotte and Charles, 1979; Three Foolish Tales, 1979; Nothing Sticks Like a Shadow, 1984; The Silver Whistle, 1988; Will You Come Back for Me?, 1988.

ABOUT: Contemporary Authors, Vol. 69; (New Revision Series), Vol. 11; Something About the Author, Vol. 14.

ANN TURNER

December 10, 1945–

AUTHOR OF *The Way Home*, etc.

Autobiographical sketch of Ann Warren Turner:

THERE WAS NEVER A TIME I can remember when I did not want to become a writer. I was one of those children who propped themselves on their noses in the middle of books—they smelt good, felt good, and went down like cling peaches. We had a tradition in our family of loving books so much that you didn't even bother to take your coat off when you came home from school, but just sat in the chair, muffled and coated, reading the book you'd been looking forward to all day.

I spent a lot of my childhood outside, making up games and dreaming. There was a special rock at the end of our field, shaded by a maple tree, where I'd sit and watch leaf patterns move across the grey rock. Or I'd lie on my back in the field watching spring come to the trees on the field's edge; first red, then a tinge of green, then green-green. I also had a favorite pine tree which I climbed and rode a branch when the wind blew, pretending I was flying.

My two brothers and I grew up in an old New England house, supposedly part of the underground railway. In the attic was a hiding place that had a roll of birch bark along its side. Whether it hid slaves or not, we never knew, but I'd imagine myself an escaping slave, lying in the hiding place, my heart pounding.

I was lucky to have a father who was a printer and a mother who was an artist. We were always making collages or linoleum cuts, painting horses, and sculpting clay. It never occurred to me that I might grow up and not draw, not paint. One of my goals is to someday paint again and illustrate one of my own books.

I first trained to be a teacher, along with my new husband, in 1967. But I soon decided that I would rather *write* books than teach them. My first book was about vultures, illustrated by my mother, and was a special collaboration. After some nonfiction books, my first novel came out in 1980, *A Hunter Comes Home*. That novel came from a picture I'd seen in Audubon magazine, and really is a novel about how a child can love and hate his parents.

I've written nonsense poetry for young children, poetry for slightly older children, historical novels, and illustrated poems based on history. Poetry seems to be an ongoing theme in my life, and probably goes back to all those hours spent dreaming in the pine tree and watching leaf shadows on a rock. I still like writing about children in other times. Maybe it's a way of asking questions: What would I do if I were alive in the 1870s and went West, only to have everything eaten by grasshoppers? What would I do if I lived in England in 1348 and were accused of being a witch? What would I do if I moved into a new house and discovered that a witch lived in my woods?

When I start a book, I rarely know where it will end up. It's like getting in a car, starting it up, and driving slowly (sometimes *very* slowly) down the road. I take note of where I'm going and write it down—but where will I end up? Sometimes writing goes fast and easily. It almost slips out like a seal pup out of its mother. At other times it is tortuous and slow, going back over the same chapter again and again, trying to get it right. I find that if I don't have my beginnings right, that the rest of the book doesn't follow naturally.

Kids sometimes ask me why I write and is it fun and do I make a lot of money at it? (Where is my Rolls Royce parked?) I write because I love to do it, because writing is one of the most exciting things I know. To sit down and have a story come spooling out under my fingers—that is magic! It is a little like being at a movie—watching the action on the screen—and yet being an actor *in* the movie. I guess I also write to share with others the child that is inside me—that ten-year-old who dreamed, painted, and pretended to be an escaped slave.

———

Ann Turner was born in Northhampton, Massachusetts. She attended rural schools in Williamsburg and received her B.A. degree in English from Bates College in Maine in 1967. She studied one year abroad at Oxford University, England, and was awarded an M.A.T. degree by the University of Massachusetts in 1968. She was married June 3, 1967 and has one child, born in 1987. Ann Turner has been a high school English teacher as well as a writer, and has worked at a home for young women with drug problems.

Vultures was named an Honor Book by the New York Academy of Sciences in 1974. Two books have been named Notable Books for their year of publication, *A Hunter Comes Home* in 1980 and *Dakota Dugout* in 1985.

SELECTED WORKS: Houses for the Dead, 1978; Rituals of Birth, 1978; A Hunter Comes Home, 1980; The Way Home, 1982; Dakota Dugout, 1985; 3rd Girl from the Left, 1986; Tickle a Pickle, 1986; Street Talk, 1986; Time of the Bison, 1987; Nettie's Trip South, 1987; Will You Come Back for Me?, 1988; Grasshopper Summer, 1989; Heron Street, 1989.

SELECTED WORKS WRITTEN WITH MARION G. WARREN: Vultures, 1973.

ABOUT: Contemporary Authors, Vol. 69; (New Revision Series), Vol. 14; Something About the Author, Vol. 14.

JEAN URE

January 1, 1943–

AUTHOR OF *See You Thursday*, etc.

Autobiographical sketch of Jean Ure, who also writes under the pen names "Ann Colin", "Jean Gregory", and "Sarah McCulloch":

BORN IN CATERHAM, SURREY (England), I now live in a three-hundred-year-old house in Croydon (part of Greater London) with one husband, three dogs, two cats, no kids.

In common with the most compulsive writers, I can't remember a time when I haven't wanted to "be a writer". My first recorded outpouring, at the age of four:

M'Daddy had a boot lace,
M'Daddy did lose it,
And when the rain began to pour,
There it was a-hanging on the door.

I stopped writing poetry pretty soon after

Ure: *EW er*

that and took up the novel instead. I wrote my first novel when I was six. It was about a little girl called Carol who went off to collect her friends for a party. The novel went on for two pages of a scrapbook and was a long list of all my favourite names—Carlotta, Bianca, Natasha, Patricia. . . . (No boys' names: at six years old I was instinctively sexist.)

When I was nine, I told my first "writer's lie": I told a little friend that I had had a story published in a magazine. The story was called "Jam Pot Jane." Maybe one of these days I shall actually get around to writing it. . . .

I wrote a great many novels before I had my first one published. They were all written in exercise books stolen from the school stationery cupboard and were mostly no more than a couple of chapters long, since after a couple of chapters I would either lose interest or couldn't think how to continue. They were all, without exception, derivative.

When I was fourteen I wrote a wish-fulfilment book called *Dance for Two*. This was all about a girl called Colleen who was desperate to learn ballet but wasn't allowed to on account of the family finances being straitened. I was Colleen and I never was allowed to; but Colleen, being part of my daydreams, got lucky: she ended up dancing the leading role in "Coppélia" with her childhood sweetheart (the Hero).

Writing this book was a very cathartic exercise and a great solace to me. It was published in the U.K. when I was sixteen and a year or so later in the States. In the U.K. version my hero is described as being small of stature: in the American version this had to be deleted . . . in America in the sixties it seemed that heroes couldn't be small.

Having a book published while I was only sixteen was a bit of a double-edged blessing, since a year later I rose up, grandly declaring myself A Writer, and flounced out of school to pursue this vocation. Over the next few years, "being A Writer" consisted mainly of scrubbing floors, waiting at table, selling groceries, having fits of temperament in people's offices . . . I also did a short spell nursing, a short spell at the BBC, a short spell at NATO, a short spell at UNESCO, a short spell at pretty well everything that didn't require any actual qualification. In 1965 I decided that it was about time I got some more learning, so I went to the Webber-Douglas Academy of Dramatic Art, in London, where I met my husband, who is an actor.

For some years I translated French books into English and wrote so-called "romantic novels" for a living—"so-called" because things happened in them which were not supposed to happen. Not in the romantic novel: not in those days. It worried my poor editor tremendously. Ultimately I found the formula just too frustrating, but it certainly taught me my craft.

After my romantic novel period I wrote a series of Georgian romances under my wee Scots granny's name of Sarah McCulloch. I greatly enjoyed these as they allowed me to pretend that I was Jane Austen. It wasn't until 1980 that I really emerged as myself, with a book for young adults called *See You Thursday*—still one of my personal favourites. (I have since written a sequel called *After Thursday* and am currently engaged on a third, to be called *Tomorrow Is Also a Day*.)

People often ask me why I write. I do so primarily for my own satisfaction—I am very much a writer who writes from "within" rather than "without," by which I mean that I tend to look inwards into myself rather than outwards at the world for my inspiration. Nonetheless, I always bear the reader very much in mind. If I have any conscious aim—though it becomes conscious only when I'm forced to stop and think about it—it's to stimulate and entertain, and hopefully, for the receptive few, to unlock the door to that same lifetime of spiritual and intellectual nourishment which was unlocked for me over forty years ago by a book called *Little Women* . . . as dear to me now as it ever was then!

———

Jean Ure spent 1965 and 1966 at Webber-Douglas Academy and was married in 1967. She is a member of the Society of Authors and translates books from French to English. *See You Thursday* was named a Best Book for Young Adults by the American Library Association in 1983 and was a Junior Literary Guild selection; *Supermouse* was also a Junior Literary Guild selection.

SELECTED WORKS: See You Thursday, 1983; Supermouse, 1984; What If They Saw Me Now, 1984; You Two, 1984; If It Weren't for Sebastian, 1985; The Most Important Thing, 1986; You Win Some, You Lose Some, 1986. After Thursday, 1987; The Other Side of the Fence, 1988.

ABOUT: Something About the Author, Vol. 48.

BETTY VANDER ELS

October 3, 1936–

AUTHOR OF *The Bombers' Moon*, etc.

Autobiographical sketch of Betty Vander Els:

I WAS BORN in Chengtu in the far west of China, and shortly thereafter began to move—China, India, Canada, the United States, and across the countries in between. I didn't stop until I reached Shaftsbury, Vermont, at age thirty-three. War, revolution, changes in my parents' occupations, then changes in my own work tossed me from place to place. I saw many kinds of people, from all sorts of backgrounds, involved in different ways of living. For the most part, I felt like an observer who never really understood the rules. But I could see that it was often difficult for people to imagine lives different from their own. When I decided to learn to write stories, I knew my background and training would be valuable, but not in the usual ways. My university studies were in nursing. However, it was an unusual course that included much literature and history. After practicing nursing for a few years, I married and had four children, to whom I read book after book after book. All that reading aloud was great fun and a marvellous way to learn how words work.

But when I began to write, I discovered that storytelling is a gift and a skill that needs years of practice. *Cricket Magazine*

accepted a few of my stories, enough to encourage me to go on working.

When I wrote the first draft of *Bombers'
Moon*, I wondered: Will modern American
children be interested in the hurly-burly of
World War II China? I remembered an ancient Chinese poet who read his work to listeners in the marketplace. If they didn't
understand, he went home and revised his
poem until they did. That seemed wise to
me. My 'marketplace' was a willing sixth
grade. Their comments and suggestions
were very encouraging, and I held them in
mind as I revised and revised. I continue to
read my work to children when it reaches
a certain point, and continue to find their
comments most valuable.

After *Bombers' Moon* was published, I
was obliged to go back into nursing; I expected to find that work that was so practical and obviously necessary would make the
dreaming and imagining essential to writing seem silly. It didn't. The opposite occurred. I realized that, yes, my nursing was
valuable in bringing physical health; but
stories and those who wrote them made
physical health worth having.

I still feel like an observer who doesn't really understand the rules, so, to keep in
touch, I read constantly. My own children
are grown, so now I borrow children from
school, because I want to write about these
children in 1988. We cook or garden or explore, and I listen to their stories of times
they've been scared or excited or amused.
Yesterday we made corn bread and talked
about the drug problems and car crashes of
some high-school students. And we talked
about birthday parties and about horseback
riding just as the sun rises. I grew up in one
kind of hurly-burly, they are growing up in
another. But I think we can meet at the core
of our experiences.

SELECTED WORKS: The Bombers' Moon, 1984; Leaving Point, 1987.

GABRIELLE VINCENT

AUTHOR AND ILLUSTRATOR OF *Ernest and
Celestine*, etc.

Biographical sketch of Gabrielle Vincent:

GABRIELLE VINCENT was born in Brus-
sels, Belgium. She is a private person and
says that to know her, one must read her
books. These are many in a series about Ernest, a bear, and Celestine, a mouse.

Told completely in dialogue, each story
is simple, concerning a problem that either
the paternal bear or childlike mouse creatively solves with much mutual love. In
Ernest and Celestine, Celestine loses a toy
bird in the snow. When Ernest finds it, it is
beyond hope. After trying to replace it with
other toys, he finally sews Celestine a new
version of the original. In *Bravo, Ernest and
Celestine*, it is Celestine who solves the
problem, which is how to pay to fix a leaking roof. She persuades Ernest to play his violin while she sings, and they succeed as
street musicians, only to use the money to
buy each other presents, instead of a new
roof. Ernest tells Celestine, however,
"'Don't worry. . . . We'll go out again
tomorrow.'" These are typical plots. Vincent has also produced two wordless books
that are smaller in format and equally simple in plot.

Vincent's line-and-wash paintings have
received much acclaim. She has been
praised for her characterization and sim-
plicity as well as the expressiveness she con-
veys in her paintings. Her books have
received awards in many countries, including Germany, France, Japan, and Holland.

Two of her books have been named Notable Books by the American Library Association: *Ernest and Celestine's Picnic* in 1982
and *Breakfast Time, Ernest and Celestine*
in 1985. *Smile, Ernest and Celestine* was
named a Best Illustrated Book of 1982 by
The New York Times. The Ernest and Celestine books have been translated into over
twelve languages. Another series about a
Koala bear named Pic-Nic has not been

GABRIELLE VINCENT

translated into English. Gabrielle Vincent lives in France.

SELECTED WORKS WRITTEN AND ILLUSTRATED: Bravo, Ernest and Celestine, 1982; Ernest and Celestine, 1982; Ernest and Celestine's Picnic, 1982; Smile, Ernest and Celestine, 1982; Merry Christmas, Ernest and Celestine, 1984; Breakfast Time, Ernest and Celestine, 1985; Ernest and Celestine's Patchwork Quilt, 1985; Where Are You, Ernest and Celestine?, 1986; Feel Better, Ernest!, 1988; Ernest and Celestine at the Circus, 1989.

ABOUT: Children's Literature Review, Vol. 13.

BARBARA BROOKS WALLACE

December 3, 1922–

AUTHOR OF *Peppermints in the Parlor*, etc.

Autobiographical sketch of Barbara Brooks Wallace:

THERE WERE ONLY two people present when I was born, my mother and myself. It was nine o'clock on a Sunday morning in a bedroom of our house in Soochow, China. My father, in a near state of collapse as he attempted to climb into his clothes downstairs in the living room, had at least man-

aged to send a servant to church for our missionary doctor. By the time the doctor arrived, however, my mother had calmly produced, cleaned, oiled, and wrapped me, so all the doctor had to do was give us his blessing, prescribe for my father, and leave.

I feel that my mother delivering me by herself and with such dispatch is rather remarkable, and so I'm reporting it even though it had nothing whatsoever to do with why I have become a writer of books for children. But then, nothing seems to me to have much to do with that, and when I was struggling to produce my first publishable book, I was often in despair over my depressingly few credentials.

To begin with, I don't remember the first thing about wanting to write as a child. As a matter of fact, I had a horribly cramped, left-handed way of writing and just the act of putting pencil and paper itself was a punishment. As a result of both these things, I did no writing except in school, so naturally published no sonnets at five, or a first novel at fourteen. And even though I read the print off my *Tiger Tim Annuals* from England that arrived faithfully under the Christmas tree each year, as well as the huge bundles of Los Angeles *Times* comics (joy!) that arrived from Grandmother in the United States every six months, I was not an avid reader of everything I could get my hands on, which I understood to be a major portent of ONE WHO WILL SOMEDAY WRITE.

My professor of freshman English at Pomona College encouraged me to write. Then I transferred to U.C.L.A. and, instead of English or creative writing courses, I brilliantly decided to take an international relations curriculum so I could go overseas and have lots of adventures to write about. I ended up going to secretarial school so I could get a job.

Several years later, when our son entered kindergarten, I entered Santa Monica City College to take creative writing. And what better to do than write a story set in the place where I had spent my childhood, China? Lots of things, apparently, because I produced a disastrous unpublishable fantasy.

Four published books later, I wrote *Can Do, Missy Charlie*. I was very pleased to have it selected by the Junior Literary Guild, but still do see it as a quaint, old-fashioned story, reminiscent of the idyllic life we lived in China as children, closely guarded by over-zealous amahs, taken to the seashore every summer, generally protected from all the horrors of local wars, the sight of heads being lopped off in the streets, the dirt, and the disease. My friends think I should write again about China, especially about the time my sister and I were allowed out of our parents' sight to vacation with our Shanghai American School Latin teacher in the summer resort of Peitaho, and the Japanese "incident" left us stranded there. We didn't see our parents again until, courtesy of a U. S. Navy destroyer and a troop transport, we steamed into Manila harbor in September. It seems as if I didn't have to go to U.C.L.A. to study international relations so I could go overseas to have an adventure. I had one lurking in my past all along. But I see this as one incident, not a book. And anyway, one thing I've learned is that you don't need to have an adventure to tell a story.

My wish for my writing future, at least it's my wish right now, is that I will only be inspired to write fantasies, melodramas, or somewhat improbable humorous stories, and that I will be struck down if I ever write anything that doesn't have a happy ending.

But back to the matter of credentials for writing for children. A little girl once said to me, "How do you know so much about how it feels to be eleven?" My mother replied, "That's because she still *is* eleven!"

I wonder if that would pass for a credential?

Barbara Brooks Wallace was married on February 27, 1954, and has one child. She attended Pomona College from 1940 to 1941 and received her B.A. degree from the University of California at Los Angeles in 1945. She has worked as a script secretary in radio, as a secretarial school teacher, and as a radio time salesperson. She is a member of the Children's Book Guild of Washington, D.C. and of the National League of American Pen Women.

Peppermints in the Parlor won the 1983 William Allen White Children's Book Award. Both *The Contest Kid Strikes Again* and *Miss Switch to the Rescue* were broadcast as ABC television specials.

SELECTED WORKS: Claudia, 1969; Trouble with Miss Switch, 1971; Victoria, 1972; Can Do, Missy Charlie, 1974; The Secret Summer of L.E.B., 1974; Julia and the Third Bad Thing, 1975; The Contest Kid Strikes Again (rev. ed), 1980; Peppermints in the Parlor, 1980; Hawkins and the Soccer Solution, 1981; Miss Switch to the Rescue, 1983; The Barrel in the Basement, 1985; Shadow on the Snow, 1985; Argyle, 1987.

ABOUT: Contemporary Authors (First Revision), Vol. 29-32; (New Revision Series), Vol. 29; The International Authors and Writers Who's Who, 1977; Something About the Author, Vol. 4; Who's Who of American Women, 1981-1982; The Writer's Directory 1984-1985.

IAN WALLACE

March 31, 1950–

ILLUSTRATOR OF *Very First Last Time*, etc.

Autobiographical sketch of Ian Wallace:

MY LOVE of story and storytelling did not come to me like a sky bolt out of a thunderous cloud, nor did it arrive one night, a ghostly apparition rising at the foot of my bed. Rather, that singular love came in the age-old way that it has for children since time immemorial, in the security and comfort of home, from the resonant voice of a parent or grandparent.

In those days, growing up in Niagara Falls, Ontario, my maternal grandparents visited infrequently. They lived on the west coast of Canada, and while they were a long way from heading toward the "poor house," money was not readily available to make yearly trips across the country. However, when they did travel east for those wonderful prolonged stays, their arrival brought with it the sound of magic.

That distinctive sound manifested itself every time my two brothers and I sat spellbound at our grandparents' feet listening to those two Saxon voices telling stories of a time long ago and a place so far away that we were transported out of our bodies. Yet each time that we were reintroduced to those tales, our grandparents told them with such drama and humour that we experienced them as if hearing them for the first time.

Here is my favorite story to the best of my recollection but severely edited:

When my grandfather was twelve years of age, he left school for the last time to enter the mines that had been dug in the rolling hills surrounding his home near Gloucestershire, England. Being a small boy for his age, he was given the task of entering the narrowest openings in the rock face where older and much larger miners could never have entered.

At the end of his first day on the job, his hands were soaked with blood from skin

that had been torn open from chipping away at the rock.

An older miner recognized his pain. "You know what you do with them, lad?" he asked in a voice that told my grandfather that he already knew the answer.

"No," my grandfather replied Without hesitation the miner said, "You piss on 'em!"

Believing implicitly in what the miner had told him and yet with great reluctance, my grandfather "pissed" on his hands. My brother's and my response as boys was to break into rolling fits of laughter that was soon hotly pursued by a cauterizing sensation that rushed down our spines.

For my grandfather's part, as a boy, the bleeding ceased after the stinging ended. The skin healed over and his hands toughened, allowing him to return to that rock face for many succeeding years.

I tell you that story because it is part of my family heritage and by virtue of the fact that it has stayed close to my soul all of these years. I assure you that this tale has given me the confidence to enter the darkened tunnels that authors and illustrators must enter in their never-ending search for a story—a quest in which we strive to discover those words and pictures, those nuggets of precious metal that illuminate human truths.

————

Born in Niagara Falls, Ontario, Canada, Ian Wallace attended the Ontario College of Art from 1969 to 1973, graduating in 1973. He also studied there as a postgraduate student from 1973 to 1974. He has been a staff writer at Kids Can Press in Toronto and an information officer at the Art Gallery of Ontario in Toronto. He has been a free-lance artist and author since 1974 and is a member of the Writers' Union of Canada. He has received grants from the Ontario Arts Council in 1985 and 1986, and from Canada Council Grants, in 1980, 1981, 1983, 1986, and 1987.

Chin Chiang appeared on the 1986 International Board on Books for Young People Honour List for illustration. The book also won the 1984 IODE Best Children's Book of the Year Award from the Education Secretary, Municipal Chapter of Toronto IODE (Imperial Order of the Daughters of the Empire), and the 1985 Amelia Howard Francis Gibbon Award from the Canada Library Association for Best Illustrated Book. *Very First Last Time* was an American Library Association Notable Book of 1987 and was a Junior Literary Guild selection. The book also was named a Children's Choice Book of 1987 by a joint committee of the Children's Book Council and the International Reading Association. It received the "White Raven Book" Prize at the Bologna Book Fair.

SELECTED WORKS WRITTEN AND ILLUSTRATED: Julie News, 1974; The Christmas Tree House, 1976; Chin Chiang and the Dragon's Dance, 1984; The Sparrow's Song, 1987; Morgan the Magnificent, 1988.

SELECTED WORKS WRITTEN AND ILLUSTRATED WITH ANGELA WOOD: The Sandwich, 1975.

SELECTED WORKS ILLUSTRATED: Very Last First Time, by Jan Andrews, 1986; Builder of the Moon, by Tim Wynne-Jones, 1989.

ABOUT: Canadian Children's Literature 48, 1987; Contemporary Authors, Vol. 107; Emergency Librarian Feburary 1985; In Review April 1979; Quill and Quire February 1985; Something About the Author, Vol. 53.

MILDRED PITTS WALTER

1922–

AUTHOR OF *The Girl on the Outside*, etc.

Bigraphical sketch of Mildred Pitts Walter:

MILDRED PITTS WALTER, was born in De Ridder, Louisiana, and received her bachelor of Arts degree in English from Louisiana's Southern University. She furthered her education in California, where she attended the University of California at Los Angeles, California State College, and the University of Southern California. She received her Master's degree in Education from the Antioch Extension in Denver, Colorado.

For many years Walter taught elementary school in the Los Angeles Unified School District. She was a member of the Board of Directors of the American Civil Liberties Union of Southern California, and with her late husband, Earl Lloyd Walter, City Chairman of the Congress of Racial Equality, worked toward desegregation of the Los Angeles school system. Walter has travel extensively throughout the United States and to China. In 1977, she journeyed to Lagos, Nigeria as a delegate to the African and Black Festival of the Arts. She has also served as a consultant to the Western Insterstate Commission of Higher Education, in Boulder, Colorado, and as a consultant, teacher, and lecturer at Metropolitan State College in Denver.

Walter published her first book, *Lillie of Watts*, in 1969, and from then on has spent much of her time writing.

Her writing for children ranges across a wide spectrum, from picture books to middle readers to young adult novels, and her efforts have been distinguished by an im-

MILDRED PITTS WALTER

pressive array of awards and honors. Her picture books include *My Mama Needs Me*, illustrated by Pat Cummings and chosen as a Reading Rainbow book, and *Brother to the Wind*, illustrated by Leo and Diane Dillon. *Brother to the Wind* was named an American Library Association Notable Book in 1985, and an NCTE Teacher's Choice. In *School Library Journal*, Gale P. Jackson called *Brother to the Wind* "a gem. The collaboration of a fine storyteller and two gifted illustrators has produced an incredibly beautiful book that shines with its creator's love of story . . . Walter's writing is imaginative, engaging, and filled with metaphors of flight and fancy and the infinite wonders of life." *Ty's One-Man Band*, illustrated by Margot Tomes, was an Irma Simonton Black Award runner-up in 1980. *Justin and the Best Biscuits in the World*, a book for middle readers illustrated by Catherine Stock, was a Coretta Scott King Award winner in 1987. *Because We Are* and *Trouble's Child* both novels, were Coretta Scott King Award Honor Books, in 1984 and 1986 respectively.

Walter's concern for racial equality has manifested itself in much of her work, including *The Girl on the Outside*. It is an account of the integration of Central High School in Little Rock, Arkansas, in 1957. Elizabeth Muther in the *Christian Science Monitor* called it "well crafted and focused, sizzling with details appropriate to her teen audience . . . It tells just how far the nation has come, and—because of its sensivity to the feelings of both races [involved in the dispute]—just how much farther we may hope to come together." The novel was named a *Christian Science Monitor* Best Book and an ALA Notable Book of 1982.

Walter's latest book, *Mariah Loves Rock*, a novel for young adults, was published in 1988. She now lives in Denver, Colorado.

SELECTED WORKS: Lillie of Watts, 1969; Lillie of Watts Take a Giant Step, 1971; Ty's One-man Band, 1980; The Girl on the Outside, 1982; Because We Are, 1983; My Mama Needs Me, 1983; Trouble's Child, 1985; Brother to the Wind, 1985; Justin and the Best Biscuits in the World, 1986; Mariah Loves Rock, 1988.

ABOUT: Rollock, Barbara. Black Authors and Illustrators of Children's Books; Something About the Author, Vol. 45.

SHIGEO WATANABE

March 20, 1928–

AUTHOR OF *What a Good Lunch!*, etc.

Autobiographical sketch of Shigeo Watanabe:

WHEN I WAS BORN there were three siblings. By the time I became five years old the number of siblings grew to five. That year my mother died. My father married a woman with two children who became my siblings as well. After then, four more siblings were born. Can you tell me how many siblings I have altogether? My father was a very broad-minded man and whenever any one of his relatives or friends was confronted by living problems he would say "Leave your kids with us. We have already so many that a few more won't make any difference!" So, my stepmother had to work very hard in feeding the children and keep-

Shigeo Watanabe

ing the house clean. I remember one night she fainted after she had done all the washing in the bathroom. There was, of course, no washing machine those days in Japan.

My father was a photographer by trade. In his spare time he loved to tell stories to children. He told stories not only to his own children but also to others in schools and kindergartens. In summer evenings when the air had cooled off, people in the neighborhood used to bring out their bamboo benches in the street and play *shogi*, Japanese chess. Then my father became very popular among the neighborhood children. It was a thrilling and chilling experience to hear him tell, in the dark, a ghost story written by Lafcadio Hearn. When I was in fifth or sixth grade I stood up in front of my classmates and told stories in a way I learned from my father. These are happy memories of my childhood.

Our house was burnt down in a big fire that swept away the whole town when I was twelve years old. And once again after the war the photographer's family home lay in ruins: a dozen children, no house in which to live, nothing to feed the children, and no work to earn his living.

I won a Fulbright Scholarship in 1954

that brought me to a library school in the U.S.A. and to the New York Public Library. Some children exlaimed when they saw me in a children's room. "Where are you from?" "How come? You are a man!" It's no wonder they were surprised; I was not only a Japanese but I realized I was the only man among more than a hundred qualified children's librarians working for the NYPL at that time. Thanks to this, I became very popular among young patrons. I enjoyed telling stories to them. Some children thought I was telling them in Japanese while I thought I was telling them in perfect English. I was chosen one of the best storytellers of the year in the library.

After the happy experiences at the NYPL I came home and started teaching in a library school in Tokyo. That was thirty years ago. I married a Japanese girl and in due course of time three sons were born.

My childhood memories, studies in children's books, library and teaching experiences, and fortunate encounters with eminent authors and artists have helped me to write books for children. I have translated over a hundred American and English children's books into Japanese. While I am doing this I always enjoy a feeling of going back and forth between realms of different cultures, not only in terms of verbal symbols, but also of images, sounds, feelings, and emotions.

I have written nearly a hundred books, including many picture books illustrated by Japanese artists. It is always a great joy to create a story. To do this my children and wife are everlasting sources of inspiration. Whenever I share any incident with my family, my childhood emotion returns within and helps me to see, listen to, feel, and understand as a child, and I am urged to write it. I am grateful to the family in which I was brought up and to the one my family is bringing up.

———

Shigeo Watanabe was born in Shizuoka, Japan. He received his B.A. degree from

Keio University in Tokyo in 1953. He also received an M.S.L.S. degree from Case Western Reserve University in 1955. He was a children's librarian at NYPL from 1955 to 1957, and was Associate Professor at Keio University from 1957 to 1959 and Professor from 1970 to 1975. He has been visiting lecturer at the University of Illinois, Western Michigan University, Pratt Institute, and the Library of Congress. He was Vice President of the International Board on Books for Young People from 1976 to 1978, and is a member of the Japan Library Association. In 1977, he delivered the May Hill Arbuthnot Lecture, administered by the American Library Association.

How Do I Put It On? was named an ALA Notable Book of 1979, and *What a Good Lunch!* was designated a Children's Choice Book of 1981 by a joint committee of the Children's Book Council and the International Reading Association. Shigeo Watanabe's translation of Howard Pyle's *Otto of the Silver Hand* apppeared on the IBBY Honour List in 1984.

SELECTED WORKS: How Do I Put It On?: Getting Dressed, 1979; What a Good Lunch!: Eating, 1980; Get Set! Go!, 1981; I Can Ride It!: Setting Goals, 1982; I'm the King of the Castle!: Playing Alone, 1982; Where's My Daddy?, 1982; I Can Build a House!, 1983; I Can Take a Walk, 1984; Daddy, Play with Me, 1985; I Like to Take a Bath, 1987; It's My Birthday!, 1988.

ABOUT: Bookbird February 1976; Children's Literature Review, Vol. 8; Contemporary Authors, Vol. 112; Something About the Author, Vol. 32; Vol. 39; Top of the News April 1976; Spring 1977.

ANN E. WEISS

March 21, 1943–

AUTHOR OF *Lies, Deception and Truth*, etc.

Autobiographical sketch of Ann Edwards Weiss:

MANY GOOD THINGS happened to me when I was a child, and one was that people read to me. I can't remember a time when

I wasn't snuggled up next to my mother, father, or grandfather, listening to a story.

Another good thing happened when I was six years old and my aunt got a book— one of her childhood favorites—from her attic, promising to read it after dinner. I begged to hear it on the spot, but my aunt was firm: cook first, read later. So I opened the book and began picking out one familiar word here, another there. Suddenly I was recognizing more and more words and all at once, the words turned into sentences and then paragraphs. Before I knew it, I was on page twenty. All those years of sitting beside adults, watching the pages as they read, had paid off!

A third good thing occurred about four years later: another aunt and my uncle gave me a book that had been autographed by its author. It seemed marvelous to me—a real writer had touched the very volume I was holding—but I wanted more. I wanted one day to meet a writer of children's books in person.

That ambition suggested pursuing a career in publishing. After graduating from high school (Rockland High School, in Rockland, Massachusetts, where I grew up), I majored in English literature at Brown

University. At the end of my senior year, I applied for a secretarial position at several New York publishers. (Being a secretary is often the way one starts out in publishing.) Once again, something good happened. Not only did I turn out to be a poor typist, I was an even worse speller—perhaps the only person who ever flunked spelling tests at four major publishing houses. Desperate, I applied for a job as a "writer-in-training" at Scholastic Magazines. You don't have to spell to write and I got the job.

At Scholastic, I learned the basics of writing for young people. My job there was doing news stories and other articles for the company's fourth-grade classroom magazine. I also did some editing of other writers' work, which was fun. In addition, I fulfilled my ambition of meeting authors. I did more than meet them, I became engaged to one, a science writer named Malcolm Weiss. About a year after Malcolm and I married, our daughter Margot was born. At the same time, I started my first book, *Five Roads to the White House*.

Five Roads was tough to write. A hundred-page book is harder to organize than a twenty-line magazine story. But I struggled on and finished that project, and another and another. By 1988 I had begun work on my twenty-fifth book.

It's work I love. I've written about the nuclear arms race and the Supreme Court, about lies and the truth, about prisons, welfare, the news media, medical ethics, and much more. Writing about something is a wonderful way to learn about it and to educate yourself about issues and problems you once hardly knew existed.

After I'd been at Scholastic for seven years, Malcolm, Margot, and I moved to rural Maine. Our second daughter, Rebecca, was born and until Margot left for college, we all lived here on twenty acres of land in a farmhouse built in 1810. I enjoy gardening and taking walks in the countryside, but most of all, I enjoy writing. I type on a computer now, so mistakes don't matter.

And I let my editors worry about the spelling.

———

Ann E. Weiss was born in Newton, Massachusetts. She received her B.A. degree in 1965 and was married January 31, 1966. She has received the Christopher Award three times: in 1975 for *Save the Mustangs*, in 1984 for *The Nuclear Arms Race*, and in 1989 for *Lies, Deception and Truth*. Many of her books have been named Notable Children's Trade Books in the Field of Social Studies by a joint committee of the Children's Book Council and the National Council on the Social Studies, each in their year of publication: *Save the Mustangs!*, *The School on Madison Avenue*, *God and Government*, *The Supreme Court*, and *Prisons. School* was also a Junior Literary Guild selection. *The Vitamin Puzzle* and *The Nuclear Question* were named Outstanding Science Trade Books for Children, in 1976 and 1981 respectively, by a joint committee of the CBC and the National Science Teachers Association.

SELECTED WORKS: Five Roads to the White House, 1970; We Will Be Heard: Dissent in the United States, 1972; Save the Mustangs!: How a Federal Law Is Passed, 1974; The American Congress, 1977; News or Not?, 1977; The School on Madison Avenue: Advertising and What It Teaches, 1979; The Nuclear Question, 1981; God and Government: The Separation of Church and State, 1982; The Nuclear Arms Race: Can We Survive It?, 1983; Over-the-Counter Drugs, 1984; The Supreme Court, 1987; Lies, Deception and Truth, 1988; Prisons: A System in Trouble, 1988.

SELECTED WORKS WITH MALCOLM WEISS: The Vitamin Puzzle, 1975.

ABOUT: Contemporary Authors, Vol. 45; (New Revision Series), Vol. 1; Vol. 11; Something About the Author, Vol. 30.

NICKI WEISS

January 25, 1954–

AUTHOR AND ILLUSTRATOR OF *Menj!*, etc.

Autobiographical sketch of Nicki Weiss:

NICKI WEISS

ONE RAINY DAY when I was eleven and at sleep-away camp for the summer, I was sick. I sat bundled up before the fireplace in my bunk. I watched the flames snapping and crackling in the hearth, and for a moment they looked like trees blowing in a wild wind. The next moment they seemed to be people frantically dancing. The next they appeared to be stormy waves in the ocean. I sat there for hours, watching the constant flow of changing images in the flames, one leading into the next, various expressions of the one fire.

Sometimes when I am thinking about life and what we are about, I think of that roaring fire. Like the flowing images in the flames, our lives are made up of one experience following into the next, each experience different from the one before but connected to it, forever in a state of changing. It is as if life were a path, a journey, the only thing certain being that one step leads to the next.

When I was young I had no idea that I would one day write and illustrate children's books. As a child I was always curious about the differences between ways people lived, the differences in cultures. My own parents were refugees from Vienna during World War II, and I was aware of the distinctions between my European-style household and the homes of my friends. When I was seventeen I went to live for a summer in France, with a family in the mountains. They spoke no English, so I learned to speak French rather quickly. The next summer I went to live with a Sioux Indian family on a reservation in South Dakota, where I learned to bead and how to speak a little Lakota, the Sioux language. In college I decided to study other languages so I could find out more about other cultures, and studied German, Spanish, and Chinese. I also returned to France to live for a short period.

A path can have unexpected twists and turns, and I soon found myself journeying into the art world. I became a textile designer, designing fabric for shirts, and I loved learning how to use the paints, airbrushes, and other tools and techniques for the work. After a few years I felt there was another way to express myself, that I wanted to draw, so I put together a small portfolio of drawings. I planned to only illustrate other people's stories, but someone who saw my drawings pointed out that they already told wordless stories, that I had my own stories right there.

I had never looked at my drawings that way. So I sat down and started to write my own stories, which I've been doing ever since. Then I began going to schools and libraries to read to children, and I liked it so much that I decided to become a nursery school teacher. I had a class of three year olds for one year, at which point my path took another turn, and I found myself living in Israel. For years I had wanted to travel there, to learn the language, to be part of the culture, so I went. For the past five years I have divided my year between living in Jerusalem and living in New York.

In this fire that is my life, the flames have expressed themselves in many other ways too: having a bread-baking business, being involved in the movement for animal rights, working for the homeless, working with deaf children. At this point in time I make books, and I love being able to express in them how I see life from my point of view. I am also aware that the rest of my life is before me, and the path will offer new opportunities for change and expression. I wonder what they will be.

———

Nicki Weiss was born in New York City. She received her B.A. degree from Union College in Schenectady, New York, in 1976. She also attended the School of Visual Arts for a year. She taught school at the Walden School in New York, and has been a children's author and illustrator since 1981.

If You're Happy . . . was a Book-of-the-Month Club selection.

SELECTED WORKS WRITTEN AND ILLUSTRATED: Menj!, 1981; Waiting, 1981; Chuckie, 1982; Hank and Oogie, 1982; Maude and Sally, 1983; Weekend at Muskrat Lake, 1984; Battle Day at Camp Delmont, 1985; Princess Pearl, 1986; If You're Happy and You Know It, 1987; Barney Is Big, 1988; Where Does the Brown Bear Go?, 1988; Dog-Boy-Cap-Skate, 1989; Sun-Sand-Sea-Sail, 1989.

ABOUT: Contemporary Authors, Vol. 108; Something About the Author, Vol. 33.

NADINE BERNARD WESTCOTT

June 24, 1949–

Adapter and Illustrator of *I Know an Old Lady Who Swallowed a Fly*, etc.

Autobiographical sketch of Nadine Bernard Westcott:

MY FIRST RECOLLECTION of drawing was doing sketches on the back of restaurant paper placemats. My parents would often take us to a local restaurant where it seemed to be an interminable length of time before dinner arrived. To alleviate my boredom and stave off hunger, I'd draw still lifes of my napkin and water glass. This lasted throughout my youth, but the trend was to continue into later life. No matter

what else I was doing, drawing remained a form of recreation as well as therapy. Today, I find myself fortunate enough to do it as a full-time profession.

I grew up in the quiet suburb of Fair Haven, New Jersey. I had several good friends and always one or two cats. I didn't care for dolls as such, but the few that I had I sacrificed their clothes to my favorite cat, a Siamese. I would put little dresses and bonnets on him, wheel him around in my doll carriage and make a bed for him in my clothes drawer. Strangely enough, he didn't object. These memories must have influenced me, for I tend to include cats in many of my illustrations. Cats play off well against the human characters in an illustration either by doing something humorous themselves or, by the use of their facial expressions, giving their commentary on what the humans are doing.

Except for a brief moment of fame when I won second prize in a contest for coloring the back of a Cheerios box, I never thought of taking art seriously enough to pursue it as a career. I spent my first two years in college studying to be an elementary school teacher. When I found myself spending more time on my elective art courses than studying, I switched my major to fine arts.

Upon graduation from college, I moved to Kansas City, Missouri, to work as a greeting card artist for Hallmark. I worked there among dozens of talented artists, was exposed to numerous styles and techniques and learned a great deal about the greeting card business.

Eventually though, I missed New England and decided to move to Vermont to the same town where I had spent every summer since I was ten years old. There, I met and married my husband, Bill, had our daughter, Becky, and in 1979 started Hartland Greeting Card Company.

Between my greeting card deadlines, I wrote and illustrated my first children's book. This first attempt resulted in a deluge of rejection slips. But thanks to the foresight and patience of one particular editor, I got a start. I've enjoyed it ever since.

I usually choose books that have the two elements I enjoy most in a story—humor and chaos. The main character almost always solves his dilemma with perseverance and humor.

If children can identify with the characters in my books and it makes them laugh, then perhaps in some small way, these children will learn that to be able to laugh at oneself is an important lesson to learn in life.

———

Nadine Bernard Westcott graduated from Syracuse University with a B.F.A. degree in 1971. She was married in 1975 and has a daughter. She lives in Woodstock, Vermont.

I Know an Old Lady Who Swallowed a Fly was named a Children's Choice book of 1981 by a joint committee of the Children's Book Council and the International Reading Association.

SELECTED WORKS WRITTEN AND ILLUSTRATED: The Giant Vegetable Garden, 1981; Getting Up, 1987; Going to Bed, 1987.

SELECTED WORKS ADAPTED AND ILLUSTRATED: I Know an Old Lady Who Swallowed a Fly, 1981; The Lady with the Alligator Purse, 1988; Skip to My Lou, 1989.

SELECTED WORKS ILLUSTRATED: The Hey Hey Man, by Sid Fleischman, 1979; The Emperor's New Clothes, by Hans Christian Andersen, 1984.

BARBARA WILLIAMS

JANUARY 1, 1925–

AUTHOR OF *Albert's Toothache*, etc.

Autobiographical sketch of Barbara Williams:

I WAS WRITING STORIES long before I could write my name. As a preschooler I would scribble in a tablet for hours, and

then "read" the stories I'd written to my mother as she ironed my father's shirts and handkerchiefs.

All of my grade-school teachers instantly diagnosed my overenthusiasm, and all of them except one (but that's another anecdote I won't go into) prescribed the same therapy: they assigned me the task of being classroom correspondent for the "School News and Views" column of a downtown Salt Lake City newspaper. That was how I earned my first byline at age five and continued to see my name in print regularly throughout my grade-school years.

Meanwhile (perhaps because paper was cheap and readily available in those Depression years), the same newspaper began another feature for children: a Sunday supplement devoted entirely to the contributions of students under the age of fourteen. I would spend the preceding Sunday at my father's desk, typing stories, articles, poems, party suggestions, and recipes as fast as I could move my right index finger over the keyboard and never stopping to change a sentence or correct a misspelling. It's no wonder at the end of the year I was praised as the "most prolific contributor" of the *Tribune Junior*. However, I was also praised as the contributor who submitted the "neatest" manuscripts, a fact that surprised my teacher, who had given me a check on my report card for "neatness in desks," and my mother, who secretly suspected I shared my bedroom with a family of rodents.

All of this fervor on behalf of the Salt Lake City *Tribune* did not interfere with my other writing projects. In our neighborhood I was the writer, director, casting supervisor, and hence the star of every theatrical production. And at school I was unofficially acknowledged as the classroom playwright, to whom all the teachers turned for fast (if boring and trite) dramatic manuscripts. I was also the editor of the underground school newspaper, which my cohorts and I titled *The Keyhole Tattler.*

Thus I wrote while others played. Throughout grade school, junior high school, high school, and even college, I sat at my typewriter while my friends swam, rode horses, climbed trees, threw balls, or hit them with bats and racquets. I was too uncoordinated to play at anything, though in time—and with considerable effort—I learned to strike a typewriter keyboard with all ten fingers.

Despite this preoccupation with writing, however, it never occurred to me that I would grow up to become a writer. I always insisted (it was fun to insist about such matters in the thirties and forties because people were invariably shocked to hear outrageous statements from a young girl) that I was going to become a lawyer when I grew up. My father, after all, was a lawyer, and so was the heroine of my favorite soap opera, "Portia Faces Life." More importantly, the young man I dated from the ninth grade on wanted to become a lawyer, and I wanted to be with him. Eventually we were married, but neither one of us became lawyers. He is a college professor who writes on the side. I am a writer who teaches on the side. We don't make as much money as most lawyers do, but we enjoy our occupations enormously.

One of the side benefits of our writing/

teaching careers has been the opportunity to travel. My husband has conducted tours to Europe for college students, has taught classes at U.S. Air Force bases abroad, and has given speeches and seminars in Hawaii and Alaska as well as in numerous mainland states. On many of these occasions he has taken the family with him. I, too, enjoy my opportunities to visit schools throughout the United States and participate in workshops and conferences.

Our four children are now grown and are rapidly increasing the size of our family by providing us with beautiful grandchildren.

––––––

Born in Salt Lake City, Barbara Williams received her B.A. and M.A. degrees from the University of Utah in 1946 and 1947 respectively. She was married July 5, 1946. She taught grammar, composition, and introductory literature there for twelve years, publishing two textbooks in freshman composition. She now teaches occasional classes in creative writing. Williams has also written plays, articles, short stories, and poetry. *Chester Chipmunk's Thanksgiving* won a 1979 Christopher Award. The Utah Arts Council awarded her a 1986 publication prize for *Beheaded, Survived. Albert's Toothache* was named a Notable Book of 1974 by the American Library Association. Five of Barbara Williams' books were chosen to be Children's Choice Books in their years of publication by a joint committee of the Children's Book Council and the International Reading Association; they include: *Jeremy Isn't Hungry, Where Are You . . . , and So What If I'm a Sore Loser?.* Four of her books were named Junior Literary Guild selections: *Albert's Toothache, Cornzapoppin'!, Someday, Said Mitchell, and Jeremy Isn't Hungry.*

SELECTED WORKS: Albert's Toothache, 1974; Kevin's Grandma, 1975; Cornzapoppin'!, 1976; Someday, Said Mitchell, 1976; Chester Chipmunk's Thanksgiving, 1978; Jeremy Isn't Hungry, 1978; Where Are You, Angela von Hauptmann, Now That I Need You?, 1979; Breakthrough: Women in Archaeology, 1980; So

What If I'm a Sore Loser?, 1981; Mitzi and Frederick the Great, 1984; Mitzi and the Elephants, 1985; Beheaded, Survived, 1987.

ABOUT: Contemporary Authors, Vol. 49; (New Revision Series), Vol. 1; Vol. 17; Something About the Author, Vol. 11; Who's Who, 1974-1975,

PAULA WINTER

October 25, 1929–

AUTHOR AND ILLUSTRATOR OF *The Bear and the Fly*, etc.

Autobiographical sketch of Paula Cecilia Winter:

I GREW UP in the Bronx and went to a Catholic grade school. Our first books were about saints, and to my mother's consternation, I decided to become one. Day after day I failed. I've often wondered why I took the religious teaching so seriously. None of my classmates did. That became especially clear to me when one of them hit me on the head with a brick.

After my desire for sainthood abated I got into something more realistic. I wanted a dog. My father was adamantly opposed to the idea, but when we visited my godmother after one of her dogs had puppies, she shrewdly suggested that we borrow one and bring it back on our next visit. After a week even my father was smitten. Bijou was with us till she died eighteen years later.

There were no brothers or sisters, but ever since kindergarten I've always had one very close friend. It hasn't always been the same person. Eventually it was my husband who became my best friend, but in grade school it was Joan. The two of us and Bijou loved to go hiking. Our favorite starting points were the Bronx Park and the George Washington Bridge, where we would climb down the Palisades and walk along the Hudson. On the Jersey treks we were frequently joined by a police dog, a fan of Bijou's no doubt, though I could never understand why. She paid no attention to

Paula Winter

him. Having come to us so young I don't think she ever knew she was a dog. Often Joan and I got so absorbed in our sightseeing we forgot that the return trip would take just as long. My mother was forever calling the police and reporting us missing. Once they actually found us and we got a ride home. At this point I'm sure she must have wished I'd go back to trying for sainthood.

At home my favorite pastimes, when not cavorting with Bijou, were reading and drawing. The high school I went to was Washington Irving, chosen for its three hours a day of art and its location in Manhattan, which gave me new territory to explore. Upon graduation I got a scholarship to study at the School for Art Studies. It doesn't exist anymore, but I had a great time painting there for about three years. Then it was time to get a job. After an assortment of them I settled down with fashion illustration and continued studying art at The Cooper Union night school.

In 1958 I married Harold Berson. He had a really severe case of wanderlust and we took many long and wonderful trips together, to Morocco, Spain, France, Italy, Yugoslavia, Greece, Turkey, and Tunisia. He was an author-illustrator and many of these countries became the settings for his books. We did on-the-spot drawing almost everywhere including back home in New York. We also both loved books and collected them avidly, especially art and picture books. By the time they had invaded even the closets in the kitchen where the dishes are supposed to be I suspected that we might have too many. Hal assured me it was just that our apartment was too small, and of course he was right. For many years I was mainly a painter, which I loved, but I also always wanted very much to do picture books. It was a big thrill when I finally did. It's an art form that I especially love, and I hope to do more of them.

———

Paula Winter attended The Cooper Union night school from 1952 to 1955. Her art has appeared in group shows at galleries such as the Eggleston Gallery in New York in 1951 and the Leonard Hutton Gallery in New York in 1960.

The Bear and the Fly was named a Notable Book of 1976 by the American Library Association and a Best Illustrated Book of the Year 1976 by *The New York Times.* Both *Bear* and *Sir Andrew* have been made into filmstrips.

SELECTED WORKS WRITTEN AND ILLUSTRATED: The Bear and the Fly, 1976; Sir Andrew, 1980.

SELECTED WORKS ILLUSTRATED: Crazy Brobobalou, by Jan Wahl, 1973; Where's Your Baby Brother, Becky Bunting?, by Hanne Tierney, 1979; The Forgetful Bears, by Lawrence Weinberg, 1981; The Forgetful Bears Give a Wedding, by Lawrence Weinberg, 1984.

ABOUT: Contemporary Authors, Vol. 107; Kingman, Lee and others, comps. Illustrators of Children's Books 1967-1976; Something About the Author, Vol. 48. Who's Who in America 1986-1987.

ASHLEY WOLFF

ASHLEY WOLFF

January 26, 1956–

Author and Illustrator of A Year of Beasts, etc.

Biographical sketch of Jenifer Ashley Wolff:

ASHLEY WOLFF was born in Boston, Massachusetts. The daughter of a professor and a porcelain restorer, she grew up in Vermont. She received her B.F.A. degree from the Rhode Island School of Design in 1979. She was married on September 6, 1980 and lives in San Francisco with her husband, son, and their border collie.

For a year in 1979, she was a staff artist at the *Valley Voice* in Middlebury, Vermont. She has held the same position at the *Pacific Sun* in Mill Valley, California.

She has also painted *trompe l'oeil* murals in Vermont, San Francisco, and Marin County, California.

Ashley Wolff enjoys portraying family life in her books. Her first picture book, *A Year of Birds*, was illustrated in block print style, a famliar style in her work. In her *Horn Book* review of *A Year of Beasts*, Mary M. Burns writes, "The use of substantial areas of velvety black . . . focuses attention on the action, recalling the handsome nursery books of the late-nineteenth and early-twentieth centuries. Yet the rhythm of the composition and the variations in perspective are both dynamic and contemporary in feeling."

A Year of Birds was named a 1984 Notable Book by the American Library Association. *The Bells of London* was named a Junior Literary Guild selection and was exhibited at the 1985 International Children's Book Fair in Bologna, Italy. *Block City* was named a 1989 Notable Children's Trade Book in the Field of Social Studies by a joint committee of the Children's Book Council and the National Council on the Social Studies.

SELECTED WORKS WRITTEN AND ILLUSTRATED: A Year of Birds, 1984; The Bells of London, 1985; Only the Cat Saw, 1985; A Year of Beasts, 1986.

SELECTED WORKS ILLUSTRATED: Block City, by Robert Louis Stevenson, 1988; Who Is Coming to Our House?, by Joseph Slate, 1988.

ABOUT: Contemporary Authors, Vol. 118; Something About the Author, Vol. 50.

AUDREY WOOD

1948–

AUTHOR OF *King Bidgood's in the Bathtub*, etc.

Biographical sketch of Audrey Wood:

AUDREY WOOD was born in Little Rock, Arkansas. Her earliest memories are of living in Sarasota, Florida, near the winter quarters of the Ringling Brothers Circus, where her father, an art student, repainted sets and where she enjoyed the acquaintance of the circus workers. She remembers them telling her stories, and she later became a storyteller to her two younger sisters.

When she was two, her family moved to San Miguel, Mexico, in a trailer. They traveled with a band of gypsies, and the young child learned Spanish as her first language. She was reading both English and Spanish at the age of three, and the family lived in Mexico until she was five.

"Since the fifteenth century," Wood writes, her family was a family of artists. Her father showed her how to use materials, and her mother was an excellent storyteller. There were lots of books in the home, and as early as fourth grade, she knew that she wanted to write and illustrate children's books, which she now sees as "a composite of many disciplines—art, music, drama, literature, and even dance."

Her mother enrolled Wood in Montessori school because of her early ability to read. She herself later chose to attend Mount St. Mary's Girls Academy, a Roman Catholic school, even though she wasn't Catholic. At age fifteen she became active in an arts organization in Arkansas that exposed her to artists from Europe and from New York.

During the late 1960s, she moved to Berkeley, California, were she met Don Wood. They were married November 21, 1969, and traveled in the Yucatan and other parts of Mexico, and Guatemala. She and her husband owned and operated a book and import shop in Arkansas from 1970 to 1975, and then the two moved to Santa Barbara, California. Their son was born in 1973. Wood became a full-time author and illustrator of children's books in 1978.

Her second book, *Moonflute*, was illustrated by Don Wood. After her manuscript was accepted and a list of possible illustrators sent to her, she suggested her husband for the job, and his samples were accepted.

Audrey Wood has some advice for those who ask where she gets her story ideas. "I have a number of simple methods that I use today, as a professional, and they are the same methods I used to amuse myself and my sisters when I was a child. Here are a few examples.

"Keep a simple diary or journal. A diary need be nothing more than a few notes scribbled in a blank book each day, or even each week. You can include quick descriptions of your life and your surroundings, as well as observations such as what makes you feel happy, sad, thoughtful, angry, foolish, or whatever. Paste in pages of magazine articles, poems, notes from friends, or cartoons. The function of a diary is to record any and all things that *interest you* and therefore might lead to a story.

"If you are a child and you keep a diary, it may be very valuable to you later as a writer. With a diary, you will never forget what it feels like to be a child.

"Become an Imagineer. Find a quiet time each day, perhaps when you are resting in bed, or before you go to sleep. Think about a wonderful place where you would like to be. Close you eyes and begin to create a world of your own. Make up characters. See them doing things, having adventures. Allow your imagination to take you anywhere. It's like watching a movie.

"Although stories may not develop directly from this exercise, being able to imagine worlds and let your mind run free is a great help during the actual writing process.

"With a friend, sit down and begin to tell a story. The first person begins, 'Once upon a time . . . ' and continues until she runs out of ideas. Then the next person picks up the story and takes it from there.

"If you are an adult, search through your childhood memories and rediscover what it felt like to live in the world of a child, the joys, the fears, and the dreams."

Audrey Wood has one son. She is a member of the Society of Children's Book Writers.

King Bidgood's in the Bathtub was named a 1986 Caldecott Honor Book by the American Library Association. It was also a 1985 ALA Notable Book and received a certificate of merit from the Society of Illustrators in 1985. *The Napping House* was a 1984 ALA Notable Book. It won the 1984 Golden Kite Award for illustration from the Society of Children's Book Writers and was named a *New York Times* Best Illustrated Book of 1984. The Southern California Council on Literature for Children and Young People conferred their 1985 illustration award on *The Napping House*, and it was named a 1985 Children's Choice Book by a joint committee of the International Reading Association and the Children's Book Council. *The Napping House* and *King Bidgood* were made into filmstrips.

SELECTED WORKS WRITTEN AND ILLUSTRATED: Magic Shoelaces, 1980; Tooth Fairy, 1985; Detective Valentine, 1987; Tugford Wanted to Be Bad, 1988.

SELECTED WORKS WRITTEN: Moonflute, 1980; Tickleoctopus, 1980; Twenty-four Robbers, 1980; The Napping House, 1984; King Bidgood's in the Bathtub, 1985; The Three Sisters, 1986; Heckedy Peg, 1987; Elbert's Bad Word (co-illustrated), 1988; The Horrible Holiday, 1988.

SELECTED WORKS WRITTEN WITH DON WOOD: The Big Hungry Bear, 1984.

ABOUT: Horn Book September/October 1986; Something About the Author, Vol. 44; Vol. 50.

DON WOOD

May 4, 1945–

ILLUSTRATOR OF *King Bidgood's in the Bathtub*, etc.

Autobiographical sketch of Don Wood:

AS A CHILD, I didn't draw portraits, nor did I paint picturesque landscapes to hang on the wall. I drew stories.

There was never enough paper for me to draw on. In those days fresh laundry arrived wrapped in a crisp, tan paper. Often the sheets of tan wrapping paper were quite large, since they contained a stack of sheets and tablecloths. Sometimes they covered the entire kitchen table.

My mother solved the problem of my paper shortage by suggesting I draw on the tan laundry paper. It worked beautifully. I remember opening the closet where the ironing board was kept and there, on a shelf in the back, was a steadily growing stack of neatly folded laundry paper she had saved for me. What riches. It was more than I could use in a lifetime.

With this new, and larger paper, I could draw my stories as long as I wanted to. In fact I no longer had to divide them up into pages. I would spread out a huge sheet of paper, start the action wherever I wanted, and let it go in any direction. Needless to say, only I understood the story when it was finished, but I enjoyed myself immensely.

In my art classes in high school, and especially in college, I began to learn what the world expected from ambitious, young artists. The world, at that time, expected single works of art, preferably with no story to them at all. Unfortunately, I listened to what the world expected, and forgot what I wanted. You would be surprised at how easy it is to do this. I stopped drawing stories, and began to make single works of art with almost no stories.

Naturally, after many years of working this way, I became unhappy with my art. I gave up art for six years. For someone who has been drawing as long as he can remember, this was a serious step.

Finally I started drawing and painting again, but this time I drew and painted stories. I've been happy as an artist ever since then. Isn't it strange that in the fourth grade I knew more about what I wanted as an artist, than I did as a young adult with a Master of Fine Arts degree.

Nearly every day I work at illustrating children's picture books and I enjoy it immensely. When I wake up in the morning I think, "I get to go to work today," not "I have to go to work today."

I paint in a small studio in our backyard shaded by a large palm tree that my son and I transplanted when it was just a wild seedling growing in our lawn. Because Santa Barbara has a mild climate, there are always flowers blooming around the studio. I especially like the big, red calla lillies and the mysterious jasmine that only blooms at night.

My wife Audrey also writes and illustrates children's books. She loves animals, so there are always a number of them around. Gizmo, one of our cats, is usually with me when I paint. If you look closely, you can always find one or two of her cat hairs in each of my paintings. Fortunately, they don't show up in the books. Audrey's big, forty-year-old desert tortoise lives in a pen right next to my studio, and when I walk between the studio and the house I pass five aviaries. Two of them are filled with hundreds of colorful finches. The others contain larger, more exotic birds such as the fiery cherry-head parrots that quack like ducks every night when the sun goes down.

All in all, it's the sort of place where I could illustrate books a long time, and I think I'll try to do just that.

———

Born in Atwater, California, Don Wood was raised on a farm in the central San Joaquin Valley where fruits and vegetables were grown. He and his brother worked eighteen-hour shifts when they were thirteen years old, and Wood was impressed that his father's hard work and ambition resulted in their family's continued prosperity, from very humble beginnings. His mother died when he was in the second grade, and his father remarried.

Wood received a B.A. degree from the University of California in Santa Barbara in 1967 and an M.F.A. degree from the California College of Arts and Crafts in 1969. He has been an editorial illustrator, a graphic designer, and, since 1976, a magazine and book illustrator. He and his wife owned and operated a book store and import shop from 1970 to 1975, and he has worked as a logger, a sailmaker, and a substitute teacher. He has one son, born in 1973.

His work has been exhibited at a show at New York City's Metropolitan Museum of Art, "The Artist as Illustrator," and has appeared on the cable TV series "Faerie Tale Theatre." It was also included in the Society of Illustrators Annual Exhibition in 1986.

King Bidgood's in the Bathtub was named a 1986 Caldecott Honor Book by the American Library Association. It was also a 1985 ALA Notable Book and received a certificate of merit from the Society of Illustrators in 1985. *The Napping House* was a 1984 Notable Book, and won the 1984 Golden Kite Award for illustration from the Society of Children's Book Writers. It was also named a *New York Times* Best Illustrated Book of 1984. The book also received the 1985 Southern California Council on Literature for Children and Young People Award for illustration, and was named a 1985 Children's Choice Book by a joint committee of the International Reading Association and the Children's Book Council. *The Napping House* and *King Bidgood* were both made into filmstrips.

SELECTED WORKS WRITTEN WITH AUDREY WOOD AND ILLUSTRATED: The Big Hungry Bear, 1984.

SELECTED WORKS WRITTEN BY AUDREY WOOD AND ILLUSTRATED: Moonflute, 1980; Quick as a Cricket, 1982; The Napping House, 1984; King Bidgood's in the Bathtub, 1985; Heckedy Peg, 1987.

SELECTED WORKS WRITTEN BY AUDREY WOOD AND CO-ILLUSTRATED: Elbert's Bad Word, 1988.

ABOUT: Horn Book September/October 1986; Something About the Author, Vol. 44; Vol. 50.

BETTY REN WRIGHT

June 15, 1927–

AUTHOR OF *The Dollhouse Murders*, etc.

Autobiographical sketch of Betty Ren Wright:

JUST THE OTHER DAY I found the notebook that made me decide—at the age of seven—that I wanted to be A WRITER. It's a black loose-leaf, and across the front is lettered *Betty Ren's Poems*. For three years I filled the lined pages and thought about how wonderful it was to be writing a book.

The wonder has never ended. Poetry remained my primary interest until I reached Milwaukee-Downer College and Miss Frances Hadley, most remarkable and encour-

Betty Ren Wright

aging of teachers. I began contributing to the college literary magazine, and gradually short stories took the place of poetry.

Soon after graduation, in 1949, I became an editorial assistant in a large midwestern publishing company. Gradually I was drawn into the world of children's books, until I found I was living a peculiar kind of double life. Juvenile books, particularly picture books, filled my days, while adult magazine fiction took my spare time (early in the morning/late at night).

My first published short stories appeared in *Alfred Hitchcock's Mystery Magazine.* Later I wrote for *Redbook, The Ladies' Home Journal, Young Miss, Seventeen,* and many other publications. At the same time I continued to edit juvenile manuscripts, and I wrote a number of picture-storybooks of my own. Picture books were fun; I loved sending a story to an illustrator and seeing how his imagination and talent enriched it.

From 1968 to 1976 I was managing editor of juvenile books. I traveled, met a lot of fascinating people, lived in a cozy, sun-filled apartment in a haunted house—and continued to write in every free minute.

The year 1976 brought a bicentennial celebration for the United States, and it was a memorable year in my personal life as well. One sunny day—in Wisconsin's loveliest month, October—I married George Frederiksen, a Wisconsin artist and former art director. Our wedding reception was held in the brick and redwood house where we've lived ever since, surrounded by woods and fields. On that afternoon I became a country person instead of a city person, and a wife, stepmother, and stepgrandmother as well. My husband's three children were grown, married, and no longer in need of mothering, but grand-mothering turned out to be a special joy. (The five we began with have become eight.)

Two years later I decided to step out from behind my editing desk and become a full-time wife-and-free-lance-writer. We fixed up an efficient, professional-looking office in one bedroom, but I seldom work there. My favorite writing place is the breakfast nook in the kitchen, with Belle, our black standard poodle, at my feet and Nougat, our orange tiger cat, curled up in the top of the typewriter-paper box. It's a handy spot for keeping an eye on the bird feeder and occasional deer that wanders out of the woods, for making coffee, and for watching whatever's in the oven.

With hours of available writing time at last, I expected to concentrate on short stories, but I enjoy reading books for ten- to fourteen-year-olds, so I decided to try my hand at one first. *Getting Rid of Marjorie* was the result; it's a story about a stepgrand-mother who experienced all the bad things that, happily, did *not* happen to me. I enjoyed writing it so much that I started another book at once. Often my books turn out to be ghost stories, since I've always enjoyed supernatural tales myself, but I like to write other kinds of books as well. I still write an occasional short story, but I think—no, I'm sure—I've found the audience I enjoy most.

————

Betty Ren Wright was born in Wakefield, Michigan. She received her B.A. degree from Milwaukee-Downer College (now part of Lawrence University) in 1949. She also studied at the University of Wisconsin and at Breadloaf Writers' Conference at Middlebury College. She worked at Western Publishing Company from 1949 to 1978. She was married October 9, 1976. She is a member of Allied Authors, the Society of Children's Book Writers, the Council for Wisconsin Writers, and Phi Beta Kappa. She received the Lawrence University Alumni Service Award for contributions to children's literature in 1973.

Wright's books have won many children's book awards that are voted upon by children. Six of her books have been named Junior Literary Guild selections: *The Secret Window, The Dollhouse Murders, Christina's Ghost, The Summer of Mrs. MacGregor, A Ghost in the Window*, and *The Pike River Phantom. Dollhouse Murders* was nominated for a 1984 Edgar Allan Poe Award by the Mystery Writers of America. *Ghosts Beneath Our Feet* was named a 1985 Children's Choice Book by a joint committee of the Children's Book Council and the International Reading Association. *Why Do I Daydream?* and *Christina's Ghost* were also Children's Choice Books, in 1982 and 1986 respectively. The latter won the 1985 Council for Wisconsin Writers Juvenile Award. *My Sister Is Different* was named a 1981 Notable Children's Trade Book in the Field of Social Studies by a joint committee of the National Council on the Social Studies and the CBC.

SELECTED WORKS: The Day Our TV Broke Down, 1980; I Like Being Alone, 1981; My Sister Is Different, 1981; Why Do I Daydream, 1981; Getting Rid of Marjorie, 1981; The Secret Window, 1982; The Dollhouse Murders, 1983; Ghosts Beneath Our Feet, 1984; Christina's Ghost, 1985; The Summer of Mrs. MacGregor, 1986; A Ghost in the Window, 1987; The Pike River Phantom, 1988.

ABOUT: Something About the Author, Vol. 48.

ARTHUR YORINKS

August 21, 1953–

AUTHOR OF *Hey, Al*, etc.

Biographical sketch of Arthur Yorinks, who also writes under the pen name "Alan Yaffe":

ARTHUR YORINKS was born in Roslyn, New York. When he was six, he began seven years' training as a classical pianist with Robert Bedford, who influenced him with his professionalism and perfectionism. He also cultivated a love of art while watching his mother, a fashion illustrator, draw and paint. Partly because his siblings were older than he, he spent a lot of time alone as a child. As a teenager, he traveled to Manhattan with a friend, seeing art in galleries and museums.

In high school, Yorinks discovered the art of picture books, particularly the work of Tomi Ungerer, William Steig, and Maurice Sendak. At sixteen, he presented himself at Sendak's door with a bundle of stories, and the bold encounter led to a long friendship.

Yorinks graduated from high school a year early, and decided not to go to college. He did attend the New School for Social Research and Hofstra New College in 1971. He began to study ballet and acting, and performed and wrote for The American Mime Theatre. From 1972 to 1979, he was an instructor in theatre arts at Cornell University in Ithaca, New York. In 1979, he founded the Moving Theatre, writing and serving as Artistic Director. His plays were produced at Hunter College Playhouse, at the Cornelia Street Cafe, and at South Street Theatre, among other theaters, in the seventies and eighties. Yorinks also has written librettos for several operas, with "Leipziger Kerzenspiel" produced at Mount Holyoke College in 1984 and "The Juniper Tree" produced at the American Repertory Theater in Cambridge, Massachusetts in 1985. He also wrote the libretto for "The Fall of the House of Usher," composed by Philip Glass.

ARTHUR YORINKS

During this time, he attempted to place his stories with a publisher, but even though he sold one, the story languished without an illustrator for a long time, to Yorinks' great frustration.

It was Maurice Sendak who suggested that Richard Egielski, illustrator of Yorinks' Caldecott Medal-winning *Hey, Al*, and Yorinks collaborate on books. *Sid and Sol* was their first book together, followed by *Louis the Fish*, *It Happened in Pinsk*, *Hey, Al*, and *Bravo Minski*. Yorinks is a great reader and drew upon Kafka's *The Metamorphosis*, in which a man is changed into an insect, for the story of *Louis the Fish*. The author has also said that his books begin "on a psychological level," and he also has said that music is very important to his writing. Alice Bregman Miller, writing in *The New York Times*, calls Yorinks' dialogue in *Company's Coming* "as well timed as the best comedy act." The book is illustrated by David Small.

Arthur Yorinks has also written a full-length story ballet commissioned by the Hartford Ballet Company, and is working with Maurice Sendak to develop the Sundance Children's Theater, a national children's theater associated with Robert Redford's Sundance Institute. He is married and lives in New York City. In addition to winning the 1987 Caldecott Medal given by the American Library Association, *Hey Al* was also named a 1986 ALA Notable Book. A video called "Story by Arthur Yorinks, Pictures by Richard Egielski" became available from Farrar, Straus and Giroux in 1987. *Louis the Fish* was named a Reading Rainbow Book. *Company's Coming* was a 1988 ALA Notable Book.

SELECTED WORKS: Sid and Sol, 1977; Louis the Fish, 1980; It Happened in Pinsk, 1983; Hey, Al, 1986; Bravo, Minski, 1988; Company's Coming, 1988.

SELECTED WORKS AS ALAN YAFFE: The Magic Meatballs, 1979.

ABOUT: Contemporary Authors, Vol. 106; New York Times Book Review January 10, 1988; Sendak, Maurice. Caldecott & Co.: Notes on Books and Pictures; Something About the Author, Vol. 33; Vol. 49.

PAUL O. ZELINSKY

February 14, 1953–

RETELLER   AND   ILLUSTRATOR   OF *Rumpelstiltskin*, etc.

Autobiographical sketch of Paul O. Zelinsky:

BEFORE I WAS grown up, what I wanted the most was to be grown up. Still, one of the nicer parts of not being was the luxury of changing my mind about what I would become when I finally got to be grown up.

I had a lot of ideas, and making children's books wasn't among them. I was going to be a ventriloquist or an astronomer or an architect, and design houses growing out of mountainsides or arching over waterfalls. I would be a painter, write musical comedies, learn all there was to know about every animal on earth. I would work in natural history museums making dioramas where elk and lemmings graze on the arctic tundra, bathed in a pink twilight glow. I would make the elk, and the lemmings, I would make the tundra, I would set up the pink lights. It strikes me that most of my plans involved being someone who makes things. To this day making things remains one of the greatest pleasures I know.

I was born in one suburb of Chicago and grew up mostly in the next one over. But my father, who was a college professor, would often take a year off to teach somewhere else, so my family moved quite a bit. I was regularly the new kid in a strange class, making a few friends and losing them again at the end of the year. My drawing, though, was a constant; it could never be left behind, and it needed no one but me. And I drew easily, and always. So I was usually the class artist, wherever the class happened to be.

Every couple of years I would imagine a new civilization, sometimes human, sometimes not, and fill it with interesting residents. I liked to illustrate my papers for school, sometimes even my exams. I would try keeping my notebooks neat and clean, but they would always end up decorated from top to bottom. When it got really bad I tried to hide my pen from myself, but that never quite worked. In high school I learned printmaking and made etchings and linoleum cuts to accompany the stories we were reading in English class, and poems my friends wrote. Why I didn't see all this as leading up to a career in illustration, I will never know. It wasn't until college, when I took a course in the history and making of children's books (it was the first class Maurice Sendak taught), that I said to myself, "I've been doing this all along!" and, collaborating with a writer in the class, started trying to get published. It wasn't long before we had a story accepted, and then it wasn't long before the accepting publisher was bought and dissolved by a larger publisher, and it wasn't until five years later, with an M.F.A. in Painting and a fast-fading desire to be a painting teacher, that I set out for New York to be an illustrator. This time things went a little better, and they've gone better ever since.

I've been able to illustrate books that are so different from one another that I always get to learn new things: new materials and ways of drawing, and all sorts of information. When you illustrate a book there's a lot you have to know. You wouldn't put a telephone on George Washington's bedside table, for instance. But would you show a lantern? Or a candle? What would it look like? Should there be a tablecloth? What would the rugs be like? The paintings on the wall? The frames? You can see that just to draw George Washington's bedside it would be best to know a lot about how people lived in Revolutionary America. I've had to learn about Victorian New England this way, and Imperial Russia. I've had to buy mice and borrow cats to learn enough about how those animals look and act. And I feel as if I know, at least until I forget it, all there is to know about the development of the spinning wheel.

It's a great deal of fun, this work. I learn things. I make things. And I feel I still get to change my mind all the time about what I want to do— my mind changes with every new book I take on. And when I realize that there are people around the country who will read my books and (I hope) enjoy the pictures, I think: How could I have been so lucky!

———

Paul O. Zelinsky was born in Evanston, a suburb of Chicago. He received a B.A. degree from Yale College in 1974 and an M.F.A. degree from Tyler School of Art in 1976. He was married December 31, 1981. He is a member of the Graphic Artists Guild and the Society of Children's Book Writers.

Hansel and Gretel was an American Library Association Caldecott Honor Book for 1985. *Rumpelstiltskin* was a 1987 Caldecott Honor Book.

Emily Upham's Revenge was nominated for a 1979 Edgar Allan Poe Award by the Mystery Writers of America. *The Maid and the Mouse* was selected for the Horn Book Graphic Gallery, a showcase of excellent books honored by *The Horn Book Magazine*. It was also a *New York Times* Best Illustrated Book of 1981.

The Sun's Asleep was a Bratislave Biennale selection, as was *Rumpelstiltskin*. Both the latter and *Mrs. Lovewright* were Reading Rainbow Books. *Ralph S. Mouse* won a 1982 Golden Kite Award for fiction. *Dear Mr. Henshaw* won the 1984 Newbery Award from the ALA and a 1984 Christopher Award. *Mrs. Lovewright* was also a *New York Times* Best Illustrated Book, of 1985.

Zelinsky's ALA Notable Books include *How I Hunted the Little Fellows* in 1979, *Hansel and Gretel* in 1984, and *Rumpelstiltskin* in 1986. Two of his books were named Children's Choices by a joint committee of the International Reading Association and the Children's Book Council: *Maid and the Mouse* in 1982, and *Mrs. Lovewright* in 1986. *How I Hunted the Little Fellows*, *The Maid and the Mouse*, and *Rumpelstiltskin* also appeared in AIGA Book Shows.

SELECTED WORKS ADAPTED OR RETOLD AND ILLUSTRATED: The Maid and the Mouse and the Odd-Shaped House, 1981; The Lion and the Stoat, 1984; Rumpelstiltskin, 1986.

SELECTED WORKS ILLUSTRATED: Emily Upham's Revenge, by Avi, 1978; How I Hunted the Little Fellows, by Boris Zhitkov, 1979; What Amanda Saw, by Naomi Lazard, 1981; Ralph S. Mouse, by Beverly Cleary, 1982; The Sun's Asleep Behind the Hill, adapted by Mirra Ginsberg, 1982; Dear Mr. Henshaw, by Beverly Cleary, 1983; Zoo Doings: Animal Poems, by Jack Prelutsky, 1983; Hansel and Gretel, retold by Rika Lesser, 1984; The Story of Mrs. Lovewright and Purrless Her Cat, by Lore Segal, 1985; The Random House Book of Humor for Children, selected by Pamela Pollack, 1988.

ABOUT: Contemporary Authors, Vol. 121; Horn Book May/June 1986; November/December 1976; Something About the Author, Vol. 33; Vol. 49.

DIRK ZIMMER

October 2, 1943–

AUTHOR AND ILLUSTRATOR OF *The Trick-or-Treat Trap*, etc.

Autobiographical sketch of Dirk Zimmer:

I WAS BORN October 2, 1943— "as a very small child," as one of my favored artists, the Dadaist Kurt Schwitters, puts it in his autobiography. My father died when he was thirty-three and I was three years old, which caused me, according to my mother's recollection, to bang my fist on the kitchen table somewhere in a peaceful little place in the Austrian Alps, exclaiming: Now *I'm* the master of the house—where is my cider, where is my beer?!

From the beginning my mother encouraged my urge and talent to do what my father had been dreaming of as a profession for himself if it had not been made impossible by Hitler's Germany and WW II: to draw and paint. So I started to draw picture-stories before I was able to read and write (my older sister helped me out with that; ach, where is she now?) and I still consider the visual aspect of information as more than just a decorative supplement for a "superior" text (remarks the sulking illustrator). As a Visual Chauvinist I declare: Language Is The Source of People's Alien-

Z/mmER

ation From Nature! Ah, but here—look at this beautiful picture with its bright colors and crisp lines. That's something else! (I could go on like this: What? You don't agree? That's because you're full of language! But I don't want to get into a serious fight over this. . . .)

My first LOVE was Pippi Longstocking, although there were certain problems I had to think through first before I would propose marriage to a person like Pippi (she could lift her horse with one arm and two policemen at the same time with her other arm; now, how would I look compared to that?). Then I got into Doctor Dolittle for a while, and when I finally found out that these and other stories and pictures (like the work of Wilhelm Busch and illustrated versions of the Grimms' fairy tales and Tove Jansson's "Moomins" and Disney Comics and more and more stuff) were made and thought out by humans and not by some angels and goblins and the like, I was really thrilled. It was like an illumination (which reminds me: TV was entirely unheard of and unlooked at at that time)!

I hated school; there were not many good teachers left after the war . . . In short, I couldn't wait to get out of it. I decided not to go on to finish high school.

I left school after ten years and was eventually accepted at the Academy of Fine Arts in Hamburg, West Germany, where I studied painting under Professor Thiemann, a student of Kandinsky and Klee at the Bauhaus. It was a grand old time, a never-ending party and quite productive in spite of all the fun and sweet confusion. When I finished there, which was in 1969, I took a trip to the United States for the first time. I painted for a gallery in Munich, trying to continue my own variation of Dadaism and Surrealism, a heavy brew and a impossible to keep up as a life style. Soon my head was dangling down like an overweight bud from an undernourished flower (this was indeed the era of the flower children; but I was far away from childlike things).

———

In America, Dirk Zimmer met Andy Warhol, who, he says, "did NOT" tell him to stop painting conventional pictures, but Zimmer stopped painting, anyway. He spent three years doing film work, starting in West Berlin, doing "underground stuff" with Super-8mm film. For two years he worked on the filming of the Valley Curtain Project of the artist Christo, the hanging of a huge curtain near Rifle, Colorado. A period of inactivity and being a "lucky bum" followed in West Berlin, and Zimmer ended up in the U.S. without a portfolio, merely a small journal filled with writings from Genesis, Jung, Nietsche, and Crumb, decorated with his tiny drawings. He procured work as an illustrator based on the journals, beginning with his first children's book in 1978. He now lives in New York State.

Bony-Legs, Estaban and the Ghost, and *In a Dark, Dark Room* were named Notable Books by the American Library Association in their years of publication.

SELECTED WORKS WRITTEN AND ILLUSTRATED: The Trick-or-Treat Trap, 1982.

SELECTED WORKS ILLUSTRATED: Felix in the Attic,

by Larry Bograd, 1978; Egon, by Larry Bograd, 1980; Mean Jake and the Devils, by William H. Hooks, 1981; The Star Rocker, by Joseph Slate, 1981; The Sky Is Full of Song, edited by Lee Bennett Hopkins, 1983; Esteban and the Ghost, by Sibyl Hancock, 1983; Bony-Legs, by Joanna Cole, 1983; In a Dark, Dark Room and Other Scary Stories, by Alvin Schwartz, 1984; Poor Gertie, by Larry Bograd, 1986; The Naked Bear: Folktales of the Iroquois, edited by John Bierhorst, 1987; The Iron Giant, by Ted Hughes, 1988; Windy Day: Stories and Poems, edited by Caroline Feller Bauer, 1988; John Tabor's Ride, by Edward Day, 1989.

LISBETH ZWERGER

May 26, 1954–

Illustrator of *Little Red Cap*, etc.

Autobiographical sketch of Lisbeth Zwerger:

I WAS BORN in Vienna, Austria, roughly halfway between the so-called Blue Danube in one direction, and the Big Wheel of *The Third Man* fame in the other.

My parents, both of whom were artistic, encouraged me throughout my childhood to paint and draw, and I spent much of my free time doing both, either alone or working on a 'project' with my younger sister. One of our early works, a four-meter-long mural depicting animals in a jungle, still hangs in my parents' home.

Like all children in Austria, I grew up in a world of fairy tales; in a way they are very much a part of our tradition. I read many stories as a child and I think it was inevitable that my love for drawing and the strong influence of stories from writers such as the Grimms, Hoffman, and Andersen should lead me to illustration. I think even as a child I always much preferred to illustrate than, say, to draw something direct from nature.

As I grew older I began to drift away from illustration, I did the occasional drawing here and there, but it wasn't until I attended The High School of Applied Arts in Vienna that I really became involved again.

Sadly my rediscovered enthusiasm soon began to fade under the constant criticism from my teachers. They were very anti-illustration and I soon found myself in the uncomfortable position of not agreeing with their ideas of what I should be doing. They wanted me to do one thing while I wanted to do something else. They tried hard to push all thoughts of illustrating from my mind and I drifted into a phase of boredom and disillusionment. This time I dropped out of college and gave up drawing altogether.

About a year later I was shown a book illustrated by Arthur Rackham and suddenly I knew what I wanted to do. Seeing those illustrations gave me the 'push' that I needed, but above all they gave me the courage to go ahead and illustrate again.

My first published book was E.T.A. Hoffman's *The Strange Child*, and this was followed by other 'classics' from well-known writers. At first it seemed to me that the list of possible stories for me to illustrate was endless, but slowly a certain pattern of choice began to emerge; I became very selective and found many stories to be unsuitable. I tried hard to get away from the sweet-Princess-who-through-her-good-deeds-manages- to-marry-a-handsome-Prince type of story, and concentrate more on stories with a strong, likeable character. A character with whom I can identify and whom I can feel something for.

Consequently, finding the right story has proved to be quite difficult at times, and is probably my biggest problem, but all in all it is a nice problem to have, and the only answer is to keep on searching, keep on drawing, and above all keep on reading!

———

In the work of Heath Robinson, Dulac, Beatrix Potter, and Ernest Shepard, Lisbeth Zwerger sees examples of literature and illustration complimenting one another. She also says that suitable stories for her to illustrate are, to her, pieces of literature rather than good messages for children. She is married to an Englishman and lives in Vienna. She collects picture books and books on old photography and textiles.

The books Lisbeth Zwerger illustrates have won many awards in Austria, and she has won the Golden Apple at the International Biennal of Illustration at Bratislava in 1985, for *The Selfish Giant*. She has also been nominated for the 1986 Hans Christian Andersen Award. Three of her books have been named *New York Times* Best Illustrated Books of the Year: *The Gift of the Magi* in 1982, *The Legend of Rosepetal* in 1985, and *Little Red Cap* in 1983. *Little Red Cap* was also chosen to appear in the Graphic Gallery, a showcase of excellent books honored by *The Horn Book Magazine. Hansel and Gretel* was named a Notable Book of 1980 by the American Library Association.

SELECTED WORKS ILLUSTRATED: Hansel and Gretel, by the Grimm Brothers, 1980; Thumbeline, by Hans Christian Andersen, 1980; The Seven Ravens, by The Grimm Brothers, 1981; The Gift of the Magi, by O. Henry, 1982; The Swineherd, by Hans Christian Andersen, 1982; Litte Red Cap, by the Grimm Brothers, 1983; The Nightingale, by Hans Christian Andersen, 1984; The Selfish Giant, by Oscar Wilde, 1984; The Strange Child, by E.T.A. Hoffman, 1984; The Deliverers of Their Country, by Edith Nesbit, 1985; The Legend of Rosepetal, by Clemens Brentano, 1985; The Canterville Ghost, by Oscar Wilde, 1986; The Nutcracker, by E.T.A. Hoffman, 1987; A Christmas Carol, by Charles Dickens, 1988.

Authors and Illustrators Included in This Series

The following list indicates the volume in which each individual may be found:

J—THE JUNIOR BOOK OF AUTHORS, second edition (1951)

M—MORE JUNIOR AUTHORS (1963)

3—THIRD BOOK OF JUNIOR AUTHORS (1972)

4—FOURTH BOOK OF JUNIOR AUTHORS AND ILLUSTRATORS (1978)

5—FIFTH BOOK OF JUNIOR AUTHORS AND ILLUSTRATORS (1983)

6—SIXTH BOOK OF JUNIOR AUTHORS AND ILLUSTRATORS (1989)

Picture Credits

Arnold Adler, Carole S. Adler; *Charles Adams*, Douglas Hill; *Richard Allen*, Allen Say; *Australia Council*, Ruth Park; *Donna L. Bessant*, Ashley Wolff; ©*Bildt News*, Etienne Delessert; *Liz Bordow*, Thacher Hurd; *George Calvert*, Patricia Calvert; *David Carlstrom*, Nancy White Carlstrom; *Paul Carter*, Dorothy Hinshaw Patent; ©*1986 Brian Crimmins*, Tor Seidler; *Susie Cushner*, Jan Brett; *Carole Cutner*, Jan Ormerod; ©*Arthur Montes De Oca 1988*, Gloria D. Miklowitz; *Mary Ellen Dronzek*, Kevin Henkes; *Lennart Edling*, Barbro Lindgren; *Nadine Edris*, Paul B. Janeczko; *Madeleine Ellis*, Audrey Wood; *Roberta Bryan Fair*, Corinda Bryan Cauley; *Sally Foster*, Colby Rodowsky; *Gene Furr*, Suzanne Newton; *George Gray Photography*, James Haskins; *Ed Gilford*, Bijou Le Tord; ©*1987 Elizabeth Gilliland*, Lillian Morrison; *David Godlis*, David Adler; *Jay Golden*, Miriam Chaikin; ©*1988 Duff Gummere*, Dirk Zimmer; *Jay Hague*, Judith St. George; *Van Hallan*, Thomas Locher; *Sally Stone Halvorson*, Susan Shreve; *Kevin Hatt*, Henrik Drescher; *Donal Holway*, Susan Beth Pfeffer; *Raymond Houte*, Betty Ren Wright; *Robert Hudson*, Mavis Jukes; *Art Hupy*, Ted Rand; *Betsy Imershein*, James Howe; *Norman P. Jacob*, Mary Downing Hahn; ©*1988 Keith E. Jacobson*, Marylin Hafner; *M. Janek*, Peter Sis; *J.P. & Co.*

Photographers, Tony Johnson; *Tzvi King*, Lloyd Bloom; ©*1988 Judy Klyn*, Felicia Bond; *Christopher Knight*, Kathryn Lasky; *Gerry Levinson*, Riki Levinson; *Ralph Lewin*, Jerry Pinkney; ©*Joel Marion*, Jan Greenberg; *Doug Martin*, Dean Hughes; *Daniel Marzani*, Charlotte Pomerantz; *Benner McGee*, Bruce McMillan; ©*Gertraud Middelhauve/Verlag Koln*, Helme Heine; *Teresa Miller*, Barbara Ann Porte; *Judith Nulty*, Patricia MacLachlan; *Charles Osgood*, ©*1988 Chicago Tribune Company*, Russell Freedman; *A. Earl Pamfilie*, Judith Hendershot; *Wil Panich*, Jamie Gilson; ©*1986 Mary Randlett*, B. Helen Berger; *Marilyn Sanders*, Sue Alexander; *Andrew Sciavlino*, Chris Conover; *Andrew Sharmat*, Mitchell Sharmat; ©*1987 Lauren Shay*, Janet Taylor Lisle; *Howard Evan Smith*, Robert Kimmel Smith; ©*Lisl Steiner*, Jay Bennett; *David Sweet*, Raffi; *Charles Trentelman*, Margaret Rostowski; *Stephen Troetouides*, Demi; *Shirley Waldron*, "Hadley Irwin"; *Annie Wells*, Ivy Ruckman; ©*Lauren Wojtyla*, Richard Egielski, Arthur Yorinks; *Reassurance Wonder*, Barry Moser; ©*Diane Woods*, George Ancona; *Deborah Yaffe*, Joanne Ryder; *Charles Yerkow*, Lila Perl; *Bo Zaunders*, Roxie Munro; *George Zebrowski*, Pamela Sargent.